THE AMERICAN MUSICAL THEATRE SONG ENCYCLOPEDIA

Thomas S. Hischak

Foreword by Gerald Bordman

GREENWOOD PRESS
Westport, Connecticut • London

Library of Congress Cataloging-in-Publication Data

Hischak, Thomas S.
    The American musical theatre song encyclopedia / Thomas S.
   Hischak ; foreword by Gerald Bordman
        p.   cm.
    Includes bibliographical references (p.   ) and index.
    ISBN 0–313–29407–0
    1. Musicals—Encyclopedias.   2. Popular music—Encyclopedias.
  I. Title.
  ML102.M88H59   1995
  782.1′4′0973—dc20   94–40853

British Library Cataloguing in Publication Data is available.

Library of Congress Catalog Card Number: 94–40853
ISBN: 0–313–29407–0

First published in 1995

Greenwood Press, 88 Post Road West, Westport, CT 06881
An imprint of Greenwood Publishing Group, Inc.

Printed in the United States of America

The paper used in this book complies with the
Permanent Paper Standard issued by the National
Information Standards Organization (Z39.48–1984).

10 9 8 7 6 5 4 3 2 1

For Mark and Karen

Contents

Foreword

On a television panel several years before his all-too-early death, Alan Jay Lerner made what might have seemed for him a rather curious comment. He suggested that a musical play's book usually underpins the entertainment's initial success, but that the show's melodies determine whether or not the musical will endure for the longer haul. The statement was curious for a number of reasons. First of all, Lerner was not a first-class librettist. The lone masterpiece of a book musical that he created, *My Fair Lady*, he did by brilliantly adapting an already-accepted non-musical classic, *Pygmalion*. His written-from-scratch librettos were invariably flawed, so the notable success of these musicals might be more readily attributed to their splendid productions, their fine casts, or their often beautiful, catchy melodies. Furthermore, despite still-ubiquitous elevator music and the sale of albums re-singing many of these old melodies, Lerner, above all, should have recognized that music alone can't do the trick. That falls, instead, to the singular magic that occurs when the right melody becomes attached to the right lyric.

Those great song-and-dance entertainments that survive decade upon decade survive in no small measure not because of their dances or librettos or what have you, but because of their songs. (Indeed, in recent years old songs from various scores have been recompiled to provide the words and music for new-fangled librettos.) Lerner's failure to mention a song's words, and to speak solely of music as the prod to longevity, is especially surprising since he himself was probably the best lyricist of his generation. Time and again each new coterie of critics (or faddists, if you will) bewail how rickety yesterday's librettos have become but how well the old songs hold up. Even the nauseatingly over-lauded Hammerstein librettos are now heard to creak occasionally. But whatever era or genre of musical theatre we talk about, the songs of its shows are what leap to mind most quickly.

Of course, librettos run on for pages and even the most dedicated musical-theatre buff could not be expected to commit them to memory. At best, a line here, a line there, or the gist of a plot are all that can be conveniently retained. Yet casual playgoers as well as ardent buffs will easily commit to memory a minute long song, words and music. For all of that, the source and history of some interesting but relatively obscure numbers can escape casual musical-theatre lover and student alike.

Now, thanks to Tom Hischak, devotées of theatrical songs will have a convenient single-volume work on hand to answer their questions or resolve any arguments. The work is a careful labor of love, which covers not only songs from recent Broadway musicals, but delves back knowingly into the nineteenth century. Not just Sondheim and Styne-Comden-and-Green are here, but Porter, the Gershwins, Kern and his best lyricists, Herbert and his wordsmiths, and even De Koven and his associates. Yet as careful as Tom's attention has been, the reader may feel something unimportant has been included to the exclusion of something unfortunately overlooked. If so, write to Tom, in care of his publisher, so that a second edition of this book, which is bound to become a standard, can rectify any oversights. Meanwhile, read, enjoy, learn and sing along.

Gerald Bordman

Preface

Over the past few decades, the time-worn questions Who wrote that song? and What musical did it come from? have been answered by a series of books that charted the origins of musical theatre songs. These weighty volumes have unearthed and categorized thousands of song titles, including many long out-of-print or lost forever. The works of Richard Lewine and Alfred Simon and that of Robert Lissauer have been of particular value in this area. But pinpointing the authors and sources for theatre songs is, in many ways, rather unsatisfying. The nature of a musical theatre song is different from that of a Tin Pan Alley or "Your Hit Parade" song. The musical theatre number is conceived, written and produced as part of a whole. While it may eventually stand on its own and join the ranks of popular hits, its immediate purpose is clear: it must "work" in the show. Whether it is part of an improbable, silly musical comedy, a loosely structured musical revue or a tightly knit integrated musical play, the theatre song must justify its existence, or it is cut. The history of the American musical is filled with examples of superb songs that were dropped before opening or discarded songs that finally worked in a later show. The nature of the musical show dictates that this be so; Tin Pan Alley has no such limitations.

Theatre composers and lyricists have always had to be playwrights as well as songwriters, even if they did not contribute to the libretto. This may sound rather high-minded, but, in fact, it is commercially pragmatic. A theatre song may advance plot, develop character, set a mood, create tension or fulfill a number of admirable requirements. But just as often a song is needed to highlight a star, provide jokes, offer a chorus of pretty girls, add a touch of romance, supply an opportunity for dance or even fill in during scenery changes backstage. These latter reasons are as much a part of musical playwriting as the former ones. All are necessary to make the whole musical work.

This book is about how hundreds of famous and not-so-famous songs have functioned in the American musical. In addition to identifying the authors and the source of the song, *The American Musical Theatre Song Encyclopedia* hopes to *explain* the song: what kind of song it is, what it is about and what purpose it has in the show, as well as who originally sang it, what the song's history is and what may be unique about this particular number. It is a book about songs as little pieces of playwriting for the musical theatre.

In order to contain all this information within a practical one-volume work, songs have been discriminately chosen. Of the thousands of songs written for the stage over the past 130 years, I have selected some 1800 that hopefully represent all the majors shows, authors, genres and eras. Considerations include the song's popularity, its high quality, historical importance, individual uniqueness and its association with a particular performer. The selections chosen come from musicals as early as *The Black Crook* in 1866 and continue through the 1993-1994 theatre season ending with *Passion*. American works and artists are emphasized over foreign ones, but songs from British and other imports that had a reasonable impact on Broadway are included. European operettas, such as the works by Gilbert and Sullivan, are not included, though they often performed in Broadway theatres. The song entries are presented alphabetically, but the "Musicals" list at the end of the book includes all the songs discussed from a particular show. The dates and number of performances used throughout are those of the New York City engagements.

Musical numbers that do not utilize lyrics (such as "*Carousel* Waltz" or "Slaughter on Tenth Avenue") are not included, nor are songs written for films (such as the scores for *Singin' in the Rain* or *Meet Me in St. Louis*) even though they later were heard on Broadway. Also, song titles are often a matter of confusion. I have chosen what is generally considered the most common title for a song when its official title is somewhat obscure. The "Alternate Song Titles" list after the entries section identifies many such songs.

In describing the types of songs, there are some musical theatre terms that may need explanation. While a love duet, torch song or chorus number may be widely familiar, there are other types that are not. "I am" songs, pastiche numbers, ballads and other terms relating to musical theatre songs are described in the Glossary.

I wish to acknowledge continued help from the staff at the Cortland Memorial Library at the State University of New York College at Cortland and the Cortland Free Library in Cortland, New York. I also wish to recognize the help of my assistant Mark Robinson, the useful comments and suggestions by Richard Norton, and my public thanks to Cathy Hischak for her endless patience with me and the manuscript. I also gratefully acknowledge the guidance of my editor at Greenwood Publishing, Alicia S. Merritt. Finally, I acknowledge the guidance and enthusiasm of Gerald Bordman who went through the manuscript carefully, making corrections and suggestions; without his help the result would have been a less accomplished book.

Glossary of Theatre Music Terms

ballad   A term with too many meanings in music and literature. In modern popular music it is any sentimental or romantic song, usually with the same melody for each stanza. Ballads are often the big sellers in a musical, the songs that can move listeners without benefit of character or plot. Most ballads written since World War Two have a foxtrot (4/4) base. A *narrative ballad* is more like poetry's definition of the term: a song that tells a story.

character song   Any musical number that is concerned with revealing a character's personality or reaction to the events of the plot. A person's first character song in a show is often his or her "I am" song. Character songs tend not to travel as well outside the context of the musical as ballads often do.

charm song   A musical number that is less about character development than it is about utilizing the characters' warmth and/or comic entertainment value. Charm songs are often expendable plotwise but are usually audience favorites.

chorus   A group of characters that sing or dance together; hence, a vocal chorus made up of singers or a chorus line made up of dancers. In today's musical theatre these two groups are usually the same. The chorus is sometimes called the *ensemble* or the *company* in the list of who sings what in a musical show. Chorus is also another term for the refrain of a song, although that definition is not used in this book.

eleven o'clock number   A special, show-stopping song that comes late in the second act of a two-act musical show. The actual time at which the number occurs is not as important as its powerful impact in bringing the show to life before the climax or finale. A ballad, comic number, torch song or any other type of song may turn into an eleven o'clock number, either by intention or not.

"I am" song Often a solo, but any song that introduces a character or group of characters early in a musical show by revealing their wishes, dreams, confusions and so on. Sometimes called an "I wish" song as well. "I am" songs became requisite with the advent of the integrated musical play, but many musicals before *Oklahoma!* (1943) have "I am" songs that function in the same way.

interpolation A song added to a show, either before or after opening, that is usually not written by the same songwriters that wrote the rest of the score. Songs may be interpolated into a musical for a variety of reasons: to improve a weak score, to please a star, to take advantage of a hit Tin Pan Alley song and so on.

list song Any song, serious or comic, that is structured as a list of examples or a series of items. Sometimes called a "laundry list" song, although the result, hopefully, is much more interesting than that.

lyric A line from a song or the entire set of lines written for a song. A lyric is written by a lyricist, as opposed to a librettist who writes the book or dialogue for a musical. The plural form *lyrics* refers to the words to all the songs a lyricist has written for a score; one writes the *lyric* for a song and the *lyrics* for a score. In this book, when a songwriter is not referred to specifically as a lyricist or a composer, it can be assumed that he or she wrote both music and lyric for the song.

pastiche song Any musical number that echoes the style, either musically or lyrically, of an earlier era. Such songs are written to spoof the past or to recapture the period for the setting of the new work.

refrain The main body of a song; that is, the section that follows the verse and repeats itself with the same melody and/or lyric. The most familiar part of a popular song is usually the refrain section. The refrain is also called the *chorus*, but the latter term is too often confused with that of a group of singers, so it is not used in this book.

release A section of the refrain that departs from the repeated melody and explores a new musical line that may or may not have been suggested in the main melody. The release helps keep a song from being too predictable or monotonous.

reprise The repeating of all or part of a song later in the show, either by the same or different characters. Reprises differ from *encores* in that the latter are repeats that are sung immediately after a song is first sung. While reprises are still common, the extended use of encores waned with the coming of the integrated musical.

soliloquy   A solo in which the character is alone and reveals his or her thoughts, confusions, concerns and so on. The most effective soliloquies are songs that show a character debating two sides of an issue or trying to come to a decision.

specialty number   A song that highlights a performer's unique talents rather than the character or plot. Not all songs written for a particular star are specialty numbers, but in revues and pre-*Oklahoma!* shows they often were.

torch song   In popular music a torch song is usually a sentimental song involving unrequited love, but musical theatre torch songs may be comic or sarcastic as well. Often in musical comedy a ballad that follows any disagreement between the lovers might be considered a torch song even though the situation is hardly weighty and the two get back together soon after.

verse   The introductory section of a song. The melody is usually distinct from that of the refrain that follows, and verses tend to be shorter. Most songs written in this century are more known for their refrains than for their verses, so songwriters tend to lavish less attention on verses. On the other hand, many songs gain their full potency from an effective verse that sets up the song's main ideas or images. During the nineteenth century, the verses to popular songs were usually quite lengthy and often contained the main body of the piece. Around the time of World War One, verses became more like introductions with the refrains becoming the focal point of the number. In the last thirty years verses, which were once considered a required section of every popular song, have been written less and less for theatre songs.

Songs

A

"Adelaide's Lament" is arguably the funniest female solo in the American musical theatre. Frank Loesser wrote the sensational character number for Miss Adelaide (Vivian Blaine) to sing in *Guys and Dolls* (1950), and it never fails to stop the show. Originally Loesser planned Adelaide as a nightclub stripper who sang about how she always catches cold while working. Later the cold developed into a more psychosomatic ailment due to Adelaide's continual disappointment in love, and the song ended up being a sympathetic but hysterical portrait of a far-from-stereotypic woman. Worth noting is Loesser's unusually wordy lyric and his two alternating melodies: a ponderous strain for the highly scientific explanations Adelaide reads from a book and a bouncy, melodic section for her own personal observations.

"Adrift on a Star" is a lovely ballad from the unsuccessful *The Happiest Girl in the World* (1961), a musical version of Aristophanes' *Lysistrata* using music by Jacques Offenbach. General Kinesias (Bruce Yarnell) and his wife Lysistrata (Dran Sietz) are caught in the crossfire of the battle of the sexes in ancient Athens and sing this engaging duet about how they depend on each other's love to make sense of a confusing and arbitrary world. E.Y. Harburg wrote the tender lyric and set it to Offenbach's "Barcarolle."

"Adventure" is a hilarious specialty number for Nancy Walker in *Do Re Mi* (1960) by Jule Styne (music) and Betty Comden and Adolph Green (lyric). Kay Cram (Walker) consoles her husband Herbie (Phil Silvers) on his latest business disaster by revealing her preference for living a life of ups and downs with him rather than the safe, upper-middle-class world of unhappy women who should be jealous of her.

"After the Ball" is the familiar narrative ballad that has remained one of the most popular theatre songs throughout the past one hundred years. Charles

K. Harris wrote the music and lyric about an old man who tells his niece why he never wed: at a fancy dress ball he saw his sweetheart kiss another man, so he left the ball and the girl and never saw her again. It was only years later that he learned that the man she kissed was her long-lost brother. Harris wrote the heart-tugging ballad in 1892 for a vaudeville singer who forgot the words during the first performance and the song failed to get any notice. When the popular musical comedy *A Trip to Chinatown* toured Milwaukee in 1892, Harris paid the singing star J. Aldrich Libby to insert the number in the second act. For the entire three verses and three refrains the audience was silent and remained so right after the song; Harris thought he had written a dud. Then the audience rose to its feet and cheered for five minutes. "After the Ball" was included in every production of the show after that, and the song went on to sell five million copies of sheet music. It was also a popular vaudeville staple, and John Philip Sousa included the song in every concert he conducted after 1893. In the 1927 landmark musical *Show Boat*, Magnolia Ravenal (Norma Terris) sang the song in her nightclub performance on New Year's Eve of 1905, and it made Magnolia a star. While the song today is known mainly for its refrain, it is still one of the most recognized tunes in American popular culture.

"After You, Who?" contains one of Cole Porter's smoothest and most unforced lyrics, filled with "you" and "who" sounds that give the song a resonance even on the printed page. The gentle ballad was sung by Fred Astaire in *Gay Divorce* (1932), his last Broadway show before heading to Hollywood, never to return to the stage again. Andrea Marcovicci made a memorable recording of "After You, Who? in 1990.

"Agony" is one of Stephen Sondheim's finest comic duets, a mock-operetta number from *Into the Woods* (1987) with a grandiose barcarolle flavor. Cinderella's Prince (Robert Westenberg) and his brother, Rapunzel's Prince (Chuck Wagner), sing this lush harmonized duet about unrequited love. One prince laments that Cinderella ran from him and he cannot find her, and the other longs for Rapunzel, who is in an unreachable tower. In the musical's second act, with each prince now married to the maiden of his earlier dreams, the two brothers reprise the song, this time describing the agony of boredom with marriage and their longing for new romantic adventures.

"Ah, Paris!" is a delicious pseudo-French Follies number from Stephen Sondheim's *Follies* (1971) that was sung by the aged but spirited Solange La Fitte (Fifi D'Orsay). The number is a playful list song in which Solange outlines all the places she has seen, only to conclude that none compares to her beloved Paris. Millicent Martin sang the comic song in the Broadway revue *Side by Side by Sondheim* (1977).

"Ah, Sweet Mystery of Life" is not only Victor Herbert's most famous composition but to many it represents American operetta more than any other single song. The rapturous duet was written for *Naughty Marietta* (1910), where it was sung by lovers Captain Dick Warrington (Orville Harrold) and Marietta d'Altena (Emma Trentini) in the operetta's finale. Actually, fragments of the song are heard earlier in the show as the "Dream Melody" that Marietta recalls from a dream she had, and she says she will marry the man who can finish the song. (A similar leitmotif technique was used with the song "My Ship" in *Lady in the Dark* thirty years later.) Rida Johnson Young wrote the lyric for Herbert's music, which is rather simple with mostly short notes and a rhythm that does not linger as in most operetta love songs. No one working on the original production thought the song would be popular and it was listed only as the "Finale" in the program on opening night. Gordon MacRae and Lucille Norman recorded a popular version of the duet in the 1950s.

"Ain't Got No" is a bitter-comic list song from *Hair* (1968) that rebelliously proclaims all the things, both important and trivial, that are denied the young generation. Galt MacDermot (music) and Gerome Ragni and James Rado (lyric) wrote the energetic number, and it was sung in the 1967 Off-Broadway production by Claude (Walker Daniels), Berger (Gerome Ragni), Woof (Steve Dean), Hud (Arnold Wilkerson) and the ensemble. On Broadway it was sung by Woof (Steve Curry), Hud (Lamont Washington), and Dionne (Melba Moore), all of whom were black, so the song took on a more specific form of frustration. Nina Simone had a best-selling recording of "Ain't Got No."

"Ain't It Awful, the Heat?" is the bluesy, atmospheric opening song from the operatic *Street Scene* (1947) by Kurt Weill (music) and Langston Hughes (lyric). The seriocomic number was sung by four residents of the New York City tenement (Helen Arden, Ellen Repp, Wilson Smith and Hope Emerson) as they discuss the heat wave that has hit the city. The song does for *Street Scene* what "Summertime" did to set the mood for *Porgy and Bess* (1935), another operatic treatment of life in a specific neighborhood. "Ain't It Awful, the Heat?" was also sung by the ensemble in the Off-Broadway revue *Berlin to Broadway With Kurt Weill* (1972).

"Ain't It de Truth?" is a potent character song from *Jamaica* (1957) in which the island beauty Savannah (Lena Horne) argues that life is short, so the true philosophy is to live it to its fullest now. Harold Arlen composed the swinging, engaging music, and E.Y. Harburg wrote the concise, piquant lyric that has a sensual subtext to it. Arlen and Harburg had written the number for Horne fourteen years earlier for the film version of *Cabin in the Sky,* and the song was recorded and shot but left on the cutting-room floor. When Horne was cast in *Jamaica,* they resurrected the song and added it to the score.

"Ain't Misbehavin'" is the hit song from the revue *Hot Chocolates* (1929) that successfully transferred from a nightclub to Broadway where it ran over six months. The famous rhythm ballad was written by Thomas "Fats" Waller and Harry Brooks (music) and Andy Razaf (lyric), and in the show it was sung by Margaret Simms, Paul Bass and Russell Wooding's Jubilee Singers. In addition to its contagious use of changing harmony, the song has, as Gerald Bordman has stated, "plaintive undertones that hint at the stylings of much of the music that would come out of Broadway for the next few years." Razaf's lyric is noteworthy for its slyness and comic self-awareness. In the orchestra for *Hot Chocolates* was Louis Armstrong, making his New York City debut, who played a trumpet solo version of the song and first gained the attention of the critics. Later he recorded the solo as part of a Seger Ellis and His Orchestra single. Of the many recordings of "Ain't Misbehavin'," the most popular was Waller's vocal and piano solo, which established the number as his theme song throughout his career. The song was heard in no less than four films and was sung by the cast of five in the Broadway Waller revue *Ain't Misbehavin'* (1978).

"Alice Blue Gown" is one of America's favorite waltz songs, a lovely number from *Irene* (1919) that referred to the light blue color favored by Alice Roosevelt Longworth, Teddy's daughter. The Irish shop girl Irene O'Dare (Edith Day) sang the number as a sort of "I am" song, quietly reflecting on an almost new dress once given to her and how she wore it over and over until it "wilted." Harry Tierney wrote the Irish-flavored music, and Joseph McCarthy provided the lyric that was, like Irene, simple and frugal but charming.

"All Aboard for Broadway" is a thrilling production number from George M. Cohan's *George Washington, Jr.* (1906). Of the many Cohan songs saluting show business and his favorite street, this is one of the most infectious. In the bio-musical *George M!* (1968) it was sung by Joel Grey, Jerry Dodge, Bernadette Peters and Betty Ann Grove as the Four Cohans.

"All Alone," one of Irving Berlin's autobiographical songs and among his most famous ballads, was interpolated into the last edition of the *Music Box Revue* (1924), where it was performed by Oscar Shaw and Grace Moore singing on telephones at each end of a darkened stage. Berlin wrote the song about the loneliness he felt before he was allowed to marry Ellin MacKay, the heiress he was in love with. After John McCormack sang "All Alone" on the radio, over a million copies of the recording were sold. Connee Boswell's recording was very popular as well. The song also sold one million copies of sheet music and 160,000 player-piano rolls.

"All Alone Monday" is a romantic song about loneliness from the Bobby Clark and Paul McCullough vehicle *The Ramblers* (1926). Movie actress

Ruth Chester (Marie Saxon) and her sweetheart Billy Shannon (Jack Whiting) sang the duet that recounted loneliness endured during each day of the week. Harry Ruby (music) and Bert Kalmar (lyric) wrote the appealing song.

"All at Once You Love Her" is a Latin-flavored ballad from *Pipe Dream* (1955), the least known of all the Rodgers and Hammerstein musicals. William Johnson, as the marine biologist Doc, sang it to Suzy (Judy Tyler); then Jerry La Zarre sang it in Spanish with Doc translating. In the second act of the show, Madame Fauna (opera star Helen Traubel) reprised the beguiling number. Perry Como's recording of the song was very popular even though *Pipe Dream* was soon forgotten. Jason Graae and Martin Vidnovic sang the number as a duet in the Broadway revue *A Grand Night for Singing* (1993).

"All 'er Nothin' " is one of Rodgers and Hammerstein's finest comedy songs, a delicious duet from *Oklahoma!* (1943) between Ado Annie (Celeste Holm) and Will Parker (Lee Dixon) about marital fidelity. Richard Rodgers' music uses a swaggering, vamp tempo that gives the song a comical hick quality, and Oscar Hammerstein's lyric finds rural wit in these two lovable wooden-headed characters.

"All Fall Down" is a searing narrative ballad from the short-lived *Romance in Hard Times* (1989) by William Finn. In a New York City soup kitchen, Zoe (Alix Korey) sings this absorbing saga about her family, college friends and husband, all of whom fell from success when the Great Depression hit. The song was recorded by Korey in 1990.

"All for the Best" is a nimble duet for Jesus (Stephen Nathan) and Judas (David Haskell) from *Godspell* (1971) by Stephen Schwartz. The dandy vaudeville turn was done as a contrapuntal duet playing Jesus' soothing soft shoe against Judas' frenzied list song that described the benefits of being rich in this world.

"All Hail the Political Honeymoon" is a rousing march that welcomes new governor Pieter Stuyvesant (Walter Huston) of New Amsterdam in *Knickerbocker Holiday* (1938). Kurt Weill wrote the robust music, and Maxwell Anderson provided the pungent lyric.

"All I Ask of You" is the sweeping love duet from the British import *The Phantom of the Opera* (1988) by Andrew Lloyd Webber (music) and Charles Hart and Richard Stilgoe (lyric). On the roof of the Paris Opera House, opera singer Christine Daae (Sarah Brightman) is comforted by Raoul (Steve Barton), and they sing this melodic duet in which all they ask is love from each other. A few moments later the Phantom (Michael Crawford) jealously reprises the song just before he sends the chandelier crashing to the stage.

"All I Care About (Is Love)" is a debonair song and dance number from *Chicago* (1975) in which shyster lawyer Billy Flynn (Jerry Orbach) explains his philosophy of life. The John Kander (music) and Fred Ebb (lyric) song is mock sentimental and ridiculously casual. It is also a unique "I am" song in that the character is lying about himself and everyone knows it.

"All I Need (Is One Good Break)" is the title character's eager "I am" song from *Flora, the Red Menace* (1965), the first score by John Kander (music) and Fred Ebb (lyric). Flora Meszaros (Liza Minnelli), a recent graduate from art school, tries to get a job as a fashion designer during the hard days of the Depression. As she fills out another job application, Flora and the other struggling artists sing ambitiously about the break that is just around the corner.

"All I Need Is the Girl" is a charming if somewhat pathetic song and dance number by a would-be Fred Astaire-type hoofer in *Gypsy* (1959). Tulsa (Paul Wallace) has been rehearsing a nightclub act about a top-hatted debonair gent who dances with a beautiful girl all in white. He demonstrates the routine for Louise (Sandra Church), who joins him in the dance section playing the elusive girl. Jule Styne composed the alternately snappy and dreamy music, and Stephen Sondheim provided the appropriately clichéd lyric.

"All of These and More" is an enraptured love song in which the lovers list the various forms of joy each feels when the other is near. The duet is from *The Body Beautiful* (1958), a musical about boxing that was the first collaboration between Jerry Bock (music) and Sheldon Harnick (lyric), and it was sung by Steve Forrest, Mindy Carson and the ensemble.

"All of You" is the popular love song from *Silk Stockings* (1955), Cole Porter's last Broadway musical. Don Ameche sang the sensual ballad to the Russian official Ninotchka (Hildegarde Neff) in order to soften her stiff bureaucratic facade. The number is also a list song in which he catalogues all of her features like a geographer studying a map.

"All That Jazz" is the intoxicating opening number from *Chicago* (1975) and the most popular song to come out of the show. John Kander (music) and Fred Ebb (lyric) wrote the red-hot number that captured the Roaring Twenties with all of its sass and decadence. Chita Rivera and the ensemble sang the song in the original production, and Liza Minnelli later recorded it. Karen Ziemba, Jim Walton and Bob Cuccioli also sang "All That Jazz" in the Off-Broadway revue *And the World Goes 'Round* (1991).

"All the Children in a Row" is a powerful musical sequence from *The Rink* (1984) by John Kander (music) and Fred Ebb (lyric). The world-weary Angel (Liza Minnelli) recalls her days in the youth movement in California: the antiwar marches, the drug scene and, in a flashback scene, her lover Danny (Scott Ellis), who lived wild and died young. The song has startling imagery, including that of long lines of young people in the California sun seeking self-fulfillment.

"All the Livelong Day (I Hear America Singing)" is the vibrant opening number in *Working* (1978), the Broadway revue about America's work force. Stephen Schwartz adapted Walt Whitman's poem, added his own lyric and wrote the music for the song, which was sung by the ensemble.

"All the Things You Are" is the unforgettable ballad from Jerome Kern's last Broadway musical, *Very Warm for May* (1939), and one of his most beloved songs. Oscar Hammerstein wrote the lyric for the scintillating number, and it was sung by Hiram Sherman, Frances Mercer, Hollace Shaw and Ralph Stuart as a musical selection in a summer stock show within *Very Warm for May*. Later in the musical it is reprised by the young apprentice Kenny (Ray Mayer). The song is one of the most perfect blendings of words and music in the American musical theatre. Hammerstein's lyric is enthrallingly romantic without crossing over into mawkishness. Kern's music, in the words of musicologist Alec Wilder, is "ingenious and daring." Kern wrote the odd but effective key and tempo changes for his own satisfaction and often stated that he never thought the song could become popular because it was too complex for the layman's ear. But "All the Things You Are" went on to be very popular, appearing in three films and recorded by artists ranging from Gordon MacRae to Jessye Norman to Ann Hampton Calloway. Its sheet music and record sales kept it on "Your Hit Parade" for eleven weeks, and in 1964 a poll of American composers chose this song most often as their all-time favorite.

"All Through the Night" is one of Cole Porter's most popular love songs and one of several that have a distinctive Latin undercurrent to them. The serenade's melody is rather complex, with many unexpected key changes that keep it interesting throughout its unusual length (sixty-four measures). "All Through the Night" was first sung by William Gaxton and Bettina Hall in *Anything Goes* (1934), where it was added when Gaxton objected to singing Porter's "Easy to Love" in the same spot.

"Allah's Holiday" is a sumptuous song with an Asian flavor from *Katinka* (1915) by Rudolf Friml (music) and Otto Harbach (lyric). Olga (Edith Decker), the wife of the Russian ambassador, sings this exotic number, which became very popular in its day.

"Almost Like Being in Love" is the only un-Scottish number from *Brigadoon* (1947), a zesty Broadway ballad with a sophisticated lyric by Alan Jay Lerner and energetic music by Frederick Loewe. It was sung by the New Yorker Tommy Albright (David Brooks), and he was joined by the Scottish lassie Fiona (Marion Bell) for an exhilarating duet. It became the most popular song from the show, with dozens of recordings over the years, perhaps most intriguing a 1953 hit by Nat "King" Cole and a lovely 1991 recording by his daughter Natalie Cole.

"Alone at a Drive-In Movie" is a camp torch song from *Grease* (1972) by Jim Jacobs and Warren Casey. Danny Zuko (Barry Bostwick) and Sandy Dumbrowski (Carole Demas) have a lovers' quarrel in his car at the drive-in theatre, and she leaves him all alone to sing this amusingly maudlin number done to the accompaniment of werewolves howling from the movie screen.

"Alone Together" is a brooding, romantic ballad from the revue *Flying Colors* (1932) by Howard Dietz (lyric) and Arthur Schwartz (music). Jean Sargent sang the alluring number; then Clifton Webb and Tamara Geva did a sinuous dance together. In the number's theatrical climax, Norman Bel Geddes' movable set receded upstage as scenery and dancers disappeared from sight. Schwartz's music for the song is both brooding and melodic, with an unusual structure that adds to its haunting quality. Jo Stafford made an exceptional recording of "Alone Together" in 1944 and Judy Garland's rendition of it is superb.

"Alone Too Long" is a wistful ballad from the period musical *By the Beautiful Sea* (1954) by Arthur Schwartz (music) and Dorothy Fields (lyric). When the old Shakespearean actor Dennis Emery (Wilbur Evans) and the ex-vaudevillian Lottie Gibson (Shirley Booth) take a boat ride through Coney Island's tunnel of love, he sings this poignant song about his lonely bachelor life. Nat "King" Cole made a popular recording of the song, which is sometimes titled "I've Been Alone Too Long."

"Always," one of Irving Berlin's most famous ballads, was the most substantial song he wrote for the Marx Brothers' vehicle *The Cocoanuts* (1925), but it was cut before opening because librettist George S. Kaufman disliked it so. (He mockingly called it "I'll Be Loving You -- Thursday.") The song was an old trunk tune of Berlin's that he had written years earlier. When it was dropped from *The Cocoanuts*, he gave it to his bride Ellin MacKay as a wedding present, and it became a Tin Pan Alley hit. While the lyric and the lazy waltzlike music strike many as mawkish, the song does have a unique shift from F major to A major that is far from routine. In addition to the dozens of recordings over the years, "Always" is heard in every production of Noël Coward's comedy classic

Blithe Spirit (1941), where the song is used as a running joke throughout the play.

"Always Do As People Say You Should" is a coy comic number from the operetta *The Fortune Teller* (1898) by Victor Herbert (music) and Harry B. Smith (lyric). The Hungarian ballet student Irma (Alice Nielsen) sings the playful song of injured innocence.

"Always True to You in My Fashion" is the comic argument of fickle Lois Lane (Lisa Kirk) in Cole Porter's *Kiss Me, Kate* (1948) as she tries to convince her boyfriend that all her previous (and future) love affairs could not in any way affect her feelings for him. The song's title and premise come from Ernest Dowson's poem "Cynara," but Porter's lyric gives the number a sassy, urbane flavor that epitomizes New York in the 1940s. Jo Stafford made a very successful recording of the song.

"Amazons' March" is a buoyant choral number from *The Black Crook* (1866) that was sung by the bare-limbed ballet dancers who portrayed the notorious Amazons. Giuseppe Operti wrote the merry march, but it is not clear if the number was in the landmark production on opening night or if it was added later in the long run, as was much of the score. The song was reconstructed and recorded by New World Records in 1978.

"America" is the droll Latin American rhythm song from *West Side Story* (1957) that sarcastically praises the attributes of the island of Manhattan over those of the island of Puerto Rico. Leonard Bernstein composed the scintillating music, Stephen Sondheim wrote the sparkling lyric, and the song was introduced by Anita (Chita Rivera), Rosalia (Marilyn Cooper) and the girlfriends of the Sharks.

"The American Dream" is a stinging tribute to American materialism from the British import *Miss Saigon* (1991) with music by Claude-Michel Schönberg and lyric by Richard Maltby, Jr., who adapted the French lyric by Alain Boublil. The Engineer (Jonathan Pryce) is about to get his visa to the United States and fantasizes about an America where money can buy anything and everything.

"Among My Yesterdays" is a beautifully evocative ballad from *The Happy Time* (1968) by John Kander (music) and Fred Ebb (lyric). Jacques Bonnard (Robert Goulet) returns to the small French Canadian town of his youth, and as he walks down the streets, memories of the past fill his head.

"And I Am All Alone" is a little-known ballad by Jerome Kern that admirers place among his very best. It was written with lyricist P. G. Wodehouse for their first full score together, *Have a Heart* (1917). Ruddy Schoonmaker (Thurston Hall) and his wife Peggy (Eileen Van Biene) are on a second honeymoon in an attempt to save their faltering marriage. In this lovely duet they conjure up visions of blissful happiness that quickly dissolve, and they each find themselves all alone. The harmonies in Kern's music are unusual and quite effective, and an unexpected pause before the final musical phrase gives the song a unique sense of dramatic songwriting. The ballad was recorded soon after the show opened by the tenor Henry Burr, who used the pseudonym of Irving Gilette on the label.

"And I Am Telling You I'm Not Going" is the eruptive lament from *Dreamgirls* (1981) that closed the first act and opened up the career of singer Jennifer Holliday. When the manager (Ben Harney) of the rhythm and blues trio the Dreams tells Effie Melody White (Holliday) that he's replacing her in the act with a prettier and thinner singer, she launches into this gospel-style tirade. Henry Krieger (music) and Tom Eyen (lyric) wrote the number, and Holliday's single from the cast album was a best-seller.

"And I Was Beautiful" is the absorbing ballad of recollection sung by the mad Countess Aurelia (Angela Lansbury) in *Dear World* (1969), the musicalization of Jean Giraudoux's *The Madwoman of Chaillot*. Jerry Herman wrote the tender song that conjures up images from the countess' past, concluding that such memories make her still feel beautiful.

"And This Is My Beloved" is an intoxicating quartet from *Kismet* (1953), the *Arabian Nights* musical that uses themes by Alexander Borodin. The poet Hajj (Alfred Drake) questions his daughter Marsinah (Doretta Morrow) about her true love, the Caliph (Richard Kiley), while on the opposite side of the stage the man discussed is singing descriptive praises of Marsinah to the Wazir of Police (Henry Calvin). The four voices blend together in an intricate and totally captivating quartet. Robert Wright and George Forrest wrote the lyric and adapted Borodin's Second String Quartet in D into a memorable stage piece.

"The Angelus" is the title for two different hymnlike songs from two different Victor Herbert operettas. In his early work *The Serenade* (1897), with a lyric by Harry B. Smith, the inspirational number was sung by the desperate Dolores (Jessie Bartlett Davis), who has been locked up in a convent by her wicked guardian. Her simple, prayerful rendition of the song was then reprised with help from a full orchestra, chorus and pipe organ. In Herbert's later *Sweethearts* (1913), with a lyric by Robert B. Smith, a similarly radiant song is delivered by the princess-in-disguise Sylvia (Christie MacDonald) as she hears the faraway chimes of the angelus bells and sings a soft melody with long phrases beautifully varied. Prince Franz (Thomas Conkey) joins her, and this "Angelus" becomes a duet. Both songs were quite popular in their respective eras, proving that even a hymn could be a hit if it was impressive enough.

"Another Autumn" is a chilling ballad from *Paint Your Wagon* (1951), the Alan Jay Lerner (lyric) and Frederick Loewe (music) musical about gold prospecting in California. Julio (Tony Bavaar), a young Mexican prospector, sings the heartfelt song about the sad realization that fall is here and he will have to face another winter alone without love.

"Another Hundred People" is an effervescent ballad about the life of single people in Manhattan from the landmark musical *Company* (1970) by Stephen Sondheim. New Yorker Marta (Pamela Myers) sits on a park bench and sings this expansive song about living in the city of strangers where personal communication and lasting relationships fail at a frantic pace. Sondheim's music is a surging re-creation of the nervous energy of the city, and the lyrics evoke striking images of the alienated nature of urban life. In the Broadway revue *Side by Side by Sondheim* (1977), the song was sung by Julia McKenzie.

"Another Life" is a deeply felt ballad of yearning for success from the short-lived *Dance a Little Closer* (1983) by Charles Strouse (music) and Alan Jay Lerner (lyric). Liz Robertson, as the ambitious Cynthia, sang the eager number in which a girl living in poverty dreams of a completely different kind of life.

"Another National Anthem" is an ironic and incendiary song from the controversial *Assassins* (1991) by Stephen Sondheim. This song of protest and pain is sung by the Balladeer (Patrick Cassidy) and the various infamous figures in American history, from John Wilkes Booth (Victor Garber) to John Hinckley (Greg Germann), who have assassinated or tried to assassinate U.S. presidents. These confused and tragic figures sing of an America of discontent and disillusion and argue that there must be a separate anthem to be sung for all of society's misfits. Sondheim's march music has harsh undertones, and his lyric cynically acknowledges the power of those outside the American dream.

"Another Op'nin', Another Show" is the lively opening chorus number of Cole Porter's *Kiss Me, Kate* (1948). It was sung by Annabelle Hill and the cast of the musical version of *The Taming of the Shrew* that is in out-of-town tryouts in Baltimore. The number has become a show-biz anthem of sorts.

"Another Suitcase in Another Hall" is the poignant song from the British import *Evita* (1979) sung by Juan Peron's sixteen-year-old mistress (Jane Ohringer) when she is replaced by his new flame Eva Duarte. Although she never expected her affair with Peron to last very long, the mistress is at a loss what to do next and sings this touching ballad while Che (Mandy Patinkin) sings encouraging comments on the side. Andrew Lloyd Webber wrote the simple folklike music, and Tim Rice provided the perceptive lyric.

"Another Time, Another Place" is a moving ballad from the short-lived *Kwamina* (1961), the experimental musical about Africa by Richard Adler. Eve (Sally Ann Howes), a white doctor from England, and Kwamina (Terry Carter), a native who has been educated in Europe, are in love but realize that they must part. She sings how their kind of love would only be possible in a different place in a future time. Robert Goulet made a popular recording of the emotional song.

"Any Dream Will Do" is the optimistic ballad that ends *Joseph and the Amazing Technicolor Dreamcoat* (1982) by Andrew Lloyd Webber (music) and Tim Rice (lyric). Biblical Joseph (Bill Hutton) has been reunited with his father Jacob and his eleven brothers and sings joyfully of how all the past suffering has led to this happy ending.

"Any Old Place With You" was the first song by the team of Rodgers and Hart to be heard in a Broadway show and to be published. It was interpolated into the Lew Fields vehicle *A Lonely Romeo* (1919), where the nimble duet was sung by Alan Hale and Eve Lynn. Lorenz Hart's lyric already shows amazing cleverness as he rhymes all the places the lovers could be happy, from Timbuktu to Philadelphia to Abyssinia. Richard Rodgers, only sixteen years old, wrote a melody that is very engaging. He was even so bold as to devise a verse of thirty-two bars and a refrain of sixteen bars, the opposite of the usual practice at the time.

"Any Place I Hang My Hat Is Home" is the free and easy credo of the uncommitted Della Green (Ruby Hill) in the Harold Arlen (music) and Johnny Mercer (lyric) period musical *St. Louis Woman* (1946). Della is the belle of St. Louis and the girlfriend of bar owner Biglow Brown (Rex Ingram), but she sings that she belongs to no one and could pick up and leave at any time.

"Anyone Can Whistle" is the tender and beguiling title song from the 1964 experimental musical by Stephen Sondheim. Nurse Fay Apple (Lee Remick), who is very controlled and rational but yearns for passion in her life, sings the poignant ballad about her inability to love. With its simple, straightforward music and gentle, revealing lyric, the song is one of Sondheim's most emotional. Too often accused of being overcontrolled and rational himself, Sondheim proved with "Anyone Can Whistle" that he could write with as much heart as brains. In the Broadway revue *Side by Side by Sondheim* (1977), David Kernan sang the song.

"Anything Can Happen in New York" is a zesty song about Manhattan that is as satirical as it is affectionate. The song was written by Richard Lewine (music) and Arnold B. Horwitt (lyric) for the revue *Make Mine Manhattan* (1948). The ensemble sang the number, which listed the many unexpected things you might find in New York, like someone who was actually born there.

"Anything for Him" is an enthralling song of love and destruction from *Kiss of the Spider Woman* (1993) by John Kander (music) and Fred Ebb (lyric). Cellmates Molina (Brent Carver) and Valentin (Anthony Crivello) each have parallel thoughts on the night before Molina is released. Valentin knows that if he makes love to his cellmate, then Molina will deliver an important message for him when he gets out. Molina, on the other hand, admits to himself that he loves Valentin and that he will do whatever he asks. Added to the duet are sections sung by the Spider Woman (Chita Rivera), who contemplates the inevitable death that is quickly approaching.

"Anything Goes," the contagiously sprightly title song from the 1934 Cole Porter hit musical, contains some of Porter's slyest as well as most cynical views on modern society and its new set of morals. The lyric work is so invigorating that it is often overlooked how pulsating and vibrant the melody is: one of the great rhythm songs of the American theatre. Ethel Merman, as the former evangelist Reno Sweeney, introduced the song, and soon the ensemble (and all America) joined with her in singing it. The oft-recorded number was a hit once again in 1967 due to a best-selling record by the group Harper's Bizarre.

"Anything You Can Do (I Can Do Better)" is arguably Irving Berlin's finest comic duet, a stinging, delightful battle of wills between Annie Oakley (Ethel Merman) and Frank Butler (Ray Middleton) in *Annie Get Your Gun* (1946). The number was an afterthought and came about when director Joshua Logan suggested at a production meeting that the two characters quarrel in song to liven up Act Two. Berlin wrote the song in fifteen minutes in the taxicab on the way home from the meeting. It is essentially a list song in which the competing sharpshooters alternate in their claims to superiority. The music climbs up the scale as their boasts get more inflated. The whole piece was a theatrical triumph that also showed for the first time that Berlin was capable of writing character songs in the Rodgers and Hammerstein style.

"Applause" is the exuberant title song from the 1970 musical based on the classic film *All About Eve* with music by Charles Strouse and lyrics by Lee

Adams. In Joe Allen's bar, Bonnie Franklin and the "gypsies" sang and danced the thrilling testament to live theatre, and although the number was peripheral to the plot and none of the major characters were in the scene, the song became the hit of the show. Also memorable about the original staging was a sequence in the number where songs and characters from current Broadway musicals, from *Fiddler on the Roof* to *Oh! Calcutta!*, were capsulized in the dance.

"The Apple Doesn't Fall (Very Far From the Tree)" is a waggish comic duet from *The Rink* (1984) by John Kander (music) and Fred Ebb (lyric). A quarreling mother (Chita Rivera) and daughter (Liza Minnelli) find that they have some things in common, although most of them are weaknesses of character.

"April in Paris" is the beloved ballad by Vernon Duke (music) and E.Y. Harburg (lyric) that magically combines the love for a city with the realization that the love for a person is what makes springtime and Paris so special. The song was written for the revue *Walk a Little Faster* (1932), where it was sung by Evelyn Hoey. Duke's music is boldly different from the standard format both melodically and harmonically. Harburg's lyric is beguiling with its short, haikulike phrases that paint a picture with a series of specific, unforgettable images. Few paid much attention to the ballad at first, probably because Hoey had laryngitis on opening night and barely got through the song. It wasn't until the number was recorded by chanteuse Marian Chase and others that it caught on and became one of the most popular of all 1930s ballads. A jazz version of "April in Paris" by Count Basie and His Orchestra in 1955 was very popular.

"April Showers" was the big hit from *Bombo* (1921), where Al Jolson sang it and made it one of his many signature songs. Louis Silvers wrote the forthright, melodic music, and B.G. DeSylva provided the heartfelt lyric that Jolson milked with his customary fervor. He recorded the song soon after *Bombo* opened, and then again in 1932, 1946 and 1949.

"April Snow" is a gentle ballad from *Up in Central Park* (1945), the musical about New York City in the 1870s by Sigmund Romberg (music) and Dorothy Fields (lyric). The sweet song was sung by Rosie Moore (Maureen Cannon), the daughter of a Boss Tweed grafter who is in love with a muckraking journalist. In its nostalgic melody and old-fashioned lyric it reminded audiences of the delicate kind of songs Romberg had written in the 1920s. Barbara Cook made a scintillating recording of "April Snow" in 1993.

"Aquarius" was one of the top-selling hits to emerge from *Hair* (1968) and the signature song for a young generation looking for a better world. The number is a hymn of sorts that summons visions of harmony for the new zodiacal age. Galt MacDermot composed the bewitching music, and Gerome Ragni and James Rado wrote the exultant lyric. In the 1967 Off-Broadway version the whole company sang it, but after the song became popular on the radio, it was turned into the opening number for the Broadway production and was sung by Ron (Ronald Dyson) and the ensemble. Of the many who recorded "Aquarius," the Fifth Dimension had the biggest hit with it.

"Are You Havin' Any Fun?" is a lively song of celebration that echoed the festive temperament of the nation at the end of the Depression. The Sammy Fain (music) and Jack Yellen (lyric) song was introduced in *George White's Scandals* (1939), where it was sung by Ella Logan in her thick Scottish brogue as she cavorted about hedonistically in a sailor costume. The number was reprised later in the show by the Kim Loo Sisters and the Three Stooges with a chorus of girls who had the words to the song printed on their hats so that the audience could sing along. In addition to Logan's recording, the song was a hit for the Tommy Dorsey Orchestra (vocal by Edythe Wright).

"Are You Sure?" is a jubilant song from *The Unsinkable Molly Brown* (1960) by Meredith Willson and one that recalls some of the vivacious patter numbers from his earlier *The Music Man* (1957). Molly (Tammy Grimes) crashes a party for the high society of Denver and delivers this revival-like song asking if the Lord hasn't already answered their prayers. The song was recorded by Tex Williams in 1960.

"Arthur in the Afternoon" is a cunning, sexy number sung by Liza Minnelli in *The Act* (1977) by John Kander (music) and Fred Ebb (lyric). As part of her nightclub act, Michelle Craig (Minnelli) sings how her dreary life has been resuscitated by a cup of coffee each morning and an hour with virile Arthur each afternoon. Karen Ziemba sang the racy number in the Off-Broadway revue *And the World Goes 'Round* (1991).

"Artificial Flowers" is the deliberately cloying sentimental ballad from *Tenderloin* (1960) that satirizes the tear-stained sort of song popular at the end of the nineteenth century. Jerry Bock wrote the tenderhearted music, and Sheldon Harnick provided the delicately tragic lyric about an orphan named Annie who earned her living making artificial flowers until she froze to death and went to heaven, where she finally found genuine flowers. Ron Husmann, as a newspaper reporter, sang the sob ditty as an audition to get into the muckraking Reverend Brock's church choir. Bobby Darin recorded the song before *Tenderloin* opened and had a success with it.

"As Long As He Needs Me" is the hit ballad from the British import *Oliver!* (1963), a gripping testament to love for a man who is unworthy of such affection. Lionel Bart wrote the languishing music and lyric, and it was sung by Georgia Brown as the steadfast Nancy. The song has been recorded often (Dionne Warwick and Shirley Bassey each had hit singles with it), sometimes as "As Long As She Needs Me" to accommodate male singers.

"As Time Goes By," the beloved song standard that Dooley Wilson sang in the film classic *Casablanca* (1942), was heard on Broadway a decade earlier but failed to catch on. The Herman Hupfeld ballad was interpolated into *Everybody's Welcome* (1931), where it was sung by Frances Williams. Rudy Vallee made a recording soon after but it was only moderately successful. After the film version came out, the Vallee recording was reissued and it became a hit. Since then it has become one of the most recorded and performed songs in American popular culture.

"Ascot Gavotte" is the droll ensemble number sung by the spectators at the Ascot races in *My Fair Lady* (1956). Frederick Loewe composed the elegantly proper music, and Alan Jay Lerner wrote the ridiculously restrained lyric in which the upper classes clipped their words and swallowed their enthusiasm. The song is that rare thing in theatre: a chorus number that is actually witty.

"Ask the Man in the Moon" is a comic trio from the *Mikado*-like satiric operetta *Wang* (1891). The conniving regent of Siam called Wang (DeWolf Hopper), the young prince Mataya (a trouser role played by Della Fox) and a French colonel (Samuel Reed) sang the slapstick number that posed comic questions, then referred one to the man in the moon for the answers. Although the story is set in the Orient, the music by Woolson Morse and the lyric by J. Cheever Goodwin were both anachronistic, even making several references to contemporary New York City. *Wang* was so popular that forty years later, when the real king of Siam visited America, it is said that he requested to hear "Ask the Man in the Moon" and other songs from the score played for him.

"At Liberty in Thebes" is an outlandishly funny production number from the Off-Broadway *Olympus on My Mind* (1986) that takes a camp outlook on Greek mythology. Charis (Peggy Hewett), having been tricked into believing that her husband no longer loves her, cuts loose with the male chorus in this raucous number about her newfound sexual freedom. Grant Sturiale composed the vivacious music, and Barry Harman provided the farcical lyric.

"At Long Last Love" is a romantic ballad by Cole Porter that takes the form of a series of questions the lover asks himself about this new sensation. Clifton Webb sang the unusual list song in *You Never Know* (1938). The song is unique in the way the wry, sophisticated lyric is tempered by a very tender, straightforward melody.

"At My Side" is a warm ballad from the flop musical *Welcome to the Club* (1989) about alimony jail by A.E. Hotchner (lyric) and Cy Coleman (music and lyric). It was sung by Samuel E. Wright and Scott Waara as they recalled their ex-wives. The song was reprised as a romantic duet by Waara and Jodi Benson later in the show.

"At the Ballet" is a beguiling trio from *A Chorus Line* (1975) in which auditionees Sheila (Carole Bishop), Bebe (Nancy Lane) and Maggie (Kay Cole) recall how the graceful beauty of ballet was an escape for them from their wretched homelife. Marvin Hamlisch composed the sensitive music, and Edward Kleban wrote the evocative lyric.

"At the Red Rose Cotillion" is a lovely piece of pastiche that Frank Loesser wrote for the period musical *Where's Charley?* (1948). The scintillating waltz was sung by college student Jack (Byron Palmer) and his sweetheart Kitty (Doretta Morrow) at the Oxford University ball scene near the end of the show.

"At the Roxy Music Hall" is a satiric number from *I Married an Angel* (1938) that used song and dance to make fun of the overblown opulence of Radio City Music Hall. George Balanchine choreographed the number with Vivienne Segal and Audrey Christie playing the entire Rockettes chorus line, and Vera Zorina performed a "modern" dance fraught with symbols, her dancing partner missing his head. Richard Rodgers (music) and Lorenz Hart (lyric) provided the daffy song section in which Christie sang of the glories of the music hall, from the mighty theatre organ to the huge bathrooms. Years later Dorothy Loudon made a fun recording of the song.

"Auf Wiedersehn" is the melting Sigmund Romberg farewell song that was his first hit and made a stage star out of the young Vivienne Segal. In *The Blue Paradise* (1915) the Viennese flower seller Mizzi (Segal) must bid farewell to her beloved Rudolphe (Cecil Lean), who is going to America to make his fortune. Their tearful duet captivated audiences and Romberg's career took a turn toward fame. Herbert Reynolds wrote the song's tender lyric.

"Auto Da Fe (What a Day!)" is an acerbic musical number about the Spanish Inquisition from the satiric *Candide* (1956). In a marketplace in Lisbon, Candide (Robert Rounseville) and Dr. Pangloss (Max Adrian) are tried by the Grand Inquisitor for believing in the goodness of man in this best of all possible worlds. They are found guilty, and the chorus sings how perfect a day it is for a hanging as the execution is prepared. Leonard Bernstein composed the acutely merry music, and Richard Wilbur and John Latouche wrote the mordant lyric. In the original 1956 production, the number was identified as the "Lisbon Sequence." For the 1974 greatly revised revival of *Candide*, Stephen Sondheim wrote an alternate lyric that made the song more farcical and, consequently, easier to laugh at, and titled it "Auto Da Fe."

"Autumn in New York" is the famous paean to love and New York City by Vernon Duke, one of his few songs for which he wrote both the music and the lyric. It was written for the revue *Thumbs Up!* (1934) as the finale with J. Harold Murray singing the number in front of a series of shifting screens depicting scenes of Manhattan. Like Duke's earlier "April in Paris," the ballad received little attention at first, and it was not until years later that a recording by Louella Hogan launched the song's popularity. Duke's music is smooth and, as James R. Morris stated, "rhythmically free, almost conversational in tone." Sarah Vaughan's 1956 recording is perhaps the finest of the many made over the years.

"Avalon" is a melodramatic ballad that Al Jolson interpolated into the score of *Sinbad* (1918) after opening night. Vincent Rose (music) and B.G. DeSylva and Jolson himself (lyric) wrote the song about the memory of a love affair on Santa Catalina island. The melody was close enough to the aria "E lucevan le stelle" in *Tosca* that Giacomo Puccini sued the songwriters and won $25,000. The song appeared in three films and was often recorded, most memorably by Nat "King" Cole in 1959 (with Count Basie's Orchestra) and by his daughter Natalie Cole in 1991.

"Away From You" is Richard Rodgers' last memorable song, a soaring ballad written for the short-lived *Rex* (1976). Sheldon Harnick provided the tantalizing lyric for this duet sung by King Henry VIII (Nicol Williamson) and Anne Boleyn (Penny Fuller). The song was recorded by Sarah Brightman in 1989.

"A-Weaving" is the sentimental ballad that singer Charlotte Sweet (Mara Beckerman) sings in her music-hall debut in the Off-Broadway mock-Victorian musical *Charlotte Sweet* (1982). Gerald Jay Markoe (music) and Michael Colby (lyric) wrote the high-pitched pastiche number about a girl, a weaver by trade, who languishes and dies as she looms away. A similar Victorian spoof, with an equally dire tale to tell, was Bock and Harnick's earlier "Artificial Flowers" from *Tenderloin* (1960).

B

"The Babbitt and the Bromide" is a unique comic song from the Gershwins' *Funny Face* (1927) that stopped the show each night. The number is a patter song set to George Gershwin's polka melody in which two stuffy gentlemen, played by Adele and Fred Astaire, have a series of stiff-upper-lip conversations filled with nothing but clichés. When they meet again in heaven, their conversation remains unchanged. At the end of the number the Astaires did their famous "run-around dance," a circular movement that got larger and larger until they danced out of sight. Ira Gershwin considered his lyric for this song to be among the best of the hundreds that he penned during his career.

"Babes in Arms" is the driving title song of the 1937 musical by Richard Rodgers (music) and Lorenz Hart (lyric). This fervent march was sung by a very young Alfred Drake, Mitzi Green, Ray Heatherton and all the gang of kids who want to put on the big show.

"Babes in the Wood" is a plaintive ballad that became the hit song of *Very Good Eddie* (1915) by Jerome Kern (music) and Schuyler Greene (lyric). Eddie Kettle (Ernest Truex) is on his honeymoon but gets separated from his bride. When he and the newlywed Elsie Darling (Alice Dovey), who has also misplaced her spouse, find themselves comforting each other in a thunderstorm, they promise to be "twice as good" as the "babes in the wood" in this charming song that became quite popular in its day.

"Babette" is a clever character song from *On the Twentieth Century* (1978) by Cy Coleman (music) and Betty Comden and Adolph Green (lyric). Movie star Lily Garland (Madeline Kahn) cannot decide whether to appear in the new drawing-room play *Babette* or in the religious pageant *The Passion of Mary Magdalene*. She starts to enact one play, then moves to the other, until the two radically different pieces start to blend together in musical and dramatic chaos.

"Baby, Dream Your Dream" is a pleasing duet from *Sweet Charity* (1966) that urges one to pursue one's heart's desire, but do it with caution. Cy Coleman (music) and Dorothy Fields (lyric) wrote the waggish number, and it was sung by Charity Hope Valentine's dance hall chums Nickie (Helen Gallagher) and Helene (Thelma Oliver).

"Baby, Talk to Me" is the adoring ballad for the adult couple in the youth-oriented *Bye Bye Birdie* (1960) by Charles Strouse (music) and Lee Adams (lyric). Dick Van Dyke, as rock and roll singer Conrad Birdie's manager Albert, sang the alluring song on the telephone, backed up by a male quartet, to his secretary Rose (Chita Rivera) after they had had a lovers' quarrel and she had left him for a bunch of Shriners.

"The Babylove Miracle Show" is the title of a thrilling extended musical sequence from *The Grass Harp* (1971) that takes the form of a revival. The flamboyant lady evangelist Babylove (Karen Morrow) sings the song series with Dolly (Barbara Cook), Collin (Russ Thacker), Catherine (Carol Brice) and the company, covering everything from faith healing to romantic advice and ending with everyone singing a song called "I Believe in Babylove." Claibe Richardson composed the intoxicating music, and Kenward Elmslie wrote the vibrant lyric.

"Bali Ha'i" is the most exotic musical number from *South Pacific* (1949) and one of the most hypnotic of all Richard Rodgers (music) and Oscar Hammerstein (lyric) songs. The Polynesian black marketeer Bloody Mary (Juanita Hall) sings the enchanting ballad to convince Lieutenant Cable (William Tabbert) to go to the nearby island called Bali Ha'i so she can get fresh provisions for her business. Yet what starts out as a con job turns into one of the American theatre's most hauntingly beautiful songs. It is said that Hammerstein brought the lyric to Rodgers at the dinner table, and before the meal was finished the melody was completed. The music conjures up an Asian flavor by holding on to a dissonant note before mounting upward to resolve the musical phrase. There is also a rippling effect in the accompaniment that suggests ocean waves lapping onto the island's beaches. As for Hammerstein's lyric, it is simple, restrained and evocative; using Bloody Mary's limited English, he managed to create a poetic marvel. Perry Como had a best-selling recording of the oft-recorded number. "Bali Ha'i" is the standard by which all dreamy place-ballads are judged.

"Ballad for Americans" is a stirring song of patriotism from the revue *Sing for Your Supper* (1939) that was a morale builder during World War Two.

Earl Robinson (music) and John Latouche (lyric) wrote the cantata as "The Ballad of Uncle Sam" for the show, where it was sung by Gordon Clarke and the ensemble as the finale. With a title change it was soon recorded by Paul Robeson, Bing Crosby and others and it became very popular. Robinson's music is quietly hymnlike but powerful, and Latouche's lyric offers hope for the future as it extols the richness and diversity of the people that make up America.

"The Ballad of Booth" is a dynamic musical scene from the Stephen Sondheim Off-Broadway musical *Assassins* (1991). The Balladeer (Patrick Cassidy) sings the tale of John Wilkes Booth (Victor Garber) with acute comments that review the famous assassin's actions much as a critic would review a performance. The scene then reveals the wounded Booth with co-conspirator David Herold (Marcus Olson), and as the army surrounds them, the impassioned Booth dictates his fiery accusations about Lincoln to the frightened Herold. Sondheim uses traditional folk music and balladlike storytelling techniques, but the effect is a powerful contemporary theatre piece.

"The Ballad of Guiteau" is a farcical number from *Assassins* (1991) that is filled with ironic enthusiasm. Charles Guiteau (Jonathan Hadary) is about to be executed for the assassination of President James Garfield, but he does a lively cakewalk song and dance proclaiming his righteousness and praising the Lord, whom he is about to meet face to face. The Balladeer (Patrick Cassidy) sings the story of Guiteau's crime and trial while the happy convict interrupts him by singing and dancing up and down the steps to the gallows. Stephen Sondheim wrote the amusing and insidious number using nineteenth-century-style music and a lyric based on the real Guiteau's writings.

"The Ballad of Sweeney Todd" is the chilling narrative ballad that frames Stephen Sondheim's *Sweeney Todd, the Demon Barber of Fleet Street* (1979). The song, sung by the ensemble at the top, at the end and at points throughout the musical, tells the story of the murderous barber and also comments on the events. This recurring song is the most Kurt Weill-like number in the very Brechtian show, and Sondheim even uses sections of Gregorian chant and themes from the Latin Mass for the Dead to give his story a dark, gothic quality.

"Bambalina" is the unlikely hit song from the early Vincent Youmans effort *Wildflower* (1923). The number is a sort of musical chairs in song: it tells the story of an old fiddler named Bambalina who played for country dances but would occasionally stop abruptly to upset the dancing folk. The fiery heiress Nina Benedetto (Edith Day) sang the perky tune with the chorus girls, and they danced a step they called the Bambalina. Youmans wrote the lively music, and Otto Harbach and a young Oscar Hammerstein provided the narrative lyric.

"Bandana Days" is the festive ensemble number from the landmark black musical *Shuffle Along* (1921) by Eubie Blake (music) and Noble Sissle (lyric). Arthur Porter led the chorus in this nostalgic song, which longed for the old plantation days in the South, with a lusty subtext. Blake recorded the song in 1921.

"Bang!" is an animated duet that Stephen Sondheim wrote for *A Little Night Music* (1973), but it was cut before opening. The number is a crafty battle of wits between a man and a woman in which images of sex and war are interchanged; sexual love becomes a military skirmish and both parties end in satiated defeat . The song was later heard in the Off-Broadway revue *Marry Me a Little* (1981), where it was sung by Suzanne Henry and Craig Lucas, and in the revue *Putting It Together* (1993), where Rachel York and Michael Rupert sang it.

"Barcelona" is a complete musical scene from the landmark musical *Company* (1970) by Stephen Sondheim. After a night of energetic lovemaking, the bachelor Robert (Dean Jones) awakes to find his one-night stand, the airline stewardess April (Susan Browning), getting ready to leave for her flight to Barcelona. Robert halfheartedly asks her to stay and tries to say endearing things to her even though he can't recall her name correctly. April considers staying, and the wry duet concludes with her accepting his false affections; then he despairs at playing this foolish game too well. Joanne Gordon has pointed out the Pinteresque quality of Sondheim's dialogue/lyric in this song, and the humorously piquant nature of the number is reminiscent of Harold Pinter's comic plays.

"Barnum and Bailey Rag" is a lively tribute to the circus team but also to the up-and-coming master of rag tunes, Irving Berlin. George M. Cohan wrote the snappy number for his revue *Hello, Broadway!* (1914), where the ensemble sang it as the rousing Act One finale. Cohan's lyric work is particularly clever as he comes up with rapid patter phrases to create a ragging rhythm. In the bio-musical *George M!* (1968) the song was sung by the company as part of the epilogue.

"The Baseball Game" is a delicious musical scene from the Off-Broadway *Falsettoland* (1990) in which all seven of the musical's characters end up at a Little League game. Jason (Danny Gerard) and other Jewish boys "who cannot play baseball" are playing the game as his mother Trina (Faith Prince) and stepfather Mendel (Chip Zien) watch eagerly. Also there are his father Marvin (Michael Rupert) and two lesbian neighbors (Heather MacRae and Janet Metz); then Marvin's ex-lover Whizzer (Stephen Bogardus) unexpectedly shows up to urge Jason on.   William Finn wrote the animated music and quick-witted lyric in which several conversations and private thoughts overlap to hysterical and revealing effect.

"Baubles, Bangles and Beads" is the atmospheric hit ballad from the *Arabian Nights* musical *Kismet* (1953) that used themes by Alexander Borodin for its score. The poet's daughter Marsinah (Doretta Morrow) visits the bazaar in ancient Baghdad and sings this beguiling list song about all the finery she sees there. Robert Wright and George Forrest wrote the lyric and adapted a movement from Borodin's String Quartet in D into a lovely theatre number. The song became very popular, due mostly to a best-selling Peggy Lee recording, but successful records were also made by the Kirby Stone Four, Julie Andrews and a distinctive jazz version by Jonah Jones.

"Be a Lion" is the enthralling song Dorothy (Stephanie Mills) sings to the Cowardly Lion (Ted Ross) to encourage him to be brave and journey with her to see *The Wiz* (1975). Charlie Smalls wrote the captivating duet, which was more in the Broadway ballad style than most of the rock/soul score.

"Be a Performer!" is an animated song from *Little Me* (1962) by Cy Coleman (music) and Carolyn Leigh (lyric) that mixes show biz and public justice. Vaudeville bookers Bernie and Bennie Bucksbaum (Joey Faye and Mort Marshall) try to convince Belle Poitrine (Virginia Martin), who is on trial for murder, to cash in on her notoriety and go on their vaudeville circuit.

"Be a Santa" is a snappy number from *Subways Are for Sleeping* (1961) by Jule Styne (music) and Betty Comden and Adolph Green (lyric). Unemployed Tom Bailey (Sydney Chaplin) gets a seasonal job as a street-corner Santa Claus, and he and the chorus sing about the fragile person inside the jolly costume.

"Be Italian" is a zesty tarantella from *Nine* (1982) in which the seasoned prostitute Sarraghina (Kathi Moss) gives her advice to all would-be lovers: act like an Italian. In a flashback sequence the filmmaker Guido Contini (Raul Julia) recalls when he was a young boy (Cameron Johann) and he and three of his friends (Jadrien Steele, Patrick Wilcox and Christopher Evans Allen) went to a secluded beach where Sarraghina told them about lovemaking. The five of them join in a merry quintet with lively music and a robust lyric by Maury Yeston.

"Be Kind to Your Parents" is a touching duet from the operatic *Fanny* (1954) by Harold Rome. Fanny (Florence Henderson) sings the gentle song to her twelve-year-old son Cesario (Lloyd Reese), who longs to go off to sea just as his biological father once did.

"Be Like the Bluebird" is a comic ditty sung by Moon-Face Martin,

Public Enemy Number Thirteen, in Cole Porter's *Anything Goes* (1934). Comedian Victor Moore introduced this song of idiotic optimism, which teaches one to tweet like a bird when disaster strikes. Porter himself recorded the song in 1935.

"Be on Your Own" is a surging song of farewell from *Nine* (1982) by Maury Yeston. Luisa (Karen Akers) is weary of her husband Guido (Raul Julia) and his many extramarital affairs, so she sets him free in this stinging song of anger and regret.

"The Bear, the Tiger, the Hamster and the Mole" is a comic song about male and female relationships in the other species. It was written by David Shire (music) and Richard Maltby, Jr., (lyric) for an unmarried biology teacher in *Baby* (1983) who considers raising a child alone; but the character and the song were cut. The number was later heard in the Off-Broadway revue *Closer Than Ever* (1989), where it was sung by Lynne Wintersteller.

"The Beast in You" is a sparkling character song from *Goldilocks* (1958) with music by Leroy Anderson and lyric by Joan Ford and Walter and Jean Kerr. Maggie Harris (Elaine Stritch) sings the riotous song to her fiancé George Randolph Brown (Russell Nype) about how he always takes the side of everyone else but her, never letting the beast in him out to defend her.

"A Beat Behind" is an inventive song and dance routine from *The Goodbye Girl* (1993) by Marvin Hamlisch (music) and David Zippel (lyric). The out-of-shape dancer Paula (Bernadette Peters) starts taking dance classes again but finds that all the other students seem so much younger and that she's always a beat behind them and the music. Paula sings of her frustration while the instructor (Scott Wise) and the other hoofers comment on the rigors of being a dancer on Broadway today.

"Beat Out Dat Rhythm on a Drum" is the Americanized version of the famous "Gypsy Song" from Georges Bizet's opera *Carmen* as heard in the Broadway musical *Carmen Jones* (1943). At Billy Pastor's cafe, Frankie (June Hawkins) urges the dance band's drummer to join her in the captivating number, beating out only the rhythm because she says she doesn't need any tune to dance. Oscar Hammerstein wrote the exhilarating lyric set to Bizet's music.

"Beautiful Girls" is the melodic pastiche number from *Follies* (1971) that introduces the aging Weismann Girls as they descend the staircase at a Follies reunion. Stephen Sondheim wrote the lush version of Irving Berlin's "A Pretty Girl Is Like a Melody" that has a double-edged lyric hyperbolizing the now-faded chorus of women. The song was sung by the old tenor Roscoe (Michael Bartlett) and the ensemble.

"Beauty School Dropout" is the comic highlight of the popular 1950s musical *Grease* (1972). The number is an outrageous dream sequence in which Frenchy (Marya Small) imagines a guardian angel called Teen Angel (Alan Paul) appearing and advising her what to do since she flunked out of beauty school. The Jim Jacobs and Warren Casey song was made even funnier by the appearance of a chorus of angels, dressed in plastic sheets and with their hair done up in giant plastic rollers, who doo-wahed in the background.

"Because, Because" is a catchy chorus number from *Of Thee I Sing* (1931) sung by the photographers as they snap pictures of the beautiful contestants for the job of First Lady of the land. While the girls flaunt the dimples on their knees, the shutterbugs assure them that each and every one of them has won their heart even though only one will win the prize. Later in the show the gold digger Diana Deveraux (Grace Brinkley) reprises the number with an altered lyric, explaining how her heart was broken by President John P. Wintergreen. George Gershwin wrote the vamplike music that ingeniously repeats the same musical phrase, and Ira Gershwin provided the facetious lyric.

"Because You're You" is a ballad from the comic operetta *The Red Mill* (1906) that the Governor of Zeeland (Neal McCay) sings to woo the young Bertha (Aline Crater), even though he is engaged to another. Victor Herbert composed the lovely music, and Henry Blossom wrote the seductive lyric. Gordon MacRae made an expert recording of the song.

"Been a Long Day" is a musical scene from *How to Succeed in Business Without Really Trying* (1961) rather than a traditional show song. Frank Loesser wrote the satiric music and lyric that examined the thoughts of six characters at the end of a day at the office. While waiting for the elevator, Finch (Robert Morse) and Rosemary (Bonnie Scott) reveal their desires and fears to the audience as Smitty (Claudette Sutherland) facilitates the conversation by prompting the young couple. A bit later J.B. Biggley (Rudy Vallee) and Hedy La Rue (Virginia Martin) wait for the same elevator as the conniving Frump (Charles Nelson Reilly) subtly blackmails them into giving him a promotion. Loesser, in his musical notation, wittily labeled the number a "trio for mezzo, pezzo and futz."

"Before I Gaze at You Again" is a delicate ballad from *Camelot* (1960) by Alan Jay Lerner (lyric) and Frederick Loewe (music) that was added at the last minute to help clarify a character's position in the love triangle. Queen Guenevere (Julie Andrews) is beginning to secretly fall in love with Lancelot. Alone before his investiture ceremony, she sings this winsome solo hoping that Lancelot will go away so that she can try to forget him.

"Before I Kiss the World Goodbye" is an agreeable song of determination from the unsuccessful *Jennie* (1963), the last musical scored by Howard Dietz (lyrics) and Arthur Schwartz (music). Mary Martin, as a Laurette Taylor-like actress at the turn of the century, sang the number at the close of each act, vowing not to retire but to continue on and live life to the fullest.

"Before I Met You" is a playful duet from the Princess Theatre musical *Oh, Lady! Lady!!* (1918) by Jerome Kern (music) and P.G. Wodehouse (lyric). Sweethearts Mollie (Vivienne Segal) and Bill (Carl Randall) sang the lively two-step number in which each confesses to the other that they had previous loves: she had a childhood crush on actor John Drew, and he in his youth was infatuated with singer Lillian Russell.

"Before the Parade Passes By" never got nearly as popular as the title number from *Hello, Dolly!* (1964), but it was this song that best encapsulated the theme and spirit of the musical. Dolly Levi (Carol Channing) sings it at the end of the first act when she decides to marry Horace Vandergelder and re-enter the world of the living. The song then escalates into a chorus number with a parade that Dolly literally does not let pass by without her joining it. It is probably the finest song in the Jerry Herman score, yet the number has often been attributed to others. The songwriting team of Charles Strouse and Lee Adams was summoned by producer David Merrick when *Hello, Dolly!* was in trouble out of town. The team recommended that a number be added for Dolly to sing at the crucial decision moment, and Bob Merrill, another songwriter summoned by Merrick, suggested the title. But it was Herman who wrote the song, and it always remained one of his favorites. Chita Rivera sang the number in the Broadway revue *Jerry's Girls* (1985).

"The Begat" is a satirical gospel number from *Finian's Rainbow* (1947) about the population explosion. The bigoted Senator Billboard Rawkins (Robert Pitkin), who has been turned into a black man by the magic of a leprechaun's pot of gold, wanders the roads of Missitucky, the victim of his own segregation laws. He meets up with three Passion Pilgrim Gospellers (Lorenzo Fuller, Jerry Laws and Lewis Sharp), a foursome whose baritone member has run off with a woman, and joins them in singing this merry blues quartet. The comic number is a list song that traces procreation from Adam up to folks in Scranton, Pennsylvania, and, in Cole Porter fashion, has fun with double entendres throughout. E.Y. Harburg wrote the ingenious lyric, and Burton Lane composed the Broadwayized spiritual.

"Begin the Beguine" is one of the most bewitching of all theatre songs and a unique piece even by Cole Porter's high standards. He claimed to have gotten its tribal-like musical accompaniment from a war dance he heard in the

Indonesian islands during a world cruise with writer Moss Hart. Later Porter said he got the "beguine" dance from Martinique natives performing in a Parisian dance hall. One thing is certain: it was first sung by June Knight as a renowned dancer in *Jubilee* (1935) and then danced by her and Charles Walters. In 1972 musicologist Alec Wilder declared "Begin the Beguine" to be the longest popular song ever written (108 measures), and the record still stands. But its length is only part of its singularity. The ballad has no verse and drives ahead without benefit of a distinct stanza or a clear-cut release that relieves the surging melody. It is also one of the most difficult Cole Porter songs to sing, a situation that kept it from gaining widespread popularity at first. Xavier Cugat made the first recording, but it was not until Artie Shaw's swing version in 1938 that the song achieved the fame it deserved. Eddy Heywood and His Orchestra had a hit recording of "Begin the Beguine" in 1944 that sold over a million copies.

"Being Alive" is the penetrating ballad that climaxes the landmark musical *Company* (1970) by Stephen Sondheim. The bachelor Robert (Dean Jones) finally realizes that waiting for the perfect girl and the perfect marriage is futile and reconciles with himself that to be truly alive one must share one's life with someone. The song was the third one that Sondheim had written for the important self-recognition scene. "Marry Me a Little" was deemed too inconsequential for the moment, and "Happily Ever After" was found to be too negative. "Being Alive" was a compromise of sorts, but it is still a powerful, captivating number and works very well for the character and the show. David Kernan, Julia McKenzie and Millicent Martin sang the song in the Broadway revue *Side by Side by Sondheim* (1977), and in the Off-Broadway revue *Putting It Together* (1993) it was sung by Stephen Collins, Michael Rupert, Julie Andrews and Rachel York.

"Being Good (Isn't Good Enough)" is a soaring ballad from *Hallelujah, Baby!* (1967) by Jule Styne (music) and Betty Comden and Adolph Green (lyric). Georgina (Leslie Uggams) wants to make it in show business, but being black means that talent is not enough in order to succeed. Sally Mayes made a memorable recording of the song in 1994.

"Belly Up to the Bar, Boys" is the impelling drinking song from *The Unsinkable Molly Brown* (1960) by Meredith Willson. Out to seek her fortune, Molly (Tammy Grimes) gets a job as a singer at the Saddle Rock Saloon, where her entire repertoire consists of this one song. She was aided in the lively number by the bartender Christmas Morgan (Joseph Sirola) and the Colorado miners. A curious novelty recording of the song was made in 1960 by the Guy Lombardo Orchestra with bandleaders Stan Kenton, Billy May and Nelson Riddle singing the lyrics.

"Bess, You Is My Woman Now" is the rhapsodic duet from the folk opera *Porgy and Bess* (1935) and one of the most moving love songs in the American theatre. The crippled Porgy (Todd Duncan) and the scarlet woman Bess (Anne Brown) sing the passionate number after Bess's lover Crown runs off and Porgy now claims her as his own. George Gershwin's music is a complex mixture of blues and operatic bravado, while the lyric by Ira Gershwin and DuBose Heyward is simple, colloquial and highly poetic in its primitive imagery. Duncan and Brown recorded the duet in 1940, and many other recordings by opera singers have been made over the years. Distinctly different is a 1976 recording of "Bess, You Is My Woman Now" by Ray Charles and Cleo Laine.

"The Best of All Possible Worlds" is the musical credo of the venerable philosopher Dr. Pangloss in *Candide* (1956) with music by Leonard Bernstein. In the original production Pangloss (Max Adrian) sang a lyric by John Latouche in which he instructed the about-to-be-wed couple Candide and Cunegonde that everything that happens in the world is for a good reason. In the 1974 revised version Stephen Sondheim provided a new lyric, and the scene was changed to a private classroom where Pangloss (Lewis J. Stadlen) taught a similar lesson to his young pupils Candide, Cunegonde, Maximilian and Paquette. In both versions Bernstein's vibrant music makes for a flavorful number in the operetta mode.

"The Best of Times" is the snappy, insistently hummable song from Jerry Herman's *La Cage aux Folles* (1983). The song is a nightclub number in which the female impersonator Albin (George Hearn) and his old friend Jacqueline (Elizabeth Parrish) lead the ensemble in celebrating the moment. The song is similar to Herman's earlier "It's Today" from *Mame* (1966).

"The Best Thing for You (Would Be Me)" is a pleasing romantic duet from Irving Berlin's *Call Me Madam* (1950). Ethel Merman, as American ambassador Sally Adams, sang the number with Paul Lukas, as Foreign Minister Cosmo, as they find themselves in a mature romance.

"The Best Thing of All" is the materialistic credo of the greedy title character in the operatic *Regina* (1949), the musicalization of Lillian Hellman's drama *The Little Foxes*. The wheeler-dealer Regina Giddens (Jane Pickens) sings the pungent aria written by Marc Blitzstein in which she states that to want and to take is the best thing of all.

"The Best Things in Life Are Free" is the engaging optimistic ballad by B.G. DeSylva and Lew Brown (lyric) and Ray Henderson (music) that was introduced in *Good News!* (1927). At Tait College, football hero Tom

Marlowe (John Price Jones) tries to encourage his low-born but high-IQ tutor Connie Laine (Mary Lawlor) that money is not everything. For a pie-in-the-sky kind of song, "The Best Things in Life Are Free" is rather poignant and can be sung sincerely as well as cheerfully. The song was an immediate hit and enjoyed newfound popularity during the Depression years.

"Bewitched, (Bothered and Bewildered)" eventually became the most famous song from Rodgers and Hart's *Pal Joey* (1940), but its success was a long time in coming. The song was introduced by Vivienne Segal as the lady-about-town Vera Simpson as she wakes up from a night of sex and booze with her gigolo Joey Evans (Gene Kelly). Richard Rodgers' music is appropriately languid, and Lorenz Hart's lyric is perhaps the most cynical and jaded he ever wrote. Unlike Cole Porter's naughty, sly approach to sex, Hart's lyrics are hardened and coarse in "Bewitched, Bothered and Bewildered," as the song is often titled. Even with some expurgated lyric changes, the song didn't get radio play because of a fight being waged at the time between ASCAP (the American Society of Composers, Authors and Publishers) and the broadcast stations. The song first became popular in France in the 1940s and entered the mainstream of American song by the end of the decade, becoming a "Your Hit Parade" champ in the 1950s. Pianist Bill Snyder and His Orchestra made a recording of "Bewitched" in 1950 that sold over a million copies, and over the years there have been memorable recordings by Sarah Vaughan, Ella Fitzgerald, Julie Andrews, Lena Horne, Barbra Streisand, Doris Day, Karen Akers, Linda Ronstadt and Carly Simon.

"Bidin' My Time" is a lethargic quartet from the Gershwins' *Girl Crazy* (1930) written in a lazy hillbilly style. The number was sung by four idle cowboys (Marshall Smith, Ray Johnson, Del Porter and Dwight Snyder) who also performed the song on a harmonica, Jew's harp, ocarina and tin flute. George Gershwin wrote the laid-back melody, and Ira Gershwin provided the meandering lyric that manages to mention "Tip Toe Through the Tulips," "Singin' in the Rain" and half a dozen other popular standards of the day. In the revised version of *Girl Crazy* called *Crazy for You* (1992), the number was sung by the Manhattan Rhythm Kings (Brian M. Nalepka, Tripp Hanson and Hal Shane) and the men's ensemble.

"The Big Back Yard" is an exciting march Sigmund Romberg wrote for *Up in Central Park* (1945) that was reminiscent of his old operetta numbers from the 1920s. The composer came out of semiretirement to write the music for Dorothy Fields's lyrics in this musical about corruption in 1870s New York City. The rousing paean to Central Park was sung by the muckraking journalist John Matthews (Wilbur Evans) and the chorus.

"The Big Black Giant" is an odd but interesting number from *Me and Juliet* (1953) that looks at the theatre audience from the actor's point of view. Bill Hayes, as the assistant stage manager of the show-within-the-show, sang the Richard Rodgers (music) and Oscar Hammerstein (lyric) song that describes a theatre audience as the sometimes weeping, sometimes laughing, sometimes coughing "giant" that always seems to be basically the same despite its fluctuating moods.

"Big 'D' " is the energetic musical tribute to Dallas, Texas, from Frank Loesser's *The Most Happy Fella* (1956). Herman (Shorty Long) and Cleo (Susan Johnson), two transplanted Texans who meet in California's Napa Valley, recognize each other immediately by their accent and jump into the zestful western song with the chorus joining in.

"Big Spender" is the deadpan seduction song sung by the lethargic dance-hall hostesses in *Sweet Charity* (1966) by Cy Coleman (music) and Dorothy Fields (lyric). Nickie (Helen Gallagher) and Helene (Thelma Oliver) led the jaded girls of the Fan-Dango Ballroom in this monotone bump-and-grind invitation to dance for a fee and director-choreographer Bob Fosse staged the number in a sexy and satirical fashion. Peggy Lee had a hit recording of "Big Spender" in 1966.

"Bigger Isn't Better" is a dandy "I am" song for the twenty-five-inch General Tom Thumb (Leonard John Crofoot) in *Barnum* (1980) by Cy Coleman (music) and Michael Stewart (lyric). As P.T. Barnum's newest attraction, Tom sings this fun list song recounting all of the small people and creatures throughout history who made quite a big impact. In Joe Layton's clever staging of the original production, little Tom was joined at the end of the song by Jumbo, the world's largest elephant; but in David Mitchell's ingenious scenic design, all that could be seen was the bottom half of Jumbo's four feet.

"The Bilbao Song" is a zesty drinking song that was written in 1929, became a hit in the 1960s and was not heard on Broadway until 1977. Kurt Weill (music) and Bertolt Brecht (lyric) wrote the number for their gangster satire *Happy End*, which was produced in Berlin in 1929. Lotte Lenya recorded it in the 1950s, and in 1961, with an English lyric by Johnny Mercer, it was a hit record for Andy Williams. Hal Watters and Jerry Lanning sang a Michael Feingold version of the song in the Off-Broadway revue *Berlin to Broadway With Kurt Weill* in 1972, and finally *Happy End* was produced on Broadway in 1977 (with the Feingold lyrics). In the musical, Bill Cracker (Bob Gunton) sings to his henchmen in his Chicago speakeasy about the good old days when he ran a gin joint in Bilbao. As they all join in, Bill keeps forgetting the words they used to sing and mumbles his way through passages while the orchestra continues on.

"Bill" is one of the musical theatre's finest torch songs and contains the most famous lyric by P.G. Wodehouse. He wrote the song with composer Jerome Kern for the Princess Theatre musical *Oh, Lady! Lady!!* (1918), where the engaged Mollie (Vivienne Segal) sang it to her mother to explain her affection for Willoughby Finch, nicknamed Bill. The song was cut before opening for various reasons: it was too slow for its Act One position, Segal's voice didn't seem right for it, and Carl Randall, who played Bill, was so dashing and likable a man that the song didn't make much sense. Kern and Wodehouse held onto the song and gave it to Marilyn Miller to sing in *Sally* (1920), but again the number didn't work and was cut. "Bill" was finally heard on Broadway, in a slightly revised form, in Kern and Oscar Hammerstein's *Show Boat* (1927), where Helen Morgan, as the dissipated Julie, sang it in a Chicago nightclub as she perched on an upright piano and made both the song and herself famous. The number remained her trademark throughout her career. Kern's melody for "Bill" is leisurely and reflective so it is Wodehouse's lyric that gives the song its punch. The tone is not maudlin or morose, as torch songs traditionally were, but rather self-aware with even a touch of self-mockery. Julie describes the weaknesses of Bill with half a smile, then concludes with the famous pause before the phrase "I don't know" that leads into "because he's just my Bill." Wodehouse took the model for the old lament song and broke it, writing the first conversational torch song. Although "Bill" was listed in the opening-night program of *Show Boat* as having a lyric by Wodehouse, most accredited the authorship to Hammerstein, who wrote the rest of the score's lyrics and who made only minor changes in the original "Bill" lyric. Hammerstein took great pains on several occasions to point out that Wodehouse was the true lyricist and even took out a newspaper ad once to clarify the point.

"Billie" is the infectious title song from the 1928 musical by George M. Cohan that would be his last Broadway score. Billie (Polly Walker), a secretary at a chewing-gum factory, sings the waltzing number that describes how she loves her name even though it was given to her by her parents, who expected a boy. Jill O'Hara sang the charming song in the bio-musical *George M!* (1968).

"Bird Upon the Tree" is a captivating duet from the operatic *Juno* (1959), Marc Blitzstein's musicalization of Sean O'Casey's *Juno and the Paycock* (1924). Juno Boyle (Shirley Booth) and her daughter Mary (Monte Amundsen) see the stalwart women of Ireland, rather than the bragging men, as the salvation of their land and sing this allegorical song about a bird caught in a nest, then set free by a violent storm.

"The Birth of the Blues" is the popular B.G. DeSylva and Lew Brown (lyric) and Ray Henderson (music) standard that was the centerpiece of the first-act finale of *George White's Scandals* (1926), one of the most memorable production numbers of the era. On a staircase leading to heaven's gate sat a chorus of angels witnessing a battle between the blues and classical music while the American blues form tried to enter paradise. Representing the classics were the Fairbanks Twins symbolizing Schubert and Schumann, Willie Howard as Beethoven and Eugene Howard as Liszt. On the other team were the McCarthy Sisters personifying "The Memphis Blues" and "St. Louis Blues." Harry Richman sang "The Birth of the Blues," with its unforgettable images of a breeze creating melody and the wail from a prison becoming the blue note that would distinguish the new form. As part of the blues argument, a section of George Gershwin's "Rhapsody in Blue" was sung as a lyric song. The production number climaxed as the blues were accepted and the pearly gates opened on the final thrilling notes of the song. The years since have proven that "The Birth of the Blues" needs no such spectacle to be a powerful, evocative song.

"Black and Blue" is the haunting, disturbing ballad by Thomas "Fats" Waller and Harry Brooks (music) and Andy Razaf (lyric) that was first heard in the revue *Hot Chocolates* (1929). Quite unusual for a popular song, the number is a lament and a protest song. When sung with the verse, the number is a lovelorn torch song sung by a dark-skinned black woman who has been rejected because her man prefers lighter-skinned women. But "Black and Blue" is usually performed without the verse, and the song becomes one about general racial injustice. Razaf's lyrics, which play on the various meanings of "black" and "blue," are restrained yet powerful. The music by Waller and Brooks is old-fashioned and melodic in the verse and then moves into a blues format for the famous refrain. Edith Wilson introduced the song in the revue and made a recording of it, verse and refrain both. Other memorable recordings were made by Louis Armstrong, Ethel Waters, Gene Krupa, Dinah Washington, Roy Eldridge and Frankie Laine. The song was sung by the five-member cast of the Broadway revue *Ain't Misbehavin'* (1978), and by Ruth Brown, Linda Hopkins, Carrie Smith, Jimmy Slyde and Bunny Briggs in the revue *Black and Blue* (1989).

"Black Bottom" is the song that launched a new dance step when dimple-kneed Ann Pennington and the chorus performed it in *George White's Scandals* (1926). B.G. DeSylva and Lew Brown (lyric) and Ray Henderson (music) wrote the song that described the dance supposedly from the mudlands of the South (the title refers to the muddy river bottom). The dance itself was a new variation of the Charleston devised by producer-director George White that required dragging one's foot as if in oozy mud.

"Blah, Blah, Blah" is a wry musical commentary on lyricwriting by the Gershwin brothers that took a half a century before it was heard on Broadway. George Gershwin's melody was used in songs cut from *East Is West* (1928) and

Show Girl (1929) before Ira Gershwin wrote the satirical lyric about the inanity of love songs that say nothing but are always sure to rhyme "moon" with "croon" and "month of May" with "clouds of gray." "Blah, Blah, Blah" was used in the 1931 film *Delicious* and was finally sung on Broadway in the "new Gershwin musical" *My One and Only* (1983) where it was performed by aviator Billy Buck Chandler (Tommy Tune).

"Blame It on the Summer Night" is an evocative ballad from the short-lived *Rags* (1986) by Charles Strouse (music) and Stephen Schwartz (lyric). New York immigrant Rebecca (Teresa Stratas) sings the bluesy number that has an ethnic flavor to it as she realizes she is falling in love with the labor organizer Saul. Karen Akers made a sparkling recording of the song in 1991.

"Blow, Gabriel, Blow" is a rousing revival number that may seem out of place in the ocean liner setting of *Anything Goes* (1934) even though a former evangelist (Ethel Merman) sang the number. But anything went in this Cole Porter musical, and the song stopped the show each evening. Merman's rendition of the number was unforgettable, and the song was associated with her thereafter.

"Blow High, Blow Low," the spirited sea chantey that Richard Rodgers (music) and Oscar Hammerstein (lyric) wrote for *Carousel* (1945), is the villain Jigger Craigin's colorful but bitter commentary about a sailor's life and how he is never totally understood on land. Murvyn Vye and the male chorus introduced the foot-stomping number, which is a less optimistic companion to the show's previous song "June Is Bustin' Out All Over."

"Blue, Blue, Blue" is the silly Act Two opening number from the short-lived *Let 'Em Eat Cake* (1932) by George Gershwin (music) and Ira Gershwin (lyric). The song was sung by the presidential staff who are repainting the White House blue, the color of heaven, they state. The title also refers to the fascist "Blue Shirts" that are taking over in this highly satiric musical. Musicologist Alec Wilder pointed out that the music is very puzzling, "like no song I've ever heard." Gershwin uses a monotonous series of repeated notes while the piano part moves into a concerto form. "Blue, Blue, Blue" was not recorded until 1987, when virtually the whole score was reconstructed by the Brooklyn Academy of Music.

"The Blue Room" is an early Rodgers and Hart love song and one of their best. It was sung in *The Girl Friend* (1926) by Sammy White and Eva Puck as lovers who pictured their little home once they are wed and the blue room that will be their secluded hideaway from the rest of the world. Lorenz Hart provided the lively lyric that rhymes "trousseau" with "Robinson Crusoe," and Richard

Rodgers wrote a superb melody that keeps returning to the same two notes even as it builds its theme with their surrounding notes.

"Blue Skies" is the perennial song favorite by Irving Berlin in which the lyric explores the various implications of the word "blue," from a color to a bird to a feeling. The verse starts in a minor key to give it a bluesy tone, then shifts to a major key as the singer welcomes the optimistic title image. Berlin wrote the song for Belle Baker, who was about to open in Rodgers and Hart's *Betsy* (1926) but had no satisfactory solo. She brought the song to producer Florenz Ziegfeld, who quickly interpolated the number despite his agreement with the songwriting team. The song caused such an uproar on opening night that Baker was forced to sing twenty-four encores. "Blue Skies" immediately became a best-seller, with recordings by Al Jolson and many others, and it has always been a favorite of jazz musicians because the music lends itself well to improvisation. Willie Nelson's recording of the song sold over a million copies.

"Bobby and Jackie and Jack" is the cunning pastiche number from *Merrily We Roll Along* (1981) for which Stephen Sondheim wrote this revue song in the style of an early 1960s Off-Broadway showcase. The subject of the song is the newly elected John Kennedy, and the number mocks the new presidential family with a lighthearted affection that was typical of the period. Because we all know the sad fate of these three famous people, the song has an uncomfortable subtext that is not accidental. The Irish-flavored comic song was performed by Frank (Jim Walton), Charley (Lonny Price), Beth (Sally Klein) and Ted (David Loud).

"Body and Soul" is the jazzy, morose torch song by Johnny Green (music) and Edward Heyman, Robert Sour and Frank Eyton (lyric) that gained attention when it was interpolated into the revue *Three's a Crowd* (1930). The song was already popular in Europe, where producer Max Gordon heard it and added it to his Broadway revue. Libby Holman sang the masochistic number about the misery of being in love, and then Clifton Webb and Tamara Geva danced to the music. Green's distinctive musical line, which was both innovative and appealing, set the style for many other 1930s songs. Also of interest are the complex verse and release and the song's unusually wide range. Although there is nothing directly lewd about the song, the sensual effect of "Body and Soul" kept radio stations from playing it in the 1930s. Coleman Hawkins made a jazz recording of the song that is considered a classic in the field, and the number is one of the most popular choices by jazz improvisational soloists. There is also a surprisingly effective recording by Martha Raye made early in her career. In the Broadway revue *Black and Blue* (1989) the song was sung by Ruth Brown.

"Bon Voyage" is a larkish ensemble song from *Candide* (1956) that uses various operetta techniques to create a stylish and farcical production number. The Governor of Buenos Aires (William Olvis) has sold Candide (Robert Rounseville) a less-than-seaworthy ship to travel in to Europe. As everyone on shore watches the boat flounder and sink in the harbor, the Governor leads the chorus in a rousing and ironic farewell song. Leonard Bernstein wrote the lively music, and Richard Wilbur provided the mock-operatic lyric. Nicolai Gedda sang the number in the 1991 complete recording of the *Candide* score.

"Bongo on the Congo" is a delectable comic trio from *Sitting Pretty* (1924) by Jerome Kern (music) and P.G. Wodehouse (lyric) that stopped the show each night with so many encores that, as one critic wrote, it "threatened to ruin the audience." At a swank country home in New Jersey, Horace Peabody (Dwight Frye) and his jewel thief Uncle Jo (Frank McIntyre) sing to Judson Waters (Eugene Revere) about big-game hunting in an African country called Bongo set on the River Congo where a man with less than twenty-four wives is considered a bachelor. Music historian and conductor John McGlinn recorded the facetious number with Jason Graae, Paul V. Ames and Merwin Goldsmith in 1989.

"Book Report" is an entertaining quartet that makes up an entire musical scene in the "Peanuts" musical *You're a Good Man, Charlie Brown* (1967) by Clark Gesner. Assigned to write a book report of at least one hundred words on "Peter Rabbit," each of the four schoolchildren approaches the task in his or her characteristic way: Charlie Brown (Gary Burghoff) worries about when he should write the report, Linus (Bob Balaban) psychoanalyzes the animal characters' subtextual motivations, Lucy (Reva Rose) counts the words to determine how close she is to the minimum, and Schroeder (Skip Hinnant) can only keep his interest in the story by loosely comparing it to "Robin Hood."

"Boom-Boom" is a hilarious pastiche of a Maurice Chevalier number from the 1930s that Sid Caesar sang in *Little Me* (1962) by Cy Coleman (music) and Carolyn Leigh (lyric). At the Skylight Roof nightclub, the French entertainer Val du Val (Caesar) and the chorus girls sing the racy ditty where the repeated "boom-boom" is used for all kinds of double entendres. Later in the musical, when Belle Poitrine (Virginia Martin) is entertaining the doughboys in the trenches, she reprises the song, but the "boom-boom" means something quite different.

"Boom Ditty Boom" is a nonsense song performed by the ensemble in *70, Girls, 70* (1971), the raucous musical about old folks by John Kander (music) and Fred Ebb (lyric). The rhythmic number was used to denote the pulsating heartbeat of the retirement home and how the place is growing in wealth and comfort as the aged residents take to burglary to augment their meager pensions.

"Bosom Buddies" is Jerry Herman's most famous comic duet, a backbiting pledge of eternal friendship from *Mame* (1966). Old friends Mame Dennis (Angela Lansbury) and Vera Charles (Beatrice Arthur) sing the acerbic eleven o'clock number that never fails to please. Leslie Uggams and Chita Rivera sang the number in the Broadway revue *Jerry's Girls* (1985).

"The Boston Beguine" is a daffy comic number from the revue *New Faces of 1952* in which new face Alice Ghostly, as a frustrated Bostonian searching for true romance, laments her sorry plight in Bean Town. The music and lyric, both of which had fun spoofing Cole Porter's "Begin the Beguine," were by Sheldon Harnick in the days before he teamed up with Jerry Bock.

"Both Sides of the Coin" is a frenzied patter song in the style of Gilbert and Sullivan from *The Mystery of Edwin Drood* (1985) by Rupert Holmes. The tormented John Jasper (Howard McGillin) sings about his dual Dr. Jekyll and Mr. Hyde personality as the music-hall Chairman (George Rose) reflects about the duality of the actor and the character he plays. The two men join in a furious tongue-twisting patter that speeds up with each stanza.

"The Bowery" is the famous song that came from the early landmark musical comedy *A Trip to Chinatown* (1891) by Percy Gaunt (music) and Charles H. Hoyt (lyric). Although the song was not in the original score, the producer added it soon after the opening, and its popularity helped the show run an astonishing 657 performances. The hypochondriac Welland Strong (Harry Conor) sang the number as a reminiscence of New York City's Bowery district as he confided in some partying couples in a San Francisco restaurant. "The Bowery" was among the earliest theatre songs to become best-sellers in the sheet-music trade and has remained a familiar favorite throughout the last one hundred years.

"A Bowler Hat" is a quietly devastating song from *Pacific Overtures* (1976) that shows the loss of a culture as it is assimilated into the modern world. The former samurai Kayama (Isao Sato) has been made governor since the arrival of Americans on the shores of Japan. In this song he sings of the Western objects he has acquired (a bowler hat, a pocket watch, cigars, a monocle, even a cutaway coat) and reflects on the loss of his traditional beliefs and lifestyle. By the end of the song Kayama has been transformed into a lonely alcoholic who no longer knows quite who he is. Stephen Sondheim wrote the provocative number that utilizes a Western waltz in the music and haikulike imagery in the lyric.

"The Boy Friend" is the daffy title song from the 1954 British import that pastiched the bubble-headed musicals of the 1920s. At Madame Dubonnet's finishing school for girls, Polly (Julie Andrews) and her classmates (Stella Claire, Dilys Lay, Ann Wakefield and Millicent Martin) sing the tingling paean to what every perfect young lady dreams about: a boy friend. They are joined by three local boys (Joe Milan, Buddy Schwab and Jerry Newby) who do a fast step with the girls. Sandy Wilson wrote the playful music and lyrics.

"The Boy From . . ." is a hilarious spoof of the popular Latin hit "The Girl From Ipanema" that was sung by Linda Lavin in the Off-Broadway revue *The Mad Show* (1966). Mary Rodgers wrote the silly bossa nova music, and Stephen Sondheim (under the pseudonym Esteban Ria Nido) provided the farcical lyric about a girl who is in love with a gay man but cannot understand why he behaves so oddly toward her.

"A Boy Like That/I Have a Love" from *West Side Story* (1957) is not quite a duet nor a contrapuntal number but rather two powerful solos sung in succession that end with a brief duet. Anita (Chita Rivera) angrily sings about Tony, who killed Bernardo; then Maria (Carol Lawrence) argues that her love for Tony is stronger than any other force in her life. The final duet section has the two women admitting the power their love has over them. This number is the only one from the score in which Stephen Sondheim wrote a completed lyric before Leonard Bernstein composed the music; consequently, the song has a more conversational and abrupt quality to it than the others.

"Boy! What Love Has Done to Me!" is a comic song using the familiar "Can't Help Lovin' Dat Man of Mine" syndrome. Ethel Merman, as the prairie gal Kate Fothergill, sang the number in the Gershwins' *Girl Crazy* (1930) about how her loser husband has turned her into a slave, but she still loves him. George Gershwin's music is filled with unexpected shifts of emphasis from melody to harmony and back again, and Ira Gershwin's comic lyric is top drawer.

"Bring All the Boys Back Home" is a satirical production number from *Two Gentlemen of Verona* (1971) that has a deadly serious subtext. In the rock version of Shakespeare's tale, the Duke of Milan (Norman Matlock) brags how he started a war so that it would help the economy and, now that he's up for re-election, he'll remain popular by promising to bring the troops home. With America deeply engaged in Vietnam, the song by Galt MacDermot (music) and John Guare (lyric) could not help but be interpreted by the audience in a modern context.

"Bring Him Home" is the high tenor solo from the British import *Les Misérables* (1987) that Jean Valjean (Colm Wilkinson) sings at night at the silent barricade, praying for the safety of young Marius (David Bryant). Claude-

Michel Schönberg wrote the music, and Herbert Kretzmer adapted the French lyric by Alain Boublil and Jean-Marc Natel. The tenor Mandy Patinkin made an effective recording of the song in 1994.

"Broadway Baby" is a marvelous pastiche number in the style of DeSylva, Brown and Henderson that Stephen Sondheim wrote for *Follies* (1971). Ethel Shutta, who had actually been in the *Ziegfeld Follies*, belted out the song in the character of the old trooper Hattie Walker. An eager, optimistic comic song filled with clichés about making it big on Broadway, the number was even funnier and somewhat more ludicrous by its being performed by an old lady with the enthusiasm of a young gold digger. In the Broadway revue *Side by Side by Sondheim* (1977), the number was sung by Julia McKenzie.

"Broadway, My Street" is a pastiche of one of those rousing tributes to the Great White Way that George M. Cohan used to write. This version was written by John Kander (music) and Fred Ebb (lyric) for *70, Girls, 70* (1971), where it was sung by a chorus of veteran performers celebrating their return to Broadway.

"The Broadway, Opera and Bowery Crawl" is one of the surviving musical numbers from *The Black Crook* (1866), America's first musical comedy extravaganza. Giuseppe Operti (music) and Philip Stoner (lyric) wrote the witty song about the sluggish afternoon "crawl" performed by Broadway dandies, opera-house stuffed shirts and Bowery tipplers. It is more than likely that the song was added sometime after the opening since the score, a collection of readily available songs, changed frequently during the show's long run. New World Records reconstructed and recorded the number in 1978 with Thomas Bankston singing it.

"Brother, Can You Spare a Dime?" is one of the first theatre songs to have a potent sociological message, and it still remains one of the most powerful of the genre. Jay Gorney (music) and E.Y. Harburg (lyric) wrote it for the revue *Americana* (1932), where it was sung by Rex Weber and a male chorus as they waited in a breadline. The song is fascinating in its restraint that still allows for a forceful message. The singer is not as bitter as he is dazed and confused. He thought America was a great country, he worked hard, won praise, went to war, saved the world; now he begs for a dime. Gorney used strains from a Russian-Jewish lullaby in his chantlike music that casually sneaks up on you until it becomes a howl of lost faith. Harburg's lyric develops from a distant "they" to the personal "I" using some indelible images along the way. The result is one of the greatest of protest songs and one that manages to be highly personal as well. The song was deemed too serious for the usually escapist nature of the Shubert brothers' revues and was nearly cut in rehearsals. The

Depression was at its lowest point when *Americana* opened, and the audience immediately seized on the gripping number. Just as many were disturbed by the song, and the Republican administration was particularly worried with an election less than a month away. Attempts were made to ban the song from radio play, but it was already spreading due to popular recordings of it by Bing Crosby and Al Jolson. "Brother, Can You Spare a Dime?" became the unofficial theme song of the Depression era, but it is a work that has managed to retain its potency through the decades. In 1985 Tom Waitts sang a slightly revised version as an anthem for the homeless and unemployed, and today the number is the fundraising theme song for the National Coalition of the Homeless. Of the many recordings, a 1989 rendition by Mandy Patinkin is perhaps the most passionate.

"Brother Trucker" is the chant of truck drivers from *Working* (1978), the musical revue about America's work force. James Taylor wrote the music and lyric, and it was sung by Joe Mantegna, Bob Gunton, David Patrick Kelly and Matt Landers.

"Brotherhood of Man" is the spirited mock-revival number from *How to Succeed in Business Without Really Trying* (1961) that makes a satiric plea for all men to love one another, something the musical proved was not necessary to achieve success. Frank Loesser wrote the keyed-up song with a bit of gospel and Dixieland thrown in for good measure, and it was sung by Robert Morse, Sammy Smith, Ruth Kobart and the company.

"Brown October Ale" is an exciting drinking song from *Robin Hood* (1891), the most celebrated American operetta of the nineteenth century. Reginald DeKoven composed the compelling music, Harry B. Smith provided the robust lyric, and it was sung by Little John (W.H. MacDonald) and the merry men. The number is sometimes listed as "The Song of Brown October Ale."

"Brush Up Your Shakespeare" is the famous eleven o'clock number from *Kiss Me, Kate* (1948). The nonintegrated number is a hilarious patter song, with the two gangsters (Harry Clark and Jack Diamond) giving musical advice on how to win the hearts of women by quoting from the Bard. Cole Porter's melody is routine, but his lyric power is at its peak here. His use of arch rhymes in this song has never been surpassed.

"Buckle Down, Winsocki" is the school song that is widely remembered from *Best Foot Forward* (1941), the academic musical about fictional Winsocki Prep School. Ralph Blane and Hugh Martin wrote the music and lyric for the rousing pep-rally song that student Chuck (Tommy Dix) and Old Grad (Stuart Langley) led the ensemble in singing. During World War Two a revised version called "Buckle Down, Buck Private" became popular. The robust melody is still a favorite of marching bands today.

"The Bus From Amarillo" is a touching narrative ballad from *The Best Little Whorehouse in Texas* (1978) by Carol Hall. Miss Mona Stangley (Carlin Glynn), the proprietor of the infamous Chicken Ranch, recalls the time she tried to change the direction of her life, but after one stop she got off the Amarillo bus.

"A Bushel and a Peck" is a facetious pastiche number from *Guys and Dolls* (1950) that ultimately became the show's most popular song in recordings and radio airplay. Frank Loesser wrote the satirical down-on-the-farm song as the nightclub act for Miss Adelaide (Vivian Blaine) and the Hot Box Farmerettes. Perry Como, Doris Day and Betty Hutton were among the many who made successful recordings of the daffy song.

"Bustopher Jones" is the "I am" song for the fat and educated cat that prowls the clubs of St. James Square in the British import *Cats* (1982). Andrew Lloyd Webber set T.S. Eliot's poem to lazy but elegant music during which Bustopher (Stephen Hanan) struts about wearing white spats. Fellow felines played by Anna McNeely, Bonnie Simmons and Donna King led the company in the musical tribute to the stout cat.

"But in the Morning, No" is one of several Cole Porter songs that had trouble with the censors; in this case, the salacious aspects of the piece were so subtle that you can only admire the puritans' sense of detection. But the Porter wit always seemed to indicate something naughty, so their suspicions were acute. Ethel Merman and Bert Lahr sang the song in *DuBarry Was a Lady* (1939), but because it was denied radio play, the number never became well known. In the delectable duet, King Louis XV of France (Lahr) and the famous concubine DuBarry (Merman) offer each other a series of activities (swimming, riding, football, poker), with each refusing to do so in the morning because that's the time they are "in low." The anachronistic lyric is offset by Porter's gavottelike melody, in keeping with the period milieu of the show. A daffy recording of the number was made by Ronny Graham and Kaye Ballard.

"But Not for Me" is the beloved torch song by the Gershwins that was first heard in *Girl Crazy* (1930). It was sung by the forlorn postmistress of Custerville, Arizona, Molly Gray (Ginger Rogers), who knows that love is all around her, but none of it seems to be for her. Then the taxi driver-turned-sheriff Gieber Goldfarb (Willie Howard) reprises the number as a comic piece to cheer Molly up, doing imitations of Maurice Chevalier, Al Jolson and Eddie Cantor singing the song. George Gershwin's lovely music is rather atypical of his style, but, as musicologist Alec Wilder stated, it is a "masterpiece of control and understatement from beginning to end, verse and chorus." Ira Gershwin's lyric is both sentimental and self-aware, with a memorable metaphor that compares Molly's gloom to that of a Russian play. Distinctive recordings of the song have been made by Judy Garland, Ella Fitzgerald and Linda Ronstadt. In the revised version of the show called *Crazy for You* (1992) the postmistress Polly Barker (Jodi Benson) sings the ballad.

"Butler in the Abbey" is a Gilbert and Sullivan pastiche from the short-lived *Darling of the Day* (1968) by Jule Styne (music) and E.Y. Harburg (lyric). In the climactic trial scene from the musical, the famous artist Priam Farll (Vincent Price), who was thought dead but in reality had his butler buried in Westminster Abbey in his place, argues with the court about the dangers of letting the truth out. He describes the reactions all the great poets and artists buried there will have when they find out that a mere butler is in their sacred midst. In English operetta fashion Priam sings the verses and the court echoes him during the refrains. Styne captures a Sullivan-like flavor in his music, but the scene is unique for the youthful, vibrant lyrics by the seventy-two-year-old Harburg. "Butler in the Abbey" was the last new Harburg lyric to be heard on Broadway.

"Button Up Your Overcoat" is the breezy standard to come out of *Follow Thru* (1929), the musical about championship golf by B.G. DeSylva and Lew Brown (lyric) and Ray Henderson (music). At the Bound Brook Country Club, the vivacious Angie Howard (Zelma O'Neal) pursues the shy Jack Martin (Jack Haley), the son of a chain-store millionaire. They both end up singing this sly cautionary song that suggested healthy food, early nights, no drinking and other insincere advice.

"Buy Yourself a Balloon" was a specialty number for Beatrice Lillie in the revue *The Show Is On* (1936). Herman Hupfeld wrote the comic song, which Lillie sang perched on a scenery moon that swung out over the audience and allowed her to toss garters to the men below. The number was spoofed years later in *Mame* (1966) with the song "The Man in the Moon."

"By Goona-Goona Lagoon" is a sultry pastiche of all those South Seas ballads that offered swaying palms and romantic moonlight. Jerome Moross (music) and John Latouche (lyric) wrote the wonderful parody for *The Golden Apple* (1954), where it was sung by the tropical siren Lovey Mars (Bibi Osterwald) and her enticing Sirenettes as they lured Ulysses and his men into their clutches.

"By My Side" is a tender folk song from the Off-Broadway sensation

Godspell (1971) in which two of Jesus' disciples (Peggy Gordon and Gilmer McCormick) led the ensemble in a gentle pledge of fidelity. It is the only song in the score not written by Stephen Schwartz; Gordon composed the sensitive music, and Jay Hamburger wrote the delicate lyric.

"By Myself" is one of the most intriguing songs by the team of Howard Dietz (lyric) and Arthur Schwartz (music), a unique song by any standards. Schwartz's beguiling melody is limited to one octave, yet the song feels expansive and wide-ranged with rich textured harmonies. Dietz's lyric is debonair, detached yet heartfelt: a torch song with a cool facade. The number was written for *Between the Devil* (1937), where it is sung by the bigamist Peter Anthony (Jack Buchanan) as he is pursued by bobbies through the foggy London streets. Fred Astaire made a memorable recording of "By Myself" in 1952 and Carly Simon recorded a distinctive rendition in 1990.

"By Strauss" is a dandy takeoff on schmaltzy Viennese waltzes that was featured in the revue *The Show Is On* (1936). The singer despairs at hearing all the modern-sounding music of Berlin, Porter, Kern and Gershwin and asks for a good old-fashioned waltz like Strauss used to write. George Gershwin wrote the flowing 3/4 time music (one of the very few waltzes he ever wrote), and Ira Gershwin provided the jocose lyric that rhymed "free 'n' easy" with "Viennesy." The song was sung in the revue by Grace Barrie and danced by Mitzi Mayfair and the chorus. Sadly, "By Strauss" was the last song by George Gershwin to be heard on Broadway in his lifetime.

"By the Light of the Silvery Moon," the perennial favorite of glee clubs and barbershop quartets, was first heard in vaudeville, where Georgie Price sang the crooning ballad; but its Broadway debut came with Ziegfeld's *Follies of 1909*, where Lillian Lorraine sang it. Gus Edwards composed the melodic music, and Edward Madden wrote the memorable lyric in which all the rhymes in the song save one rhyme with "moon." Of the many recordings over the years, the most successful was an instrumental version by Ray Noble and His Orchestra in 1941 that sold over one million records.

"By the Mississinewah," one of Cole Porter's naughtiest songs, is a playful little duet about bigamy. Ethel Merman and Paula Lawrence sang it as two Indian squaws who share their wigwam with the same brave in *Something for the Boys* (1943). The Indiana river of the song's title allowed Porter to play with all sorts of "iss" and "wah" sounds in the lyric. For the published version, the song was changed to a solo lament by a squaw who anxiously awaits her chief's return home. Kaye Ballard and Bibi Osterwald made a delicious recording of the duet.

"By the Saskatchewan" is an operatic duet from *The Pink Lady* (1911) by Ivan Caryll (music) and C.M.S. McLellan (lyric). In the enchanted forest of Compeigne, Desiree (Ida M. Adams) and Bebe (John E. Young) have met, have fallen in love and now wonder if it is possible to remain true to an old love back home on the Saskatchewan River when you've found a new one on the banks of the Seine.

"By the Sea" is a delicious pastiche of a Victorian music-hall ditty from Stephen Sondheim's *Sweeney Todd, the Demon Barber of Fleet Street* (1979). Mrs. Lovett (Angela Lansbury) sings the jaunty song in which she imagines how pleasant it would be if she and Mr. Todd (Len Cariou) could retire to a seaside resort town together, coyly suggesting that a romance will develop between them there.

"Bye and Bye" is a romantic duet from *Dearest Enemy* (1925) that became a musical standard at the time. Helen Ford and Charles Purcell introduced the song by Richard Rodgers (music) and Lorenz Hart (lyric) in which the lovers imagine a future life together.

"Bye, Bye, Baby" is the hit ballad from *Gentlemen Prefer Blondes* (1949) by Jule Styne (music) and Leo Robin (lyric). The appealing farewell song is sung by millionaire Gus Esmond (Jack McCauley) to his fiancée Lorelei Lee (Carol Channing) before she sails for Europe on the *Ile de France*. He makes her promise to behave herself on the trip, and then she and the ensemble join him in singing the number. In the 1974 revised version called *Lorelei*, the ballad was sung by Peter Palmer, Channing and the chorus.

C

"Cabaret" is the seemingly jubilant title number from the 1966 musical by John Kander (music) and Fred Ebb (lyric) and the most popular song to come out of the show. Although the song is usually performed as an optimistic call to party life, in the context of *Cabaret* it is highly ironic and, in its middle patter section, very sardonic. The number is sung by Sally Bowles (Jill Haworth) in the Berlin Kit Kat Klub on the eve of World War Two. Of the many recordings of the song, the biggest hits were ones by Herb Alpert and the Tijuana Brass, a single by Marilyn Maye, and Liza Minnelli's concert and film rendition.

"Cabin in the Sky" is the warm and appealing title song from the 1940 "Negro folk musical" by Vernon Duke (music) and John Latouche (lyric). Petunia Jackson (Ethel Waters) and her husband "Little Joe" (Dooley Wilson) sing the fond duet in which they imagine heaven to be a humble little cabin. Ella Fitzgerald made a hit recording of the song.

"Cadillac Car" is an ambitious musical sequence from *Dreamgirls* (1981) that chronicles the social history of the black man's upward mobility in America as it parallels the growth of the characters in the story. Henry Krieger (music) and Tom Eyen (lyric) wrote the captivating number, sung by the whole cast, that uses recitative, pop songs and dramatic Broadway melody to achieve its startling effect.

"California, Here I Come" is the surging "westward ho" song most often associated with Al Jolson. The number was written by Joseph Meyer (music) and B.G. DeSylva and Jolson himself (lyric) and Jolson added it to the 1923 tour of *Bombo*, where his robust rendition of the song made it popular. Jolson's 1946 recording of "California, Here I Come" was a hit all over again and the number was used as the theme song for two groups: Abe Lyman and his Orchestra and the California Ramblers.

"A Call From the Vatican" is a sexy comic number from *Nine* (1982) by Maury Yeston in which the actress Carla (Anita Morris) simulates making love while talking to her lover Guido (Raul Julia) on the phone. Since Guido's wife Luisa (Karen Akers) is with him when the phone rings, he tells her it is a monsignor from the Vatican on the line. Director Tommy Tune staged the number with Carla going through erotic contortions while perched on a scenery block wearing a see-through leotard designed by William Ivey Long.

"Camelot" is the beguiling title number from the 1960 musical by Alan Jay Lerner (lyric) and Frederick Loewe (music). King Arthur (Richard Burton) describes the whimsical nature of his kingdom to prospective bride Guenevere (Julie Andrews) in his effort to convince her to stay. The charming list song does convince her, and the number develops into a duet that solidifies their relationship. At the end of the musical, Arthur reprises part of the song to the young boy Tom (Robin Stewart) to teach him the ideals that Camelot once stood for. The song was a favorite of John F. Kennedy's and, after his death, became a symbol of his character and accomplishments.

"Can-Can," the sprightly title song from Cole Porter's 1953 musical, is more clever than most dance songs. Its lyric has all kinds of fun with variations on the word "can" and plenty of playful internal rhymes. The melody is also one of Porter's liveliest. The number was introduced by Lilo, Gwen Verdon and the ensemble and was soon being played by dance bands across the country.

"Can That Boy Foxtrot" is a sexy, hilarious song that Stephen Sondheim wrote for Yvonne DeCarlo to sing in *Follies* (1971), but it was cut and replaced with "I'm Still Here." Later the devilish number was sung as a duet by Millicent Martin and Julia McKenzie in the Broadway revue *Side by Side by Sondheim* (1977). The song is filled with crafty innuendo as it relates the awful qualities of a jerk who is good for nothing but sex. Sondheim's lyrics have rarely been more clever, with delectable internal rhymes scattered throughout.

"Can This Be Love?" is a beguiling ballad about romantic confusion from *Fine and Dandy* (1930) by Kay Swift (music) and Paul James (lyric). The sweet ingenue Nancy Ellis (Alice Boulden) sang the engaging song, which became a recording favorite of big bands, in particular that of Woody Herman, who had a hit with the number.

"Can't Help Lovin' Dat Man" is the bluesy, rhythmic torch song from *Show Boat* (1927) by Jerome Kern (music) and Oscar Hammerstein (lyric) and one of the many hits from the landmark musical. Julie LaVern (Helen Morgan) recalls a "colored folk song" from her youth and sings it with Magnolia (Norma Terris), Queenie (Tess Gardella), Joe (Jules Bledsoe) and Windy (Allan

Campbell). Unknown to the others, Julie is a mulatto, so the song's ethnic heritage is more than appropriate. Also, the lyric fits with the character and situation, for Julie is in love with her troublesome husband Steve, but she can't say why. Later in *Show Boat*, Magnolia sings the song as her audition for a music hall job. When the manager tells her the number is too sad, she does a lively, jazzed-up version of the song. Morgan recorded the torch song in 1927 and again in 1932, and among the later recordings of "Can't Help Lovin' Dat Man" were memorable ones by Lena Horne and Barbra Streisand.

"Can't We Be Friends?" is an appealing torch song that Libby Holman sang in the innovative revue *The Little Show* (1929). The lyric is by Paul James, and the music was composed by Kay Swift in one of her rare forays into writing for Broadway. Frank Sinatra had a popular recording of the song in 1955.

"Captain Hook's Waltz" is a dandy comic number for Hook (Cyril Ritchard) and his pirates in *Peter Pan* (1954). Jule Styne (music) and Betty Comden and Adolph Green (lyric) wrote the insidious song, which celebrates the Captain's infamy and even lets the man reveal his tender inside, only to find it as pleasantly wicked as the surface.

"Carolina in the Morning" is the perennial standard by Walter Donaldson (music) and Gus Kahn (lyric) that was interpolated into *The Passing Show of 1922*. It was introduced by the comedy brothers Willie and Eugene Howard and immediately caught the public's fancy. Donaldson's music is simple, with a melody that cleverly moves back and forth between the same two notes, and Kahn's lyric is warm and evocative, even though he admitted at the time that he'd never been to North or South Carolina. "Carolina in the Morning" was used in four films and the oft-recorded song was given a unique rendition by Barbara Cook in concert and on record.

"Cast of Thousands" is an engrossing musical monologue from the intimate Off-Broadway show *Three Postcards* (1987) with music and lyrics by Craig Carnelia. A waiter (Brad O'Hare) in a New York City restaurant sings a chronicle of his life up to that point, recalling some of the many people and places that have played a part in his past. The lyric is superb, and the images chosen are very vivid.

"Castle of Dreams" is the romantic duet from the popular *Irene* (1919) by Harry Tierney (music) and Joseph McCarthy (lyric). Shop girl Irene O'Dare (Edith Day) and rich Long Islander Donald Marshall (Walter Regan) sang the number, which borrowed liberally from Chopin for its melody.

"Celebration" is the title song and the mysterious invocation number that opened and concluded the 1969 allegorical musical by Tom Jones (lyric) and Harvey Schmidt (music). Potemkin (Keith Charles) and the Revelers sing the bewitching song that urges the audience to ignore those who say the world is ending and instead to celebrate life and its possibilities.

"Cell Block Tango" is a hilarious chorus number from *Chicago* (1975) in which Velma Kelly (Chita Rivera) and her fellow murderesses sing about why each killed the man who had it coming to him. John Kander composed the Latin-flavored music, and Fred Ebb provided the pungent lyric.

"A Certain Girl" is a sprightly trio from *The Happy Time* (1968) by John Kander (music) and Fred Ebb (lyric). Crusty old Grandpere (David Wayne), the family black sheep Jacques (Robert Goulet) and the young Bibi (Michael Rupert) sing the praises of that one special girl who can change your life.

"C'est Magnifique" is Cole Porter's sultry tribute to Parisian love, a smooth and charming number from *Can-Can* (1953). It was sung by Lilo, as dance-hall owner Madame Pistache, to a rather cautious official, played by Peter Cookson, who joined her in singing the duet. Porter's music is so authentic and so familiar that many think the song is an actual period French composition.

"C'est Moi" is the playful mock aria that serves as Lancelot's "I am" song in *Camelot* (1960) by Alan Jay Lerner (lyric) and Frederick Loewe (music). The French Lancelot (Robert Goulet) arrives in England to join the Round Table and sings this jocular number listing all the qualities that a superior knight should have; to each virtue he admits that he fills the bill splendidly.

"Chain of Love" is an enchanting ballad from the offbeat musical *The Grass Harp* (1971) by Claibe Richardson (music) and Kenward Elmslie (lyric). The spinster Dolly Talbo (Barbara Cook) sings the reflective number in which she summarizes her life as a series of warm memories linked by love.

"Chain Store Daisy" is a seriocomic character song from the labor revue *Pins and Needles* (1937) by Harold Rome. Ruth Rubenstein sang the touching number about a Vassar grad who can only get work selling ladies' foundation garments at Macy's. Although the witty Rome score did not get an original cast recording, Rubenstein recorded this number in 1938.

"Chanson" is a simple ballad used as a leitmotif throughout the ill-fated *The Baker's Wife*, which closed in 1976 before it got to New York. The cafe owner's wife Denise (Teri Ralston) introduces the show with the melodic song, singing how quickly one's life can change. Sections of the ballad were reprised at different points in the story, and then it was used at the finale. Stephen Schwartz wrote the enticing music and lyric.

"Charleston" is the song that launched the dance that captivated the nation like no other during the 1920s. It was written by Jimmy Johnson and Cecil Mack for the all-black musical *Runnin' Wild* (1923), where Elisabeth Welch sang and danced the zesty number. The liberated, frantic, high-stepping dance became so popular that it replaced the shimmy as the predominant step of the jazz age and, in many ways, symbolized the era itself.

"Chief Cook and Bottle Washer" is the jocular "I am" song for Anna (Chita Rivera) in *The Rink* (1984) by John Kander (music) and Fred Ebb (lyric). After years of being housewife, mother and proprietor of an amusement-park skating rink, Anna sings that she is selling out and moving on with her life.

"Children and Art" is the poignant ballad from *Sunday in the Park With George* (1984) in which the aged Marie (Bernadette Peters) looks back on life and sees children and art as the only two things that go on forever. Stephen Sondheim wrote the gentle, evocative number which has a waltzing, bluesy flavor to it and knowing, delicate lyrics.

"Children of the Wind" is a passionate ballad about the struggles of immigrants to reach America from the short-lived *Rags* (1986). Charles Strouse composed the expansive music, Stephen Schwartz wrote the penetrating lyric, and Teresa Stratas, as the newly arrived immigrant Rebecca, sang the soaring number.

"Children Will Listen" is the bittersweet ballad that concludes the fairy-tale musical *Into the Woods* (1987) by Stephen Sondheim. The Witch (Bernadette Peters) and the ensemble sing this haunting song about parents and children and the accepting of responsibility that comes with growing up and growing wise. Sondheim's music is mournful yet elegant, and his lyric has a tranquil tone to it that is very telling. Betty Buckley and Barbra Streisand each made touching recordings of the song.

"Chin Up, Ladies" is a diverting comic number from Jerry Herman's first musical, *Milk and Honey* (1961), that was sung by a group of American widows touring Israel looking for husbands. The marchlike song was led by Yiddish theatre favorite Molly Picon.

"Chinatown, My Chinatown" is the durable song favorite by Jean Schwartz (music) and William Jerome (lyric) that salutes New York City's

Chinatown district. Although it was written and published in 1906, the song did not catch on until it was interpolated after opening into the Eddie Foy vehicle *Up and Down Broadway* (1910) to replace another Chinatown number. Ernest Hare, as a police officer, sang the number with the chorus (which included young songwriters Irving Berlin and Ted Snyder). Popular recordings of the song over the years include ones by the Mills Brothers, Louis Prima, Fletcher Henderson and Tommy Dorsey and the Clambake Seven.

"Christmas at Hampton Court" is a lively trio written by Richard Rodgers (music) and Sheldon Harnick (lyric) for the unsuccessful *Rex* (1976) about King Henry VIII of England. The merry number, which opened the second act, was performed by the king's three children: Elizabeth (Penny Fuller), Edward (Michael John) and Mary (Glenn Close).

"Chrysanthemum Tea" is a unique musical number from *Pacific Overtures* (1976) in which the passage of time and a change of power occur during a song. At the court of the Shogun (Mako), his wife (Freda Foh Shen) serves him tea each day and asks what he will do about the foreign ships anchored in the bay. A soothsayer, some priests and the samurai are consulted, but still the Shogun does nothing. On the fourth day the wife confesses that she has been poisoning his tea, and as he dies she concludes that when the Shogun is weak, then the tea must be strong. Stephen Sondheim wrote the fascinating number, which was very funny and ingeniously dramatized the events of the story.

"The Church Around the Corner" is a waltzing romantic song with a purely American temperament from *Sally* (1920), a number Jerome Kern (music) had written with P.G. Wodehouse (lyric) for an earlier unproduced musical. Rosalind (Mary Hay) and Otis (Walter Catlett) sing the lively duet about the frugal wedding and humble lifestyle they will have together. Wodehouse's lyrics are silly, cozy and touching. Kern's music is very simple, written entirely in quarter notes except for the last note of each musical sentence, but totally captivating. The song has been listed in no less than four different ways over the years, from "Little Church Around the Corner" to "Church 'Round the Corner."

"City Mouse, Country Mouse" is a winning character number about the advantages of life on the farm from *Plain and Fancy* (1955), the musical about the Pennsylvania Amish by Albert Hague (music) and Arnold B. Horwitt (lyric). Emma Miller (Nancy Andrews) and the Amish women sing the comic number comparing country life with city living as they prepare a wedding dinner in Emma's kitchen.

"Civilization" is a novelty number that Elaine Stritch sang in the intimate revue *Angel in the Wings* (1947) by Bob Hilliard and Carl Sigman. The comic song found dissatisfaction with modern civilization and urged a return to the wilds of the jungle. The sly ditty, sometimes titled "Bongo, Bongo, Bongo (I Don't Want to Leave the Congo)," was a surprise hit, with a popular recording by Danny Kaye with the Andrews Sisters and orchestral best-sellers by Louis Prima and Woody Herman.

"Clap Yo' Hands" is an intoxicating revival number from the Gershwins' *Oh, Kay!* (1926) sung and danced by Larry Potter (Harlan Dixon) and the ensemble at a Long Island mansion. George Gershwin wrote the rhythmic music, and the compelling lyric is by Ira Gershwin with help from Howard Dietz. The number is unusual in that the title never occurs in the song; the repeated phrase used throughout is "clap-a yo' hand," but Ira Gershwin felt that this was an ineffective song title. An early recording of the number was made by Claude Hulbert in 1927.

"Class" is a crass comic song from *Chicago* (1975) about how crass the world has become. Murderess Velma Kelly (Chita Rivera) and the prison Matron (Mary McCarty) sing this waggish duet in which they list all the vulgarities of modern life. John Kander composed the harmonious melody, and Fred Ebb wrote the amusingly sour lyric.

"Cleanin' Women" is the bitter, determined cry of a black woman who is one of the faceless cleaners in America's work force. Micki Grant wrote the powerful music and lyric, and it was sung by Lynne Thigpen in the revue *Working* (1978).

"Cleopatterer" is a comic ditty from *Leave It to Jane* (1917), the early college musical by Jerome Kern (music) and P.G. Wodehouse (lyric). Georgia O'Ramey, as the sultry Flora, sang the song while she did a whirling Egyptian dance that stopped the show each night. The song details the ways she hopes to use the legendary queen's sexual and political talents to mesmerize men. "Cleopatterer," with its arch rhymes and risqué subtext, is considered one of Wodehouse's finest comic lyrics and foreshadows the wit and playfulness of the later lyricists Lorenz Hart, Ira Gershwin and Cole Porter, all of whom stated that Wodehouse was their inspiration.

"Climb Ev'ry Mountain" is the inspirational number that ends each act of *The Sound of Music* (1959) and gives the musical its driving force. The famous song is first sung by the Mother Abbess (Patricia Neway) to convince Maria (Mary Martin) to return to the Von Trapp family. It is reprised at the end of the show by the nuns at the convent when the family flees the Nazis by literally climbing the mountains and crossing into Switzerland. Richard Rodgers' music does its own climbing the scales in the tradition of his earlier "You'll Never Walk Alone" and "Something Wonderful," and Oscar Hammerstein's lyric skillfully mixes nature imagery with lofty phraseology. The number is also one of the more difficult songs in the Rodgers and Hammerstein repertoire to sing and is often relegated to opera singers. Tony Bennett had a best-selling record of the song.

"Close as Pages in a Book" is a duet from the last years of Sigmund Romberg's career and contains the melodic temperament of a ballad while retaining the operetta flavor of his early career. The song was written for the period musical *Up in Central Park* (1945) with lyrics by Dorothy Fields. The muckraking reporter John Matthews (Wilbur Evans) falls in love with Rosie Moore (Maureen Cannon), who is the daughter of one of Manhattan's corrupt elite. But politics aside, they offer each other a pledge of everlasting love in this ardent duet. Benny Goodman's Orchestra made a hit recording of the song and years later Barbara Cook made a distinctive recording of it.

"Close Every Door" is a tender ballad from the raucous *Joseph and the Amazing Technicolor Dreamcoat* (1982) by Andrew Lloyd Webber (music) and Tim Rice (lyric). Biblical Joseph (Bill Hutton) has been thrown into an Egyptian prison, where he sings this song of hope, knowing that he and his people have been promised by God a land of their own.

"A Cockeyed Optimist" is Nellie Forbush's "I am" number in *South Pacific* (1949) and one of the most vibrant examples of this song type in the musical theatre. Nellie (Mary Martin) is an American hick in an exotic world surrounded by war; yet she has confidence in life and, indirectly, love. Richard Rodgers provided a cheery melody for the heroine's introductory song, and Oscar Hammerstein's lyric is sassy and all-American, a rich contrast to the dignified European sound he gives Emile (Ezio Pinza). The song is so famous that some of the clichés Hammerstein invented for the lyric have become idiomatic. A sample of the team's craftsmanship: the high note for the word "far" wobbles and nearly slides down the scale when Nellie talks of the end of the world and how it hasn't "far to go." Julie Andrews made a memorable recording of the song.

"The Cocoa Bean Song" is the incendiary opening number from *Kwamina* (1961), the unusual musical by Richard Adler about a West African nation on the verge of independence. Ako (Robert Guillaume), an overseer at a cocoa bean plantation, urges the workers to keep up the production pace while Scott Gibson, Gordon Watkins and the natives chant in multipart harmony about how the different kinds of beans reflect the different kinds of people there are. Adler's blending of African rhythms into a Broadway score format is quite expert throughout the score, but never more so than in this enthralling number.

"Cocoanut Sweet" is an enchanting ballad from *Jamaica* (1957) that uses tropical forms of nature to express love. Harold Arlen composed the intoxicating music, E.Y. Harburg wrote the atmospheric lyric, and the song was sung by the island beauty Savannah (Lena Horne) and wise old Grandma Obeah (Adelaide Hall).

"Coffee Break" is a frantic chorus number from the satirical *How to Succeed in Business Without Really Trying* (1961). Bud Frump (Charles Nelson Reilly), Smitty (Claudette Sutherland) and the other office workers sing this delirious paean to the necessity of caffeine in the workplace. Frank Loesser wrote the clever lyric and the unconventional music set to a traditional cha-cha tempo, and Bob Fosse choreographed the number with chaotic dance steps and contorted body movements.

"Coffee in a Cardboard Cup" is a frenzied comic song from *70, Girls, 70* (1971) by John Kander (music) and Fred Ebb (lyric). Senior citizens Melba (Lillian Hayman) and Fritzi (Goldye Shaw) stop the plot of the musical to sing to the audience about what they consider wrong with the world today: fast food, rude waitresses, people in a hurry, Minute Rice, plastic spoons and coffee-to-go in a cardboard cup. Mandy Patinkin recorded the hyperactive song, and it was sung by the ensemble in the Off-Broadway revue *And the World Goes 'Round* (1991).

"Color and Light" is a captivating musical scene from *Sunday in the Park With George* (1984) by Stephen Sondheim that reflects on art and life and how they sometimes do not overlap. In his studio the painter George Seurat (Mandy Patinkin) works at his canvas, singing quick, blunt notes and lyrics that match the dabbing motion of his pointillist style. In the next room his mistress Dot (Bernadette Peters) applies her makeup as she prepares to go out on a night on the town. She considers her half-dressed body in the mirror as George scrutinizes his painting. She fantasizes about being a Follies girl and then decides it would be a life too full of color and light. Meanwhile George sings out the colors he is applying to his canvas. The number climaxes with a duet in which Dot sings of her unexplained love for George as he rhapsodizes over what the painting may become. The musical sequence is one of Sondheim's most inventive and remarkable, filled with shifting rhythms and piquant lyric craftsmanship.

"Colorado Love Call" is the melodic spoof of the famous "Indian Love Call" duet as pastiched in the Off-Broadway send-up *Little Mary Sunshine* (1959) by Rick Besoyan. Mary Potts (Eileen Brennan), the proprietress of the Colorado

Inn, and Captain "Big Jim" Warington (William Graham) of the U.S. Forest Rangers sing the rhapsodic number in which they praise each other and their beloved Colorado.

"Colored Lights" is the reflective ballad that opens the John Kander (music) and Fred Ebb (lyric) musical *The Rink* (1984). The world-weary Angel (Liza Minnelli) thinks back on her too many lovers in too many places, yet she cannot find any colored lights in her life. Kander's music shifts back and forth from a playful calliope melody to a slower, wistful theme, and Ebb's lyric is both intimate and painful. Karen Mason sang the ballad in the Off-Broadway revue *And the World Goes 'Round* (1991).

"The Colors of My Life" is the romantic ballad from *Barnum* (1980), a quiet, enticing number that became somewhat popular. When his wife Chairy wants him to give up the humbug business and settle down to a respectable trade, P.T. Barnum (Jim Dale) explains to her his vision of the world as one filled with color and excitement rather than security and conformity. When she is alone, Chairy (Glenn Close) reprises the song and reflects on the colors of her life: plain, everyday, honest colors. In the second act, right before Chairy dies, they both reprise the warm Cy Coleman (music) and Michael Stewart (lyric) song.

"Come A-Wandering With Me" is a vibrant gypsy number from *The Gay Life* (1961) that Elizabeth Allen sang and stopped the show with. The night before his wedding, Anatole (Walter Chiari) runs across his old flame, the gypsy Magda (Allen), in a Viennese cafe, and she entices him to renew their former passion and high life together. Howard Dietz (lyric) and Arthur Schwartz (music) wrote the inflammatory number.

"Come Back to Me" is a sprightly song of yearning from the ESP musical *On a Clear Day You Can See Forever* (1965) by Alan Jay Lerner (lyric) and Burton Lane (music). Psychiatrist Mark Bruckner (John Cullum) uses extrasensory control to summon the missing Daisy Gamble (Barbara Harris) back to him. Lane's music is very compelling, and Lerner's lyric, an ingenious list of the ways that she might use to return, is first-rate. Johnny Mathis made a hit recording of the song.

"Come Down, Ma Evenin' Star" was the song forever associated with the legendary Lillian Russell, who sang it in the Weber and Fields burlesque *Twirly Whirly* (1902). The wealthy dowager Mrs. Bond (Russell) despairs that being a shining star of the social set can never have the timeless luster of the real stars up in the heavens, so she summons one of them to her. The story behind the song is quite theatrical: Composer John Stromberg wrote the ballad for Russell, then changed his mind, not showing it to anyone else. A few weeks later he committed suicide in his apartment, and the sheet music was found in his pocket and quickly added to the score. On opening night Russell broke down and wept as she tried to sing it. Soon it became her signature song, and she recorded it in 1912, the only existing record she ever made. Robert B. Smith wrote the lyric for Stromberg's swan song.

"Come On Feet Do Your Thing" is a riveting number from *Ain't Supposed to Die a Natural Death* (1971), the revue about life and death in the black ghetto by Melvin Van Peebles. Although the title suggests another happy hoofing song for a black tap dancer, the number is actually a surging account of a man, played by Sati Jamal, desperately running from the police and begging his feet not to quit on him now.

"Come Play Wiz Me" is a prankish comic duet from *Anyone Can Whistle* (1964) by Stephen Sondheim that uses mock French 101 vernacular in a sexy and silly manner. Nurse Fay Apple (Lee Remick) disguises herself as the sultry "Lady from Lourdes" and tries to seduce Dr. Hapgood (Harry Guardino) as a screen above translates the caricatured French for the audience.

"Come Rain or Come Shine" is the hit ballad from *St. Louis Woman* (1946) and one of Harold Arlen's most famous compositions. Johnny Mercer wrote the scintillating lyric that is romantic yet colloquial. The song was sung as a duet promising eternal love by gal-about-town Della Green (Ruby Hill) and jockey Little Augie (Harold Nicholas). Arlen's music is unusual in that it has no verse and starts in one key only to end in another. He also uses a repeated note to wondrous effect, a device rarely found in his work. Margaret Whiting, Judy Garland and Joe Williams (with Count Basie's Orchestra) each made a popular recording of the oft-recorded ballad.

"Come to Me, Bend to Me" is an enchanting romantic serenade from *Brigadoon* (1947) by Alan Jay Lerner (lyric) and Frederick Loewe (music). Charlie Dalrymple (Lee Sullivan) is not allowed to meet with his betrothed Jean MacLaren (Virginia Bosler) before the wedding, so he woos her from afar with this hauntingly beautiful ballad. Lerner's lyric is simple but evocative, and Loewe's music has a madrigal-like quality to it. The song was made popular by Al Jolson's radio performance of it, and it remained one of Loewe's personal favorites throughout his life.

"Come to the Masquerade" is a ravishing ballad from the Off-Broadway period musical *Man With a Load of Mischief* (1966) by John Clifton (music and lyric) and Ben Tarver (lyric). The British manservant Charles (Reid Shelton) sings the enticing waltz not about a masked ball but rather about a lifestyle of deception in which people merely play at the game of love rather than experience it.

"Come to the Moon" is a contagious musical invitation to love from *Demi-Tasse Revue* (1919) by George Gershwin (music) and Ned Wayburn and Lou Paley (lyric). Paul Frawley, Lucille Chalfont and the chorus sang the rhythmic number. In 1992 conductor John McGlinn reconstructed the original orchestrations and recorded it with Brent Barrett and the Ambrosian Chorus.

"Come Up to My Place" or, as it is sometimes listed, the "Taxi Number" is a hilarious song from *On the Town* (1944) by Leonard Bernstein (music) and Betty Comden and Adolph Green (lyric). Sailor Chip (Cris Alexander) has only twenty-four hours' leave to see all the sights of New York City, but when he gets into the taxicab driven by Hildy (Nancy Walker), she's more interested in romance; besides, Chip's tour book is so out-of-date that the attractions he wants to see are all torn down or forgotten. Bernstein's chaotic music parallels the stopping and starting of the cab in New York traffic, and Comden and Green's lyric is sassy and playful throughout.

"Comedy Tonight" is the well-known announcement song from *A Funny Thing Happened on the Way to the Forum* (1962) that opens the show and sets the farcical style of the antics to follow. It is also the song that saved the musical from failure. While the musical farce was trying out in Washington, D.C., it was not pulling together at all, and Jerome Robbins was brought in to advise and contribute his services. *Forum* opened with a pleasant soft-shoe song called "Love Is in the Air," and Robbins suggested it be replaced by a more raucous number that told the audience what kind of show they were going to see. Stephen Sondheim wrote "Comedy Tonight," everything fell into place, and the show was a hit. Sondheim's music for the song is marchlike and vigorous, and the lyric playfully lists all the things the show will and will not be about. In the original production the number was sung by Zero Mostel and the company, and in the Broadway revue *Side by Side by Sondheim* (1977) it was sung by Millicent Martin and Julia McKenzie.

"Comes Once in a Lifetime" is a pleasant song of advice from *Subways Are for Sleeping* (1961) by Jule Styne (music) and Betty Comden and Adolph Green (lyric). Angie McKay (Carol Lawrence) and Tom Bailey (Sydney Chaplin) sing the duet that teaches one to seize the day and find happiness now.

"Coming Together, Going Together" is a musical sequence from the Off-Broadway revue *Oh! Calcutta!* (1969) that foreshadows *A Chorus Line* six years before the famous musical. A group of actors audition for a revue that will contain a lot of nudity, and each reveals his or her anxieties, hopes, ambitions and even love of ballet. The song was written by the Open Window, which consisted of Stanley Walden, Robert Dennis and Peter Schickele.

"Company" is the complex, captivating title song that opens the 1970 landmark musical by Stephen Sondheim. Set to the insistent tempo of a telephone's busy signal, the number uses a montage of phrases and sounds to introduce both the central character Robert (Dean Jones) and the subtextual character of New York City itself. As all his friends sing and speak to Robert in fragments, the musical's themes of miscommunication, loneliness and alienation are also introduced. Then Robert himself sings about his friends and the need for company. The title implies both companionship and the ensemble of performers in a musical. Sondheim's music is in the jazzy Broadway style, with a bit of blues suggested here and there. The lyric is so masterfully written that scraps of dialogue, images and phrases all combine to speak with one voice by the time the song reaches its climactic finish. In the Broadway revue *Side by Side by Sondheim* (1977), a section of "Company" was sung by Millicent Martin, Julia McKenzie and David Kernan.

"The Company Way" is a jolly credo of subservience in the corporate structure that is both shrewd and accurate. Frank Loesser wrote the number for *How to Succeed in Business Without Really Trying* (1961), where it is sung by Mr. Twimble (Sammy Smith), the veteran head of the mailroom, to the office clerks Finch (Robert Morse) and Frump (Charles Nelson Reilly).

"Coney Island Boat" is an appealing list song from the period musical *By the Beautiful Sea* (1954) by Arthur Schwartz (music) and Dorothy Fields (lyric). The ensemble at Coney Island sings of all the joys of vacationing at the famous beach resort, while the ex-vaudevillian Lottie Gibson (Shirley Booth) sings "In the Good Old Summertime." The new song becomes a delightful countermelody for the old standard, and together they re-create the turn-of-the-century atmosphere very effectively.

"Conga!" is a furious Latin number from *Wonderful Town* (1953) by Leonard Bernstein (music) and Betty Comden and Adolph Green (lyric). Ruth (Rosalind Russell), desperate for a story that will get her a newspaper job, goes to the Brooklyn Navy Yard to interview some naval cadets from Brazil, but all they want to do is dance the conga. What results is a frenzied song and dance, with Ruth singing out questions as the amorous sailors toss her about in Donald Saddler's wild choreography. Of particular interest are the many 1930s names and references in the lyric, all of which rhyme.

"Consider Yourself" is the rousing music-hall-like song from the British import *Oliver!* (1963) by Lionel Bart that became quite popular. The

Artful Dodger (David Jones) and the ensemble sings the romping number as runaway Oliver Twist (Bruce Prochnik) is introduced to London's world of crime.

"Conversation Piece" is an exciting and unusual piece of theatre music from *Wonderful Town* (1953) in which dialogue and music do not blend together but upset one another in a cynical way. Five New Yorkers (Rosalind Russell, George Gaynes, Edith Adams, Cris Alexander and Dort Clark) try to hold a conversation with each other, but awkwardness abounds. Whenever one speaks, another starts and seems to stop him as the music fills in the dead spots with sly commentary. Finally everyone tries to speak at once, and the music goes berserk with trills and squawks. Betty Comden and Adolph Green wrote the funny, accurate lyric, and Leonard Bernstein composed the adventurous music. The comic number was one Bernstein was particularly proud of all his life.

"Cool" is perhaps Leonard Bernstein's most experimental vocal number in *West Side Story* (1957), a chaotic, jazz-influenced song filled with the kind of tension that he put in the show's dance music. Riff (Mickey Calin) tells the Jets, who have been called hoodlums, to keep cool and save all their anger for the rumble instead of taking it out on each other. Stephen Sondheim wrote the slang-filled lyric, and Jerome Robbins choreographed the eruptive dance that the song led into.

"Cool, Cool, Considerate Men" is a tongue-in-cheek minuet from *1776* (1969) sung by the Pennsylvania delegate John Dickinson (Paul Hecht) and the other conservative members of the Continental Congress, who urge the others to stick to the right. The elegant music and droll lyric are by Sherman Edwards.

"Corner of the Sky" is the fervent "I am" song for the title character in *Pippin* (1972) by Stephen Schwartz. Charlemagne's son Pippin (John Rubinstein) sings the song of yearning in which he seeks to find life's answers as well as his own "corner of the sky." The Jackson Five made a hit recording of the number.

"Could I Leave You?" is a scathing character song from *Follies* (1971) and arguably the most stinging number Stephen Sondheim has ever written. The wealthy but discontented Phyllis Stone (Alexis Smith) answers the song title's musical question for her husband Ben (John McMartin) in this acute list song that explains all the reasons she can and will leave him. As the song builds, the tempo speeds up, the barbs and rhymes increase, and the number becomes a venting of years of anger and frustration. What makes the song bearable for the audience is the high level of wit in Sondheim's lyric. The number was also sung by Julie Andrews in the Off-Broadway revue *Putting It Together* (1993) and, with quite a different twist to it, by David Kernan in the Broadway revue *Side by Side by Sondheim* (1977).

"Could You Use Me?" is a comic duet from the Gershwins' *Girl Crazy* (1930) in which comedy and romance go hand in hand. East Coast playboy Danny Churchill (Allen Kearns) tries to convince Arizona town postmistress Molly Gray (Ginger Rogers) of his usefulness because, as he states, he can certainly use her. George Gershwin wrote the flavorful music, and Ira Gershwin provided the sparkling lyric. In the revised version of the musical called *Crazy for You* (1992), the playboy is Bobby Child (Harry Groener) and the postmistress is Polly Barker (Jodi Benson), but the comic sentiments are the same.

"Could've Been a Ring" is a rustic comic duet by Frank Loesser from the unsuccessful *Greenwillow* (1960) that illustrated that he could write a funny song for rural folks as competently as he wrote for city swells in *Guys and Dolls* (1950). Gramma Briggs (Pert Kelton) and old Thomas Clegg (Lee Cass) almost got married many years back; now in old age the quarrelsome couple recalls what might have happened if they had wed.

"Country House" is an acerbic duet that Stephen Sondheim wrote for the 1987 London revival of *Follies*. The wealthy Ben Stone and his wife Phyllis discuss the possible things they might do to save their marriage, from buying a country house to having a baby, but with no success. The song was heard in New York in the Off-Broadway revue *Putting It Together* (1993), where it was sung by Stephen Collins and Julie Andrews.

"The Country's in the Very Best of Hands" is a tuneful sarcastic number from the comic-strip musical *Li'l Abner* (1956) by Gene de Paul (music) and Johnny Mercer (lyric). Abner Yokum (Peter Palmer) and Marryin' Sam (Stubby Kaye) return to Dogpatch from Washington, D.C., and report on the fine sort of government they found there. Mercer's lyric craftily captures the spirit of cartoonist Al Capp's political humor.

"The Cradle Will Rock" is a song rallying the working man to face the inevitable eruption in the American social system, stating that the storm will come, the cradle will rock. The left-wing number was the title song from Marc Blitzstein's controversial 1938 music-drama. It was sung by Howard Da Silva as the fiery labor organizer Larry Foreman. The marchlike song, along with most of the score, was recorded in 1938, the first full recording in this country of an American musical.

"Crazy Rhythm" is the showstopping jazz number from *Here's Howe* (1928) that was one of the finest rhythm songs of its era. Roger Wolfe Kahn and Joseph Meyer composed the compelling music, Irving Caesar wrote the vivacious lyric, and it was sung by Ben Bernie, Peggy Chamberlain and June O'Dea. Benny Goodman, Doris Day, Gene Nelson and Skitch Henderson are among the many who made successful recordings of "Crazy Rhythm" over the years.

"Crinoline Days" is a nostalgic pastiche number Irving Berlin wrote for the 1922 edition of the *Music Box Revue*. Grace La Rue sang the lovely song, which conjured up visions of the good old days. As she sang, the platform she was standing on rose higher and higher until her giant hoopskirt filled the whole stage. Paul Whiteman's Orchestra made a popular recording of the song.

"Cross Your Heart" is a romantic duet for the young lovers Polly (Mary Lawlor) and Richard (Clarence Nordstrom) in *Queen High* (1926). The Lewis E. Gensler (music) and B.G. DeSylva (lyric) ballad was a hit before the show opened in New York because of the lengthy tryout run in Philadelphia where the song first caught on. Among the recordings made include ones by Ed Smalle, Vaughan DeLeath and the Roger Wolfe Kahn Orchestra (vocal by Henry Burr).

"Crossword Puzzle" is a comic character song about a woman who lost her lover because she was much better at doing the crossword than he was. The nimble David Shire (music) and Richard Maltby, Jr., (lyric) number was sung by Loni Ackerman in the Off-Broadway revue *Starting Here, Starting Now* (1977).

"Cry, the Beloved Country" is a stirring song of anguish from *Lost in the Stars* (1949) by Kurt Weill (music) and Maxwell Anderson (lyric). The chorus, led by Frank Roane, sang this heartfelt song about South Africa as the minister Stephen Kumalo (Todd Duncan) visited his son Absalom in jail and married him to his common-law wife Irina. The song is more a lament than a cry of bitterness as the people weep for their land torn apart by prejudice and greed. The title comes from Alan Paton's powerful novel, on which *Lost in the Stars* is based.

"Cuddle Up a Little Closer, Lovey Mine" is an endearing love song from *Three Twins* (1908) with music by Karl Hoschna and lyric by Otto Hauerbach (later Harbach). Alice Yorke as Kate Armitage sang the intimate song, which then became an elaborate production number that dramatized the seven ages of lovers, from infancy to old age. *Three Twins* was Hoschna and Harbach's first Broadway show and this song became their first hit.

"A Cup of Coffee, a Sandwich and You" was an American song interpolation into the British import *The Charlot Revue of 1926* (1925). Gertrude Lawrence and Jack Buchanan sang and danced the gentle love duet by Joseph Meyer (music) and Al Dubin and Billy Rose (lyric) that celebrated life's simple, everyday pleasures. Lawrence and Buchanan recorded the number as well.

"Cupid and I" is a leisurely waltz from Victor Herbert's operetta *The Serenade* (1897) that made the twenty-year-old Alice Nielsen a star. Yvonne (Nielsen), the eager ballet dancer in Madrid, sings the tantalizing number, which even includes some ingenious syncopation in the music. Harry B. Smith wrote the lyric for the Herbert melody.

D

"Dames at Sea" is the zesty title song from the 1968 Off-Broadway spoof of early Hollywood musicals by Jim Wise (music) and George Haimsohn and Robin Miller (lyric). The song was a number within the show *Dames at Sea* being performed on a battleship because the company had lost its theatre. The ensemble sang the silly song in which the lusty sailors complain that it is not enough to have a girl in every port; they want women when at sea as well, and tap-dancing cuties enter to oblige them.

"Dance a Little Closer" is the enticing title song from the short-lived 1983 musical by Charles Strouse (music) and Alan Jay Lerner (lyric). Harry (Len Cariou), Cynthia (Liz Robertson) and guests at the Barclay-Palace Hotel in the Austrian Alps sang and danced to the delectable number, and the whole company reprised it at the end of the show. Strouse's melody for the song was taken from a forgotten number called "Let Me Sing My Song" (with a lyric by Lee Adams) that was used in *A Broadway Musical* (1978), a musical that, like *Dance a Little Closer*, closed after one performance.

"Dance: Ten; Looks: Three" is a slick comic song from *A Chorus Line* (1975) for Val (Pamela Blair), the busty auditionee who makes no secret that she's had silicone injections to advance her career and her sex life. Marvin Hamlisch composed the jazzy number, and Edward Kleban provided the hilarious lyric. The song's title refers to the kind of evaluations Val got before she discovered the importance of "Tits and Ass" (which the song is often called).

"Dancing in the Dark" is arguably the most famous song by the team of Howard Dietz (lyrics) and Arthur Schwartz (music), the masters of revue scores, and was written for *The Band Wagon* (1931). Schwartz's intoxicating music seems expansive, yet it has a narrow range and mostly uses repeated notes. Dietz's lyric is just as engaging, even if it does refer to the song itself as a waltz when it is written in 4/4 time. John Barker introduced the number in the revue while Tilly Losch danced on a raked, mirrored floor that seemed to move with the changing colored lights. Of the many recordings of the song over the years, none was more popular than Artie Shaw's 1941 version, which sold over a million disks.

"Dancing on the Ceiling" is a delightful song by Richard Rodgers (music) and Lorenz Hart (lyric) that producer Florenz Ziegfeld cut before the opening of the Ed Wynn vehicle *Simple Simon* (1930). The number was later heard in the London musical *Evergreen* (1930), where it was sung by Jessie Matthew and Sonnie Hale. Eventually the song caught on, and British bandleader Jack Hylton had a popular recording of it. Hart's lyric has a dreamy quality as the singer imagines her lover dancing on the ceiling over her bed. In fact, Hart came up with the idea for the lyric after hearing Rodgers' melody and proclaiming that it had a feeling of weightlessness. Jeri Southern made an effective recording of the song in 1952 and Frank Sinatra had a hit with it in 1955.

"Dat's Love" is the heroine's seductive song about the lawlessness of love in *Carmen Jones* (1943), lyricist Oscar Hammerstein's Americanization of Georges Bizet's *Carmen* that retains the general plot and music of the original. Carmen Jones works in a parachute factory in a Southern town during World War Two. One day she taunts Corporal Joe, slyly warning him that if she falls in love with him, it will mean his destruction. The song uses the famous "Habanera" selection from Bizet's opera, but Hammerstein's sultry lyric sits on the melody well. Muriel Smith and Muriel Rahn, in opera fashion, alternated in singing the title role.

"The Day Before Spring" is the alluring title song from the 1945 fantasy musical by Alan Jay Lerner (lyric) and Frederick Loewe (music). Irene Manning sang the reflective ballad about a woman who was depressed but then found love on the first day of spring; now she has forgotten the day before spring.

"Day by Day" is the hit prayer-ballad from the long-running Off-Broadway musical *Godspell* (1971). Robin Lamont and the ensemble sang the gentle revival song, and Stephen Schwartz wrote the infectious music. He also wrote the lyric, which was based on librettist-director John-Michael Tebelak's original, which was based on a prayer by St. Richard of Chichester that was adapted from a twelfth-century prayer. That is an awful lot of authors for one of the musical theatre's simplest and most repetitive song lyrics. The single cut from the original cast album was a best-seller, and the Fifth Dimension also had a hit with "Day By Day."

"Dear Friend" is a song that appears in different guises throughout the charming *She Loves Me* (1963). Amalia Balash (Barbara Cook) and Georg Nowack (Daniel Massey) have been corresponding with each other without knowing each other's identity except as "dear friend." The song is used in various letters they write back and forth but reaches its most poignant moment at the end of Act One when Amalia, alone in a cafe after having been stood up by her friend, asks herself where he can be. Jerry Bock composed the lovely waltz-tempo music, and Sheldon Harnick wrote the delicate lyric.

"Dear Old Syracuse" is the homesick Antipholus' paean to his hometown in Rodgers and Hart's *The Boys From Syracuse* (1938), a jazzy number that then turns into a delightful soft-shoe. Lorenz Hart's lyric, as in the rest of the score, has great fun mixing ancient world references with a contemporary sassy manner. Richard Rodgers' music is similarly clever as it moves from a subdued verse to a swinging refrain. Eddie Albert introduced the number with the aid of Jimmy Savo and the dancing ensemble.

"Dear One" is a tender quartet from *Kiss of the Spider Woman* (1993) by John Kander (music) and Fred Ebb (lyric). The prisoner Molina (Brent Carver) imagines his mother (Merle Louise) comforting him as Valentin (Anthony Crivello), his cellmate, conjures up the vision of his lover Marta (Kristi Carnahan). The four voices combine in tender music and gentle words for the show's most lyrical moment.

"Dear Tom" is a letter song from a woman to her ex-husband that is devoid of bitterness or sentimentality. The number was written by Gretchen Cryer (lyric) and Nancy Ford (music) for the Off-Broadway *I'm Getting My Act Together and Taking It on the Road* (1978), in which pop singer Heather Jones (Cryer) examines her life as she rehearses her new act. In the letter she apologizes for trying too hard to be Mrs. Perfect for him and then manipulating things so that he'd leave her.

"Dear World" is the insisting, tuneful title number from the 1969 Jerry Herman musical based on Jean Giraudoux's *The Madwoman of Chaillot*. The song, which gives instructions to a sick civilization on how to get better again, is more George M. Cohan than French fantasy, but the melody is unquestionably catchy. Angela Lansbury, as the mad Countess Aurelia, and the ensemble sang the number as the first-act finale.

"Deep Down Inside" is a foot-stomping hoedown number from *Little Me* (1962) by Cy Coleman (music) and Carolyn Leigh (lyric). Belle (Virginia Martin) tells the old miser Amos Pinchley (Sid Caesar) that there must be some good in him deep down inside and sings this spirited song with Pinchley Jr.

(Mickey Deems) and the chorus.

"Deep in My Heart, Dear" is the thrilling waltz duet for the lovers in the operetta *The Student Prince* (1924) by Sigmund Romberg (music) and Dorothy Donnelly (lyric). Prince Karl Franz (Howard Marsh), studying with the students in old Heidelberg, and the tavern waitress Kathie (Ilse Marvenga) have fallen in love at first sight and sing this intoxicating duet together in the moonlight. Although the music is more Viennese waltz than German, the number was a sensation on opening night and has remained an operetta favorite. Allan Jones had a successful recording of the song as a solo and Robert Rounseville and Dorothy Kirsten recorded a lovely duet version.

"Democracy March" is a very satirical, highly potent chorus number from the antiwar musical *Johnny Johnson* (1936) by Kurt Weill (music) and Paul Green (lyric). At the unveiling of a new statue dedicated to peace, the townspeople sing of the brave efforts by George Washington, Abraham Lincoln and Woodrow Wilson to preserve peace, and they protest against the war going on in Europe. Then word arrives that the president has declared war against Germany, and the chorus immediately shifts into a war chant with patriotic fervor. A shortened version of the number was performed by the ensemble in the Off-Broadway revue *Berlin to Broadway With Kurt Weill* (1972).

"Den of Iniquity" is the song performed in the spot usually reserved for a sweet romantic duet for the two lovers in a musical comedy. But there was little sweetness in *Pal Joey* (1940), where this number was first sung, so Richard Rodgers (music) and Lorenz Hart (lyric) came up with an appropriately cynical and knowing duet for the situation. The Chicago socialite Vera Simpson (Vivienne Segal) has been having an affair with the younger nightclub singer Joey Evans (Gene Kelly). She has set him up in an apartment (their little den of iniquity) and is even backing his career. The duet reveals their sensual, narcissistic relationship, and the song is perhaps the closest the team ever came to a fully integrated musical number.

"Dentist!" is an outrageous comic song from the Off-Broadway hit *Little Shop of Horrors* (1982) in which the sadomasochist Orin (Franc Luz) explains that dentistry is the ideal profession for him. In the pastiche rock and roll number Orin was backed up by Ronnette (Sheila Kay Davis), Chiffon (Leilani Jones) and Crystal (Jennifer Leigh Warren). Alan Menken composed the eruptive music, and Howard Ashman wrote the hilarious lyric.

"Dere's a Cafe on de Corner" is a sprightly but passionate duet from *Carmen Jones* (1943) that uses the exhilarating "Seguidilla" from Georges Bizet's *Carmen*. Oscar Hammerstein wrote the alluring lyric in which the prisoner Carmen convinces her guard Corporal Joe (Luther Saxon) to set her free and promises to meet him at Billy Pastor's cafe. Muriel Smith and Muriel Rahn, in opera fashion, alternated in singing the title role.

"The Desert Song" is the haunting title number from the exotic 1926 operetta by Sigmund Romberg (music) and Otto Harbach and Oscar Hammerstein (lyric). The leader of the Moroccan Riffs, known only as the Red Shadow (Robert Halliday), sang the smoldering song to Frenchwoman Margot Bonvalet (Vivienne Segal) as he enticed her to come away with him to the beckoning Sahara. Mario Lanza and Judith Raskin recorded an expert duet version of the number. The song is also frequently listed as "Blue Heaven."

"Diamonds Are a Girl's Best Friend" is the cunning credo of Lorelei Lee in *Gentlemen Prefer Blondes* (1949) and the signature song for Carol Channing, who sang it in the original production and in the 1974 revised version called *Lorelei*. In the Jule Styne (music) and Leo Robin (lyric) comic song, Lorelei explains the fleeting nature of compliments and affections compared with the permanency of jewels that never lose their luster. Although the song has always belonged to Channing, Pearl Bailey made a fun recording of it.

"Diary of a Homecoming Queen" is the musical chronicle of a popular high-school girl as she grows older and must hang onto adolescent memories in order to face the disappointments in her current life. Craig Carnelia wrote the potent number, and Maureen Silliman sang it in *Is There Life After High School?* (1982).

"Diga Diga Doo" is a playful jungle song from the revue *Blackbirds of 1928* by Jimmy McHugh (music) and Dorothy Fields (lyric). In an African setting, Adelaide Hall and a chorus of girls in feathered Zulu costumes sang the antic number, which is sometimes listed as "Digga Digga Do." Duke Ellington recorded the song on two different occasions, and the Mills Brothers had a hit recording of it in 1932.

"Dinah" is the perennial song favorite that became a hit when it was interpolated into the Eddie Cantor vehicle *Kid Boots* (1923) where he sang it. Harry Akst composed the catchy melody, and Sam Lewis and Joe Young wrote the lighthearted lyric. The number had been heard previously at a New York nightclub where Ethel Waters first sang it. She later sang it in *Africana* (1927) and *Blackbirds of 1930*, and her recording of the song is still considered a jazz classic. Just as accomplished were an early Louis Armstrong recording and a 1931 record with the Mills Brothers singing with Bing Crosby. The young singer Fanny Rose Shore sang it on her first radio appearance and it went over so well she changed her name to Dinah Shore.

"Disneyland" is a touching ballad from the unsuccessful *Smile* (1986) by Marvin Hamlisch (music) and Howard Ashman (lyric). Doria (Jodi Benson), a teenage contestant in the Young America Miss Pageant, recounts her unhappy home life and her fantasy of escaping to a perfect, artificial world. After *Smile* flopped, both Ashman and Benson went to Disney for real and made the film *The Little Mermaid* (1989). Benson recorded the song in 1994.

"Dites-Moi," the opening number of Rodgers and Hammerstein's *South Pacific* (1949), is as unlikely an opening to a Broadway musical as the same team's gentle beginning for *Oklahoma!* (1943). Two Eurasian children, Jerome (Michael DeLeon) and Ngana (Barbara Luna), sing a thirty-second song entirely in French, do a quick minuet step together, then exit. Yet the brief scene sets up the whole musical play. Just as their names are European and Polynesian, the children suggest the play's thematic conflict by doing a European song and dance on a South Pacific island. In the song the boy asks the mademoiselle if life is beautiful because he is in love with her. The answer will only come at the end of the musical when the adults must face the question, as well as the conflict of cultures that has kept them apart.

"Dixie Moon" is an effective number from the early black musical *The Chocolate Dandies* (1924). The Eubie Blake (music) and Noble Sissle (lyric) song was sung by the ensemble. In the Broadway revue *Eubie* (1978) the number was sung by Mel Johnson, Jr., and the company.

"Do Do Do" is a lighthearted romantic duet from the Gershwins' *Oh, Kay!* (1926) that contains all the silliness of a jazz-age love song. Kay Denham (Gertrude Lawrence) and Jimmy Winter (Oscar Shaw) have pretended to be married to fool a revenue officer and have kissed passionately in front of him to pull off the scheme. Now that they are alone, Kay and Jimmie ask each other to repeat the kiss just for themselves. George Gershwin's music is a merry variation on repeated notes, just as Ira Gershwin uses repeated words for playful effect. Taken away from the musical's context, "Do Do Do" was considered too risqué by some and had trouble getting played on the radio. Lawrence recorded the song as a solo in 1926 and with Harold French as a duet in 1927.

"Do I Hear a Waltz?" is an engaging waltz by the master of the form, Richard Rodgers. It was sung by the American tourist Leona (Elizabeth Allen) in the 1965 musical of the same name. Stephen Sondheim wrote the appealing lyric that expressed the yearnings of a spinster in Venice who believes she will discover true love when it is accompanied by a waltz.

"Do It Again" is a saucy little song by George Gershwin (music) and B.G. DeSylva (lyric) that was interpolated into *The French Doll* (1922). Irene Bordoni sang the suggestive number that had so many double entendres that it was long banned from radio play. Paul Whiteman's Orchestra did make an instrumental recording, though, that was a hit. Although it is an early Gershwin piece, the music is very adventurous, with unexpected changes in rhythm and harmony throughout the song.

"Do-Re-Mi" has become such a widely accepted musical teaching tool that audiences watching revivals of *The Sound of Music* (1959) often imagine it to be an old favorite that Rodgers and Hammerstein interpolated into their show. It is not a particularly stimulating lyric, but then neither is "every good boy does fine." The simple melody using ascending steps on a diatonic scale may seem like it wrote itself, but it took a composer of Richard Rodgers' experience to trust the obvious. Oscar Hammerstein's lyric is likewise obvious, but postulant Maria (Mary Martin) would probably find the punning of "fa" for "far" quite droll. In the musical the number is used by Maria to teach the seven Von Trapp children about music and to break down their cool military demeanor; the song succeeds on both counts. Mitch Miller and Anita Bryant each had hit recordings of "Do-Re-Mi" in the 1960s.

"Do We?" is a supple duet from *70, Girls, 70* (1971) about sex after seventy. Walter (Gil Lamb) and Eunice (Lucie Lancaster) are engaged to be married, and although they are old, they know what we in the audience are thinking. They break into a merry song and dance about the question on everyone's mind, but conclude that a lady and a gentleman just don't tell certain things. John Kander composed the tuneful music, and Fred Ebb wrote the crafty lyric.

"Do You Love Me?" is a charm song from *Fiddler on the Roof* (1964) that became as famous as ballads from other musicals sometimes become. Jerry Bock (music) and Sheldon Harnick (lyric) wrote the touching duet in which Tevye (Zero Mostel) tries to find out if Golde (Maria Karnilova), his wife of twenty-five years, loves him. After some argument and recalling of memories from the past, the unsentimental Golde finally admits that she supposes she does.

"Doin' the New Low-Down" is the snazzy song and dance that Bill "Bojangles" Robinson performed in the revue *Blackbirds of 1928* that launched his career. Jimmy McHugh (music) and Dorothy Fields (lyric) wrote the sparkling number that celebrated a new jazzy dance step. Robinson recorded the song with Don Redman and His Orchestra, and years later Pearl Bailey made a memorable recording of it.

"Doin' the Old Yahoo Step" is a jocular pastiche number from the clever revue *Lend an Ear* (1948) with songs by Charles Gaynor. In the first-act finale the entire cast parodied 1920s musicals with a hysterical minimusical called "The Gladiola Girl." Part of that number was a Charleston spoof in which Carol Channing and the company did the "Yahoo." It was the Broadway debut for Channing as well as for Gower Champion, who choreographed the silly, lovable number.

"Doin' What Comes Natur'lly" is Annie Oakley's "I am" song from Irving Berlin's *Annie Get Your Gun* (1946), explaining how she and her kinfolk have always relied on instinct rather than education. It was the first song Berlin wrote for the score, as an experiment to see if he could pull off the hillbilly quality of the character. Taking Oscar Hammerstein's advice to omit the final "g" in all the "ing" words, Berlin quickly wrote the number and then agreed to do the show. The song was sung by Ethel Merman and Annie's younger siblings in the show. Both Dinah Shore and Doris Day made hit recordings of it.

"Don Jose of Far Rockaway" is a buffoonish comedy number from *Wish You Were Here* (1952), the musical about the Catskills adult Camp Kare-Free by Harold Rome. Itchy (Sidney Armus), the camp's clownish social director, sang the farcical number that made several references to the urban world that the campers came from.

"Donny Didn't, Donny Did" is a fascinating choral number from *The Pink Lady* (1911) by Ivan Caryll (music) and C.M.S. McLellan (lyric). In the forest of Compeigne, a satyr is running loose and stealing kisses from young ladies. When the antiques dealer Dondidier (Frank Lalor) is suspected as the satyr, the forest residents debate whether "Donny" is or isn't the kissing criminal. The concerted number was led by La Comtesse (Louise Kelly), Madame Didier (Alice Hegeman), Lucien (Jack Henderson) and Didier (Frank Lalor) as they moved up and down an elegant staircase, making and denying charges concerning Donny.

"Don't Be a Woman If You Can" is a tricky comic number from the unsuccessful *Park Avenue* (1946) by Arthur Schwartz (music) and Ira Gershwin (lyric). In this daffy trio, Mary Wickes, Martha Errolle and Ruth Matteson advise the audience not to be born female and proceed in an extended patter section to list their reasons, mostly dealing with nail polish, perfume, hairdos and fur coats. Although written at the end of his Broadway career, Gershwin's lyric is top drawer, with dozens of allusions to 1940s people, products and fads. The song's title was inspired by a colorful Tin Pan Alley character named Dave Clark who once praised a Broadway show by saying, "Don't miss it if you can."

"Don't Bother Me, I Can't Cope" is the witty title song from the 1972 all-black revue with music and lyrics by Micki Grant. The ensemble sang this astute number that took a tongue-in-cheek look at the pressures of modern society.

"Don't Cry for Me, Argentina" is the hit song from the British import *Evita* (1979), a dark and curious number that seems unlikely for popularity. It is used in fragments throughout the musical, but its complete rendering is at the top of the second act when Eva Peron (Patti LuPone) appears on the balcony of the Buenos Aires presidential mansion and sings to the people that she will not forget them now that she and her husband are in power. Andrew Lloyd Webber composed the graceful music, and Tim Rice wrote the politically effective but emotionally suspect lyric. British recordings of the song by Elaine Paige and Julie Covington were both very popular in this country.

"Don't Ever Leave Me" is the romantic duet from *Sweet Adeline* (1929), the "gay nineties" musical by Jerome Kern (music) and Oscar Hammerstein (lyric). Addie Schmidt (Helen Morgan), a Broadway star with humble beginnings, sings this plea for permanence with society figure James Day (Robert Chisholm). Judy Kaye and Davis Gaines recorded the number in a restored version in 1992.

"Don't Forget 127th Street" is a robust chorus number from *Golden Boy* (1964) by Charles Strouse (music) and Lee Adams (lyric) that managed to be both exhilarating and sly. Johnny Brown and the residents of Harlem wish boxing contender Joe Wellington (Sammy Davis, Jr.) good luck as he leaves the neighborhood for the big time. What results is an incendiary song and dance that outlines with comic bitterness all the ills of living in Harlem, the place white folks think black people love.

"Don't Let It Get You Down" is a playful song of advice from *Hold on to Your Hats* (1940) by Burton Lane (music) and E. Y. Harburg (lyric). Jack Whiting sang the number, which cautioned about taking love too seriously or else you'll be down in the dumps. Lane's catchy melody line is interrupted throughout the song by a bluesy retard that was played by the brass section. Fifty years later Michael Feinstein and Lane recorded the witty number together.

"Don't Marry Me" is the comic plea of Sammy Fong (Larry Blyden) to his "picture bride" from China (Miyoshi Umeki) in Rodgers and Hammerstein's *Flower Drum Song* (1958). The waggish duet was added in Boston when Larry Storch was replaced by Blyden, who felt that the character needed a strong comic number in his efforts to get out of his contracted marriage. In the Broadway revue *A Grand Night for Singing* (1993), the song was sung as a quartet by Martin Vidnovic, Jason Graae, Victoria Clark and Lynne Wintersteller.

"Don't Quit While You're Ahead" is a delightful Victorian music-hall pastiche from *The Mystery of Edwin Drood* (1985) by Rupert Holmes. The Princess Puffer (Cleo Laine) leads the company in this tuneful song about seeking out all of life's opportunities.

"Don't Rain on My Parade" is a surging song of determination from *Funny Girl* (1964) by Jule Styne (music) and Bob Merrill (lyric). In a bold and stubborn move, Fanny Brice (Barbra Streisand) quits the *Ziegfeld Follies* to pursue the man she loves, refusing to listen to the objections of others who are dampening her chance for happiness. Streisand sang the song on film and in concert and Diana Ross recorded it as well.

"Don't Tell Mama" is a slick nightclub number for Sally Bowles (Jill Haworth) and the Kit Kat Klub girls in *Cabaret* (1966) by John Kander (music) and Fred Ebb (lyric). The playful song has more a British music-hall flavor than a German one, but Sally, who is English, sings the number as a seemingly proper young lady who, instead of going to finishing school, is strutting her stuff in a sleazy nightclub. Although the pastiche number is done as a cabaret ditty, it also serves as Sally's "I am" song.

"Don't Wanna Be No Superstar" is the boast of the three stand-up comics (Scott Bakula, Jerry Colker and John Kassir) in the Off-Broadway musical *Three Guys Naked From the Waist Down* (1985). The lively number by Michael Rupert (music) and Colker (lyric) lists all the banalities of being famous, but it's clear the three aspiring entertainers would gladly suffer them all.

"Doomed, Doomed, Doomed" is a riotous rag from *The Golden Apple* (1954) that satirizes both ancient mythology and modern science. Miss Minerva (Portia Nelson) leads the ensemble in this doomsday description of the universe and concludes that we are nothing but specks of cosmic dust and doomed to disappear without a trace. Jerome Moross composed the scintillating music, and John Latouche wrote the sly lyric.

"The Door of Her Dreams" is a lovely waltz number in the Eastern European style even though it is sung in the Canadian Rockies, the setting for *Rose-Marie* (1924). Mary Ellis, the operetta's title heroine, sang the song with the chorus. Rudolf Friml wrote the pleasing music, and Otto Harbach and Oscar Hammerstein provided the dreamy lyric.

"Down by the Erie Canal" is a rompish number by George M. Cohan for his revue *Hello, Broadway!* (1914). The song was used in a spectacular production number that started out with Louise Dresser and the chorus in front of the curtain singing the song as they shook tambourines. Then a boy in the balcony took up the song, then an old man in a box, and finally the curtains on stage parted to reveal colorful Venetian gondolas flowing along the Erie Canal. The song was sung as "Down by the Erie" by Jonelle Allen, Susan Batson and the ensemble of the bio-musical *George M!* (1968).

"Down in the Depths (On the Ninetieth Floor)" was a tender moment in an otherwise raucous and silly show, Cole Porter's *Red, Hot and Blue!* (1936). Ethel Merman sang the torch song as "Nails" O'Reilly, a former manicurist who is now a wealthy Manhattan widow, who looks out from her penthouse and envies all those in the vibrant city who have found love. Although it was an atypical song choice for Merman, it was long associated with her.

"Down With Everyone's Who's Up" is a slapstick chorus number from the dark satire *Let 'Em Eat Cake* (1933). Political agitator Kruger (Philip Loeb) rouses the masses with this nonsense list song that is against everyone from Stravinsky to Minsky. George Gershwin wrote the eruptive music, and Ira Gershwin provided the acerbic lyric. In the musical the song is linked to a less irate number called "Union Square" in which the populace gathers in the fresh air of Union Square to cure all the problems of mankind. Neither number was ever recorded until 1987, when virtually the whole score was finally put on record by the Brooklyn Academy of Music with David Garrison as Kruger.

"Down With Love" is a satirical song that starts by assaulting romance and ends up lampooning love songs themselves. The number was written by Harold Arlen (music) and E.Y. Harburg (lyric) for the offbeat *Hooray for What!* (1937), where it was sung by Jack Whiting, June Clyde and Vivian Vance. Arlen's music is upbeat and rhythmic and contrasts playfully with Harburg's caustic lyric that explodes love clichés left and right. Modern interpretations of the number by Barbra Streisand in the 1970s and Julie Wilson in the 1980s brought the song back to the attention of the public.

"Dream Babies" is an enchanting ballad from *The Me Nobody Knows* (1970), the arresting revue based on the writings of New York ghetto school kids. Gerri Dean sang the haunting number by Gary William Friedman (music) and Will Holt (lyric) about the optimistic dreams of children living in a bitter environment.

"Dressing Them Up" is the animated "I am" song for the window dresser Molina (Brent Carver) in *Kiss of the Spider Woman* (1993) by John Kander (music) and Fred Ebb (lyric). Molina explains to his new cellmate Valentin (Anthony Crivello) his high standards in dressing the mannequins at the department store where he worked before being arrested. The song is both flamboyant and sincere as the character's serious concern about seemingly trivial things is revealed.

"Drinking Song" from the operetta *The Student Prince* (1924) is the musical theatre's most famous drinking song and one that had a particular popularity later during Prohibition. At the Inn of the Three Golden Apples, the students from Heidelberg University were led by Raymond Marlowe in the lusty salute to love and drink and, specifically, the beautiful waitress Kathie (Ilse Marvenga). Before opening, the producing Shubert brothers wanted the song cut and replaced with a number for a chorus line of pretty females, but composer Sigmund Romberg, lyricist Dorothy Donnelly and their lawyer fought the producers and won. In the original production, thirty-six full-throated male voices sang the rousing number (sometimes listed as "Drink, Drink, Drink"), and it was such a hit that the Shuberts made sure all their subsequent operettas had a strong male chorus in them.

"Drop That Name" is an entertaining chorus number from *Bells Are Ringing* (1956) in which lyricists Betty Comden and Adolph Green get to show off their talent for comically rhyming proper names. Jule Styne wrote the zippy music, and the song was sung by Judy Holliday and the social-climbing partygoers who can't help but toss the names of celebrities into every conversation.

"Drums in My Heart" is an exciting spiritual-like number from the short-lived *Through the Years* (1932) by Vincent Youmans (music) and Edward Heyman (lyric). Reginald Owen sang the surging song, which achieved some popularity after the show's twenty-performance run.

"Duet for One (The First Lady of the Land)" is an ambitious musical sequence from the ill-fated *1600 Pennsylvania Avenue* (1976) by Leonard Bernstein (music) and Alan Jay Lerner (lyric). Patricia Routledge gave a tour de force performance in the number by portraying outgoing first lady Julia Grant on the inauguration day of President Grant's successor Rutherford Hayes. As the swearing-in proceeded, Routledge, with a quick change of wig and attitude, became the jubilant new first lady Lucy Hayes and then continued to switch back and forth between the characters as the ceremony and song climaxed. The score for *1600 Pennsylvania Avenue* was never recorded, but the entire "Duet for One" sequence was put on record in 1991 with Judy Kaye singing the double role.

"Dulcinea" is the ravishing ballad Don Quixote (Richard Kiley) sings in *Man of La Mancha* (1965) when he first sees the sluttish Aldonza (Joan Diener) and imagines her to be the Lady Dulcinea. The delectable number is reprised near the end of the musical when Aldonza sings it to the dying Quixote to help restore his memory. The muleteers also reprise the song with a mocking version to taunt Aldonza. Mitch Leigh composed the delicate music, and Joe Darion wrote the impassioned lyric.

"D'Ye Love Me?" is one of the hits to come out of *Sunny* (1925) by Jerome Kern (music) and Otto Harbach and Oscar Hammerstein (lyric). Circus bareback rider Sunny Peters (Marilyn Miller) sang the gentle, lullabylike number, which was pliable enough in its musical construction to be used as a waltz at one point and as a foxtrot at another. Jack Donahue did a dance routine to the song that stopped the show each evening. The number was originally listed as "Do You Love Me?" but used the slangy title when it was published and has been known as "D'Ye Love Me?" ever since.

E

"Each Tomorrow Morning" is the resolute "I am" song for the mad Countess Aurelia (Angela Lansbury) in the Jerry Herman musical *Dear World* (1969). The pleasantly demented lady explains how she lives day to day, refusing to admit the passage of time. The song was also used for a ballet sequence for the whole cast and was later reprised by Kurt Peterson as the young Julian.

"Eadie Was a Lady" is the exciting song that Ethel Merman sang as the show-within-the-show number in *Take a Chance* (1932). In a New Orleans dive, Merman and a chorus of girls dressed like sailors sang the narrative ballad about bordello operator Eadie, who has passed on but whose memory is celebrated in the electric song. Richard Whiting and Nacio Herb Brown wrote the fervent music, and B.G. DeSylva and Roger Edens provided the sassy lyric. Lillian Roth made a hit recording of the song.

"The Eagle and Me" is a soaring ballad in which a slave yearns for freedom in *Bloomer Girl* (1944), the Civil War-era musical by Harold Arlen (music) and E.Y. Harburg (lyric). Pompey (Dooley Wilson), an escaped slave on the Underground Railroad, explains to his master why he ran off. It is a passionate plea, filled with nature images and examples of animals roaming unconfined, but it is not a pathetic or subservient song. Pompey seeks to change things rather than endure them. Harburg's lyric is poetic but boldly confrontational. Instead of submitting to greater powers, as in "Ol' Man River," or grieving over a tragic situation, as in Irving Berlin's "Supper Time," "The Eagle and Me" gently but clearly demands freedom. Harburg biographers Harold Meyerson and Ernie Harburg called it "the first theatre song of the fledgling civil rights movement." The ballad enjoyed some popularity and was recorded on occasion. Of particular interest is Lena Horne's 1988 recording that clearly interprets the number as a civil-rights anthem.

"Ease on Down the Road" is the vibrant Motown version of "We're Off to See the Wizard" from the black reworking of *The Wizard of Oz* called *The Wiz* (1975). Charlie Smalls wrote the exhilarating number that was sung by Dorothy (Stephanie Mills), the Scarecrow (Hinton Battle), the Tinman (Tiger Haynes) and the Lion (Ted Ross) as they travel to see the all-powerful Wiz. The most popular song to come from the show, "Ease on Down the Road" had a hit recording by the group Consumer Rapport.

"Easier to Love" is a discerning ballad from *Baby* (1983) by David Shire (music) and Richard Maltby, Jr., (lyric). Alan McNally (James Congdon), who has been married for many years and has grown children, sings of how simple and open the love for a young child is as compared to the complex and mysterious love for a wife.

"Easter Parade," one of Irving Berlin's all-time hit songs, was introduced in the lavish revue *As Thousands Cheer* (1933), but the melody had been used fifteen years earlier for an unsuccessful song called "Smile and Show Your Dimple." Berlin rewrote the lyric for the nostalgic rotogravure section of the revue in which Marilyn Miller and Clifton Webb sang it as they stepped out of an old sepia photograph and paraded down Fifth Avenue. Among the many recordings of "Easter Parade" were ones by Guy Lombardo and Harry James, each one selling over a million copies.

"Easy Street" is a jazzy 1930s pastiche number from *Annie* (1977) that contrasted nicely with all the sweetness that ran through most of the show. The conniving Miss Hannigan (Dorothy Loudon) sings the Charles Strouse (music) and Martin Charnin (lyric) song with her low-life brother (Bob Fitch) and his floozie (Barbara Erwin) as the three of them plan to use the orphan Annie to find a spot for them on easy street.

"Easy Terms" is a heart-rending ballad from the British import *Blood Brothers* (1993) by Willy Russell. The impoverished single mother Mrs. Johnstone (Stephanie Lawrence) sings about how you cannot really call things your own in this world. She sings it to her babies in a pram as the creditors repossess her furniture; then the song is reprised with even deeper implications when Mrs. Johnstone gives up one of her twin babies because she cannot afford to keep it.

"Easy to Be Hard" is the beguiling hit ballad from *Hair* (1968), the "tribal love-rock musical" by Galt MacDermot (music) and Gerome Ragni and James Rado (lyric). The song concerns indifference in the world, but, more specifically, it is sung by Sheila (Lynn Kellogg) to her lover, who cares about mankind but treats individual people shamelessly. In the 1967 Off-Broadway version, the ballad was sung by Suzannah Evans, Linda Compton, Paul Jabara and the company. The group Three Dog Night made a best-selling recording of the song in 1969.

"Easy to Love" is the beloved Cole Porter ballad known to many from the movies, but it was originally written for the nautical Broadway musical *Anything Goes* (1934). Planned as the romantic duet for William Gaxton and Bettina Hall, the number was replaced by "All Through the Night" when Gaxton objected to singing the difficult high notes in "Easy to Love." The song was interpolated into the 1988 Broadway revival of *Anything Goes*, where it was sung by Howard McGillin.

"The Echo Waltz" is a silly, likable production number from *Dames at Sea* (1968), the Off-Broadway spoof of the early Hollywood musicals by Jim Wise (music) and George Haimsohn and Robin Miller (lyric). Mona Kent (Tamara Long), the star of the show, sings this reverberating number with Joan (Sally Stark) and Ruby (Bernadette Peters), while the rest of the ensemble echoes them with ridiculous glee.

"Economics" is a swinging ragtime quartet from the experimental *Love Life* (1948) by Alan Jay Lerner (lyric) and Kurt Weill (music). The inventive number was a lesson on what is and what is not good economics, concluding that what is good for the economy is bad for love. The song was introduced by a black quartet (John Diggs, Joseph James, James Young and William Veasey) in the original production, and Dorothy Loudon recorded it years later.

"Edelweiss" is the gentle, graceful folk song that Richard Rodgers (music) and Oscar Hammerstein (lyric) wrote for *The Sound of Music* (1959), although many assumed it was an old Austrian piece of folklore once sung by the real Von Trapp family. An edelweiss is an Austrian alpine flower and a simple but potent symbol of national pride. The Captain (Theodore Bikel) and his family sing the number at the Salzburg Music Festival near the end of the musical. Originally it was planned that they reprise one of the earlier songs from the score, but it was later felt that the Captain should use the festival as a way of displaying his Austrian patriotism to the Nazis occupying his homeland. Hammerstein, already quite ill and only nine months from death, worked on the short, fervent lyric at home; it was the last song lyric that he ever wrote.

"Eileen" is the waltzing title song from the 1917 operetta that was Victor Herbert's personal favorite. Irish rebel Captain Barry O'Day (Walter Scanlan) sang the slow and alluring waltz about his beloved Eileen Mulvaney (Grace Breen). Henry Blossom wrote the lyric for Herbert's Irish melody.

"El Capitan's Song" is a robust march from John Philip Sousa's operetta *El Capitan* (1896) and one of his most memorable compositions. Comic star DeWolf Hopper played the swaggering Viceroy of Peru who disguises himself as the bandit El Capitan. This boastful song was sung by Hopper on his grand entrance and then later became a rousing orchestral march for the rebel forces. Sousa wrote the music and, with Tom Frost, the lyric. It was sung by Trey Wilson and the ensemble in the 1980 Broadway revue *Tintypes*.

"Elegance" is a festive quartet from *Hello, Dolly!* (1964) that opens the second act with a good-natured spoof of high society. The Jerry Herman song was performed by Cornelius (Charles Nelson Reilly), Irene Malloy (Eileen Brennan), Barnaby (Jerry Dodge) and Minnie Fay (Sondra Lee) as they use the fashionable method of transportation: walking (and a little dancing as well). The song's authorship is sometimes attributed to Bob Merrill, who was among the songwriters producer David Merrick called in to "doctor" the show out of town, but Merrill refuses to acknowledge that he wrote it.

"The Elephant Song" is a comic song about death from the raucous *70, Girls, 70* (1971) by John Kander (music) and Fred Ebb (lyric). Ida (Mildred Natwick) tells the audience of her experience at the zoo when her favorite elephant died. She wanted to know where the body of the deceased elephant goes, but no one on the zoo staff would answer her question. She still wants to know, so she asks the audience the musical question "Where does an elephant go?"

"Embraceable You" is one of the Gershwin brothers' most endearing ballads, an indelible blending of music and lyrics in a number that is expressive without being sentimental. It was written for the unproduced *East Is West* but was first heard in *Girl Crazy* (1930) when playboy Danny Churchill (Allen Kearns) and prairie postmistress Molly Gray (Ginger Rogers) finally admit they are in love. George Gershwin's music is simple, economic and totally captivating, with some very unusual but subtle innovations in the melody line. Ira Gershwin's lyric is enticing and sits on the music beautifully, especially when he finds repeated words to go with the music's repeated notes. "Embraceable You" is one of the most recorded of the brothers' songs and was a personal favorite of Ira Gershwin. It was used in no less than eight movie musicals, and has been recorded by Nat "King" Cole, Judy Garland, Michael Feinstein and many others. In the revised version of *Girl Crazy* called *Crazy for You* (1992), the duet is sung by playboy Bobby Child (Harry Groener) and postmistress Polly Barker (Jodi Benson).

"Empty Chairs at Empty Tables" is the poignant ballad from *Les Misérables* (1987) in which Marius (David Bryant) mourns for all his fellow students who died on the barricade during the unsuccessful uprising. Claude-Michel Schönberg wrote the simple folklike music, and Herbert Kretzmer adapted the French lyric by Alain Boublil and Jean-Marc Natel.

"Empty Pockets Filled With Love" is a pleasant love duet from Irving Berlin's unsuccessful *Mr. President* (1962) that uses a contrapuntal countermelody in the refrain. Jack Haskell, as a Secret Service agent, and Anita Gillette, as the president's daughter, sang the "double" song that was reminiscent of Berlin's earlier "You're Just in Love" but not nearly as lovable. *Mr. President* was Berlin's last Broadway score.

"The Enchanted Train" is an inviting song that is a tribute to, of all trains, the Long Island Railroad. The charming number was sung by Gertrude Bryan and Rudolf Cameron in *Sitting Pretty* (1924), who saw the train as highly romantic because it was the commuter line that brought him home from work to their bungalow on Long Island. Jerome Kern composed the tingling music, and P.G. Wodehouse wrote the playful lyric. Paige O'Hara and Davis Gaines recorded a restored version of the duet in 1989.

"Epiphany" is the ferocious diatribe that Sweeney Todd (Len Cariou) delivers in a fit of bitter revenge in *Sweeney Todd, the Demon Barber of Fleet Street* (1979) by Stephen Sondheim. When Todd misses his opportunity to slit the throat of Judge Turpin and revenge his dear wife, he bursts into this musical nervous breakdown that creates the demon murderer of the legend. Sondheim uses terse phrases with few rhymes in the lyric, and the pounding, Prokofiev-like music reflects the chaotic turbulence within the character.

"Erbie Fitch's Twitch" is a larkish music-hall pastiche from the Victorian-era musical *Redhead* (1959) by Albert Hague (music) and Dorothy Fields (lyric). Essie Whimple (Gwen Verdon) dons a tweed outfit complete with bowler hat and cane and, in a colorful cockney dialect, does a song and dance turn at the Odeon Music Hall. Director-choreographer Bob Fosse's staging of the electric number and Verdon's performance are what made it memorable.

"Evelina" is a comic-romantic duet that was the hit song from *Bloomer Girl* (1944) by Harold Arlen (music) and E.Y. Harburg (lyric). The Southern gentleman Jefferson Calhoun (David Brooks) woos the emancipated Yankee suffragette Evelina Applegate (Celeste Holm), who is attracted to him despite the fact that her father wishes for the marriage for business reasons. As Calhoun melodically praises her, Evelina replies with sarcastic commentary, and the duet turns into a playful, kidding conversation in song. Arlen's music is very unusual, ignoring traditional song structure, and Harburg's lyric is equally unique, with curious rhyming used throughout.

"Every Day a Little Death" is a bittersweet duet about the humiliation of love from *A Little Night Music* (1973) by Stephen Sondheim. When the Countess Charlotte Malcolm (Patricia Elliot) tells the young bride Anne Egerman (Victoria Mallory) that both of their husbands are having affairs with the actress Desiree, the two women sing this beguiling number about the everyday heartaches that slowly destroy one. The song is melodic and elegant even while it is melancholy. Martin Gottfried also pointed out that the topic for the number is unique, there being "no precedent for life's painful pinpricks being the subject of a show tune." In the Off-Broadway revue *Putting It Together* (1993), the duet was sung by Julie Andrews and Rachel York.

"Every Day Is Ladies' Day With Me" is a dandy comic number from Victor Herbert's *The Red Mill* (1906), more a musical comedy than the composer's usual operetta milieu. When the Governor of Zeeland (Neal McCay) arrives in town to marry the burgomaster's daughter, he is accompanied by a bevy of beautiful girls. He makes no apologies and sings this lively march number. Henry Blossom provided the lyric for Herbert's merry music, and years later Gordon MacRae made a memorable recording of the song.

"Every Little Movement (Has a Meaning of Its Own)" is the captivating song from *Madame Sherry* (1910) that still remains a standard, particularly as a dance number. It was written by Karl Hoschna (music) and Otto Harbach (lyric) and was used throughout the show as a kind of leitmotif. Dance instructor Lulu (Frances Demarest) sings the number as a dance lesson for her young pupils at the Sherry School of Aesthetic Dancing. Later in the show she meets the wealthy Venezuelan Leonard Gomez (John Reinhard) and sings the number to him as a love song, the clever lyric taking on a new meaning. The song is also used as a romantic duet and dance by the school's principal Edward Sherry (Jack Gardner) and the fresh-from-the-convent-school Yvonne (Lina Abarbanell).

"Every Street's a Boulevard in Old New York" is a cheery tribute to Manhattan from *Hazel Flagg* (1953) by Jule Styne (music) and Bob Hilliard (lyric). The mayor of New York (Jack Whiting) sings and dances this soft-shoe number for the city representatives who are arguing over what street the parade for Hazel Flagg (Helen Gallagher) ought to be held on.

"Everybody Has the Right to Be Wrong" is a 1960s pop ballad by James Van Heusen (music) and Sammy Cahn (lyric) from *Skyscraper* (1965). Peter L. Marshall, as the young architect Timothy Bushman, sang the song about human fallibility; later in the show it was reprised by the dreamy Georgina, played by Julie Harris in her only musical role. The song enjoyed some popularity due to a recording by Frank Sinatra.

"Everybody Loves Louis" is an artful comic song from *Sunday in the Park With George* (1984) by Stephen Sondheim. In order to make her ex-lover, the artist George Seurat, jealous, the model Dot (Bernadette Peters) sings the praises of her new lover, Louis the baker. Sondheim's music is buoyant with a sassy French liveliness, and his lyric playfully uses double entendres equating baking and lovemaking.

"Everybody Ought to Have a Maid" is the audience favorite from *A Funny Thing Happened on the Way to the Forum* (1962) that stops the show whenever the musical farce is performed. Stephen Sondheim wrote the vaudeville turn about the advantages, practical and sexual, of having a maid in the house, and it was sung by the dirty old men Senex (David Burns), Pseudolus (Zero Mostel), Hysterium (Jack Gilford) and Marcus Lycus (John Carradine). Although it is the least integrated number in the show, the song captures the bawdy, carefree spirit of the musical with its prankish double entendres, clever repetition and double and triple rhymes. As Martin Gottfried stated, it is "the only old-fashioned showstopper that Sondheim would ever write." The song was performed by Stephen Collins, Christopher Durang and Michael Rupert in the Off-Broadway revue *Putting It Together* (1993).

"Everybody Rejoice" is an effervescent chorus number interpolated into *The Wiz* (1975), the all-black retelling of *The Wizard of Oz*. When Dorothy (Stephanie Mills) destroys Evillene (Mabel King), the Wicked Witch of the West, by accidentally melting her with water, all the enslaved Winkies join Dorothy in celebrating their newfound freedom. Although Charlie Smalls wrote the score for *The Wiz*, this number had music and lyric by Luther Vandross.

"Everybody Says Don't" is a driving song about nonconformity from the short-lived Stephen Sondheim musical *Anyone Can Whistle* (1964). Oddball psychiatrist Dr. Hapgood (Harry Guardino) sings this testament to breaking the rules and being free to experience life fully. The song was sung by Millicent Martin, Julia McKenzie and David Kernan in the Broadway revue *Side by Side by Sondheim* (1977), and Barbra Streisand recorded the number in a personalized rendition in 1993.

"Everybody Step" was the rousing first-act finale of the first edition of the *Music Box Revue* (1921) by Irving Berlin. The song has some of Berlin's most vibrant use of syncopated tempo, and his split, abrupt rhyming in the lyric is equally zippy. The dance number was sung by the three Brox Sisters, who invited everybody to join in the new-style syncopated steps. The song became very popular in the dance-crazy 1920s, helped no doubt by a best-selling Paul Whiteman Orchestra recording.

"Everybody's Got a Home But Me" is an agreeable ballad from *Pipe Dream* (1955), Rodgers and Hammerstein's least-known show. The number is the "I am" song for the lonely drifter Suzy (Judy Tyler). Richard Rodgers wrote one of his pleasing melodies that climb the scale comfortably, and Oscar Hammerstein's lyric is filled with touching domestic images. Despite the show's quick disappearance, the song became somewhat popular due to a hit recording by Eddie Fisher.

"Everybody's Got the Right (To Be Happy)" is a jaunty Broadway-style number with a deeply troubled subtext from the controversial *Assassins* (1991) by Stephen Sondheim. At a fairground shooting gallery, the Proprietor (William Parry) invites passersby to take a shot at images of U.S. presidents. The cheery music and lyric suggest that all discontentment and frustration will be relieved by taking aim at infamy. Different assassins from history come to the booth and join in singing this disturbingly satiric number.

"Everyone Hates His Parents" is a wily soft-shoe number from *Falsettoland* (1990) by William Finn. The adolescent Jason (Danny Gerard) has upset his parents by refusing to go through with their bar mitzvah plan for him; so his stepfather-psychiatrist Mendel (Chip Zien) reveals to him in song and dance that everyone hates his parents, but you grow up, have kids, they hate you and you warm up to your own parents.

"Everything Beautiful Happens at Night" is a pleasing ballad about the magic of the evening from *110 in the Shade* (1963) by Tom Jones (lyric) and Harvey Schmidt (music). The enchanting number was sung by Toby (George Church), Jimmie (Scooter Teague), Snookie (Lesley Warren) and the townspeople.

"Everything's Coming Up Roses" is Mama Rose's determined song of optimism sung at a moment of temporary defeat in *Gypsy* (1959). When her daughter June runs off and elopes with Tulsa, Mama Rose (Ethel Merman) decides that she'll make her other daughter Louise (Sandra Church) into a vaudeville star. Jule Styne wrote the explosive music, which, in part, was from a song he and lyricist Sammy Cahn had written for *High Button Shoes* (1947) but was dropped before opening. Stephen Sondheim wrote the lyric for "Everything's Coming Up Roses," giving a desperate edge to the eager words that makes the song so powerful.

"Ev'ry Time We Say Goodbye" may be an atypical Cole Porter ballad in its melody and lyric, but it is still one of his finest efforts. The unusual shifts in key give the song's melody a haunting quality, and the sentiment of the lyric is straightforward and deeply heartfelt. The most famous moment of this farewell song is near the end, when the lyric states how one's emotion moves from "major to minor" and the music shifts into a minor chord on the phrase. Nan Wynn introduced the ballad in the revue *Seven Lively Arts* (1944) and Benny Goodman's Orchestra (vocal by Peggy Mann), Stan Kenton, Lena Horne and others made popular recordings of it.

"Ev'rything I've Got (Belongs to You)" is a delightfully wicked comic duet that Richard Rodgers (music) and Lorenz Hart (lyric) wrote for *By Jupiter* (1942). The rhythmic number is sung by Queen Hippolyta (Benay Venuta) and King Sapiens (Ray Bolger), who trade verbal barbs and acerbic putdowns with great panache.

"Exactly Like You" is the warm Jimmy McHugh (music) and Dorothy Fields (lyric) ballad that Harry Richman and Gertrude Lawrence sang in the *International Revue* (1930). The number was also sung by Ann Jillian and the girls' chorus in the Broadway revue *Sugar Babies* (1979), and Barbara Cook made a delectable recording of it in 1993.

F

"F.D.R. Jones" is an inspirational number from the revue *Sing Out the News* (1938) by Harold Rome. Rex Ingram and the people of Harlem sang the exuberant tribute to then-president Roosevelt at a christening where a black baby is named after him. The song became popular nationwide, and both Ella Fitzgerald and Cab Calloway made hit recordings of it.

"Fabulous Feet" is one of several energetic dance numbers in *The Tap Dance Kid* (1983), the contemporary musical about black dancers by Henry Krieger (music) and Robert Lorick (lyric). Uncle Dipsey (Hinton Battle), a professional dancer-choreographer, sang and danced this celebratory number with the ensemble. Danny Daniels choreographed the show-stopping number in which the dancers tapped away while wearing sneakers.

"The Face on the Dime" is a quiet but powerful tribute to the recently deceased Franklin Roosevelt that was written by Harold Rome for the postwar military revue *Call Me Mister* (1946). Lawrence Winters sang the moving song about the former commander- in-chief whose likeness was etched on a newly minted coin.

"Falling in Love With Love" is one of Richard Rodgers' most beloved waltzes. Lorenz Hart wrote the adult and knowing lyric that gives the love song a surprisingly somber mood. The number was written for *The Boys From Syracuse* (1938) where it was sung by Adriana (Muriel Angelus) and her household maidens as they weaved a tapestry. Rodgers manages to work a methodically repeating pattern into the music that suggests the monotony of toiling, yet the song moves beautifully and has enchanted listeners for decades in various recordings and productions.

"Fancy Forgetting" is an enticing waltz pastiche from the British import

The Boy Friend (1954). The venerable Madame Dubonnet (Ruth Altman) and her old flame Percival Browne (Eric Berry) recall a waltz that they danced to in Paris years ago and revel in this operatic duet followed by a grand ballroom dance routine. Sandy Wilson wrote the rhapsodic music and lyric.

"Fanny" is the appealing title song from the 1954 operatic musical by Harold Rome. Marius (William Tabbert) sings to Fanny (Florence Henderson) that as much as he loves her, his yearning to go to sea is even greater. The song became very popular due to producer David Merrick's strong promotion and hit recordings by Eddie Fisher and Fred Waring's Pennsylvanians.

"Far From the Home I Love" is the tender ballad from *Fiddler on the Roof* (1964) that Hodel (Julia Migenes) sings to her father (Zero Mostel) before leaving her village to find her fiancé in Siberia. Jerry Bock (music) and Sheldon Harnick (lyric) wrote the score's most operatic song for this scene because Migenes had a much fuller voice than most of the performers cast in the show. It is a graceful piece of writing, expansive yet colloquial.

"Faraway Boy" is a devoted, evocative ballad from the unsuccessful *Greenwillow* (1960) by Frank Loesser. Dorrie (Ellen McCown) has loved and lost the only man in her life; in a dreamy soliloquy she imagines herself telling some future lover that she will always have a warm spot in her heart for her first love.

"Farewell Letter" is a musical missive from Stephen Sondheim's *Passion* (1994) that turns into a duet for two lovers parting ways. The married Clara (Marin Mazzie) writes to her lover Giorgio (Jere Shea) that they must break off their affair until her son is older and they can risk any scandal. Giorgio, reading her letter, is shocked that her love could be so practical and compromising when he loves her passionately and without conditions. The number blends into a confrontational duet in which both realize that their love was not so special and perfect as they once thought.

"The Farmer and the Cowman" is the lively song and dance number that opens the second act of *Oklahoma!* (1943). The Richard Rodgers (music) and Oscar Hammerstein (lyric) song uses the structure of a country reel rather than a traditional musical theatre production number. It was introduced by Aunt Eller (Betty Garde) and Andrew Carnes (Ralph Riggs) with the ensemble.

"Farming" is a specialty number that Danny Kaye sang in Cole Porter's *Let's Face It* (1941). The comic list song concerned the latest trend of celebrities buying farms and pretending to get back to nature, and the lyric drops names indiscriminately. The song's music is distinctive in that it shows the influence the swing era was having on Porter's compositional skills.

"Fascinating Rhythm" is the song that brought the vibrant jazz age to Broadway. The Gershwin brothers wrote it for their first collaboration, *Lady, Be Good!* (1924), where it was sung and danced by Adele and Fred Astaire with Cliff "Ukelele Ike" Edwards. George Gershwin's tricky rhythms and his highly sophisticated syncopation made "Fascinating Rhythm" amazingly fresh. Audiences did not have to understand the song's unusual beat and rapid changes in meter to know that they were hearing something new. Ira Gershwin's lyric is also noteworthy, filled with double rhymes and rhymes on the penultimate note of each phrase in order to keep up with the brisk music. Adele and Fred Astaire recorded the number in 1926 with George Gershwin at the piano.

"Fasten Your Seat Belts (It's Gonna Be a Bumpy Night)" is an acerbic number from *Applause* (1970) whose title was taken from the most famous line in the film *All About Eve*, the basis for the musical. Margo Channing (Lauren Bacall) is feeling a bit insecure about her career and her love life, so she gets drunk at her own party, causing an awkward reaction among the partygoers. Charles Strouse wrote the appropriately idiosyncratic music, and Lee Adams provided the cunning lyric.

"Fatherhood Blues" is a comic frolic from *Baby* (1983) about the joy and panic of becoming a father. Expectant father Alan (James Congdon) and the young, single father-to-be Danny (Todd Graff) sing a contagious song of excitement while the hoping-to-be-a-father Nick (Martin Vidnovic) and the weary dad with kids Dean (Dennis Warning) add their hopes and comments. David Shire composed the jubilant music, and Richard Maltby, Jr., wrote the sprightly lyric.

"Fathers and Sons" is a moving, reflective musical monologue from *Working* (1978), the short-lived revue about America's work force. Stephen Schwartz wrote the music and lyric, and Bob Gunton sang the powerful number in which a man starts thinking of his grown-up son, then recalls his own father, seeking forgiveness from them both.

"Feeling Good" is a stirring ballad of yearning for freedom from the allegorical musical *The Roar of the Greasepaint -- The Smell of the Crowd* (1965) by Leslie Bricusse and Anthony Newley. Gilbert Price, as "the Negro," stopped the show with his soaring rendition of the song that celebrated the freedom of creatures in nature and envied their ability to escape bondage.

"Feeling I'm Falling" is one of Ira Gershwin's most alliterative lyrics, a sassy love duet that playfully uses a series of "f" sounds in the refrain. George Gershwin wrote the nimble music, and it was sung by Gertrude Lawrence and

Paul Frawley in the unsuccessful *Treasure Girl* (1928).

"Feelings" is a charming character song from "The Diary of Adam and Eve" playlet in *The Apple Tree* (1966) by Jerry Bock (music) and Sheldon Harnick (lyric). The first woman (Barbara Harris) is having conflicting emotions about the first man (Alan Alda) and concludes that these new feelings are all part of a new human sensation called "hell."

"Feet, Do Yo' Stuff" is a vibrant 1920s jazz pastiche number from *Hallelujah, Baby!* (1967) by Jule Styne (music) and Betty Comden and Adolph Green (lyric). At a Harlem nightclub for white patrons, the dancing team of Tip & Tap (Winston DeWitt Hemsley and Alan Weeks) pull the stops out and do a Nicholas Brothers-like routine with limber limbs and big smiles. They are supported by a chorus of Congo Cuties wearing peacock feathers and little else.

"A Fellow Needs a Girl" is a gentle ballad from the experimental musical *Allegro* (1947) by Richard Rodgers (music) and Oscar Hammerstein (lyric). The hero's parents (William Ching and Annamary Dickey) sing the homespun song as they contemplate what kind of girl their college-bound son will someday marry, hoping he will be as happy as they are. Frank Sinatra and Perry Como both made hit recordings of the ballad, and years later Julie Andrews made an expert recording of it.

"Fighting for Pharaoh" is a simple but eloquent antiwar song from the revue *Don't Bother Me, I Can't Cope* (1972). Alex Bradford, Bobby Hill, Alberta Bradford and Charles Campbell sang the powerful Micki Grant song that pleads for change so that our children's history books will not need to include any more wars.

"Find Me a Primitive Man" is the musical plea sung by Evelyn Hoey in Cole Porter's *Fifty Million Frenchmen* (1929) as she wearies of the Arrow Collar type of man and longs for a mate who carries a club rather than belongs to one. Hoey stopped the show each evening with this comic lament with the help of Billy Reid, Lou Duthers and the ensemble. In the 1991 reconstructed recording of the *Fifty Million Frenchmen* score, the song was sung by Kim Criswell with Michael Taranto, Christopher May, David Montgomery and Steven Katz.

"Finding Words for Spring" is an alluring ballad from *Baker Street* (1965), the Sherlock Holmes musical by Marian Grudeff and Raymond Jessel. The stage star Irene Adler (Inga Swenson) sings the lovely song in response to the cool, calculated comments Holmes (Fritz Weaver) has made about her stolen love letters.

"Fine and Dandy" is the tangy title song from the 1930 musical by Kay Swift (music) and Paul James (lyric) about the goings-on at the Fordyce Drop Forge and Tool Factory. General Manager Joe Squibb (comedian Joe Cook) and the sweet ingenue Nancy Ellis (Alice Boulden) sing the upbeat duet that trumpets happiness with a syncopated beat. The song was one of the first, but far from the last, in a line of rousing anti-Depression numbers that proliferated throughout the 1930s. During the 255-performance run, James added and revised the lyric in the song to include topical references and to lampoon other shows currently running on Broadway. Barbra Streisand made a memorable recording of the number.

"Finishing the Hat" is a riveting ballad from *Sunday in the Park With George* (1984) about love and art and how one is sacrificed for the other. The artist George Seurat (Mandy Patinkin) reflects on his art and his love for Dot (Bernadette Peters), who has left him. His sense of loss mingles with his sense of creation in this beguiling ballad by Stephen Sondheim.

"The First Man You Remember" is a touching number from the British import *Aspects of Love* (1990) in which old age and youth meet for a moment of happiness. The elderly George Dillingham (Kevin Colson) sees his fourteen-year-old daughter Jenny (Danielle DuClos) dressed up like an adult woman for the first time and sings this tender song about wanting to be the first man she remembers and the last one she will forget. Jenny joins him in the song, treating the old man as a young beau and going into a sweeping dance for him. Andrew Lloyd Webber wrote the appealing foxtrot music, and Charles Hart and Don Black provided the emotional lyric.

"First Thing Monday Mornin' " is a compelling chorus number from *Purlie* (1970) by Gary Geld (music) and Peter Udell (lyric). The cotton pickers in a rural Georgia community open the show's second act with this rhythmic song that starts out lethargically as the men procrastinate about everything, but soon they grow in power and conviction and end up eager to change the world.

"The First Time" is the carefree Zorbá's "I am" song from the John Kander (music) and Fred Ebb (lyric) musical *Zorbá* (1968). Herschel Bernardi, as the colorful title character, sang the animated number about how he always approaches every experience as if it is happening for the first time.

"Flahooley" is the playful title song from the satiric 1951 musical by Sammy Fain (music) and E.Y. Harburg (lyric) about big business in America. The toy company B.G. Bigelow, Inc., introduces its latest product, a laughing doll named Flahooley, that will compete with all the crying dolls on the market.

Employees Griselda (Fay DeWitt) and Miss Buckley (Marilyn Ross) lead the company executives in singing the praises of the new doll. The seemingly innocent situation is made acutely sarcastic by Harburg's stinging lyric that calls for the need to laugh in this crazy world, arguing that a country that cannot laugh at itself is already bound in chains. Harburg himself had been blacklisted by the House Un-American Activities Committee for his highly leftist lyrics and had been labeled subversive, so the subtext in "Flahooley" was very powerful.

"Flair" is a lighthearted frolic about how style is everything. David Shire (music) and Richard Maltby, Jr. (lyric) wrote the zippy number, and it was sung by George Lee Andrews in the Off-Broadway revue *Starting Here, Starting Now* (1977).

"Flaming Agnes" is a specialty number that Mary Martin sang in *I Do! I Do!* (1966) by Tom Jones (lyric) and Harvey Schmidt (music). Agnes (Martin), furious at the news that her husband has had an extramarital affair, digs out a huge feathered hat that she has been hiding for years and struts about the stage singing how she will become a sexually scintillating creature everyone will call Flaming Agnes.

"Flings" is a show-stopping comic number from *New Girl in Town* (1957) by Bob Merrill and a showcase for the comic talents of Thelma Ritter. The crusty old Marthy Owen (Ritter) and her two cronies (Lulu Bates and Mara Lundi) sarcastically lament how old age takes its toll on lovemaking and conclude that romantic flings have to be flung by the young. Pearl Bailey made a sassy recording of the song.

"Foolish Heart" is a waltzing ballad in the style of a Victor Herbert operetta from the musical fantasy *One Touch of Venus* (1943) by Kurt Weill (music) and Ogden Nash (lyric). The goddess Venus (Mary Martin) sings the lilting number to museum owner Whitelaw Savory (John Boles), who loves the come-to-life statue. Years later Lotte Lenya, Weill's widow, made an intriguing recording of the song.

"Fools Fall in Love" is a breezy love song by Irving Berlin from *Louisiana Purchase* (1940). Berlin employs an unusual structure in the music, resulting in a very flowing and unique melody. William Gaxton and Vera Zorina introduced the number as two opportunists who have fallen in love despite themselves.

"For My Mary" is a quaint pastiche number from the short-lived *Rags* (1986) that captures the essence of the turn-of-the-century ballad form. Charles Strouse (music) and Stephen Schwartz (lyric) wrote the simple romantic song that immigrant Ben (Lonny Price) plays on a gramophone for his beloved Bella (Judy Kuhn), singing along and changing the lyrics to fit her description.

"Forever" is the pastiche love duet between Charlotte Sweet (Mara Beckerman) and Ludlow Ladd Grimble (Christopher Seppe) in the Off-Broadway music-hall melodrama *Charlotte Sweet* (1982). Michael Colby provided the mock-Victorian lyric, and Gerald Jay Markoe composed the turn-of-the-century music. The number was reprised by the lecherous Barnaby Bugaboo (Alan Brasington), who covets Charlotte for his music-hall troupe.

"Forty-Five Minutes From Broadway" is the witty title song from the 1906 musical by George M. Cohan. Slick New Yorker Kid Burns (Victor Moore) is in New Rochelle tending to business when a local girl, Mary Jane Jenkins (Fay Templeton), suggests that they go out together for a night on the town. Burns wryly suggests that that might be difficult to do in such a hick town that's forty-five minutes by train from Times Square, and he and the ensemble sing the tuneful, funny song. Quite naturally, the New Rochelle Chamber of Commerce took offense at the song, but it became widely popular all the same. In the bio-musical *George M!* (1968), the number was sung by Loni Ackerman and Joel Grey.

"Four Jews in a Room Bitching" is the hilarious opening number from the Off-Broadway musical *March of the Falsettos* (1981) by William Finn. Marvin (Michael Rupert), his son Jason (James Kushner), his lover Whizzer (Stephen Bogardus) and his psychiatrist Mendel (Chip Zien) introduce themselves in this frantic song in which their neuroses and "worst sides" are revealed with comic ferocity.

"Four Little Angels of Peace" was a topical number from the revue *Pins and Needles* (1937) by Harold Rome that remained topical during the show's two-and-a-half-year run by altering its lyric as it was influenced by current events. This biting comic song featured Adolf Hitler, Benito Mussolini, Anthony Eden and an unnamed Japanese leader, all played by members of the International Ladies Garment Workers Union dressed as angels and justifying their aggressive takeovers with playful innocence. Figures such as Neville Chamberlain and Joseph Stalin later became members of the quartet, replacing political leaders no longer in the news.

"Frank Mills" is the odd but engaging narrative ballad from *Hair* (1968) by Galt MacDermot (music) and Gerome Ragni and James Rado (lyric). Crissy (Shelley Plimpton) sings about the ups and downs, ins and outs of being a teenager in love with the wrong sort of man. The story has more than its fair share of non sequiturs, and the lyric, which eschews rhyming, has a wistful quality to it.

"Franklin Shepard, Inc." is a frenzied musical scene from *Merrily We Roll Along* (1981) in which Stephen Sondheim creates a character's nervous breakdown in song and dialogue. While on a television talk show, songwriter Charley (Lonny Price) explains how he and his collaborator Frank (Jim Walton) work together. But the partnership is falling apart, all of Charley's anxieties, bitterness and disappointments regarding Frank take over, and he explodes in a seriocomic tirade in song.

"Freddy, My Love" is an appealing rock and roll quartet from *Grease* (1972) that pastiches the girl groups of the 1950s. At a pajama party in her bedroom, Marty (Katie Hanley) tells her girlfriends Jan (Garn Stephens), Frenchy (Marya Small) and Betty Rizzo (Adrienne Barbeau) about what she writes in her letters to her boyfriend Freddy, who's in the Marines. Jim Jacobs and Warren Casey wrote both music and lyric for the dreamy pop song.

"Free" is the antic "I am" song for the conniving slave Pseudolus (Zero Mostel) in *A Funny Thing Happened on the Way to the Forum* (1962) by Stephen Sondheim. When the young master Hero (Brian Davies) promises to set Pseudolus free if he helps him get Philia as his bride, the delighted slave launches into this comic tribute to the glories and lucrative advantages of freedom. Sondheim's music is very much in the vaudeville style, but with a dissonant strain that gives the song its comic edge.

"Free at Last" is an impassioned song of freedom sung by the runaway slave Jim (Ron Richardson) and the chorus in the *Huckleberry Finn* musical *Big River* (1985). Country composer-singer Roger Miller wrote the stirring song for this, his only Broadway musical.

"The Friendliest Thing" is a very direct song of seduction from *What Makes Sammy Run?* (1964) that leaves little room for double entendre. Laurette (Bernice Massi), the studio boss's daughter, tries to bed eager film executive Sammy Glick (Steve Lawrence) with this sultry number by Ervin Drake. Eydie Gorme made a successful recording of the song.

"Friends" is an appealing character song from "The Diary of Adam and Eve" section of *The Apple Tree* (1966) by Jerry Bock (music) and Sheldon Harnick (lyric). Eve (Barbara Harris) is lonely in the Garden of Eden because she and Adam (Alan Alda) are not getting along. Then she looks into a pool of water and finds a true friend in her own reflection, one who never turns her back on her.

"Friendship," the most famous song from *DuBarry Was a Lady* (1939), is

Cole Porter at his most lighthearted. The vivacious comic duet, sung by Ethel Merman and Bert Lahr, has a mock-hillbilly melody and accompaniment with a lyric that uses Ira Gershwin-like nonsense words to accentuate the beat. Merman and Lahr stopped the show each evening as they improvised comic bits within the song in their efforts to break each other up. The song is also a highlight in many revivals of *Anything Goes,* into which it is often interpolated. Jo Stafford, with Tommy Dorsey's Orchestra, and Kay Kyser and His Orchestra each had best-selling recordings of the song.

"From This Moment On" is the biggest hit to come from the score of Cole Porter's *Out of This World* (1950), but, ironically, it was cut from that show before opening because co-director George Abbott thought it was slowing down the story. Priscilla Gillette and William Eythe sang the jubilant love song in Philadelphia but didn't create too many sparks. It was through subsequent recordings and its interpolation into the 1953 film version of *Kiss Me, Kate* that the song caught on with the public.

"Fugue for Tinhorns" is the unforgettable comic trio from *Guys and Dolls* (1950) that sets the witty, cockeyed mood for the whole show. The Frank Loesser song was sung by three horseplayers--Nicely-Nicely Johnson (Stubby Kaye), Rusty Charlie (Douglas Deane) and Benny Southstreet (Johnny Silver)-- as they peruse the racing forms and pick the day's bets. Loesser's use of a classical music form (the song is indeed a fugue) for such delightful low-lifes summarizes what makes *Guys and Dolls* so wonderful. Originally Loesser wrote the fugue at a much slower tempo with a different lyric to be sung by Nathan Detroit (Sam Levene), Sky Masterson (Robert Alda) and Sarah Brown (Isabel Bigley), but for various reasons (one being that Levene could not sing) it took its present form before opening.

"Fun to Be Fooled" is an entrancing ballad from the revue *Life Begins at 8:40* (1934) by Harold Arlen (music) and Ira Gershwin and E.Y. Harburg (lyric). The contemplative song is about how we are fooled by life, but, in the case of love, such foolishness can be fun. Arlen's straightforward Kern-like music uses short musical phrases in the refrain that are matched by Gershwin and Harburg's succinct lyric phrases. "Fun to Be Fooled" was sung in the revue as a duet by Frances Williams and Bartlett Simmons and years later Julie Wilson made a distinctive recording of the song.

"Funny Face" is the breezy title song from the 1927 Gershwin brothers' musical that starred Adele and Fred Astaire. Frankie Wynne (Adele) and her guardian Jimmie Reeve (Fred) sang this playful number in which they mocked as lightly as they praised each other's facial features while he pulled her around the stage in a toy wagon. George Gershwin composed the flavorful music, and Ira

Gershwin wrote the sassy lyric. The song was sung in the rewritten version of *Funny Face* called *My One and Only* (1983) by airplane mechanic Mickey (Denny Dillon) and the Russian Prince Nikolai (Bruce McGill).

G

"The Game" is a slapstick comedy number for the baseball players in *Damn Yankees* (1955) by Richard Adler and Jerry Ross. The Washington Senators are finally on a winning streak, so the team members decide they've got to forget about women and concentrate on the game. Rocky (Jimmy Komack) and Smokey (Nathaniel Frey) lead the players in this raucous song in which they conjure up visions of seduction only to drop them to think about baseball.

"A Game of Poker" is a cynical duet from the ambitious but unsuccessful *Saratoga* (1959) by Harold Arlen (music) and Johnny Mercer (lyric). The two opportunists Clio Delaine (Carol Lawrence) and Clint Maroon (Howard Keel) sing the song about love as a hit-or-miss affair with the odds of a card game. A little later in the show they reprise the number in counterpoint to the lovely ballad "Love Held Lightly" sung by Odette Myrtil.

"The Games I Play" is a fascinating musical soliloquy from *March of the Falsettos* (1981) in which Whizzer (Stephen Bogardus) tries to describe his love/hate relationship with Marvin. William Finn wrote the delicate music and the ambivalent but penetrating lyric.

"Gary, Indiana" is a pleasant vaudeville soft-shoe from *The Music Man* (1957) that pastiches the kind of ditty popular at the turn of the century. Meredith Willson wrote the lighthearted music and lyric, and they were sung by the introverted youth Winthrop Paroo (Eddie Hodges).

"Gavotte" is a luscious quartet from *Candide* (1956) with two contrasting melodies that create a sparkling operetta pastiche. At a Venice gambling casino, the wily Old Lady (Irra Petina) complains to Candide (Robert Rounseville) and Cunegonde (Barbara Cook) about her family troubles. As they sympathize with her in song, the slaphappy Dr. Pangloss (Max Adrian) keeps winning at roulette and naming all the lovely ladies that flock to him and his newfound wealth. Leonard Bernstein composed the delightful double melody, and Richard Wilbur and Dorothy Parker wrote the playful lyric for the number, which is sometimes listed as "Venice Gavotte." The music from the double song was retained for the 1974 revised revival of *Candide,* and Stephen Sondheim wrote a new lyric for a new plot situation, retitling the number "Life Is Happiness Indeed."

"Gee, Officer Krupke!," one of the modern musical theatre's greatest comic songs, is also the most telling song in *West Side Story* (1957) because its satiric look at urban squalor and discontented youth is what the show is all about. The number is a musical mockery of modern administration in which the gang members act out the ridiculous efforts of the judge, social worker and psychiatrist who have to deal with problem juveniles. Action (Eddie Roll) and Snowboy (Grover Dale) lead the Jets in the farcical charade that provides the necessary comic relief in Act Two. Yet Leonard Bernstein's music is clownish only on the surface. His notation reads "in a fast vaudeville," and he even adds a can-can effect to part of the harmony later in the number; but there are prevalent harsh tones in the music as well. It is Stephen Sondheim's ingenious lyric that turns the juveniles' tension and frustration into outlandish comedy.

"The Gentleman Is a Dope" is a bittersweet torch song from the experimental Richard Rodgers (music) and Oscar Hammerstein (lyric) musical *Allegro* (1947). Lisa Kirk, as a Chicago nurse in love with her boss, ponders her predicament as she tries to hail a cab home from work. She comes to the conclusion that the man is not for her and that she'd best walk home. The tough-minded song made Kirk a Broadway star, and Jo Stafford made a popular recording of it. In the Broadway revue *A Grand Night for Singing* (1993), "The Gentleman Is a Dope" was sung by Alyson Reed.

"Gentleman Jimmy" is a zippy Charleston number from *Fiorello!* (1959) by Jerry Bock (music) and Sheldon Harnick (lyric). It was used as a campaign song for the incumbent Mayor James Walker and was sung and tapped by Eileen Rodgers and the chorus girls as they rehearsed for the big political rally. In contrast to Fiorello's homespun campaign song "The Name's LaGuardia," this sophisticated rhythm number uses Irving Berlin-like syncopation and a simple-minded lyric that flaunts clichés with typical political optimism.

"Get Happy" is the first Harold Arlen song to become a hit and one of his most joyous compositions. He wrote the hallelujah number with lyricist Ted Koehler (their first collaboration) for the short-lived *9:15 Revue* (1930), where it was sung by Ruth Etting on an inexplicable beach setting with the cast all in bathing suits and the stage covered with sand. Despite the show's short run, sheet-music sales made "Get Happy" a hit, and it launched Arlen's career. The song is often associated with Judy Garland, who recorded it and sang it on film and in concerts.

"Get Me to the Church on Time" is the exhilarating music-hall turn from *My Fair Lady* (1956) sung by the dustman-turned-gentleman Alfred Doolittle (Stanley Holloway) on the night before the wedding that will make him respectable. Alan Jay Lerner (lyric) and Frederick Loewe (music) wrote the eleven o'clock number in the Edwardian sing-along style, and it has always proved to be an audience favorite. Julius LaRosa had a best-selling record of the song in 1957.

"Get Out of Town" is the tender ballad from the sprightly Cole Porter musical *Leave It to Me!* (1938) that was introduced by Tamara, who wished that her old flame William Gaxton would leave her and her heartache alone. Frances Langford made a popular recording of the song, as did the Eddy Duchin and Lawrence Welk orchestras.

"Get Yourself a Geisha" is a comic number from the revue *At Home Abroad* (1935) by Howard Dietz (lyric) and Arthur Schwartz (music). In a Japanese garden, Beatrice Lillie and a chorus of Oriental maidens sang the satiric song on how to cope with life in the exotic East.

"Getting Married Today" is the show-stopping seriocomic number from *Company* (1970) showing a bride having a nervous breakdown on her wedding day. As a church choir soloist (Teri Ralston) and the groom Paul (Steve Elmore) sing rhapsodically about the great event, the hyperactive bride Amy (Beth Howland) launches into a Gilbert and Sullivan-like tongue-twisting patter song listing all the reasons she should not get married today. Stephen Sondheim wrote the scintillating number with music that ranges from the operatic to the contemporary and a lyric that hilariously follows the altar-wary bride's hysterical stream of consciousness. Millicent Martin, Julia McKenzie and David Kernan sang the number in the Broadway revue *Side by Side by Sondheim* (1977), and in the Off-Broadway revue *Putting It Together* (1993) it was sung by Julie Andrews and the ensemble.

"Getting to Know You," the charm song Anna sings with the royal children in *The King and I* (1951), was a late addition to the show, prompted by Richard Rodgers (music) and Oscar Hammerstein (lyric), who felt that the first act needed a lighter moment. The song's melody and some of the lyric came from a number cut from *South Pacific* (1949) and replaced by "Younger Than Springtime." "Getting to Know You" is very simple and even predictable, but it is supposed to be a school lesson for Siamese children learning English. Gertrude Lawrence introduced the song, which became one of Rodgers and

Hammerstein's most recognized pieces.

"Giannina Mia" is a vibrant Neapolitan number from Rudolf Friml's operetta *The Firefly* (1912), much in the line of Victor Herbert's "Italian Street Song" from *Naughty Marietta* (1910), both of which were sung by Emma Trentini. In *The Firefly* Nina Corelli (Trentini) disguises herself as the Italian pickpocket Antonio and sings this festive love song as a street singer. Otto Harbach wrote the enchanting lyric and years later Jeanette MacDonald made a popular recording of the song.

"Giants in the Sky" is a wondrous ballad by Stephen Sondheim from *Into the Woods* (1987). Having escaped from the giant's castle by way of his magic beanstalk, Jack (Ben Wright) expresses his fear and amazement at what has occurred and reflects on how his whole outlook on life has changed. Sondheim's music is expansive, and the lyric is filled with ambivalent imagery. Mandy Patinkin made a riveting recording of the song in 1990.

"A Gift Today" is a curiously touching yet cynical number from *I Can Get It for You Wholesale* (1962) by Harold Rome. At the bar mitzvah party for Sheldon Bushkin (Steve Curry), the show-off Harry Bogen (Elliott Gould) gives him a huge check and sings about the spiritual gifts that money can bring. The other guests join in singing the melodic, ethnic-sounding song that reminds one of "Sunrise, Sunset" from *Fiddler on the Roof* (1964), but with a crass undercurrent.

"Gifts of Love" is a ravishing duet from the unsuccessful *The Baker's Wife* (1976) that never made it to New York. The baker Amiable (Topol, later Paul Sorvino) and his young wife Genevieve (Patti LuPone) sing the song, but each is in a different mind track: he is in the kitchen rhapsodizing how lucky he is to have such a beautiful wife, while she is up in the bedroom revealing her lack of love for Amiable; but she promises herself that she will smile at him and treat him well, and he will believe these gestures to be gifts of love. Stephen Schwartz wrote the entrancing music and lyric.

"Gimme Love" is an eruptive production number from *Kiss of the Spider Woman* (1993) by John Kander (music) and Fred Ebb (lyric). In a fantasy sequence from the movies, Aurora (Chita Rivera) appears in a feathered costume in a bird cage at a nightclub and sings and dances with the male chorus about her lack of interest in revolutions or earthquakes or bullfights; all she wants is to make love. Molina (Brent Carver) joins in singing the vibrant Latin song, and, in Rob Marshall and Vincent Paterson's original choreography, the number becomes a frenzied fantasy-turned-nightmare that closes the first act.

"The Girl Friend," the lively title song of the 1926 Rodgers and Hart musical, is a Charleston number that allowed Eva Puck and Sammy White to kick up their heels to the audience's delight. Lorenz Hart showed that he could provide a witty lyric even for a busy dance number, and Richard Rodgers' music has a gleeful melody that giddily climbs up the scale against a chromatic bass line that recalls the best of George Gershwin. Years later British composer-lyricist Sandy Wilson spoofed this sort of number in his title song for *The Boy Friend* (1954).

"A Girl Is on Your Mind" is a captivating concerted number from *Sweet Adeline* (1929) that makes for a thrilling musical sequence utilizing the principal male characters in the show (Robert Chisholm, Max Hoffman, Jr., John D. Seymour and Jim Thornton) and the male chorus. In a turn-of-the-century New York City tavern, the men gather to forget that special girl who cannot be forgotten. They question each other's strange behavior and offer each other consoling drinks but always come to the same realization: some girl is always on your mind. At one point in the nearly seven-minute sequence, Addie (Helen Morgan) appears and sings a similar lament from the feminine point of view. Jerome Kern wrote the stirring, blues-flavored music, and Oscar Hammerstein provided the succinct lyric. *Sweet Adeline* had a disappointingly short run due to the stock-market crash a month after it opened, and "A Girl Is on Your Mind" seemed to fade from memory. But conductor John McGlinn's 1992 recording with the reconstructed orchestrations, using the alternate title "Some Girl Is on Your Mind," brought the song newfound recognition. The recording featured Cris Groenendaal, Brent Barrett, George Dvorsky, Davis Gaines and Judy Kaye.

"The Girl Is You and the Boy Is Me" is the hit love song from the 1926 edition of *George White's Scandals*. The number was written by B.G. DeSylva and Lew Brown (lyric) and Ray Henderson (music) and was cooed by Harry Richman and Frances Williams.

"Girl of the Moment" is a pastiche of the lavish Florenz Ziegfeld-like production numbers that glorified a beautiful lady. In this case it was Gertrude Lawrence in the experimental *Lady in the Dark* (1941) by Kurt Weill (music) and Ira Gershwin (lyric). A chorus of adoring men sang the lush song to Liza Elliott (Lawrence) in a ritzy nightclub in the "Glamour Dream" fantasy sequence of the show. The song is reprised a bit later as what the authors called "an oratorio with Bach-like harmonies" as Liza's portrait is being painted for the latest U.S. stamp. Finally the number turns into a bolero as the portrait is revealed as rather unflattering, and the crowd sings and dances in a mocking fashion. In the Off-Broadway revue *Berlin to Broadway With Kurt Weill* (1972), "Girl of the Moment" was sung by Jerry Lanning and Hal Watters.

"The Girl on the Magazine Cover" is the elegant ballad from Irving Berlin's *Stop! Look! Listen!* (1915) that celebrates feminine beauty. The lavish production number featured Harry Fox singing in front of a huge *Vogue* magazine cover as four show girls literally walked off the page into real life. The music for "The Girl on the Magazine Cover" is among Berlin's more operatic-sounding, with the unique trait that he repeats the opening melodic phrase only twice in the whole song.

"The Girl That I Marry" is a melodic ballad from Irving Berlin's *Annie Get Your Gun* (1946) sung by Frank Butler (Ray Middleton) to impress Annie Oakley (Ethel Merman) with his vision of the perfect woman: someone soft, feminine and everything Annie is not. The simple but enticing song has a waltz tempo and a melody that remains all within one octave; yet it is a rich and flavorful ballad that became one of the many hits from the show. Frank Sinatra's recording of the song was particularly popular.

"Girls Like Me" is an absorbing "I am" song for Angie McKay (Carol Lawrence) in *Subways Are for Sleeping* (1961) by Jule Styne (music) and Betty Comden and Adolph Green (lyric). Angie works in a tall, crowded office building in Manhattan, but she is lonely and in need of love.

"Give a Little, Get a Little" is a sassy number from the revue *Two on the Aisle* (1951) with music by Jule Styne and lyric by Betty Comden and Adolph Green. Dolores Gray and the chorus sang the frolicsome song.

"Give a Man Enough Rope" is a jaunty country song that expresses the philosophy of Will Rogers (Keith Carradine) in *The Will Rogers Follies* (1991). Cy Coleman (music) and Betty Comden and Adolph Green (lyric) wrote the appealing number, and it was sung by Rogers and the four Drugstore Cowboys: John Ganun, Troy Britton Johnson, Jerry Mitchell and Jason Opsahl.

"Give It Back to the Indians" is one of Lorenz Hart's most nimble lyrics, a list song cataloging how impossible New York City has gotten to live in. Richard Rodgers wrote the pulsating melody, and it was introduced by Mary Jane Walsh in *Too Many Girls* (1939). The song is, in many ways, a playful reversal on the team's earlier ballad "Manhattan." Ella Fitzgerald made a delightfully sassy recording of the song.

"Give My Regards to Broadway," one of the most beloved songs of the American theatre, is George M. Cohan's paean to both the theatre and the America he loved. The song was written for *Little Johnny Jones* (1904), where it was featured in the show's famous "transformation" scene. Jockey Johnny Jones (Cohan) is in Southampton, England, where he bids farewell to his friends returning to New York. He cannot go with them because he has been wrongly accused of throwing the Derby and is waiting to be cleared. Johnny asks the travelers to remember him to his beloved Manhattan with the famous song. Then the lights fade out to denote the passage of a few hours, and Johnny is discovered alone on the pier watching the ship sail off in the distance. Suddenly a rocket is fired from the ship, the signal that evidence to clear his name has been discovered, and the despondent Johnny explodes in a high-kicking reprise of the song. A shortened version of the number was performed in the 1968 bio-musical *George M!*, in which Joel Grey played Johnny.

"Glad to Be Unhappy" is one of Rodgers and Hart's finest torch songs, a simple but heartfelt number from *On Your Toes* (1936). Richard Rodgers' melody is straightforward and unadorned, and Lorenz Hart's lyric, like the paradoxical title, is painfully self-aware. It is also worth noting that the verse is nearly as long as the refrain and just as potent. In the show, "Glad to Be Unhappy" was sung as a duet by Doris Carson and David Morris. Over the years it has been sung by artists as varied as Lena Horne, Frank Sinatra, Barbara Cook and the Mamas and the Papas.

"The Glamorous Life" is a sparkling number from *A Little Night Music* (1973) for a trio of characters and the chorus that has a lighthearted operetta flavor while it shrewdly comments on such a romanticized lifestyle. The touring actress Desiree (Glynis Johns) writes short letters home to her daughter Fredrika (Judy Kahan) and her mother Madame Armfeldt (Hermione Gingold) telling them about her tour and commenting on the unglamorous aspects of a theatrical life. In between stanzas of the songs are sections where Fredrika and Armfeldt express their views on the gypsy existence of Desiree. Stephen Sondheim's waltzing music for both sections is enthralling, and his lyric is as succinct as it is flowing.

"Glitter and Be Gay," the most famous song from *Candide* (1956), became popular as an instrumental piece due to its prominence in the oft-performed concert favorite Overture to *Candide*. (The melody has also been the theme song for Dick Cavett over the years.) In the musical, Cunegonde (Barbara Cook) has become a woman of lax virtue, serving as the mistress of two different men. In the mock-coloratura aria, Cunegonde begins by lamenting her low state and self-shame to a slow waltz tempo; then, as she looks at all the riches bestowed on her by her wealthy lovers, she gains strength and breaks into a lively allegro section climaxing with a frenzied series of "ha ha ha"s. Leonard Bernstein composed the delectably bombastic music, and Richard Wilbur wrote the clever depressed/jubilant lyric. Cook's recording of "Glitter and Be Gay" is definitive but Dawn Upshaw recorded an admirable version in 1994.

"The Glow-Worm" is the popular novelty song that enjoyed two different eras of success. The song was first heard in the Lew Fields vehicle *The Girl Behind the Counter* (1907), where it was sung by May Naudain. Paul Lincke composed the snappy melody, and Lilla Cayley Robinson wrote the lyric that was based on a 1902 German song. The number was interpolated into the show after opening and became a hit, due mostly to early recordings by Lucy Isabelle March and the Victor Orchestra. As the decades passed the song faded away, but in 1952 Johnny Mercer wrote a witty new lyric and the song became popular all over again, due this time to a best-selling recording by the Mills Brothers.

"Go Visit" is a dandy soft-shoe number from *70, Girls, 70* (1971) by John Kander (music) and Fred Ebb (lyric). The bellhop Eddie (Tommy Breslin) and his spry grandmother (Henrietta Jacobson) sing and dance the vaudevillian duet about the necessity of visiting your grandmother. One section of the song is contrapuntal, with each singer moving at a different tempo, and the number has a jazz section as well in which old age and youth dance together.

"The God-Why-Don't-You-Love-Me Blues" is the hilarious but disturbing comedy number from *Follies* (1971) that pastiches the slapstick vaudeville routines of the past. Stephen Sondheim wrote the clownish number in which Buddy (Gene Nelson), in baggy pants and derby, sings a comic lament about his two loves, his wife Sally and his mistress Margie, both of whom he cannot love if they are foolish enough to love him. Buddy is assisted by two chorus girls (Suzanne Rogers and Rita O'Connor) who play floozie versions of Sally and Margie, and the trio launches into a burlesque routine in which Buddy's heartache is the recurring joke. The song, which is sometimes called "Buddy's Blues," was sung by David Kernan, Millicent Martin and Julia McKenzie in the Broadway revue *Side by Side by Sondheim* (1977).

"God's Country" is a tongue-in-cheek patriotic number from the satirical *Hooray for What!* (1937) by Harold Arlen (music) and E. Y. Harburg (lyric). Jack Whiting and the ensemble sang the lighthearted flag-waver that contrasted life in the United States with that under the Fascist and Communist governments in Europe. Harburg's lyric has particular fun with allusions to several 1930s celebrities' names and products, from Gypsy Rose Lee to Jello.

"God's Green World" is a zestful song set to a rhythmic Latin beat from the early Alan Jay Lerner (lyric) and Frederick Loewe (music) effort *The Day Before Spring* (1945). Bill Johnson sang the expansive number that encouraged one to get up, get out and see the world.

"The Gods on Tap" is a raucous production number from the Off-Broadway camp musical *Olympus on My Mind* (1986) by Barry Harman (lyric) and Grant Sturiale (music). In ancient Greece, Delores (Elizabeth Austin) leads Jupiter (Martin Vidnovic), Mercury (Jason Graae) and the chorus in this toe-tapping song, which credits the celestial beings for Thebes' recent military victory over Sparta.

"Going Up" is the infectious title song from the 1917 aviation musical by Louis Hirsch (music) and Otto Harbach (lyric). Robert Street (Frank Craven), a braggart who has written a best-selling book about flying but has never actually flown, and his sweetheart Grace Douglas (Edith Day) lead members of the cast (Ruth Donnelly, Marion Sunshine and Donald Meek) in this merry song that became quite popular.

"Golden Days" is an irresistible male duet from the operetta *The Student Prince* (1924) by Sigmund Romberg (music) and Dorothy Donnelly (lyrics). Prince Karl Franz (Howard Marsh) and his tutor Dr. Engel (Greek Evans) are about to leave for Heidelberg to begin studies when the old man recalls his own student days there, and the two men sing the nostalgic song of lost youth. Mario Lanza made a memorable recording of the song.

"Gonna Build a Mountain" is a revival-like song of ambition from the British import *Stop the World -- I Want to Get Off* (1962) by Leslie Bricusse and Anthony Newley. When Littlechap (Newley) arrives in the industrial city of Sludgepool to manage his father-in-law's factory, he sings this optimistic song and soon has all the ensemble doing a rousing mock-gospel number. Because the musical had been a hit in London for a year before the New York opening, this and other songs from the show were already well known in America and remained popular throughout the decade.

"Gooch's Song" is a comic gem from Jerry Herman's *Mame* (1966) in which the unmarried and pregnant Agnes Gooch (Jane Connell) explains what happened when she took the advice of Mame's earlier song "Open a New Window." The song is also known as "What Do I Do Now?," as Agnes repeatedly asks in the number.

"Good Clean Fun" is a hilariously naive comedy song from *Tenderloin* (1960) in which the muckraking Reverend Brock (Maurice Evans) outlines all the innocent games of childhood that ought to be played instead of patronizing the vice dens of the Tenderloin district. Jerry Bock composed the zesty music, and Sheldon Harnick wrote the amusing list song's lyric that includes over two dozen period games, from spoons to Queen of Sheba to the parson's cat.

"Good Morning Starshine" is the sweet, optimistic ode to nature from *Hair* (1968) by Galt MacDermot (music) and Gerome Ragni and James

Rado (lyric). In the 1967 Off-Broadway production, the soft and entrancing song was sung by Sheila (Jill O'Hara) and the company. In the Broadway version, Sheila (Lynn Kellogg) and Dionne (Melba Moore) sang it with the ensemble. A top-selling single was recorded by the singer Oliver.

"Good News" is the vivacious title song from the 1927 college musical by B.G. DeSylva and Lew Brown (lyric) and Ray Henderson (music). At Tait College, the high-kicking co-ed Flo (Zelma O'Neal) leads the students in this revivalistic number that promises that good news is on the way because all the lucky signs are there. The song was one of five from the DeSylva-Brown-Henderson score to become a standard.

"Good Thing Going" is a wistful song from *Merrily We Roll Along* (1981) that Stephen Sondheim wrote in the style of an early 1960s pop ballad. The songwriters Frank (Jim Walton) and Charley (Lonny Price) play their new song at a party given by a wealthy backer. The ballad is a beautifully restrained lament about a love affair that started so well but soon faded because each took for granted the good thing they had going for them. In a bitter reprise of the number, the songwriters sing the song again, but the partygoers, who had been so enthusiastic, lose interest in the lovely ballad and return to their gossip and small talk. Frank Sinatra made a popular recording of the number and most recently Mandy Patinkin recorded it.

"Good to Be Alive" is the rompish comic song that recurs throughout the Off-Broadway musical farce *Lucky Stiff* (1988) by Stephen Flaherty (music) and Lynn Ahrens (lyric). The whole cast, at one time or another, joins in singing this silly salute to life. The number is all the more ironic since one of the musical's major characters is a stuffed corpse.

"Goodbye, Becky Cohen" was the first of many songs Irving Berlin wrote for producer Florenz Ziegfeld. The song was heard in the *Follies of 1910* and was sung by Fanny Brice in her *Follies* debut. The character number is a comic ditty that allowed Brice to employ her incomparably funny Yiddish dialect.

"Goodbye Broadway, Hello France" is a World War One song by Billy Baskette (music) and C. Francis Reisner and Benny Davis (lyric) that was very popular in its day. The number was written for the revue *The Passing Show of 1917*, where it was sung by the ensemble as the stirring finale of the show.

"Goodbye Girls, I'm Through" is a snappy song of joyous amazement that is sung by a lover who realizes his philandering days have been cut short by true love. Ivan Caryll (music) and John Golden (lyric) wrote the number during the Philadelphia tryouts for *Chin-Chin* (1914) just to cover a costume change, but audiences made it into a hit. Although *Chin-Chin* was a vehicle for the comedians Dave Montgomery and Fred Stone, the song was sung by Douglas Stevenson as Aladdin in the fantasy musical.

"Goodbye, Old Girl" is a tender farewell ballad from *Damn Yankees* (1955) by Richard Adler and Jerry Ross. Middle-aged Joe Boyd (Robert Shafer) has agreed to let the devil make him young so that he can play baseball, but before he leaves, he writes a note to his wife Meg. At the end of the song the devil makes Joe young, and the song is reprised, with youthful exuberance, by the new Joe Hardy (Stephen Douglass).

"Goodnight, My Someone" is the enchanting lullaby that serves as the "I am" song for Marian Paroo (Barbara Cook) in *The Music Man* (1957) by Meredith Willson. The ostracized librarian sings the touching song as she wishes upon a star, and her piano pupil Amaryllis (Marilyn Siegel) plunks out the melody as she practices the piano. The music for "Goodnight, My Someone" is the same as that for "Seventy-Six Trombones" but at a much slower tempo. Both songs are reprised near the end of the musical, with Harold Hill (Robert Preston) singing the tender lullaby and Marian the rousing march version.

"Goodtime Charley" is the engaging title song from the 1975 musical about Joan of Arc (Ann Reinking) helping the Dauphin (Joel Grey) to become the future King Charles VII of France. The Larry Grossman (music) and Hal Hackaday (lyric) song was sung by the Dauphin, recounting how he would rather just enjoy life than become king.

"Grand Imperial Cirque de Paris" is an enthralling chorus number from *Carnival* (1961) that illustrated director-choreographer Gower Champion's exciting sense of showmanship. Jacquot (Pierre Olaf) sings to the lethargic carnival performers that their run-down circus will one day be as famous as the "Grand Imperial Cirque de Paris." As his enthusiasm grows, so does the production number, until the performers are aglow with energy and the whole cast is joined arm in arm in a jubilant kickline. Bob Merrill wrote both music and lyric for the vibrant number.

"Grand Knowing You" is a dashing farewell song that was sung with great aplomb by the dashing Jack Cassidy in *She Loves Me* (1963). The bon vivant Mr. Kodaly (Cassidy) has been fired from his job for having an affair with the boss's wife but he leaves in great style, dispatching farewells to his off-and-on lover Miss Ritter and his fellow employees. Jerry Bock composed the tangy soft-shoe-style music, and Sheldon Harnick wrote the grandiose lyric.

"Grand Old Ivy" is Frank Loesser's rousing pastiche song from *How to Succeed in Business Without Really Trying* (1961) that lampoons college fight songs. The march-tempo number is supposedly the school song for Old Ivy, from which J.B. Biggley (Rudy Vallee) had graduated. Corporate climber Finch (Robert Morse) finds this out and makes Biggley believe that he also is a "Groundhog," joining him in singing this silly song. Ironically, the jocular number spoofed the very sort of college songs that Vallee was famous for crooning on the radio in the 1930s.

"The Grass Is Always Greener" is one of Kander and Ebb's funniest songs, a hilarious duet from *Woman of the Year* (1981) in which the housewife Jan Donovan (Marilyn Cooper) and the celebrity Tess Harding (Lauren Bacall) envy each other's lifestyle. John Kander's purposely monotonous music (for Jan's monotonous life) accents Fred Ebb's sparkling lyric, and the number stopped the show each evening. Brenda Pressley and Karen Mason sang the duet in the Off-Broadway revue *And the World Goes 'Round* (1991).

"Great Day" is the effervescent title song from the short-lived 1929 musical by Vincent Youmans (music) and Billy Rose and Edward Eliscu (lyric). The plantation slave Lijah (Lois Deppe) and the farm hands sang the lively come-to-meeting song, and Youmans wrote some very unusual music in his somewhat subdued approach to a rhythm number. Paul Whiteman's Orchestra made a hit instrumental recording of the song.

"Green Finch and Linnet Bird" is a frenzied aria from *Sweeney Todd, the Demon Barber of Fleet Street* (1979) by Stephen Sondheim. The cloistered ward Johanna (Sarah Rice) sings the highly melodic ballad to a caged singing bird with whom she feels she has much in common. Sondheim's music is a rapid, trilling piece with chirping accompaniment, and the lyric is ornately Victorian in its sentiment.

"Green-Up Time" is a jaunty welcome song to spring from the concept musical *Love Life* (1948) by Alan Jay Lerner (lyric) and Kurt Weill (music). Nanette Fabray introduced the cheery number that might have enjoyed more popularity if there had not been an ASCAP strike at the time that prohibited the score from being recorded and broadcast over the air. Regardless, Buddy Clark made a successful recording of the song later on, and Weill's widow Lotte Lenya recorded a distinctive version of it as well.

"Grizabella" is the beguiling "I am" song for the Glamour Cat (Betty Buckley) of the song title in the British import *Cats* (1982). Andrew Lloyd Webber set T.S. Eliot's poem to haunting music that suggested Grizabella's almost mystical presence as the faded beauty roamed the scenes of her past glory.

"Guido's Song" is the unusual "I am" song for the confused filmmaker Guido Contini (Raul Julia) in *Nine* (1982) by Maury Yeston. Guido sings of the many paradoxes within him: he wants to be old/young, to be married/single, to stay put/travel, and so on. But he admits that he has never met anyone like himself and proceeds to sing a duet with himself in two different voices.

"Gun Song" is a gripping number sung by four infamous assassins in Stephen Sondheim's Off-Broadway musical *Assassins* (1991). Leon Czolgosz (Terrence Mann), John Wilkes Booth (Victor Garber), Charles Guiteau (Jonathan Hadary) and Sara Jane Moore (Debra Monk) sing about all the people needed to create a gun and how one person's little finger can fire the weapon and change history. The song was sung by the cast of five in the Off-Broadway revue *Putting It Together* (1993).

"Guys and Dolls," the sparkling title song from the 1950 musical classic, is sung by two secondary characters, Nicely-Nicely Johnson (Stubby Kaye) and Benny Southstreet (Johnny Silver), as they note the effect women have on men. The Frank Loesser song is filled with prankish rhymes, delicious examples and a highly animated melody. The entire company reprises the number at the show's wedding finale.

"Gypsy Love Song" is the most famous number from Victor Herbert's operetta *The Fortune Teller* (1898) and the most well-known gypsy song to come from Broadway. Eugene Cowles, as the gypsy musician Sandor, sang the haunting lullaby in the original production, and in 1906 he recorded it, one of the first recordings of a Broadway song by its original interpreter. Harry B. Smith wrote the lyric for Herbert's bewitching melody, and the song became the composer's first major hit. The number reappeared on Broadway in the 1946 hybrid Herbert musical *Gypsy Lady*, and Mario Lanza had a popular recording of it in the 1950s.

H

"Hair" is the electric title song from the 1968 "tribal love-rock musical" by Galt MacDermot (music) and Gerome Ragni and James Rado (lyric). The eruptive rock number celebrates boys wearing long hair as a sign of freedom, yet the lyrics are more comic than ardent. The song was sung on Broadway by Claude (Rado), Berger (Ragni) and the company; in the 1967 Off-Broadway version, the role of Claude was played by Walker Daniels. The Cowsills had a best-selling recording of the song in 1969.

"Half a Sixpence" is the engaging title song from the 1965 British import by David Heneker. The young apprentice Arthur Kipps (Tommy Steele) and the working-class Ann Pornick (Polly James) sing this touching duet after they find a sixpence, break it in half and each keep a half as a token of their simple love.

"The Half of It, Dearie, Blues" is a smooth ragtime lament from the Gershwins' first show together, *Lady, Be Good!* (1924). Fred Astaire, as the vaudevillian Dick Trevor, sang the song to his beloved Shirley (Kathlene Martyn) and then danced a solo, his first public dance routine without his sister Adele. George Gershwin wrote the genial music, and Ira Gershwin provided the mock-blues lyric.

"Hallelujah!" is one of Vincent Youmans' most performed songs and, surprisingly, the first one he ever wrote. While in naval training during World War One, Youmans composed the lively number, but it was never heard until he used it with a lyric by Leo Robin and Clifford Grey in the nautical musical *Hit the Deck!* (1927). The song was sung as a revival number in the show, with Stella Mayhew performing it in blackface. "Hallelujah!" has been recorded many times and is a particular favorite of Navy bands.

"Hallelujah, Baby!" is the keyed-up title song from the 1967 musical by Jule Styne (music) and Betty Comden and Adolph Green (lyric). Georgina (Leslie Uggams) finally has her own nightclub act, a foot-stomping gospel number that celebrates her new independence. She is supported in the lively song by the energetic dance team of Tip & Tap (Winston DeWitt Hemsley and Alan Weeks).

"Hammacher Schlemmer, I Love You" is a mocking love song from the revue *The Little Show* (1929) by Howard Dietz (lyric) and Arthur Schwartz (music) and the first song the celebrated team ever wrote together. The ardent lover (Clifton Webb) sings his affections for the famous tool company as if it were an intoxicating lady. The company of the title didn't seem to mind the attention; that Christmas they sent the authors a box of tools with a card reading "Dietz and Schwartz, we love you."

"A Handbag Is Not a Proper Mother" is a delectable comic duet from *Ernest in Love* (1960), the Off-Broadway musical version of Oscar Wilde's *The Importance of Being Earnest*. When Jack Worthing (John Irving) informs Lady Bracknell (Sara Seegar) that he is an orphan and as an infant he was found in a handbag, she launches into this ludicrous lesson in Victorian morals and standards. Lee Pockriss wrote the appealing music, and Anne Croswell provided the witty lyric.

"Handful of Keys" is a thrilling, frenzied number from the popular revue *Ain't Misbehavin'* (1978) celebrating the music of Thomas "Fats" Waller. The melody goes back to 1933, when Waller wrote it as a piano piece. Richard Maltby, Jr., and Murray Hamilton added the vibrant lyric celebrating the joys of tickling the ivories, and the number was sung by the revue's cast of five.

"Hang Up" is a vivacious mock-gospel number from *By the Beautiful Sea* (1954) by Arthur Schwartz (music) and Dorothy Fields (lyric). Ruby Monk (Mae Barnes) leads the residents of a Coney Island boardinghouse in this animated lesson that teaches one to hang up if the devil calls on the phone or tries other ways to get into your life.

"Happiness" is the simple but touching finale for the Off-Broadway "Peanuts" musical *You're a Good Man, Charlie Brown* (1967) by Clark Gesner. At the end of a typical day in the life of Charlie Brown (Gary Burghoff), the show's six characters each reflect on the little everyday things that make life beautiful.

"Happiness" is the opening duet from Stephen Sondheim's *Passion* (1994) and a musical motif that is used throughout the operatic score. The Italian soldier Giorgio (Jere Shea) and his lover Clara (Marin Mazzie) sing the direct and unrhymed love song, which takes the form of a postcoital conversation rather than a traditional rhapsodic series of refrains. As unusual as the song itself was director-librettist James Lapine's staging of the number with the two lovers singing the duet in the nude. Later in the show, the unattractive, unloved Fosca (Donna Murphy) sings fragments of "Happiness" as she slowly begins to win the heart of Giorgio.

"Happy Birthday" is a pathetic musical scene from *Zorbá* (1968) in which the dying courtesan Hortense (Maria Karnilova) has visions of her sixteenth birthday when her mother promised her that she would dance through life. Now old and unwanted, Hortense breaks into a childlike dance before she collapses and dies in the arms of Zorbá (Herschel Bernardi). John Kander composed the fragile music, and Fred Ebb wrote the poignant lyric.

"Happy Talk" is the charming little ditty that Bloody Mary (Juanita Hall) sings to Lieutenant Cable (William Tabbert) in *South Pacific* (1949) to try and convince him to marry her daughter Liat. The Richard Rodgers (music) and Oscar Hammerstein (lyric) song is childlike in melody and words, for Bloody Mary has a limited English vocabulary, but there is a desperation to please that is disarming.

"The Happy Time" is the calliopelike title song that opens the nostalgic 1968 musical set in French Canada. Jacques Bonnard (Robert Goulet) is a professional photographer who returns to his hometown to remember the happy times of the past. Members of the family join in singing the song as photographs about the stage capture moments from the past. Jacques and the ensemble reprise the song at the end of the show as well. John Kander composed the engaging music, and Fred Ebb wrote the evocative lyric.

"Happy to Make Your Acquaintance" is a charm song from the operatic *The Most Happy Fella* (1956) by Frank Loesser that takes the form of an etiquette lesson in English. Rosabella (Jo Sullivan) teaches the Italian vineyard owner Tony (Robert Weede) how to make a gracious introduction, and then they try it out on her visiting friend Cleo (Susan Johnson).

"Hard Candy Christmas" is a wistful number from *The Best Little Whorehouse in Texas* (1978) in which the "girls" at the Chicken Ranch contemplate their future now that the bordello has been closed down and they must move on. Carol Hall wrote the tender music and lyric.

"Harlem on My Mind" is a sultry, slow blues number by Irving Berlin that is also very crafty in its twofold persona. Ethel Waters introduced the song in the revue *As Thousands Cheer* (1933), where she portrayed a Josephine Baker-like expatriate in Europe who wearies of the Paris nightlife and longs for her old upper-Manhattan haunts. Berlin manages to mix a Parisian flavor with bits of honky-tonk in an amazing manner. Waters' recording of the song was a hit, as were those by Gertrude Niesen and Thelma Carpenter, and years later Bobby Short made a distinctive recording as well.

"Harrigan" is the catchy George M. Cohan number that is one of the most recognized tunes in American popular culture. Cohan wrote and titled the song "H-A-Double R-I-G-A-N" for his musical *Fifty Miles From Boston* (1908), in which James C. Marlowe sang the rousing tribute to the character Harrigan (George Parson), a rough-and-tumble Irish American. Using the name was Cohan's own tribute to his idol, Edward Harrigan of the pioneering team of Harrigan and Hart. The twosome had developed strong immigrant characters in their nineteenth-century musical comedies and had laid the groundwork for the all-American shows Cohan specialized in. The opening night of *Fifty Miles From Boston* was particularly emotional because the aged and forgotten Ned Harrigan was in the audience as Cohan's guest. Joel Grey sang the song as "Harrigan" (as it was published and forever after known) in the bio-musical *George M!* (1968).

"Has Anybody Here Seen Kelly?" is a popular British music hall ditty, but by the time it was heard on Broadway it sounded like an all-American classic. C.W. Murphy and Will Letters wrote the original song that was popular in England, and the producers of the Broadway musical *The Jolly Bachelors* (1910) decided to interpolate it into the show for Nora Bayes to sing. The American lyricist William J. McKenna revised the British lyric, changing all the geographical and topical references to American places and names, and the song was a hit. Bayes, as a girl impatiently waiting for her boyfriend Kelly to show up, stopped the show with the number, and she later recorded it.

"Haunted Heart" is a surging love ballad from the revue *Inside U.S.A.* (1948) by Howard Dietz (lyric) and Arthur Schwartz (music) and the last of the seven Broadway revues they scored together. In a San Francisco waterfront setting, John Tyers and Estelle Loring sang this entrancing song of romantic obsession while Valerie Bettis danced with the male chorus. Perry Como made a hit recording of the number soon after, and Andrea Marcovicci recorded an intriguing version in 1990.

"Have I Told You Lately?" is a touching love song for an older married couple in *I Can Get It for You Wholesale* (1962) and a sort of precursor of "Do You Love Me?" from *Fiddler on the Roof* (1964). Meyer Bushkin (Ken Le Roy) and his wife Blanche (Bambi Linn) sing the gentle duet in which they find comfort in each other's love even after years of marriage. Harold Rome wrote the effective music and lyric.

"Have You Met Miss Jones?" is a love song from Rodgers and Hart's political satire *I'd Rather Be Right* (1937) and the hit from the show. Richard Rodgers' music is both sad and romantic as the melody climbs up the scale in a winning manner. Lorenz Hart's lyric is rather subdued for him and very touching. The duet was written to provide a less talky way for the young lovers (Austin Marshall and Joy Hodges) to meet, and the song did much more than solve the problem. Ella Fitzgerald made a memorable recording of the song.

"He Always Comes Home to Me" is an artful comic number from the short-lived *Dance a Little Closer* (1983) with an exceptional score by Charles Strouse (music) and Alan Jay Lerner (lyrics). The wealthy Englishwoman Cynthia Brookfield-Bailey (Liz Robertson) explains that despite her husband's many extramarital flings, he returns to her at the end of each one of them. Strouse's waltz melody is both eloquent and amusing, and Lerner's wry humor recalls his best lyricwriting.

"He Had Refinement" is one of the finest comic character songs of the postwar theatre, a delectable number sung by Shirley Booth in the period musical *A Tree Grows in Brooklyn* (1951) by Arthur Schwartz (music) and Dorothy Fields (lyric). The childlike Aunt Cissy (Booth) recalls her husband, the bigamist Harry Swanswine, who was, she argues, very classy even if a bit suspect in his morals. Fields's lyric, in one of her finest comic numbers, manages to keep Cissy deliciously sincere, while her recounting of past events is hilariously ambiguous.

"He Hasn't a Thing Except Me" is a comic number from the *Ziegfeld Follies of 1936* in which Fanny Brice lampooned her famous torch song "My Man." In the revue Brice was seen leaning against the requisite lamp post looking forlorn. The lamp post walked off, and she sang this mock lament about her louse of a husband who has no money, no charm, no looks: nothing but a doting wife. Vernon Duke composed the pseudo-blues music, and Ira Gershwin wrote the shrewd lyric.

"He Loves and She Loves" is a dreamy love song from the Gershwins' *Funny Face* (1927), sung by aviator Peter Thurston (Allen Kearns) and his sweetheart Frankie Wynne (Adele Astaire). George Gershwin wrote the melodic music, and Ira Gershwin provided the simple romantic lyric. The song was a last-minute addition to the score, used to replace "How Long Has This Been Going On?"after it was cut during tryouts. Sarah Vaughan made a stunning recording of "He Loves and She Loves" in 1983, and that same year, in the rewritten version of *Funny Face* called *My One and Only*, the song was sung by aviator Billy Buck Chandler (Tommy Tune) and aquatic star Edith Herbert (Twiggy) in a movie palace as they watched a romantic silent film together.

"He Was Too Good to Me" was dropped from Rodgers and Hart's *Simple Simon* (1930) before opening, but it is an accomplished torch song with a wry lyric. Only Lorenz Hart could devise such an imaginative and ambiguous lyric as when the jilted one concludes that he "was too good to be true." Richard Rodgers' music is just as intriguing, providing a sweeping melody within a very narrow range (one note more than an octave). It was sung by Lee Morse in the pre-Broadway tryouts, but the song was cut when Morse was. Carly Simon recorded it beautifully in 1990.

"Heart" or, as most know it, "You Gotta Have Heart" is an exhilarating showstopper from *Damn Yankees* (1955) with music and lyrics by Richard Adler and Jerry Ross. Benny Van Buren (Russ Brown), the manager of the Washington Senators baseball team, sings the tuneful song of encouragement to his losing team. The number starts out as a solo; then players Rocky (Jimmy Komack), Smokey (Nathaniel Frey) and Vernon (Albert Linville) join him in a barbershop quartet version of the song. Soon all the players join in, and only after an encore does the audience let the show continue. Later in the musical the song was reprised by Jean Stapleton, as an eager Senators fan, and three children (Ronn Cummins, Jackie Scholle and Cherry Davis). The Four Aces and Eddie Fisher both made hit recordings of the song. At the funeral of Jerry Ross, who died at the age of twenty-nine soon after *Damn Yankees* opened, the lyric for "Heart" was read, taking on a whole new meaning.

"The Heart Is Quicker Than the Eye" is a nimble character song from *On Your Toes* (1936) by Richard Rodgers (music) and Lorenz Hart (lyric). The duet is a comic piece of advice given by a wealthy arts patroness (Luella Gear) to a young hoofer in love (Ray Bolger).

"Heat Wave" is a very atypical Irving Berlin song but a hit all the same. Ethel Waters, delivering a weather report in the revue *As Thousands Cheer* (1933), introduced the saucy number. Berlin's music swings, but in a lazy, languid manner, and has a very unusual patter-section melody. Also, his lyric is rather risqué and borders on the Cole Porterish. The word "heat," for example, is used with varied meanings. "Heat Wave" remains one of Berlin's most theatrical pieces and one that illustrates his seemingly limitless versatility.

"The Heather on the Hill" is the bucolic hit ballad from *Brigadoon* (1947) by Alan Jay Lerner (lyric) and Frederick Loewe (music). New Yorker Tommy Albright (David Brooks) and the Scottish lass Fiona (Marion Bell) sing the lyrical duet about taking a stroll through the flowering Highlands. The popular song has been recorded many times, including a single by the original singers Brooks and Bell.

"Heaven in My Arms" is an enchanting ballad from the short-lived *Very Warm for May* (1939) by Jerome Kern (music) and Oscar Hammerstein (lyric). The number was sung by three of the young apprentices (Jack Whiting, Frances Mercer and Hollace Shaw) at Winnie's Barn, a summer stock theatre. The lovely but mostly neglected score was the last Kern wrote for Broadway.

"Heaven on Earth" is a soaring ballad from the Off-Broadway mythological musical *Olympus on My Mind* (1986) by Barry Harman (lyric) and Grant Sturiale (music). Jupiter (Martin Vidnovic) has disguised himself as the mortal Amphitryon so that he can seduce the man's wife Alcmene (Emily Zacharias). He sings to her that together they will make a little bit of heaven on earth, and she agrees, the two of them joining for an enticing duet.

"Hello Again" is the beguiling title number from the 1994 Off-Broadway musical by Michael John LaChiusa. The song is heard as a musical scene of loveless lovemaking between the Whore (Donna Murphy) and the Soldier (David A. White) and then is reprised by the whole cast at the end of the show.

"Hello, Dolly!" is the most popular song to come out of Broadway in the 1960s and was the undisputed highlight of the 1964 musical that took its title from the zesty number. Jerry Herman wrote the catchy turn-of-the-century-style number as a welcome song for Dolly Levi (Carol Channing) as she makes a grand entrance at the Harmonia Gardens Restaurant. Channing sang it with a chorus of waiters and cooks, and it stopped the show as few shows have ever been stopped. Much of the song's popularity can be attributed to Louis Armstrong's 1964 recording, which sold over a million copies. Within a year there were over seventy different recordings in the United States and over thirty-five in Europe. With an altered lyric, the song became "Hello, Lyndon" and was used as the official campaign song for Johnson's bid for the presidency. Herman's melody has been a matter of some controversy; it is similar to that of a 1915 song "Here Comes Tootsie" by Herman Finck, and uncomfortably close to a 1948 song by Mack David called "Sunflower." After the success of the show, David and his publishers sued Herman and won.

"Hello, Frisco!" is the hit song from the 1915 edition of the *Ziegfeld Follies* by Louis Hirsch (music) and Gene Buck (lyric). Although the big news from San Francisco that year was the fair, this song celebrated the recent inauguration of transcontinental telephone service. Ina Claire and Bernard Granville sang the tangy number. The song was heard again on Broadway in 1976 when it was interpolated into the revival of Hirsch's *Going Up!*, where it was sung by Pat Lysinger and four "aviators."

"Hello, Young Lovers" is Anna's affectionate ballad in *The King and I* (1951), a soaring number that reveals the character's passionate heart while retaining her British reserve. The Richard Rodgers (music) and Oscar Hammerstein (lyric) song is a sweeping and melodic aria, but, in fact, the music is quite limited (only one half step above an octave) because the original Anna, Gertrude Lawrence, had a narrow voice range. But the way the waltz climbs up the scale, taking chromatic steps and climaxing at the end of the refrain, is thrilling. Of the many performers who recorded the number, perhaps the most unique interpretation was that by Mabel Mercer in 1951. "Hello, Young Lovers" was not popular only with female singers; Perry Como made a best-selling recording in the 1950s, and Paul Anka had a hit with it in 1960.

"Here Am I" is an optimistic ballad that is one of Jerome Kern's most unique, if lesser-known, songs. He wrote it with lyricist Oscar Hammerstein for *Sweet Adeline* (1929), where it was sung by beer-hall singer Addie Schmidt (Helen Morgan) and her pal Dot (Violet Carson). Kern's music is very unusual in its structure and has a striking F-sharp beginning even though the song is written in E-flat. Also of interest are the remarkable harmonies used throughout. Conductor John McGlinn reconstructed the original orchestrations in 1992 and recorded the number with Judy Kaye and Rebecca Luker singing the duet.

"Here and Now" is an expansive ballad of enthusiasm from *The Girl Who Came to Supper* (1963) by Noël Coward. Mary Morgan (Florence Henderson), an American chorus girl mixing with visiting royalty in London, sang the exuberant number.

"Here I'll Stay" is a buoyant duet from the experimental "musical vaudeville" *Love Life* (1948) and the only song to become popular from the superb score by Alan Jay Lerner (lyric) and Kurt Weill (music). Sam Cooper (Ray Middleton) and his wife Susan (Nanette Fabray) decide that the outside world and all its glamours are not for them; they'll stay together at home and in love. Jo Stafford made a hit recording of the idyllic number, and many years later Karen Akers recorded it.

"Here in My Arms (It's Adorable)" is a soaring romantic duet from the early Rodgers and Hart musical *Dearest Enemy* (1925) and one that became a standard. It was introduced by Helen Ford, as a colonial New Yorker, and Charles Purcell, as a British officer occupying Manhattan during the Revolutionary War. Richard Rodgers' music is grandiose and a bit challenging for musical comedy; in the refrain it has a stretch of an octave and a fifth, something more expected in operetta. Lorenz Hart's lyric eschews the sentimental and is all the more charming for that.

"Here's Love" is the festive title song from the 1963 musical based on the film favorite *Miracle on 34th Street*. Meredith Willson wrote the compelling list song in which Kris Kringle (Laurence Naismith) leads the ensemble in wishing the gift of love for all opposing nations, companies, neighbors and so on.

"Here's That Rainy Day" is a memorable torch song from the six-performance flop *Carnival in Flanders* (1953) by James Van Heusen (music) and Johnny Burke (lyric). Dolores Gray, as the mayor's wife Cornelia who single-handedly must save the town from Spanish invasion, sang the lament and gave the limping show its one bright spot. The ballad was a popular staple in nightclubs throughout the 1950s, and later was recorded by Frank Sinatra, Ann Hampton Calloway and others.

"Here's to Dear Old Us" is a slaphappy tribute to friends from the musical farce *Ankles Aweigh* (1955) by Sammy Fain (music) and Dan Shapiro (lyric). Betty Kean, Lew Parker and Gabriel Dell led the ensemble in the rousing self-congratulatory number.

"Here's to Your Illusions" is the unusual but appealing love song from the most unusual *Flahooley* (1951) by Sammy Fain (music) and E.Y. Harburg (lyric). Toy inventor Sylvester Cloud (Jerome Courtland) and his sweetheart Sandy (Barbara Cook) sing the beguiling duet that welcomes love that is blind to reality and plans that are just illusions. Years later Andrea Marcovicci made a distinctive recording of the song.

"Hernando's Hideaway" is the mock-Latin tango from *The Pajama Game* (1954) that became a popular favorite of orchestras in the 1950s. Richard Adler and Jerry Ross wrote the song when director George Abbott suggested a sexy number for the nightclub scene. Carol Haney, as the seductive Gladys, sang and danced the song with John Raitt and the chorus. Abbott staged the first part of the number in total darkness, then a match was lit, then another, and the dance continued lit only by flickering matches. "Hernando's Hideaway" had popular recordings by Archie Bleyer and His Orchestra and Guy Lombardo's Orchestra.

"He's Only Wonderful" is a melodic song of encouragement from the big-business satire *Flahooley* (1951) by Sammy Fain (music) and E.Y. Harburg (lyric). Sandy (Barbara Cook) sings the ballad about her sweetheart, toy developer Sylvester Cloud (Jerome Courtland), and then they sing the number together as a duet.

"Hey, Good-Lookin' " is Cole Porter's version of a way-out-West cowboy song, written for *Something for the Boys* (1943), which took place in Texas. Ethel Merman and Bill Johnson did the hootin' and hollerin', and the number was reprised later in the show by Bill Callahan and Betty Bruce. The song is different from the 1951 Hank Williams hit that used Porter's opening line and melody.

"Hey, Look Me Over!" is the robust "I am" song for the heroine in *Wildcat* (1960) and the big hit from the show by Cy Coleman (music) and Carolyn Leigh (lyric). Wildcat Jackson (Lucille Ball) arrives in oil-rich Centavo City with her crippled sister Jane (Paula Stewart), and they sing this eager march. The cheery music and optimistic lyric are ideal for political conventions, and the number has proven a useful theme song for more than one campaign, including Edward Kennedy's 1962 senatorial bid. The Peter King Chorale made a hit recording of the number.

"Hey There," the hit ballad from *The Pajama Game* (1954), was nearly cut before opening, but the songwriters Richard Adler and Jerry Ross couldn't come up with anything they liked better, so it stayed. John Raitt, as the factory superintendent Sid Sorokin, sang the song in his office while his Dictaphone recorded it. Then he played back the tape, commenting on himself and eventually singing a duet with himself. It was Adler's idea to double the song, a gimmick that had been used in pop music with the recent invention of multitrack recording. (Both Patti Page and Kay Starr had made records singing duets with themselves.) The song is very lyrical, with a dreamy Mozartian melody and lush romantic lyrics. Among the many who made hit recordings of it were Johnnie Ray, Rosemary Clooney and Sammy Davis, Jr.

"Hey There, Good Times" is the toe-tapping showstopper from *I Love My Wife* (1977) that was sung by the band rather than the cast. Throughout the musical, John Miller, Michael Mark, Joseph Saulter and Ken Bichel acted as a Greek chorus of four, commenting on the action, playing musical instruments and singing some of the songs. This dandy old-time number was a banjo-plucking delight and immediately became an audience favorite. Cy Coleman wrote the tuneful music, and Michael Stewart provided the sprightly lyric.

"Hic Haec Hoc" is a musical theatre curiosity, a chorus number from *Ben Franklin in Paris* (1964) in which an ensemble of French monks joyfully sing (in Latin, of course) as they toil in the monastery vineyard. Mark Sandrich, Jr., (music) and Sidney Michaels (lyric) wrote the unusual but somehow memorable number.

"High and Low" is a lovely duet from the revue *The Band Wagon* (1931) by Howard Dietz (lyric) and Arthur Schwartz (music). Roberta Robinson and John Barker sang the flowing, contemplative ballad.

"High Flying Adored" is a melodic song of worship and derision from the British import *Evita* (1979) by Andrew Lloyd Webber (music) and Tim Rice (lyric). When Eva Peron (Patti LuPone) becomes First Lady of Argentina, she celebrates her exalted role and political triumph while Che (Mandy Patinkin) cynically marvels at her rapid rise to fame, warning her not to look down because it is quite a height to fall from.

"High Hat" is the exhilarating dance number from *Funny Face* (1927) that created the debonair, tuxedoed style of performance that would forever be associated with Fred Astaire. In the show Jimmie Reeve (Astaire) donned formal wear with top hat and, with his hands in his pockets, casually tapped away while two dozen men in black tie echoed his stamping feet. The song, by George Gershwin (music) and Ira Gershwin (lyric), argued that if you treat girls with "high hat" style they'll always come around. From that point on no Broadway show, movie or television program with Fred Astaire would be complete without a "High Hat" kind of number.

"His Love Makes Me Beautiful" is a hilarious production number from *Funny Girl* (1964) that pastiched the *Ziegfeld Follies* spectaculars of the early decades of this century. In a lavish wedding number, a tenor (John Lankston) sings the praises of the bride-to-be as gorgeous chorines in bridal wear descend the requisite staircase. But when Fanny Brice (Barbra Streisand) appears as the bride in question, she is noticeably pregnant under her wedding gown and coyly moves down the staircase as the nonplused tenor carries bravely on. Finally she sings the syrupy song, which becomes outrageously risqué given her circumstances. Jule Styne wrote the Berlin-like music, and Bob Merrill provided the facetious lyric.

"Holding to the Ground" is a beguiling soliloquy from *Falsettoland* (1990) in which Trina (Faith Prince) keeps trying to adjust her life to the always surprising circumstances that surround her. She must now deal with the fact that her ex-husband's male lover has AIDS, and she is trying to keep her sanity as the rules keep changing. William Finn wrote the urgent music and perceptive lyric.

"Home" is the soaring ballad that concludes *The Wiz* (1975), the black retelling of *The Wizard of Oz*. As Dorothy (Stephanie Mills) clicks her heels and returns to Kansas, she sings this enthralling song by Charlie Smalls. With no scenery or special effects, Mills's powerhouse voice created a stunning climax that was as dazzling as any spectacular musical finale.

"Homework" is not about academics but rather the seriocomic lament of a newspaper reporter who longs to marry her true love, quit her job and work at home. Mary McCarty sang the appealing character song in Irving Berlin's *Miss Liberty* (1949).

"Honey Bun" being sung and danced by Mary Martin in an oversized sailor suit is one of the American musical theatre's most enduring images. In Rodgers and Hammerstein's *South Pacific* (1949), Nellie Forbush (Martin) entertains the American servicemen with this silly ditty at the "Thanksgiving Follies." After she sings the lighthearted paean to a pretty and young swinging doll, Nellie is joined by Luther Billis (Myron McCormick) in drag with a grass skirt and cocoanut breasts, who dances to the reprise of the song. The cross-dressing number is a piece of comic relief for the soldiers and for the main characters, who, by the time the song comes around, have all separated from their romantic partners. In the Broadway revue *A Grand Night for Singing* (1993), "Honey Bun" was sung by Martin Vidnovic and the ensemble.

"Honey in the Honeycomb" is a wry ballad from the "Negro folk musical" *Cabin in the Sky* (1940). Vernon Duke (music) and John Latouche (lyric) wrote the beguiling song, which was sung by the devil's temptress Georgia Brown (Katherine Dunham).

"The Honeymoon Is Over" is a seriocomic duet sung by a couple in marital trouble in *I Do! I Do!* (1966). Michael (Robert Preston) and Agnes (Mary Martin) trade complaints about each other and realize that each had better be on the alert for trouble. Tom Jones wrote the tangy lyric, and Harvey Schmidt composed the furious music.

"Hoops" is an unusual comic duet from the renowned revue *The Band Wagon* (1931) by Howard Dietz (lyric) and Arthur Schwartz (music). Adele and Fred Astaire played two naughty French children in a Paris park who play with their toy hoops and sing proudly of the ways they terrorize adults. The dance team did their famous "run-around" dance exit for the final time (it was Adele Astaire's last public performance), and the ingenious staging by Hassard Short had the stage revolve as the "children" ran through the park. The Astaires recorded the song with Leo Reisman's Orchestra in 1931.

"Hooray for Captain Spaulding" is the comic song that introduced Groucho Marx's character in *Animal Crackers* (1928) and became his signature song for the rest of his life. As the great African explorer Spaulding, Marx made his entrance carried in by natives as the chorus sang his praises and he gladly joined in the song. Harry Ruby wrote the daffy music, and Bert Kalmar provided the prankish lyric.

"The Hostess With the Mostes' on the Ball" is the snappy "I am" song for the new ambassadress Sally Adams (Ethel Merman) in Irving Berlin's *Call Me Madam* (1950). The character was based on Washington socialite Perle Mesta, whom President Truman had recently named ambassador to Luxembourg, thereby setting the premise for the musical comedy.

"Hottentot Potentate" is a clever comic number from the revue *At Home Abroad* (1935) by Howard Dietz (lyric) and Arthur Schwartz (music). In an African jungle, Ethel Waters sings how she brought everything she learned in Harlem to the Congo, where she now rules as the potentate of all the natives.

"House of Flowers" is the warm and romantic title song from the 1954 musical by Harold Arlen (music) and Truman Capote (lyric). Although the show's title refers to a Caribbean house of prostitution where each of the girls is given the name of a flower, this song is a tender duet between Royal (Rawn Spearman) and Ottilie (Diahann Carroll) in which he describes to her his home, which is, literally, overflowing with flowers, birds and other vibrant signs of life.

"How Are Things in Glocca Morra?" is the wistful ballad from *Finian's Rainbow* (1947) that was not only the biggest hit from a show filled with hits but became the most popular theatre song of that season. Burton Lane (music) and E.Y. Harburg (lyric) wrote the pseudo-Irish reverie that is sung by Sharon McLonergan (Ella Logan) as she thinks back on the homeland she has left to come to America with her father. Lane's music is graceful and nostalgic, while Harburg uses nature images and melodic place names to create an enchanting world called Glocca Morra. (There is no actual place of that name; Harburg made it up, saying it sounded Irish.) Coming near the beginning of the show, "How Are Things in Glocca Morra?" not only established Sharon's character (it is her "I am" song) but set up the airy, magical atmosphere that the subsequent fantasy requires. Cynics have pointed out that the little brook mentioned in the lyric would have to be longer than most rivers in Europe to hit all the towns listed in the song. Logan's Scottish burr gave the ballad an unreal quality, but she sold the number winningly, and audiences warmed up to it immediately. The song became a national favorite due to an early Dick Haymes recording.

"How Beautiful the Days" is an exhilarating Verdi-like quartet from Frank Loesser's operatic *The Most Happy Fella* (1956). Tony (Robert Weede), Maria (Mona Paulee), Rosabella (Jo Sullivan) and Joe (Art Lund) sing the evocative number, which has a mixture of English and Italian lyrics.

"How Can Love Survive?" is a merry, cynical duet for the Baroness

(Marion Marlowe) and her friend Max (Kurt Kasznar) in *The Sound of Music* (1959) about the impossibility of true love in a millionaire's life. Richard Rodgers wrote an insistent, frolicsome melody to go with Oscar Hammerstein's sophisticated, acrid lyric, and the song provides a necessary contrast to all the nuns and children that occupy most of the musical. Because the number was not included in the popular film version, it is not much known today.

"How Can You Tell an American?" is a satirical number from the Kurt Weill (music) and Maxwell Anderson (lyric) spoof of early Manhattan called *Knickerbocker Holiday* (1938). Brom Broeck (Richard Kollmar) is a rugged individualist who loves his freedom and shuns all authority. He and Washington Irving (Ray Middleton) sing this swinging song claiming that the unwillingness to follow the orders of powerful leaders is what makes the American spirit. Despite its preachy anti-FDR sentiments, the song is quite fun, recalling the Gershwins' style in *Strike Up the Band* (1930) and *Of Thee I Sing* (1931). The song was also sung by the ensemble in the Off-Broadway revue *Berlin to Broadway With Kurt Weill* (1972).

"How Do You Speak to an Angel?" is an emotional ballad from *Hazel Flagg* (1953) by Jule Styne (music) and Bob Hilliard (lyric). The sophisticated New Yorker Wallace Cook (John Howard) sings the song about the Vermont girl Hazel (Helen Gallagher), whom he thinks is dying of radiation poisoning and with whom he has fallen in love. Both Eddie Fisher and Gordon MacRae made successful recordings of the song.

"How Long Has This Been Going On?" is a poignant song about the discovery of love that the Gershwins wrote for *Funny Face* (1927). The number was sung as a duet by Adele Astaire and Stanley Ridges before it and Mr. Ridges were cut during tryouts and replaced by "He Loves and She Loves." But Florenz Ziegfeld liked the song and put it in his production of *Rosalie* (1928), where it was sung by the soubrette character Mary (Bobbe Arnst) as a solo. In both cases the song is inspired by a first kiss, with George Gershwin's music and Ira Gershwin's lyric expressing delighted wonderment. It took a long time for the song to become the popular standard it is today. Not until Peggy Lee and Lee Wiley recorded it decades later did it start to catch on. Recordings were also made by Julie Andrews, Michael Feinstein and, most memorably, by Ella Fitzgerald who recorded it six different times. In the "new Gershwin musical" *My One and Only* (1983), the song was again a duet, sung by Captain Billy Buck Chandler (Tommy Tune) and swimming champion Edith Herbert (Twiggy) at the end of the show.

"How Lovely to Be a Woman" is a charming "I am" song for the teenager Kim McAfee (Susan Watson) in the youthful *Bye Bye Birdie* (1960) by

Charles Strouse (music) and Lee Adams (lyric). The appealing number celebrates the joy and bewilderment of adolescence from a teenager's point of view.

"How the Money Changes Hands" is a dandy production number from *Tenderloin* (1960) in which various characters at a Tenderloin district haunt sing about the circular path money takes from grocer to dentist to landlord to mayor, all ending up in the purchasing of vice. Maurice Evans, Eileen Rodgers, Christine Norden, Eddie Phillips, Lee Becker and the ensemble sang the rompish Jerry Bock (music) and Sheldon Harnick (lyric) song as the first-act finale.

"How to Handle a Woman" is a tender ballad from *Camelot* (1960) in which King Arthur (Richard Burton) feels he is losing touch with Guenevere and tries to recall the advice his old teacher Merlin once gave him about women. Alan Jay Lerner (lyric) and Frederick Loewe (music) wrote the beguiling number, which had a hit recording by Johnny Mathis.

"How'd You Like to Spoon With Me?" was Jerome Kern's first commercially successful song, a lighthearted frolic he wrote with lyricist Edward Laska that was interpolated into the British import *The Earl and the Girl* (1905). The saucy duet was sung by Georgina Caine and Victor Morley, supported by six beautiful girls on flowered swings who swung out over the audience. The authors had written the song a few years earlier, but prospective producers thought that "spoon" was too vulgar a word for theatre audiences.

"How's Chances?" is a gleeful rhythm ballad by Irving Berlin from the popular revue *As Thousands Cheer* (1933). Marilyn Miller, as millionairess Barbara Hutton, wooed Prince Mdivani (Clifton Webb) with the easygoing number, and he returned the compliment by singing and dancing it as well. Leo Reisman and His Orchestra (with a Clifton Webb vocal) made a popular recording of the song.

"Hugette Waltz" is a poignant solo from the operetta *The Vagabond King* (1925) by Rudolf Friml (music) and Brian Hooker (lyric). The French prostitute Hugette (Jane Carroll) is in love with the dashing outlaw Francois Villon (Dennis King), and sings this heartrending waltz about her unrequited love. Years later Lucille Norman made a memorable recording of "Hugette Waltz." The song is sometimes listed as "Waltz Hugette."

"Hulla-Baloo-Balay" is a tantalizing narrative ballad from the Off-Broadway period musical *Man With a Load of Mischief* (1966) by John Clifton (music and lyric) and Ben Tarver (lyric). The manservant Charles (Reid Shelton), who is staying with his master at a nineteenth-century inn, sings the tale of a young man who longed to go to sea but didn't understand the ways of the world until his heart was broken by a gypsy maid. The song has the flavor of an old English ballad, with its repeating title phrase accenting each verse of the tale.

"Human Again" is a spirited production number from *Beauty and the Beast* (1994) in which all the enchanted objects in the Beast's castle savor the expectation of the spell being broken. Alan Menken (music) and Howard Ashman (lyric) wrote the French-flavored song for the 1991 film version's original score, but it was cut in production. On stage it was sung by Lumiere (Gary Beach), Madame de la Grande Bouche (Eleanor Glockner), Cogsworth (Heath Lamberts), Mrs. Potts (Beth Fowler), Chip (Brian Press), Babette (Stacey Logan) and the ensemble.

"The Human Heart" is an absorbing ballad from the Caribbean musical *Once on This Island* (1990) by Stephen Flaherty (music) and Lynn Ahrens (lyric). Erzulie (Andrea Frierson), the Goddess of Love, and the storytellers sing the captivating song about how all people are connected in part by love.

"Humming" is a jocular number from *Carnival* (1961) that featured the special talents of Kaye Ballard. The magician's assistant (and sometimes mistress) Rosalie sings with Mr. Schlegel (Henry Lascoe) about her lover's frequent infidelities. She always knows when he has been unfaithful by his humming, so she plans to cut loose herself and come back humming to see how he likes it. Bob Merrill wrote the witty music and lyric.

"A Hundred Million Miracles" is the most Asian-sounding number from *Flower Drum Song* (1958), the Rodgers and Hammerstein musical about Chinese-Americans in San Francisco. Miyoshi Umecki, as the newly arrived immigrant Mei Li, sang the fragile song along with some of the citizens of Chinatown. Oscar Hammerstein's lyric combines Eastern philosophy with homespun warmth, and Richard Rodgers' music is highly evocative, its eight-note drumbeat serving as the musical signature for the show from overture to finale. In the Broadway revue *A Grand Night for Singing* (1993), Alyson Reed sang the song.

"Hundreds of Girls" is a jolly, satirical song from *Mack and Mabel* (1974) that celebrated silent filmdom's "bathing beauties" in a self-mocking way. Robert Preston, as movie director Mack Sennett, sang the delightful Jerry Herman song, and a line of beachside chorines did a merry dance to it.

"Hurry! It's Lovely Up Here" is an enticing character song from *On a Clear Day You Can See Forever* (1965) by Alan Jay Lerner (lyric) and Burton Lane (music). Daisy Gamble (Barbara Harris) sings the number to a potted plant in a psychiatrist's office to show him how she talks to plants to encourage them to grow. Lane's music is warm and seductive, and Lerner's lyric craftsmanship is at its best here, particularly in the playful internal rhymes.

"Hymn for a Sunday Evening" is a droll comic song from *Bye Bye Birdie* (1960) that is a tongue-in-cheek tribute to TV's popular "The Ed Sullivan Show." Charles Strouse composed the acutely reverent music, Lee Adams wrote the waggish lyric, and it was sung by Mr. McAfee (Paul Lynde) and his family when they find out that they are going to appear on the renowned variety show.

"A Hymn to Him" is the official title of the comic song from *My Fair Lady* (1956) known to most as "Why Can't a Woman Be More Like a Man?" After Eliza has run off, Henry Higgins (Rex Harrison) sings to his friend Colonel Pickering (Robert Coote) and his housekeeper Mrs. Pearce (Phillipa Bevans) of his astonishment at the illogical behavior of women. Frederick Loewe wrote the march-tempo melody, and Alan Jay Lerner devised the ingenious lyric in which Higgins' bombastic pomposity is actually endearing: he defeats his every argument with his examples, but his confusion is sincere.

I

"I Ain't Down Yet" is the heroine's eager "I am" song from Meredith Willson's *The Unsinkable Molly Brown* (1960). The ever-enthusiastic Molly (Tammy Grimes) sings this song at various points in the story to boost her own morale. At the beginning of the show she sings it with her three brothers (Sterling Clark, Bill Starr and Bob Daley), and later Molly and her husband Johnny (Harve Presnell) sing it as a duet. Dinah Shore recorded the number in 1960.

"I Am Easily Assimilated" is a delectable Latin-flavored character number from *Candide* (1956). A wily Old Lady (Irra Petina) convinces the naive Cunegonde (Barbara Cook) that they must adapt to new places and situations. Since they are now trapped in Buenos Aires, the Old Lady suddenly becomes Spanish, attracting the attention of two local senores and proving how quickly she can assimilate into a new culture. Leonard Bernstein wrote the vibrant music and, with his wife Felicia Montealegre, the jocular lyric as well. Christa Ludwig sang the number in the 1991 complete recording of the *Candide* score.

"I Am Going to Like It Here" is the delicate "I am" song for Mei Li (Miyoshi Umeki), the newly arrived immigrant from China in *Flower Drum Song* (1958). Oscar Hammerstein wrote the fragile lyric that takes a sonnet form and, for the most part, eschews rhymes. Richard Rodgers' music evokes a simple Asian melody yet is firmly in the Broadway style.

"I Am Loved" is a rapturous ballad from Cole Porter's *Out of This World* (1950). Priscilla Gillette introduced the declarative love song, which has a surprisingly simple and straightforward lyric for a Porter number.

"I Am What I Am" is the valiant character song that Albin (George Hearn) sings at the end of the first act of Jerry Herman's *La Cage aux Folles*

(1983). When his lover Georges (Gene Barry) demands that Albin not be around when his son's future in-laws visit, the temperamental Albin replies with this heartbreaking number that pleads for acceptance as it declares pride in his homosexuality.

"I Believe in You" is the only popular song to come out of *How to Succeed in Business Without Really Trying* (1961), and it only became well known as a sentimental love ballad removed from its original context in the show. The Frank Loesser song is actually a biting testimony to self-love sung by the hero to the hero. Corporate climber Finch (Robert Morse) sings to his image in a mirror in the executive washroom as the other businessmen sing a counterpoint melody about how they "Gotta Stop That Man" to the accompaniment of the electric shavers they are using as they look into their own mirrors. Without a lyric change, "I Believe in You" was often recorded as a touching song of love and encouragement.

"I Built a Dream One Day" is the hit ballad from the Sigmund Romberg operetta *May Wine* (1935). Oscar Hammerstein wrote the evocative lyric for Romberg's lovely melody, and it was sung by Walter Slezak, Walter Woolf King and Robert C. Fischer.

"I Cain't Say No" is Ado Annie's famous "I am" song from *Oklahoma!* (1943) and the model for dozens of comic numbers for secondary characters in later musicals. Celeste Holm introduced the number, in which the fickle and flirtatious Ado Annie recounts how she finds all men attractive, so she encourages them all. Richard Rodgers wrote the zesty country music, and Oscar Hammerstein provided the memorable comic lyric. Victoria Clark sang "I Cain't Say No" in the Broadway revue *A Grand Night for Singing* (1993).

"I Can Cook Too" is a jazzy tour de force comedy number for Nancy Walker in *On the Town* (1944) by Leonard Bernstein (music) and Betty Comden and Adolph Green (lyric). Hildy (Walker), a New York City taxi driver who has fallen for the sailor Chip (Cris Alexander), gets him to her apartment to cook him dinner and sings of her culinary skills, which are thinly disguised metaphors for her romantic prowess. Barbara Cook made a lively recording of the song.

"I Can Do That" is an energetic tap solo from *A Chorus Line* (1975) for the auditioning dancer Mike (Wayne Cilento) by Marvin Hamlisch (music) and Edward Kleban (lyric). Mike recalls how he used to watch his sister take dance classes until one day he realized "I Can Do That" himself and his love affair with dance began.

"I Can Dream, Can't I?" is the popular ballad from the short-lived

Right This Way (1938) by Sammy Fain (music) and Irving Kahal (lyric). Mimi Chester (Tamara), the common-law wife whose mate wants to go official, sang the song that got little attention at the time but eventually became a popular favorite. Of the many recordings over the years, one by the Andrews Sisters in 1949 remained on the Top Ten for seventeen weeks.

"I Can Have It All" is a caustic number from the comic-strip musical *Doonesbury* (1983) by Elizabeth Swados (music) and Gary Trudeau (lyric). Boopsie (Laura Dean), who longs to be a professional cheerleader, leads the ensemble in this funny song of ambition about how a woman can handle a career, love life, kids, the works.

"I Can See It" is a stirring duet of contrasting optimism and cynicism from *The Fantasticks* (1960) by Tom Jones (lyric) and Harvey Schmidt (music). The eager Matt (Kenneth Nelson) sets out to see the world and learn what he can of its grandeur. Meanwhile the bandit El Gallo (Jerry Orbach) sings of the cruelty and misery of the outside world and how it will teach Matt a lesson. Each fervently sings his viewpoint, and the song climaxes in a scintillating ironic duet. Barbra Streisand successfully recorded the number as a solo.

"I Can't Be in Love" is a funny soliloquy from *Goldilocks* (1958) on a familiar theme, but the highly analytical approach the character takes is unique. Movie producer Max Grady (Don Ameche) is starting to fall in love with his nemesis, actress Maggie Harris (Elaine Stritch), and the idea causes him to list all the reasons why he isn't in love, using a multiple-choice test form. Leroy Anderson wrote the frantic music, and the quick-witted lyric is by Joan Ford and Walter and Jean Kerr.

"I Can't Do the Sum" is a bright and childlike song from Victor Herbert's *Babes in Toyland* (1903) with a lyric by Glen MacDonough. The two "babes," Alan (William Norris) and Jane (Mabel Barrison), lead the children's chorus in this merry number about the difficulty of math, the simple rhythm tapped out by chalk on schoolroom slates.

"I Can't Get Started (With You)" is a delightful pseudo-comic lament from the *Ziegfeld Follies of 1936* that became the hit of the show. The number is a wry list song in which the unrequited lover catalogues his many accomplishments and admirable qualities (all amusing exaggerations) but despairs that he cannot win her heart. Vernon Duke composed the enticing music, and Ira Gershwin wrote the witty lyric. In the revue the number was sung by Bob Hope, with Eve Arden as his hardhearted sweetheart. In the return engagement of the same revue in 1937 the song was sung by Bobby Clark, with Gypsy Rose Lee as the object of his affection. An interesting footnote: it was when Hollywood producers saw Hope sing this number that they signed him for the movies. "I Can't Get Started" is among Duke's most recorded songs and Buddy Rich had a best-selling record of it. A single by trumpeter-band leader Bunny Berrigan, who played and sang the song in the recording, is considered a jazz classic, and the number became his theme song.

"I Can't Give You Anything But Love" is one of the handful of gems to come out of *Blackbirds of 1928*. This perennial favorite was first sung by Aida Ward and then by Lois Deppe and Adelaide Hall in the all-black revue by Jimmy McHugh (music) and Dorothy Fields (lyric). The songwriters said that their inspiration for the song came when they saw a poor couple staring into the window at Tiffany's and overheard the boy say the title line to the girl. The two songwriters rushed home and completed the song in one hour. It was originally called "I Can't Give You Anything But Love, Lindy" and was sung by Patsy Kelly and Bert Lahr in *Harry Delmar's Revels* (1928), but it was cut soon after opening and became a hit in the later *Blackbirds of 1928*. Recordings by Louis Armstrong, Benny Goodman, Ethel Waters and Thomas "Fats" Waller helped make the song popular, and it has remained a standard over the decades. Most recently the number was successfully recorded by Barbara Cook. Years after Waller's death, his son Maurice claimed that his father composed the music and sold it outright to McHugh; the question has never been satisfactorily resolved. Andre De Shields and Charlaine Woodard sang "I Can't Give You Anything But Love" in the Broadway revue *Ain't Misbehavin'* (1978), Mickey Rooney sang it in *Sugar Babies* (1979), and Angela Hall and Eugene Fleming performed it with the dancing ensemble in the revue *Black and Blue* (1989).

"I Could Be Happy With You" is a pastiche love duet from the British import *The Boy Friend* (1954) that captures the inanity of 1920s songs like "I Want to Be Happy" from *No, No, Nanette* (1925) but also has their charm and innocence as well. Lovely Polly Browne (Julie Andrews) meets handsome delivery boy Tony (John Hewer), and before long they are singing the lovable duet and enjoying a tap routine together. Sandy Wilson wrote the silly but appealing music and lyric.

"I Could Have Danced All Night" is the popular lyrical ballad from *My Fair Lady* (1956) and one of the most recorded and performed songs from the Alan Jay Lerner (lyric) and Frederick Loewe (music) score. Eliza Doolittle (Julie Andrews) sings the jubilant song in a state of elation after having mastered phonetics and pleasing Professor Higgins (Rex Harrison). The song was never a favorite of Lerner's, for he felt it was too flowery and genteel for the rough-edged Eliza; but audiences have loved it from the start. Of the many recordings of the ballad, including chart records by Rosemary Clooney and Dinah Shore, perhaps the most successful was one by Sylvia Syms.

"I Could Write a Book" has become a Rodgers and Hart romantic favorite, but in the context of *Pal Joey* (1940), where it was first sung, the number is a smooth but phony declaration of love used by Joey Evans (Gene Kelly) to woo the innocent Linda (Leila Ernst). The scene was played on Jo Mielziner's famous pet-shop setting with the actors looking into the window from the street. Richard Rodgers' melody is intoxicating, and Lorenz Hart's lyric is seductive; no wonder Linda fell for it. The song has been recorded many times, most notably by Frank Sinatra, who also sang it in the watered-down 1957 film version.

"I Didn't Know What Time It Was" is a popular love song from *Too Many Girls* (1939), the college musical by Richard Rodgers (music) and Lorenz Hart (lyric). This ballad has a reverberating melody that stays with you, and the Hart lyric makes the most of the colloquial title phrase, turning it into a wonderfully romantic expression. The duet was introduced by Richard Kollmar and Marcy Westcott and soon became a standard. Perhaps the most memorable recording was that by Ella Fitzgerald.

"I Do Not Know a Day I Did Not Love You" is the number that provided a bright moment in the weak Richard Rodgers musical *Two By Two* (1970). The ballad is a soaring love song worthy of much more popularity than it has received. Martin Charnin wrote the lyric for Rodgers' fluttering melody, and it was sung by Walter Willison as Noah's son Japheth, who is falling in love with his sister-in-law Rachel (Tricia O'Neil). The two of them reprise the beautiful ballad later in the show.

"I Don't Believe in Heroes Anymore" is the disillusioned cry of a stand-up comic who has found fame but also disaster and grief. The Michael Rupert (music) and Jerry Colker (lyric) ballad was sung by Scott Bakula in the Off-Broadway musical *Three Guys Naked From the Waist Down* (1985).

"I Don't Care" is the sassy, free-spirited ditty that was Eva Tanguay's signature song throughout her career. The Harry O. Sutton (music) and Jean Lenox (lyric) number was first heard on Broadway in *The Blonde in Black* (1903) where Blanche Ring sang it. But when Tanguay interpolated the number into the tour of *The Sambo Girl* (1905), the song became popular and she continued to sing it in vaudeville and in clubs. Tanguay became so identified with the song that she was commonly known as "The I Don't Care Girl." The number was sung by the ensemble in the Broadway revue *Tintypes* (1980).

"I Don't Know How to Love Him" was a hit single before *Jesus Christ Superstar* (1971) opened on Broadway because the "concept album" had been a best-seller. In the show the ballad is sung by Mary Magdalene (Yvonne

Elliman) about the confused state of her affections for Jesus of Galilee, who seems unlike any other man she's ever known. Andrew Lloyd Webber (music) and Tim Rice (lyric) wrote the impressionable number. Elliman's recording from the original cast album was very successful, as was a later single by Helen Reddy.

"I Don't Remember You" is an enchanting ballad from *The Happy Time* (1968) by John Kander (music) and Fred Ebb (lyric). Jacques Bonnard (Robert Goulet) returns to his hometown in French Canada, where he sees Laurie Mannon (Julie Gregg), a woman he was once in love with. He sings this beguiling song as he tries to block out his memories of her, only to have them surface more potent than before. Bob Cuccioli sang the ballad in the Off-Broadway revue *And the World Goes 'Round* (1991).

"I Don't Think I'll Fall in Love Today" is a comic love song from the Gershwin brothers' short-lived *Treasure Girl* (1928). The money-hungry Ann Wainwright (Gertrude Lawrence) and put-upon fiancé Neil Forrester (Paul Frawley) sing this song of romantic caution by George Gershwin (music) and Ira Gershwin, whose lyric is particularly witty.

"I Dreamed a Dream" is a heartfelt song of remembering times past from the British import *Les Misérables* (1987). Factory worker Fantine (Randy Graff) recalls the man she fell in love with one summer who left her when autumn came and Fantine found herself with a child on the way. Claude-Michel Schönberg wrote the soaring music, and Herbert Kretzmer adapted the French lyric by Alain Boublil and Jean-Marc Natal. "I Dreamed a Dream" had a hit recording by Neil Diamond.

"I Enjoy Being a Girl" is nightclub singer Linda Low's zestful "I am" song in *Flower Drum Song* (1958), a vibrant testament to this Chinese-American's assimilation into American culture. The Richard Rodgers (music) and Oscar Hammerstein (lyric) number bubbles with enthusiasm that many find cloying but for a 1950s woman discovering her New World charms as she tosses off the ancient Chinese view of females, it is quite appropriate. Pat Suzuki introduced the song, and it has been heard everywhere, particularly at beauty pageants and fashion shows.

"I Feel at Home With You" is a daffy love duet for the secondary pair of lovers in *A Connecticut Yankee* (1927), the anachronistic musical comedy by Richard Rodgers (music) and Lorenz Hart (lyric). Evelyn La Belle-Ans (June Cochrane) and Sir Galahad (Jack Thompson) sing the affectionate number in which they realize they have much in common, such as a lack of wit or brains.

"I Feel Pretty" is the frolicsome trio from *West Side Story* (1957) sung by Maria (Carol Lawrence) to her girlfriends Rosalia (Marilyn Cooper) and Consuelo (Reri Grist) about her elation at being in love. Leonard Bernstein composed the Latin-flavored music, and Stephen Sondheim wrote the clever lyric. When fellow lyricist Sheldon Harnick saw the number in tryouts, he pointed out that Maria's internal rhymes and intricate phrases were perhaps too clever for a newly arrived Puerto Rican immigrant. Sondheim agreed and wrote a new lyric, but the rest of the production team loved the original words and insisted that they not be changed. The most recent recording of "I Feel Pretty" was a captivating one by Dawn Upshaw in 1994.

"I Found a Million Dollar Baby (In a Five and Ten Cent Store)" is the hit song from Billy Rose's *Crazy Quilt* (1931) featuring Fanny Brice. The playful number was written by Harry Warren (music) and Mort Dixon and Rose (lyric), and Brice sang it in top hat and tails with Phil Baker and Ted Healy. As in many Depression-era songs, the use of financial hyperbole to express happiness or love gives the number its extra kick, and the song's popularity survived the era. Among the many who recorded the number was Bing Crosby, who recorded it twice.

"I Get a Kick Out of You" is the first song audiences hear in Cole Porter's *Anything Goes* (1934), a very unusual spot for a torchy love song sung by a major star. But Ethel Merman, as sharp-tongued, big-hearted Reno Sweeney, sang it in the show's prologue and carried it off. The song is a Porter favorite, both for its breezy melody, which starts each section by leisurely climbing scales, and for its succinct lyric, which mixes cynicism and heartbreak. (The reference to cocaine in the refrain kept the song off the radio until an unauthorized "perfumes of Spain" was substituted.) It should also be pointed out that "I Get a Kick Out of You" contains what is arguably Porter's finest verse, and the song, when sung without this verse, loses much of its richness. Merman recorded the song, as did Eileen Rodgers and Patti LuPone, both of whom played Reno in New York revivals of the show.

"I Get Carried Away" is a slapstick, mock-operatic duet from *On the Town* (1944) with music by Leonard Bernstein and lyric by Betty Comden and Adolph Green. At the Museum of Natural History, the anthropologist Claire de Loon (Comden) and the sailor Ozzie (Green) meet in front of a dinosaur skeleton and find that they both are compulsive addicts about everything. By the time they finish their over-rhapsodic duet, they have accidentally destroyed the dinosaur.

"I Get Embarrassed" is a convivial comic duet from the period musical *Take Me Along* (1959) by Bob Merrill. Uncle Sid (Jackie Gleason) gets down on his knees to propose marriage to the stiff and proper Lily (Eileen Herlie), and as his endearments get more and more ribald, she breaks into bouts of embarrassment and gleeful joy.

"I Got a Marble and a Star" is a blues number from the operatic *Street Scene* (1947) by Kurt Weill (music) and Langston Hughes (lyric). Creighton Thompson, as the apartment building's black janitor Henry, sang the dreamy ballad.

"I Got a Song" is the show-stopping number from *Bloomer Girl* (1944) sung by a jail full of slaves who have been caught up North on the Underground Railroad. Alexander (Richard Huey), a three-hundred-pound runaway, is joined by Pompey (Dooley Wilson), Augustus (Herbert Dilworth) and the chorus in passing the time while waiting to be shipped back to the South. Alexander boasts that he knows all kinds of songs and, encouraged by his fellow inmates, sings his railroad song, woman song, bullfrog song and finally a freedom song. Harold Arlen composed the lazy blues music, and E.Y. Harburg wrote the sometimes cynical, sometimes expansive lyric.

"I Got Life" is an exuberant number from *Hair* (1968) that celebrates what makes life worth living, most of which has to do with the freedom to wear long hair and use the body for whatever pleases. The inventive anthem was sung by Claude (Walker Daniels) and his Mom (Marijane Maricle) in the 1967 Off-Broadway production. On Broadway it was sung by Claude (James Rado) and the company. Galt MacDermot composed the driving music, Gerome Ragni and James Rado wrote the defiant lyric, and Nina Simone made a hit recording of the song.

"I Got Lost in His Arms" is Annie Oakley's enchanting ballad from Irving Berlin's *Annie Get Your Gun* (1946). The song uses the device of a series of repeated notes that ascend the scale, then descend suddenly and effectively as the lyric concludes the thought. Ethel Merman introduced the song and made a hit single recording of it, as did Tony Bennett, Jane Frohman and others.

"I Got Love" is an impassioned ballad from *Purlie* (1970) by Gary Geld (music) and Peter Udell (lyric) that Melba Moore stopped the show with each evening and that made her a star. Lutiebelle (Moore) is in love with the "newfangled preacher" Purlie (Cleavon Little) and expresses her joy in this jubilant number that combines traditional Broadway ballad with gospel expressiveness. Because Lutiebelle is an uneducated farm girl, she uses mounting repetition much in the manner of Nellie Forbush's "A Wonderful Guy" in *South Pacific* (1949). In fact, Udell's lyric for this song can be considered the black equivalent to the expressive Oscar Hammerstein song.

"I Got Lucky in the Rain" is an affectionate number from *As the Girls Go* (1948), the musical about the first woman president by Jimmy McHugh (music) and Harold Adamson (lyric). The show was really a vehicle for the inspired comic Bobby Clark, who played the First Husband, but this delectable duet was sung by his son Kenny (Bill Callahan) and his sweetheart Kathy Robinson (Betty Jane Watson).

"I Got Plenty o' Nuttin' (An' Nuttin's Plenty fo' Me)" is the song of contentment that Porgy (Todd Duncan) sings in *Porgy and Bess* (1935) as he basks in the newfound happiness that comes with loving Bess (Anne Brown). George Gershwin wrote the cheerful "banjo song" music, and Ira Gershwin and DuBose Heyward collaborated on the easygoing lyric. Ira Gershwin was slated to do all the lyrics for the score, with Heyward writing the libretto based on his play *Porgy*. But when Ira came up with the title "I Got Plenty o' Nuttin'," Heyward immediately countered with "An' Nuttin's Plenty fo' Me." Under Ira's tutelage, Heyward collaborated on this song and the two duets "I Loves You, Porgy" and "Bess, You Is My Woman Now," as well as writing "My Man's Gone Now," "Summertime," "A Woman Is a Sometime Thing" and "I'm on My Way."

"I Got Rhythm," one of Ethel Merman's signature songs, was first heard in the Gershwins' *Girl Crazy* (1930), where, as the western prairie gal "Frisco" Kate Fothergill, she blasted her way to stardom with the song. George Gershwin's music is a brassy set of variations on a rising and falling five-note phrase with some surprising rhythm changes throughout. Ira Gershwin's lyric has surprisingly few rhymes and is slangy and colloquial ("I got rhythm" instead of "I have rhythm"), but, in its overpowering way, it is still a love song of sorts. Merman's interpretation was far from subtle, as she belted out and held a high C for sixteen bars while the ensemble sang a full second refrain. "I Got Rhythm" was also used in the updated *Crazy for You* (1992), where Jodi Benson, as postmistress Polly Barker, and the company sang it as a first-act finale. George Gershwin adapted the song into one of his most performed concert pieces, "Variations on I Got Rhythm" for piano and orchestra. "I Got Rhythm" has been recorded many times throughout the decades, with a surprise hit by the Happenings in 1967 that sold over a million records.

"I Got the Sun in the Morning (And the Moon at Night)" is a thrilling swing number from Irving Berlin's *Annie Get Your Gun* (1946). Annie Oakley (Ethel Merman) sings of her satisfaction with the simple things in life, charming the high-society folk who join her in singing it. The joyful song has a contagious tempo, a very unique release and a beguiling tag at the end.

"I Gotta Right to Sing the Blues" is the famous torch song by

Harold Arlen (music) and Ted Koehler (lyric) that is actually written in a blues style, each of its eight-bar phrases punctuated with blue notes. The confessional number was sung by Lillian Shade in the revue *Earl Carroll Vanities* (1932) and eventually became a standard. Popular recordings of the song were made by Louis Armstrong, Billie Holiday, Benny Goodman, Ethel Merman, Cab Calloway, Lena Horne, Dorothy Lamour and trombonist-conductor Jack Teagarden, who made it his theme song.

"I Guess I'll Have to Change My Plan" is the popular, debonair torch song by Howard Dietz (lyric) and Arthur Schwartz (music) from the revue *The Little Show* (1929). Clifton Webb has just found out that the girl he loves is already married, but he decides to adjust his plans and woo her anyway. Schwartz's breezy melody had been written years before when he and Lorenz Hart worked at a summer camp and wrote a number called "I Love to Lie Awake in Bed." Dietz's ingenious new lyric makes the song both detached and alluring at the same time; it also has amusing insight and flowing images throughout. Surprisingly, the song did not catch on right away. Not until the number became popular in England as "The Blue Pajama Song" (in reference to the hero's lyric where he regrets buying blue pajamas before he ever won the girl's heart) did it gain attention here. Paul Whiteman, Rudy Vallee and Frank Sinatra each made hit recordings of the song.

"I Guess I'll Miss the Man" is a tender little torch song amidst all the razzle-dazzle of *Pippin* (1972) by Stephen Schwartz. The Lady Catherine (Jill Clayburgh) has nursed the moody Pippin (John Rubinstein) back to health and fallen in love with him. But Pippin wants more out of life than domestic bliss and leaves her. Catherine, without help of scenery, costumes and full orchestra, insists on singing this simple folk song in which she laments the less-than-perfect Pippin.

"I Had Myself a True Love" is the absorbing arialike solo from *St. Louis Woman* (1946) by Harold Arlen (music) and Johnny Mercer (lyric). Lili (June Hawkins), the discarded mistress of the bar owner Biglow Brown (Rex Ingram), cannot get over her love for him and sings this stirring torch song. It is an unusually long song (sixty-four measures) and one that blends the operatic with a painful blues style. Barbra Streisand made a dramatic recording of the song in the 1960s.

"I Happen to Like New York" was added to the score of Cole Porter's *The New Yorkers* (1930) after opening. In fact, Porter was sailing to Monte Carlo and wired the song back to New York from the ship mid-ocean. This sly but heartfelt paean to Manhattan was introduced by Oscar "Rags" Ragland, who played a comic gangster named Mildew. Considered by many to be the finest Broadway anthem to the city, "I Happen to Like New York" has been recorded dozens of times, most memorably by Frank Sinatra and Bobby Short.

"I Hate Men" is Kate's "I am" song in the musical version of *The Taming of the Shrew* within Cole Porter's *Kiss Me, Kate* (1948). Although the character and the setting are Italian Renaissance, Porter's lyric is filled with delightful anachronisms as Kate drops the names Betty Grable, Jack the Ripper and the dog Lassie. Patricia Morison introduced the song, which has remained a favorite character song for sopranos ever since.

"I Have Dreamed" was a last-minute addition to the score of *The King and I* (1951), a beguiling duet by Richard Rodgers (music) and Oscar Hammerstein (lyric) that brought the secondary lovers into the show's second act. The slave Tuptim (Doretta Morrow) and her lover Lun Tha (Larry Douglas) sing the penetrating ballad, which seems operatic but is, in Eastern fashion, a repetition of the same musical section until it climaxes in a new melody fragment. In the Broadway revue *A Grand Night for Singing* (1993), "I Have Dreamed" was sung by the company as the finale.

"I Just Can't Wait" is a facetious comic song from *Subways Are for Sleeping* (1961) by Jule Styne (music) and Betty Comden and Adolph Green (lyric). Charlie Smith (Orson Bean) confesses to Martha Vail (Phyllis Newman), who spends most of the time clad only in a towel since she's been evicted from her apartment, that he loves her and "just can't wait" to see her with her clothes on.

"I Know About Love" is an unusual "I am" song from *Do Re Mi* (1960), the musical about the jukebox industry. Music businessman John Henry Wheeler (John Reardon) knows all about love songs and the kind that sell; but he admits he knows nothing about love itself. Jule Styne (music) and Betty Comden and Adolph Green (lyric) wrote the appealing song.

"I Know Him So Well" is the hit ballad from the British import *Chess* (1988) by Benny Anderssen and Bjorn Ulvaeus (music) and Tim Rice (lyric). As the Hungarian refugee Florence (Judy Kuhn) sings of her lover, the Russian chess champion Anatoly, his wife Svetlana (Marcia Mitzman) echoes the same sentiments. Elaine Paige and Whitney Houston (with her mother Cissy Houston) both made popular recordings of the song.

"I Know That You Know" is a lively rhythm song from *Oh, Please!* (1926) by Vincent Youmans (music) and Anne Caldwell (lyric). Beatrice Lillie and Charles Purcell sang the playful duet that utilizes Youmans' favorite musical device of repeated notes made enticing by insistent chord changes. The song has been recorded many times over the years, including an exceptional Benny Goodman arrangement and one by Nat "King" Cole.

"I Know Things Now" is an ambivalent character song from *Into the Woods* (1987) by Stephen Sondheim. Little Red Riding Hood (Danielle Ferland), having escaped from the wolf, sings the seriocomic number about the need to heed parents and be cautious; yet she admits that the temptation for adventure is still great and that knowledge isn't everything.

"I Left My Heart at the Stage Door Canteen" is the hit song from Irving Berlin's military revue *This Is the Army* (1942), which raised money for the Army Emergency Relief Fund. The bittersweet number about the loneliness of a soldier far from home was sung by Earl Oxford, and several recordings were made during the war years. Sammy Kaye and His Orchestra (vocal by Don Cornell) had a best-selling recording of the song.

"I Like the Likes of You" is a stammering love song by Vernon Duke (music) and E.Y. Harburg (lyric) from the *Ziegfeld Follies of 1934*. A likable but befuddled lover sings praises to his sweetheart but keeps getting sidetracked, twisting himself into verbal knots. By the time the singer reaches the release, the music and the lyrics get as tongue-tied as the unfortunate hero. The number was sung by Brice Hutchins (who later changed his name to Bob Cummings) to Judith Barron, and then Vilma and Buddy Ebsen danced to the song.

"I Love a Cop" is a charming character song from *Fiorello!* (1959) in which Dora (Pat Stanley) expresses her thrill and consternation at having fallen for Floyd the policeman. Sheldon Harnick's lyric captures Dora's beguiling situation poignantly, and Jerry Bock's music, with its erratic jumps up and down the scale, melodically expresses her alternating misery and joy. The song is reprised later in the show with a different lyric when Dora tries to comfort Floyd after he is rejected from enlisting because of his flat feet.

"I Love a Piano" is one of Irving Berlin's first ragtime songs, a vibrant, witty number that uses the piano as a metaphor for a lovely woman and lovemaking. Throughout the song Berlin "rags" the words, turning "piano" into a one-syllable word, then stretching it out over several notes longer for comic effect. The song was introduced by Harry Fox and the chorus in *Stop! Look! Listen!* (1915), where the production number featured a keyboard that stretched across the stage and six pianists played the song on six pianos. Billy Murray recorded "I Love a Piano" in 1915, Arthur Schutt had a hit with it in 1934, and years later it was recorded by Judy Garland, Barbara Cook and others.

"I Love Louisa" is a bouncy song set to a calliope tempo that was the first-act finale of the revue *The Band Wagon* (1931). Arthur Schwartz composed the engaging ompah-pah music, and Howard Dietz wrote the zesty lyric that praised the charms of Louisa even over that of drinking German beer. Adele and Fred Astaire sang the song with the chorus on an elaborate Bavarian merry-go-round that filled the stage, the first use of a revolving stage in a Broadway musical. The inspiration for the song was a chambermaid named Louisa at the St. Moritz Hotel in New York, where Dietz and Schwartz wrote most of the score.

"I Love My Wife" is a frolicsome tribute to marriage sung and danced by Robert Preston in *I Do! I Do!* (1966) by Tom Jones (lyric) and Harvey Schmidt (music). Newlywed Michael (Preston) cannot contain his joy in being married to Agnes (Mary Martin), so he jumps out of bed and, while she sleeps, does a jubilant soft-shoe in his bare feet with a top hat and cane.

"I Love My Wife" is the simple and tender title song from the 1977 musical about wife swapping by Cy Coleman (music) and Michael Stewart (lyric). After all their fantasies have worn out, husbands Wally (James Naughton) and Alvin (Lenny Baker) realize that it is their wives that they truly love. Frank Sinatra made a hit recording of the ballad.

"I Love Paris," the biggest hit to come from Cole Porter's *Can-Can* (1953), is perhaps the finest of his many songs about his favorite city. The song is written in a minor key that gives the melody a haunting quality, and Porter's lyric is simple and unadorned, lacking any witticisms. Lilo sang the ballad in front of a backdrop by designer Jo Mielziner that illustrated a dreamy panorama of Paris rooftops. In fact, Porter stated that he was inspired to write the song when he saw Mielziner's evocative design sketches for the show. Popular instrumental recordings of "I Love Paris" were made by Les Baxter and Michel Legrand.

"I Love Thee, I Adore Thee" is the rhapsodic recurring serenade that unifies Victor Herbert's operetta *The Serenade* (1897). Carlos Alvarado (W.H. MacDonald) and Dolores (Jessie Bartlett Davis) sang the intoxicating song as a romantic duet, but later in the show it became a comic number as a monastery full of monks chanted it a cappella. At another point in the operetta, Dolores is locked away in a convent, and strains of the same serenade are used to guide Carlos in his rescue of her. Harry B. Smith wrote the lyric for Herbert's soaring music. "I Love Thee, I Adore Thee" reappeared on Broadway in the hybrid Herbert musical *Gypsy Lady* (1946).

"I Love to Dance" is a dancing duet from *Ballroom* (1978), the musical by Billy Goldenberg (music) and Alan and Marilyn Bergman (lyric). The number is sung by Bea Asher (Dorothy Loudon), a lonely widow, and Al Rossi (Vincent Gardenia), a middle-aged married man she has fallen in love with.

"I Love What I'm Doing" is a vibrant "I am" song for Dorothy Shaw (Yvonne Adair), the brunette friend of Lorelei Lee in *Gentlemen Prefer Blondes* (1949). Jule Styne (music) and Leo Robin (lyric) wrote the sprightly number in which the carefree flapper exalts having fun over having money. Tamara Long played Dorothy and sang the song in the 1974 revised version of the musical called *Lorelei*.

"I Love You" is a romantic duet from *Little Jessie James* (1923) that not only saved the show but went on to become the most popular song of the season. Harry Archer composed the music, Harlan Thompson wrote the lyric, and it was sung by Ann Sands and Jay Velie. Paul Whiteman's Orchestra, which played in the pit for the show, made a hit recording of the number.

"I Love You" may seem too simple a title for a Cole Porter song, but it was no accident that the witty composer-lyricist settled for such a simple name. The story goes that actor-director Monty Woolley made a bet with Porter that he couldn't write a successful song with such a trite title. Another version of the story says that it was producer Mike Todd who proposed the wager. Regardless, Porter came up with a lovely ballad in which different elements of nature (April breezes, the dawn, birds and so on) whisper the time-worn phrase to lovers. With its delectable Latin-flavored melody, "I Love You" was the hit of *Mexican Hayride* (1944), where it was sung by Wilbur Evans. Bing Crosby recorded it with the John Scott Trotter Orchestra, and within weeks it was the best-selling song in America. Subsequent recordings by Jo Stafford, Perry Como and others were also popular.

"I Love You" is a comic love song from *Little Me* (1962) that manages to be more a putdown than a declaration of romance. The rich snob Noble Eggleston (Sid Caesar) proposes marriage to the common-as-dirt Belle Schlumpfert (Virginia Martin) even though he is wealthy and she is riffraff. Belle and an echoing chorus join him in the satirical number by Cy Coleman (music) and Carolyn Leigh (lyric).

"I Love You This Morning" is a snappy duet from the early Lerner and Loewe fantasy *The Day Before Spring* (1945). Bill Johnson and Irene Manning sang the sweet number, for which Frederick Loewe composed the cheery music and Alan Jay Lerner wrote the simple-minded lyric. Blossom Dearie made a lively recording of the song.

"I Loved You Once in Silence" is a poignant ballad from *Camelot*

(1960) that Guenevere (Julie Andrews) sings to Lancelot (Robert Goulet) in their love scene together just before they are discovered and accused by Mordred. Alan Jay Lerner wrote the elegant lyric, and Frederick Loewe composed the graceful music.

"I Loves You, Porgy" is a ballad of love and affirmation from the folk opera *Porgy and Bess* (1935). Threatened by the villainous Crown, Bess (Anne Brown) and Porgy (Todd Duncan) sing this beautiful duet promising each other that nothing will come between them. George Gershwin composed the flowing music, and Ira Gershwin and DuBose Heyward collaborated on the tender lyric. Nina Simone's 1959 recording of the song sold over a million copies.

"I Married an Angel," the title song from the 1938 Rodgers and Hart musical fantasy, was actually written in 1933 for a proposed film musical of the same story that never was made. When the Hungarian tale was turned into a Broadway musical, the team rescued the song and named the show after it. Richard Rodgers' agreeable melody and Lorenz Hart's dreamy lyric made the song a standard, usually sung as a hyperbolic tribute to a spouse. But in the show it was sung by Dennis King, who had literally married an angel.

"I May Be Gone a Long, Long Time" is a tearful World War One favorite that was introduced in the revue *Hitchy Koo* (1917). Albert von Tilzer (music) and Lew Brown (lyric) wrote the heartfelt ballad, and it was sung by Grace La Rue.

"I Might Fall Back on You" is a vaudeville turn for the *Cotton Blossom* performers Ellie (Eva Puck) and Frank (Sammy White) in *Show Boat* (1927). Jerome Kern (music) and Oscar Hammerstein (lyric) wrote the lively polka that pastiches the kind of duo act that was popular in the nineteenth century. Janet Pavek and Kevin Scott recorded a lively version of the duet in 1956, and Paige O'Hara and David Garrison sang it in John McGlinn's 1988 complete recording of the score.

"I Never Has Seen Snow" is a sensitive ballad from *House of Flowers* (1954) that approaches the operatic in its full-flavored music by Harold Arlen but is also very restrained and controlled. The song was sung by the innocent young Ottilie (Diahann Carroll), who mentions the many things she has not experienced, but she is sure her love for Royal (Rawn Spearman) is real. Truman Capote, in his only Broadway musical venture, wrote the captivating lyric with help from Arlen. The song is unusual in that the release combines melodies from both the refrain and the verse.

"I Never Know When (To Say When)" is a bluesy torch song from *Goldilocks* (1958) with music by Leroy Anderson and lyric by Joan Ford and Walter and Jean Kerr. Sharp-tongued Maggie Harris (Elaine Stritch) has gone too far once again, and it looks like she has scared off the only man she's ever loved. Karen Akers recorded the song in 1990.

"I Never Wanted to Love You" is a provocative ballad from *March of the Falsettos* (1981) in which all five characters in the musical profess the confused state of love they are in. Trina (Alison Fraser) sings to her ex-husband Marvin (Michael Rupert) that she is not ashamed of having loved him, while her new husband Mendel (Chip Zien) tries to express his love for her. The young Jason (James Kushner) reveals his love/hate for his father, who abandoned him, while Marvin and his lover Whizzer (Stephen Bogardus) argue that it was never their choosing to fall in love with each other. William Finn wrote both the music and the lyric for the expansive quintet.

"I Read" is the melancholy "I am" song for the unattractive, unloved Fosca (Donna Murphy) in Stephen Sondheim's *Passion* (1994). When the sickly Fosca meets the Italian Captain Giorgio Bachetti (Jere Shea) for the first time, she explains that her passion for reading is not to educate herself or to learn about life but rather to forget what she knows of life and to escape to different worlds. With its unrhymed lyric and minor keys, the song is as uncompromisingly morose as the desperate character who sings it.

"I Really Like Him" is a simple but charming character song for the buffoonish Sancho (Irving Jacobson) in *Man of La Mancha* (1965) by Mitch Leigh (music) and Joe Darion (lyric). When asked by Aldonza (Joan Diener) why he stays with the lunatic Quixote, Sancho can only come up with this blubbering tribute.

"I Say It's Spinach (And the Hell With It!)" is a zesty noses-up-at-the-Depression song by Irving Berlin that was sung by Katherine Carrington and J. Harold Murray in *Face the Music* (1932). The dizzy, optimistic number was inspired by a Peter Arno *New Yorker* cartoon in which a wealthy child refuses a plate of broccoli, stating "I say it's spinach . . . and the hell with it!" Michael Feinstein made a playful recording of the song in 1987.

"I See Your Face Before Me" is one of the loveliest ballads by the team of Howard Dietz (lyric) and Arthur Schwartz (music). The haunting song is from *Between the Devil* (1937), where it was sung by Evelyn Lane and later in the show was reprised as a duet by Jack Buchanan and Adele Dixon. Schwartz's music uses a repeated note to dazzling effect, and Dietz's lyric is completely captivating as the memory of the lover becomes almost ghostlike in its power to beguile. "I See Your Face Before Me" was most recently recorded by Carly

Simon.

"I Still Believe" is a passionate duet for two women at opposite ends of the world who share a similar determination in the British import *Miss Saigon* (1991). Although it has been three years since her GI lover Chris has left, Kim (Lea Salonga) still has faith that one day he will send for her. In America, Chris's wife Ellen (Liz Callaway) ponders the elusive nature of her husband since he returned from Vietnam but believes that one day their love will be what it once was. Claude-Michel Schönberg wrote the music, and Richard Maltby, Jr., adapted the original French lyric by Alain Boublil.

"I Still Believe in Love" is a torchy ballad in a pop mode that Marvin Hamlisch (music) and Carole Bayer Sager (lyric) wrote for *They're Playing Our Song* (1979). Lucie Arnaz, as the lyricist Sonia Walsk who's had two unsuccessful romances in a row, sang the teary number.

"I Still Get Jealous" is an old-fashioned romantic duet for the very married Mr. and Mrs. Longstreet (Jack McCauley and Nanette Fabray) in the period musical *High Button Shoes* (1947). Jule Styne (music) and Sammy Cahn (lyric) wrote the sentimental song that led into a charming soft-shoe for the couple. The Harry James, Guy Lombardo and Jimmy Dorsey orchestras all made successful recordings of the song, and the McCauley-Fabray cut from the original cast recording was also popular. Gordon MacRae's recording with the Paul Weston Orchestra sold over a million copies in 1947. Jason Alexander and Faith Prince performed the number in *Jerome Robbins' Broadway* (1989).

"I Still See Elisa" is a gentle folk song by Alan Jay Lerner (lyric) and Frederick Loewe (music) from *Paint Your Wagon* (1951), the musical about the California gold rush. The old prospector Ben Rumson (James Barton) recalls his deceased wife in the soft and delicate ballad.

"I Talk to the Trees" is a popular romantic ballad from *Paint Your Wagon* (1951) that uses imagery from nature to create an absorbing and potent view of love. Alan Jay Lerner wrote the evocative lyric, Frederick Loewe composed the winsome music, and it was sung by Tony Bavaar and Olga San Juan as two young lovers in a California mining town.

"I Think I Can Play This Part" is a song used throughout *The Goodbye Girl* (1993) by the struggling actor Elliot Garfield (Martin Short). Sections of the number are heard as he sings about his role in *Richard III* and later as an apology after his fiasco of a performance in the part. The song takes on a new meaning when Elliot goes rowing on Central Park Lake with the young Lucy (Tammy Minoff) and tries to convince her that he'd make an ideal husband for her mother and a good stepfather for her. Marvin Hamlisch wrote the appealing music, and David Zippel provided the flexible lyric.

"I Waltz Alone" is a creepy number for the cynical Doctor Otternschlag (John Wylie) in *Grand Hotel* (1989) with music and lyric by Robert Wright and George Forrest. The heroin-addicted physician sings the languid waltz as night descends on the Grand Hotel and he finds himself hidden in his room in a drugged stupor. Karen Akers, who was in *Grand Hotel* but didn't sing the song, recorded it later.

"I Wanna Be Loved by You" is the hit song from *Good Boy* (1928), a musical by Harry Ruby and Herbert Stothard (music) and Bert Kalmar (lyric). The flapper Pansy McManus (Helen Kane, the "boop-a-doop girl") sang (and squeaked) the duet with the tap-dancing Bobby D'Arnell (Dan Healy). It was the kind of song that could be written and embraced only in the carefree 1920s, although it has far from disappeared. Of the many parodies of the baby-talk song written over the years, Sandy Wilson's "It's Never Too Late to Fall in Love" from *The Boy Friend* (1954) is perhaps the most accurate and enjoyable.

"I Wanna Get Married" is a sultry comic number for the striptease queen Bubbles La Man (Gertrude Niesen) in *Follow the Girls* (1944). Phil Charig wrote the music and Dan Sharpiro and Milton Pascal provided the risqué lyric. Niesen stopped the show with her suggestive rendition of the song, later recording it with Harry Sosnik's Orchestra. Years later Pearl Bailey made a frolicsome recording of the number.

"I Want a Man" is a superior torch song from the innovative but unsuccessful *Rainbow* (1928) by Vincent Youmans (music) and Oscar Hammerstein (lyric). Out in the Wild West, the ubiquitous Lotta (Libby Holman) tries, with little success, to win gambler Captain Stanton (Allan Prior) away from his wife. Holman's languorous rendition of the song brought her her first attention on Broadway and launched her career. Youmans' music is in a sort of jazz-influenced operetta style, foreshadowing the kind of sound Harold Arlen would pursue later, and the tone is not unlike that of George Gershwin's *Porgy and Bess* a decade later.

"I Want It All" is an eager trio for three expectant mothers in *Baby* (1983) by David Shire (music) and Richard Maltby, Jr., (lyric). In a doctor's waiting room, the young and pregnant Lizzie (Liz Callaway) and the hoping-to-get-pregnant Pam (Catherine Cox) break into a vivacious song about all the things they dream of getting out of life. The older, experienced Arlene (Beth Fowler) cautions them that having a baby limits one's possibilities, but then she admits that in her dreams she "wants it all" too.

"I Want to Be a Popular Millionaire" is a jovial character song from George M. Cohan's *Forty-Five Minutes From Broadway* (1906). Tom Bennett (Donald Brian) believes he has just inherited his rich New Rochelle uncle's fortune and sings to the gentlemen of the press of his plan to live life and spend money in a manner different from that of his late relative.

"I Want to Be Bad" is a comic character song from *Follow Thru* (1929), the musical about golf by B.G. DeSylva and Lew Brown (lyric) and Ray Henderson (music). The determined flapper Angie Howard (Zelma O'Neal) sings this musical confession with all the shame that the Roaring Twenties could afford. There was a popular recording of the snappy number by Helen Kane, the "boop-a-doop girl."

"I Want to Be Happy" was, along with "Tea for Two," a late addition to *No, No, Nanette* (1925), and both songs ended up being the hits of the show. Bible publisher Jimmy Smith (Charles Winninger) and his ward Nanette (Louise Groody) sing the idiotically cheerful song, which philosophically teaches that one cannot be happy unless everyone else is happy too. The duet then turns into a production number, with all of Nanette's friends singing and dancing the song. Later in the show, "I Want to Be Happy" is briefly reprised by the three women Jimmy has been supporting from afar: Winnie from Washington (Mary Lawlor), Betty from Boston (Beatrice Lee) and Flora from Frisco (Edna Whistler). Vincent Youmans composed the sparkling music, and Irving Caesar wrote the zesty lyric. Because *No, No, Nanette* played in Chicago a year before coming to New York, the whole country was already singing the song by opening night. Of the various recordings made of the number, the most unique were two popular orchestral ones recorded in 1958 by Tommy Dorsey and by Enoch Light, who added "Cha Cha" to the title and played the song accordingly.

"I Want to Be Seen With You Tonight" is a jazzy, affectionate duet from *Funny Girl* (1964) by Jule Styne (music) and Bob Merrill (lyric). After her successful opening night in the *Ziegfeld Follies*, Fanny Brice (Barbra Streisand) tells the dashing Nick Arnstein (Sydney Chaplin) that he'd be bored at the neighborhood party in her honor. But Nick is attracted to the funny young star and claims he'd be proud to go with her.

"I Want to Be With You" is a passionate love song from the boxing musical *Golden Boy* (1964) by Charles Strouse (music) and Lee Adams (lyric). The lovely duet was sung by Sammy Davis, Jr., as the young contender Joe Wellington, and Paula Wayne, as his girlfriend Lorna. Nancy Wilson made a hit recording of the song.

"I Want to Hear a Yankee Doodle Tune" is a George M. Cohan rouser that, in this rare instance, was not introduced in a Cohan musical. *Mother Goose* (1903) was a revue spectacular that was based on a London hit, but the producers interpolated songs by American authors to fill out the score. The march-like number was also featured in the bio-musical *George M!* (1968), where it was sung by Joel Grey and the ensemble at the end of the epilogue.

"I Want to Walk to San Francisco" is an appealing rock song from the pioneering Off-Broadway rock musical *The Last Sweet Days of Isaac* (1970) by Gretchen Cryer (lyric) and Nancy Ford (music). The ensemble sang this upbeat number about how we isolate ourselves from the world, stating how revealing it would be to walk all the way to California and savor each day it took to get there rather than fly there in a few hours.

"I Want What I Want When I Want It" is a pompous character song from the operetta *Mlle. Modiste* (1905) by Victor Herbert (music) and Henry Blossom (lyric). The gruff and narrow-minded Comte de St. Mar (William Pruette) sings the robust comedy song to show that he will not relax his stubborn ways. Trey Wilson sang the boisterous number in the Broadway revue *Tintypes* (1980).

"I Was Born in Virginia" is the show-stopping comic "I am" song from *George Washington, Jr.* (1906) by George M. Cohan. Dolly Johnson (Ethel Levey), the niece of a U. S. senator, proudly boasts of her Southern lineage as she belts out this spirited song. So memorable was Levey's rendition of the number that it became known as "Ethel Levey's Virginia Song." Jamie Donnelly played Levey and sang the number in the bio-musical *George M!* (1968).

"I Whistle a Happy Tune" is the childlike song that opens *The King and I* (1951) and serves as the "I am" song for the British governess Anna (Gertrude Lawrence). To ease their anxiety about moving from England to Siam, Anna and her son (Sandy Kennedy) sing the simple ditty. The Richard Rodgers melody is tuneful and jaunty, in contrast to the characters' stressful condition, and Oscar Hammerstein came up with a suitably optimistic lyric that may seem cloying outside of the song's context in the musical.

"I Will Follow You" is the musical promise of a young Israeli to his American wife in *Milk and Honey* (1961). Jerry Herman wrote the sensitive ballad, and it was sung by Tommy Rall.

"I Wish I Could Forget You" is a sung letter from Stephen Sondheim's *Passion* (1994), a show filled with musical missives; but this musical scene uses letterwriting in an unusual way. The sickly, unattractive

Fosca (Donna Murphy) dictates the letter to the handsome soldier Giorgio (Jere Shea) that is addressed to herself. The letter, supposedly coming from Giorgio, emotionally relates the powerful effect she has had on him and how she has forced him to re-examine love now that he has met her. The scene is both pathetic and hypnotic as the unwilling Giorgio writes what Fosca wants him so desperately to feel.

"I Wish I Were in Love Again" is a memorable comic duet from *Babes in Arms* (1937) that lists all the aches and heartaches of romance, but, the lovers admit, they miss it. Richard Rodgers provided the bouncy music, and Lorenz Hart wrote the lyric that sits precariously on the line between cynicism and exultation. The lively duet was introduced by Rolly Pickert and Grace MacDonald, and there was a best-selling recording by Mickey Rooney and Judy Garland taken from the soundtrack of the 1948 film *Words and Music.* More recently, the number was recorded as a solo by Ella Fitzgerald and Julie Andrews.

"I Wish It So" is a scintillating ballad from *Juno* (1959), Marc Blitzstein's operatic version of Sean O'Casey's *Juno and the Paycock* (1924). The young Mary Boyle (Monte Amundsen) sings to her mother Juno (Shirley Booth) about the unrest she is feeling and how she longs for love. Blitzstein incorporated lines from the Irish poet Thomas Moore's "Molly, My Dear" into the lyric to give it some authentic flavor. Although *Juno* had a short run, "I Wish It So" managed to live on and became a popular audition song in the 1960s. Judy Kaye recorded the ballad in 1986, and Dawn Upshaw made a distinctive version in 1994.

"I Wonder What the King Is Doing Tonight" is the piquant "I am" song for young King Arthur (Richard Burton) in *Camelot* (1960) by Alan Jay Lerner (lyric) and Frederick Loewe (music). In this opening song of the show, Arthur acts out the gossip going through his kingdom on the day that his betrothed is to arrive. He then tells the audience the truth: he is scared and wants to hide. It is a charming number, and nonsinger Burton was able to adjust his Shakespearean skills to create a real and intriguing musical comedy character.

"I Wonder Who's Kissing Her Now" is the durable song of sentiment that sold over three million copies of sheet music in the early decades of the century. Henry Woodruff sang the ballad in *The Prince of Tonight* (1909), and soon it was played and sung in parlors across America. Will M. Hough and Frank R. Adams wrote the heart-tugging lyric, but the authorship of the music was a matter of some deception. Harold Orlob composed the melody "for hire" for singer Joseph Howard, who claimed the music as his own for many years, performing the song in clubs and on radio throughout his career. Orlob sued for rightful credit in 1947 and won, the song thereafter listing both men as the composer.

"I Won't Grow Up" is the adamant musical lesson that Peter (Mary Martin) teaches the lost boys in *Peter Pan* (1954). Mark Charlap (music) and Carolyn Leigh (lyric) wrote the eager number in which the boys vow never to embrace the evils of adulthood. But at the end of the musical all but Peter sing a reprise of the number in which they promise they *will* grow up.

"I Won't Send Roses" is the pleasing romantic ballad from Jerry Herman's short-lived musical *Mack and Mabel* (1974). It is sung by silent-movie director Mack Sennett (Robert Preston) to his up-and-coming star Mabel Normand (Bernadette Peters), explaining that a love affair with him promises none of the niceties of romance. The song is later reprised by Mabel when she accepts his very uncommitted love, declaring that she doesn't need roses. Leslie Uggams sang the song in the Broadway revue *Jerry's Girls* (1985).

"Ice Cream" is one of the theatre's most prized musical stream-of-consciousness pieces. In *She Loves Me* (1963), Amalia Balash (Barbara Cook) has received a visit and a gift of vanilla ice cream from her quarrelsome co-worker Georg (Daniel Massey). After he leaves, Amalia proceeds to write a letter to her anonymous "dear friend," but her mind keeps wandering back to Georg and her realization that he seemed so different today. Jerry Bock wrote the delectable music, and Sheldon Harnick provided the insightful lyric.

"I'd Be Surprisingly Good for You" is an unromantic love duet from the British import *Evita* (1979) by Andrew Lloyd Webber (music) and Tim Rice (lyric). The ambitious Eva Duarte (Patti LuPone) and the politically powerful Juan Peron (Bob Gunton) meet for the first time and immediately see the advantages of combining forces. The number moves from flattery to seduction, with both political and sexual undertones throughout.

"I'd Do Anything" is a fun music-hall turn from the British import *Oliver!* (1963) in which the have-nots parody the gentility of the haves. In Fagin's London hideout, Nancy (Georgia Brown) and the Artful Dodger (David Jones) demonstrate for Oliver Twist (Bruce Prochnik) and the boys how the wealthy behave, and they sing this mockingly polite duet. Lionel Bart wrote the tuneful music and the wry lyric.

"Ida, Sweet as Apple Cider" is the popular little ditty often associated with Eddie Cantor, who sang it in vaudeville and on the radio throughout his career. Eddie Leonard wrote the music, Eddie Munson provided the slaphappy lyric, and it was sung by Leonard to Queenie Smith in *Roly-Boly Eyes* (1919). Red Nichols and His Five Pennies made a recording that sold over a million copies.

"If Ever I Would Leave You" is the hit ballad from *Camelot* (1960), a lush love song in which Sir Lancelot (Robert Goulet) examines the four seasons of the year to determine in which one he could leave Guenevere; he decides that none of them will do and he must stay. Alan Jay Lerner (lyric) and Frederick Loewe (music) wrote the popular song, which had many recordings, including a pop version by Goulet himself.

"If He Walked Into My Life" is the well-known ballad from *Mame* (1966) by Jerry Herman. In the show the torch song is sung by Mame Dennis (Angela Lansbury) after a fight with her nephew Patrick (Jerry Lanning), but the number became popular in several recordings as a more romantic song of regret and longing. Leslie Uggams sang the number in the Broadway revue *Jerry's Girls* (1985).

"If I Can't Love Her" is a soul-searching solo for the Beast (Terrence Mann) in the Broadway musical version of Disney's *Beauty and the Beast* (1994). The tormented prince-turned-beast fights off despair and considers his ability to fall in love with Belle (Susan Egan) in this stirring first-act-finale song. The number was written for the stage by Alan Menken (music) and Tim Rice (lyric).

"If I Had a Fine White Horse" is an engaging pastiche of an old English folk song from *The Secret Garden* (1991) by Lucy Simon (music) and Marsha Norman (lyric). The Yorkshire housemaid Martha (Alison Fraser) encourages the sour orphan Mary Lennox (Daisy Eagan) to go out and play, singing the imaginary adventures she herself would have if she didn't have to stay indoors and work all day.

"If I Had a Million Dollars" is a captivating ensemble number from the revue *The Me Nobody Knows* (1970) by Gary William Friedman (music) and Will Holt (lyric). The musical is based on the writings of ghetto school kids in New York City. In this song each character submits his or her plan on how to spend a fortune, from the outrageous to the heartbreaking.

"If I Had My Druthers" is the lethargic "I am" song for Abner Yokum (Peter Palmer) in the comic-strip musical *Li'l Abner* (1956) by Gene de Paul (music) and Johnny Mercer (lyric). Abner and the young men of Dogpatch sing about their wish of a life of idleness and seek to raise laziness to a fine art.

"If I Loved You" is mostly remembered as the big romantic ballad from *Carousel* (1945), and recordings by Frank Sinatra, Perry Como, Bing Crosby and even the 1960s team of Chad and Jeremy have kept the song popular. But in *Carousel* the song is a twelve-minute musical scene that mixes song and dialogue in a brilliant manner that has rarely been equaled. Billy Bigelow (John Raitt) and Julie Jordan (Jan Clayton) have only met that evening, and in this musical sequence we see them tease each other, then bully and threaten. Finally they are drawn to each other in a way that is dangerous and exciting. Richard Rodgers' music is lyrical in an operatic way, yet there is also a terrible urgency in the piece. Oscar Hammerstein, as in his previous "Make Believe" and "People Will Say We're in Love," manages to create a highly romantic lyric without any direct declarations of love. "If I Loved You" may be the fulfillment of Hammerstein's dream of song, story and character coming together in one sustained piece of music drama. In the Broadway revue *A Grand Night for Singing* (1993), the song was sung as a solo by Victoria Clark.

"If I Ruled the World" is an entrancing ballad from the short-lived British import *Pickwick* (1965), the musicalization of Charles Dickens' *The Pickwick Papers*. The genial Mr. Pickwick (Harry Secombe) is mistaken for a political candidate when he enters a small English town. Not wishing to disappoint anyone, he goes along with it and sings this stirring campaign song about a utopian society filled with love. Cyril Ornadel (music) and Leslie Bricusse (lyric) wrote the song, which enjoyed some popularity due to a recording by Tony Bennett.

"If I Sing" is a tender song that is about the very song being written. Lyricist Richard Maltby, Jr., took a melody by his collaborator composer David Shire and played it for his father, a bandleader who was too old and infirm to play music anymore. The song is dedicated to his father's gift of music, and in the lyric Maltby is playing it for his father. Richard Muenz sang the number in the Off-Broadway revue *Closer Than Ever* (1989), and Karen Akers recorded the song in 1991 with a revised lyric about a mother who used to play the piano.

"If I Were a Bell" is a slaphappy musical declaration of freedom from *Guys and Dolls* (1950) brought to the surface by a bit of alcohol and an intensely romantic setting. Gambler Sky Masterson (Robert Alda) has brought the straightlaced Sarah Brown (Isabel Bigley) to Havana to win a bet. After a few disguised drinks she lets loose in this jubilant Frank Loesser song in which she compares herself to a ringing bell, a singing bird and a whole list of exuberant things. Doris Day, Dinah Shore and Frankie Laine were among those who made successful recordings of the lighthearted song.

"If I Were a Rich Man" is one of the most famous "I am" songs in the American theatre, a brilliant tour de force for the dairyman Tevye in *Fiddler on the Roof* (1964). Jerry Bock (music) and Sheldon Harnick (lyric) wrote the song after Zero Mostel was cast as Tevye, putting in mock Hebrew incantations and the sounds of scattering chickens that they knew he could elaborate on. As Tevye lists all the things he would have and things he would do if he were wealthy, the imagery expands and grows until it becomes ridiculous (the staircase going down would be longer than the one going up) and touching at the same time. Although the number is a character song, that didn't keep Herb Alpert and the Tijuana Brass from having a hit instrumental version of it.

"If I Were You" is a breezy soft-shoe number for the nimble, light-footed Ray Bolger in *All American* (1962) by Charles Strouse (music) and Lee Adams (lyric). Professor Fodorski (Bolger) proposes to the Dean of Women (Eileen Herlie), and when she accepts, the duet turns into an entertaining dance opportunity for Bolger.

"If Love Were All" is the memorable Noël Coward ballad that pretends to scoff at life but has a deeply unsettling subtext. The song was first sung on Broadway in the British import *Bitter Sweet* (1929), where Manon, played by the chanteuse Mireille, sang it as a rehearsal piece in a Vienna cafe. Of particular interest are Coward's very unusual rhyme scheme and the somewhat autobiographical lyric that describes his life as nothing more than "a talent to amuse." The song has been recorded by Judy Garland, Bobby Short, Dorothy Loudon, Sarah Brightman and others and was sung by Barbara Cason in the Off-Broadway revue *Oh! Coward!* (1972).

"If Momma Was Married" is a wry waltz duet for the frustrated daughters of Rose (Ethel Merman) in *Gypsy* (1959) by Jule Styne (music) and Stephen Sondheim (lyric). June (Lane Bradbury) and Louise (Sandra Church) imagine how much simpler life would be if their mother got out of show business, married Herbie and stayed married.

"If My Friends Could See Me Now" is a vibrant character song for Charity Hope Valentine (Gwen Verdon) when she finally has a stroke of good luck in *Sweet Charity* (1966). Charity finds herself in the plush apartment of the Italian movie star Vittorio Vidal (James Luisi) and launches into this number that is as bubbly as the champagne she is served. Cy Coleman (music) and Dorothy Fields (lyric) wrote the zesty song and Verdon stopped the show with her top-hat-and-cane dance routine.

"If the Rain's Got to Fall" is a gleeful production number from the British import *Half a Sixpence* (1965) with music and lyrics by David Heneker. Arthur Kipps (Tommy Steele) is going to meet with his new love on Sunday, so he asks that if it must rain, let it be on Monday or Wednesday or any day but Sunday. He is joined by his male friends (Grover Dale, Will Mackenzie and Norman Allen) and a chorus of girls as the song blossoms into a lighthearted romp.

"If the World Were Like the Movies" is a touching soliloquy from *My Favorite Year* (1992) by Stephen Flaherty (music) and Lynn Ahrens (lyric). The dashing movie star Alan Swann (Tim Curry) reveals that his life is not nearly as glamorous as his films and wonders how much better things would be if one could control one's personal affairs with the neat and rewarding precision of a movie.

"If There Is Someone Lovelier Than You" is the memorable serenade by Howard Dietz (lyric) and Arthur Schwartz (music) from their unsuccessful attempt at operetta, *Revenge With Music* (1934). The Spanish gentleman Carlos (Georges Metaxa) woos the married Isabella (Ilka Chase) with this graceful ballad. Schwartz, who had originally written the melody for a radio serial, once stated that this was his favorite of all his songs.

"If This Is Goodbye" is a sweeping duet from *Anya* (1965), the short-lived musical about the Russian princess Anastasia who may or may not have survived the revolution. Anya (Constance Towers) and the former Prince Bounine (Michael Kermoyan) sing the farewell song, which lyricists Robert Wright and George Forrest adapted from Sergei Rachmaninoff's Second Piano Concerto.

"If This Isn't Love" is the larkish love song from *Finian's Rainbow* (1947) by Burton Lane (music) and E.Y. Harburg (lyric) that was a hit in a show filled with hits. Labor organizer Woody Mahoney (Donald Richards) and Irish immigrant Sharon McLonergan (Ella Logan) sing the vigorous ballad with the chorus, proclaiming the obvious by listing ridiculous alternatives. If these two people are not in love, then winter is summer and the whole world has gone crazy. Lane's music, the most brassy, Broadway-sounding in the show, is electric, and Harburg's lyric sparkles with arch rhymes, silly syllogisms and explosive phrases.

"If You Believe" is the soulful ballad of faith from *The Wiz* (1975), the black reworking of *The Wizard of Oz* by Charlie Smalls. Glinda (Dee Dee Bridgewater), the Good Witch of the South, sings the enthralling number to Dorothy (Stephanie Mills), telling her that the magic slippers will take her home if she truly believes they can. Johnny Mathis had a hit recording of the song.

"If You Could See Her," also known as "The Gorilla Song," is the most stinging of all the Kit Kat Klub numbers in *Cabaret* (1966) by John Kander (music) and Fred Ebb (lyric).The Master of Ceremonies (Joel Grey) sings the shrewdly affectionate song dancing with a lady gorilla (Jere Admire), telling the audience how no one understands how deep his love for her is. Commenting on the anti-Semitism going on outside the nightclub, the Emcee concludes the song with the acid remark that looking through his eyes, she doesn't look Jewish at all. When the song was recorded, the last line of the lyric referred to the gorilla as a meeskite (Yiddish for ugly) rather than risk offending the purchasers of the original cast album.

"If You Hadn't, But You Did" is an inspired comic number from the revue *Two on the Aisle* (1951) by Jule Styne (music) and Betty Comden and Adolph Green (lyric). Dolores Gray belted out the rapid patter song that listed all the reasons why she bumped off her husband. Sally Mayes recorded the number under the title "If" in 1994.

"If You Knew Suzie Like I Know Suzie" is the comic ditty that became the trademark song for Eddie Cantor even though it was written for Al Jolson in the hopes of his popularizing it. Joseph Meyer (music) and B.G. DeSylva (lyric) wrote it for the Jolson vehicle *Big Boy* (1925), but the song didn't go over well, so Jolson dropped it soon after opening and gave it to Cantor to try out. The wide-eyed Cantor was perfect for the silly number, and he continued to perform it throughout his career.

"If You Want to Die in Bed" is a cynical song about survival during difficult times from the British import *Miss Saigon* (1991). The Engineer (Jonathan Pryce), who has arranged to escape from Communist Vietnam, sings the provocative number about grabbing any opportunity that comes along to save yourself. Claude-Michel Schönberg wrote the music, and Richard Maltby, Jr., adapted the French lyric by Alain Boublil.

"If You're in Love, You'll Waltz" is the romantic duet from the operetta *Rio Rita* (1927) by Harry Tierney (music) and Joseph McCarthy (lyric). Feisty Rita Furguson (Ethelind Terry) and Texas Ranger Captain James Stewart (J. Harold Murray) sang the waltzing duet along the banks of the Rio Grande.

"I'll Always Remember the Song" is a lively polka from *Romance, Romance* (1988) by Barry Harman (lyric) and Keith Herrmann (music). Two Viennese aristocrats, Alfred (Scott Bakula) and Josefine (Alison Fraser), have disguised themselves as working-class folk and recall the wonderful time they had dancing the polka and falling in love.

"I'll Be Hard to Handle" is a jaunty comic song from *Roberta* (1933) sung by the plucky Clementina Scharwenka (Lyda Roberti) about her independent ways. Jerome Kern composed the snappy music, and Otto Harbach, who wrote the lyrics for the rest of the score, let his nephew Bernard Dougall pen the sly lyric for this song.   Liz Robertson sang the number in the Broadway revue *Jerome Kern Goes to Hollywood* (1986).

"I'll Be Here Tomorrow" is the defiant credo of the resourceful Jewish refugee S.L. Jacobowsky (Joel Grey) in *The Grand Tour* (1979). The touching Jerry Herman song chronicled all the places Jacobowsky had lived, each time forced to move due to persecution; but his incurable optimism has taught him that he will survive. After his misadventures during the course of the musical, Jacobowsky reprises the song as he sets off for yet another new home.

"I'll Be Seeing You," the beloved torch song and favorite of the World War Two era, is probably the finest song to come out of a show that lasted only fourteen performances. The show was *Right This Way* (1938), a musical about a common-law marriage that goes official and loses its luster; the score introduced "I Can Dream, Can't I?" and this standard. Sammy Fain composed the unforgettable music, and Irving Kahal wrote the delicate lyric. Tamara, as the common-law wife Mimi, sang the number, and, surprisingly, it caused no sparks. The song sat for five years unpublished and unrecorded. When it did catch on the appeal was passionate; it remained on the "Hit Parade" for twenty-four weeks, and during the war years no song better captured the wistful yearning of women waiting for their men to return. Among the many recordings were best-sellers by Hildegarde, Frances Langford and Frank Sinatra with the Tommy Dorsey Orchestra, as well as a recent recording by Mandy Patinkin.

"I'll Build a Stairway to Paradise" is the jazzy hit song from *George White's Scandals of 1922* with music by George Gershwin and lyric by B.G. DeSylva and Ira Gershwin. The electric song was the lavish first-act finale, with fifty girls climbing twin staircases up to heaven as Winnie Lightner sang the revivalistic number with Paul Whiteman's Orchestra. The song's idea was DeSylva's, and he and Ira Gershwin wrote a number called "A New Step Every Day" in 1919. Later George Gershwin was brought in as composer, and the lyric was rewritten into the version that became a hit. Musically, the song is very unusual, with some daring accentuations, an intriguing melody with a five-step ascent and a five-step descent, and some very subtle enharmonic changes. Ira Gershwin never thought the song would become popular because of the complexity of the music, but dance bands immediately picked up on it, and soon sheet-music sales soared. The song is also known as "Stairway to Paradise."

"I'll Buy You a Star" is an enchanting ballad from the period musical *A Tree Grows in Brooklyn* (1951) by Arthur Schwartz (music) and Dorothy Fields (lyric). The undependable Johnny Nolan (Johnny Johnston) sings to his wife Katie about the life of luxury they will have together. Neither Katie nor the audience believes him, but his earnest, affectionate demeanor is nonetheless enthralling.

"I'll Follow My Secret Heart" is a tender waltz by Noël Coward from the British import *Conversation Piece* (1934), where it was sung by Yvonne Printemps. Coward boasted that he'd written the song in one sitting when he was drunk, composing it in the key of G-flat, a key in which he'd never even played before. The popular ballad was recorded by Lee Wiley, Lily Pons, Hildegarde and others.

"I'll Go Home With Bonnie Jean" is the robust character song from *Brigadoon* (1947) that captures a Scottish flavor while remaining a solid Broadway production number. The about-to-be-wed Charlie Dalrymple (Lee Sullivan) sings about his romantic wanderings of the past but joyfully vows that from now on it will only be he and his new wife Jean. Alan Jay Lerner wrote the playful lyric, and Frederick Loewe composed the spirited Highland music.

"I'll Know (When My Love Comes Along)" is one of those musical theatre situations where the boy and the girl start the song in disagreement, then slowly get interested in each other as the number progresses. Frank Loesser wrote this beguiling duet for *Guys and Dolls* (1950) where gambler Sky Masterson (Robert Alda) and mission sister Sarah Brown (Isabel Bigley) each describe the kind of person meant for them. Sarah Vaughan, Billy Eckstine, Sammy Davis, Jr., and Fran Warren were among the singers who made popular recordings of the song.

"I'll Never Be Jealous Again" is a clownish duet from *The Pajama Game* (1954). Time-study expert Hines (Eddie Foy, Jr.) loves the flighty Gladys (Carol Haney) but is (rightfully) jealous of her flirting ways. In this daffy song, secretary Mabel (Reta Shaw) quizzes Hines on his trust in Gladys with hilarious results. Richard Adler and Jerry Ross together wrote the jocular music and lyric.

"I'll Never Fall in Love Again" is the popular ballad by Burt Bacharach (music) and Hal David (lyric) from their only Broadway show, *Promises, Promises* (1968). Chuck Baxter (Jerry Orbach) and Fran Kubelik (Jill O'Hara) have each been stung by love and, individually on opposite sides of the stage, vow not to repeat the experience. The simple pop folk song seemed even more contemporary because O'Hara, in 1960s style, accompanied herself on the guitar as she sang. Of the many recordings of the hit song, the ones by Dionne Warwick and the Carpenters were the most popular.

"I'll Never Say No" is the ardent love ballad from *The Unsinkable Molly Brown* (1960) by Meredith Willson. "Leadville" Johnny (Harve Presnell) sings the song to Molly (Tammy Grimes) to get her to marry him, and then they sing it as an engaging duet. Jack Jones recorded the number with the Guy Lombardo Orchestra in 1961.

"I'll See You Again" is arguably Noël Coward's most popular song, a lovely farewell waltz from his operetta *Bitter Sweet* (1929) that originated in London. The number is first heard as a music exercise for Sarah Millick (Evelyn Laye) and her teacher Carl Linden (Gerald Nodin) and then recurs throughout the musical as a kind of leitmotif. Mario Lanza's recording of "I'll see You Again" was popular and Bobby Short recorded a very distinctive rendition of the ballad.

"The Illegitimate Daughter" is a comic number from the musical satire *Of Thee I Sing* (1931) sung by the French Ambassador (Florenz Ames) and the ensemble as they trace the ancestral lineage of the jilted Diana Deveraux (Grace Brinkley) all the way back to an illegitimate nephew of Napoleon. George Gershwin wrote the French-flavored patter music, and Ira Gershwin devised the farcical lyric.

"I'm a Jonah Man" is the comic-sad lament by an unlucky outcast that Bert Williams made famous. The Alex Rogers song was written around 1900 but did not become well known until it was interpolated after opening into *In Dahomey* (1903), where Williams sang it. The song is sometimes titled "Jonah Man," under which title it was sung by Catherine Wright in the Broadway revue *Tintypes* (1980).

"I'm Always Chasing Rainbows" is a popular ballad that seems to resurface every few decades when new audiences rediscover it. The entrancing song of wistful yearning was written for *Oh, Look!* (1918), where Harry Fox, as the down-and-out Stephen Baird, stopped the show each evening when he sang it. Sheet-music sales surpassed the one million mark, and the song was performed everywhere. Although it never fell into obscurity, the ballad had a boost in the 1940s when a Perry Como recording put it at the top of "Your Hit Parade" for twelve weeks. Broadway audiences got to hear the song again when Debbie Reynolds sang it in the 1974 revival of *Irene*. Joseph McCarthy wrote the dreamy lyric, and Harry Carroll adapted Chopin's "Fantaisie-Impromptu" into a hit theatre song, the first pop best-seller to be based on a classical piece of music.

"I'm an Indian, Too" is a mock tribal number that Annie Oakley (Ethel Merman) sings after she is invited into the Sioux nation in Irving Berlin's *Annie Get Your Gun* (1946). The song, which includes phony Indian lyrics and rhyming tribal names, has a predictable tom-tom beat with a scaling release that tops off the joke beautifully.

"I'm an Ordinary Man" is Henry Higgins' hilarious "I am" song from *My Fair Lady* (1956) by Alan Jay Lerner (lyric) and Frederick Loewe (music). Rex Harrison introduced the comic tour de force number in which Higgins reveals his eruptive nature by alternating between a serene patter song about his gentlemanly ways and a bombastic aria about the ills of womankind.

"I'm Breaking Down" is a frenzied musical soliloquy from the Off-Broadway musical *In Trousers* (1979) by William Finn. Finding out that Marvin, her husband and the father of her son, is gay and is leaving her for his male lover Whizzer, the Wife (Alison Fraser) has a comic nervous breakdown in song. The frantic number was used in the later Broadway production *Falsettos* (1992), where it was sung by Barbara Walsh as the wife, now named Trina.

"I'm Falling in Love With Someone" is an aria from the Victor Herbert operetta *Naughty Marietta* (1910) that has become a favorite of tenors over the decades. It is sung by Captain Dick Warrington (Orville Harrold) as a confessional soliloquy in which he realizes that his friendship with Marietta d'Altena (Emma Trentini) is turning into romance. The song was immediately popular, with Harrold having to give four encores on opening night. Rida Johnson Young wrote the lyric for Herbert's music, which has a unique opening section and an unusual leap of a ninth in the refrain. The rather difficult composition here and in other songs from *Naughty Marietta* is due to the fact that Herbert wrote the score for the Manhattan Opera Company rather than for traditional Broadway singers. Mario Lanza and Gordon MacRae each made popular recordings of the song.

"I'm Flying" is the exhilarating song that Peter Pan (Mary Martin) sings as he shows off his lighter-than-air abilities in *Peter Pan* (1954). He is soon joined by the three Darling children (Kathy Nolan, Robert Harrington and Joseph Stafford), and all four fly off to Neverland. Mark Charlap (music) and Carolyn Leigh (lyric) wrote the thrilling number that became one of Broadway's (and later television's) warmest memories. The number was performed by Charlotte d'Amboise as Peter in *Jerome Robbins' Broadway* (1989) with Donna Di Meo, Linda Talcott and Steve Ochoa.

"I'm Getting Tired So I Can Sleep" is a delicate Irving Berlin ballad from the all-soldier revue *This Is the Army* (1942). The music has a languid lullaby quality to it, and the lyrics yearn for sleep not out of weariness but because the singer wishes to dream of the one he left behind. In the revue Stuart Churchill sang the number in a barracks setting. Jimmy Dorsey's Orchestra made a hit recording of it and many years later Richard Chamberlain recorded it.

"I'm Glad to See You've Got What You Want" is a touching duet from the allegorical musical *Celebration* (1969) by Tom Jones (lyric) and Harvey Schmidt (music). Angel (Susan Watson) and Orphan (Michael Glenn-

Smith) have seen their wishes come true: she is covered in diamonds, and he is going to get his garden back. Yet they seem less than happy as they politely congratulate each other, knowing that life must be more than wishes coming true.

"I'm Going Back (To the Bonjour Tristesse Brassiere Company)" is an inflammatory specialty number for Judy Holliday in *Bells Are Ringing* (1956) by Jule Styne (music) and Betty Comden and Adolph Green (lyric). Ella Peterson (Holliday) decides to quit her job as a telephone answering service operator and breaks into this nostalgic rag in the Al Jolson style.

"I'm Gonna Wash That Man Right Outa My Hair" is a joyous and wild romp for Nellie Forbush (Mary Martin) and one of the highlights of *South Pacific* (1949) due mainly to the novelty of the character's shampooing her hair on stage. It was Martin's idea to take the title of the song literally, and authors Richard Rodgers (music) and Oscar Hammerstein (lyric) thought it more than appropriate for the character. The song itself is a bluesy but silly combination of a torch song and a comic number. Later in the show Emile de Becque (Ezio Pinza) reprises the song as he mimics Nellie and her famous shampoo. In the Broadway revue *A Grand Night for Singing* (1993), the number was sung by Victoria Clark, Alyson Reed and Lynne Wintersteller.

"I'm Just Wild About Harry" is the high-stepping musical tribute to Harry Walton (Roger Matthews), who is running for mayor in the landmark black musical *Shuffle Along* (1921). The popular song was sung by Harry's girlfriend Jessie (Lottie Gee) and the citizens of Jimtown. Authors Eubie Blake (music) and Noble Sissle (lyric) had originally written the number as a waltz, but it was soon determined that white audiences would have trouble accepting such a European sound in an all-black show, so they revised it into the rousing cakewalk that is known today. The oft-recorded song was featured in three films. In the Broadway revue *Eubie* (1978), the song was sung by Lynnie Godfrey, Janet Powell and the female ensemble.

"I'm Like a New Broom" is a nimble song of optimism from the period musical *A Tree Grows in Brooklyn* (1951) by Arthur Schwartz (music) and Dorothy Fields (lyric). No-good Johnny Nolan (Johnny Johnston) promises his fiancée Katie that he'll change his ways once they are married. The song is so engaging that one can almost believe him.

"I'm Not at All in Love" is a lighthearted waltz from *The Pajama Game* (1954) with music and lyric by Richard Adler and Jerry Ross. Union organizer Babe Williams (Janis Paige) sings with the girls at the factory that she has no romantic interest in the new superintendent Sid Sorokin (John Raitt), but we all know otherwise.

"I'm Not Saying a Word" is a gentle ballad in the 1960s pop style from the British import *Blood Brothers* (1993) by Willy Russell. Edward Lyons (Mark Michael Hutchinson) is in love with Linda (Jan Graveson) but knows she loves another, so he sings of his affection for her without saying what he really feels.

"I'm on My Way" is the closing number in *Porgy and Bess* (1935), a song of hope and determination sung by Porgy (Todd Duncan) as he sets off in his goat cart to find his beloved Bess in far-off New York City. George Gershwin composed the fervent music, and DuBose Heyward wrote the optimistic lyric.

"I'm Only Thinking of Him" is an amusing trio from *Man of La Mancha* (1965) sung by Don Quixote's relatives in the church confessional. The niece Antonia (Mimi Turque) and her housekeeper (Eleanore Knapp) tell the Padre (Robert Rounseville) of their frustrations with the lunatic relative, and all three concur that no matter what the course of action, they are only thinking of his welfare. The number is reprised with Dr. Carrasco (Jon Cypher) joining the three as he decides to fetch Quixote home. Mitch Leigh wrote the mock-operatic music, and Joe Darion provided the humorous lyric.

"I'm Past My Prime" is a breezy lament for the over-the-hill seventeen-year-old Daisy Mae (Edith Adams) in *Li'l Abner* (1956). Because she hasn't gotten Abner Yokum to marry her yet, Daisy Mae despairs and tells her troubles to Marryin' Sam (Stubby Kaye), who joins her in this droll duet. Gene de Paul wrote the languid music, and Johnny Mercer provided the wry lyric.

"I'm Still Here" is one of Stephen Sondheim's most accomplished songs, a character number that is also a chronicle of American life over the past decades. The song (a last minute replacement for "Can That Boy Foxtrot") was sung by Yvonne De Carlo as the worldly-wise Carlotta Campion in *Follies* (1971). As Carlotta relates the ups and downs of her career, the song mirrors the changing tastes of the American public over the years, moving from innocence to camp and then to nostalgia. A Sondheim lyric has never been more piquant, and his bluesy, languid music gives the song a world-weary quality. In the Broadway revue *Side by Side by Sondheim* (1977), the captivating number was sung by Millicent Martin.

"I'm the First Girl in the Second Row (In the Third Scene of the Fourth Number)" is a delicious character song for Nancy Walker in the musical *Look, Ma, I'm Dancin'!* (1948). Hugh Martin wrote the playful number, which was sung by brewery heiress Lily Malloy (Walker), who underwrites a ballet company and eventually gets to strut her stuff.

"I'm the Greatest Star" is the young Fanny Brice's ambitious "I am" song from *Funny Girl* (1964) by Jule Styne (music) and Bob Merrill (lyric). Fanny (Barbra Streisand) belts out her unqualified self-rave review to hoofer Eddie Ryan (Danny Meehan) even though she's yet to make even the chorus line in a show. One section of the number is used as a leitmotif throughout the score, most noticeably in the later "Don't Rain on My Parade."

"Imagine" is a pleasing little ballad that weaved in and out of the "Peter's Journey" ballet section of *Babes in Arms* (1937). Richard Rodgers (music) and Lorenz Hart (lyric) wrote the dreamy song that catalogued all the things the young characters imagined happening to them in the future. The song was introduced by Wynn Murray, Alex Courtney, Clifton Darling, James Gillis, Robert Rounseville and Duke McHale.

"The Impossible Dream" is the hymnlike ballad that became one of the most popular theatre songs of the 1960s. It was sung by Richard Kiley as the knight errant Don Quixote in *Man of La Mancha* (1965) with music by Mitch Leigh and lyric by Joe Darion. Quixote, who is spending a night's vigil in preparation for his dubbing, explains to Aldonza (Joan Diener) about "The Quest," as the song is titled in the show. With its lush, idealistic lyric and absorbing chromatic passages in the music, the ballad was a showstopper from the first preview. At the end of the show the number is reprised by Aldonza and the ensemble. Jack Jones, Roger Williams, Jim Nabors, Andy Williams, Robert Goulet and the Hesitations are among the many who made successful recordings of the song.

"In a Little While" is a diverting romantic duet from the fairy-tale musical *Once Upon a Mattress* (1959) by Mary Rodgers (music) and Marshall Barer (lyric). The lovers are Lady Larkin (Anne Jones) and Sir Harry (Allen Case), and the title refers to the fact that the unmarried Larkin is pregnant and soon everyone will know their secret.

"In Buddy's Eyes" is one of the finest subtext songs of the American theatre, a beautifully written piece that means the opposite of what the character sings. Stephen Sondheim wrote the song for *Follies* (1971), where Sally (Dorothy Collins) sings it to her old flame Ben (John McMartin) about how happy her life has turned out with her husband Buddy (Gene Nelson). Sally sings cheerfully about her everyday hobbies and activities, but Sondheim's dissonant music, with a dry woodwind accompaniment, and her overly eager lyric belies her optimistic facade and reveal a woman deeply unhappy.

"In Egern on the Tegern See" is a pastiche of an old-style operetta number that Jerome Kern (music) and Oscar Hammerstein (lyric) wrote for *Music in the Air* (1932). The Bavarian prima donna Frieda Hatzfeld (Natalie Hall) is coaxed into singing her big number from an old operetta, and she obliges with this nostalgic aria filled with images of moonlight on the water and soft caressing breezes. Nancy Andrews recorded the song in the 1960s. The number was spoofed in the pastiche musical *Little Mary Sunshine* (1962) with a song entitled "In Izzenschnooken on the Lovely Essenzook Zee."

"In My Own Lifetime" is the stirring ballad from *The Rothschilds* (1970) by Jerry Bock (music) and Sheldon Harnick (lyric). Family patriarch Meyer Rothschild (Hal Linden) sings of his hopes to live long enough to see the day when the Jews of Europe will not be confined to designated urban ghettos.

"In Our Hands" is a moving song of optimism about the future sung by the teenage contestants of a beauty pageant in the musical *Smile* (1986). Marvin Hamlisch wrote the engaging music, and Howard Ashman provided the succinct lyric that remains clearheaded but hopeful.

"In the Good Old Summertime" is the popular favorite that opened the door for other songs about the seasons of the year. The memorable George Evans (music) and Ren Shields (lyric) number was heard in vaudeville at the turn of the century, but didn't catch on until Blanche Ring sang it in *The Defender* (1902). Music publishers were reluctant to print the song, arguing that performers could only appropriately sing it three months out of the year. But once it was published it sold over a million copies of sheet music and a flood of seasonal songs followed. "In the Good Old Summertime" was also heard on Broadway in *In Posterland* (1902), and the 1904 musical *The Good Old Summertime* was built around the song. Years later the number was heard in *By the Beautiful Sea* (1954), where Shirley Booth sang it as a countermelody to the ensemble's "Coney Island Boat."

"In the Heart of the Dark" is a gentle ballad from the unsuccessful *Very Warm for May* (1939), the last Broadway musical by composer Jerome Kern. Oscar Hammerstein wrote the romantic lyric for this nocturnal reverie, which was sung by Carroll (Hollace Shaw) and later reprised by Liz (Frances Mercer). The music, with its repeated notes and quarter-note triplets, is very atypical of Kern and recalls a Cole Porter kind of melody, just as Hammerstein's lyric is reminiscent of Porter's "All Through the Night." Barbara Cook made a lovely recording of "In the Heart of the Dark" in the 1960s.

"In the Name of Love" is a typically zesty Cy Coleman song that was heard in the musical flop *Welcome to the Club* (1989). Marcia Mitzman, as a recent divorcée, sang the upbeat list song by A.E. Hotchner (lyric) and Coleman (music and lyric) about the downbeat side of divorce.

"In the Shade of the New Apple Tree" is a swinging love song with a sentimental lyric from the offbeat *Hooray for What!* (1937) by Harold Arlen (music) and E.Y. Harburg (lyric). Jack Whiting and June Clyde sang the nostalgic number that used old-fashioned imagery redefined for an up-to-date love song. The combination so impressed film producer Arthur Freed that he signed Arlen and Harburg to score the film *The Wizard of Oz* based on this one song.

"Indian Love Call" is the most popular song from the long-running operetta *Rose-Marie* (1924) and possibly the American theatre's most parodied number. Fur trapper Jim Kenyon (Dennis King) and Rose-Marie (Mary Ellis) find love in the Canadian Rockies, and their expansive love duet is a primeval call of the wild. Although Rudolf Friml's music is far from authentic Indian, the unusual chromatics in the piece make it distinctly non-European in style. Otto Harbach and Oscar Hammerstein wrote the lyric, which unabashedly turns the word "you" into a resounding mating call that echoed throughout the decades. A recording of the duet by Nelson Eddy and Jeanette MacDonald in 1936 sold over a million records, and country singer Slim Whitman had a million-seller with his 1952 solo version of the song. Also memorable was a 1938 recording by Artie Shaw's Orchestra (vocal by Tony Pastor).

"Intermission Talk" is Rodgers and Hammerstein's wry look at theatre audiences, a part-waltz, part-dialogue number from *Me and Juliet* (1953), the team's only musical comedy effort. In the song we hear the comments of audience members at the intermission of the play-within-the-play; topics range from opinions on how the show is going to income tax woes, dislike of these modern plays that are too serious, misquoted lines and confused songs, and the conclusion that the theatre is dying for sure. Oscar Hammerstein's lyric includes sly references to several shows currently running on Broadway (including their own *The King and I*), and Richard Rodgers' melody is foolishly bouncy. The animated "Intermission Talk" is a fun insight into how the famous team viewed their audience.

"Irene" is the infectious title song from the 1919 musical by Harry Tierney (music) and Joseph McCarthy (lyric). Mrs. Marshall (Florence Hills) and the ensemble sang the entrancing number as a way of proving Irene's bogus royal lineage.

"Is Anybody There?" is an electric musical soliloquy from *1776* (1969) in which statesman John Adams (William Daniels), at the lowest point in his campaign to declare independence from Britain, envisions a new country that will one day celebrate its difficult beginnings with fireworks. The song was more than mere hindsight on the part of Sherman Edwards, who wrote the music and the lyric. Adams' sentiments come directly from his actual letters to his wife, and the song's title is from the war-weary George Washington, who posed the succinct question in a letter to the sluggish Continental Congress in Philadelphia.

"Is There Anything Better Than Dancing?" is a graceful song for the title couple in the short-lived *Nick and Nora* (1991). Barry Bostwick, as amateur sleuth Nick Charles, and Joanna Gleason, as his society wife and partner Nora, sang the smooth number by Charles Strouse (music) and Richard Maltby, Jr., (lyric).

"The Isle of Our Dreams" is a passionate duet from *The Red Mill* (1906) by Victor Herbert (music) and Henry Blossom (lyric). In a Holland setting, the lovely Gretchen (Augusta Greenleaf) is in love with Captain Van Damm (Joseph M. Ratliff) but betrothed to another. They plan to elope that night, and in this romantic number they long to sail off together to the paradise of the song title. Lucille Norman and Gordon MacRae made a memorable recording of the duet.

"Isn't It a Pity?" is a captivating if obscure Gershwin ballad from the unsuccessful *Pardon My English* (1933). Josephine Huston and George Givot sang the number as a duet in which two people regret not having met years before and falling in love then. George Gershwin's music is very enchanting, and Ira Gershwin's lyric seems like rhymed conversation. Although the song was published, it rarely surfaced after *Pardon My English* closed. Years later it was often sung by Mabel Mercer, who considered it one of her favorite Gershwin songs, and Mel Tormé. Michael Feinstein and Rosemary Clooney recorded the song for the first time as a duet in 1987.

"It" is an out-of-place but delectable comedy number from the operetta *The Desert Song* (1926) by Sigmund Romberg (music) and Otto Harbach and Oscar Hammerstein (lyric). Amidst the exotic musical strains of the North African desert, Benjamin Kidd (Eddie Buzzell) and the soubrette Susan (Nellie Breen) sing this dandy tribute to "It" girl Clara Bow, Elinor Glyn and other sirens who were in vogue during the flapper era. The song is unique in its shrewd lyric, which was far from the usual fare in operetta.

"It Ain't Etiquette" is one of Cole Porter's lesser-known comic ditties but one of his funniest. Bert Lahr and Jean Moorhead sang the daffy duet in

DuBarry Was a Lady (1939), and while it was obviously tailored to Lahr's special talents, the lyric stands on its own as a witty list of all the don'ts of high society. Years later Ronny Graham made a playful recording of the comic song.

"It Ain't Necessarily So" is the cynical song sung by the philosophical Sportin' Life (John W. Bubbles) in *Porgy and Bess* (1935). At the picnic on Kittiwah Island, Sportin' Life tries to shock the church-going residents of Catfish Row with this irreverent number that suggests that some stories in the Bible (David and Goliath, Jonah and the whale, Moses being found in the stream, Methuselah's age and the devil himself) are not true. The ensemble joins him in the scat-sound responses, giving the effect of a mock-revival number. George Gershwin composed the thrilling music that alternates from a lethargic blues tempo to a rousing gospel one, and Ira Gershwin wrote the funny, acerbic lyric. In rehearsal Bubbles had trouble singing the song's tricky rhythms, particularly the slow triplets in the music. It wasn't until the conductor tapped out the pattern and Bubbles was able to tap dance the rhythm that the song worked. Paul Robeson, Lawrence Tibbett, Cab Calloway and Martha Raye are among those who made successful recordings of the number. In 1952 Ira Gershwin adapted his lyric to include snide references to Eisenhower and Nixon, and it was used as the campaign song for Adlai Stevenson's unsuccessful bid for president.

"It All Depends on You" is the first song written by the illustrious team of DeSylva, Brown and Henderson. The Al Jolson vehicle *Big Boy* (1925) needed another song for its star, so B.G. DeSylva and Lew Brown wrote the lyric about romantic dependency, Ray Henderson provided the music, and the new team was born. Both Jolson and Ruth Etting made popular recordings of the song and in 1972 George Burns recorded it.

"It Couldn't Please Me More" is an appealing charm song for the elderly lovers in *Cabaret* (1966) by John Kander (music) and Fred Ebb (lyric). The Jewish fruit merchant Herr Schultz (Jack Gilford) presents his beloved Fraulein Schneider (Lotte Lenya) with the gift of a pineapple from his shop, and she gratefully sings this sweet duet with him. The sentimental song has a nice lazy foxtrot tempo, with some Hawaiian musical phrases thrown in for comic accent.

"It Depends on What You Pay" or "The Rape Song" is a thrilling comic number from the Off-Broadway musical *The Fantasticks* (1960) in which the bandit El Gallo (Jerry Orbach) explains to the two fathers (William Larsen and Hugh Thomas) the different kinds of abduction he can provide for a price. The hilarious list song includes the military, Gothic, Indian, comic, drunken or Venetian variety, and soon the fathers join him in the rousing flamenco number.

The song was the last one added to the score; authors Tom Jones (lyric) and Harvey Schmidt (music) were so impressed with Orbach's comic talents that they took what was originally just a speech of El Gallo's and turned it into this full-blown showstopper. Over the years since the musical opened, the many references to rape in the lyric have caused problems with some audiences even though the three men are talking about a classical abduction rather than a sexual crime. In 1990 Jones wrote a new lyric for a national touring production of *The Fantasticks*, but the song stayed the same in the original Off-Broadway company. In 1991 the title was changed to "The Abduction Song."

"It Isn't Working" is a shrewd comic number from *Woman of the Year* (1981) by John Kander (music) and Fred Ebb (lyric). Tess and Sam have only been married a short time, but already their friends Gerald (Roderick Cook), Chip (Daren Kelly) and Helga (Grace Keagy) join the chorus in the nasty observation that the marriage isn't working.

"It Never Entered My Mind" is one of those amazing Rodgers and Hart torch songs that uses a colloquial expression as a springboard to explore all sorts of emotions. The song is one of rueful contemplation, and Richard Rodgers' music shifts from major to minor keys inventively. Lorenz Hart's lyric is painfully subdued, including the famous observation of being uneasy in an easy chair. Shirley Ross introduced the song in *Higher and Higher* (1940) and recorded it that same year, but it wasn't until recordings by Frank Sinatra, Mabel Mercer and others that it became a standard. Both Benny Goodman and Larry Clinton also recorded orchestral versions that were popular, and years later Ella Fitzgerald and Linda Ronstadt each gave memorable interpretations of the number.

"It Never Was You" is a very lyrical romantic duet from the satirical *Knickerbocker Holiday* (1938) by Kurt Weill (music) and Maxwell Anderson (lyric). The freedom-loving Brom Broeck (Richard Kollmar) loves Tina Tienhoven (Jeanne Madden), but, on a trumped-up charge, he is condemned to hang. The two lovers do have time for this engaging duet in the Romberg-like operetta style. Weill's music, as usual, breaks away from the standard thirty-two-bar formula and manages to parody operetta even as it pleases. Eddy Duchin and Ray Herbeck each made successful orchestral recordings of the song, and Weill's widow Lotte Lenya made a distinctive version as well.

"It Only Takes a Moment" is the only duet in *Hello, Dolly!* (1964) and one of the score's gentlest numbers. The Jerry Herman love song is sung by Cornelius Hackl (Charles Nelson Reilly) and Irene Malloy (Eileen Brennan) near the end of the musical. Leslie Uggams also sang it in the Broadway revue *Jerry's Girls* (1985).

"It Takes a Woman to Take a Man" is a comic number from *As the Girls Go* (1948) that the inspired clown Bobby Clark stopped the show with each night. As Waldo Wellington, the husband of the first female president of the nation, Clark sang the clever song by Jimmy McHugh (music) and Harold Adamson (lyric).

"It Was Good Enough for Grandma" is a sly feminist cry for freedom from *Bloomer Girl* (1944) by Harold Arlen (music) and E.Y. Harburg (lyric). The emancipated Evelina Applegate (Celeste Holm) and the girls sing this merry marchlike song arguing that the old-fashioned ways for women are not good enough for them. Harburg's animated lyric is witty, with a subtext of real anger under the lighthearted defiance.

"It Would Have Been Wonderful" is a humorous duet from *A Little Night Music* (1973) that takes the form of twin soliloquies. Fredrik Egerman (Len Cariou) and Count Carl-Magnus Malcolm (Laurence Guittard) find themselves together at the country house of their mistress Desiree and coldly size each other up with a curt "sir!" Then, in alternating lyrics, each contemplates how he wishes Desiree was not so desirable so that he could extricate himself from her. Stephen Sondheim wrote the amusing lyric and the intriguing music, which moves from a ponderous pacing tempo when they consider all the faults Desiree could have had to a lush, melodic strain when they recall her delectable qualities.

"It Would Have Been Wonderful" is a pleasing torch song from the Off-Broadway sequel *Annie Warbucks* (1993) by Charles Strouse (music) and Martin Charnin (lyric). Marguerite MacIntyre, as Oliver Warbuck's secretary Grace, sang the touching number after it became clear that the billionaire would never marry her because of their age difference.

"Italian Street Song" is a zesty character song from Victor Herbert's *Naughty Marietta* (1910) and an operetta favorite over the decades. Marietta d'Altena (Emma Trentini) sings of her youth in Naples and vocally captures the excitement and buoyancy of an Italian street celebration with her "zing, zing, zi-zi-zi-zi-zi-zing boom ay!" Rida Johnson Young wrote the festive lyric for Herbert's melody. The song, a coloratura classic, is particularly difficult to sing because of its required vocal precision and lyrical purity.

"It's a Chemical Reaction, That's All" is the chilly analytical description of love given by the Russian comrade Ninotchka in Cole Porter's *Silk Stockings* (1955). Hildegarde Neff played the icy lady who argued a scientific reason for Don Ameche's attraction to her.

"It's a Fine Life" is an animated music-hall ditty from the British import *Oliver!* (1963) by Lionel Bart. Two of London's low-lifes, Nancy (Georgia Brown) and Bet (Alice Playten), sing the catchy sing-along about the ups and downs of a life of crime, with Fagin (Clive Revill) and his boys joining in. Later in the show the number is reprised by Bill Sikes (Danny Sewell), Nancy, Fagin and the boys.

"It's a Long Way to Tipperary" is the World War One favorite by Jack Judge and Harry Williams that was interpolated into the Al Jolson vehicle *Dancing Around* (1914) to liven up a weak score. Later that same season it was added to *Chin-Chin* (1914), where it was sung by the popular comics Dave Montgomery and Fred Stone. Early recordings of the song by the American Quartet and by John McCormack were very popular and the song became a nationwide hit.

"It's a Lovely Day Today" is a sprightly love duet from Irving Berlin's *Call Me Madam* (1950) that is a simple but exhilarating testament to romantic companionship. The number was introduced by Russell Nype, as an American diplomatic aide, and Galina Talva, as a princess in the mythical country of Lichtenburg.

"It's a Lovely Day Tomorrow" is an appealing Irving Berlin song from *Louisiana Purchase* (1940), where Irene Bordoni, as Mme. Boudelaise, sang it to Vera Zorina, as Marina Van Linden, in order to cheer her up. Berlin's hymnlike melody is reminiscent of Jerome Kern, and the song manages to beguile, all within a one-octave range. Mary Martin made a popular recording of the number.

"It's a Perfect Relationship" is the pleasing "I am" song for telephone answering service operator Ella Peterson (Judy Holliday) in *Bells Are Ringing* (1956) by Jule Styne (music) and Betty Comden and Adolph Green (lyric). Ella confesses she's in love with playwright Jeff Moss, whom she talks to on the phone all the time, but always disguised as a little old lady he calls "mom." Ella sees it as an ideal situation, yet she suspects there may be more to love than such a safe and secure relationship.

"It's a Simple Little System" is a prankish comic number from *Bells Are Ringing* (1956) about an illegal betting ring that uses an innocent answering service as a front. Racketeer Sandor (Eddie Lawrence) explains the system to his boys: horse races are given code names of classical composers so that bookies can place bets by pretending to order records through the answering service. Betty Comden and Adolph Green wrote the jocular lyric, and Jule Styne composed the playful music, which uses sections of classical pieces to illustrate the simple little system.

"It's All Right With Me" is one of Cole Porter's most haunting torch songs, a beautifully sustained composition with an insistent rhythm and a melody that shifts expertly from major to minor keys. Peter Cookson introduced the memorable ballad in *Can-Can* (1953), and it has remained a Porter standard ever since.

"It's an Art" is the musical boast of a proud waitress (Lenora Nemetz) in *Working* (1978), the revue about America's work force. Stephen Schwartz wrote the engaging music and knowing lyric.

"It's Delightful to Be Married" is a humorously droll number that became Anna Held's signature song during her short and tragic life. Held wrote the lyric and set it to a popular French melody by Vincent Scotto. She first sang it in *The Parisian Model* (1906) as she held up a hand mirror to the faces of the men in the audience. Carolyn Mignini sang the number in the Broadway revue *Tintypes* (1980).

"It's De-Lovely" is a Cole Porter favorite that uses word invention in a lyric in the style of Ira Gershwin's "'S Wonderful." The duet was introduced by Ethel Merman and Bob Hope in *Red, Hot and Blue!* (1936), where they managed to kid each other with a list of "de" words, many of them original concoctions by Porter. When all five refrains are sung, the song chronicles the saga of a romance from lovers on a moonlit night to a wedding to a honeymoon to the birth of a baby boy to his growing up and becoming the toast of the social set. Merman recorded the song, and there was also a successful record by Eddy Duchin and His Orchestra.

"It's Good to Be Alive" is a captivating song of optimism from *New Girl in Town* (1957) that avoids any sentimentality. Streetwalker Anna Christie (Gwen Verdon) starts to feel better about life as she sails out to sea on her father's barge. The song is later reprised by the stoker Mat Burke (George Wallace) after he falls in love with Anna. The Bob Merrill song was the hit ballad of the show and was popular for a while.

"It's Got to Be Love" is one of Rodgers and Hart's most jaunty efforts, a love song that swings and bounces along both musically and lyrically. Lorenz Hart's lyric lists all the things this condition is not (tonsillitis, the morning after, fallen arches, indigestion); therefore it must be love. Richard Rodgers' melody is very contagious and refuses to disappear even after only one hearing. The song was sung as a duet and danced by Doris Carson and Ray Bolger in *On Your Toes* (1936). Hal Kemp and His Orchestra made a best-selling recording of the number.

"It's Me" is a snappy comic duet from Rodgers and Hammerstein's only musical comedy, *Me and Juliet* (1953). An actress (Joan McCracken) in her dressing room explains to another cast member (Isabel Bigley) that in real life she is dull and uninspired; but give her a role to play on stage and she becomes vibrant and alluring. Richard Rodgers wrote the lively music, and Oscar Hammerstein provided the playful lyric. In the Broadway revue *A Grand Night for Singing* (1993), the song was sung as a trio by Alyson Reed, Jason Graae and Martin Vidnovic.

"It's Never Too Late to Fall in Love" is a hilarious duet from the pastiche musical *The Boy Friend* (1954), a British import by Sandy Wilson. When the young flapper Dulcie (Dilys Lay) has a spat with her boyfriend, the elderly Lord Brockhurst (Geoffrey Hibbert) suggests she try a more mature vintage of romance with him. Wilson's frolicsome music and witty lyric, Dulcie's intermittent "boop a doop"s and the chorus coming in for the occasional "whack a do"s make this the show-stopping eleven o'clock number of the musical.

"It's Not Too Late" is an appealing duet from *Romance, Romance* (1988) by Barry Harman (lyric) and Keith Herrmann (music). In nineteenth-century Vienna the jaded aristocrat Alfred (Scott Bakula) wonders if it is still possible to find true romance in life. Meanwhile the society lady Josefine (Alison Fraser) ponders the same question, and as each character dresses in their respective homes, they both sing a vigorous duet deciding there is still time to find love. In the modern section of the musical, New Yorkers Sam (Bakula) and Monica (Fraser) agree that although they have been married to their respective spouses for some time, they still believe in the possibility of romance, and they reprise the song with an updated lyric and a contemporary rock tempo.

"It's Not Where You Start (It's Where You Finish)" is a lavish production number from *Seesaw* (1973) that stopped the show each evening, and the song was the only one from the musical that enjoyed any popularity outside of the theatre. The would-be choreographer David (Tommy Tune) and the dancers performed this old-fashioned cakewalk of a number that viewed life with the sort of silly optimism found in songs of the Depression. It was more than pastiche since the show's lyricist, the prolific Dorothy Fields, had penned several of those kinds of songs in the 1930s. *Seesaw* was her last Broadway show, but her lyric craftsmanship in "It's Not Where You Start" is as youthful and scintillating as her debut in 1928. Cy Coleman composed the contagious music, and Michael Bennett and Tune staged the number with a stage full of multicolored balloons to celebrate the song's optimism. Barbara Cook gave the song a unique interpretation in a 1993 recording.

"It's Raining on Prom Night" is a tongue-in-cheek song from *Grease* (1972) that pastiches teenage torch songs of the 1950s. Sandy (Carole Demas) listens to the mock tearjerker being sung by Kathi Moss on the radio, and she joins in sympathetically as she thinks of losing Danny Zuko. Jim Jacobs and Warren Casey wrote both the music and lyric for the fun number.

"It's Superman" is a surprisingly affectionate tribute to the Man of Steel sung by Lois Lane (Patricia Marand), who secretly loves him in the comic-strip musical *It's a Bird, It's a Plane, It's Superman!* (1966) by Charles Strouse (music) and Lee Adams (lyric). The catchy song is reprised in the second act as various characters await the arrival of or plot to destroy the elusive Superman.

"It's the Going Home Together" is a warm romantic duet from the clever Homeric spoof *The Golden Apple* (1954) by Jerome Moross (music) and John Latouche (lyric). Ulysses (Stephen Douglass) returns home to Angel's Roost, Washington, from the Spanish-American War, and he and his wife Penelope (Priscilla Gillette) sing this graceful song that celebrates domestic bliss.

"It's the Hard-Knock Life" is a dandy, toe-tapping number for the orphan girls in *Annie* (1977) by Charles Strouse (music) and Martin Charnin (lyric). Annie (Andrea McArdle) and her six cohorts (Shelley Bruce, Janine Ruane, Danielle Brisebois, Robyn Finn, Donna Graham and Diana Barrows) sing of their plight as orphans during the Depression and mock the orphanage matron Miss Hannigan with a good deal of energy and good-natured aplomb.

"It's Time for a Love Song" is a lyrical number from the short-lived *Carmelina* (1979) by Alan Jay Lerner (lyric) and Burton Lane (music). Opera singer Cesare Siepi, as Vittorio, the Italian suitor to Carmelina (Georgia Brown), sang the lovely ballad about his long-standing affection for the attractive widow. Michael Feinstein recorded the song in 1991.

"It's Today" is Mame Dennis' lively "I am" song from Jerry Herman's *Mame* (1966), a blindly optimistic number that celebrates the moment. It was sung by Angela Lansbury, as the indomitable aunt of the title, and her guests at one of her frequent parties. The melody is the same as that of an earlier Herman song, "There's No Tune Like a Show Tune," from the Off-Broadway musical *Parade* (1954).

"It's You Who Makes Me Young" is a vivacious but hollow song of celebration by the wealthy Rich (Ted Thurston) in the Tom Jones (lyric) and

Harvey Schmidt (music) allegorical musical *Celebration* (1969). Rich sings and dances the song with the Revelers to the pretty girl Angel (Susan Watson), whom he has covered in diamonds.

"I've Come to Wive It Wealthily in Padua" is Petruchio's "I am" song in the musical version of *The Taming of the Shrew* being performed in Cole Porter's *Kiss Me, Kate* (1948). The first two lines of the song come directly from Shakespeare, and other parts of the lyric reflect back on the original with a clever mix of the Elizabethan and the modern. Alfred Drake sang the number, with the male chorus repeating the title phrase à la Gilbert and Sullivan.

"I've Confessed to the Breeze" is a coy love duet written by Vincent Youmans (music) and Otto Harbach (lyric) for *No, No, Nanette* (1925) but dropped from the score before opening. It was sung by Nanette (Louise Groody) and her beau Tom (Jack Barker), who, in their timidity, tell nature about their love for one another before they have the courage to tell each other. Although the number was cut during the frantic preopening tryouts, "I've Confessed to the Breeze" was added to the long-running London production and was used in the popular 1970 Broadway revival, where it was sung by Susan Watson and Roger Rathburn.

"I've Got a Crush on You" is a Gershwin standard that came from the brothers' short-lived *Treasure Girl* (1928), where it was sung by Clifton Webb, Mary Hay and the ensemble. Since it was too good to disappear forever, the Gershwins put it in *Strike Up the Band* (1930), where it was sung by Gordon Smith and Doris Carson. In both shows George Gershwin's music was played at a quick tempo, and Ira Gershwin's lyric came across as glib and sassy. It wasn't until years later, when Lee Wiley sang the number in a slower, more sincere tempo and the recording became popular that the song emerged as we know it today. Among the many who recorded the number was Frank Sinatra, who had his first popular single with the song.

"I've Got Five Dollars" was a popular Depression song with a sly sense of humor. Richard Rodgers (music) and Lorenz Hart (lyric) wrote it for *America's Sweetheart* (1931), where it was sung by Gus Shy and Harriet Lake (who later changed her name to Ann Sothern). The song is a marriage proposal of sorts in which the boy offers the girl all he's got in the world (which isn't much) as they acidly comment on Depression times.

"I've Got My Captain Working for Me Now" is, in its way, a follow-up to Irving Berlin's earlier "Oh! How I Hate to Get Up in the Morning." In that song an enlisted man dreams of murdering the bugler who plays reveille early each morning. "I've Got My Captain Working for Me Now" is a postwar boast in which a jubilant ex-GI gets his sweet revenge in civilian life. Eddie Cantor introduced the comic song in the *Ziegfeld Follies* (1919).

"I've Got Rings on My Fingers (And Bells on My Toes)" is the flavorful little ditty that was most often associated with Blanche Ring throughout her career. She first sang the Maurice Scott (music), R.P. Weston and F.J. Barnes (lyric) song in *The Midnight Sons* (1909) and it became the hit of the show. Ring recorded the number in 1910, then reprised it in *The Yankee Girl* (1910), *When Claudia Smiles* (1914) and yet again in *Right This Way* (1934). The song is sometimes titled "Mumbo Jumbo Jijiboo J. O'Shea," which begins to make sense when one realizes that the outlandish lyric describes an Irish girl getting married to an Oriental nabob on St.Patrick's Day.

"I've Got to Be Me" is the popular ballad of self-integrity that has been a favorite of lounge singers wherever tuxedos are sold. It was written by Walter Marks for *Golden Rainbow* (1968), where the shiftless hotel owner Larry Davis (Steve Lawrence) sings the soaring plea to be accepted as he is. Of the many recordings made of the ballad, the one by Sammy Davis, Jr., was the most successful.

"I've Got You on My Mind" is a sparkling Cole Porter romantic duet where the lovers exchange a list of each other's shortcomings but are resigned to the fact that they can't shake the mental image of the other. Fred Astaire and Claire Luce sang it in *Gay Divorce* (1932), and Astaire's later recording of the song was very popular.

"I've Got Your Number" is a breezy seduction song and a soft shoe favorite from *Little Me* (1962) by Cy Coleman (music) and Carolyn Leigh (lyric). Belle Poitrine (Virginia Martin) is propositioned by old but agile admirer George Musgrove (Swen Swenson), who then breaks into a slinky mating dance.

"I've Gotta Crow" is the boastful "I am" song that Peter (Mary Martin) sings in *Peter Pan* (1954) when he regains his shadow and feels more than a little proud of himself. Mark Charlap (music) and Carolyn Leigh (lyric) wrote the robust song, which Peter sings with Wendy (Kathy Nolan).

"I've Grown Accustomed to Her Face" is one of the musical theatre's most restrained love songs, a gentle but penetrating ballad sung by Henry Higgins in *My Fair Lady* (1956). Knowing that George Bernard Shaw's Higgins is not a romantic character, Alan Jay Lerner wrote a lyric that reflected the man's dogged approach to love. Frederick Loewe composed the graceful melody, and nonsinger Rex Harrison gave the song a touching interpretation. In the original score, the number includes an eruptive interlude in which Higgins imagines a destitute Eliza who will regret ever having left him, but once his anger is vented, the character returns to the torch song, making it all the more effective. Rosemary Clooney's recording of the number was very popular in 1956.

"I've Just Seen Her" is an expansive ballad from the college musical *All American* (1962) by Charles Strouse (music) and Lee Adams (lyric). Football player Edwin Brickner (Ron Husmann) has just snuck into the women's dorm to see his beloved Susan (Anita Gillette). He realizes with joy that he's seen her for the first time without her makeup on and he loves her all the more.

"I've Never Been in Love Before" is the only outright love song in *Guys and Dolls* (1950), a warm and romantic duet free of the comic cynicism found in most of the Frank Loesser score. Sky Masterson (Robert Alda) and Sarah Brown (Isabel Bigley) confess their love for each other after they have returned to New York City from Havana. The song became very popular, helped by hit recordings by Dick Haymes, Doris Day, Billy Eckstine, Margaret Whiting and others.

"I've Told Ev'ry Little Star" is the simple but absorbing ballad from *Music in the Air* (1932) that became very popular. Jerome Kern (music) and Oscar Hammerstein (lyric) wrote the number as the song that an old Bavarian music teacher writes with the young schoolmaster Karl Reder (Walter Slezak), based on a melody they have heard a bird singing. The timid Karl first sings the affectionate song as part of the Edendorf Choral Society recital. Later Karl and his sweetheart Sieglinde (Katherine Carrington) sing it as a duet when they audition the song for a music publisher in Munich. Hammerstein's lyric is particularly touching, with the singer asking why he's told all of nature and all his friends about his love but he hasn't told her. Kern got the main musical phrase for the song, the story goes, from a bird he heard singing outside his window while visiting Nantucket. The ballad had successful recordings by Eddy Duchin, Irene Dunne and others, and in 1961 Linda Scott made a single that hit the Top Ten. It was also sung by the ensemble in the Broadway revue *Jerome Kern Goes to Hollywood* (1986).

J

"Jealousy Duet" is a vibrant, sarcastic number from *The Threepenny Opera* with music by Kurt Weill and lyric by Bertolt Brecht, adapted and translated by Marc Blitzstein for the long-running 1954 Off-Broadway version. Polly (Jo Sullivan) and Lucy (Beatrice Arthur) both love Macheath (Scott Merrill) and argue over him in front of his jail cell. The mock-opera duet has the two women competing in furious alternating verses, then they break into perfect harmony for the oversentimental refrains. Margery Cohen and Judy Lander sang the stinging number in the Off-Broadway revue *Berlin to Broadway With Kurt Weill* (1972).

"Jeanette and Her Little Wooden Shoes" is a famous wooden-shoe song, written as an excuse for a traditional clog dance, from the operetta *Sweethearts* (1913) by Victor Herbert (music) and Robert B. Smith (lyric). Hazel Kirke, Lionel Walsh, Frank Belcher and Robert O'Connor sang the silly tale of a girl whose loud "clip-clop-clopping" of her shoes could be heard for miles and foiled her plans for a discreet elopement.

"Jet Song" is the inflammatory "I am" song for the gang of "white" street kids in *West Side Story* (1957) by Leonard Bernstein (music) and Stephen Sondheim (lyric). Riff (Mickey Calin) and the Jets sing the boastful song that blends street talk, jazzlike rhythms and modern dance in a manner essential to making the rest of the musical work on stage.

"Jilted" is a mock torch song from the satirical *Of Thee I Sing* (1931) by George Gershwin (music) and Ira Gershwin (lyric). Diana Deveraux (Grace Brinkley) testifies at the Senate impeachment hearings how President John P. Wintergreen broke her heart by not marrying her as he had promised. The Senate joins in sympathetically, proclaiming that the sexy gold digger is now a mere wilted flower due to Wintergreen and vowing to impeach him.

"Joe Worker" is a powerful ballad of social consciousness from the controversial *The Cradle Will Rock* (1937) by Marc Blitzstein. Ella (Blanche Collins) finds out that her brother, who has been hurt in a factory accident, will get no compensation because the company doctor has been paid off to say the worker was drunk at the time. Ella launches into this song asking what it will take for the average Joe to get wise to the situation. The song, along with most of the score, was recorded in 1938, the first full recording in this country of an American musical.

"Joey, Joey, Joey" is the haunting ballad from Frank Loesser's *The Most Happy Fella* (1956) that became popular for its mysterious, enchanting melody and dreamy lyric. Art Lund, as the restless ranch foreman Joe, introduced the number in which Joe sings of the voices that call to him to travel and find his own happiness. The oft-recorded song had its biggest hit with a Peggy Lee single in 1956.

"Johanna" is a beautiful serenade from *Sweeney Todd, the Demon Barber of Fleet Street* (1979) and one of Stephen Sondheim's few outright love songs. When the sailor Anthony Hope (Victor Garber) sees the lovely Johanna (Sarah Rice) on her balcony, he bursts into this intoxicating ballad with straightforward amorous lyric and serenely melodic music. In the second act of the musical, the song becomes a quartet with a new lyric and countermelodies. Anthony wanders the streets of London looking for Johanna, who, imprisoned in an insane asylum, yearns for him in song. At the same time Sweeney Todd (Len Cariou) is casually slitting the throats of his customers as he sings of his daughter Johanna, and the Beggar Woman (Merle Louise) rushes through the neighborhood voicing her suspicions about the strange smoke coming from Mrs. Lovett's pie shop. This complex quartet is one of the oddest and most bewitching of all musical theatre scenes.

"Johnny One-Note" is one of the handful of standards to come out of Rodgers and Hart's *Babes in Arms* (1937), and it is the most vivacious number in the show. Richard Rodgers' music has a great deal of fun sustaining the one note Johnny sings, and Lorenz Hart's lyric bounces along at a furious pace. Wynn Murray introduced the keyed-up number and got help from Douglas Parry, Alfred Drake, the Nicholas Brothers and the chorus of "babes" putting on their big show.

"Johnny's Song" is a delicate ballad by Kurt Weill (music) and Paul Green (lyric) from the antiwar music drama *Johnny Johnson* (1936). The sculptor Johnny (Russell Collins) has gone to war and been wounded, confined to a mental institution, psychoanalyzed and released. He now sells nonmilitary toys in his war-hungry village and sings this disturbing song of innocence, revealing Johnny's undying hope for mankind. The number is also known as "Listen to My Song" and was sung under that title by Hal Watters in the Off-Broadway revue *Berlin to Broadway With Kurt Weill* (1972).

"The Joker" is a jazzy song of despair from the allegorical musical *The Roar of the Greasepaint -- The Smell of the Crowd* (1965) by Leslie Bricusse and Anthony Newley. The have-not Cocky (Newley) has been outsmarted in love by the authoritarian Sir (Cyril Ritchard), so Cocky explodes with this self-mocking tirade about how life needs losers and fools, but no one pays attention to their breaking hearts.

"Jubilation T. Cornpone" is a foot-stomping production number from *Li'l Abner* (1956) sung by Marryin' Sam (Stubby Kaye) and the citizens of Dogpatch about their cowardly founder. Gene de Paul wrote the catchy music, and Johnny Mercer provided the prankish lyric, which, he stated years later, was among his favorites of all his hundreds of songs.

"A Jug of Wine" is a sassy number from *The Day Before Spring* (1945), an early Lerner and Loewe effort. Patricia Marshall sang the droll song in which, taking its cue from the poet, true romance needs only wine, a loaf of bread and "thou, baby!" Frederick Loewe composed the honky-tonk melody, and Alan Jay Lerner wrote the Ira Gershwin-like lyric filled with slang.

"Jump Jim Crow!" is an atypical number from the sentimental operetta classic *Maytime* (1917) by Sigmund Romberg (music) and Rida Johnson Young (lyric). At Mme. Delphine's nightclub, the ensemble sing and dance a shocking new step that is all the rage in "modern" New York City.

"June Is Bustin' Out All Over" is the famous chorus number from *Carousel* (1945) and one of the most recognized songs by Richard Rodgers (music) and Oscar Hammerstein (lyric). The effervescent number celebrates the arrival of summer in New England; it is also a fertile rite of spring as the boys' and girls' choruses compete in singing and dancing. Christine Johnson as Nettie, a sort of Mother Earth character, led the merriment.

"Just a Housewife" is the frantic, touching musical lament from *Working* (1978) in which a woman tries to justify her job of being what society looks on as "just a housewife." The music and lyric are by Craig Carnelia, and it was sung by Susan Bigelow and the women of the ensemble.

"Just a Little Joint With a Jukebox" is a wistful but sly number from the prep-school musical *Best Foot Forward* (1941) by Ralph Blane and Hugh Martin. At Winsocki Prep School, the Blind Date (Nancy Walker) and Hunk Hoyt (Kenneth Bowers) lead the students in this musical tribute to the local watering hole. Walker's performance in *Best Foot Forward* and in this number in particular set her career in motion.

"Just for Today" is a touching eleven o'clock number from the unsuccessful *Her First Roman* (1968), Ervin Drake's musical version of Shaw's *Caesar and Cleopatra*. Cleopatra (Leslie Uggams) sings the dramatic number in which she yearns to return to the innocence of her childhood. Unfortunately for Uggams and the audience, the song was interrupted each evening by the revelation of the body of her hefty servant Ftatateeta, who was hard to miss, and then continued without a chance of recovering itself.

"Just Imagine" is a dreamy ballad from the college musical *Good News!* (1927) and one of the hits to come from a show filled with hits. B.G. DeSylva and Lew Brown (lyric) and Ray Henderson (music) wrote the gentle song of wishful thinking that was sung by Tait College students Shirley Vernon, Mary Lawlor, Ruth Mayon and fellow coeds.

"Just in Time" is the best-selling ballad from *Bells Are Ringing* (1956) by Jule Styne (music) and Betty Comden and Adolph Green (lyric). Jeff Moss (Sydney Chaplin) sang it in a lighthearted song and dance style in Central Park to entertain passersby. Styne's melody is perhaps the simplest he ever wrote, being basically confined to only two notes until the release, but it became one of his most famous songs. Among the many recordings of the ballad was a big seller by Tony Bennett, and a highly unusual version by Barbra Streisand.

"Just One of Those Things" took a while to catch on, but it eventually became a Cole Porter standard, its reference to "gossamer wings" making it perhaps the epitome of Porter sophistication. The song is a free-wheeling farewell to a lover with no regrets and the snappy music keeps away any torch-song sentiment. It was introduced by June Knight and Charles Walters in *Jubilee* (1935), and although the song was published soon after opening night, it did not become popular until the 1940s. "Just One of Those Things" was featured in five films and Ella Fitzgerald and Lena Horne each made distinctive recordings of the number.

"Just One Way to Say I Love You" is a romantic duet from Irving Berlin's *Miss Liberty* (1949). While it never became a standard, it has all the charm and simplicity of his 1920s and 1930s ballads. Unfortunately, the 1949 audiences found it too old-fashioned after the arrival of the Rodgers and

Hammerstein musicals. Eddie Albert, as an American newspaper reporter in Paris, sang it with Allyn McLerie, a French model he believed posed for the Statue of Liberty. Jo Stafford and Perry Como both made moderately popular recordings of the song.

"Just You Wait" is Eliza Doolittle's musical tirade to the offstage Henry Higgins in *My Fair Lady* (1956) by Alan Jay Lerner (lyric) and Frederick Loewe (music). Julie Andrews introduced the impassioned, farcical revenge song in which Eliza imagines her pompous teacher condemned and shot by a royal firing squad. The song is a dazzling example of how Lerner can start with an emotion and develop it into delectable narrative.

"Just You Watch My Step" is the eager anthem of the go-getter college kids in *Leave It to Jane* (1917). Jerome Kern composed the infectious, toe-tapping music, P.G. Wodehouse wrote the zippy lyric, and it was sung by Stub (Oscar Shaw), Louella (Arlene Chase) and the spirited students at Atwater College.

K

"Ka-lu-a" is a pseudo-Hawaiian ballad from *Good Morning, Dearie* (1921) by Jerome Kern (music) and Anne Caldwell (lyric) that was extremely popular in its day and still shows up occasionally. Society dandy Billy Van Courtlandt (Oscar Shaw) and a chorus of girls sang the romantic memory song about a moonlit night in the tropics. Hawaiian songs had been the rage for a few years, and this alluring number was among the most popular, becoming a best-seller in piano rolls and recordings. The title is sometimes listed as "Kailua."

"Kansas City" is cowboy Will Parker's account of life in the big city from Rodgers and Hammerstein's *Oklahoma!* (1943). The song and dance number is a vibrant example of how the new integrated musical worked. Will (Lee Dixon) sings about his recent trip to Kansas City and how they've gone about as far as progress will allow. He then demonstrates some newfangled dance steps he saw in the city. Before long the others are imitating him, and the result is a chorus of cowboys dancing that makes logical sense. Many know the Richard Rodgers (music) and Oscar Hammerstein (lyric) song as "Everything's Up to Date in Kansas City." The number was sung by the company of the Broadway revue *A Grand Night for Singing* (1993).

"Katie Went to Haiti" is a specialty number for Ethel Merman as a nightclub act in Cole Porter's *DuBarry Was a Lady* (1939). The racy narrative ballad tells the story of an American floozie who travels to the Caribbean, where she finds a world of easy living (and easy virtue) and stays. Merman performed the number with a chorus line of girls in native costumes and fruit baskets on their heads, a forerunner to the Hollywood vision of Latin America during the 1940s. The song served as the inspiration for Porter's next musical, *Panama Hattie* (1940).

"Keep Smiling at Trouble" is an Al Jolson standard that he introduced in *Big Boy* (1925) and sang throughout his long career. Lewis E. Gensler wrote the music and B.G. DeSylva and Jolson provided the carefree lyric.

"Kickin' the Clouds Away" is a snappy song that provided a thrilling dance number in *Tell Me More* (1925). Phyllis Cleveland, Esther Howard, Lou Holtz and the female ensemble sang the showstopper, in which Sammy Lee's choreography utilized outrageous acrobatics. George Gershwin wrote the sparkling music, and B.G. DeSylva and Ira Gershwin provided the energetic lyric. An interesting footnote: *Tell Me More* was originally titled *My Fair Lady*, but the producers changed it because it didn't sound commercial enough. Roscoe Lee Browne, as a bootlegging Harlem minister, and the ensemble sang and danced "Kickin' the Clouds Away" in the "new Gershwin musical" *My One and Only* (1983).

"The Kid Inside" is the reflective, truthful opening number from *Is There Life After High School?* (1982) with music and lyric by Craig Carnelia. The ensemble sang the knowing song about the high-school student deep inside each of us who will not allow us to let go of the past.

"Kids" is a comedy song favorite from *Bye Bye Birdie* (1960) by Charles Strouse (music) and Lee Adams (lyric) that expresses the parents' point of view in the youth-oriented musical. Paul Lynde and Marijane Maricle, as the hassled Mr. and Mrs. McAfee, sang the facetious number, which was set to a Charleston-like melody to illustrate just how out of touch these adults were.

"King Herod's Song" is a flamboyant song and dance turn from *Jesus Christ Superstar* (1971) by Andrew Lloyd Webber (music) and Tim Rice (lyric). When Jesus (Jeff Fenholt) is brought before Herod (Paul Ainsley), the latter taunts the "King of the Jews" with this outrageous, honky-tonk number asking for miracles (such as walking across his swimming pool) to prove his claim.

"Kiss Her Now" is the Madwoman's advice to the young Julian in *Dear World* (1969), the musical version of Jean Giraudoux's *The Madwoman of Chaillot*. The fervent ballad by Jerry Herman was sung by Angela Lansbury. The number was also sung by Leslie Uggams and Kirsten Childs in the Broadway revue *Jerry's Girls* (1985).

"A Kiss in the Dark" is the last great Victor Herbert waltz, an enchanting number from *Orange Blossoms* (1922), the last musical produced during the composer's lifetime. Kitty (Edith Day) sings to her godfather (Pat Somerset) about a mysterious but thrilling kiss she received from a stranger one night when she was visiting Deauville. B.G. DeSylva wrote the appealing lyric for the popular waltz which Mario Lanza recorded with success.

"Kiss Me Again" is one of Victor Herbert's most beloved waltzes, a lovely number from the operetta *Mlle. Modiste* (1905) with a lyric by Henry Blossom. Fifi (Fritzi Scheff) works in a hat shop in Paris and goes into an extended musical sequence called "If I Were on the Stage" as an audition for a wealthy American. In one section, to show off her emotional talents, she sings the memorable "Kiss Me Again." In rehearsals Scheff wanted the song cut, claiming it was written too low for her, and producer Charles Dillingham agreed. But Herbert refused, and the song not only became the hit of the operetta but was forever associated with Scheff as she revived the role five times in New York over the next twenty-five years. Carolyn Mignini sang the waltzing number in the Broadway revue *Tintypes* (1980).

"Kiss Me and Kill Me With Love" is a mocking plea for affection from the musical farce *Ankles Aweigh* (1955). Jane Kean and Mark Dawson sang the pseudo-Latin song by Sammy Fain (music) and Dan Shapiro (lyric).

"Kiss of the Spider Woman" is the bewitching title song from the 1993 musical by John Kander (music) and Fred Ebb (lyric). The Spider Woman (Chita Rivera), who is the personification of death, sings about her fatal powers and how sooner or later all men, no matter how successful or secure, will be caught in her web and submit to her deadly kiss. In the dynamic original staging by Harold Prince, the Spider Woman sang the song alone, perched in the midst of a giant web that filled the stage. Because it took so long for *Kiss of the Spider Woman* to reach Broadway, the title song was first heard in New York in the Off-Broadway revue *And the World Goes 'Round* in 1991, where it was sung by Bob Cuccioli.

"The Kiss Waltz" is a delectable number from the operetta *The Pink Lady* (1911) in which the saucy Angele (Alice Dovey) teaches the men of France the true art and science of kissing. Ivan Caryll composed the waltz, and C.M.S. McLellan provided the flippant lyric. The same melody was used later in the operetta with more ardent lyrics and called "My Beautiful Lady."

"Knowing When to Leave" is an engaging musical soliloquy from *Promises, Promises* (1968) by Burt Bacharach (music) and Hal David (lyric). Fran Kubelik (Jill O'Hara), stuck in an affair with a married man, debates her position and the possibility of finding new love.

"K-ra-zy for You" is a jazzy love song from the Gershwins' short-lived *Treasure Girl* (1928). Clifton Webb, Mary Hay and the ensemble sang and danced the sleek number by George Gershwin (music) and Ira Gershwin (lyric). The song resurfaced sixty-four years later when it inspired the title for the "new Gershwin musical comedy" *Crazy for You* (1992) and was sung in the new show by the would-be hoofer Bobby Child (Harry Groener).

L

"The Ladies Who Lunch" is probably the most sardonic number ever to become an eleven o'clock showstopper. Stephen Sondheim wrote the stinging solo for *Company* (1970), where the hard-boiled Joanne (Elaine Stritch) sang it as a contemporary sort of saloon song. At a Manhattan restaurant Joanne gets a bit drunk and verbally assaults the upper-middle-class lifestyle, in particular the affluent women who try to bring meaning to their dreary lives. She sarcastically toasts the different types and ends up including those like herself who drink too much in order to compensate for unfulfilled lives. The song is unusual in its structure: a series of refrains that build in volume, intensity and bitterness until the number climaxes in an ugly cry of despair. Stritch's performance was riveting, and a Sondheim lyric has never been more devastating.

"The Lady Is a Tramp" is a song so purely Rodgers and Hart that it is difficult to imagine any other team getting away with it. Richard Rodgers' music is free and rolling, like the character who sings it, and Lorenz Hart's lyric sparkles with abandon: a delectable song about Hobohemia that has not lost any of its verve over the years. The song, first sung by Mitzi Green in *Babes in Arms* (1937), was one of several standards to come out of the show. Lena Horne, Ella Fitzgerald and Diana Ross are among those who recorded "The Lady Is a Tramp" and Buddy Greco and His Orchestra made an instrumental recording of it in 1961 that sold over a million copies.

"Lady of the Evening" is a graceful Irving Berlin ballad not very well known today, but it was very popular after its introduction in the second edition of the *Music Box Revue* (1922). Irish tenor John Steele sang the haunting song, which uses a unique simile in its lyric (one's cares are folded up and steal away at night like nomadic Arabs) and an elegant melody that has an Oriental flavor in the verse. The song was not, as its title might imply, about prostitution; Steele sang it in a romantic setting with moonlit roofs behind him.

"The Lambeth Walk" is the show-stopping dance number that had been a favorite of British audiences for fifty years before Broadway got to join in the fun. The song was written by Noel Gay (music) and Douglas Furber (lyric) for the 1937 London musical *Me and My Girl*, in which the song and dance comic Lupino Lane, as the pugnacious Cockney Bill Snibson, led all the bluebloods in the high-strutting number. The musical was never seen in New York until the 1986 revised edition, in which Robert Lindsay played Bill and "The Lambeth Walk" was the song of the year. Director Mike Ockrent and choreographer Gillian Gregory staged the number in music-hall style, with the cast dancing in the aisles and the audience encouraged to sing along.

"The Land of My Own Romance" is one of Victor Herbert's finest love songs, a luscious solo for the title character in *The Enchantress* (1911). On her first entrance, the opera singer and mystic Vivien Savary (Kitty Gordon) sings this waltzing number as a sort of "I am" song. Harry B. Smith wrote the lyric for Herbert's captivating music. Opera singer Beverly Sills made a memorable recording of the song which is sometimes titled "In the Land of My Own Romance."

"Larger Than Life" is an engrossing "I am" song for the young TV writer Benjy Stone (Evan Pappas) in *My Favorite Year* (1992). Benjy recalls growing up feeling abandoned when his father ran off, but he always found excitement at the RKO movie palace. His favorite film star was the swashbuckling Alan Swann (Tim Curry), who is now going to be a guest on the TV show Benjy writes for. Stephen Flaherty composed the thrilling music, and Lynn Ahrens wrote the perceptive, evocative lyric.

"The Last Night of the World" is the jazzy, romantic duet for the lovers Kim (Lea Salonga) and Chris (Willy Falk) in the British import *Miss Saigon* (1991). With the final days of the American occupation of Saigon at hand, Chris and Kim passionately sing to the sound of a solo saxophone and love each other as if the world were to end tomorrow. Claude-Michel Schönberg wrote the emotional music, and Richard Maltby, Jr., adapted the original French lyric by Alain Boublil.

"The Last Round-Up" is one of the few popular Western songs to come from Broadway. Billy Hill wrote the cowpoke ballad and it was interpolated into the *Ziegfeld Follies* (1934), where Don Ross sang it and then Willy Howard did a hilarious reprise of it in a Yiddish dialect. The number had been heard previously at the Paramount Theatre, where Joe Morrison sang it, and later had a hit recording with the George Olson Orchestra. The song was one of Bing Crosby's earliest hits, and it was also successful for Rudy Vallee, Arthur Tracy, Richard Himber and Conrad Thibault. Roy Rodgers made the biggest hit recording of "The Last Round-Up" and it launched his career.

"Lazy Afternoon" is a languid, seductive song from *The Golden Apple* (1954) that brought Kaye Ballard to the attention of critics and audiences alike. Helen (Ballard), the sultry farmer's daughter, gets an eyeful of the handsome traveling salesman Paris (Jonathan Lucas) and sings this bluesy ode to a hot summer's day as she undresses him with her eyes and hands. John Latouche wrote the provocative lyric, and Jerome Moross composed the beguiling music, whose melodic line lazily spirals downward in a tantalizing way. The ballad became very popular even though *The Golden Apple* had a disappointingly short run. Sarah Vaughan and Vic Damone are among the many who recorded it.

"Leaning on a Lamp Post" is an appealing character song from the British import *Me and My Girl* (1986), the new edition of the 1937 London hit that had never been produced on Broadway before. Cockney-born Bill Snibson (Robert Lindsay) has inherited a fortune but is losing his Lambeth girlfriend Sally (Maryann Plunkett) in the process so he stands outside her house and leans on a lamp post, singing and hoping she'll come by. Noel Gay wrote the breezy music and lyric.

"Learn to Be Lonely" is an absorbing soliloquy from the short-lived *A Doll's Life* (1982), the musical sequel to Henrik Ibsen's *A Doll's House*. Having left her husband only to find herself caught in the affections of another man, Nora (Betsy Joslyn) sings this provocative song about learning to live independently even if it means living in loneliness. Larry Grossman (music) and Betty Comden and Adolph Green (lyric) wrote the knowing number.

"Leave de Atom Alone" is a political song from *Jamaica* (1957) that was decades ahead of its time. The native woman Ginger (Josephine Premice) and some fellow islanders sing the comic song that traces man's foolishness from Adam in the Garden of Eden up to the hydrogen bomb. They warn that this latest folly could be the greatest of all and advise to leave nature as it is. Harold Arlen composed the calypsolike music, and E.Y. Harburg wrote the succinct lyric that, in his unique style, spoke of catastrophic things in comic terms.

"Leave It to Jane" is the catchy title song from the 1917 college musical by Jerome Kern (music) and P.G. Wodehouse (lyric). When the students at Atwater College have a dilemma, they turn to the president's daughter Jane (Edith Hallor), who leads the ensemble in this merry number. The song is particularly contagious because of the simple 4/4 time that has a subtle syncopation in its melody and countermelody.

"Leave It to the Girls" is a jocular comic number from the musical sequel *Annie Warbucks* (1993) by Charles Strouse (music) and Martin Charnin (lyric) demonstrating that when real evil must be done, one can only depend on females. Commissioner Harriet Doyle (Arlene Robertson) and her ex-con daughter Florence (Donna McKechnie) sing the farcical song as they plan to bump off billionaire Daddy Warbucks and his adopted daughter Annie.

"Leavin's Not the Only Way to Go" is an engaging trio in the country-western style from *Big River* (1985), the *Huckleberry Finn* musical by Roger Miller. Huck (Daniel H. Jenkins), the runaway slave Jim (Ron Richardson) and Mary Jane Wilkes (Patti Cohenour), each in his or her own thoughts, sing this tender farewell song in unison.

"Left All Alone Again Blues" is the catchy hit song from Jerome Kern's *The Night Boat* (1920) that was very modern in its harmonies and even suggested a jazz flavor at times. As performed in the show, Stella Hoban sang the song while the ensemble sang a countertune, an old lilting number called "The Blue Bells of Scotland." Anne Caldwell wrote the new lyric, and Marion Harris recorded "Left All Alone Again Blues" even before the show opened in New York.

"Legalize My Name" is a breezy comic song from *St. Louis Woman* (1946) that Pearl Bailey stopped the show with each evening. The barmaid Butterfly (Bailey) has been wooed by an amorous jockey (Fayard Nicholas), but she's holding back until he offers marriage. Harold Arlen wrote the smooth, easy-going music that is offset by Johnny Mercer's funny lyric. Gertrude Niesen made a popular recording of the number.

"Let Me Entertain You" is a simple little tap number that is used throughout *Gypsy* (1959) to give unity to the episodic story of Gypsy Rose Lee. Under the title "May We Entertain You" it is used as the audition song for Baby June (Jacqueline Mayro) and little Louise (Karen Moore). Later June sings "Let Me Entertain You" as part of her vaudeville act. Near the end of the play, grown-up Louise (Sandra Church) reprises the song as her striptease number that raises her through the ranks of burlesque to the big time. Jule Styne composed the pleasurable music, and Stephen Sondheim wrote the flexible lyric that was sweetly appropriate for a kids' song and slyly suggestive as a stripper's invitation.

"Let the Sunshine In" is the stirring finale for *Hair* (1968), the "tribal love-rock musical" by Galt MacDermot (music) and Gerome Ragni and James Rado (lyric). The number was called "The Flesh Failures" on Broadway and was sung by Claude (Rado), Sheila (Lynn Kellogg), Dionne (Melba Moore) and the company. Due mainly to the best-selling recording by the Fifth Dimension, the song is now known as "Let the Sunshine In."

"Let's Be Buddies" is that rare thing in a Cole Porter show: a sweet, sentimental song with no cynical undercurrent. The show was *Panama Hattie* (1940), in which Ethel Merman, as bar girl Hattie Maloney, loves Philadelphia millionaire Nick Bullett (James Dunn) but must win the affections of his little girl (Joan Carroll) by a previous marriage. Merman and Carroll finally hit it off and stopped the show with the charming "Let's Be Buddies." Because Carroll was only eight years old and labor laws prohibited her from singing or dancing on a professional stage, she had to talk-sing her part of the duet.

"Let's Do It (Let's Fall in Love)," one of Cole Porter's earliest list songs and one of his best, is a prime example of his ability to stay just one step ahead of the censors. (The parenthetical part of the title allowed radio stations to air the song without difficulty.) The song was a last-minute replacement for the similar "Let's Misbehave" in *Paris* (1928), Porter's first success, where it was sung by Irene Bordoni and Arthur Margetson. "Let's Do It" catalogues over thirty members of the animal kingdom as well as humans from Siam to Boston, and it is the playful rhyming of the names that distinguishes the song.

"Let's Fly Away" is a sportive duet from Cole Porter's *The New Yorkers* (1930) that is the flip side of his "Take Me Back to Manhattan" from the same show. Charles King and Hope Williams introduced this musical plea to escape the city and return to nature. Just as famous as the song itself is Noël Coward's parody, which was published and performed with Porter's good-natured approval.

"Let's Go Back to the Waltz" is the musical suggestion Nanette Fabray made in Irving Berlin's unsuccessful *Mr. President* (1962). As the First Lady, she interrupts a White House ball where the newfangled twist is being danced; the much-longed-for waltz takes over, and Berlin is on familiar ground again. But as the First Lady exits, the twist resumes, and it sounded the swan song for America's most popular songwriter. *Mr. President* was Berlin's last Broadway show.

"Let's Have Another Cup of Coffee," one of the most famous of the sprightly optimistic Depression theme songs, was written by Irving Berlin as a satirical number for *Face the Music* (1932). Katherine Carrington and J. Harold Murray, as formerly wealthy socialites, sang the cheery song as they dined at the Automat with the hoi polloi. Enric Madriguera and his Hotel Baltimore Orchestra had a hit record with the number and years later Michael Feinstein made a fine recording of it.

"Let's Misbehave" is a Cole Porter song that leaves little room for an innocent interpretation, which is probably why it was dropped from *Paris* (1928) and replaced with the more ambiguous "Let's Do It (Let's Fall in Love)." "Let's Misbehave" was published the year before *Paris* opened and was performed in the Paris cafe La Revue des Ambassadeurs, where Irving Aaronson and His Commanders played it and later recorded it.

"Let's Not Talk About Love" is a comic list song by Cole Porter that allowed Danny Kaye to rattle off multi-syllabic sciences in the manner that he had recited Russian composers in "Tschaikowsky." In *Let's Face It* (1941) Eve Arden sang that she wanted to discuss romance, to which Kaye replied with a list of all the things he'd rather talk about. Kaye's recording of the song was very popular.

"Let's Not Waste a Moment" is the musical plea of a middle-aged tourist in Israel to the American widow whom he loves in *Milk and Honey* (1961). Jerry Herman wrote the heartfelt ballad, and it was sung by former opera star Robert Weede.

"Let's See What Happens" is a simple and tender waltz from the short-lived *Darling of the Day* (1968) by Jule Styne (music) and E.Y. Harburg (lyric). The working-class widow Alice Chalice (Patricia Routledge) meets Priam Farll (Vincent Price), a famous artist disguised as a butler, and she sings this cautious but optimistic ballad about the possibility of love.

"Let's Take a Walk Around the Block" is a gentle soft-shoe number from the revue *Life Begins at 8:40* (1934) by Harold Arlen (music) and Ira Gershwin and E.Y. Harburg (lyric). Two impoverished New Yorkers in love (Earl Oxford and Dixie Dunbar) dream of all the exotic places they'll travel to but, in the meantime, are content to take a Manhattan stroll. Arlen's music is quiet and melodic, and the Gershwin-Harburg lyric builds beautifully to a warm and comic climax in each refrain.

"Let's Take an Old-Fashioned Walk" is the only song from Irving Berlin's *Miss Liberty* (1949) to become a hit, a pleasant nostalgic number sung by an American newspaper man (Eddie Albert) who woos a French model (Allyn McLerie) on the sidewalks of Paris. Berlin's lyrics were indeed old-fashioned, but the charming melody made the number popular. Perry Como, Frank Sinatra and Doris Day all had recordings of the song on the charts.

"Liaisons" is a droll soliloquy from *A Little Night Music* (1973) by Stephen Sondheim that Hermione Gingold sang with her customary disapproving style. The aged courtesan Madame Armfeldt (Gingold) tries to recall her famous lovers from the past but keeps getting sidetracked by her own commentary on the sad state of love and love affairs today.

"Lida Rose" is an engaging barbershop quartet pastiche number from Meredith Willson's *The Music Man* (1957) that is so authentic-sounding that many assumed it was a genuine example from the musical's 1912 period. The lilting song was harmonized by the four town aldermen, played by the celebrated quartet the Buffalo Bills (Bill Spangenberg, Al Shea, Wayne Ward and Vern Reed). They then reprised the song with the wistful ballad "Will I Ever Tell You?" sung by Marian Paroo (Barbara Cook), the two songs blending contrapuntally.

"Life Is" is the robust opening number for *Zorbá* (1968) in which the Chorus Leader (Lorraine Serabian) and the members of a bouzouki circle each contribute their opinions as to the meaning of life. Finally the Leader steps forward and proclaims that life is what you do while you're waiting to die, and that leads into the story of Zorbá the Greek. John Kander (music) and Fred Ebb (lyric) wrote the festive number that, like much of the show's score, was very atypical of their usual Broadway work.

"Life Is Happiness Indeed" is a "new" song for the 1974 revival of *Candide* that uses two Leonard Bernstein melodies from the original's "Gavotte." Stephen Sondheim wrote a new lyric for the contrapuntal number that introduced the four main characters of the satiric epic. Candide (Mark Baker) and Cunegonde (Maureen Brennan) sing their lyrical "I am" songs while Maximilian (Sam Freed) introduces himself with a contrasting melody. Then Paquette (Deborah St. Dare) joins in, making for a delicious comic quartet in gavotte tempo.

"Life Is Just a Bowl of Cherries" is one of the most famous of the many chins-up Depression antidotes that came out of Broadway during the 1930s. This one was written by Lew Brown (lyric) and Ray Henderson (music) for the 1931 edition of *George White's Scandals*. Ethel Merman, who had gained recognition in *Girl Crazy* the year before, was rushed into the George White revue right before opening and stopped the show with her brassy rendition of the new hit number. Bing Crosby, Rudy Vallee and Merman herself all made successful recordings of the number, which became the theme song for the "Maxwell House Show Boat" radio program.

"The Life of the Party" is a merry sing-along number from *The Happy Time* (1968) sung and danced by David Wayne, as the prankish Grandpere Bonnard, in a red top hat recalling his romantic and social conquests of the past. John Kander (music) and Fred Ebb (lyric) wrote the zippy song, and Wayne stopped the show each night performing it.

"Life Story" is a penetrating musical soliloquy sung by a woman who looks back on her life and her mistakes and questions them both, all the while assuring us that she's not complaining. David Shire (music) and Richard Maltby, Jr., (lyric) wrote the provocative song, and it was sung by Lynne Wintersteller in the Off-Broadway revue *Closer Than Ever* (1989).

"Life Upon the Wicked Stage" is a sparkling comic song from *Show Boat* (1927) in which the showgirl Ellie (Eva Puck) and the chorus girls mockingly lament the rigors of show business. The lilting melody by Jerome Kern and the shrewd lyric by Oscar Hammerstein recall the sassy musical comedy numbers from the Princess Theatre shows a decade earlier. Of particular interest is the song's frothy lyric filled with clever rhyming, something Hammerstein usually eschewed in his work. Janet Pavek made a sly recording of the song in 1956, and Paige O'Hara sang it in John McGlinn's comprehensive recording of *Show Boat* in 1988.

"Life's a Funny Proposition After All" is an engaging, atypical George M. Cohan song from *Little Johnny Jones* (1904) that is more reflective than exclamatory. While the American jockey Johnny Jones (Cohan) is on the chase through San Francisco's Chinatown to rescue his beloved Goldie Gates (Ethel Levey), he stops for a moment to contemplate the ironies of life. Cohan quietly talk-sang the number with a lyric that is more rambling and cerebral than his usual short-phrased proclamations. Cohan recorded the number in 1911, one of his rare ventures into a recording studio.

"Light Sings" is a stirring song from *The Me Nobody Knows* (1970), a revue based on the writings of ghetto school kids in New York City. Devin Lindsay led the ensemble in this enticing number by Gary William Friedman (music) and Will Holt (lyric).

"Like Him" is an intriguing character duet from *The Tap Dance Kid* (1983) by Henry Krieger (music) and Robert Lorick (lyric). The overweight teenager Emma (Martine Allard) and her mother (Hattie Winston) argue in song about the sibling rivalry Emma has toward her younger brother Willie, trying to sort out the difference between liking someone and loving them.

"Like It Was" is a wistful ballad from the short-lived *Merrily We Roll Along* (1981) by Stephen Sondheim. Mary (Ann Morrison), a jaded alcoholic author, longs for the old days when her friendship with Charley (Lonny Price) and her unrequited love for Frank (Jim Walton) made her life worth living. Julie Andrews sang the poignant number in the Off-Broadway revue *Putting It Together* (1993).

"Lily's Eyes" is an enthralling duet from *The Secret Garden* (1991) by Lucy Simon (music) and Marsha Norman (lyric). Archibald Craven (Mandy Patinkin) and his brother Neville (Robert Westenberg) both notice that the orphan niece Mary Lennox (Daisy Eagan) has the same hazel eyes as Archibald's deceased wife Lily. In the sweeping operatic duet Archibald recalls Lily, while Neville reveals the unrequited love he had for her as well.

"Limehouse Blues" is the hit song from *Andre Charlot's Revue of 1924*, a British import that introduced Gertrude Lawrence to Broadway. She sang the alluring number about life in London's Chinatown district, and it became her signature song for a while. Philip Braham wrote the bewitching music, and Douglas Furber provided the exotic lyric.

"Lionnet" is a poignant aria from the operatic *Regina* (1949), Marc Blitzstein's musicalization of Lillian Hellman's drama *The Little Foxes*. The fading Southern belle Birdie (Brenda Lewis) sings of her youth and growing up on the family plantation called Lionnet, then looks at how pathetic her life is now. The number is sometimes listed as "Birdie's Aria."

"Listen to the Music" is an intoxicating pastiche number from the Off-Broadway musical *Hello Again* (1994) that captures the sound of 1912, the time period for this song. On the deck of the *Titanic*, the Husband (Dennis Parlato) seduces the Young Thing (John Cameron Mitchell) and insists they listen to the band play rather than to the screams of the passengers who realize the ship is sinking. Michael John LaChiusa wrote the engrossing music and lyric.

"Listen to the Rain on the Roof" is a tingling rhythm number from *Follies* (1971) that cheerfully pastiches the naive, optimistic theatre songs of the 1920s. The playful number is performed by the old dancing partners Emily and Theodore Whitman (Marcie Stringer and Charles Welch) at a Follies reunion. The sprightly music and lyric were written by Stephen Sondheim.

"A Little Bit in Love" is a languorously smooth ballad from *Wonderful Town* (1953) by Leonard Bernstein (music) and Betty Comden and Adolph Green (lyric). Edith Adams, as the overpopular Eileen, introduced the song, and Julie Andrews was among those who later recorded it.

"A Little Brains -- A Little Talent" is the supple "I am" song for Lola (Gwen Verdon), the devil's sexy helper in *Damn Yankees* (1955). Mr. Applegate (Ray Walston) has summoned Lola to seduce baseballer Joe Hardy, but warns her that it will not be an easy job. Lola responds in song, boasting of her many past conquests over the centuries. Richard Adler and Jerry Ross wrote the rhythmic music and witty lyric, made up almost completely of internal rhymes. The number was a last minute addition to the score, put in during the out-of-town tryouts. Verdon had so little rehearsal with the song and was so nervous about it that the stage manager had to whisper the lyric to her from behind a curtain.

"Little Do They Know" is a funny chorus number that reveals a different side of show business. In the Liza Minnelli vehicle *The Act* (1977), Gayle Crofoot, Roger Minami and the other disgruntled dancers sing what it is like having to support a big star in a show. John Kander wrote the nimble music, and Fred Ebb provided the satiric lyric.

"Little Girl Blue" is a simple, evocative Rodgers and Hart ballad that is intoxicating all the same. Lorenz Hart builds his lyric easily and smoothly, but the effect is powerful: count on your fingers, count the raindrops, don't count on love. Richard Rodgers' melody sticks to a narrow range, returning to a haunting three-note combination, and then he moves into a circuslike waltz in the patter section. The song came from a circus of sorts: Billy Rose's mammoth musical extravaganza *Jumbo* (1935), where it was sung at the end of the first act by Gloria Grafton in a blue-lit dream sequence where she imagines she is a child again being entertained by a circus. Mabel Mercer recorded the song and sang it for several years in her nightclub act. Margaret Whiting and Ella Fitzgerald made memorable recordings of "Little Girl Blue" and, more recently, Carly Simon and Linda Ronstadt recorded lovely versions.

"A Little Girl From Little Rock" is the crafty "I am" song for gold digger Lorelei Lee (Carol Channing) in *Gentlemen Prefer Blondes* (1949) by Jule Styne (music) and Leo Robin (lyric). In the comic number, Lorelei tells of her rise from a simple Arkansas girl to a woman of the world. Channing repeated her sly rendition of the song in the 1974 revised version of the musical called *Lorelei*. Among those who recorded the song were Ethel Merman and Dorothy Shay, the "Park Avenue hillbilly."

"Little Girls" is the farcical "I am" song for Miss Hannigan, the matron of the Municipal Orphanage, in *Annie* (1977). Charles Strouse wrote the jazzy music, Martin Charnin provided the slapstick lyric that listed the ways girl orphans have driven her nuts, and Dorothy Loudon sang it as a maniacal tour de force that ranged from mock opera to bump and grind.

"Little Green Snake" is a seriocomic song about alcoholism from the period musical *Take Me Along* (1959) by Bob Merrill. The boozing Uncle Sid (Jackie Gleason) uses vivid images to describe the consequences of his drinking, the result being a comic showcase for Gleason with a very sober subtext.

"Little Hands" is a touching duet from the short-lived *Anya* (1965), the musical about the Russian princess Anastasia using musical themes by Sergei Rachmaninoff. When Anya (Constance Towers) convinces the Dowager Empress (Lillian Gish) that she is indeed the surviving princess, they sing this song from childhood. Actually, Gish, in her only musical, talked the lyric while Towers harmonized. Robert Wright and George Forrest wrote the tender lyric and adapted Rachmaninoff's "Vocalise."

"Little Jazz Bird" is a breezy narrative song from *Lady, Be Good!* (1924) that tells the tale of a songbird who accidentally flew into a jazz club one day, and from that time on all he wanted to sing was syncopated blues. Cliff "Ukelele Ike" Edwards sang the tuneful George Gershwin (music) and Ira Gershwin (lyric) number. The song was included in the all-Gershwin score for *My One and Only* (1983), where it was sung by Tommy Tune and Twiggy; the number was cut before opening but retained on the original cast recording.

"Little Lamb" is a tender character song for the neglected Louise (Sandra Church) in *Gypsy* (1959) by Jule Styne (music) and Stephen Sondheim (lyric). On Louise's birthday she quietly gathers her humble gifts and sings to them with understanding; like her they seem sad and confused. The piquant song was cut by director Jerome Robbins during rehearsals because he felt it was slowing down the show. "Little Lamb" was restored to the score only after the authors brought the songwriters' union in and threatened legal action.

"A Little More Mascara" is the insightful "I am" song for the flamboyant female impersonator Albin (George Hearn) in Jerry Herman's *La Cage aux Folles* (1983). As he puts on his makeup for a performance, the depressed Albin gets his old confidence back, arguing that all one needs is a little glamour to face the world.

"Little Old New York (Is Good Enough for Me)" is a snappy tribute to Manhattan from *Tenderloin* (1960) by Jerry Bock (music) and Sheldon Harnick (lyric). The frolicsome number was sung by Eileen Rodgers, Lee Becker and the low-life citizens of the Tenderloin district, who warn the muckraking Reverend Brock (Maurice Evans) to keep his hands off their city. At the end of the show Brock moves his campaign to Michigan, where the rabble reprises the song as "Little Old Detroit."

"A Little Priest" is the hilarious, off-color duet about the intricacies of cannibalism that closes the first act of *Sweeney Todd, the Demon Barber of Fleet Street* (1979). Once Sweeney Todd (Len Cariou) decides to go on a murdering spree, the pragmatic Mrs. Lovett (Angela Lansbury) suggests there might be a practical use for all the bodies. More than just a sick joke, the unique song is the comic manifestation of the dog-eat-dog mentality of the gruesome tale. Stephen Sondheim wrote the clever list song in which Todd and Lovett pretend to sample different items on the menu covering a multitude of occupations from priest to greengrocer. The music, in lilting waltz time, is quirky and harsh at times, and the lyric is in the style of a lowly music-hall turn filled with outrageous rhymes and puns. In the Off-Broadway revue *Putting It Together* (1993) the song was sung by the five-member cast.

"Little Rag Doll" is a delicate song of lament from the Off-Broadway *Man With a Load of Mischief* (1966) by John Clifton (music and lyric) and Ben Tarver (lyric). At a nineteenth-century wayside inn, a Maid (Alice Cannon) has enjoyed a one-night dalliance with a Lord (Raymond Thorne) who drops her the next morning. She sings this touching song, longing for the simple things in life and wondering whatever happened to her little rag doll she had as a child.

"Little Red Hat" is a raucous comic duet from *110 in the Shade* (1963) by Tom Jones (lyric) and Harvey Schmidt (music). Jimmie Curry (Scooter Teague) and Snookie (Lesley Warren) sing this rural but racy number about their date together and how he managed to win her treasured little red hat away from her.

"The Little Things You Do Together" is a caustic number about marital discord that is used as commentary on the plot in the concept musical *Company* (1970). Stephen Sondheim wrote the sardonic number in which Joanne (Elaine Stritch) and other members of the cast make scathing comments on marriage's little foibles, although they wryly include divorce and child rearing among the trivial "little things." Julia McKenzie and David Kernan sang the number in the Broadway revue *Side by Side by Sondheim* (1977).

"Little Tin Box" is arguably the finest comedy song in the whole Jerry Bock (music) and Sheldon Harnick (lyric) repertoire. This hilarious number from *Fiorello!* (1959) is about the famous Seabury Hearings in which corrupt New York City officials were exposed. Ben Mario (Howard Da Silva) and his political hacks act out how the Tammany crooks will defend themselves, claiming they gave up streetcars, returned empty bottles and passed up lunches to build up their nest eggs at home in a little tin box. The music has a folksy, barbershop style to it and a soft-shoe tempo that makes the outrageously naive arguments all the funnier. The song was a last-minute addition to the score and stopped the show each night.

"The Little White House (At the End of Honeymoon Lane)" is one of the many theatre songs from the 1920s in which the young lovers extol the simple life of domestic bliss they hope to achieve. This "love nest" song was written by James F. Hanley (music) and Eddie Dowling (lyric) for *Honeymoon Lane* (1926), where Dowling himself sang it. Popular recordings were made by Frank Munn, Johnny Marvin and Fred Warings' Pennsylvanians.

"Live, Laugh, Love" is a relaxed, debonair pastiche song from *Follies* (1971) that eventually explodes into the chaotic climax of the musical. Stephen Sondheim wrote the breezy, Fred Astaire-like number for the Loveland fantasy sequence of the show, and it is sung by millionaire Ben Stone (John McMartin) dressed in white top hat and tails and backed by a white-tuxedoed chorus line. While the lyric claims that life is easy and a lighthearted approach to love is all that is necessary, there is dissonance in the music that suggests that Ben is lying to himself. Soon he forgets his lines and, as the chorus continues with the false lyric, Ben falls apart. The number ends in total musical and verbal confusion as the past and present collide and all the characters' illusions are destroyed.

"Liza" is a tantalizing Gershwin song from the Florenz Ziegfeld extravaganza *Show Girl* (1929). Ruby Keeler sang and tapped the song as a minstrel number with Nick Lucas and one hundred girls perched on the requisite Ziegfeld staircase as Duke Ellington's Orchestra played. On opening night Al Jolson stood up in the audience and sang the song to his new bride Keeler and made the George Gershwin (music) and Ira Gershwin and Gus Kahn (lyric) ballad famous. The song is sometimes titled "All the Clouds'll Roll Away." "Liza" remained one of George Gershwin's favorite pieces for the rest of his too-short life.

"Loads of Love" is the heroine's jazzy "I am" song in *No Strings* (1962) with both music and lyric by Richard Rodgers. Diahann Carroll, as fashion model Barbara Woodruff, sang the cynical, self-aware number that recalled Rodgers' work with Lorenz Hart.

"London Is a Little Bit of All Right" is a music-hall turn from *The Girl Who Came to Supper* (1963) by Noël Coward. The vibrant cockney Ada Cockle (Tessie O'Shea) led King Nicholas III of Carpathia (Sean Scully) and the ensemble in this festive tribute to her home town.

"The Lonely Goatherd" is an energetic pastiche song Richard Rodgers (music) and Oscar Hammerstein (lyric) wrote for *The Sound of Music* (1959), creating a yodeling alpine ditty that was also pure Broadway. In the stage version, Maria (Mary Martin) sings the frolicsome narrative to the seven Von Trapp children late at night in order to take their minds off the thunderstorm raging outside.

"Lonely Heart" is a charming ballad that Irving Berlin wrote for the popular revue *As Thousands Cheer* (1933), which used the format of a newspaper to cue its songs and sketches. This number was in the letters-to-the-lovelorn section of the paper, and Franklin Munn sang the song as a letter writer seeking advice for the heartbroken.

"Lonely House" is a penetrating song of loneliness from the urban opera *Street Scene* (1947). The student Sam Kaplan (Brian Sullivan) may live in a crowded apartment building filled with the noise of neighbors, but he is as forlorn as a man in dismal solitude. Langston Hughes wrote the provocative lyric, and Kurt Weill composed the melancholy music that blends Broadway blues and opera arioso. The lament was also sung by Hal Watters in the Off-Broadway revue *Berlin to Broadway With Kurt Weill* (1972).

"Lonely Room" is a lesser-known song from *Oklahoma!* (1943) and one that is too often dropped in revivals of the show, but it is Jud Fry's principal character number and one that adds a dark and painful quality to the musical. Richard Rodgers (music) and Oscar Hammerstein (lyric) felt that the moody Jud (Howard Da Silva) ought not to be a stereotypic villain, so they wrote this unsettling soliloquy for him to sing once he is left alone in his room in the smokehouse. In the number Jud mocks his life and his own ugliness but ends up more determined than ever to take Laurey to the box social. The song does not diminish Jud's wickedness, but it makes him seem all the more combustible. The operatic aria uses a great deal of dissonance and a series of lowering chords to create the appropriate creepiness and sense of danger.

"Lonely Town" is a mournful ballad from the otherwise jubilant *On the Town* (1944), filled with a lovely and longer-than-traditional melodic strain in the music by Leonard Bernstein and a beguiling lyric by Betty Comden and Adolph Green. John Battles, as the sailor Gabey looking for love in New York City, sang the endearing song, which led into an extended dance sequence devised by Jerome Robbins. Mary Martin, Frank Sinatra and Mel Tormé were among the artists who recorded the song.

"Long Before I Knew You" is a haunting love song from *Bells Are Ringing* (1956) that embraces the idea of déjà vu, just as Rodgers and Hart's "Where or When" had decades earlier. Playwright Jeff Moss (Sydney Chaplin) and telephone operator Ella Peterson (Judy Holliday) sing the ballad about their love that existed even before they met. Ironically, Jeff doesn't know that Ella is the operator he often speaks with, so he actually did know her before he met her. Jule Styne wrote the alluring music, and Betty Comden and Adolph Green provided the appealing lyric.

"Look at Me, I'm Sandra Dee" is an acrid comic number from *Grease* (1972) by Jim Jacobs and Warren Casey in which Betty Rizzo (Adrienne Barbeau) makes fun of virginal Sandy Dumbrowski in order to get Danny Zuko to take her to the dance. Later in the show Sandy (Carole Demas) reprises the song with a different lyric as she decides to change her image. The lyric for the song refers to such period personalities as Doris Day, Sal Mineo, Troy Donahue, Rock Hudson and Annette Funicello as well as Sandra Dee.

"Look at That Face" is a beguiling number from the allegorical musical *The Roar of the Greasepaint -- The Smell of the Crowd* (1965) that is sung as a song of affection and then one of derision. To encourage the lowly Cocky (Anthony Newley) to keep playing "the game," Sir (Cyril Ritchard) praises the fellow's facial features for their uniqueness and charm. Then the urchins, led by Sally Smith, sing about Cocky's foolish and homely face and put him back in his place. Leslie Bricusse and Newley wrote the catchy song, which was somewhat popular and recorded, though usually with the more flattering lyric.

"Look for a Sky of Blue" is a pastiche of the famous "Look for the Silver Lining" and other optimistic songs of the 1920s from the Off-Broadway spoof *Little Mary Sunshine* (1959) by Rick Besoyan. Mary Potts (Eileen Brennan), the proprietress of the Colorado Inn, is about to be evicted, but she keeps her chin up and sings this bubble-headed song of hope with the forest rangers who adore her.

"Look for the Silver Lining" is the biggest song hit from the long-running *Sally* (1920) and one of the musical theatre's most recognized songs. The millionaire Blair Farquar (Irving Fisher) sings the optimistic ballad to the downhearted dishwasher Sally (Marilyn Miller), who then joins him in singing it. B.G. DeSylva wrote the hopeful lyric, and Jerome Kern composed the simple, almost hymnlike melody. The song's popularity is possibly due to its delectable ambiguity: it conjures up impressions of longing and sadness as much as it instills a feeling of hope and joy. "Look for the Silver Lining" is also a purely theatrical song in that it requires no scenery or costumes to create the dramatic situation of the number. The oft-recorded song was featured in no less than four movie musicals.

"Look to the Rainbow" is the enchanting, inspiring ballad from *Finian's Rainbow* (1947) that sounds like an authentic Irish folk song. Burton Lane (music) and E.Y. Harburg (lyric) wrote the lovely number for Sharon McLonergan (Ella Logan) to sing to Woody Mahoney (Donald Richards) explaining the whimsical nature of her father Finian and what he always taught her about following the dream. What the old man says may be blarney, the song suggests, but it is inspirational blarney. Lane's music is both wistful and urgent, and Harburg's lyric is perhaps the most expansive and poetic he ever wrote. Surprisingly, the song never became as popular as might be expected, probably due to its being overshadowed by "How Are Things in Glocca Morra?"

which Logan sang right before "Look to the Rainbow" in the show. But it is a superior ballad and one that best summarizes the talent and philosophy of Harburg. Fran Warren, who played Sharon in the road company of *Finian's Rainbow*, made a successful recording of the song, and in 1987 Aretha Franklin did a soul version that was very effective.

"Look What Happened to Mabel" is a bouncy song and dance number from Jerry Herman's short-lived musical *Mack and Mabel* (1974) about the silent movie era. Mabel Normand (Bernadette Peters) sees herself on the screen for the first time and is amazed at the transformation the camera has made of her. Herman's music starts slowly and sluggishly as the projector clicks away, then builds into a joyous number for Mabel and the ensemble. Chita Rivera sang the song in the Broadway revue *Jerry's Girls* (1985).

"Look Who's Alone Now" is a pleasing, torchy number from the quick flop *Nick and Nora* (1991) by Charles Strouse (music) and Richard Maltby, Jr., (lyric). Barry Bostwick, as the amateur sleuth Nick Charles, sang the touching song after a spat with his society wife Nora.

"Look Who's Dancing" is a contagious polka from *A Tree Grows in Brooklyn* (1951) by Arthur Schwartz (music) and Dorothy Fields (lyric). Katie Nolan (Marcia Van Dyke) and her sister Cissy (Shirley Booth) sing the lively number with the chorus as Katie begins married life with Johnny.

"Look Who's in Love" is the romantic duet from *Redhead* (1959) by Albert Hague (music) and Dorothy Fields (lyric). Sleuthing partners Essie Whimple (Gwen Verdon) and Tom Baxter (Richard Kiley) set out to solve a murder at the Simpson Sisters' Waxworks and soon realize they are in love with each other.

"Looking for a Boy" is a wistful ballad from the Gershwins' *Tip-Toes* (1925) in which vaudevillian "Tip-Toes" Kaye (Queenie Smith) yearns for a boy who is looking for a girl to love. George Gershwin composed the tender music that has a Brahms-like quality, and Ira Gershwin wrote the direct, poignant lyric. Sarah Vaughan made a superb recording of the number in 1983.

"The Lorelei" is the title of at least three theatre songs, all on the same subject. In Germanic folklore, the Lorelei was a Rhine maiden who sang to passing ships, luring men to their destruction. Jerome Kern (music) and Anne Caldwell (lyric) wrote a trio version for *Sally* (1920), where it was sung by Walter Catlett, Mary Hay and Stanley Ridges. Noël Coward wrote a "Lorelei" for the London revue *This Year of Grace* (1928), but it wasn't included when the show came to Broadway later that year. The best of the "Lorelei" songs is a sultry, comic one with simple, charming music by George Gershwin and a delicious lyric by Ira Gershwin. They wrote it for the unsuccessful *Pardon My English* (1933), where it was sung by the team of (Carl) Randall and (Barbara) Newberry with the ensemble. A song on the same subject but titled "The Siren's Song" was written by Kern (music) and P.G. Wodehouse (lyric) for *Leave It to Jane* (1917).

"Lorna's Here" is a bluesy ballad by Charles Strouse (music) and Lee Adams (lyric) for their most atypical show, the boxing musical *Golden Boy* (1964). Paula Wayne, as Lorna, sang the alluring song about her decision to stick with young boxer Joe Wellington (Sammy Davis, Jr.).

"Losing My Mind" is an entrancing torch song from *Follies* (1971) that pastiches the Gershwin-style laments heard in the 1920s and 1930s. Stephen Sondheim wrote the emotional number for the Loveland fantasy section of the musical, and it was sung by Sally (Dorothy Collins) as a brooding, seductive movie queen dressed in a sequined gown. Although the intention was to present an ironic, distant commentary on Sally's main folly in life, the song appealed to audiences for its heartfelt power and has remained a favorite of singers as a serious torch song. Sondheim's music is evocative and alluring, and his lyric is masterfully restrained as he uses the idea of hours, days, weeks going by slowly, all adding to the endless loneliness the singer expresses. In the Broadway revue *Side by Side by Sondheim* (1977), the song was sung by Julia McKenzie, and Barbara Cook made a powerful recording of the number in the 1980s.

"Lost and Found" is a seductive song sung by the oversexed Mallory Kingsley (Rachel York) in the movie-within-a-play in *City of Angels* (1989). The private eye Stone (James Naughton) has been looking all over L.A. for the missing heiress Mallory only to return to his bungalow and find her waiting naked in his bed. She then sings the sultry Cy Coleman (music) and David Zippel (lyric) song to Stone, suggesting he claim what he has found.

"Lost in the Stars" is the delicate title song from the 1949 musical drama about South Africa by Kurt Weill (music) and Maxwell Anderson (lyric). The minister Stephen Kumalo (Todd Duncan) has been searching for his son in Johannesburg and finds him in jail accused of murder. Kumalo sings this poignant song about how we are so lost that maybe God cannot find us to hear our prayers. The number was written years earlier for a project called *Ulysses Africanus* that fell through. "Lost in the Stars" was recorded by Lotte Lenya, Weill's widow, and was sung by Jerry Lanning in the Off-Broadway revue *Berlin to Broadway With Kurt Weill* (1972).

"A Lot of Livin' to Do" is the sparkling rhythmic number from *Bye*

Bye Birdie (1960) that celebrates a youthful, optimistic view of a life of unrestrained joy. The Charles Strouse (music) and Lee Adams (lyric) song is more jazz than rock and roll, but it fits rock idol Conrad Birdie (Dick Gautier) as he and the teenagers of Sweet Apple, Ohio, do a night on the town. Herb Alpert and the Tijuana Brass made a successful recording of the song under the title "Gotta Lotta Livin' to Do."

"Louisiana Hayride" is a jubilant rural song from the revue *Flying Colors* (1932) that utilized a Southern gospel style. Howard Dietz (lyric) and Arthur Schwartz (music) wrote the flavorful number, which was sung by Clifton Webb, Tamara Geva and the cast on a rousing hayride that closed the revue's first act. The number was made all the more effective by the use of film footage projected behind that gave the illusion that the wagon was actually moving.

"Louisiana Purchase" is the animated title song from the 1940 Irving Berlin hit musical about Southern politics. The song has a big-band sound, complete with touches of Latin and blues flavors. A young and vivacious Carol Bruce and the male chorus sang the thrilling number, which celebrated New Orleans.

"Lounging at the Waldorf" is a sleek and funny number that was featured in the 1978 revue *Ain't Misbehavin'* celebrating the music of Thomas "Fats" Waller. He composed the song in 1936 as an instrumental, and Richard Maltby, Jr., wrote the cunning lyric when he put together the popular revue. The number was sung by Armelia McQueen, Charlaine Woodard, Ken Page and Nell Carter.

"Love Can't Happen" is a passionate love song from *Grand Hotel* (1989) in which the Baron (David Carroll) expresses his astonishment to the celebrated ballerina Elizaveta Grushinskaya (Lilianne Montevecchi) that he could actually fall in love. Maury Yeston wrote the captivating music and lyric, and Carroll recorded the song as a single but died before the cast album was completed.

"Love Changes Everything" is the simple and catchy number that runs throughout *Aspects of Love* (1990), the British import by Andrew Lloyd Webber (music), Don Black and Charles Hart (lyric). The Englishman Alex Dillingham (Michael Ball) sings the ballad at the top of the show as he remembers the events of the story. Then the same melody reappears throughout the musical as a kind of leitmotif, the lyric changing to fit the various situations.

"Love, Don't Turn Away" is a ravishing ballad from *110 in the Shade*

(1963) that also serves as the heroine's "I am" song. Lizzie Curry (Inga Swenson) is getting older and seems to be heading toward spinsterhood, but she sings that she's still ready and willing for love to enter her life. Tom Jones wrote the wistful lyric, and Harvey Schmidt composed the endearing music.

"Love for Sale" is a passionate solo from the operetta *The Vagabond King* (1925) that is sung by the Parisian prostitute Hugette (Jane Carroll). Rudolf Friml composed the fervent music, and Brian Hooker wrote the heartbreaking lyric. Unlike Cole Porter's later song of the same title, the character in this operetta is more pathetic than sensual.

"Love for Sale" is famous for being Cole Porter's most censored song, the tantalizing ballad of a prostitute seeking every kind of love but "true love." There is no regret or pathos detected in the streetwalker as she offers her wares, and it is this amoral distancing that makes the song so potent. "Love for Sale" was first sung by Kathryn Crawford, as a white prostitute, and her three girlfriends standing outside of Reuben's Restaurant in *The New Yorkers* (1930). When some objected to the number, the producers changed the song's setting to a street outside the Cotton Club in Harlem and recast the part with Elizabeth Welch, a black singer. Unlike Porter's "My Heart Belongs to Daddy" and "Let's Do It (Let's Fall in Love)," this song was not open to possible innocent interpretations and for many years it was denied radio play. But after enough time passed, Libby Holman, Dinah Washington, Billie Holiday and others made successful recordings of the song.

"Love Held Lightly" is a fragile ballad from the ambitious but unsuccessful *Saratoga* (1959) that was, sadly, Harold Arlen's last Broadway musical. Belle Piquery (Odette Myrtil) sang the delectable song as a solo, then reprised it as a countermelody to the cynical "A Game of Poker" sung by Carol Lawrence and Howard Keel. Johnny Mercer wrote the absorbing lyric for Arlen's music.

"Love Is a Dancing Thing" is a flowing ballad from the revue *At Home Abroad* (1935) by Howard Dietz (lyric) and Arthur Schwartz (music). Woods Miller sang the bewitching song, and it was danced by Paul Haakon and Nina Whitney. There is an "interlude" section in Schwartz's music that contains a Debussy-like musical phrase.

"Love Is in the Air" is a pleasant soft-shoe song that Stephen Sondheim wrote as an opening number for *A Funny Thing Happened on the Way to the Forum* (1962), but it was cut before opening night and replaced by the more raucous "Comedy Tonight." The gentle "Love Is in the Air" was finally heard on Broadway in the revue *Side By Side By Sondheim* (1977), where it was sung by

David Kernan.

"Love Is Like a Firefly" is the zesty, philosophical song from *The Firefly* (1912), the popular operetta by Rudolf Friml (music) and Otto Harbach (lyric). Nina Corelli (Emma Trentini) sings this lighthearted look at love to her old friend Suzette (Ruby Norton) to disguise her unhappy home life.

"Love Is Sweeping the Country" is the energetic campaign song from *Of Thee I Sing* (1931), a swinging march number sung by campaign manager Jenkins (George Murphy), his assistant Miss Benson (June O'Dea) and the ensemble at a political rally for John P. Wintergreen. George Gershwin's syncopated music is bold and melodic, and Ira Gershwin's lyric is facetiously bright and optimistic. There is a delightful patter section in the song that has a slight Chinese flavor to it; this is because George Gershwin used a melody from their unproduced Oriental musical *East Is West*.

"Love Is the Best of All" is one of Victor Herbert's most accomplished compositions, a captivating number from the operetta *The Princess Pat* (1915) with a lyric by Henry Blossom. Eleanor Painter, as the heroine of the title, sang the number on her first entrance. Herbert used a mazurka strain in one of the stanzas (to point up Pat's European background) and then added choral responses for the lovely refrain which contains one of his finest waltzes.

"Love Is the Reason" is a bittersweet list song from *A Tree Grows in Brooklyn* (1951) in which the endearing Aunt Cissy (Shirley Booth) chronicles life's many oddities and pitfalls, claiming that love is the cause of them all. Arthur Schwartz (music) and Dorothy Fields (lyric) wrote the piquant number.

"Love, Look Away" is an intoxicating ballad by Richard Rodgers (music) and Oscar Hammerstein (lyric) written for *Flower Drum Song* (1958). The number is a torch song sung by Helen Chao (Arabella Hong), a secondary character in the musical; consequently, it was not nearly as effective as it ought to have been. The music starts high and maintains a grasping, heartfelt quality throughout the song. In the Broadway revue *A Grand Night for Singing* (1993), the song was sung by Jason Graae.

"Love Makes Such Fools of Us All" is a lyrical pastiche number from *Barnum* (1980) that captures the essence of a nineteenth-century ballad. The song was sung by the "Swedish nightingale" Jenny Lind (Marianne Tatum), first in Swedish, then in English. Cy Coleman composed the entrancing waltz melody, and Michael Stewart wrote the beguiling lyric.

"Love Makes the World Go Round" is the more familiar title for the song that is officially the "Theme From *Carnival*," the 1961 musical by Bob Merrill. The show was based on the film *Lili* (1953) that boasted the hit single "Hi Lili, Hi Lo." But Merrill came up with the equally simple and charming "Love Makes the World Go Round" for *Carnival*, and it also became a hit. The song is first heard played on a single concertina where the show's overture would be. As the sun rises, the members of the French carnival troupe straggle on stage pulling their wagons, set up their tents, and, as the song progresses, gradually become a circus parade. Lili (Anna Maria Alberghetti) and the puppets sing the song as the first-act finale, and the number is reprised at the end of the show as well.

"Love Me or Leave Me" is one of the theatre's great torch songs, so it seems surprising that the number was written for the musical farce *Whoopee* (1928). It was introduced by Ruth Etting, who, playing the movie-star-on-the-run Leslie Daw, sang the song in front of the curtain while scenery was being changed, and managed to stop the show with it. Etting also sang the number in *Simple Simon* (1930), in her nightclub act and everywhere else, and the song was forever identified with her. Walter Donaldson (music) and Gus Kahn (lyric) wrote the number, which has been recorded often over the years. Benny Goodman's Orchestra, Lena Horne, Doris Day and Sammy Davis, Jr., all made hit recordings of the torch song.

"Love Me Tonight" is the tremulous duet from the operetta *The Vagabond King* (1925) by Rudolf Friml (music) and Brian Hooker (lyric). The swashbuckling outlaw Francois Villon (Dennis King) and the aristocratic Katherine de Vaucelles (Carolyn Thomson) sing the romantic number, which is often confused with a Rodgers and Hart song with the same title from the 1932 film musical of the same name.

"The Love Nest" is a nostalgic little ditty that swept the nation in the early 1920s. The song was written by Louis Hirsch (music) and Otto Harbach (lyric) for *Mary* (1920), where Jack Keene (Jack McGowan), who hopes to make his fortune by selling "portable houses," sings the sweet ballad of domestic bliss to the secretary Mary (Janet Velie). Because *Mary* had an extensive tour before coming to Broadway, "The Love Nest" was already a hit on opening night. The melody for the song is most remembered today as the theme song from George Burns and Gracie Allen's radio and television show.

"The Love of My Life" is a farcical character song from *Brigadoon* (1947) for the man-hungry lass Meg Brockie (Pamela Britton), who has found the one true love of her life many times, but in each case her love was not returned. The number is far from a torch song: Meg is proud of her pursuits and sings of them to the New Yorker Jeff Douglas (George Keane), who is going to be the next real love of her life. Alan Jay Lerner wrote the prankish lyric, and Frederick Loewe composed the pseudo-Scottish music.

"Love Song" is an intoxicating ballad from the experimental *Love Life* (1948) by Alan Jay Lerner (lyric) and Kurt Weill (music). A comic hobo played by Johnny Thompson introduced the expansive song about a man who has traveled the world and heard every song, but he sings only of love. The number was also sung by the ensemble in the Off-Broadway revue *Berlin to Broadway With Kurt Weill* (1972).

"Love Stolen" is a wicked and engaging ballad from the backwoods musical *The Robber Bridegroom* (1976) by Robert Waldman (music) and Alfred Uhry (lyric). The bandit Jamie Lockhart (Barry Bostwick) sings of how much sweeter life is when done on the sly and confesses that the only kind of love for him is that stolen from the cookie jar.

"Love Will Find a Way" is an enticingly optimistic duet from the landmark black musical *Shuffle Along* (1921) by Eubie Blake (music) and Noble Sissle (lyric). Mayoral candidate Harry Walton (Roger Matthews) and his girlfriend Jessie (Lottie Gee) sang the spirited romantic song.

"Love Will See Us Through (Till Something Better Comes Along)" is a silly but affectionate pastiche number from *Follies* (1971) in which Stephen Sondheim wrote an optimistic duet in the early Jerome Kern style. The song was performed in the Loveland fantasy section of the musical by Young Buddy (Harvey Evans) and Young Sally (Marti Rolph), where it was reprised contrapuntally with the pastiche duet "You're Gonna Love Tomorrow."

"Love-Line" is a beguiling number from *Bajour* (1964), the musical by Walter Marks about gypsies in contemporary New York. The sinuous gypsy Anyanka (Chita Rivera) reads the palms of anthropologist Emily Kirsten (Nancy Dussault) and Lt. Lou MacNiall (Robert Burr), planting the idea of love in both of their minds while stealing Lou's watch, wallet and pistol.

"Lovely" is a romantic ballad from *A Funny Thing Happened on the Way to the Forum* (1962) that mocks romantic ballads through its wonderfully insipid lyrics. Stephen Sondheim wrote the song for the beautiful slave Philia (Preshy Marker) and the enamored Hero (Brian Davies) to sing in the spot usually reserved for the traditional love duet. Later in the show Pseudolus (Zero Mostel) sings it with Hysterium (Jack Gilford) to convince the nervous slave that his bridal disguise is quite becoming. Sondheim's music is flowing and melodic, but his lyric is empty-headed and askew, making the farcical song work. Rachel York sang the number in the Off-Broadway revue *Putting It Together* (1993).

"Lover, Come Back to Me" was called by one critic at the time a "hot torch psalm," and that fairly describes the passionate yet gentle quality of the song. Sigmund Romberg (music) and Oscar Hammerstein (lyric) wrote the number for the star Evelyn Herbert to sing in the operetta *The New Moon* (1928), but she rejected it, saying she wanted an aria to sing, not a ballad. Romberg rewrote the ending, giving Herbert three high notes to sing, and the soprano was satisfied. In the operetta it is sung by the aristocratic Marianne on the deck of the ship *The New Moon* and is later reprised by her lover, the rebel Robert Misson (Robert Halliday). The song was an immediate hit, selling over one million copies of sheet music. Later Billie Holiday and Mario Lanza recorded it, and Rudy Vallee made a hit record with it, making "Lover, Come Back to Me" a favorite on his radio show. It is worth pointing out that the release section of the song is based on Tschaikowsky's piano piece "June Barcarolle."

"Lovers on Christmas Eve" is a charming song about married love from *I Love My Wife* (1977) by Cy Coleman (music) and Michael Stewart (lyric). Wally (James Naughton) and his wife Monica (Joanna Gleason) sing the playful list song that considers the romantic atmosphere of all the holidays and concludes that Christmas Eve is the best.

"Lovin' Is a Lowdown Blues" is a sad but seductive song from *Jelly's Last Jam* (1992), the concept bio-musical about jazz pioneer Jelly Roll Morton. The three Hunnies (Mamie Duncan-Gibbs, Stephanie Pope and Allison M. Williams), who act as a sensual Greek chorus throughout the musical, sing this bluesy lament while Jelly (Gregory Hines) and Anita (Tonya Pinkins) make love. Susan Birkenhead wrote the smooth lyric set to Morton's music.

"Luck Be a Lady" is the exhilarating song and dance number from *Guys and Dolls* (1950) set in an underground sewer beneath Broadway. Sky Masterson (Robert Alda) sings the driving Frank Loesser song as he tries to win the crap game, thereby guaranteeing a full house of sinners at the local mission. Almost as memorable as the song were the scenery by Jo Mielziner and the exciting choreography by Michael Kidd. Barbra Streisand made one of the few recordings of a woman singing the song.

"Lucky Day" is an exuberantly joyous number by B.G. DeSylva and Lew Brown (lyric) and Ray Henderson (music) that was one of a handful of hits from the 1926 edition of *George White's Scandals*. Harry Richman, with straw hat and cane, sang the rousing song surrounded by beautiful girls dressed as a wishbone, horseshoe, four-leaf clover and other symbols of luck. Later on the number became the theme song for the radio show "Your Hit Parade." The song is sometimes titled "This Is My Lucky Day."

"Lucky in Love" is the popular love song from the college musical *Good News!* (1927) by B.G. DeSylva and Lew Brown (lyric) and Ray Henderson (music). Tait College's football star Tom Marlowe (John Price Jones) and intelligent coed Connie Laine (Mary Lawlor) sing the jaunty but romantic duet, arguing that luck in love is even better than luck in gambling.

"Lucky to Be Me" is an alluring ballad from *On the Town* (1944) by Leonard Bernstein (music) and Betty Comden and Adolph Green (lyric). John Battles, as the sailor Gabey standing in Times Square awaiting the arrival of Ivy Smith (Sono Osato), sang the endearing song, and the chorus of New Yorkers passing by joined in. Mary Martin made a successful recording of the song.

"Lud's Wedding" is a sparkling duet from the ill-fated *1600 Pennsylvania Avenue* (1976) by Leonard Bernstein (music) and Alan Jay Lerner (lyric). Lud (Gilbert Price) and Seena (Emily Yancy), black servants in the White House, recall their courtship days, how Lud proposed and their wedding day. The music has a jazzy rhythmic quality that accentuates the folklore lyrics beautifully. The musical score was never recorded, but Sarah Brightman, Ritchie Pitts and the Stephen Hill Singers recorded the number in 1989.

"Lullaby" is the title of two popular nineteenth-century songs, each with its roots in the musical theatre. A 1880s lullaby by Harry Paulton and Edward Jakobowski, sometimes called "Dear Mother, In Dreams I See Her," was one of the best-loved songs of its generation. It was first heard in the comic opera *Erminie* (1886), where it was sung by Pauline Hall, as the heroine of the title, as she recalled her deceased mother. The gentle song became the hit of the year and remained popular for the next fifty years. Joseph K. Emmet wrote a "Lullaby" in the 1870s that is still sung today, remembered mostly as the melody for the child's song "Go to Sleep, My Baby." Emmet sang it as he accompanied himself on the guitar in the sentimental musical *Fritz, Our Cousin German* (1870), although one cannot be sure it wasn't added later in the run; theatre programs at the time did not list musical numbers and the song was not copyrighted until 1878. Emmet also sang the lullaby in the musical sequels *The New Fritz, Our Cousin German* (1878) and *Fritz in Ireland* (1879). The song, which has one of the most famous melodies to come from the American stage, is often titled "Emmet's Lullaby."

"The Lusty Month of May" is a spirited frolic for the ensemble in *Camelot* (1960) with sprightly music by Frederick Loewe and a zestful lyric by Alan Jay Lerner. Julie Andrews, as Queen Guenevere, led the company in the tangy number that celebrates spring's joys, wholesome and "un."

M

"Ma Belle" is a sweeping ballad from Rudolf Friml's swashbuckling operetta *The Three Musketeers* (1928). It was customary to give a solo to an Irish-type tenor in a secondary role when the hero of the operetta was a baritone. In this case the musketeer Aramis (Joseph McCauley) was the tenor and he sang the luscious song, stopping the show with it each night. Clifford Grey wrote the lyric, and opera star Robert Merrill later made a hit recording of the song.

"Ma Blushin' Rosie (Ma Posie Sweet)" is the most famous song to come out of the Weber and Fields music-hall shows. The John Stromberg (music) and Edgar Smith (lyric) Negro-dialect song was introduced in the satirical *Fiddle-Dee-Dee* (1900) by Fay Templeton with a chorus of girls costumed in polka dots. Al Jolson's 1946 recording of the Southern ballad sold over a million records. The song is sometimes titled by its first line "Rosie, You Are My Posie."

"Macavity" is a jazzy number from the British import *Cats* (1982) that describes the Mystery Cat Macavity (Kenneth Ard), who breaks every law (including that of gravity) and gets away with it because whenever a crime is discovered, he's gone. Fellow cats Demeter (Wendy Edmead) and Bombalurina (Donna King) sang the song, which was T.S. Eliot's poem set to dissonant music by Andrew Lloyd Webber.

"Mack the Knife" is one of the biggest hits to come from the theatre during the 1950s even though the song was German and had been written back in 1928. Kurt Weill (music) and Bertolt Brecht (lyric) wrote the sinister number for the original 1928 production of *The Threepenny Opera* in Berlin. The song was called "Moritat" (German for "murder deed") and was a dissonant version of a German street song. *The Threepenny Opera* was first translated and produced on Broadway in 1933 (where the song was titled "The Legend of Mackie Messer"), but it quickly closed and the song was forgotten. The 1954 Off-Broadway version, with Brecht's lyric translated and adapted by Marc Blitzstein, was a hit, and as "Mack the Knife" the song was sung by the Street Singer (Gerald Price). In 1955 alone, "Mack the Knife" was recorded twenty times, the most successful being the version by Louis Armstrong. The number has also been successful for Dick Hayman, Frank Sinatra, Ella Fitzgerald and Bobby Darin. Jerry Lanning and the ensemble sang it in the Off-Broadway revue *Berlin to Broadway With Kurt Weill* (1972). The song is sometimes titled "The Theme From *The Threepenny Opera*."

"Mad" is a hyperactive comic song from the one-performance flop *Dance a Little Closer* (1983) that showed that lyricist Alan Jay Lerner still had a dazzling lyric wit in this, his last Broadway musical. Charles Strouse wrote the frantic music for the facetious comic song in which Harry Aikens (Len Cariou) lists in rapid-fire tempo all the things about modern life that he despises, from phone answering machines to picture books about Marilyn Monroe. Three chorus girls (Cheryl Howard, Alyson Reed and Diane Pennington) sang a countermelody in the background in which they explained to the audience that Harry was furious really because he was "mad" about a certain woman.

"Mad About the Boy" is a Noël Coward ballad that gushes with pathos without losing its stiff upper lip. The song was first heard in the London revue *Words and Music* (1932), and was performed on Broadway in *Set to Music* (1939), a revue built around the talents of Beatrice Lillie. She sang it with Penelope Dudley Ward, Gladys Henson and Laura Duncan, and the song was later recorded by Belle Baker, Lena Horne, Gertrude Lawrence, Dinah Washington and Lillie herself. In the Off-Broadway revue *Oh! Coward!* (1972), "Mad About the Boy" was sung by Barbara Cason.

"Mad Dogs and Englishmen" is perhaps the most Noël Cowardish of all Noël Coward songs, a witty number about how the indefatigable English refuse to adjust to the ways and means of the rest of the world. Beatrice Lillie introduced the comic song in *The Third Little Show* (1931) as she sat in a rickshaw wearing a pith helmet. The ditty is essentially a list song that chronicles how different nationalities react to the tropical climate, but only mad dogs and Englishmen go out in the midday sun. Coward wrote the song, the story goes, while motoring from Hanoi to Saigon. His recording of the number was a best-seller, as was a record by Danny Kaye, who also did the song on the radio, on television and in the movies. Barbara Cason, Roderick Cook and Jamie Ross sang the comic number in the Off-Broadway revue *Oh! Coward!* (1972).

"Maggie Murphy's Home" is the waltzing song favorite about simple New York City life in the 1890s. David Braham (music) and Edward Harrigan (lyric) wrote the number for the Harrigan and Hart musical comedy *Reilly and the Four Hundred* (1890), where it was sung by fifteen-year-old Emma Pollack, as Maggie Murphy, and the ensemble. The song was the hit of the show, and became Pollack's theme song for the rest of her career. Ada Lewis scored a hit with the number years later in vaudeville. New World Records revived the song in 1978 with a recording by Max Morath, Lois Winter, Rose Marie Jun, Phil Olson and Charles Magruder. The old ballad was again heard on Broadway in the 1985 bio-musical *Harrigan and Hart*, where it was sung by Trudi Roche, Harry Groener, Clent Bowers and the company.

"Magic Moment" is a thrilling ballad from *The Gay Life* (1961), the musical about Viennese high society by Howard Dietz (lyric) and Arthur Schwartz (music). The neglected Liesl (Barbara Cook) has loved the devilish Anatole (Walter Chiari) since she was a child and sings this enthralling song about the day when he will grow to love her.

"Magic to Do" is the bewitching opening number from *Pippin* (1972) in which the Leading Player (Ben Vereen) and his company of traveling commedia dell'arte actors, singers, dancers, jugglers and magicians invite the audience to let them amuse them for an hour or two. Stephen Schwartz wrote the alluring music and lyric, and director-choreographer Bob Fosse staged the dynamic number that began with only the actors' hands being lit.

"Make a Miracle" is an ambitious piece of musical theatre writing that made it clear that Broadway newcomer Frank Loesser was a talent to reckon with. Loesser wrote the comic duet for *Where's Charley?* (1948) and used offbeat counterpoint and intricate rhyming to turn the number into a complete musical scene. The Victorian young lady Amy (Allyn McLerie) has been reading a book about a future world filled with new inventions (telephones, horseless carriages, breakfast cereals that explode and so on) and sings about them coyly as Charley (Ray Bolger) woos her with his song, asking Amy to forget the miracles of the future and make a miracle now by marrying him.

"Make Believe" is the rhapsodic duet from *Show Boat* (1927) and one of the American theatre's greatest love songs. The young and impressionable Magnolia Hawks (Norma Terris) and riverboat gambler Gaylord Ravenal (Howard Marsh) have just met but are attracted to each other. Rather than break into a duet, as accepted in operetta, the two tease each other and pretend to be lovers singing to each other. The subtext is clear and the moment is, lyrically and characterwise, thrilling. Jerome Kern's music is very melodic with wonderful harmonic surprises, such as the interesting triplets in the refrain. Oscar Hammerstein's lyric is both passionate and playful. Of the many duet versions of "Make Believe," perhaps the finest are the 1956 recording by Robert Merrill and Patrice Munsel and the 1966 version with Barbara Cook and Stephen Douglass. The song is sometimes listed as "Only Make Believe."

"Make It Another Old-Fashioned, Please," the hit song from Cole Porter's *Panama Hattie* (1940), gave Ethel Merman a chance to sing a torch song, be it more cynical and shrewd than compassionate. Porter's music has a lazy, drunken quality that makes it memorable, if rather difficult to sing.

"Make Our Garden Grow" is the absorbing finale for *Candide* (1956), a brilliantly inspiring choral number that teaches the characters in the musical epic that the answer to life is work, dedication and tending one's own garden. Leonard Bernstein composed the elegant music, and Richard Wilbur wrote the poignant lyric. The song was sung by Candide (Robert Rounseville) and Cunegonde (Barbara Cook) and then by the ensemble, a section of it done a cappella.

"Make Someone Happy" is the popular ballad from *Do Re Mi* (1960) and the only hit to come from the Jule Styne (music) and Betty Comden and Adolph Green (lyric) score. Jukebox businessman John Henry Wheeler (John Reardon) sings the tingling song to singer-waitress Tilda Mullen (Nancy Dussault) as his prescription for romantic bliss. Among the many recordings of the song was a best-seller by Perry Como.

"Make the Man Love Me" is a gentle ballad from the period musical *A Tree Grows in Brooklyn* (1951) by Arthur Schwartz (music) and Dorothy Fields (lyric). Katie (Marcia Van Dyke) sings the tender plea about the undependable Johnny Nolan (Johnny Johnston), who then responds in song, turning the number into a lovely duet. Barbara Cook recorded a sterling version of "Make the Man Love Me" in 1993.

"Makin' Whoopee" is the cunning comic song that Eddie Cantor sang in *Whoopee* (1928) and was forever after associated with. The enticing music is by Walter Donaldson, the popular Tin Pan Alley composer in one of his rare forays into Broadway musicals, and Gus Kahn wrote the sassy, satiric lyric. The hypochondriac Henry Williams (Cantor) sings to a sextet of lovely ladies his views on marriage: what starts as nerves and lust soon turns to dreary married life and eventual infidelity, with both partners out looking for new "whoopee." The song's euphemistic title had been coined by columnist Walter Winchell not long before, and Cantor's wide-eyed rendition of the number brought out all the naiveté and salaciousness of the expression. He recorded the song several times, first in 1928, and Paul Whiteman's Orchestra made a hit recording of it with a vocal by the Rhythm Boys. In the 1950s both Frank Sinatra and Nat "King" Cole recorded popular versions.

"Mama Will Provide" is a zesty calypso number from the Caribbean musical *Once on This Island* (1990) by Stephen Flaherty (music) and Lynn Ahrens (lyric). Asaka (Kecia Lewis-Evans), the Mother of the Earth, and the storytellers sing the spirited song about how Mother Nature will take care of Ti Moune (La Chanze) on her journey to the big city.

"Mame," the spirited title number from the 1966 musical by Jerry Herman, was an obvious attempt to capture the theatrical moment as "Hello, Dolly!" had done two years before; it must have worked, because the song became popular. In the show, Mame Dennis (Angela Lansbury) returns triumphant from a fox hunt in the deep South (she brings the fox home alive) and is greeted by Charles Braswell and the ensemble in a joyous celebration in song and dance. The word "Mame" is hardly a lyrical one, but Herman manages to use the one-syllable moniker effectively, adding a Dixie flavor to the music as well. Among the many recordings of the song were ones by Bobby Darin, Herb Alpert and the Tijuana Brass and by Louis Armstrong, who had had great success with "Hello, Dolly!" earlier.

"The Man I Love," one of the Gershwin brothers' most beloved songs, has a long and troubled history, having been in and out of more shows than any other song the brothers wrote. It was written for Adele Astaire to sing at the top of *Lady, Be Good!* (1924) but was deemed too slow a start for such a jazz-flavored show and was cut in previews. Three years later the song was added to the score of the 1927 version of *Strike Up the Band*, which closed out of town. Ira Gershwin revised some of his lyrics so that "The Man I Love" could be used in *Rosalie* (1928), but it was among the many cuts made in that show during rehearsals. Max Dreyfus published the song at this time, and slowly it caught on, particularly after Helen Morgan and her singing sisters performed it everywhere. George Gershwin's music in the number is deceptively difficult to sing because of the shifting harmony that descends chromatically measure by measure to its final haunting statement. Much has been written about the justly famous release in the song, a marvelous musical achievement that many feel inspired a trend toward bold and varied releases in popular music. Ira Gershwin's lyric is straightforward and far from flowery. Yet the song succeeds because of this unusual, hypnotic quality and remains to this day one of the Gershwins' most recorded works. "The Man I Love" was heard in no less than six movie musicals, and among the many recordings over the years were memorable versions by Marion Harris, Helen Forrest (with Benny Goodman's Orchestra), Lee Wiley (with Eddie Condon's Orchestra), Barbra Streisand and Michael Feinstein who sang it as "The Girl I Love."

"The Man I Used to Be" is a breezy character song from *Pipe Dream* (1955), Rodgers and Hammerstein's least successful show. Doc (William

Johnson), an impoverished marine biologist, looks back and recalls his cocky, spirited youth. Richard Rodgers' music has an old soft-shoe tempo, and Oscar Hammerstein's lyric is cheery and revealing.

"The Man in the Moon" is a pastiche number from Jerry Herman's *Mame* (1966) that satirizes the empty-headed musical spectaculars of the 1930s. The song is sung by actress Vera Charles (Beatrice Arthur) in her new musical show about astronomy. The song and the whole production number collapse when Mame (Angela Lansbury), sitting atop a prop moon, starts to fall and ends up swinging back and forth in a farcical fashion. Dorothy Loudon also sang the song in the Broadway revue *Jerry's Girls* (1985).

"Man of La Mancha" is the driving title song from the 1965 musical by Mitch Leigh (music) and Joe Darion (lyric). The imprisoned Miguel de Cervantes (Richard Kiley) transforms himself into the cockeyed Don Quixote and begins to tell his story with this energetic number, also known as "I, Don Quixote." He is joined by his manservant (Irving Jacobson), who becomes the foolish squire Sancho, and together they set off in search of adventures and their destiny. A memorable aspect of the original staging was Jack Cole's choreography of this number in which two dancers did the rapid hoofbeats of the two adventurers' horses.

"Man Say" is an intriguing character song from *Raisin* (1973), the musicalization of Lorraine Hansberry's *A Raisin in the Sun*. At breakfast, the black chauffeur Walter Lee Younger (Joe Morton) talks of his dreams of making something of himself, but all his wife Ruth (Ernestine Jackson) says is to eat his eggs and get to work. Judd Woldin composed the eruptive music, and Robert Brittan wrote the succinct lyric.

"Man to Man Talk" is an unusual duet in that one of the characters is silent throughout the song. In the fairy-tale musical *Once Upon a Mattress* (1959) by Mary Rodgers (music) and Marshall Barer (lyric), the naive Prince Dauntless (Joe Bova) gets a lesson about the birds and the bees from the mute King (Jack Gilford), who pantomimes his lesson charades-style.

"Man With a Load of Mischief" is the enchanting title song from the 1966 Off-Broadway musical about the occupants of a nineteenth-century English wayside inn. The Lady (Virginia Vestoff) sings the song, whose title is the name of the inn but also refers to the deception she finds in the men of her class. John Clifton composed the elegant music and, with Ben Tarver, wrote the absorbing lyric.

"Mandy" is one of Irving Berlin's most recognized melodies, a compelling love song with a straightforward lyric but the song was written as a spoof of Florenz Ziegfeld's lavish tributes to womanhood. "Mandy" was originally performed in the all-soldier Broadway benefit *Yip, Yip, Yaphank* (1918), where privates John Murphy and Dan Healy did a minstrel-show routine in blackface. The cakewalk number was intended as a simple-minded marriage proposal, but subsequent uses of the song have turned it into a Berlin romantic standard. The comedy team of Van and Schenck sang it in the *Ziegfeld Follies* (1919), where it was also danced by Marilyn Miller, Ray Dooley and a tambourine-banging chorus of "Follies Pickaninnies." "Mandy" was also featured in the 1942 military revue *This Is the Army* and was a popular favorite by singer Mabel Mercer.

"Manhattan," the first hit song by Rodgers and Hart, still remains one of the most romantic paeans to New York City. The ballad was written for the unproduced *Winkle Town* in 1921 but wasn't heard on Broadway until 1925 in the first *Garrick Gaieties* revue where Sterling Holloway and June Cochrane sang it simply in front of the curtain. Richard Rodgers' music has some unexpected turns in the refrain that make it unforgettable. Lorenz Hart's lyric possesses a sly but heartfelt quality that turns the mundane (pushcarts on Mott Street, the subway, Childs Restaurant and so on) into the sublime. "Manhattan" quickly became a standard and has remained one of the most beloved of theatre songs.

"Many a New Day" is Laurey's song of independence in Rodgers and Hammerstein's *Oklahoma!* (1943); she sings it to show that she is not upset about Curly's taking another girl to the box social. Oscar Hammerstein's lyric is direct and a bit pouting, exactly how a farm girl with grit would speak. Richard Rodgers' music conveys Laurey's determination by avoiding the usual theatre-song structure and keeping the same principal melody throughout instead of breaking away with a traditional release. The song was introduced by Joan Roberts and the women's chorus, and in the Broadway revue *A Grand Night for Singing* (1993) it was sung by Victoria Clark, Alyson Reed and Lynne Wintersteller.

"March of the Falsettos" is the eerie title song from the 1981 Off-Broadway musical by William Finn. In a fantasy sequence, Marvin (Michael Rupert), his son Jason (James Kushner), his lover Whizzer (Stephen Bogardus) and his psychiatrist Mendel (Chip Zien) do a surreal march singing the lyric in falsetto voice. The song is about the many confusions of sexual identity as the four men, two of them gay, do a manly strut in a mincing voice.

"March of the Musketeers" is the boastful march of self-praise from the operetta *The Three Musketeers* (1928) by Rudolf Friml (music) and Clifford

Grey and P.G. Wodehouse (lyric). The three swashbuckling heroes (Douglass Dumbrille, Detmar Popper and Joseph McCauley) are joined by newcomer d'Artagnan (Dennis King) for this swaggering anthem.

"March of the Toys" is the grand and brassy march most associated with the Christmas season today. It was written for the stage extravaganza *Babes in Toyland* (1903) by Victor Herbert (music) and Glen MacDonough (lyric) and was sung by the two "babes," Alan (William Norris) and Jane (Mabel Barrison). "March of the Toys" is one of the most recognized melodies in American popular culture.

"March With Me" is the comic song that introduced Beatrice Lillie to Broadway when she appeared in the British import *Andre Charlot's Revue of 1924*. Ivor Novello (music) and Douglas Furber (lyric) wrote the silly march which Lillie, dressed as Britannia, sang as she led a cadre of military officers into comic chaos.

"Maria" is the first song Leonard Bernstein (music) and Stephen Sondheim (lyric) wrote for *West Side Story* (1957) when they experimented to see how they might work together. The famous ballad is perhaps the most rhapsodic number in the show and became one of the musical's most popular songs. Tony (Larry Kert) sings the heartfelt ballad after having met Maria (Carol Lawrence) at the dance at the gym. Of all the many recordings of the song, the biggest seller was one by Johnny Mathis.

"Maria" is the pleasing comic quartet from *The Sound of Music* (1959) that most know as "How Do You Solve a Problem Like Maria?" It is sung by the Mother Abbess (Patricia Neway) and her three fellow sisters (Muriel O'Malley, Elizabeth Howell and Karen Shepard) about their troublesome postulant Maria (Mary Martin). Oscar Hammerstein wrote the gentle mock-prayer lyric, and Richard Rodgers composed the tangy melody that undercut any possible solemnity. In the Broadway revue *A Grand Night for Singing* (1993), Jason Graae sang "Maria" as the comic lament of an anxious lover.

"Marian the Librarian" is the snappy seduction song that con man Harold Hill (Robert Preston) sings in *The Music Man* (1957) to try and win the attention of the aloof Marian Paroo (Barbara Cook). Composer/lyricist Meredith Willson keeps the song lively and unsentimental, with a driving rhythm that is all the more playful because the number is set in a library, where no rhapsodic or theatrical gushing is allowed.

"Marianne" is a flavorful ballad from the unsuccessful *The Grand Tour* (1979) by Jerry Herman. The enticing song is sung by a Polish colonel (Ron

Holgate) about the French girl of the song title (Florence Lacey). In the second act the number is reprised by the refugee Jacobowsky (Joel Grey).

"Marilyn Monroe" is the 1960s-like pop song that runs throughout the British import *Blood Brothers* (1993) as a kind of leitmotif. Mrs. Johnstone (Stephanie Lawrence), the impoverished single mother, sings the narrative ballad near the beginning of the musical to tell the story of her courtship, marriage and abandonment. The tone throughout is light, and the metaphors used all apply to the famous movie star of the title. She later reprises the number three more times to bring the story up to date, still utilizing the Marilyn Monroe comparisons. Willy Russell wrote the droll music and lyric.

"Marriage Type Love" is the brisk romantic number in the musical comedy being performed in the musical *Me and Juliet* (1953). Arthur Maxwell, as the star of the show-within-the-show, and the chorus sing this melodic song by Richard Rodgers (music) and Oscar Hammerstein (lyric), and the audience on stage and the audience in the theatre couldn't help humming the catchy tune during intermission.

"Married" is a tender duet for the elder lovers in *Cabaret* (1966) by John Kander (music) and Fred Ebb (lyric). Herr Schultz (Jack Gilford) proposes marriage to Fraulein Schneider (Lotte Lenya), and while she leaves to think over his offer, he sings of how marriage can bring fulfillment to a person's life. In her bedroom, Schneider also sings her thoughts, and the number ends as a charming duet sung by two lovers in different rooms but of the same mind.

"A Married Man" is a touching little solo for Dr. Watson (Peter Sallis) in the Sherlock Holmes musical *Baker Street* (1965) with music and lyric by Marian Grudeff and Raymond Jessel. Trapped by Dr. Moriarty and near almost certain death, the doctor recalls his deceased wife and the happy years they had together. Even before the show opened the song was somewhat popular due to a recording by Richard Burton in which he talk-sang the lyrics. Later Ed Ames recorded a more melodic version.

"Marry Me" is a simple but heartfelt ballad from the John Kander (music) and Fred Ebb (lyric) musical *The Rink* (1984). In a flashback sequence, "good old Lenny" (Jason Alexander) proposes to Anna (Chita Rivera) with this touching song containing no hyperbole or rhapsodizing. Jim Walton also sang it in the Off-Broadway revue *And the World Goes 'Round* (1991).

"Marry Me a Little" is a devastating love song Stephen Sondheim wrote for *Company* (1970), but it was cut before opening. The number is a desperate plea for happiness that asks for concessions and compromises because unrestricted love is too frightening a thought to comprehend. Originally the number was intended as a proposal song for Robert (Dean Jones) to sing to Amy (Beth Howland) when she decides not to marry her live-in boyfriend Paul. The song was then tried at the climax of the musical where Robert realizes he's ready for love, but that spot was eventually filled by "Being Alive." "Marry Me a Little" was finally heard as the title number in the 1981 Off-Broadway revue, where it was sung by Suzanne Henry. Michael Rupert also sang it in the 1993 revue *Putting It Together*.

"Marry the Man Today" is the quick-witted comic duet from Frank Loesser's *Guys and Dolls* (1950) that resolves the conflicts of the two romantic couples and offers a bit of philosophical advice along the way. Sarah Brown (Isabel Bigley) and Miss Adelaide (Vivian Blaine) decide that they cannot wait for their gambler boyfriends to change their ways; the only solution is to marry them immediately and change them "subsequently."

"Marry With Me" is a rollicking exclamation of love sung by the earthy servant Catherine Creek (Carol Brice) in the cult musical *The Grass Harp* (1971). Claibe Richardson composed the surging music, and Kenward Elmslie wrote the zesty lyric.

"Marrying for Love" is a gentle romantic duet for the old-fashioned European Foreign Minister (Paul Lukas) and the up-to-date American Sally Adams (Ethel Merman) in Irving Berlin's *Call Me Madam* (1950). Dinah Shore recorded the song with Lukas, Rosemary Clooney with Guy Mitchell, and Merman recorded it as a solo.

"Mary's a Grand Old Name" is the enthralling hit ballad from George M. Cohan's *Forty-Five Minutes From Broadway* (1906) that praises the unpretentious simplicity of the common name. The wisecracking secretary Kid Burns (Victor Moore) meets the maid Mary Jane Jenkins (Fay Templeton) and, finding out her name, tells her his mother was named Mary also. She assures him that it is a grand name, and together they sing about it. In the bio-musical *George M!* (1968), Josephine Alloway sang the number as "Mary," the title by which the song is commonly known today.

"The Mascot of the Troop" is one of Victor Herbert's most exciting marches, an operetta chorus number from *Mlle. Modiste* (1905). The rousing number was sung by the French soldiers, and Henry Blossom provided the lyric for Herbert's Gallic-flavored music that even broke into "La Marseillaise" at points to add some authentic color.

"The Mason" is an affectionate tribute to the man who makes a lasting testament to his craft. It was sung by David Patrick Kelly in *Working* (1978), the musical about different people's occupations. Craig Carnelia wrote the knowing music and lyric.

"Masquerade" is the stunning production number that opens the second act of the British import *The Phantom of the Opera* (1988) by Andrew Lloyd Webber (music) and Charles Hart and Richard Stilgoe (lyric). At the New Year's Eve ball in the foyer of the Paris Opera House, the costumed and masked guests descend the ornate staircase and sing this grandiose song about hiding one's face and turning life into a masquerade.

"Master of the House" is an animated comic number from the British import *Les Misérables* (1987) in which the odious Thenardier (Leo Burmester), his shrewish wife (Jennifer Butt) and the customers at the tavern sing mockingly of Thenardier's admirable qualities as proprietor and husband. The song is more British music hall than French provincial, but a playful crowd pleaser all the same. Claude-Michel Schönberg composed the music, and Herbert Kretzmer adapted the French lyric by Alain Boublil and Jean-Marc Natel.

"Matchmaker, Matchmaker" is one of the songs from *Fiddler on the Roof* (1964) that became popular outside of the show when its context was changed and modernized. Usually a light and frothy anticipation of marriage when performed in variety shows, "Matchmaker, Matchmaker" is a shrewd and revealing character song in *Fiddler on the Roof*. Two of Tevye's daughters (Julia Migenes and Tanya Everett) start by fantasizing about the husband of their dreams until the eldest daughter (Joanna Merlin) brings them back to reality by painting a picture of the dreadful men the matchmaker might bring. The song concludes on a more somber note as all three tell the imaginary matchmaker that they are in no hurry to marry and will hope and pray for a decent husband. Jerry Bock composed the melodic music, and Sheldon Harnick wrote the insightful lyric. Because two of the three women cast as the daughters had limited vocal ranges, this song is one of the easiest of all theatre numbers to sing, but it always proves richly satisfying.

"Maybe" is the warm romantic duet from the Gershwins' *Oh, Kay!* (1926). Kay Denham (Gertrude Lawrence), disguised as a maid, and wealthy Long Islander Jimmy Winter (Oscar Shaw) sing about finding true love; maybe it will be soon, maybe it will be later. George Gershwin's music is atypical for him, being more in the Jerome Kern style. The song is short (only fifty-one notes), spare and simple, but very inventive, with a lovely ascending scale that goes with the lyric's reference to paradise opening its gates. Ira Gershwin wrote the cozy lyric, and Lawrence recorded the song with Harold French in 1927.

"Maybe My Baby Loves Me" is a jolly Charleston-like ditty from *Grand Hotel* (1989) sung by two black Americans (David Jackson and Danny Strayhorn) both named Jimmy. The sprightly 1920s pastiche number was written by Robert Wright and George Forrest.

"Me" is a boastful, egocentric marriage proposal that is one of the comic highlights of the Broadway version of Disney's *Beauty and the Beast* (1994). The swaggering Gaston (Burke Moses) sings the clownish number painting a vivid picture of what married life with him will be like, while the less-than-impressed Belle (Susan Egan) makes sly comments that go over his thickheaded head. Alan Menken (music) and Tim Rice (lyric) wrote the prankish song.

"Me and My Town" is the pungent opening number from the experimental musical *Anyone Can Whistle* (1964) by Stephen Sondheim. Mayoress Cora Hooper (Angela Lansbury) and her boys (Sterling Clark, Harvey Evans, Larry Roquemore and Tucker Smith) sing this antic pastiche of a 1940s nightclub number for a big star. Cora complains about her bankrupt town and the lack of respect she gets from her citizens. The music ranges from a mock-blues lament to a jazzy exchange with the boys that breaks into a tingling patter section complete with syncopated clapping and Latin rhythms.

"Meadowlark" is the beloved ballad from the ill-fated *The Baker's Wife* that closed out of town in 1976. Genevieve (Patti LuPone), the baker's young wife, is attracted to the egocentric Dominique (Kurt Peterson), who has asked her to run off with him. In the course of this magnificent but lengthy song, Genevieve sneers at Dominique's proposal, then she recalls a childhood story about a meadowlark who died trying to please an old king. Finally, she changes her mind and rushes off to join Dominique. Stephen Schwartz wrote the intoxicating song that was pulled and then restored during the show's long out-of-town preview tour. Producer David Merrick insisted that the number was too long and at one point went into the orchestra pit and ripped up the sheet music, saying "nothing in life should last more than five minutes." Sarah Brightman, Betty Buckley and LuPone herself are among those who have made recordings of the song.

"Measure the Valleys" is a song of acceptance and encouragement from *Raisin* (1973), the musicalization of Lorraine Hansberry's *A Raisin in the Sun*. The family matriarch Lena Younger (Virginia Capers) sings the moving number by Judd Woldin (music) and Robert Brittan (lyric) about not judging a man until you have tried to understand what he has been through.

"Meeskite" is an entertaining narrative number from *Cabaret* (1966) that seems awkwardly tacked on to the story, but thematically fits right in. At the engagement party for Herr Schultz (Jack Gilford) and Fraulein Schneider (Lotte Lenya), Schultz amuses the guests with a Yiddish song about two "meeskites" (ugly persons) who meet, fall in love, and bear a beautiful child. The fable concludes with a moral (that beauty can be found even in the ugly and unwanted) that disturbs Ernst Ludwig (Edward Winter) and the other Nazi Party members at the celebration and foreshadows the anti-Semitic sentiments growing in Berlin. John Kander composed the carefree music, and Fred Ebb wrote the quaint but succinct lyric.

"Melinda" is a dreamy ballad from *On a Clear Day You Can See Forever* (1965) that is sung to a woman who may have never existed. Psychiatrist Mark Bruckner (John Cullum) is starting to fall in love with an eigthteenth-century femme fatale named Melinda Wells, whom he has discovered while hypnotizing chain-smoking Daisy Gamble (Barbara Harris). He sings the lyrical Alan Jay Lerner (lyric) and Burton Lane (music) song about the elusive woman, not quite sure if she is real or just a psychosomatic dream.

"Melisande" is a musical tall tale from *110 in the Shade* (1963) by Tom Jones (lyric) and Harvey Schmidt (music). The con man Starbuck (Robert Horton) tells the spinster Lizzie (Inga Swenson) that her name ought to be Melisande and proceeds to tell a fantastic whooper about the legend of a woman of that name. Lizzie sees right through the tale that confuses *Hamlet* with Jason and the Argonauts and other myths, but Starbuck's telling of it is wide-eyed and magical.

"Memories of You" is the popular ballad by Eubie Blake (music) and Andy Razaf (lyric) that Minto Cato introduced in *Lew Leslie's Blackbirds* (1930). Because of Cato's unusually wide range, this number written for her spans an octave and a fifth, a challenge for a popular song. She sang it with ease as a pre-Civil War slave sitting in front of her plantation cabin. Ethel Waters made the first recording of the song, but the most popular one was by Glen Gray and his Casa Loma Orchestra with a trumpet solo by Sonny Dunham; the number became his theme song. Ethel Beatty sang "Memories of You" in the Broadway revue *Eubie* (1978), and it was performed by Dianne Walker, Bernard Manners and Kevin Ramsey in the revue *Black and Blue* (1989).

"Memory" is the hit ballad from the British import *Cats* (1982) and one of the most popular theatre songs of the 1980s. Unlike the rest of the score, which utilizes T.S. Eliot's poems set to music by Andrew Lloyd Webber, the lyric for "Memory" was written by the director Trevor Nunn, who took several poetic fragments from Eliot's notebooks and fashioned a haunting ballad. The song is heard in pieces throughout the musical; finally it is sung in its entirety by Grizabella (Betty Buckley), the Glamour Cat. "Memory" is also one of the few numbers in *Cats* that is not an "I am" song or a description of another cat, a distinction that helped it stand out. Among the many recordings of the song, ones by Elaine Paige, Barbra Streisand, Michael Crawford, Betty Buckley and Barry Manilow were all popular.

"Merely Marvelous" is a song of lilting triumph from *Redhead* (1959) by Albert Hague (music) and Dorothy Fields (lyric). Essie Whimple (Gwen Verdon) has just gotten a kiss from Tom Baxter (Richard Kiley) and bursts into this joyous solo.

"Merry Little Minuet" is an acerbic novelty number from the revue *John Murray Anderson's Almanac* (1953). Orson Bean sang the list song, which described all the violence in the world and how easily the atom bomb could put an end to all of it. Both music and lyric were by Sheldon Harnick, before he teamed up with Jerry Bock, and the satirical song had a hit recording by the Kingston Trio.

"Metaphor" is a bombastic, mock-opera duet for the eager lovers in *The Fantasticks* (1960) by Tom Jones (lyric) and Harvey Schmidt (music). Matt (Kenneth Nelson) praises Luisa (Rita Gardner) with outrageous metaphors (the flame that can melt the iceberg, the star Polaris, the microscopic details within a leaf and so on) and she swoons with rapturous joy and joins him in the duet.

"The Middle Years" is an enthralling ballad from *Your Own Thing* (1968), the Off-Broadway musicalization of Shakespeare's *Twelfth Night*. Discotheque owner Olivia (Marcia Rodd) comes to grips with her own identity and approaches middle age with confidence and no further illusions about being young forever. Later in the show, the number is reprised by Sebastian (Russ Thacker), who is in love with Olivia. Hal Hester composed the expansive music, and Danny Apolinar wrote the penetrating lyric.

"Milk and Honey" is the rousing title number from the 1961 musical about the emerging nation of Israel. The Jerry Herman song celebrates the rugged, beautiful new nation and was sung by Tommy Rall and the chorus with sly commentary by Juki Arkin. The song was also sung by Leslie Uggams in the Broadway revue *Jerry's Girls* (1985).

"The Miller's Son" is a scintillating ballad sung by a minor character in *A Little Night Music* (1973) by Stephen Sondheim. The maid Petra (D. Jamin-Bartlett) has just slept with the butler Frid (George Lee Andrews). As he lies sleeping at her feet, she sings about marrying a simple miller's son, then imagines herself married to a successful businessman and, finally, fantasizes about being wed to the Prince of Wales. But each of her reveries is punctuated by a rapid, free-wheeling patter section where Petya declares that she will enjoy life to the fullest before she marries any man and life passes her by. The lyric is one of Sondheim's most accomplished, a beautifully crafted number with a theatrical triple structure, potent parallel imagery and delightful use of alliteration and internal rhyme.

"Mine" is a flavorful contrapuntal number from the unsuccessful satire *Let 'Em Eat Cake* (1933) by George Gershwin (music) and Ira Gershwin (lyric). At a political rally, President Wintergreen (William Gaxton) and his wife Mary (Lois Moran) sing the lively duet of affectionate support while the ensemble sings a countermelody commenting on the blissful state of the First Lady and her husband. "Mine" is the only number from *Let 'Em Eat Cake* to achieve any popularity. This is due to the fact that it is one of the very few nonsatirical songs in the show. It was recorded quite a few times, most successfully by Bing Crosby and Judy Garland together in 1947. The song was also interpolated into the 1952 revival of *Of Thee I Sing*, where it was sung by Jack Carson, Betty Oakes and the ensemble.

"Mira" is the delicate "I am" song for the gentle heroine Lili (Anna Maria Alberghetti) in *Carnival* (1961) by Bob Merrill. The orphan Lili arrives at the carnival looking for a job and a home and sings this gentle song about her hometown Mira where everyone knew her name.

"Miracle of Miracles" is an eager love ballad from *Fiddler on the Roof* (1964) that uses a variety of biblical images to express romantic joy. Jerry Bock (music) and Sheldon Harnick (lyric) wrote the exhilarating song for Motel the tailor (Austin Pendleton) when he finally gets permission from Tevye to marry his eldest daughter. References to the fall of Jericho, the parting of the Red Sea, the slaying of Goliath and other Old Testament events are used to describe Motel's own miracle.

"Mis'ry's Comin' 'Round" is a stirring spiritual number from *Show Boat* (1927) that was cut in the Washington out-of-town tryouts in order to trim the four-and-a-half-hour show. Jerome Kern (music) and Oscar Hammerstein (lyric) wrote the haunting song that was sung by the black chorus. The number is sometimes restored to the score in revivals of *Show Boat* and adds a fuller dimension to the black characters in the epic musical.

"Miss Byrd" is a funny, sexy romp sung by a quiet secretary who takes scandalously erotic lunch breaks. David Shire (music) and Richard Maltby, Jr., (lyric) wrote the number for the Off-Broadway revue *Urban Blight* (1987). It received more recognition, though, when it was sung by Sally Mayes in the revue *Closer Than Ever* (1989).

"Miss Marmelstein" is a delectable character song from *I Can Get It for You Wholesale* (1962) that first brought Barbra Streisand to the attention of audiences and critics alike even though the role was a minor one. Miss Marmelstein is a put-upon secretary in the garment district whom everyone takes advantage of except romantically. To all who work with her she is never "boobala" or "passion pie" but merely "Miss Marmelstein." Her frustration is both accurate and hilarious. Harold Rome wrote the playful music and the farcical lyric.

"Mister Snow" is Carrie Pipperidge's character song about her fiancé in *Carousel* (1945) by Richard Rodgers (music) and Oscar Hammerstein (lyric). Carrie (Jean Darling) describes fisherman Enoch Snow to her girlfriend Julie, praising his gentleness and even the smell of fish about him. The song is reprised later when she sings it to the girls' chorus, and Mr. Snow himself (Eric Mattson) enters and joins her in singing it.

"Moanin' in the Mornin' " is a mock-blues number from *Hooray for What!* (1937) by Harold Arlen (music) and E.Y. Harburg (lyric). Vivian Vance sang the lament as a woman who is cured of romantic illusions, has given up on love and will no longer start her mornings moaning away in grief. Julie Wilson made a stylish recording of the song.

"Moanin' Low" is the tormented torch song that Libby Holman sang in the revue *The Little Show* (1929) that made her a Broadway star. Ralph Rainger (music) and Howard Dietz (lyric) wrote the sensual number that Clifton Webb staged and danced with Holman in one of the era's most bizarre musical theatre moments. In a Harlem tenement, Holman (in blackface) sings of her rough and violent lover (Webb), who is sleeping in the bed beside her in a drunken stupor. Webb then awakes, and they dance a feverish pas de deux that ends with his strangling her to death.

"Molasses to Rum (To Slaves)" is a powerful musical number from *1776* (1969) about the slavery question during the passing of the Declaration of Independence. Edward Rutledge (Clifford David), the delegate from South Carolina, refuses to sign the document if the antislavery clause remains and accuses the Northern states of hypocrisy because they are the ones who get rich shipping molasses, rum and slaves to the colonies. Sherman Edwards wrote the music and lyric for the devastating song that uses an auctioneer's patter in the middle section to conjure up the sounds of the slave markets.

"Momma, Look Sharp" is a poignant song about the misery of war from *1776* (1969) by Sherman Edwards. A courier (Scott Jarvis) from General Washington's army delivers his letter and then tells the congressional custodian

(William Duell) and a leather apron (B.J. Slater) about the action he's seen. He sings this moving folk song about the plea of a dying soldier to his mother to come and find him. The number then turns into a delicate trio as the two listeners sing the comforting words of the mother.

"Money Isn't Everything" is a peppy waltz by Richard Rodgers (music) and Oscar Hammerstein (lyric) for their concept musical *Allegro* (1947). The satirical number, sung by Roberta Jonay and a chorus of penniless housewives during the Depression, is about riches being unnecessary (unless you're poor).

"The Money Rings Out Like Freedom" is a lively production number from *Coco* (1969), the Alan Jay Lerner (lyric) and Andre Previn (music) bio-musical about designer Coco Chanel. Katharine Hepburn, in her only Broadway musical appearance, played the title character and, with the chorus, sang this celebratory song as the Chanel fashion house became famous.

"Money to Burn" is the banjo-strumming, high-stepping showstopper from the British import *Half a Sixpence* (1965) with music and lyric by David Heneker. Arthur Kipps (Tommy Steele) celebrates his newfound wealth in a pub with his male friends, and they engage in a rousing production number that was choreographed by Onna White.

"Monkey in the Mango Tree" is a crafty calypso number from *Jamaica* (1957) that takes Darwin's theory of evolution and looks at it from the monkey's point of view. The fisherman Koli (Ricardo Montalban) and some of his fellow islanders sing the comic number about a monkey who has heard about the humans' claim to be evolved from the apes and is aghast that his descendants could live in cities and pursue possessions, commercial products and war. Harold Arlen composed the rhythmic music, and E.Y. Harburg wrote the piquant lyric.

"Monotonous" is a clever comic number from the revue *New Faces of 1952* that launched new face Eartha Kitt's career. Arthur Siegel (music) and June Carroll and Ronny Graham (lyric) wrote the wry song in which Kitt, a femme fatale lounging languorously in her penthouse, lamented her monotonous life of too much amorous attention.

"Moon in My Window" is a dreamy trio from *Do I Hear a Waltz?* (1965) in which two American tourists in Venice (Elizabeth Allen and Julienne Marie) and an Italian pensione keeper (Carol Bruce) each reflect on romance as they gaze out over the canals at night. Richard Rodgers wrote the enchanting music, and Stephen Sondheim provided the gentle lyric.

"Moonbeams" is a delicate song of prayer from *The Red Mill* (1906) by Victor Herbert (music) and Henry Blossom (lyric). Locked inside a red windmill overnight by her father in order to keep her from eloping, Gretchen (Augusta Greenleaf) sings this passionate plea to the moon to send a message to her lover so that he can rescue her. Lucille Norman made a lyrical recording of the song.

"Moon-faced, Starry-eyed" is the only popular song to come from the ambitious Kurt Weill (music) and Langston Hughes (lyric) music drama *Street Scene* (1947), yet it is the least typical number in the operatic score. A fast and swinging young couple, Mae (Sheila Bond) and Dick (Danny Daniels), sang the wild jitterbug number and energetically danced all over the street, sidewalk, stoop and even garbage cans. The 1940s jive number was successfully recorded by Freddy Martin's and Benny Goodman's orchestras.

"Moonfall" is a hauntingly beautiful pastiche of a Victorian love ballad from *The Mystery of Edwin Drood* (1985) by Rupert Holmes. The dastardly John Jasper (Howard McGillin) lusts after his innocent music pupil Rosa Bud (Patti Cohenour), so he writes a sensual song and forces her to sing it as part of her music lesson. The number is reprised later, with a different lyric, as Helena (Jana Schneider), Alice (Judy Kuhn) and Beatrice (Donna Murphy) join Rosa in a lovely quartet. At the end of the first act, "Moonfall" becomes a tempestuous duet for Rosa and Jasper.

"Moonshine Lullaby" is a lazy, easygoing number from Irving Berlin's *Annie Get Your Gun* (1946) that Annie Oakley (Ethel Merman) sings to her younger brothers and sisters to put them to sleep at night. The song has a breezy, backwoods flavor to it as the lyric recalls the old days back home in the hills. Because the moonshine of the title referred to pappy's still rather than lunar beams, the song was limited in its radio play; consequently, "Moonshine Lullaby" never became as popular as some of the other hits from this hit-packed show.

"More I Cannot Wish You" is a tender little ballad from *Guys and Dolls* (1950) by Frank Loesser that brings a moment of sincerity to all the farcical highlights of the musical's second act. The old missionary Brother Abernathy (Pat Rooney, Sr.) comforts the confused Sarah Brown (Isabel Bigley) by encouraging her to love Sky Masterson despite his less-than-saintly character.

"More Than You Know" is an adoring ballad from the short-lived *Great Day* (1929) by Vincent Youmans (music) and Billy Rose and Edward Eliscu (lyric). Mayo Methot, as the financially troubled plantation owner Emma Lou Randolph, sang the endearing song that became popular despite the show's closing after only thirty-six performances.

"A Mormon Life" is a shrewd comic number from the short-lived Jerome Kern musical *Dear Sir* (1924) that showed the promise of young lyricist Howard Dietz in his first Broadway score. Walter Catlett and a chorus of girls sang the ribald number about how dandy it would be to live the life of a multiwived Mormon. Dietz's lyric work is sparkling, rhyming "bigamy" with "polygamy" and "pig o' me."

"Morning Glow" is a stirring song of hope from the medieval musical *Pippin* (1972) by Stephen Schwartz. Having committed regicide and patricide in one fell swoop, Charlemagne's son Pippin (John Rubinstein) leads the ensemble in this entrancing number that sees the new dawn as the beginning of a new age.

"The Most Beautiful Girl in the World" is one of Richard Rodgers' finest waltz melodies. Lorenz Hart wrote a clever, knowing lyric that also manages to be romantic, and the number was sung by Donald Novis and Gloria Grafton in the stage spectacular *Jumbo* (1935). Ted Straeter, who was rehearsal pianist for the show, made "The Most Beautiful Girl in the World" the theme song for his band and recorded the waltz three times over the years.

"Most Gentlemen Don't Like Love" is Cole Porter's comic testament to the fickleness of men, stating that the only thing they want to do with love is "kick it around." Sophie Tucker and the ensemble sang it in *Leave It to Me!* (1938), and Mary Martin, who was in the show but didn't sing it, made a popular recording of the song with Eddy Duchin's Orchestra.

"Mother Machree," the popular Irish ballad by Ernest R. Ball, Chauncey Olcott (music) and Rida Johnson Young (lyric), was first heard on Broadway in *Barry of Ballymore* (1910), where Olcott sang it. The song became popular after its being interpolated into *The Isle o' Dreams* (1913), where Olcott performed it again. "Mother Machree" was a staple in all the concerts by Irish tenor John McCormack throughout his career.

"Mountain Greenery" is the Rodgers and Hart hit from the second edition of *The Garrick Gaieties* (1926), much as their "Manhattan" was in the first edition. While the latter celebrated the joys of being in the city, the former is about getting away to the country. Lorenz Hart's lyric uses unlikely word divisions to great effect. Richard Rodgers' driving rhythm builds by repeating the first three notes, then makes all sorts of dazzling harmonic shifts in the release. Sterling Holloway (who had introduced "Manhattan") and Bobbie Perkins were the first to sing "Mountain Greenery," and soon everyone was singing it. Mel Tormé, in particular, made a very popular recording years later. In 1947 Rodgers used an orchestrated version of the song as dance music for a 1920s scene in his *Allegro*.

"Mountain High, Valley Low" is a tender song of farewell from the "Chinese musical" *Lute Song* (1946) by Raymond Scott (music) and Bernard Hanighen (lyric). The scholar Tsai-Yong (Yul Brynner) must leave his wife Tchao-Ou-Niang (Mary Martin) to travel to court, but before they separate they sing this lovely duet, vowing to remain loyal to each other. Dorothy Collins and Martin herself each made popular recordings of the song, though *Lute Song* had a disappointingly short run.

"The Mounties" is the rousing march favorite from the operetta *Rose-Marie* (1924) with music by Rudolf Friml and Herbert Stothart and a lyric by Otto Harbach and Oscar Hammerstein. Sergeant Malone (Arthur Deagon) of the Canadian Mounties and his men sing the number, which started a vogue for similar kinds of chorales in operetta.

"Move On" is a soaring duet from *Sunday in the Park With George* (1984) by Stephen Sondheim and one of his most expansive and optimistic songs. The confused contemporary artist George (Mandy Patinkin) is given advice from the ghostly spectre of George Seurat's mistress Dot (Bernadette Peters) to ignore trends, forget the critics and move forward and accept life with all its possibilities. The number builds beautifully from two contrapuntal melodies to a penetrating duet with George and Dot singing together. The song is not only the climax of the musical but in many ways the summation of what Sondheim has tried to do with the musical form over the decades. Barbra Streisand made a highly personalized recording of the song.

"Move Over, New York" is the exhilarating opening number from *Bajour* (1964), the gypsy musical by Walter Marks. Johnny Dembo (Herschel Bernardi) and his tribe of gypsies rent a New York City storefront and set up shop for their illegal activities. The exciting number was cleverly staged by choreographer Peter Gennaro, with the empty store being transformed in front of the audience into a colorful display of shawls, beaded curtains and astrological and phrenological charts.

"The Movie in My Mind" is a wistful but powerful ballad from the British import *Miss Saigon* (1991) with music by Claude-Michel Schönberg and lyric by Richard Maltby, Jr., who adapted Alain Boublil's original French text. During a sordid beauty pageant to crown Miss Saigon, the prostitute-contestant Gigi (Marina Chapa) privately reveals her fantasies about marrying a GI and going to live in America. The thoughts of Kim (Lea Salonga) and the other girls are similar as they join in singing about their vision of happiness, all of it based on crass images from American TV and movies.

"Mr. Cellophane" is one of the handful of pastiche numbers in *Chicago*

(1975) by John Kander (music) and Fred Ebb (lyric). The forlorn husband Amos Hart (Barney Martin) sings the wry song about how no one notices him, even apologizing to the audience for bothering them with his invisible problem. The number is an obvious pastiche of Bert Williams' famous rendition of "Nobody" and in perfect keeping with the vaudeville nature of *Chicago*. Bob Cuccioli also sang "Mr. Cellophane" in the Off-Broadway revue *And the World Goes 'Round* (1991).

"Mr. Gallagher and Mr. Shean" is the classic and much-parodied comic song written and performed by the men of the title. The number was introduced in the 1922 edition of the *Ziegfeld Follies*, where Ed Gallagher and Al Shean, costumed as an explorer and a desert native, meet in front of an Egyptian backdrop and sing a series of non sequitur questions and comments, always calling each other by their formal titles. The comedy team performed the number often throughout their careers, adding new lyrics as they pleased. The song was parodied throughout the nation at the time, and in 1938 Bing Crosby and Johnny Mercer made a popular recording of the duet.

"Mr. Goldstone" is a vivacious list song from *Gypsy* (1959) in which the grateful Rose (Ethel Merman) thanks Mervyn Goldstone (Mort Marshall) for booking her act on the Orpheum Circuit by offering him everything on their table (egg rolls, napkins, chopsticks and so on) and then anything else she can think of. Jule Styne composed the march melody, and Stephen Sondheim provided the clever lyric that manages to list the various kinds of "stones" to add to the joyous fun.

"Mr. Monotony" is one of the most rejected songs in the annals of musical theatre. Irving Berlin wrote the odd, jazzy number for Judy Garland in the film *Easter Parade* (1948), and it was recorded and filmed but left on the cutting-room floor. He then added it to the Broadway score for *Miss Liberty* (1949), where it was deemed inappropriate for the character and was dropped. The song was sung by Ethel Merman in *Call Me Madam* (1950) for a while but was cut before opening because Merman couldn't make it work. The song disappeared until Ben Bagley rediscovered it and made a recording with Dorothy Loudon singing it in 1967. When the revue *Jerome Robbins' Broadway* opened in 1989, Debbie Shapiro sang it and the ensemble danced to its sexy, offbeat rhythms. (Robbins had choreographed *Miss Liberty*.) Ironically, after the revue had been running a few weeks, the producers cut "Mr. Monotony" in order to trim the running time of the show. There is no other song in the Berlin repertoire quite like this number. The lyric narrates a tale of a woman who can only be pleased by a certain monotonous man. The melody purposely pounds one note, then, when it almost becomes unbearable, varies a few notes or changes keys, only to begin another monotonous melody. The effect is a very moody, very unique song that would not have been out of place in a 1950s "beat" coffeehouse.

"Mr. Wonderful" is the hit song from the 1956 Sammy Davis, Jr., vehicle of the same name. Ironically, the number was not sung by Davis but by leading lady Olga James, as his fiancée, about the Davis character. Jerry Bock, in his days before he met Sheldon Harnick, wrote the music, and the unrestrained lyric is by Larry Holofcener and George Weiss. Peggy Lee, Teddi King and Sarah Vaughan each made popular recordings of the song.

"Much More" is the eager, funny "I am" song for the young Luisa (Rita Gardner) in the long-running *The Fantasticks* (1960). In the fervent aria, Luisa explains how she wants to have danger and romance in her life before she gets too old. Harvey Schmidt wrote the simple melody that climbs the scale until it bursts into comic rhapsody, and Tom Jones provided the zesty lyric. In the early 1960s Barbra Streisand recorded the song and sang it in her nightclub act; in fact, it was her signature song until she did *Funny Girl* (1964) and "People" became forever associated with her.

"Mulligan Guard" was one of New York City's most sung, whistled and hummed songs in its day, thanks to its being sung or played in several Harrigan and Hart musical comedies. The song, written by David Braham (music) and Edward Harrigan (lyric) for a vaudeville sketch in 1873, makes fun of those who like to dress up and parade about in uniform. The sketch and the song led to the Broadway show *The Mulligan Guards' Ball* (1879), where it was sung by Harrigan and his partner Tony Hart. The number caught on and was heard in some form in all the seven succeeding Harrigan and Hart musicals. The song was again heard on Broadway in the 1985 bio-musical *Harrigan and Hart*, where it was sung by Harry Groener and Mark Hamill, as the title characters, and the ensemble.

"Museum Song" is a rompish list song from *Barnum* (1980) that was also a fast-talking patter number in the style of Gilbert and Sullivan. P.T. Barnum (Jim Dale) describes the new Barnum's American Museum by rattling off a list of some of the contents with a rhyming flourish. Cy Coleman wrote the frantic music, and Michael Stewart provided the witty lyric.

"The Music and the Mirror" is a poignant song about the need to dance from *A Chorus Line* (1975) by Marvin Hamlisch (music) and Edward Kleban (lyric). Cassie (Donna McKechnie) graduated from the chorus line to featured roles, but her career hasn't worked out and she desperately wants to return to dancing. She sings this impassioned plea to Zach (Robert LuPone), the director auditioning the dancers and also her former lover. Cassie sings of returning to the dance-studio mirrors, then launches into a frenzied dance solo choreographed by Michael Bennett that reveal her frustrations and desires.

"The Music of the Night" is the seductive, eerie ballad from the British import *The Phantom of the Opera* (1988) by Andrew Lloyd Webber (music) and Charles Hart and Richard Stilgoe (lyric) that is arguably the most famous song from the popular show. The Phantom (Michael Crawford) plays the pipe organ in his underground lair and then sings the ballad hypnotically to the opera singer Christine (Sarah Brightman), asking her to submit to the power of his music.

"The Music That Makes Me Dance" is a ravishing torch song by Jule Styne (music) and Bob Merrill (lyric) written for Fanny Brice (Barbra Streisand) to sing in *Funny Girl* (1964) as a replacement for the real Brice's signature song "My Man." The beautiful ballad enjoyed only a limited amount of popularity because it was overshadowed by the show's other emotional ballad "People." Also, the song was dropped from the 1968 film version when the actual "My Man" was used. Regardless, it contains one of Styne's most haunting melodies and an impressionable lyric by Merrill. Michael Feinstein recorded the ballad in 1991.

"The Music Went Out of My Life" is the bluesy torch song that Julie Wilson sang in the infamous musical flop *Legs Diamond* (1988). Peter Allen wrote the music and lyric for the roaring 1920s pastiche number.

"Mutual Admiration Society" is the popular paean to friendship that Ethel Merman introduced in *Happy Hunting* (1956) by Harold Karr (music) and Matt Dubey (lyric). Philadelphia Mainliner Liz Livingstone (Merman) and her daughter Beth (Virginia Gibson) sang the rousing number that allowed them to praise each other with all the stops out. The song was heard on the radio and on jukeboxes across the country before the show even opened. Teresa Brewer, Eddy Arnold and Jay P. Morgan are among those who recorded it.

"My Beautiful Lady" is the waltzing hit ballad from the operetta *The Pink Lady* (1911) by Ivan Caryll (music) and C.M.S. McLellan (lyric). Lucien (William Elliott) sang the romantic serenade to Angele (Alice Dovey), as the two lovers imagined themselves as beautiful violets adorning a Parisian cafe. In a rather unusual reprise, Hazel Dawn, as the "pink lady" Claudine, accompanied herself on the violin as she also sang the number. When audiences heard the song, they were already familiar with the melody; it had been used in an earlier number called "The Kiss Waltz." From all his operettas in London and on Broadway, "My Beautiful Lady" remains Caryll's most recognized song.

"My Best Girl" is a quiet little ballad amidst all the shenanigans of the musical *Mame* (1966) by Jerry Herman. After Mame Dennis (Angela Lansbury) has been fired from her featured part in a musical show, her young nephew Patrick (Frankie Michaels) comforts her with this sweet song. It is reprised at the top of the second act by the young and the grown-up Patrick (Jerry Lanning) with an altered lyric.

"My Big Mistake" is a reflective character song for Betty Rogers (Dee Hoty) in *The Will Rogers Follies* (1991) by Cy Coleman (music) and Betty Comden and Adolph Green (lyric). As she roams the country with her husband and children on the Wild West Show circuit, Betty wonders about her life and looks back with regret and love on the day she decided to marry Will Rogers.

"My Brudder and Me" is a sportive song and dance number from the revue *Make Mine Manhattan* (1948) by Richard Lewine (music) and Arnold B. Horwitt (lyric). Danny Daniels and Sheila Bond stopped the show with this delightful number about a brother and sister who love to dance but can't afford the fancy nightclubs, so they do their hoofing on the sidewalk outside a record store. Daniels and Bond became a dance team in demand because of their appearance in this number.

"My Castle in the Air" is an early Jerome Kern (music) and P.G. Wodehouse (lyric) collaboration that was interpolated into *Miss Springtime* (1916) and became the hit of the show. This bouncy invitation to come and visit a dreamy castle at the rainbow's end was sung by George MacFarlane, who, in a very rare case for this period, actually got to record the song he had introduced on the stage. While Wodehouse's lyric for the number is dependable and routine, Kern's music has several subtle shifts in key and overriding harmony that make the song unusual.

"My Cup Runneth Over" is the hit ballad to come out of *I Do! I Do!* (1966) by Tom Jones (lyric) and Harvey Schmidt (music). The married couple Michael (Robert Preston) and Agnes (Mary Martin) are expecting the birth of their first child and sing this heartfelt duet about the deep affection they have for one another. The number was cut from the show during rehearsals when both stars were having difficulty sustaining the high note that ends the song. But the lovely piece was sorely missed, so the final note was shortened and the song was restored to the score during the Boston tryouts. Ed Ames's recording of the ballad was a top seller.

"My Darling, My Darling" is a popular romantic ballad from *Where's Charley?* (1948) with music and lyric by Frank Loesser. The enticing duet was sung by Oxford undergrad Jack Chesney (Byron Palmer) and his sweetheart Kitty (Doretta Morrow) in the early blushes of their romance. Fellow undergrad

Charley Wykeham (Ray Bolger) reprised the number near the end of the show. Buddy Clark and Doris Day made a hit recording of the song together, as did Jo Stafford, Gordon MacRae and others.

"My Favorite Things" is a merry list song written by Richard Rodgers (music) and Oscar Hammerstein (lyric), a naive but charming number from *The Sound of Music* (1959). In the stage version the song is sung by Maria (Mary Martin) for the Mother Abbess (Patricia Neway), who recalls it from her childhood and wishes to write it down. The number ends as a happy duet that solidifies the warm relationship between the two women. Aside from being popular with children's choruses, the song was a hit for Herb Alpert and the Tijuana Brass in a 1969 instrumental recording, for the Peter King Chorale and in a best-selling jazz version by John Coltrane in 1968.

"My Favorite Year" is the warm and nostalgic title number from the 1992 musical about the early days of live television. Comedy writer Benjy Stone (Evan Pappas) and the ensemble sing the song at the end of the show, recalling the year 1959 when Benjy found success, love and a new understanding of true heroism. Stephen Flaherty composed the pleasant music, and Lynn Ahrens wrote the evocative lyric.

"My First Love Song" is the timid proposal of love from the put-upon Cocky (Anthony Newley) in the allegorical musical *The Roar of the Greasepaint -- The Smell of the Crowd* (1965). While playing "the game," Cocky experiences love for the first time and sings this tender song to the Girl (Joyce Jillson), who joins him for a melodic duet. Leslie Bricusse and Newley wrote the unusual love song.

"My Funny Valentine" may be the most beloved of all of Rodgers and Hart's ballads. It is one of several hits to come out of *Babes in Arms* (1937), where Mitzi Green sang it about her true love (Ray Heatherton), whose name was Valentine. Richard Rodgers' melody for the verse is simple and unaccompanied; the refrain is a brilliant variation of the same six-note phrase that climaxes beautifully. Lorenz Hart's lyric in the verse uses archaic language ("thy," "knowest," "hast") to arrive at a slangy intimacy; in the refrain he manages to take gentle insults and turn them into highly romantic compliments. It is a song only Rodgers and Hart could have written and a marvel by any standards. Memorable versions of the oft-recorded song were made by Tony Bennett, Julie Andrews, Linda Ronstadt and Carly Simon.

"My Heart Belongs to Daddy" is the Cole Porter song that launched Mary Martin's career and was associated with her for many years. The number is a mock striptease that she sang in *Leave It to Me!* (1938) bundled in furs, sitting on a trunk in a Siberian train station. The number stopped the show, which was unexpected since Martin's was a minor character (it was her only song) and the scene was written to cover a major set change backstage. Porter's lyric is delectable in its double entendres and sly variations on the word "daddy" yet it leaves enough room for a naive, innocent interpretation. It is very unlikely that many thought the song was about fatherlove, but that conceit allowed the number to be played on the radio. Martin recorded it with Eddy Duchin's Orchestra, and there was a best-selling record by the Larry Clinton Orchestra (vocal by Bea Wain).

"My Heart Is So Full of You" is a rhapsodic love duet in the Italianate opera style from Frank Loesser's *The Most Happy Fella* (1956). Opera singer Robert Weede, as the vineyard owner Tony, and Jo Sullivan, as his young wife Rosabella, introduced the endearing number.

"My Heart Stood Still" is a romantic duet that Richard Rodgers (music) and Lorenz Hart (lyric) wrote for *A Connecticut Yankee* (1927), and it joined their growing ranks of popular hits. The song was originally heard in the London revue *One Damn Thing After Another* (1927) and then was added to *A Connecticut Yankee* for William Gaxton and Constance Carpenter to sing. Hart's lyric for the refrain is unusual in that it is comprised almost entirely of one-syllable words, a tricky feat in a serious love song.

"My Hometown" is a tribute to Hollywood from the behind-the-scenes show-business musical *What Makes Sammy Run?* (1964) with music and lyric by Ervin Drake. The ambitious New Yorker Sammy Glick (Steve Lawrence) arrives in L.A. and sings this nightclub-style song about the town that will fulfill his big-time dreams. Lawrence's recording single of the song was very popular.

"My Houseboat on the Harlem" is a deliciously sarcastic song for the comic leads in *Dear Sir* (1924), a Jerome Kern musical that introduced lyricist Howard Dietz to Broadway. Walter Catlett and Kathlene Martyn sang the witty number about the horrors of urban living, including a houseboat stuck in the Harlem River mud.

"My Husband Makes Movies" is the revealing and moving "I am" song for the filmmaker's wife in *Nine* (1982) by Maury Yeston. Luisa (Karen Akers) is being interviewed by the press about her famous husband Guido Contini and coolly explains that his sometimes eccentric behavior is due to his total immersion into the art. Then, in a private soliloquy section, Luisa recalls her once-promising acting career and how she fell in love with Guido and became a different person.

"My Joe" is a touching song of undying love from *Carmen Jones* (1943), Oscar Hammerstein's Americanization of Georges Bizet's opera *Carmen*. Cindy Lou (Carlotta Franzell) has followed her beloved Joe to Chicago after he went there to pursue Carmen Jones. In this poignant aria, which uses the music from *Carmen*'s "Micaela's Air," Cindy Lou explains to the boxer Husky Miller how deep her love for Joe is.

"My Last Love" is a breezy ballad from *What's Up?* (1943), the first Broadway collaboration of Alan Jay Lerner (lyric) and Frederick Loewe (music). Mary Roche, Larry Douglas, Lynn Gardner, Johnny Morgan and William Tabbert sang the appealing song about a new love that is superior to previous loves and the hope that this new lover will indeed be the last. The musical was never recorded, but Dorothy Loudon made a stylish recording of the song.

"My Lord and Master" is the brief but impressionable "I am" song sung by the slave Tuptim (Doretta Morrow) near the beginning of *The King and I* (1951). In the Richard Rodgers (music) and Oscar Hammerstein (lyric) ballad, Tuptim vows to obey and serve the king, but her heart belongs to another.

"My Love" is an unromantic love duet from *Candide* (1956) with elegant music by Leonard Bernstein and a droll lyric by Richard Wilbur and John Latouche. The Governor of Buenos Aires (William Olvis) propositions the enticing Cunegonde (Barbara Cook) with love without marriage, stating that undying love is a fabrication of poets. Cunegonde is shocked at the suggestion, so the Governor proposes marriage even though he's sure they'll quickly learn to loathe each other. In the 1974 revised revival of *Candide*, the serenade was used, with no lyric changes, by the Governor (Lewis J. Stadlin) to woo Maximilian (Sam Freed), who was disguised as a woman at the slave market.

"My Love Is a Married Man" is a bluesy torch song from *The Day Before Spring* (1945) that is so self-aware and witty that it avoids any self-pity. Patricia Marshall sang the number, Frederick Loewe composed the beguiling music, and Alan Jay Lerner, showing brilliant promise that would soon be fulfilled, wrote the succinct lyric.

"My Lucky Star" is the popular ballad from *Follow Thru* (1929), the musical about golf by B.G. DeSylva and Lew Brown (lyric) and Ray Henderson (music). The dashing Jerry Downs (John Barker) is being pursued by two women golf champions, but only one (Irene Delroy) is the lucky star for him. The oft-recorded song had two outstanding hits by Paul Whiteman's Orchestra and Fred Waring's Pennsylvanians.

"My Mammy" is the quintessential Al Jolson song, one he interpolated into his Broadway vehicle *Sinbad* (1918) but also sang in other shows, in concert and on film. For *Sinbad* a ramp was built from the stage far out into the audience where Jolson, in blackface and white gloves, sang the number down on one knee, surrounded by the crowd. The robust song of maternal affection was written by Walter Donaldson (music) and Sam Lewis and Joe Young (lyric). Others have recorded the number over the years, including a surprise hit single in 1967 by the Happenings.

"My Man" is the atypical but popular Fanny Brice song, a serious lament about unrequited love delivered without any of her usual self-deprecating humor. Brice sang the torch song in the 1921 edition of the *Ziegfeld Follies* standing under a lamp post dressed in drab clothes not expected in a Ziegfeld show. But Brice revealed a whole new facet to her remarkable talents, and the song became the highlight of the revue. Maurice Yvain composed the music for the French song "Mon Homme," and Channing Pollock wrote an original lyric for the ballad. "My Man" was featured in four movie musicals and among the many who made hit recordings of the ballad were Billie Holiday, Dinah Shore, Diana Ross, Peggy Lee, Barbra Streisand and Brice herself, who recorded it three times.

"My Man's Gone Now" is one of the most penetrating songs of the American theatre, a heartfelt wail of anguish from the folk opera *Porgy and Bess* (1935). Her husband killed in a crap-game knife fight, Serena (Ruby Elzy) grieves for him in this powerful arioso, with the ensemble joining in on the pervasive moans that punctuate the piece. George Gershwin composed the complex number that uses waltz time for the main section, interrupts it for a slow wailing theme, then climaxes with an ascending glissando that pierces the heart. DuBose Heyward wrote the absorbing lyric that uses the image of "ole man sorrow" to personify the widow's grief. In addition to several recording by opera singers, Sarah Vaughan and Cleo Laine each had distinctive renditions of the song recorded.

"My Most Important Moments Go By" is a wistful song from the pioneering Off-Broadway rock musical *The Last Sweet Days of Isaac* (1970) by Gretchen Cryer (lyric) and Nancy Ford (music). The hyperactive Isaac Bernstein (Austin Pendleton) and the office secretary Ingrid (Fredricka Weber) are stuck in an elevator for an hour together and start to explore the meaninglessness of their existence in this bittersweet duet.

"My Mother's Wedding Day" is an amusing character song from *Brigadoon* (1947) in which Meg Brockie (Pamela Britton) describes a raucous Scottish wedding, complete with a drunken groom, a family feud and a "bonnie brawl." Frederick Loewe composed the Highland-like music, and Alan Jay Lerner wrote the witty lyric in which he utilized and rhymed over a dozen Scottish names.

"My One and Only" is a jazzy love song from the Gershwins' *Funny Face* (1927) that was sung and tapped by Fred Astaire with Gertrude McDonald, Betty Compton and the girls' ensemble. George Gershwin wrote the lively, rhythmic music, and Ira Gershwin provided the lyric that craved romantic exclusivity but settled for lighthearted fun. The rewritten version of *Funny Face* in 1983 used the song title for the new show's title, and the number was sung and danced by the philosophical Mr. Magix (Charles "Honi" Coles) as he taught aviator Billy Buck Chandler (Tommy Tune) a thing or two about love and hoofing.

"My Own Morning" is a fervent song of determination for the heroine Georgina (Leslie Uggams) in *Hallelujah, Baby!* (1967). Working in the kitchen of a rich white family, the black servant Georgina dreams of having her own home with her own things and her own life. Jule Styne (music) and Betty Comden and Adolph Green (lyric) wrote the appealing number.

"My Romance" is a terrific love song that achieves its effect by having the lyric list all the clichés (blue lagoon, moon, stars, castles in Spain) that the lovers do not need. Richard Rodgers' music climbs up the scale in a leisurely manner, and Lorenz Hart's lyric uses the list format to arrive at a beautifully simple conclusion. Gloria Grafton and Donald Novis sang it as a duet in the Hippodrome musical extravaganza *Jumbo* (1935), and it was recorded by artists ranging from Paul Whiteman (whose orchestra played in the original show) to Ella Fitzgerald to Dave Brubeck to Carly Simon to a duet version by Dinah Shore and Frank Sinatra.

"My Ship" is the haunting, mysterious ballad used throughout *Lady in the Dark* (1941) as a leitmotif and as a key to the major character. Magazine editor Liza Elliott (Gertrude Lawrence) tells her psychoanalyst Dr. Brooks (Donald Randolph) that she vaguely recalls a nursery song from her childhood but cannot remember all of it. Throughout the musical only fragments of the melody are heard until the end, when Liza pieces it all together. When her advertising manager Charlie Johnson (MacDonald Carey) also recalls the song, Liza finally makes up her mind about marrying him. "My Ship" was the only song in the score that was sung outside the show's expressionistic dream sequences. Ira Gershwin wrote the simple but evocative lyric, and Kurt Weill composed the bewitching melody that sounded sweet and comforting at times, then menacing and pervasive at other times. Julie Andrews and Dawn Upshaw are among those who recorded "My Ship," and Margery Cohen sang the ballad in the Off-Broadway revue *Berlin to Broadway With Kurt Weill* (1972).

"My Sword and I" is the musical credo of the heroic d'Artagnan (Dennis King) in the operetta *The Three Musketeers* (1928). Rudolf Friml composed the stirring music, and Clifford Grey provided the earnest lyric.

"My Time of Day" is the shortest (only sixteen bars) and one of the quietest songs from Frank Loesser's *Guys and Dolls* (1950), a gentle, heartfelt love song to the city of New York. Gambler Sky Masterson (Robert Alda) sings the number to Sarah Brown (Isabel Bigley) as they walk down the quiet streets of Broadway at 4 a.m. The song is extremely evocative of the sounds and smells of a sleeping city and was one of Loesser's favorites of all his works.

"My Wild Irish Rose" is the beloved standard still popular today and one of the finest Irish ballads to come from America. The song was written by Chauncey Olcott, who sang it in *A Romance of Athlone* (1899), but it was when he performed it in *The Isle o' Dreams* (1913), a musical melodrama set in Ireland, that he scored a personal triumph with the song. The ballad remains among the most performed and recorded of all American songs.

N

"'N' Everything" is lyricist B.G. DeSylva's first hit song, a breezy romantic number in which the suitor runs out of poetic descriptions, so he concludes with the catchall "'n' everything." Al Jolson sang the song in *Sinbad* (1918) and propelled it to fame, initiating DeSylva's long and prolific career. The number was written by DeSylva, Gus Kahn and Jolson himself.

"Namely You" is the pleasing romantic duet for the not-so-romantic Abner Yokum (Peter Palmer) and the marriage-minded Daisy Mae (Edith Adams) in the comic-strip musical *Li'l Abner* (1956). Gene de Paul wrote the appealing music, and Johnny Mercer provided the coy lyric. Don Cherry made a popular recording of the ballad.

"The Name's LaGuardia" is the rousing campaign song sung by the optimistic candidate (Tom Bosley) and his supporters in *Fiorello!* (1959). Jerry Bock composed the foot-stomping music, and Sheldon Harnick wrote the chummy lyric that included verses in Italian and Yiddish to please LaGuardia's culturally diverse constituency. Besides being a spirited production number, the song also serves as a potent contrast to incumbent mayor James Walker's more sophisticated campaign song "Gentleman Jimmy" in the same show.

"Napoleon" is a patter song from *Have a Heart* (1917) and lyricist P.G. Wodehouse's first major comic number in a Broadway show. Vaudeville comic Billy B. Van, as the elevator boy Henry who saves the day, sang the song, which outlines all the reasons for the French general's greatness, despite the fact that he was short and stingy and had other less-than-noble attributes. Jerome Kern wrote the music, and Van recorded the song himself, a very unusual practice for the period.

"Napoleon" is a caustic comic number from *Jamaica* (1957) by Harold

Arlen (music) and E.Y. Harburg (lyric) about the fleeting quality of fame. When the assistant governor Cicero (Ossie Davis) is made governor pro tem, the island beauty Savannah (Lena Horne) brings him down a peg or two by singing this witty song about how all the great men of history have become names for commercial products: Napoleon is a pastry, Gladstone is a bag, Lincoln is a tunnel, and so on. Arlen and Harburg had written a similar number for *Hooray for What!* (1937) called "Napoleon's a Pastry" that June Clyde sang. The music is different, but many of the lyric ideas are the same. To make matters more confusing, the new "Napoleon" is sometimes listed as "Napoleon's a Pastry."

"Naughty Marietta" is the zesty title song from the 1910 Victor Herbert operetta and a kind of "I am" song for the show's heroine. Marietta d'Altena (Emma Trentini) introduces herself as a fun-loving but mischievous girl with changing moods, and Herbert's music follows her whimsical description playfully. Rida Johnson Young wrote the tangy lyric.

"Neapolitan Love Song" is what it sounds like, a rich Italian romantic number for a resonant male voice. Victor Herbert (music) and Henry Blossom (lyric) wrote this irresistibly popular song for the operetta *The Princess Pat* (1915), where it was sung by the visiting Prince Antonio de Montaldo (Joseph R. Lertora), who dreams of holding his beloved once again.

"Near to You" is a poignant ballad from *Damn Yankees* (1955) with music and lyric by Richard Adler and Jerry Ross. Young Joe Hardy (Stephen Douglass) tells Meg (Shannon Bolin) that, although her husband has left, he is still near to her in his thoughts. Meg joins in for the duet section of the song, made all the more poignant by the fact that young Joe is her husband in a disguise of sorts. For the 1994 Broadway revival, the song was turned into a trio, with Meg (Linda Stephens) singing the ballad as both Joes (Jarrod Emick and Dennis Kelly) appear and join her.

"'Neath the Southern Moon" is a passionate aria from the operetta *Naughty Marietta* (1910) by Victor Herbert (music) and Rida Johnson Young (lyric) that uses rich, tropical imagery in both its melody and lyrics. The quadroon slave girl Adah (Marie Duchene) sings the intense song asking Fortune whether her love will prove true. The number is a difficult contralto piece that requires sustained long lines more demanding than traditional operetta. Herbert wrote the score for the Manhattan Opera Company and consequently came up with the most challenging compositions of his career. Nelson Eddy had a popular recording of the song.

"Necessity" is a comic blues number from *Finian's Rainbow* (1947) sung by Dolores Martin, Maude Simmons and the other black sharecroppers, who lament how all the fun in life is destroyed by the practical things in this world, such as paying rent and getting thrown in jail. Burton Lane wrote the clever music that starts as a wailing church spiritual, then breaks into an irreverent jazz number. E.Y. Harburg wrote the insidious lyric that serves as a socioeconomic satire on labor and religion. Georgia Gibbs made a popular single recording of the song.

"Nellie Kelly, I Love You" is the waltzing love song from *Little Nellie Kelly* (1922) by George M. Cohan. Jerry Conroy (Charles King), a wisecracking Irishman, crashes a big society party to woo the working-class Nellie, the daughter of a police officer in the Bronx. There is more than just a touch of the Irish in the lilting ballad, and Cohan's lyric is soft and warm. Joel Grey, Bernadette Peters and the company sang the number in the bio-musical *George M!* (1968).

"Nesting Time in Flatbush" is a cozy comic number from *Oh, Boy!* (1917) that spoofed all those "let's settle down together in - - -" songs of the period, in particular the popular ballad "When It's Apple Blossom Time in Normandy." Jerome Kern (music) and P.G. Wodehouse (lyric) wrote the "syncopated foxtrot," which was sung by the show's comic leads, Jackie Sampson (Anna Wheaton) and Jim Marvin (Hal Forde).

"Never, Never Land" is the enchanting ballad from *Peter Pan* (1954) that Peter (Mary Martin) sings to Wendy (Kathy Nolan) describing the dreamy land where he lives. Jule Styne (music) and Betty Comden and Adolph Green (lyric) wrote the wistful number on the road before the Broadway opening, and it became the most tender moment in the show. The song is sometimes titled "Neverland" or "Never Land."

"Never Say No" is a clownish duet for the two fathers in the Off-Broadway phenomenon *The Fantasticks* (1960) by Tom Jones (lyric) and Harvey Schmidt (music). Hucklebee (William Larsen) and Bellomy (Hugh Thomas) have used reverse psychology and gotten their children to fall in love by refusing to let them see each other. The fathers are so proud of their clever plan that they break into this comic tango in which they explain how to handle kids.

"Never Will I Marry" is a surging song of resignation from the superb Frank Loesser score for the unsuccessful *Greenwillow* (1960). Gideon Briggs (Anthony Perkins) knows he is cursed to wander, so he vows not to wed any woman and break her heart. The passionate ballad has a very unusual time signature (6/4) for a popular song that gives the number an aching sense of want and despair. Barbra Streisand made a popular recording of the song.

"A New Argentina" is the inflammatory Act One finale from the British import *Evita* (1979) by Andrew Lloyd Webber (music) and Tim Rice (lyric). Juan Peron (Bob Gunton) stirs up the populace as he runs for president of the country, promising a renewed government and a better life for all. His wife Eva (Patti LuPone) encourages him throughout the number, while the rebellious student Che (Mandy Patinkin) makes left-wing comments. In Harold Prince's original staging of the number, posters, banners and placards were used to create a political rally that was very effective.

"The New Ashmolean Marching Society and Students' Conservatory Band" is a rousing march number for the students at Oxford University in Frank Loesser's *Where's Charley?* (1948). In addition to the delightfully engaging melody, Loesser came up with a droll lyric, the kind not usually found in large ensemble numbers.

"New Fangled Preacher Man" is the animated "I am" song for the unconventional minister Purlie (Cleavon Little) in *Purlie* (1970). Arriving in a small Georgia town where he has bought the Big Bethel Church, Purlie tells his new congregation that his cause is happiness for all *before* they die instead of after. Gary Geld wrote the rocking gospel music, and Peter Udell provided the shrewd lyric.

"New Sun in the Sky" is the popular song of optimism by Howard Dietz (lyric) and Arthur Schwartz (music) that was one of the hits from their revue *The Band Wagon* (1931). Fred Astaire, as a proper gentleman in top hat, white tie and tails, checked himself in front of a mirror and sang the romping song that declared good times ahead (despite the show's opening at the low point of the Depression). Astaire recorded the song with Leo Reisman's Orchestra.

"New York, New York" is the vibrant testament to Manhattan from *On the Town* (1944) and perhaps the most exhilarating of the many songs that try to capture the excitement of the city. Three sailors on twenty-four hours' leave (Cris Alexander, Adolph Green and John Battles) jump off their ship at the Brooklyn Navy Yard and anticipate the adventures that await them. Leonard Bernstein composed the jazzy, hyperactive music that contains Stravinsky-like bursts of expression, and Betty Comden and Adolph Green wrote the bombastic lyric.

"Next to Lovin' (I Like Fightin')" is a robust song celebrating life's two great pleasures from the rural musical *Shenandoah* (1975) by Gary Geld (music) and Peter Udell (lyric). The rambunctious Anderson brothers (Jordan Suffin, Joel Higgins, Robert Rosen, Ted Agress and David Russell) sing the exhilarating number as they dance and roughhouse together. Also memorable was Robert Tucker's animated choreography for the number, which included a fist fight in slow motion.

"Nice" is a sweet duet from the Off-Broadway musical farce *Lucky Stiff* (1988) in which the dog-hating Harry Witherspoon (Stephen Stout) and the animal-rights advocate Annabel Glick (Julie White) are reconciled and admit that they will miss their rivalry in the future. The charming number was written by Stephen Flaherty (music) and Lynn Ahrens (lyric).

"Nickel Under the Foot" is a searing indictment song from the controversial *The Cradle Will Rock* (1937) by Marc Blitzstein. The prostitute Moll (Olive Stanton) is brought into night court, where she sings how easy it is to talk about morals and right or wrong when one has plenty to eat and a nice place to live. The song, along with most of the score, was recorded in 1938, the first full recording in this country of an American musical.

"Night and Day," Cole Porter's most famous song, is unusual in several respects. Its melody has a rather limited range because it was written for Fred Astaire, whose voice had definite constraints. The ballad also contains an insistent series of bass notes that would normally lead to a sort of monotony; but in this case the melody line meets with the bass line at crucial moments to make the song totally satisfying. Also unique are the lyric's passionate, uncynical temperament and the lack of any of the usual Porter urbane wit. The lyric refers to the "drip drip drip" and the "tick tick tick" that denote the slow passage of time that haunts the lover. Porter said that he was inspired to use this tom-tom beat after hearing a Mohammedan call to prayer when he was in Morocco. Along with "Begin the Beguine," it is Porter's most exotic song. "Night and Day" was first heard in *Gay Divorce* (1932), where Astaire sang it to Claire Luce and then they both danced to it. The song was the hit of the show and helped override the mixed reviews. In fact, on Broadway it was informally known as the "Night and Day Show." Within months after opening, there were popular orchestral recordings by Leo Reisman and Eddie Duchin. Over the years there have been hundreds of other recordings (Astaire recorded it in 1932); perhaps most successful was a Tommy Dorsey Orchestra record with a vocal by Frank Sinatra that swept the charts in 1942.

"Night Letter" is a bewitching duet from *Two Gentlemen of Verona* (1971), the rock version of Shakespeare's tale by Galt MacDermot (music) and John Guare (lyric). Silvia (Jonelle Allen) asks Valentine (Clifton Davis) to help her write a letter to her secret love but soon ends up loving Valentine himself.

"Night of My Nights" is a rhapsodic ballad from *Kismet* (1953), the *Arabian Nights* musical that used musical themes by Alexander Borodin for its score. The Caliph of Baghdad (Richard Kiley) and his entourage sing this thrilling serenade about his beloved Marsinah (Doretta Morrow). Robert Wright and George Forrest wrote the lyric and adapted Borodin's piano piece "Serenade" into a passionate theatre song.

"Night Song" is an enthralling and evocative character song from *Golden Boy* (1964) by Charles Strouse (music) and Lee Adams (lyric). On a warm summer night, Joe Wellington (Sammy Davis, Jr.) reflects on his situation, trapped in Harlem and not knowing what he wants out of life. The absorbing "I am" song manages to capture the tension of urban youth with some striking imagery.

"The Night Was Made for Love" is a sweeping love serenade from *The Cat and the Fiddle* (1931) by Jerome Kern (music) and Otto Harbach (lyric). George Meader, as the strolling guitarist Pompineau, sang the arioso number near the beginning of the show to set a soft, romantic mood, and it was reprised in spots throughout the evening as a recurring theme song.

"Nightlife" is an eager character song from the college musical *All American* (1962) by Charles Strouse (music) and Lee Adams (lyric) that expresses the yearning of youth for some action, much as "A Lot of Livin' to Do" did in the same team's earlier *Bye Bye Birdie* (1960). Coed Susan (Anita Gillette) has been confined to her dorm room on a lovely night, and she and her roommates dream about the joys of nightlife.

"No Boom Boom" is a whimsical character song from *Zorbá* (1968) by John Kander (music) and Fred Ebb (lyric). The faded French courtesan Hortense (Maria Karnilova) entertains Zorbá (Herschel Bernardi) and Nikos (John Cunningham) with tales of her famous lovers, particularly the many admirals she knew. The song turns into a flashback as the admirals enter and woo her, but before she will accept them, they must promise not to fire their naval guns on the island of Crete.

"No Lies" is a winsome song about facing up to the reality of life from *The Best Little Whorehouse in Texas* (1978) by Carol Hall. Miss Mona (Carlin Glynn) and Jewel (Delores Hall) lead the girls at the bordello in the gospel-flavored number that says if you ask no questions you'll be told no lies.

"No, No, Nanette" is the vivacious title song from the 1925 musical comedy that typifies the frivolous 1920s more than any other show. The number is sung by the ensemble at the end of the first act when the defiant young ward Nanette (Louise Groody) decides to go to Atlantic City on her own despite the protestations of her boyfriend Tom (Jack Barker) and everyone else who never say anything but "no" to the anxious young lady. Vincent Youmans wrote the tuneful music, and Otto Harbach provided the winning lyric.

"No One Has Ever Loved Me (As Deeply as You)" is the lyrical realization of the handsome soldier Giorgio (Jere Shea) that he loves the unattractive Fosca (Donna Murphy) in Stephen Sondheim's *Passion* (1994). Near the end of the musical, Giorgio breaks off his affair with his mistress Clara and tells Fosca that her unrelenting, uncompromising love for him is the purest kind of love that can exist. The number is one of the few in the operatic score that uses traditional rhyme in the lyric.

"No One Is Alone" is an inspirational song from *Into the Woods* (1987) by Stephen Sondheim that became quite popular. The number is about how everything one does affects everyone else and how the consequences of our actions have far-reaching effects. Yet often the song is recorded as a straightforward ballad of companionship or affection. In the musical it is sung by Cinderella (Kim Crosby) to the distraught Little Red Riding Hood (Danielle Ferland). Then it is picked up by the Baker (Chip Zien) and Jack (Ben Wright) and becomes a lovely quartet. Betty Buckley and Mandy Patinkin are among those who have recorded the ballad.

"No Other Love," the only popular song to come out of Rodgers and Hammerstein's *Me and Juliet* (1953), is one of their more enticing ballads. Bill Hayes, as an assistant stage manager, and Isabel Bigley, as an actress in the show-within-the-show, sang the lovely ballad in the form of a rehearsal. The music by Richard Rodgers was already somewhat familiar to audiences, having been used for the sound track for his NBC-TV series "Victory at Sea" the year before. Oscar Hammerstein wrote the appealing lyric, and the song caught on, helped by a hit recording by Perry Como.

"No Song More Pleasing" is a delicate waltz by Richard Rodgers (music) and Sheldon Harnick (lyric) from the short-lived *Rex* (1976), the musical about King Henry VIII. The number was sung by Ed Evanko as Mark Smeaton, the court minstrel, and later reprised by the King (Nicol Williamson) and Jane Seymour (April Shawhan).

"No Strings," the title song from the 1962 musical for which Richard Rodgers wrote both music and lyrics, describes the uncommitted love affair between a writer (Richard Kiley) and a fashion model (Diahann Carroll), who sang the song together. The title also refers to the fact that Ralph Burns's orchestrations for the show used no string instruments.

"No Time at All" is the show-stopping vaudeville number from *Pippin*

(1972) in which the audience was asked to sing along with the help of a bouncing ball highlighting the lyric on a billboard-sized medieval manuscript. Stephen Schwartz wrote the pastiche song, which was sung by Pippin's grandmother Berthe (Irene Ryan) and her "boys," who advised everyone to live life to the fullest because you get old in "just no time at all."

"No Way to Stop It" is a shrewd, cynical and quite disturbing trio from *The Sound of Music* (1959), the least shrewd, cynical or disturbing of all of Rodgers and Hammerstein's musicals. The song is sung by Captain Von Trapp (Theodore Bikel), his fiancée the Baroness (Marion Marlowe) and their friend Max (Kurt Kasznar) about the need to capitulate to the Nazi takeover of Austria. Oscar Hammerstein's lyric is comic but stinging, and Richard Rodgers' music oompahs in a sprightly German way, but the effect is quite potent. The song is the turning point in the relationship between the Captain and the Baroness; they separate for political reasons. Because the number was not included in the popular film version, it is little known today, but it does give *The Sound of Music* a bite and some grit that enriches the play.

"Nobody" is the famous seriocomic trademark song for the renowned black singer-comic Bert Williams, a number he sang in several different editions of the *Ziegfeld Follies*. Williams introduced the song in vaudeville in 1905, and again when he made his *Follies* debut in the 1910 edition, the first time a black performer was starred alongside white stars. The number is the lament of a man whom no one seems to pay attention to and who, consequently, has no friend but himself. Williams wrote the music for the song and Alex Rogers provided the lyric, tailoring the words to the sad-funny character the performer had created. Phil Harris, Perry Como, Bing Crosby and Williams himself all made successful recordings of the song. It was sung by Avon Long in the Broadway revue *Bubbling Brown Sugar* (1976), and by Lynne Thigpen in *Tintypes* (1980).

"Nobody Does It Like Me" is the embracing "I am" song for the kookie New Yorker Gittel Mosca (Michele Lee) in *Seesaw* (1973) by Cy Coleman (music) and Dorothy Fields (lyric). With a history of affairs that have ended badly, Gittel proudly admits that she is an expert in messing up any possible romance but is still more than eager to try again.

"Nobody Makes a Pass at Me" is the comic lament of a young lady who has bought and used all the beauty products she's heard advertised on the radio, but her love life still hasn't picked up. The wry song was written by Harold Rome for the revue *Pins and Needles* (1937), where it was sung by Millie Weitz, who was not a professional actress or singer but a dressmaker. Barbra Streisand recorded the song in 1962.

"Nobody Steps on Kafritz" is a show-stopping comic number from the unsuccessful *Henry, Sweet Henry* (1967) by Bob Merrill. The bratty teenager Kafritz (Alice Playten) belted out this song of determined egotism, which made pint-sized Playten the new star of the moment.

"Nobody Tells Me How" is a poignant musical monologue by a veteran teacher who is told that her teaching methods are out-of-date. Mary Rodgers (music) and Susan Birkenhead (lyric) wrote the knowing song for the revue *Working* (1978), where it was sung by Bobo Lewis.

"Nobody Told Me" is an absorbing ballad from *No Strings* (1962), Richard Rodgers' first musical after the death of Oscar Hammerstein and the only one in which he wrote both music and lyrics. This poignant love duet was sung by Richard Kiley and Diahann Carroll as the interracial couple admit to each other that they are in love. Julie Andrews made a memorable recording of the song.

"Nobody's Chasing Me" is a dandy list song-torch song from *Out of This World* (1950) that stopped the show each evening, due partly to the vivacious singing and dancing of Charlotte Greenwood, who came out of retirement to play Juno in the Cole Porter musical. The lyric mentions dozens of animals, gods, goddesses and celebrities who are being chased in the name of love; but, unfortunately, she isn't. Dinah Shore's recording of the comic lament was very popular.

"Nobody's Heart (Belongs to Me)" is one of those intriguing love songs in which the character insists that he/she is pleased to be out of love, but the subtext clearly states the opposite. This demonstrative ballad by Richard Rodgers (music) and Lorenz Hart (lyric) is from *By Jupiter* (1942), where it was introduced by Constance Moore. A comic version of the song was sung later in the musical by Ray Bolger, and he stopped the show with it.

"Nodding Roses" is a delicious waltz duet from *Very Good Eddie* (1915) by Jerome Kern (music) and Schuyler Greene and Herbert Reynolds (lyric). Dick Rivers (Oscar Shaw) and Elsie Lilly (Ann Orr) finally get together near the end of the contemporary musical and sing this number together. Actually, only the refrain is in a waltz tempo, and, as a sly comment, Kern inserted some musical phrases from the recent *Der Rosenkavalier* in the piano accompaniment.

"Not a Day Goes By" is one of Stephen Sondheim's most beautiful ballads, a fragile song of total love that has a painful subtext. It was written for the short-lived *Merrily We Roll Along* (1981), where it was sung in two very different contexts. In the original production, Frank (Jim Walton) sang it to his wife Beth (Sally Klein) as a final plea of undying love when she wanted to divorce him. Later in the musical, which goes backwards in time, the song was sung on the day Frank and Beth got married. But this time it became a trio as Mary (Ann Morrison) also sang the number as a soliloquy of her unrequited love for Frank as the wedding ceremony took place. In some of the many revised versions of the show, the song is sometimes given to Beth to sing as a solo. Sondheim's melody is unpredictable and enchanting, with an extraordinary harmony line, and his lyric is ambiguously enthralling. Despite the brief run of *Merrily We Roll Along*, the song has become somewhat popular.

"Not Every Day of the Week" is a convivial duet for two awkward lovers from *Flora, the Red Menace* (1965) by John Kander (music) and Fred Ebb (lyric). Out-of-work artist Flora Meszaros (Liza Minnelli) meets the politically active Harry Toukarian (Bob Dishy), and as they stammer through some small talk, they realize that a meeting like this is not an everyday occurrence.

"Not Mine" is a tender torch song from *Hallelujah, Baby!* (1967) sung by the theatrical producer Harvey (Allan Case), who loves starlet Georgina (Leslie Uggams) but knows that her heart is for another. Jule Styne (music) and Betty Comden and Adolph Green (lyric) wrote the gentle ballad. Michael Feinstein recorded the song in 1991.

"Not While I'm Around" is an entrancing ballad of affection that soon turns into a menacing song of danger in *Sweeney Todd, the Demon Barber of Fleet Street* (1979). The young cripple Toby (Ken Jennings) sings the touching proclamation of protection to Mrs. Lovett (Angela Lansbury), whom he loves as a mother. She is amused by his chivalrous intentions, but when she realizes that Toby suspects her beloved Sweeney Todd of murdering people, Mrs. Lovett joins in the singing and mentally plots how she can silence Toby for good. Stephen Sondheim wrote the bewitching number that potently mixes warmth and evil, and Barbra Streisand made a potent recording of it.

"Nothin' for Nothin'" is a flavorful character song from the unsuccessful *Arms and the Girl* (1950), the musical that brightened up only when Pearl Bailey, in a minor role, took the stage and sang. The escaped slave named Connecticut (Bailey) works as a servant and resident philosopher in a New England household during the American Revolution. (She used to be called Virginia, but she moved.) She sings about her outlook on life in this breezy number by Morton Gould (music) and Dorothy Fields (lyric). The comic song was recorded by Bailey and by Artie Shaw (with vocal by Mary Ann McCall).

"Nothing Can Stop Me Now" is the driving, jubilant song of success from the allegorical musical *The Roar of the Greasepaint -- The Smell of the*

Crowd (1965) by Leslie Bricusse and Anthony Newley. For the first time in his life, the have-not Cocky (Newley) wins one round of "the game" over the aristocratic Sir (Cyril Ritchard), and he celebrates with this rousing number that recalls a political rally anthem. Because of the show's lengthy tour before opening in New York, "Nothing Can Stop Me Now" and other numbers from the musical were already well known and remained popular throughout the decade.

"Nothing More to Look Forward To" is a haunting song of despair from *Kwamina* (1961), the musical about modern West Africa by Richard Adler. Ako (Robert Guillaume) and Naii (Ethel Ayler) are in love, but she is betrothed to another, so Ako decides to move away. The captivating duet is both romantic and morose as they both realize that they have no more dreams left.

"November Song" is a playful comic number from *Sugar* (1972) about love and old age. Osgood Fielding, Jr., (Cyril Ritchard) and the other ancient millionaires vacationing in Miami Beach sing this song proclaiming that even "dirty old men" need love. The Jule Styne (music) and Bob Merrill (lyric) song is a takeoff on the famous ballad "September Song," which also dealt with an old man looking for love.

"Now!" is a flamboyant aria from *Song of Norway* (1944), the popular bio-musical about Edvard Grieg that used his music for the score. The flirtatious Italian prima donna Louisa Giovanni (Irra Petina) proclaims her impatience with waiting for anything and sings this comic character song that lyricists Robert Wright and George Forrest adapted from a Grieg waltz and his Second Violin Sonata in G.

"Now/Later/Soon" is a medley of three "I am" songs from *A Little Night Music* (1973) by Stephen Sondheim in which the thoughts of three characters are revealed individually and then in unison. Each soliloquy is structured around some element of time. The middle-aged lawyer Fredrik (Len Cariou) is concerned with time passing and debates whether he should try to seduce his young wife Anne (Victoria Mallory) or simply take a nap. As Anne prattles on about trivial events of her day, Fredrik considers his options in legal language set to rapid, unmelodic music and comically uses logic and rationalizing to deal with the possibility of sex. In the next room the gloomy divinity student Henrik (Mark Lambert) practices the cello and morosely contemplates his own situation: everyone always tells him to wait until "Later." He also has sex on his mind (he is secretly in love with his stepmother Anne), but his soliloquy moves slowly and mournfully, set to melancholy music. Finally, with Fredrik napping, Anne expresses her naive hope that "Soon" she will learn to love her husband in a sexual rather than a paternal manner. Her thoughts are very poetic, and her music is flowing and melodic. Sondheim then arranges for all three soliloquies to be reprised together, creating an intoxicating polyphony for three voices that is both overwhelming and fully satisfying.

"Now You Know" is a sparkling production number that concludes the first act of *Merrily We Roll Along* (1981), the short-lived musical by Stephen Sondheim. Frank (Jim Walton) is at City Hall, where his divorce is being finalized, and all his friends try to cheer him up and encourage him to keep going on. The advice is sometimes cheerfully optimistic, other times cynically pragmatic.

"Nowadays" is the smooth and sassy song and dance number from *Chicago* (1975) in which John Kander (music) and Fred Ebb (lyric) pastiched the debonair vaudeville teams of the 1920s. Roxie Hart (Gwen Verdon) and Velma Kelly (Chita Rivera) have each beat a murder rap and use their notoriety to form a headlining vaudeville act together. The hat-and-cane number explains how sin and greed are just the thing nowadays.

"Now's the Time" is the compelling finale for *Hallelujah, Baby!* (1967) by Jule Styne (music) and Betty Comden and Adolph Green (lyric). Georgina (Leslie Uggams) has found her new identity as a black woman in the 1960s and eagerly sings with the ensemble about how things can start to change now.

O

"Of Thee I Sing, (Baby)" is the spirited title song from the 1931 musical satire about love and politics. John P. Wintergreen (William Gaxton) and his wife-to-be Mary Turner (Lois Moran) lead the ensemble in singing this rousing song after he wins the presidential election. George Gershwin composed the lively, rhythmic music, which musicologist Alec Wilder described as "swinging operetta," and Ira Gershwin wrote the sparkling lyric. In the title phrase he mixes the dignified with the slangy, thereby mocking patriotic and Tin Pan Alley songs at the same time. Co-librettist George S. Kaufman objected to the word "baby" and some others feared that it might be taken as unpatriotic, but audiences loved it, and the phrase has since entered the slang vernacular. Some early recordings of the song that were popular include those by Sleepy Hall's Orchestra, Paul Small and Jane Frohman, and the Arden-Ohman Orchestra; much later Sarah Vaughan made a unique recording of the number.

"Off to the Races" is a merry music-hall number from *The Mystery of Edwin Drood* (1985) by Rupert Holmes that has, admittedly, nothing to do with the action of the musical but is too good to pass up. The Music Hall Royale's Chairman (George Rose) interrupts the tale of Edwin Drood to sing, along with Jerome Dempsey, Stephen Glavin and the company, the jolly Victorian number that they all proudly proclaim as their theatre's trademark song.

"Oh, Bess, Oh Where's My Bess?" is a beautiful trio from the folk opera *Porgy and Bess* (1935) by George Gershwin (music) and Ira Gershwin (lyric). When Porgy (Todd Duncan) returns to find his beloved Bess gone, he wails and pleads with the neighbors to tell him what they know. At the same time Serena (Ruby Elzy) and Maria (Georgette Harvey) try to convince Porgy that he is well rid of her, the three voices climaxing in a moment of terrible anguish. Usually recorded by opera singers, the number got an original interpretation by Ray Charles in 1976.

"Oh, Gee! Oh, Joy!" is one of Ira Gershwin's irresistibly slangy love songs, this one from *Rosalie* (1928), where it was sung by Marilyn Miller and Jack Donahue. George Gershwin composed the spirited music, P.G. Wodehouse co-authored the slaphappy lyric with Ira Gershwin, and the last minute addition to the score became a hit. The song has the same melody as an earlier George and Ira Gershwin number called "What Could I Do?," and music historian Robert Kimball has suggested that this earlier effort was the dummy lyric for the later "Oh, Gee! Oh, Joy!"

"Oh, Happy We" is a lyrical romantic duet from *Candide* (1956) that is exhilarating in its Leonard Bernstein music but satiric in its tongue-in-cheek lyric by Richard Wilbur. Candide (Robert Rounseville) sings of a simple life with modest joys (smiling babies, faithful dogs and so on), while his fiancée Cunegonde (Barbara Cook) imagines a life of luxury (pearls, eating peacock breast and so on). Since neither listens to the other in their joyful rapture, they both marvel at how well they are matched. In Bernstein's 1991 complete recording of the *Candide* score, the duet was sung by Jerry Hadley and June Anderson.

"Oh! How I Hate to Get Up in the Morning" is one of the most popular of all war songs and, after "Over There," the most famous World War One song. Irving Berlin wrote the simple, comic ditty as a private in Camp Upton while waiting to be shipped over to France. When he put together the all-soldier revue *Yip, Yip, Yaphank* in 1918 and it played on Broadway for thirty-two benefit performances, Berlin himself sang the sadly comic number on stage. Unlike the many hyperbolic war songs being written at the time, this one is about the drudgery of military life and took the enlisted man's point of view by dramatizing the soldier's distaste for reveille. The song's lyric manages to be good-natured and still patriotic. It also remained timely and appropriate; Berlin sang the song again in his 1942 military revue *This Is the Army*.

"Oh, I Can't Sit Down!" is a jubilant chorus number from the folk opera *Porgy and Bess* (1935). The residents of Catfish Row sing the exhilarating song as they prepare to go on a picnic at Kittiwah Island. George Gershwin composed the infectious music, and Ira Gershwin wrote the vivacious lyric.

"Oh, Johnny! Oh, Johnny! Oh!" is a popular ditty that swept the nation in 1914, selling over a million copies of sheet music. The Abe Olman (music) and Ed Rose (lyric) number was interpolated into the Anna Held vehicle *Follow Me* (1916), where it was sung by Henry Jackson. The song was a hit all over again twenty years later when a recording by Wee Bonnie Baker with the Orrin Tucker Orchestra sold over a million records, and there was also a very popular recording by Connee Boswell in the 1930s.

"Oh, Lady, Be Good!" is a lighthearted plea for affection from the Gershwins' first show together, *Lady, Be Good!* (1924). The debonair lawyer "Watty" Watson (Walter Catlett) sings the enticing number to a chorus of flappers, not asking them to behave as much as to "be good to me." The musical was slated to be called *Black-Eyed Susan,* but when the librettists heard this sprightly song, they dropped the "Oh" and adapted the song title for the show. As originally performed, George Gershwin's music was sung "slow and gracefully," but over the years the song has usually been performed at a brisker pace that does tend to diminish Ira Gershwin's tangy lyric. Lester Young's recording of the song became a jazz classic.

"Oh Me! Oh My! (Oh You!)" is a delightful ditty from *Two Little Girls in Blue* (1921), the first musical by composer Vincent Youmans and the first complete score by Ira Gershwin (who was still using the pen name Arthur Francis). The zippy song was introduced by Oscar Shaw as the shipboard passenger Robert Barker who is in love with one of the Sartoris twins, but he's not sure which one. Paul Whiteman's Orchestra made a popular recording, and years later it was recorded as a duet by Blossom Dearie and Charles Rydell. The number was sung by the ensemble in the Off-Broadway revue *Oh Me, Oh My, Oh Youmans* (1981).

"Oh, My Mysterious Lady" is an odd but charming operatic pastiche from *Peter Pan* (1954) in which Captain Hook (Cyril Ritchard) pursues a beautiful spirit in the forest that turns out to be Peter Pan (Mary Martin) in disguise. The silly Jule Styne (music) and Betty Comden and Adolph Green (lyric) number has nothing to do with the plot or the J.M. Barrie characters, but during the out-of-town tryouts it was felt that the show's two stars should have at least one song together, and the authors wanted to give Martin a chance to use her operaticlike talents for comic effect.

"Oh, Promise Me," the extremely popular wedding song, was written for the operetta *Robin Hood* (1891) by Reginald DeKoven (music) and Clement Scott (lyric). The memorable ballad was not in the score originally, but to appease the star, Jessie Bartlett Davis, it was added to the wedding scene. Maid Marian is about to be wed against her wishes to Guy of Gisborne. One of Robin's merry men, Alan-a-Dale (a trouser role traditionally played by a woman, in this case Davis), hides behind the bushes and sings to his sweetheart Annabel (Lea Van Dyke) of her vow to marry him. The song became the hit of the show and was responsible for *Robin Hood* being revived frequently over the next three decades.

"Oh, to Be a Movie Star" is the waggish "I am" song for the chimney sweep Ella (Barbara Harris), who naively dreams of Hollywood fame in the

"Passionella" musical playlet of *The Apple Tree* (1966). Jerry Bock composed the pleasing music and Sheldon Harnick wrote the wry lyric in which Ella offers to clean the movie theatre and fold up all the seats if they'll let her be a picture star.

"Oh, What a Beautiful Mornin' " is the first song Richard Rodgers (music) and Oscar Hammerstein (lyric) wrote together for their first collaboration, *Oklahoma!* (1943), and it displays all the high craftsmanship and inspired magic that the team would become famous for. The popular ballad is actually in waltz tempo, but with a leisurely, rural air to it. The lyric is drawn from Lynn Riggs's poetic stage directions for the first scene of his play *Green Grow the Lilacs* (1931), which served as the basis for the musical. Hammerstein clips off all the "g" endings (mornin' instead of morning) not only to create the midwestern colloquialisms but also to soften the words and allow for a smooth, dreamy line of verse. Alfred Drake, as the cowboy Curly, introduced the song in *Oklahoma!*'s quiet, non-chorus line opening, a surprising and rather unique innovation. Bing Crosby and Frank Sinatra are among the many who made successful recordings of the ballad, and it was sung by Martin Vidnovic in the Broadway revue *A Grand Night for Singing* (1993).

"Oh, You Wonderful Girl" is the hit love song from *The Little Millionaire* (1911) by George M. Cohan. Roscoe Handover (Sidney Jarvis), the friend of the story's villain, sang the zesty, romantic tribute. Bernadette Peters sang the number as "Oh, You Wonderful Boy" in the bio-musical *George M!* (1968).

"Ohio" is a harmonious duet from *Wonderful Town* (1953) by Leonard Bernstein (music) and Betty Comden and Adolph Green (lyric). Sisters Ruth (Rosalind Russell) and Eileen (Edith Adams) have just arrived in 1930s New York City to seek romance and fortune. But as they huddle together in their Greenwich Village apartment and listen to the blasting coming from the street as the new subway line is being built, the two get homesick and wonder "why, oh, why, oh" they left their hometown in Ohio. Although intended as a spoof on the Old Homestead sort of song, "Ohio" became a hit ballad in the 1950s, with popular recordings by Lisa Kirk and others. It is also worth noting that the main melody of the song comes directly from the third movement of Brahms's Second Piano Concerto, something that Bernstein made no attempt to hide.

"Oklahoma," the rousing title song from *Oklahoma!* (1943), minus the exclamation point for some reason, was originally planned as a solo for the cowboy Curly (Alfred Drake) to sing to his fiancée Laurey (Joan Roberts) late in the second act. But in the previews the song wasn't going over, so it was given to the whole cast as an ensemble number and it stopped the show. In fact, the imminent popularity of the song prompted the producers to change the musical's name from *Away We Go!* to *Oklahoma!*. Richard Rodgers' music boldly starts with a long sustained note for lyricist Oscar Hammerstein's "o" of "Oklahoma." It is a device similar to the long "who" for Jerome Kern's sustained note in "Who?" years before. "Oklahoma" is one of the most recognized songs in American popular culture. It was later made the official state song for Oklahoma, the only theatre song to have that distinction.

"Ol' Man River" is arguably the greatest theatre song in America, for it is surely one of the most popular, recognized and beloved. It is used throughout *Show Boat* (1927) as a kind of leitmotif but also stands firmly on its own and has retained its power decade after decade. Jules Bledsoe, as the black stevedore Joe, introduced the ballad in the original but the song is most associated with Paul Robeson, who sang it in the London production, in revivals, on film and in his concerts for many years. Essentially a folk song, "Ol' Man River" is, as its lyricist Oscar Hammerstein described it, a "song of resignation with protest implied." This ambiguity is what makes the song so haunting. Joe and the black workers along the Mississippi lament their oppression, yet they can't help feeling in awe of the mighty river that is indifferent to mankind's troubles. The ballad was at first mistaken for an authentic Negro spiritual because Jerome Kern's music captures a Southern folk flavor that few theatre songs before or since have attained. It was the first number that Kern and Hammerstein wrote for the score, and when they played it for Edna Ferber, she overcame her objections to musicalizing her novel and gave the authors permission to proceed with the show. "Ol' Man River" is not a complex song musically and has no major jumps in the melody, although it does have a wide range (an octave and a sixth) with a high ending that has always proven a challenge to singers. The release is actually a section of the verse repeated, so musically the ballad is very tight and unified; consequently, it is one of the few theatre songs that is usually sung complete, verse and refrain. Lyrically, it is Hammerstein's master achievement. He avoids lengthy phrases and hard endings (sumpin', nuthin', rollin', don') and employs few traditional rhymes. Instead he uses a series of identities and scattered soft feminine rhymes to capture the steady, rolling feel of the river flowing by. Also pure Hammerstein about the lyric is the way the singer, an uneducated dock worker, expresses himself with eloquence and dignity and still remains true to the character. Just as the Mississippi gives unity to Ferber's sprawling novel, "Ol' Man River" gives unity to the *Show Boat* score. The song is reprised several times and even shows up in altered forms, as in the opening "Cotton Blossom" theme, which is "Ol' Man River" played in reverse and speeded up to a banjo-strumming tempo. Of the hundreds of recordings of the song, those most famous and popular were Robeson's 1932 record and best-sellers by Bing Crosby (with the Paul Whiteman Orchestra) and Frank Sinatra.

"Old Deuteronomy" is the elegant song that describes the ancient and wisest of cats in the British import *Cats* (1982). Andrew Lloyd Webber set T.S. Eliot's poem to music and fellow cats Harry Groener and Terrence Mann led the company in singing about Old Deuteronomy (Ken Page), whose reputation goes back to before Queen Victoria's coronation.

"Old Devil Moon" is the bewitching ballad from *Finian's Rainbow* (1947) by Burton Lane (music) and E.Y. Harburg (lyric) that was one of the hits to come out of the show. Labor organizer Woody Mahoney (Donald Richards) wants to move on, but he stays in Rainbow Valley with Sharon (Ella Logan) because the moon has put a magic spell on him. The two then sing the invigorating duet about the seductive and dazzling power of the moon and of the developing love they have for each other. Lane's jazzy music is almost avant-garde in its melodic and harmonic jumps and its spiraling release that seems to explode with passion. It is also an extremely difficult song to sing correctly. Harburg's lyric sparkles, using rolling alliteration and assonance at times and vigorous eruptive words in other instances. Frank Sinatra and Mel Tormé are among the many who recorded the song successfully.

"Old Friend" is a penetrating ballad about true friendship from the Off-Broadway *I'm Getting My Act Together and Taking It on the Road* (1978) by Gretchen Cryer (lyric) and Nancy Ford (music). Pop singer Heather Jones (Cryer) sings the beautiful song to her manager and old friend Joe (Joel Fabiani) about the constancy of their relationship while all the things in life seem to be changing.

"Old Maid" is a powerful character song from *110 in the Shade* (1963) by Tom Jones (lyric) and Harvey Schmidt (music) and a tour de force for its star Inga Swenson. Lizzie Curry (Swenson) sings this poignant soliloquy as she pictures her future as a spinster, an embarrassment for relatives and a pathetic figure in the town. The number is, like the character, self-aware and not at all self-pitying.

"Old Wicked Willage of Wenice" is a delicious comic song from *Fioretta* (1929) in which Fanny Brice lampooned grand opera singers. The fun number was written by George Bagby (music) and G. Romilli (lyric).

"The Oldest Established (Permanent Floating Crap Game in New York)" is an irresistible comic number early in *Guys and Dolls* (1950) that introduces Nathan Detroit (Sam Levene) and sets up several important plot devices. The number is Nathan's "I am" song, but Levene's singing was so weak that Frank Loesser had to write this number in which Nicely-Nicely Johnson (Stubby Kaye), Benny Southstreet (Johnny Silver) and the chorus of gamblers sang *about* him and his activities.

"An Old-Fashioned Wife" is a melodic number from *Oh, Boy!* (1917) in which the up-to-date New Yorker Lou Ellen (Marie Carroll) promises her boyfriend George (Tom Powers) that she'll behave like a submissive wife in order to get him out of the scrape he's in. Jerome Kern composed the lovely music that has a waltz strain in it, and P.G. Wodehouse wrote the wry lyric.

"On a Clear Day You Can See Forever" is the magical, beguiling title song from the 1965 musical about ESP. The psychiatrist Mark Bruckner (John Cullum) sings the soaring ballad to the insecure Daisy (Barbara Harris) to encourage her to look at her extrasensory powers as a gift with boundless opportunities. The Alan Jay Lerner (lyric) and Burton Lane (music) song became a major hit, and both Robert Goulet and Johnny Mathis made best-selling recordings of the ballad. Lerner's lyric is one of the musical theatre's most illusive; nobody, including the show's authors, was quite sure what it referred to. Because the subject is an unexplained phenomenon, the lyric is probably appropriate. Lane later said that Lerner went through ninety-one complete lyrics for the song before he came up with this one.

"On a Roof in Manhattan" is a pleasing duet that Irving Berlin wrote for *Face the Music* (1932). In contrast to the usual format of having the lovers fantasize about living in a castle in Spain or similar exotic places, these New Yorkers (J. Harold Murray and Katherine Carrington) are content with their urban domain of the title.

"On a Sunday by the Sea" is a sprightly beach number from the period musical *High Button Shoes* (1947) by Jule Styne (music) and Sammy Cahn (lyric). Phil Silvers, as the con man Harrison Floy, led the ensemble in this catchy song at the Atlantic City seaside. The number led directly into the famous Bathing Beauty ballet (known today as the Mack Sennett ballet) choreographed by Jerome Robbins.

"On and On and On" is a vigorous march from the short-lived satire *Let 'Em Eat Cake* (1933) by George Gershwin (music) and Ira Gershwin (lyric). President Wintergreen (William Gaxton) and his wife Mary (Lois Moran) lead the "Blue Shirts" in this rhythmic number that admits that, like the military, it has nowhere to go but on and on and on. The song was not recorded until 1987, when the Brooklyn Academy of Music recorded virtually the whole score.

"On the Farm" is a harsh character song from *New Girl in Town* (1957) by Bob Merrill and a dramatic soliloquy for Gwen Verdon. Anna Christie (Verdon) was sent to a relative's farm when she was a young girl; years later she bitterly sings this Brecht-like song about how she was sexually abused and taught to fend for herself in life.

"On the S.S. Bernard Cohn" is a jaunty character song from *On a Clear Day You Can See Forever* (1965) by Alan Jay Lerner (lyric) and Burton Lane (music). Daisy (Barbara Harris) has just taken a boat ride around Manhattan with the handsome psychiatrist Mark (John Cullum) and sings joyfully about the experience.

"On the Steps of the Palace" is a beguiling soliloquy for Cinderella in Stephen Sondheim's *Into the Woods* (1987). Having run away from the handsome prince, the half-shoeless Cinderella (Kim Crosby) ponders the ambiguous feelings she has about fairy-tale love and questions whether she wants the prince to find her or not. Sondheim's lyric work in the song is unusually intricate even for him, with several triple rhymes and double-meaning words.

"On the Street Where You Live," the most accomplished ballad from *My Fair Lady* (1956) by Alan Jay Lerner (lyric) and Frederick Loewe (music), was almost cut from the show when tryout audiences seemed bored and restless during the song. Loewe, who hated the melody, wanted to get rid of it, but it was one of Lerner's favorites and he fought to retain it. The problem was soon deciphered: the song was sung by Freddy Eyensford-Hill (John Michael King), who had been seen briefly in two previous scenes, but audiences didn't remember him. To interrupt the Eliza-Higgins plot for a pretty ballad sung by a stranger put the audience in an unreceptive mood for the song. So Lerner rewrote the verse and the release of the number and added some dialogue before the scene to reintroduce the character, and the song was a hit. Among the many recordings were those by Vic Damone, Mel Tormé, Eddie Fisher and Andy Williams.

"On the Sunny Side of the Street" is one of the earliest and one of the best of the flock of cheery anti-Depression songs that flooded the airwaves in the 1930s. This one by Jimmy McHugh (music) and Dorothy Fields (lyric) came from *The International Revue* (1930), where it was sung by Harry Richman and Gertrude Lawrence. McHugh's music seems to spring forth like the joyous footsteps of a happy man, and Fields's lyric has a lift to it that is contagious. The song has proven to be a favorite of singers over the years, and jazz musicians love its liberated bounce as well. Richman recorded the number, and over the decades, both Tommy Dorsey's Orchestra and Frankie Laine had hit recordings of it. "On the Sunny Side of the Street" was featured in no less than seven film musicals, and Ann Miller and Mickey Rooney sang the song in the Broadway revue *Sugar Babies* (1979). The most recent recording, by Barbara Cook in 1993, reveals the number to be as sparklingly fresh as ever.

"On This Night of a Thousand Stars" is a melodic pastiche of a Latin American pop song from the British import *Evita* (1979) by Andrew Lloyd Webber (music) and Tim Rice (lyric). The folk singer Augustin Magaldi (Mark Syers) sings the hyperbolic love song as part of his act in a cheap tavern where he befriends the young Eva Duarte (Patti LuPone). Later, after he has become a big star, he sings part of it before a huge enthusiastic crowd at a charity benefit.

"On Your Toes," the sprightly title song from the 1936 musical, was a competition in dance between American hoofers and Russian ballet dancers. Richard Rodgers wrote the insistent, catchy melody, and Lorenz Hart provided the witty lyric that is much more clever than can be appreciated in a dance number. The gleeful song was introduced by Doris Carson, Ray Bolger, David Morris and the ensemble.

"Once-a-Year-Day!" is a rousing chorus number from *The Pajama Game* (1954) by Richard Adler and Jerry Ross. John Raitt and Janis Paige led all the workers at the Sleep-Tite Pajama Factory in this joyous production number that was choreographed by Bob Fosse.

"Once in a Blue Moon" is a graceful lullaby by Jerome Kern (music) and Anne Caldwell (lyric) that has fallen into oblivion but is greatly admired by Kern scholars. It was written for the fairy-tale musical *Stepping Stones* (1923), where it was sung by various princes and fantasy characters played by Roy Hoyer, Evelyn Herbert, John Lambert, Lilyan White and Ruth White. The song is captivatingly simple, with a sweet lyric that turns cynical in the last line and a melody that barely extends outside a single octave. The great song interpreter Mabel Mercer sang the lullaby over the years in an effort to revitalize interest in it, but it remains a mostly forgotten gem.

"Once in a Lifetime" is the soaring ballad of ambition from the British import *Stop the World -- I Want to Get Off* (1962) by Leslie Bricusse and Anthony Newley. When Littlechap (Newley) looks around and sees what a mess the world is in, he decides to go into politics and sings this expansive song about grabbing the moment and running with it. Recordings by Newley, Sammy Davis, Jr., and others helped keep this song popular throughout the 1960s.

"Once in Love With Amy" is the hit ballad from *Where's Charley?* (1948) and became Ray Bolger's signature song for many years. Frank Loesser wrote both music and lyric, and Bolger, as the cross-dressing Charley Wykeham, sang it about his true love, Amy Spettigue. The number was planned as a lighthearted soft-shoe routine to be played in front of the curtain to cover a scene change. During previews the song was not going over well, and Bolger started ad-libbing and asked the audience to join in singing the refrain. By opening night in New York, the number was a twenty-five-minute audience-participation sensation. Because of its popularity on the radio, soon audiences were entering the theatre singing it. Bolger's recording of the song was the first hit single over four minutes in length since cylinders had been replaced by disks.

"Once Upon a Time" is the indelible love ballad from *All American* (1962), the only song from the Charles Strouse (music) and Lee Adams (lyrics) score to become a hit. The tender, evocative number is sung by the show's older lovers, Professor Fodorski (Ray Bolger) and the Dean of Women (Eileen Herlie) as they look to the past and see how quickly life's romantic opportunities fade away. Tony Bennett's best-selling recording helped make the song a standard.

"Once You Lose Your Heart" is the gentle torch song from the British import *Me and My Girl* (1986) that was written in 1937 but didn't play on Broadway until fifty years later. Noel Gay wrote the music and lyric for this direct love song in which the cockney girl Sally Smith (Maryann Plunkett) describes her steadfast affection for Bill Snibson (Robert Lindsay), the cockney who has found wealth and seems to have forgotten her.

"One" is the rhythmic chorus number from *A Chorus Line* (1975) that represents the typical Broadway salute to a big star. The irony lies in the fact that the auditionees sing and dance it by themselves, and the number becomes a tribute to their own individuality. The sparkling reprise of the song at the end of the musical, with the chorus members in glittering costumes reflected in mirrors, becomes a testament to all dancers and to the Broadway musical itself. Marvin Hamlisch composed the vibrant music, and Edward Kleban provided the driving lyric.

"One Alone" is an ardent duet from the exotic operetta *The Desert Song* (1926) by Sigmund Romberg (music) and Otto Harbach and Oscar Hammerstein (lyric). The Red Shadow (Robert Halliday), the mysterious leader of the Riff revolt in North Africa, and the Frenchwoman Margot Bonvalet (Vivienne Segal) sing this rhapsodic duet in which they pledge romantic fidelity. Years later Mario Lanza had a successful recording of "One Alone."

"One Big Union for Two" is a sly little ditty that uses labor-management terminology in a love song format. Harold Rome wrote the clever number for the topical labor revue *Pins and Needles* (1937), and it was sung by the ensemble as the ultimate expression of collective bargaining.

"One Boy" is an appealing love ballad from *Bye Bye Birdie* (1960) by Charles Strouse (music) and Lee Adams (lyric). Ohio teen Kim McAfee (Susan Watson) and two of her friends (Jessica Albright and Sharon Lerit) dream of going steady as adult Rose Grant (Chita Rivera) sings her own version of romance called "One Guy."

"One Day More" is the stirring production number that ends the first act of *Les Misérables* (1987), the British import with music by Claude-Michel Schönberg and lyrics by Herbert Kretzmer, who adapted the original French text by Alain Boublil and Jean-Marc Natal. Enjolas (Michael Maguire) rallies the students in Paris to revolt, singing that there is only one day before the storm. Meanwhile Jean Valjean (Colm Wilkinson) assures his daughter Cosette (Judy Kuhn) that they will escape "tomorrow" from the clutches of the police officer Javert (Terrence Mann), who is readying the weapons to stop the students' uprising. Also featured in the act finale are the student Marius (David Bryant), who promises Enjolas he will join the battle even though he fears losing Cosette; the obnoxious Mon. and Mme. Thenardier (Leo Burmester and Jennifer Butt), who relish the chaos about to happen; and their hopeful daughter Eponine (Frances Ruffelle), who dreams that she will win the love of her beloved Marius in "one day more."

"One Extraordinary Thing" is an exhilarating number from *The Grand Tour* (1979), the unsuccessful musical by Jerry Herman. Jewish refugee S.L. Jacobowsky (Joel Grey) and his companions on the run from the Nazis disguise themselves as carnival performers and sing this lively song with a circus melody and typically optimistic Herman lyrics.

"One Hand, One Heart" is the poignant love duet from *West Side Story* (1957) in which Tony (Larry Kert) and Maria (Carol Lawrence) act out their proposed wedding ceremony, at first in jest and then with great solemnity. Stephen Sondheim wrote the simple but touching lyric, and Leonard Bernstein composed the hymnlike music that was originally written for *Candide* (1956) but never used.

"One Hundred Easy Ways (To Lose a Man)" is a show-stopping specialty number for Rosalind Russell in *Wonderful Town* (1953) by Leonard Bernstein (music) and Betty Comden and Adolph Green (lyric). Ruth Sherwood (Russell), who has never had much luck in love, gives instructions on how to destroy romance: specifically, being too intelligent, too efficient and too much like a man. Because the lyric is so self-mocking, the song is still funny in today's more politically correct climate.

"One Kiss" is the enthralling ballad from the operetta *The New Moon* (1928) by Sigmund Romberg (music) and Oscar Hammerstein (lyric). As she is preparing for a New Orleans ball, the aristocratic Marianne (Evelyn Herbert) sings the waltzing number with the other ladies of society. Although the vogue is for a young lady to have many beaux, Marianne dreams of being loved by only one man, and it is for him that she is saving her one kiss. The oft-recorded song got a more contemporary sound in Barbra Streisand's recording in the 1960s.

"One More Angel in Heaven" is an amusing pastiche of a country-western song set in biblical times for *Joseph and the Amazing Technicolor Dreamcoat*, which finally arrived on Broadway in 1982. Levi (Steve McNaughton) and his ten brothers sang this mock song of bereavement for their supposedly deceased brother Joseph. In front of their father the number is a mournful hymn but, once the old man exits, they break into a rousing hoedown version of the song. Andrew Lloyd Webber (music) and Tim Rice (lyric) wrote the prankish number.

"One More Kiss" is a ravishing pastiche number from *Follies* (1971) that Stephen Sondheim wrote in the style of a Rudolf Friml or Sigmund Romberg operetta number. The aging diva Heidi Schiller (Justine Johnson) sings her old farewell song, urging her lover to never look back at the past. Then the ghost of Young Heidi (Victoria Mallory) appears, and in her youthful, stronger voice she echoes the Old Heidi, eventually blending into an intoxicating duet. As beautiful as the number is, the ironic lyric and the sharply contrasting singers give the song a melancholy far deeper than the farewell being expressed.

"One More Walk Around the Garden" is one of the finest ballads to come out of Broadway in the 1970s, but few heard it because it is unabashedly old-fashioned and the show it was written for, *Carmelina* (1979), had a short run. Three ex-GIs (Gordon Ramsey, Howard Ross and John Michael King) return to the Italian village where they were stationed during World War Two to see the woman they loved and, they believe, had a child by. Although they are old, they feel they have one more opportunity for romance. Burton Lane composed the endearing music for the trio, and Alan Jay Lerner wrote the penetrating and haunting lyric. Michael Feinstein recorded the ballad in 1990.

"One Night in Bangkok" was the hit single from *Chess* years before it opened in London or New York because of the popular concept album that put the song in the Top Ten. Benny Anderssen and Bjorn Ulvaeus, of the rock group ABBA, wrote the surging music, and Tim Rice provided the cynical lyric about the sleazy side of the exotic Thai capital. In the 1988 Broadway production, the song was sung by temperamental American chess champion Freddie (Philip Casnoff) and the ensemble.

"One Night Only" is the song that carries the singing characters onto the charts in the record-business musical *Dreamgirls* (1981). When Effie Melody

White (Jennifer Holliday) tries to make a comeback with a single called "One Night Only," her vindictive ex-manager and ex-lover Curtis Taylor, Jr., (Ben Harney) has his trio the Dreams (Sheryl Lee Ralph, Loretta Devine and Deborah Burrell) make their own recording of the song to steal Effie's thunder. In the musical we hear both versions of the vibrant number by Henry Krieger (music) and Tom Eyen (lyric). Elaine Paige made a popular recording of the song.

"One of the Boys" is a diverting number from *Woman of the Year* (1981) in which Tess Harding (Lauren Bacall) proves she can hold her own in a man's world by singing this song with Maury (Rex Everhart) and the men. John Kander wrote the lively music, and Fred Ebb provided the robust lyric.

"One Room" is a sweet marriage proposal song from *The Rothschilds* (1970) by Jerry Bock (music) and Sheldon Harnick (lyric). The struggling but ambitious Mayer Rothschild (Hal Linden) hopes to wed Gutele (Leila Martin), who dreams of a one-room apartment where they can be happy together. But Mayer paints her a picture of great wealth and success in the future; so Gutele says she'll settle for an apartment with two rooms.

"One Wife" is an amusing song from *Kwamina* (1961), the experimental musical about modern Africa by Richard Adler. The wives of a West African village sing to the betrothed Naii (Ethel Ayler) that marriage with only one wife is wrong and impractical and that the ancient custom of polygamy is the only way a woman can get a bit of peace and quiet in this world.

"Only a Rose" is the famous duet from the swashbuckling *The Vagabond King* (1925) by Rudolf Friml (music) and Brian Hooker (lyric). The high-born Parisian Katherine de Vaucelles (Carolyn Thomson) gives the dashing outlaw-poet Francois Villon (Dennis King) a single rose, and the two burst into this rapturous duet. Mario Lanza's recording of the song was very popular.

"Only for Americans" is a shrewd comic song from Irving Berlin's *Miss Liberty* (1949) that was sung by seventy-one-year-old veteran Ethel Griffies as a French countess. The raffish list song chronicles all the French clichés (Folies Bergere, expensive sidewalk cafes, French postcards and so on) that are not for the French at all; they are only for Americans with money to waste. Berlin's melody has a pleasing European flavor to it, and the lyric is acute and delightful.

"Only Love" is a poignant torch song from *Zorbá* (1968) by John Kander (music) and Fred Ebb (lyric). The aged courtesan Hortense (Maria Karnilova) sings the tender song about how all things fade and only the possibility of love makes life bearable. The song is reprised at the end of the act by the Chorus

Leader (Lorraine Serabian) as the young scholar Nikos (John Cunningham) decides to go to the bedroom of the beautiful Widow (Carmen Alvarez).

"Only With You" is a romantic song from *Nine* (1982) that makes an ironic statement about the loveless character who sings it. Filmmaker Guido Contini (Raul Julia) sings the tender ballad to his wife, then, as she appears, to his mistress Carla and then to his star actress Claudia. Maury Yeston wrote the melodic music and the sly lyric.

"Only You" is probably the only love song ever written for two trains, and it is certainly the most rhapsodic one. Andrew Lloyd Webber (music) and Richard Stilgoe (lyric) wrote the number for the British import *Starlight Express* (1987), and it was sung by the engine Rusty (Greg Mowry) and his beloved passenger car Pearl (Reva Rice). A pop hit recording of the song was recorded by Peter Hewlett and Josie Aiello.

"Open a New Window" is Mame Dennis' musical philosophy of life, and the song led into one of the most animated production numbers in Jerry Herman's *Mame* (1966). Auntie Mame (Angela Lansbury) decides to show her young nephew Patrick (Frankie Michaels) life's many adventures. The number starts out with her singing to him as they sit on a windowsill that drifts over Manhattan; then they join a 1920s dance routine, visit a speakeasy that gets raided by the police and end up in a police paddy wagon singing the song without a regret in the world.

"Opening Doors" is a fascinating musical sequence from *Merrily We Roll Along* (1981) that is also one of the most autobiographical songs Stephen Sondheim has written. The number chronicles the early struggles of three artists: the songwriters Frank (Jim Walton) and Charley (Lonny Price) and author Mary (Ann Morrison). As the months go by, we see them writing, auditioning, revising, being rejected and finally putting together a small revue to showcase their work. The funniest and most revealing section of the number is when Frank and Charley audition one of their songs for a producer (Jason Alexander) who rejects it, asking for a tune he can hum. It is a complaint that Sondheim heard often as a beginning songwriter and one he still hears today.

"Ordinary People" is a lyrical romantic duet from the short-lived *Kwamina* (1961) by Richard Adler. Kwamina (Terry Carter) is a West African who has returned to his tribe after being educated in Europe. He is drawn to the white Englishwoman Eve (Sally Ann Howes) and she to him, but they know they can never be like other couples.

"The Other Woman" is a sassy comic number from the Off-Broadway sequel *Annie Warbucks* (1993) by Charles Strouse (music) and Martin Charnin (lyric). Faced with the prospect of Daddy Warbucks marrying, Annie (Kathryn Zaremba) runs off to the orphanage for advice and four of the orphans (Ashley Pettet, Missy Goldberg, Elisabeth Zaremba and Natalia Harris) warn her to watch out for the new woman that enters her life.

"Our Favorite Son" is the jaunty song that made for a thrilling production number in *The Will Rogers Follies* (1991) and stopped the show each night. Will Rogers (Keith Carradine) decides to go into politics and run for president as the candidate for the De Bunk Party. The Ziegfeld Girls join Will for this zany chorus number that serves as his campaign song. Cy Coleman wrote the toe-tapping music, and Betty Comden and Adolph Green provided the slaphappy lyric. More memorable, though, was director-choreographer Tommy Tune's staging, in which Will and the girls danced the whole number from a seated position.

"Our Language of Love" is the hit ballad from *Irma la Douce* (1960), the British import of the French musical about a prostitute with the proverbial heart of gold. Irma (Elizabeth Seal) and the young student Nestor (Keith Michell) sing the alluring song about how their love transcends mere words. Marguerite Monnot wrote the music and French lyric that was translated and adapted by Julian More, David Heneker and Monty Norman.

"Our Private World" is a soaring pastiche of an operatic duet sung by the flamboyant leading couple in *On the Twentieth Century* (1978). Producer-director Oscar Jaffe (John Cullum) and his old flame, movie star Lily Garland (Madeline Kahn), are on the same train heading for New York and are a quarrelsome couple when they are together. But alone in their separate compartments, each recalls their past love together in this rhapsodic number. Cy Coleman composed the expansive music, and Betty Comden and Adolph Green wrote the lush lyric. Sally Mayes made a distinctive recording of "Our Private World" as a sincere ballad in 1994.

"Our Time" is perhaps the most optimistic song Stephen Sondheim has ever written, a haunting and stirring anthem from the short-lived *Merrily We Roll Along* (1981). On a New York City rooftop in 1957, three young artists (Jim Walton, Lonny Price and Ann Morrison) watch the faint image of the Sputnik satellite in the sky and sing of a new world full of hope and progress. The imagery throughout is poignantly optimistic without being sentimental, and the characters' joyous anticipation of a future that they will build is painful and moving. The song is all the more effective because it comes near the end of the reverse-plotted musical after we've seen how sadly these three characters handle their future lives.

"Out of My Dreams" is the wistful ballad from *Oklahoma!* (1943) that leads into the famous "Laurey Makes Up Her Mind" ballet. The song was sung by Joan Roberts, as the bewildered Laurey, and the women's chorus. Richard Rodgers' music is a waltz that masterfully uses ascending and descending scales, and Oscar Hammerstein's lyric is appropriately dreamy and romanticized. The song's melody was also intermittently used in Agnes de Mille's renowned ballet that ended the first act.

"Over the Hill" is a delightful character song from *Shenandoah* (1975), the musical by Gary Geld (music) and Peter Udell (lyric) set in rural Virginia during the Civil War. The young farm girl Jenny (Penelope Milford) sings this comic lament about her fear that by the time her boyfriend gets up the courage to finally kiss her, she'll be too old to respond.

P

"Pack Up Your Sins and Go to the Devil" is the fiery Irving Berlin song that serves as the first-act finale for the second edition of the *Music Box Revue* (1922). The song's contrapuntal melodies and unusual rhyming make it a syncopated delight. In the revue, Charlotte Greenwood, dressed as a red devil in Hades dispatching jazz musicians to the flames, and the McCarthy Sisters sang the lively number. Orchestral recordings by Paul Whiteman and Emil Coleman were both popular, and years later Dorothy Loudon made a fun recording of the song.

"Pack Up Your Troubles in Your Old Kit Bag (And Smile, Smile, Smile)" is the British hit song that was equally popular with the American troops during World War One. Adele Rowland sang the Felix Powell (music) and George Asaf (lyric) marching song in *Her Soldier Boy* (1916), and the next year there were popular recordings by James F. Harrison and the Knickerbocker Quartet and by Reginald Werrenrath. The male ensemble of the British import *Oh What a Lovely War!* (1964) also sang the song.

"A Pal Like You" is a warm duet from the Princess Theatre musical *Oh, Boy!* (1917) by Jerome Kern (music) and P.G. Wodehouse (lyric). Hal Forde and Anna Wheaton sang the cozy ballad, which was published as "We're Going to Be Pals."

"Papa, Won't You Dance With Me?" is the pleasing polka number from *High Button Shoes* (1947) that stopped the show each night with its intoxicating song and dance. Mrs. Longstreet (Nanette Fabray) coaxes her husband (Jack McCauley) to join in the foot-stomping polka, and soon all the members of the ensemble are dancing. Jule Styne wrote the lively music and Sammy Cahn provided the merry lyrics. Among the recordings of the song was an early Doris Day single that was her first effort after breaking away from singing as an orchestra vocalist.

"A Parade in Town" is an odd but absorbing number from the experimental musical *Anyone Can Whistle* (1964) by Stephen Sondheim. Mayoress Cora Hooper (Angela Lansbury) has been rejected by her town, and the brassy lady reveals a vulnerable side in this touching lament. Sondheim offsets her sincerity by putting the music in a march tempo so that Cora is alternately dejected and triumphant.

"Paree, What Did You Do to Me?" is the musical question asked in Cole Porter's *Fifty Million Frenchmen* (1929) by Jack Thompson and Betty Compton as American tourists falling in love in Paris. This song inspired a 1934 Vitaphone film called *Paree, Paree* that introduced Bob Hope to the movies.

"Paris Loves Lovers" might have been just another Cole Porter paean to his favorite city, but this song from *Silk Stockings* (1955) is punctuated by Communist propaganda comments that make the Paris-lover work all the harder. Don Ameche sang it to Comrade Ninotchka (Hildegarde Neff), who supplied all the "istic" suffixes in order to puncture his balloon. But he eventually got the girl, thanks to the love song "All of You" later in the show.

"Paris Original" is a delightfully satiric number about feminine vanity and big business from Frank Loesser's *How to Succeed in Business Without Really Trying* (1961). Rosemary (Bonnie Scott) has bought an expensive new dress, a Paris original, to impress Finch (Robert Morse). But when she arrives at the office party, she sees another woman (Mara Landi) wearing the same "original," and they both sing how some irresponsible dressmaker has deceived them. As the song progresses, more women wearing the dress enter until there are twenty identical originals on stage.

"Paris Wakes Up and Smiles" is a gentle, beguiling Irving Berlin song from *Miss Liberty* (1949) sung by Johnny Thompson as a Parisian lamplighter. The first section of the song is a dreamlike hymn to the City of Light; then Allyn McLerie and the chorus join him, and it becomes a joyous greeting for a new day.

"Parisian Pierrot" is the wistful ballad that Gertrude Lawrence sang in *Andre Charlot's Revue of 1924*, the British import that introduced her to Broadway. Noël Coward wrote the delicate music and lyric, and years later Julie Andrews made a memorable recording of the song.

"The Party's Over" is the hit ballad from *Bells Are Ringing* (1956) by

Jule Styne (music) and Betty Comden and Adolph Green (lyric) that Judy Holliday sang as the disheartened Ella Peterson, who thinks she's lost the man she loves. Among the many recordings of the song, the biggest seller was one by Doris Day.

"Patterns" is a reflective soliloquy that David Shire (music) and Richard Maltby, Jr., (lyric) wrote for *Baby* (1983) but that was cut before opening. Arlene (Beth Fowler), a middle-aged woman and a mother of grown kids who finds out that she is pregnant again, looks back at the patterns her life has taken and laments that no one notices the great change that is taking place inside her. The delicate number was later heard in the Off-Broadway revue *Closer Than Ever* (1989), where it was sung by Lynne Wintersteller. The song is often restored to the score in revivals of *Baby*.

"People," the hit ballad from *Funny Girl* (1964) by Jule Styne (music) and Bob Merrill (lyric), was starting to get popular even before the show opened due to Barbra Streisand's recording of it. In fact, the number was slated to be cut (it really has nothing to do with the plot or Fanny Brice's character), but it was becoming clear that the song would be the hit of the show. Fanny (Streisand) sings the ballad to Nick Arnstein (Sydney Chaplin) about the people in her Henry Street neighborhood, but it quickly develops into a love song that aids their budding romance.

"People Will Say We're in Love" is one of Rodgers and Hammerstein's most beloved love songs and the most popular number to come out of the hit-packed *Oklahoma!* (1943). The song is essentially a list song in which Laurey (Joan Roberts) and Curly (Alfred Drake) give each other advice on how to behave to discourage the gossip that they are in love. But lyricist Oscar Hammerstein, as he had done in "Make Believe" sixteen years earlier, creates a tender love song by avoiding any direct "I love you" sentiments. The lyric, filled with buried internal rhymes and homespun imagery, is a wondrous example of subtext in theatre songwriting. Richard Rodgers wrote the music before the lyric was created (the opposite of the team's usual practice), and it has an unusually warm and meandering melody.

"Perfect Strangers" is a beguiling duet from the pastiche Victorian musical *The Mystery of Edwin Drood* (1985) by Rupert Holmes. Rosa Bud (Patti Cohenour) and Edwin Drood (Betty Buckley) have been betrothed to wed since they were children, but they break off the engagement, wishing that they had been perfect strangers to each other and had perhaps fallen in love on their own. In British pantomime style, the youthful Edwin is played by a woman, so the duet is oddly intoxicating, being sung by two women's voices. Holmes himself and Rita Coolidge made a recording of the graceful duet.

"The Phantom of the Opera" is the surging title song from the 1988 British import by Andrew Lloyd Webber (music) and Charles Hart and Richard Stilgoe (lyric). As the Phantom (Michael Crawford) takes the opera singer Christine (Sarah Brightman) to his underground lair, they sing this duet while traveling by boat on an subterranean lake surrounded by candelabras. The song is atypical of the rest of the score in that Webber's music has a driving rock and roll rhythm rather than a romantic approach.

"The Physician" is a comic lament by Cole Porter by a woman who is in love with her doctor, but all she can get out of him is medical compliments about her physiology. The song was introduced by Gertrude Lawrence in Porter's *Nymph Errant* in London in 1933, but the show was not produced in America until an Off-Broadway production in 1982, where "The Physician" was sung by Kathleen Mahoney-Bennett. Porter's lyric work in the song is particularly clever as he manages to find rhymes for multisyllabic medical terms. Pearl Bailey made a distinctive recording of the song.

"Piano Lesson" is an ingenious musical scene from *The Music Man* (1957) by Meredith Willson. Librarian-piano teacher Marian Paroo (Barbara Cook) and her mother (Pert Kelton) argue about Marion's being so particular about men, all to the rhythm of the finger exercises the pupil Amaryllis (Marilyn Siegel) is practicing on the parlor piano. The number uses few traditional rhymes, and much of the melody is simply the rising scales being practiced on the keyboard.

"The Pickers Are Comin' " is a tender ballad from the Civil War musical *Shenandoah* (1975) by Gary Geld (music) and Peter Udell (lyric). The Virginia farmer Charlie Anderson (John Cullum) sings wistfully of losing his daughter to marriage.

"Pick-Pocket Tango" is one of those unforgettable Gwen Verdon numbers that transcend the vehicle and character and become set pieces for her and her choreographer Bob Fosse. This exhilarating song and dance is from *Redhead* (1959) by Albert Hague (music) and Dorothy Fields (lyric). The Victorian Essie Whimple (Verdon) finds herself in jail, where she and the Jailer (Buzz Miller) perform the vivacious number.

"The Picture in the Hall" is a reflective ballad from the intimate Off-Broadway musical *Three Postcards* (1987) with music and lyric by Craig Carnelia. The tender song was sung by Karen Trott as K.C., a woman who recalls the wedding portrait of her parents and tries to understand what her mother was really like. Karen Akers also recorded the ballad.

"The Picture of Happiness" is a sly comic number from *Tenderloin* (1960) about the virtues of vice. Newspaper reporter Tommy Howatt (Ron Husmann) sings about virtuous women who fell to temptation and are now the picture of happiness. Jerry Bock wrote the animated honky-tonk music, and Sheldon Harnick provided the wry lyric.

"A Picture of Me Without You" is a Cole Porter list song that has so many up-to-the-minute references that one needs an almanac to decipher some of the allusions. June Knight and Charles Walters introduced the playful duet in *Jubilee* (1935), where they listed celebrities and their famous trademarks, such as Heinz and his pickle or Billy Sunday and his sinners. (A reference to Huey Long had to be deleted after his 1935 assassination.) Besides the clever rhyming, the lyric is unique in that almost every line in the five refrains starts with the word "picture." Most of the fun in "A Picture of Me Without You" is in the words, but that didn't keep orchestra leaders Johnny Green, Hoagy Carmichael and George Hall from making successful instrumental recordings of the song.

"Pine Cones and Holly Berries" is a contrapuntal Christmas song from *Here's Love* (1963) by Meredith Willson in which the secondary melody became more famous than the title one. Kris Kringle (Laurence Naismith) sings the holiday list song "Pine Cones and Holly Berries," then Macy's executives Doris Walker (Janis Paige) and Marvin Shellhammer (Fred Gwynne) sing the more memorable "It's Beginning to Look a Lot Like Christmas," making for a festive trio.

"Pirate Jenny" is a haunting, sinister ballad from *The Threepenny Opera* with music by Kurt Weill and lyric by Bertolt Brecht, translated and adapted by Marc Blitzstein for the 1954 Off-Broadway version. The prostitute Jenny (Lotte Lenya) sings the mordant number in which she imagines herself a bloodthirsty pirate. Weill's music is both alluring and disturbing as it shifts from a violent, angry patter section into a slow, evocative refrain that chills one with its sense of evil. Lotte Lenya, who had played Jenny and had sung the song in the original 1928 production in Berlin, recorded the song, and Judy Collins' version in the 1960s was very popular. "Pirate Jenny" was also sung by Judy Lander in the Off-Broadway revue *Berlin to Broadway With Kurt Weill* (1972).

"Please Hello" is a farcical yet telling musical sequence from *Pacific Overtures* (1976) in which the Western world besieges the newly opened Japan with offers of friendship and commerce. The old counselor Abe (Yuki Shimoda) is first visited by the American Admiral (Alvin Ing) who uses pidgin English and Sousa-like music to offer modern products and mutual trade. Then the British Admiral (Ernest Harada) enters and in Gilbert and Sullivan style does a fast-talking patter song expressing the best wishes of Queen Victoria and a promise of diplomatic friendship. When the Dutch Admiral (Patrick Kinser-lau) joins them, he offers chocolate and wooden shoes in a caricatured "Dutch comic" routine from the old Weber and Fields music-hall shows. The Russian Admiral (Mark Hsu Syers) offers caviar in a deep bass voice, and the French Admiral (James Dybas) wants a "detente" with everyone as he throws kisses to an Offenbach-like can-can. Stephen Sondheim wrote the delectable sequence which climaxes with all the nations joyfully embracing the East despite Abe's protests that they want to be left alone.

"**Poems**" is an engaging duet from *Pacific Overtures* (1976) that captures the simplicity of Japanese poetry and mentally evokes images from Asian painting. As Kayama (Isao Sato) and Manjiro (Sab Shimono) travel across the Japanese landscape, they make up poems to pass the time. Kayama sings of the beauty of nature and how it reminds him of his beautiful wife. Manjiro, who has been to America, sings of how the rain-washed scenery reminds him of Boston. The two poetic lines blend, and the number ends in an enthralling duet. Stephen Sondheim wrote the captivating number, and Harold Prince staged it with a series of screens that revealed different views of the moon as time passed.

"**Politics and Poker**" is a delightfully acerbic comedy number from *Fiorello!* (1959) and one of the musical theatre's most knowing songs about politics. The Jerry Bock (music) and Sheldon Harnick (lyric) song is sung by politico Ben Marino (Howard Da Silva) and his henchmen as they play five-card stud and try to decide on who to run in the next election. As possible candidates are considered and dismissed (for the lamest of reasons), the card game goes on uninterrupted, drawing keen comparisons between the two activities. Bock's beer-hall waltz melody is justly famous, and Harnick's lyric is hilarious and sharp, illustrating his mastery of the E.Y. Harburg-like wit he employed in his early shows.

"**Poor Butterfly**" is a sentimental song that lamented the fate of the Madame Butterfly character, and went on to sweep the country, selling over two million copies of sheet music. Raymond Hubbell (music) and John Golden (lyric) wrote the song, and it was featured in the Hippodrome spectacular *The Big Show* (1916), where it was sung by the Chinese-American singer Haru Onuki; her performance was lacking and the number got little notice. But early recordings by Edna Brown and by the Joseph C. Smith Orchestra became hits, and twenty-five years later Russ Columbo also had a best-selling record of the song. Other artists who had success with "Poor Butterfly" include Red Nichols, Deanna Durbin, Al Hibbler, Fritz Kreisler and, in perhaps the best interpretation of all, Sarah Vaughan. The most unusual recording was a 1963 hit by the Three Suns, which played Rimsky-Korsakov's "The Flight of the Bumblebee" contrapuntally with "Poor Butterfly."

"Poor Little Rich Girl" is Noël Coward's first song success in America, a sly number that was sung by Gertrude Lawrence in the 1925 British import *The Charlot Revue of 1926*. The number is a wry, moralistic piece about a bored wealthy woman who courts disaster and to whom virtue is very unfamiliar. The song was first heard in London in the 1925 revue *On With the Dance*. Lawrence made a popular recording of the song, as did Larry Clinton and His Orchestra and Judy Garland.

"Pore Jud Is Daid" is the comic duet for the villainous Jud Fry (Howard Da Silva) and his rival Curly (Alfred Drake) in *Oklahoma!* (1943) by Richard Rodgers (music) and Oscar Hammerstein (lyric). In hopes of encouraging Jud to commit suicide, Curly describes how moved all the members of the community will be at his funeral. An unusual feature of the song, besides its bizarre premise, is the use of a funeral march tempo and heavy recitative in a comic number.

"The President Jefferson Sunday Luncheon Party March" is a gleeful ensemble number from the short-lived *1600 Pennsylvania Avenue* (1976) by Leonard Bernstein (music) and Alan Jay Lerner (lyric). Jefferson (Ken Howard) led the march with all his guests in attendance at the White House where a buffet was made up of dishes from around the world. The score for *1600 Pennsylvania Avenue* was not recorded, but the song was recorded by John Reardon in 1981 and the number was reconstructed by conductor John McGlinn in 1992 with Davis Gaines, Linda Richardson, Tracey Miller and the Ambrosian Chorus.

"Pretty as a Picture" is a satiric song from the operetta *Sweethearts* (1913) that became popular as a sweet, sentimental favorite. Victor Herbert (music) and Robert B. Smith (lyric) wrote the number as the second-act opener, in which Petrus Van Tromp (Frank Belcher) and the chorus made fun of the female's enslavement to cosmetics in order to be picture perfect. But the music in the refrain is so graceful and entrancing that the song lost its comic edge.

"Pretty Baby" is a popular favorite that came from *A World of Pleasure* (1915), a musical with a score by Sigmund Romberg, but this interpolation was by Gus Kahn (lyric), Tony Jackson and Egbert Van Alstyne (music). The Shubert Brothers added the number to their *Passing Show of 1916*, where Dolly Brackett sang it in a baby voice with a chorus of girls dressed like dolls. The song was later a hit for Al Jolson, Eddie Cantor and others.

"A Pretty Girl" is a simple ballad from the satiric *Wang* (1891) that spoofed royal life in Siam. The young prince Mataya (Della Fox in the trouser role) sings the lovely song about his beloved Gillette, a French diplomat's daughter. The charming song by Woolson Morse (music) and J. Cheever Goodwin (lyric) had a cynical tone to it, but it became very popular in its day. In 1978 New World Records reconstructed the song and recorded Thomas Mariner singing it.

"A Pretty Girl Is Like a Melody" is the consummate *Ziegfeld Follies* song, the one that most conjures up visions of beautiful women descending a staircase. Irving Berlin wrote the elegant, graceful ballad for the 1919 edition of the *Follies*, where it was sung by John Steel. As part of the lavish production number, girls dressed as classical music selections were seen while the orchestra played fragments from Dvořák's "Humoresque," Mendelssohn's "Spring Song," Schubert's "Serenade" and others. The song was first recorded by Ben Selvin's Novelty Orchestra and has been heard since around the world, especially in fashion shows and beauty pageants.

"Pretty Lady" is an intoxicating ballad from *Pacific Overtures* (1976) by Stephen Sondheim that is so lovely and melodic that one forgets it is a crude seduction song. Three British sailors (Timm Fuji, Patrick Kinser-lau and Mark Hsu Syers) on leave in a Japanese town see a beautiful girl and, thinking she is a prostitute, woo her with this tender song. In the Broadway revue *Side by Side by Sondheim* (1977), the trio was sung by David Kernan, Millicent Martin and Julia McKenzie.

"Pretty Little Picture" is a sparkling trio from *A Funny Thing Happened on the Way to the Forum* (1962) by Stephen Sondheim. The clever slave Pseudolus (Zero Mostel) tries to convince the young and thickheaded Hero (Brian Davies) and the beautiful but vacant Philia (Preshy Marker) that they should elope, and he paints a series of pictures of what the adventure might be like. Sondheim's music is bouncy and frolicsome, and the lyric, arguably the finest one in the score, is scintillating, filled with amusing images and playful alliteration and packed with extraneous conjunctions that give the song a distinctive rhythm.

"Pretty Women," one of Stephen Sondheim's most alluring songs, is used to create the most suspenseful scene in *Sweeney Todd, the Demon Barber of Fleet Street* (1979). While the barber Todd (Len Cariou) prepares to slit the throat of his nemesis, Judge Turpin (Edmund Lyndeck), they sing this lyrical tribute to the elusiveness of women. The tense situation is made more gripping by the gentle, melodic song that celebrates the little everyday things women do that make them so wondrous. In the Off-Broadway revue *Putting It Together* (1993), the duet was sung by Stephen Collins and Michael Rupert.

"The Pricklepear Bloom" is the hilarious "I am" song for the jealous stepmother Salome (Barbara Lang) in the backwoods musical *The Robber Bridegroom* (1976). Salome is married to the rich Mississippi planter Clemment Musgrove, but he still dreams of his beautiful first wife, who died, and doesn't pay enough attention to Salome's own prickly attributes. Robert Waldman wrote the bluegrass music, and Alfred Uhry provided the colorful lyric.

"Prima Donna" is a seriocomic number from the British import *The Phantom of the Opera* (1988) that uses opera techniques to lampoon opera singers and their temperaments. The managers of the Paris Opera House, Andre (Cris Groenendaal) and Firmin (Nicholas Wyman), try to soothe the ruffled feathers of their star Carlotta Guidicelli (Judy Kaye). At the same time Raoul (Steve Barton), Madame Giry (Leila Martin) and Meg (Elisa Heinsohn) contemplate the next move by the Phantom (Michael Crawford), who is also heard commenting on the action. The thrilling number is the most complex piece in the score by Andrew Lloyd Webber (music) and Charles Hart and Richard Stilgoe (lyric).

"Progress" is a wry musical number from the experimental *Love Life* (1948) by Alan Jay Lerner (lyric) and Kurt Weill (music). This ambitious song chronicles the development of man from his natural state (when love was everything) to the industrial age (where money is everything) to economic crash. Weill's music moves from driven melodies with an anxious lyric to an easy vaudeville soft-shoe tempo with a tongue-in-cheek lyric. The number was sung by Ray Middleton, Nanette Fabray and the chorus. In the Off-Broadway revue *Berlin to Broadway With Kurt Weill* (1972), it was sung by Jerry Lanning and Hal Watters.

"Promise Me a Rose" is a touching character song from the period musical *Take Me Along* (1959) in which the spinster Lily (Eileen Herlie) reveals her deeply romantic nature under her stiff and proper exterior. Bob Merrill wrote the gentle music and lyric.

"Promises, Promises" is the surging title number from the 1968 musical by Burt Bacharach (music) and Hal David (lyric). At the end of the show, Chuck Baxter (Jerry Orbach) discontinues his practice of loaning his apartment to company executives needing a trysting place and, free from such guilty responsibilities, embraces his new-found freedom. Dionne Warwick made a best-selling recording of the pop song.

"Proud Lady" is a lusty character song from the ill-fated *The Baker's Wife* that closed out of town in 1976. Dominique (Kurt Peterson), the town's ladykiller, sees the baker's young wife for the first time and is smitten with her despite (or because of) the fact that she refuses to be interested in him. Stephen

Schwartz wrote the soaring music and the passionate lyric that has a delightful self-mocking flavor.

"Purlie" is the affectionate title song for the 1970 musical comedy about bigotry and change in the South. Lutiebelle (Melba Moore) sings the praises of the preacher Purlie (Cleavon Little), whom she is falling in love with. Gary Geld wrote the appealing music, and Peter Udell provided the loving lyric.

"Push de Button" is a rompish comic song from *Jamaica* (1957) satirizing the world of modern conveniences. The island beauty Savannah (Lena Horne) longs for a life on the isle of Manhattan because everything there is automated, from elevators to orange juice to child raising. Harold Arlen composed the pseudo-Caribbean music, and E.Y. Harburg wrote the sparkling lyric that uses a kind of pidgin English based on American television and movies.

"Put a Curse on You" is a searing number from *Ain't Supposed to Die a Natural Death* (1971), the revue about life and death in the black ghetto by Melvin Van Peebles. Minnie Gentry and the ensemble sang the indicting song that curses the white man with all the heartaches and destruction that are part of everyday life on the ghetto streets.

"Put Me in My Little Cell" is the first of several hundred lyrics P.G. Wodehouse wrote for the theatre and, as luck would have it, his first published and recorded song. It was written with composer Frederick Rosse for the London musical *Sergeant Brue*, which had a successful run on Broadway in 1905. The comic song is the amusing lament of a jailbird who, tired of the woes and responsibilities of the outside world, longs to go back to the comforts of prison. There is a very early recording of the song by tenor Billy Murray.

"Put on a Happy Face" is the most popular song to come out of *Bye Bye Birdie* (1960), a lighthearted soft-shoe number that was eons away from the rock and roll milieu of the plot but was very engaging anyway. Charles Strouse composed the tuneful music, Lee Adams wrote the breezy lyric, and Dick Van Dyke sang it to cheer up a disheartened teenager (Karin Wolf) who had just missed seeing her idol, Conrad Birdie.

"Put on Your Sunday Clothes" is the dandy chorus number from *Hello, Dolly!* (1964) in which most of the characters set off from Yonkers to Manhattan for a day of adventure. The Jerry Herman song starts as a character number for Cornelius Hackl (Charles Nelson Reilly) and Barnaby (Jerry Dodge), then includes Dolly Levi (Carol Channing) and others as they end up boarding the train for the big city. The song's catchy title, like most of the titles in the score, comes directly from Thornton Wilder's *The Matchmaker*, which inspired the musical.

"Put Your Arms Around Me, Honey" is a popular love song that was interpolated after opening into the sassy musical farce *Madame Sherry* (1910). Comedienne Elizabeth Murray sang the number by Albert Von Tilzer (music) and Junie McCree (lyric). Because of the show's record-breaking tour, the song was popular nationwide.

"Putting It Together" is the finest song ever written about the artistic process and how it must be reconciled to the business of the art. Stephen Sondheim wrote the provocative number for *Sunday in the Park With George* (1984), which was about the fine arts, but the song is a piquant view of all the arts and is especially relevant to Sondheim's career on Broadway. The contemporary artist George (Mandy Patinkin) reflects on the compromises he must swallow as he exchanges small talk at the opening of his latest sculpture, "Chromolume #7." The number is a musical scene in which song, soliloquy and dialogue explore the business of art. To illustrate the many faces the artist must wear before his patrons, critics and public, cardboard cutouts of George rose out of the floor and continued blank conversations with the partygoers while George sang to the audience of the tricky state of the art. Sondheim's music is hyperkinetic, and his lyric is cynically resigned to the way things are. In the 1993 Off-Broadway revue named after the song, "Putting It Together" was sung by the cast of five. Barbra Streisand recorded the song with an altered lyric so that it spoke of the compromises necessary in the music business.

"A Puzzlement" is the King's provocative musical soliloquy in Rodgers and Hammerstein's *The King and I* (1951) and one of the few times the character sings in the show. The King (Yul Brynner) is caught between the old ways of his father and the new ways of democratic enlightenment; he tries to rationalize the "puzzlement" he faces but can come to no firm conclusion at the end. The song is also a knowing "I am" song to which Richard Rodgers gives an exotic and regal melody, and Oscar Hammerstein's lyric provides the King with vivid images, all within his limited English vocabulary.

Q

"Questions" is a powerful, evocative song from the all-black revue *Don't Bother Me, I Can't Cope* (1972). Micki Grant wrote the music and lyrics for the vibrant score, and she herself sang this number about a black woman's confusion in the modern world.

"A Quiet Girl" is a rich and graceful ballad from *Wonderful Town* (1953) by Leonard Bernstein (music) and Betty Comden and Adolph Green (lyric). Newspaper editor Robert Baker (George Gaynes) has had a fight with the stubborn, very vocal Ruth (Rosalind Russell), so he muses in song about his ideal woman.

"Quiet Night," a lesser-known Rodgers and Hart ballad from *On Your Toes* (1936), is a lovely piece of sustained simplicity. The Richard Rodgers melody keeps harking back to its initial three-note phrase to great effect, and Lorenz Hart's lyric is so tranquil it practically whispers. The song was sung in the show by Earl MacVeigh and the ensemble, and Barbra Streisand made a memorable recording of it in 1964.

"A Quiet Thing" is one of Kander and Ebb's finest songs, a thrilling ballad from their first Broadway musical *Flora, the Red Menace* (1965). Struggling artist Flora Meszaros (Liza Minnelli) finally gets a job as a fashion illustrator for a Fifth Avenue department store and, as she revels in her good luck, realizes that the most important moments in one's life quietly come "in on tiptoe." The nineteen-year-old Minnelli's heartwarming rendition of the John Kander (music) and Fred Ebb (lyric) song launched her career. Karen Ziemba also sang the number in the Off-Broadway revue *And the World Goes 'Round* (1991).

R

"Race You to the Top of the Morning" is a heartfelt ballad from *The Secret Garden* (1991) by Lucy Simon (music) and Marsha Norman (lyric). The widower Archibald Craven (Mandy Patinkin) visits the bedroom of his sickly son Colin, and while the boy sleeps, he reads to him a book about a dragon and a maid in distress. But soon the song becomes a father's lament that he must leave the boy to a doctor's care as he goes off to face dragons of his own.

"Rackety Coo" is probably the most popular theatre song ever written about pigeons. Adele Rowland and the chorus sang the number in the operetta *Katinka* (1915) with a flock of trained pigeons performing the requisite spectacle. Rudolf Friml wrote the music, and Otto Harbach provided the birdlike lyric.

"Rags" is the powerful title number from the 1986 musical about immigrants at the turn of the century. Bella (Judy Kuhn) is weary of the optimistic lies about America that her father (Dick Latessa) still believes in. She erupts into a musical tirade explaining that all she sees in the new land is people like her dressed in rags. Charles Strouse composed the dramatic music that utilized ethnic strains and period ragtime, and Stephen Schwartz wrote the emotional lyric.

"Railbird" is an evocative ballad of yearning for adventure sung by Eugene Gant (Don Scardino) in *Angel* (1978), the short-lived musical version of Thomas Wolfe's *Look Homeward, Angel*. Gary Geld composed the enticing music, and Peter Udell wrote the absorbing lyric.

"The Rain in Spain" is a simple, unexceptional little ditty of a song, but, in the context of its placement in *My Fair Lady* (1956), it is the springboard for one of the musical theatre's most triumphant moments. The scene in which Eliza Doolittle finally begins to master the English language is not even in George Bernard Shaw's *Pygmalion* (1914), but the musical's creators Alan Jay Lerner (lyric) and Frederick Loewe (music) saw it as a major turning point and, sketching out the song in ten minutes, added it to the show right before rehearsals began. The number is prefaced by the servants' choral singing of "Poor Professor Higgins . . . Quit, Professor Higgins." Once Eliza (Julie Andrews) manages to pronounce her phonic exercises correctly, she and Henry Higgins (Rex Harrison) and Colonel Pickering (Robert Coote) burst into the fandango "The Rain in Spain" with improvised rhymes and sections of Eliza's drill sheets filled with "h" words. Finally, the three of them break into a silly tango, and the number climaxes with a joyous exultation rarely seen on the Broadway stage. Although "The Rain in Spain" was rarely recorded as a single, the cast album of *My Fair Lady* went on to become the best-selling musical score up to that point, and the song became one of the most recognized tunes in American culture.

"The Rainbow Girl" is the vibrant title song from the 1918 musical by Louis Hirsch (music) and Rennold Wolf (lyric). Billy B. Van sang the number extolling the virtues of Mollie Murdock (Beth Lydy) of the Frivolity Theatre in London. The song is sometimes listed as "My Rainbow Girl."

"Raining in My Heart" is a simple-minded but engaging number from *Dames at Sea* (1968), the Off-Broadway spoof of the early Hollywood musicals. Ruby (Bernadette Peters) sings the silly lament about how blue she feels over losing her sweetheart Dick. Jim Wise composed the engaging music, and George Haimsohn and Robin Miller wrote the pastiche lyric.

"The Rangers' Song" is the stirring male chorus number from the operetta *Rio Rita* (1927) by Harry Tierney (music) and Joseph McCarthy (lyric). Dashing Captain James Stewart (J. Harold Murray) leads the Texas Rangers in the robust march, proclaiming that "we're all pals together." Murray recorded the song soon after opening.

"Raunchy" is an eruptive comic number from *110 in the Shade* (1963) by Tom Jones (lyric) and Harvey Schmidt (music) and a showstopper for the actress playing Lizzie. Inga Swenson demonstrated her comic talents in the original production as the usually practical Lizzie Curry who cuts loose and does a mocking tribute to the kind of women who have no trouble attracting men. Her father H.C. Curry (Will Geer) makes comments throughout the song and joins her in the final bars.

"Razzle Dazzle" is a smooth-as-silk song from *Chicago* (1975) by John Kander (music) and Fred Ebb (lyric). The crooked lawyer Billy Flynn (Jerry Orbach) leads the ensemble at the courtroom in this detached song about how easily the public can be deceived. Bob Fosse staged the soft-shoe number with snapping fingers and contorted bodies and turned the trial scene into a circus act.

"The Real American Folk Song (Is a Rag)" is the first song the Gershwin brothers wrote together and lyricist Ira Gershwin's first song to be performed in public. Nora Bayes first sang it in a concert and then interpolated it into the tour of her Broadway vehicle *Ladies First* (1918). The song was not published and faded from view for forty years until Ella Fitzgerald made the first recording of the number, which was followed by the first publication of the song. Another thirty-four years passed before it was finally heard on Broadway when Brian M. Nalepka, Tripp Hanson and Hal Shane sang it in *Crazy for You* (1992). George Gershwin's music is a gentle rag that moves into syncopation when Ira Gershwin's lyric describes "a syncopated sort of meter."

"Real Live Girl" is an entrancing waltz from *Little Me* (1962) by Cy Coleman (music) and Carolyn Leigh (lyric) and a very tender number from an otherwise raucous farce of a musical. The sensitive doughboy Fred Poitrine (Sid Caesar) sings the song of romantic innocence to Belle Schlumpfert (Virginia Martin) after kissing his bride for the first time. The wistful number was later reprised by the World War One soldiers as they danced a gentle waltz in their trenches. Steve Alaimo and Jack Jones each made a popular recording of the song.

"The Red Ball Express" is a somber and powerful number from the postwar military revue *Call Me Mister* (1946) by Harold Rome. A black truck driver (Lawrence Winters), who had carried important army supplies throughout the war on the Red Ball Express, sang of his frustration when he was the only member of a group of applicants to be denied a job in the postwar employment boom because of his race.

"Red, Hot and Blue!," the title song from the 1936 Cole Porter musical comedy about politics and lotteries, celebrates the music of Berlin, Youmans and Ellington over that of Stravinsky, Chopin and Sibelius. Ethel Merman and the ensemble introduced the lively number, and Porter provided a hot, jazzy accompaniment to prove the point.

"Red Hot Chicago" is the jazzy showstopper from *Flying High* (1930), a musical about the current flying craze by B.G. DeSylva and Lew Brown (lyric) and Ray Henderson (music). Kate Smith gave a powerful rendition of the rhythmic ode to the city that (the song says) was the origin of jazz. Anyone who argues with that, Kate sang, is a "nincompoop."

"Red Sails in the Sunset" is a popular British song that was equally successful in America in the 1930s. The atmospheric number, with music by Hugh Williams (aka Will Grosz) and a lyric by Jimmy Kennedy, was interpolated into *Provincetown Follies* (1935), where Phyllis Austen sang it. Popular orchestral recordings were made by Guy Lombardo, Les Brown and Montovanni, as well as records by Bing Crosby, Louis Armstrong, Lanny Ross, Frances Langford and whistler Fred Lowery.

"Remember That I Care" is an expansive romantic duet from the operatic *Street Scene* (1947) that was sung by Brian Sullivan and Anne Jeffreys as two dreamers living in the same New York City neighborhood. Kurt Weill's music is Puccini-like yet captures an urban American flavor. Langston Hughes's lyric, suggested by Walt Whitman's poem "When Lilacs Last in the Dooryard Bloom'd," uses nature imagery to show the young dreamers' yearning to escape the city.

"Repent" is a farcical specialty number for Imogene Coca in the mock operetta *On the Twentieth Century* (1978) by Cy Coleman (music) and Betty Comden and Adolph Green (lyric). The zany religious fanatic Letitia Primrose (Coca) sang the daffy number aboard the Twentieth Century Limited on its journey from Chicago to New York.

"Reuben and Cynthia" is a witty comic number from the early landmark musical comedy *A Trip to Chinatown* (1891) by Percy Gaunt (music) and Charles H. Hoyt (lyric). The tune was an old one that Gaunt adapted, and Hoyt wrote a clever lyric that took the form of a silly conversation between Reuben and Cynthia about various matters. In the show the song was sung by the hypochondriac Welland Strong (Harry Conor), who comes to San Francisco hoping that an earthquake will rejuvenate him. Over the years the song remained popular, usually under the title "Reuben, Reuben," the expression that begins each stanza. New World Records reconstructed and recorded the number in 1978 as a duet with Gina Ferraro and William Schaeffer.

"Reviewing the Situation" is a seriocomic soliloquy for the delicious villain Fagin (Clive Revill) in the British import *Oliver!* (1963) by Lionel Bart. With his pickpocket business threatened by Oliver Twist's escape, Fagin considers going straight and argues it out to himself. But as he pictures each new lifestyle possibility, the thought frightens him into looking for alternatives. The song is reprised near the end of the show when Fagin's business is destroyed and he faces a bleak future.

"Rhode Island Is Famous for You" is a clever list song from the revue *Inside U.S.A.* (1948) by Howard Dietz (lyric) and Arthur Schwartz (music). Jack Haley sang (sometimes seriously, sometimes not) of the attractions of several American states, concluding that his sweetheart is the prized by-product of Rhode Island.

"A Rhyme for Angela" is one of Ira Gershwin's most ingenious but least known lyrics, a list song that comes up with a dozen far-from-ordinary rhymes for exotic women's names but, alas, none for Angela. The number was sung by Melville Cooper as Duke Alessandro of Florence in the short-lived *The Firebrand of Florence* (1945). Kurt Weill wrote the lively music for the facetious song.

"Ribbons Down My Back" is the quietest moment in *Hello, Dolly!* (1964), a gentle ballad sung by Irene Malloy (Eileen Brennan) as she anticipates rejoining the human race by marrying Horace Vandergelder. Jerry Herman wrote the music and lyric for the delicate song.

"Riches" is a riotous quartet from the musical folk tale *The Robber Bridegroom* (1976) by Robert Waldman (music) and Alfred Uhry (lyric). At an engagement dinner of sorts, the rich planter Clemment Musgrove (Stephen Vinovich) is trying to marry off his daughter Rosamund (Rhonda Coullet) to the disguised bandit Jamie Lockhart (Barry Bostwick), but his overbearing wife Salome (Barbara Lang) has her own designs on the young man. As Jamie sings of the treasures he hopes to get from the marriage, Rosamund tries to look as disheveled and act as ornery as possible because she loves the bandit in the woods, whom she doesn't recognize as Jamie.

"Ride Through the Night" is a fascinating chorus number from *Subways Are for Sleeping* (1961) that explores the thoughts of all those blank faces you see on the subway. Angie McKay (Carol Lawrence) and the passengers on the express car go beyond the small talk and expose their dreams and fantasies as they ride deep underground. Jule Styne (music) and Betty Comden and Adolph Green (lyric) wrote the unusual number.

"Ridin' High" is a joyous Cole Porter number long associated with Ethel Merman, who introduced it in *Red, Hot and Blue!* (1936) as "Nails" O'Reilly when she discovers that Bob Hale (Bob Hope) loves her. In addition to the raucous verse and refrain, the song also contains two patter sections in which Nails lists a bevy of famous beauties, all of whom she rates herself above because she's in love.

"The Riff Song" is a stirring chorus number from the operetta *The Desert Song* (1926) by Sigmund Romberg (music) and Otto Harbach and Oscar Hammerstein (lyric). The Moroccan leader of the Riff revolt, the Red Shadow (Robert Halliday), and his aide Sid El Kar (William O'Neal) lead their band of ruffians in this male choral number that is a call to battle. Mario Lanza made a vibrant recording of the song.

"Right as the Rain" is the popular love song from *Bloomer Girl* (1944) by Harold Arlen (music) and E.Y. Harburg (lyric) that avoids any sentimental romanticism by presenting love as a fact of nature. The Southern gentleman Jefferson Calhoun (David Brooks) and the nineteenth-century suffragette Evelina Applegate (Celeste Holm) sing the convivial ballad, assuring each other that their love is as real and tangible as the rain that falls. Arlen's music is seamless, flowing and melodic, eschewing conventional verse, refrain and release. Harburg's lyric is direct but poetic and avoids the banal by keeping the characters on a rational rather than an emotional level. The song was recorded often, and a single version by Brooks and Holm was quite popular.

"The Right Girl" is a delirious character song from *Follies* (1971) in which the unhappy Buddy Plummer (Gene Nelson) reveals his frustrations about love and self-love in a frantic song and dance. Stephen Sondheim wrote the fascinating number in which Buddy envisions conversations with his wife and then with his mistress, trying to determine who is the right girl in his life. The song climaxes in a furious dance routine filled with self-loathing.

"The Rink" is the snappy title song from the 1984 musical by John Kander (music) and Fred Ebb (lyric). The frolicsome song about the joys of roller skating at the rink was sung and skated by the six moving men (Ronn Carroll, Scott Holmes, Frank Mastrocola, Scott Ellis, Mel Johnson, Jr., and Jason Alexander) who have come to clear out the old building.

"Rio Rita" is the loving title song from the 1927 operetta by Harry Tierney (music) and Joseph McCarthy (lyric) and the biggest hit from the popular show. The song celebrates the tempestuous heroine Rita Furguson (Ethelind Terry) of the Texas Rio Grande territory and was sung by Captain James Stewart (J. Harold Murray) of the Texas Rangers and as a duet for him and Rita. At one point in the show the song was sung against another number in the score, "The River Song," to great effect. Murray recorded "Rio Rita" soon after the show opened.

"Rise 'n' Shine" is the exhilarating spiritual number from *Take a Chance* (1932), the last musical with songs by Vincent Youmans. Ethel Merman, as the brassy Wanda Brill, stopped the show with her thrilling rendition of the optimistic, anti-Depression song. Youmans wrote the cheering music, and B.G. DeSylva provided the ardent lyric. Paul Whiteman's Orchestra made a hit recording of the song, and the music was a favorite for tap dancers, jugglers, acrobats and the like in nightclubs and variety shows.

"River in the Rain" is an evocative song of nature from the *Huckleberry Finn* musical *Big River* (1985) with songs by country-western composer Roger Miller. As Huck (Daniel H. Jenkins) and the runaway slave Jim (Ron Richardson) float down the Mississippi on their raft, a light rain falls, and they sing this gentle and bucolic duet about the transcendent beauty of the Mississippi River.

"The Road to Paradise" is an expressive duet by Sigmund Romberg (music) and Rida Johnson Young (lyric) from the operetta *Maytime* (1917). Richard (Charles Purcell) and Ottillie (Peggy Wood), now married to others, meet after fifteen years and admit that they still love each other, singing this waltz that was very popular in its day.

"The Road You Didn't Take" is a perceptive character song from *Follies* (1971) that potently reveals a subtextual falsehood in the successful man who sings it. Ben Stone (John McMartin) tries to convince his old flame Sally (Dorothy Collins) that the choices that one makes in life are unavoidable and that it does no good to look back. But the way Stephen Sondheim wrote the disturbing music and the way the lyric keeps asking rhetorical questions, it is clear that Ben not only remembers his past mistakes but is haunted by them.

"Rock Island" is the rhythmic opening number of *The Music Man* (1957) by Meredith Willson. Charlie Cowell (Paul Reed) and the other traveling salesmen on board the Rock Island Railroad discuss the trade and provide exposition about the con man Harold Hill, all in time to the rhythm of the train. There is no music per se and the flavorful lyric does not rhyme, but the effect is that of a scintillating chorus number.

"Rock-a-Bye Your Baby With a Dixie Melody" is one of Al Jolson's popular Southern songs that he sang in blackface in a variety of shows, this one interpolated into the extravaganza *Sinbad* (1918), where he sang it as the Baghdad comic Inbad who disguises himself as the famous sailor. The song was written by Jean Schwartz (music) and Sam Lewis and Joe Young (lyric). Jolson used the number throughout his long career, singing it in three films and doing a recording of it as late as 1946 that sold a million copies.

"Romantic Notions" is an evocative ballad from *Romance, Romance* (1988) by Barry Harman (lyric) and Keith Herrmann (music) sung by two married couples who admit that in certain moods and at certain times they fantasize about romance outside of their marriages. The graceful number was sung by Scott Bakula, Alison Fraser, Deborah Graham and Robert Hoshour.

"Romany Life" is an exhilarating chorus number that captures the spirit of the gypsies in Victor Herbert's operetta *The Fortune Teller* (1898). Eugene Cowles, Joseph Cawthorn and a chorus of gypsies sang the song that, along with the same show's "Gypsy Love Song," is the most famous gypsy music ever written for Broadway. Harry B. Smith wrote the lyric for Herbert's Hungarian-flavored music.

"A Room in Bloomsbury" is an appealing pastiche number from the British import *The Boy Friend* (1954) by Sandy Wilson. Polly Browne (Julie Andrews) and her boy friend Tony (John Hewer) imagine a simple but loving life together in this duet that recalls 1920s songs of a similar temperament, such as "The Love Nest," "The Church Around the Corner," "Sitting Pretty" and "Tea for Two."

"A Room With a View" is a romantic ballad by Noël Coward from the revue *This Year of Grace* (1928) which was imported from London with Coward himself heading the cast. The juvenile lead Billy Milton sang the dreamy, youthful number, which producer Charles B. Cochran wanted Coward to perform. Although he felt he was too old for it, Coward tried singing it but quickly despaired, telling Cochran "It's more than I can bear and more than one should expect of any audience!" Regardless, the song went on to be one of Coward's most popular ballads. Bobby Short's recording of the number is very stylish.

"A Room Without Windows" is a swinging 1960s version of the old let's-get-away-from-it-all formula song that has been popular in musicals since the turn of the century. This one is from *What Makes Sammy Run?* (1964) by Ervin Drake and was sung by movie executive Sammy Glick (Steve Lawrence) and filmwriter Kit Sargent (Sally Ann Howes) about a secluded little hotel in Tijuana that he wants to take her to.

"Rose-Marie" is the luscious title song from the popular 1924 operetta about romance in the Canadian Rockies. This enticing tribute to the musical's heroine was written by Rudolf Friml (music) and Otto Harbach and Oscar Hammerstein (lyric) and was sung by fur trapper Jim Kenyon (Dennis King) and Sergeant Malone (Arthur Deagon) in an easy, conversational style that was unique to the operetta form. The song was popular in the 1920s and had a resurgence decades later due to a best-selling recording by Slim Whitman in 1954.

"Rose of the World" is one of Victor Herbert's most passionate declarations of love, an operetta standard that was first heard in *Algeria* (1908), where it was sung by Ida Brooks Hunt. The show was short-lived, but the song was heard again in the revised version called *The Rose of Algeria* (1909), where it was sung by Lillian Herlein. Glen MacDonough wrote the fervent lyric for Herbert's lush music.

"Roses at the Station" is a powerful soliloquy from *Grand Hotel* (1989) in which the Baron (David Carroll), dying from a gunshot wound, imagines he is at the train station waiting for his beloved Elizaveta (Liliane Montevecchi) with an armful of red roses. In the course of the dramatic number the Baron recalls his youth and being in the Great War, where he was always near to death but managed to escape until this moment. Maury Yeston wrote the absorbing music and lyric.

"Rose's Turn" is the musical climax of *Gypsy* (1959), a theatrical tour de force in which Mama Rose (Ethel Merman) has a musical nervous breakdown on stage. Abandoned by both her daughters and filled with anger and regret, Rose launches into this electric soliloquy in which she decides it's her turn to get the spotlight because all along it was her talent and drive that made her daughters what they were. Stephen Sondheim's stream-of-consciousness lyric is brassy, painful and unsentimental. Jule Styne's music is equally dynamic, with a touch of bump and grind amidst all the passion. The lengthy sequence includes sections of songs heard previously in the score, including one called "Momma's Talking Soft" that was dropped before opening but retained in "Rose's Turn."

"Row, Row, Row" is the rousing song favorite that Lillian Lorraine introduced in the *Ziegfeld Follies* (1912). The lively James V. Monaco (music) and William Jerome (lyric) song, about a romance in a rowboat, was recorded by Ada Jones in 1912 and became popular nationwide. It was sung by the ensemble in *Oh What a Lovely War!*, the British import that reached Broadway in 1964.

S

"'S Wonderful" is one of the musical theatre's most distinctive songs, a unique blending of music and lyric by the Gershwin brothers that epitomizes the sassy 1920s love song. The number was introduced in *Funny Face* (1927), where it was sung by aviator Peter Thurston (Allen Kearns) and his beloved Frankie Wynne (Adele Astaire). George Gershwin's music, with its light-footed repetition of musical phrases, is charming, but there is just as much melody in Ira Gershwin's lyric, which uses the sibilant "s" sound throughout the number in a way that can only be described as Gershwinesque. "'S Wonderful" was the hit of *Funny Face* and has remained just as popular ever since. Singers ranging from Sarah Vaughan to Michael Feinstein have recorded the playful number. In the largely rewritten version of the show called *My One and Only* (1983), the song was sung by aviator Billy Buck Chandler (Tommy Tune) and swimming star Edith Herbert (Twiggy) as they splashed about in a pool of water.

"Sabbath Prayer" is a very unusual number for a Broadway musical, a devout hymn that expresses a people's faith rather than the wishes of any one character. The graceful and moving song was sung in *Fiddler on the Roof* (1964) by Zero Mostel, Maria Karnilova and the families of the village. Jerry Bock wrote the music, which climbs the scale in a penetrating manner, and Sheldon Harnick provided the reverent lyric.

"Sadie, Sadie" is a jocular tribute to married life from *Funny Girl* (1964) and a song very close to the style of the actual Fanny Brice. Jule Styne composed the cheery music, and Bob Merrill wrote the comic lyric in which Fanny (Barbra Streisand) and her friends celebrate her marriage to Nick Arnstein (Sydney Chaplin).

"Safety in Numbers" is the less-than-discreet credo of flapper Maisie (Ann Wakefield) in the British import *The Boy Friend* (1954) by Sandy Wilson.

Finishing-school student Maisie has her wild side, which worries her boy friend Bobby (Bob Scheerer), but she explains that having many beaux is her safeguard against loneliness. To prove her point she performs this raucous song and dance with Bobby and the boys.

"The Saga of Jenny" is the show-stopping bump-and-grind number that Gertrude Lawrence, in a departure from her usual droll style, performed in *Lady in the Dark* (1941). During the "Circus Dream" sequence of the musical, Liza Elliott (Lawrence) is put on trial for failing to make up her mind whether or not to marry Kendall Nesbitt (Bert Lytell). She defends herself with this flashy narrative about a woman named Jenny who brought destruction wherever she went because she was so strong-minded. Kurt Weill composed the jazzy music, and Ira Gershwin wrote the pungent lyric. "The Saga of Jenny" was the highlight of the show, but it was a late addition to the score. Weill and Gershwin had written an intricate and dark number about the signs of the zodiac and their fatalistic powers. But the song proved too oppressive, and a lighter tone was needed, so they wrote this sassy narrative ballad. In previews it was feared that the new song, which followed Danny Kaye's spectacular specialty number "Tschaikowsky," would be anticlimactic. But "The Saga of Jenny" was an even bigger crowd pleaser and a triumph for Lawrence. Judy Lander sang the song in the Off-Broadway revue *Berlin to Broadway With Kurt Weill* (1972), and recordings were made by Lotte Lenya, Julie Andrews, Dawn Upshaw and others.

"Sail Away" is the buoyant title number from the 1961 Noël Coward musical set on a Cunard liner voyaging through the Mediterranean. Passenger Johnny Van Mier (James Hurst) and the ensemble sing the jolly advice for escaping from one's everyday woes. The song was originally heard in the London musical *Ace of Clubs* (1950); Coward took the number and built a whole new show around it. "Sail Away" was sung by Barbara Cason, Roderick Cook and Jamie Ross in the Off-Broadway revue *Oh Coward!* (1972).

"Sailors' Song" is a rousing tango from *Happy End* with music by Kurt Weill and a lyric by Bertolt Brecht, translated by Michael Feingold for the 1977 Broadway premiere of the 1929 German musical. Salvation Army worker Hallelujah Lil (Meryl Streep) gets drunk at Bill Cracker's Chicago gin joint and launches into this raucous ballad about the life of sailors. Weill's music is vibrant and very unconventional, with long and unusual refrains and a tango melody that shifts into 1920s jazz. Lotte Lenya recorded the number in the 1950s, and it was sung by the ensemble in the Off-Broadway revue *Berlin to Broadway With Kurt Weill* (1972), where it was called "Sailor Tango."

"Sam and Delilah" is a rousing Wild West version of the biblical lovers' tale that Ethel Merman sang in the Gershwins' *Girl Crazy* (1930). In a saloon in

Custerville, Arizona, prairie gal Kate Fothergill (Merman) sings this tongue-in-cheek narrative ballad, and the ensemble joins in on the chorus about the femme fatale Delilah being up to no good. George Gershwin composed the bluesy music, and Ira Gershwin wrote the satiric lyric that spoofed the "Frankie and Johnny" kind of ballad. Duke Ellington's Orchestra (vocal by Chick Bullock) and Lee Wiley both made hit recordings of the number.

"Same Sort of Girl" is a swinging foxtrot song by Jerome Kern (music) and Harry B. Smith (lyric) that was interpolated into the British import *The Girl From Utah* (1914). The Mormon wife Una Trance (Julia Sanderson) flees to London, where she falls for song and dance man Sandy Blair (Donald Brian), who sings to her how she is different from all his past loves. The song was quite successful, particularly with dance bands, and years later when Sanderson and her husband Frank Crumit had their popular 1940s radio show, "Same Sort of Girl" was a recurring favorite.

"Sands of Time" is the haunting number that opens and closes the *Arabian Nights* musical *Kismet* (1953) using musical themes by Alexander Borodin. The Iman of the Mosque (Richard Oneto) sings the beguiling song, telling the audience that only lovers know all there is to know. Robert Wright and George Forrest wrote the atmospheric lyric and adapted Borodin's "In the Steppes of Central Asia" for the theatre song.

"Saturday Night in Central Park" is a snappy tribute to New York City nightlife that takes the form of an urban hoedown. Richard Lewine (music) and Arnold B. Horwitt (lyric) wrote the popular song for the revue *Make Mine Manhattan* (1948), where it was sung by the ensemble as the first-act finale.

"Say It With Music" is the lush Irving Berlin ballad that was featured in the first edition of the *Music Box Revue* (1921) and became the theme song for the subsequent three annual editions. Using music as a metaphor for romance, the lovely number has a syncopated strain that makes for a unique blend of the old and the new. In the revue Wilda Bennett sang it with Paul Frawley, but the song was already popular before opening night because Berlin had given it to some nightclub orchestras and it was starting to catch on. Tenor John Steel and Paul Whiteman's Orchestra both made hit recordings of the song.

"Scylla and Charybdis" is a rompish vaudeville pastiche number from *The Golden Apple* (1954) that is also a takeoff on the famous Gallagher and Shean routine. Scylla (Dean Michener) and Charybdis (Jack Whiting) are two corrupt stockbrokers who are cornering the hemp market and revel in their own wickedness. Jerome Moross composed the old-time melody and John Latouche wrote the satirical lyric.

"The Sea Song" is the dandy pastiche number that opens the period musical *By the Beautiful Sea* (1954) by Arthur Schwartz (music) and Dorothy Fields (lyric). Ex-vaudevillian Lottie Gibson (Shirley Booth) and her father (Cameron Prud'homme) take over the management of a Coney Island boardinghouse and sing with the ensemble about the advantages of being near the sea. The boardinghouse was called "By the Beautiful Sea," and that phrase is used throughout the lyric, but the authors needed to distinguish their song from the famous period number of the same name, so they called it "The Sea Song."

"Seagull, Starfish, Pebble" is a tender "I am" song that introduced the simple-minded waif Gelsomina (Bernadette Peters) in the one-performance flop *La Strada* (1969) based on the Federico Fellini movie of the same name. The musical was scored by Lionel Bart, but all but three of his songs were dropped before opening. The new score, including this lovely number, had music by Elliot Lawrence and lyrics by Martin Charnin. With its title shortened to "Starfish," the song was recorded by Judy Kuhn in 1994.

"Second Hand Rose" is the delectable specialty number written for Fanny Brice for the 1921 edition of the *Ziegfeld Follies*. James Hanley (music) and Grant Clarke (lyric) wrote the seriocomic lament of a girl from Second Avenue whose life has been a series of hand-me-downs. The number is a sequel of sorts to the popular "Rose of Washington Square." For the first time Brice had a song that allowed her to interject some pathos into her wisecracking ethnic character. Although she never sang the number in the Brice bio-musical *Funny Girl* (1964), Barbra Streisand made a popular recording of the song.

"A Secretary Is Not a Toy" is a deliciously droll chorus number from *How to Succeed in Business Without Really Trying* (1961) that offered a lesson in office etiquette as it satirized the "man as boy" syndrome. Paul Reed, as the company's personnel manager, sang the musical lesson that evolved into a soft-shoe devised by choreographer Bob Fosse and set to the clatter of typewriters all in tempo. Frank Loesser originally wrote the song as a childlike waltz that the company president, J.B. Biggley (Rudy Vallee), was to sing to his employees. But Vallee refused to perform the number at Loesser's tempo, choosing rather to croon it, and the number failed in previews. It was Fosse who reconceived the piece and made it work.

"See the Light" is a narrative number that tells of the escapades of Emma Finch, who stole furs and husbands before she reformed and saw the light. The delightful ragtime pastiche song is sung by senior citizen Gert (Lillian Roth) in *70, Girls, 70* (1971) as she distracts the night watchman at Bloomingdales while her cohorts rob the store. John Kander wrote the zestful music, and Fred Ebb provided the daffy lyric.

"Seeing Things" is an enthralling duet from *The Happy Time* (1968) by John Kander (music) and Fred Ebb (lyric). Jacques Bonnard (Robert Goulet) and his old flame Laurie Mannon (Julie Gregg) try to renew their past romance, but it is soon clear that each has such a different way of looking at life that they could never be happy together.

"Seesaw" is the fervent title song from the 1973 musical about an up-and-down romance by Cy Coleman (music) and Dorothy Fields (lyric). Everybody is on a seesaw, the song states, and it's quite a ride. The song is first heard sung by the chorus at the opening of the show, then is reprised by Gittel Mosca (Michele Lee) near the end of the musical after her tottering affair with Jerry Ryan (Ken Howard) has ended.

"The Senatorial Roll Call" is a comic list song from the satirical *Of Thee I Sing* (1931) that has playful music by George Gershwin and a prankish lyric by Ira Gershwin. Vice President Alexander Throttlebottom (Victor Moore) assembles the U.S. Senate to begin impeachment hearings against President Wintergreen and calls the roll, rhyming the states' names. After half a dozen names he suspends the rest of the roll, singing that he can't be bothered when the names do not rhyme.

"Send in the Clowns" was a late addition to *A Little Night Music* (1973) by Stephen Sondheim, but it was quickly established as the centerpiece of the score. The ballad was sung by Glynis Johns as the scandalous actress Desiree after she is deserted by her old flame Fredrik (Len Cariou). The number is a torch song, yet the unsentimental lyric allows it to be interpreted in various ways, from a wistful statement on the frivolity of love to a deeply cynical ballad about the futility of life. At the end of the musical the song is reprised, with a different lyric, by Desiree and Fredrik and becomes a love duet. Because of Johns's low and rather limited voice range, the song is actually one of Sondheim's least difficult compositions to sing, having no sustained notes and several musical interludes for the singer to rest. But the number is rich in both melody and harmony, being disconcerting and satisfying at the same time. Sondheim's lyric is understated, with short phrases that paint vivid pictures, and, Desiree being an actress, the song is filled with theatre metaphors. "Send in the Clowns" was not immediately popular outside of the theatre, but by 1975, thanks to recordings by Judy Collins and Frank Sinatra, it became a hit and has remained Sondheim's most well-known song. In the Broadway revue *Side By Side By Sondheim* (1977), the number was sung by Millicent Martin.

"Sentimental Me," an early Rodgers and Hart song that later became a standard, manages to be both a love song and a spoof of a love song; surprisingly, it satisfies on both counts. Richard Rodgers (music) and Lorenz

Hart (lyric) wrote it for the satirical revue *The Garrick Gaieties* (1925), where it was sung by June Cochrane, James Norris, Edith Meiser and Sterling Holloway. In the first section of the song two overinfatuated lovers lament the hopeless state love has brought them to. In a second comic section an asthmatic old man and a rheumatic old lady compare ailments and confess their love. Successful orchestral recordings of "Sentimental Me" were made by Ben Selvin and by Arden and Ohman.

"September Song" is one of the most beloved of all theatre songs, and Walter Huston's heartfelt rendition of it is one of the musical theatre's most enduring memories. The ballad was written by Kurt Weill (music) and Maxwell Anderson (lyric) for *Knickerbocker Holiday* (1938), where the aging Governor Pieter Stuyvesant (Huston) sang about the passing of time to a young girl (Jeanne Madden) he hoped to wed. Huston had been in vaudeville but never in a Broadway musical, and he agreed to do the show if the authors wrote him a simple sentimental song within his range. When Weill asked him what his range was, Huston telegraphed that he had no range and that he would be singing on the radio that night. Weill and Anderson listened to the broadcast and in a few hours wrote the unforgettable "September Song." The lyric is provocative yet rather restrained, with only a handful of rhymes and simple imagery (change of seasons, passage of time, the shortening daylight hours and so on) that is powerful while being soothing. Weill's music, which is more Germanic than colonial American, follows the traditional thirty-two-bar form, yet the initial eight-bar theme is never repeated in exactly the same manner. Like the lyric, the music is enticing and responsive, even within the narrow range that Huston required. The oft-recorded song had popular recordings by Stan Kenton and His Orchestra, George Shearing, Bing Crosby, Jimmy Durante, Frank Sinatra (who recorded it three times), Lena Horne, Willie Nelson and the nonsinging Huston himself.

"Serenade" is the title of two different Sigmund Romberg songs, both sung by Howard Marsh in two different operettas in the 1920s. In the biographical *Blossom Time* (1921) about the life of Franz Schubert, Romberg adapted the classic composer's famous "Serenade," and Dorothy Donnelly added the romantic lyric that was sung by Marsh as Baron Shoeber. In the popular *The Student Prince* (1924), Romberg composed original music, Donnelly provided the dreamy lyric, and Marsh sang the operatic "Serenade" as Prince Karl Franz, a student in Heidelberg. Producer J.J.Shubert wanted to cut the number from *The Student Prince* because he felt it was too highbrow for their usual audiences. But Romberg and his lawyer threatened legal action, and the song remained, becoming the hit of the show. Of the many recordings of the song is a violin solo version by Efrem Zimbalist that was very popular. Romberg's "Serenade" for *The Student Prince* is sometimes titled by its first line, "Overhead the Moon

Is Beaming," to distinguish it from Schubert's "Serenade."

"Serenade" is a captivating trio from the ill-fated *The Baker's Wife* that closed out of town in 1976 before getting to New York. Stephen Schwartz wrote the harmonious number in which the lusty Dominique (Kurt Peterson) serenades the baker's house at night, praising the treasures he has brought to town. Inside, the amiable baker (Topol, later Paul Sorvino) sings his delight at such gratitude, while his wife Genevieve (Patti LuPone) knows that Dominique desires her and is using his double-meaning lyric to woo her.

"Seven-and-a-Half Cents" is the spirited chorus number sung at the union rally in *The Pajama Game* (1954). Janis Paige and Stanley Prager led the workers at the Sleep-Tite Pajama Factory in the song, which celebrated the long-term benefits of a seven-and-a-half cent raise. Richard Adler and Jerry Ross wrote the song, and the title came from the Richard Bissel book that served as the basis for the hit musical.

"The Seven Deadly Virtues" is the deliciously wicked character song for Mordred (Roddy McDowell) in *Camelot* (1960) by Alan Jay Lerner (lyric) and Frederick Loewe (music). King Arthur's bastard son Mordred has come to Camelot to make trouble and, in this stinging soliloquy, mocks the courtly virtues of courage, purity, humility, honesty, diligence, charity and fidelity. He concludes the list song by vowing never to be "cursed" by any of them.

"Seventy-Six Trombones" is the most famous march to come from the Broadway stage since the popular operettas of the 1920s. The spirited number was sung by the con man Professor Harold Hill (Robert Preston) and the ensemble in *The Music Man* (1957) by Meredith Willson and has been a favorite of marching bands ever since. In the musical, Hill paints a vivid picture of the day all the famous bands converged on the same city. His hyperbolic description rouses the citizens of River City to embrace Hill's offer to start a boys' band in the small Iowa town. The music for "Seventy-Six Trombones," at a much slower tempo, is also used for the wistful lullaby "Goodnight, My Someone" that Marian (Barbara Cook) sings earlier in the show. Near the end of the musical both songs are reprised, but Hill sings the lullaby version, while Marian sings the fervent march.

"Shaking the Blues Away" is an impelling rhythm song that Irving Berlin wrote for the 1927 edition of the *Ziegfeld Follies*. The revival-like number uses sharp rhythmic accents and rhyming open-vowel contractions to maintain its electric quality. Ruth Etting, in her *Follies* debut, sang the number with the chorus. Both Paul Whiteman and Ben Selvin made popular orchestral recordings of it.

"Shall I Tell You What I Think of You?" is Anna's funny, furious soliloquy in *The King and I* (1951), a counterpart to the King's soliloquy "A Puzzlement." Richard Rodgers' music wavers from European to Eastern tones as Oscar Hammerstein's lyric illustrates the frustration Anna (Gertrude Lawrence) is going through, trying to decide what to say to the King.

"Shall We Dance?" is the irresistible duet and dance for Anna (Gertrude Lawrence) and the King (Yul Brynner) that climaxes their relationship in *The King and I* (1951). The unconventional pair needed an unconventional way to have their big number. Songwriters Richard Rodgers (music) and Oscar Hammerstein (lyric) solved the problem with this sweeping polka that allows Anna to show the King how they dance at formal gatherings in the West. Their beguiling duet and dance is the most enduring image from the popular musical. In the Broadway revue *A Grand Night for Singing* (1993), the duet was sung by Jason Graae and Lynne Wintersteller.

"Shalom" is the warm and inviting song from *Milk and Honey* (1961) that became the show's only popular number. The song explains the many meanings of the Hebrew expression and was sung by two American tourists (former opera singers Robert Weede and Mimi Benzell) visiting Israel. Like much of the Jerry Herman score, "Shalom" is a pleasing mixture of Jewish rhythms and Broadway sounds. Robert Goulet was among those who recorded it, and Leslie Uggams sang it in the 1985 Broadway revue *Jerry's Girls*.

"She Didn't Say 'Yes' " is the lighthearted hit song from *The Cat and the Fiddle* (1931) that was sung by the American composer Shirley Sheridan (Bettina Hall) in contemporary Brussells. The "ballad of indecision" was written by Jerome Kern, whose ascending and descending pattern of eight notes gives the music a swinging, American sound, and lyricist Otto Harbach provided the sassy lyric. Elisabeth Welch sang the number in the Broadway revue *Jerome Kern Goes to Hollywood* (1986).

"She Likes Basketball" is a jubilant musical solo from *Promises, Promises* (1968) in which Chuck Baxter (Jerry Orbach) exalts in the discovery that his favorite girl likes his favorite sport. Burt Bacharach composed the energetic music, and Hal David wrote the robust lyric.

"She Loves Me" is perhaps the least characteristic song from *She Loves Me* (1963), being more American and contemporary-sounding than the rest of the Jerry Bock (music) and Sheldon Harnick (lyric) European-flavored score. But it was the only number from the musical to achieve any sort of popularity, usually when recorded in jazzed-up pop versions. "She Loves Me" was introduced by Daniel Massey as Georg Nowack when he realizes that his secret "dear friend"

Amalia Balash is finally warming up to him.

"She Touched Me" is a memorable ballad from the short-lived *Drat! The Cat!* (1965), a silly nineteenth-century musical melodrama by Milton Schafer (music) and Ira Levin (lyric). It was sung by Elliott Gould as a dim-witted policeman who is in love with Alice (Lesley Ann Warren), who is secretly a cat burglar. Later in the show Gould and Warren reprised the number with her singing "He Touched Me." It was under this title that the song became popular, due mostly to a recording by Barbra Streisand.

"Sherry!" is the bubbly title song from the 1967 musical version of *The Man Who Came to Dinner* that became somewhat popular despite the fact that the musical was not very successful; but the melody is so catchy that it is not easily forgotten even after only one hearing. Movie composer Laurence Rosenthal wrote the music, and James Lipton provided the fun lyric. In the show the song was an extended musical reunion between celebrity Sheridan Whiteside (Clive Revill) and movie star Lorraine Sheldon (Dolores Gray). The number starts out as a "Hello, Dolly!"-like tribute to "Sherry" by Lorraine then turns into a delicious chronicle of tabloid-like gossip about their friends. Both Andy Williams and Marilyn Maye made hit pop recordings of the song using an innocuous lyric that sang cheerfully about some vague male/female. "Sherry!" was finally recorded twenty-seven years later with Christine Baranski and Jonathan Freeman singing the original witty lyric.

"She's Roses" is a sweet, if dim-witted, list song for the musical cops-and-robbers spoof *Drat! The Cat!* (1965) by Milton Schafer (music) and Ira Levin (lyric). The hapless hero (Elliott Gould) sang the love song, which is overstuffed with metaphors, about his beloved Alice, and he was joined in singing it by his mother (Lu Leonard).

"Shine On, Harvest Moon," the perennial turn-of-the-century favorite, was introduced by Nora Bayes in the Florenz Ziegfeld revue *Follies of 1908*, and it was her trademark song thereafter. Bayes wrote the song with her husband Jack Norworth, and it caught on immediately, selling thousands of copies of sheet music nationwide. The nocturnal ballad was interpolated into the musical *Miss Innocence* later that same year, where Lillian Lorraine sang it, and into the 1931 edition of the *Ziegfeld Follies*, where Ruth Etting impersonated Nora Bayes and sang it.

"A Shine on Your Shoes" is the buoyant, optimistic number by Howard Dietz (lyric) and Arthur Schwartz (music) that was one of the hits from their revue *Flying Colors* (1932). Monette Moore sang of the physician's advice to relieve the blues by getting a fresh shoeshine; while he sang it, Buddy and

Vilma Ebsen tapped away to the accompaniment of Larry Adler on the harmonica.

"A Ship Without a Sail" is a melting ballad from *Heads Up!* (1929) by Richard Rodgers (music) and Lorenz Hart (lyric) that uses nautical imagery to carry out an old torch-song format. The music reminded Hart of a gondolier's song, so he wrote the seaworthy lyric that was sung by Jack Whiting, as a Coast Guard lieutenant, and a chorus of sailors. Libby Holman made a popular recording of "A Ship Without a Sail," and years later Ella Fitzgerald recorded a distinctive rendition of the song.

"Shoeless Joe From Hannibal, Mo." is an energetic hoedown number from *Damn Yankees* (1955) by Richard Adler and Jerry Ross. Gloria (Rae Allen), a newspaper sports writer, titles the rookie Joe Hardy "shoeless Joe from Hannibal, Mo." because at practice he batted without his shoes on (they were too tight) and because Joe's manager, Mr. Applegate (Ray Walston), said the new player was from the Missouri city. Gloria leads the baseball players and fans in the song, and they all go into a joyous romp choreographed by Bob Fosse.

"Shoes Upon the Table" is a threatening song from the British import *Blood Brothers* (1993) about the bad luck that can befall you if you break one of the rules of superstition. When Mrs. Johnstone (Stephanie Lawrence) is told that her separated twins will die if they ever find out the truth about their origin, the Narrator (Warwick Evans) sings this song to the audience, listing the different superstitions and warning that the devil will come knocking at your door if you break any of the rules. Throughout the musical the Narrator returns to the song whenever Mrs. Johnstone's secret enters into the plot. Willy Russell wrote the music and lyric for the absorbing song.

"The Shortest Day of the Year" is a romantic ballad from *The Boys From Syracuse* (1938) that celebrates the day of the least sunlight because it provides the longest night of the year. Richard Rodgers (music) and Lorenz Hart (lyric) wrote the dreamy number, and Ronald Graham introduced it in the show.

"Show Me" is Eliza Doolittle's furious song of impatience from *My Fair Lady* (1956) by Alan Jay Lerner (lyric) and Frederick Loewe (music). Eliza (Julie Andrews) leaves Professor Higgins' house only to discover the worshiping Freddy (John Michael King) on the doorstep singing odes to her. Fed up with words (and the men who speak them so beautifully), she bursts into the electric "Show Me" and demands some action instead of talk.

"Shy" is a farcical character song for Princess Winifred (Carol Burnett) in

Once Upon a Mattress (1959) in which "Fred" proves that she is anything but shy. Marshall Barer wrote the funny lyric, and Mary Rodgers composed the playful music in which Burnett got to sing a seven-note leap to hit her high note on the word "shy."

"Side by Side by Side" is a soft-shoe pastiche number from *Company* (1970) that opens the second act with a dandy vaudeville turn. Stephen Sondheim wrote the drolly insightful song, and it was sung and danced by the bachelor Robert (Dean Jones) and the ensemble. Robert sings of the joys of being accepted by his married friends, and they all celebrate the coziness of each individual threesome. But the extra "by side" in the music and lyrics is disconcerting and belies the relaxed, rhythmic quality of the song. From this number the cast moves immediately into the more raucous "What Would We Do Without You?" Then the musical scene climaxes with a reprise of "Side by Side by Side" with everyone matched with a partner except Robert. The song was sung by the ensemble at the end of the Broadway revue *Side by Side by Sondheim* (1977).

"The Sidestep" is a toe-tapping western number from *The Best Little Whorehouse in Texas* (1978) that made parallels between politics and dancing. When the Governor of Texas (Jay Garner) is questioned by the press about the scandalous bordello called the Chicken Ranch, he does some fancy footwork and sidesteps the issue in song and dance. Carol Hall wrote the music and lyric for the satirical song.

"Silver Moon" is a lyrical duet from the Civil War-era operetta *My Maryland* (1927) with music by Sigmund Romberg and lyrics by Dorothy Donnelly. The Yankee Captain Trumball (Nathaniel Wagner) woos the maiden Barbara Frietchie (Evelyn Herbert), and together they sing this rhapsodic duet. Paul Whiteman's Orchestra made a successful recording of the song.

"Simple" is the ironic title for one of the most complex song sequences ever written for a Broadway musical. Stephen Sondheim wrote the music and lyric for the musical scene in conjunction with librettist Arthur Laurents. The ambitious number closed the first act of *Anyone Can Whistle* (1964). In a bankrupt town filled with escaped patients from the local mental hospital, psychiatrist Dr. Hapgood (Harry Guardino) is prevailed upon by the mayoress (Angela Lansbury) to separate the lunatics from the sane citizens. The number "Simple" is Hapgood's interrogation in which he asks questions, places people in vague categories, stirs up all the citizens and concludes that they are all (including the audience) crazy. This eighteen-minute musical sequence utilizes spoken word, song and chanting as the music moves from a simple nursery-rhyme style to a march to a frenzied waltz, all with dissonant undertones that give the scene a surreal quality.

"Simple" is a graceful farewell song from *Nine* (1982) by Maury Yeston. Filmmaker Guido Contini (Raul Julia) has been promising both Carla (Anita Morris) and Claudia (Shelly Burch) that he will divorce his wife and marry them. But Claudia has found someone else and tells Guido about her new life as Carla sings about how simple love should be and leaves him with the statement that the ways to say goodbye are also simple.

"A Simple Melody" is the actual title for a song most know as "Play a Simple Melody." It was Irving Berlin's first contrapuntal number (or "double song"), a delicious duet from *Watch Your Step* (1914) that featured his first full Broadway score. Sallie Fisher sang melodically about how she yearned for a simple tune while Charles King contrasted it with his desire for ragtime. "A Simple Melody" was one of the first contrapuntal numbers in popular song, and was an immediate favorite with theatre audiences. Yet, surprisingly, the song did not cross over to become a hit and all but disappeared for forty years. A 1950 recording by Bing and Gary Crosby sold a million disks and turned the song into a Berlin standard.

"The Simple Joys of Maidenhood" is Guenevere's sly "I am" song from *Camelot* (1960), a delightfully droll number that satirizes the conventions of medieval courtly love. Forced to wed a stranger at her young age, Guenevere (Julie Andrews) prays to her patron Ste. Genevieve asking why she should miss all the simple things of youth: ardent knights competing for her, blood spilt in her name, abduction by a foreigner, a feud or even a war on her behalf. Ironically, all these events do occur before the end of the musical, but they hardly have the luster she imagines in this wily song. Frederick Loewe composed the sprightly music, and Alan Jay Lerner wrote the facetious lyric.

"Simple Little Things" is a warm ballad that celebrates life's everyday joys. Tom Jones (lyric) and Harvey Schmidt (music) wrote it for *110 in the Shade* (1963), where it is sung by Lizzie (Inga Swenson) as she explains to the con man Starbuck (Robert Horton) about her simple dreams, the sort that can come true, as opposed to his grandiose ideas.

"Sing!" is a farcical character song from *A Chorus Line* (1975) in which the tone-deaf Kristine (Renee Baughman) admits her liability and wants to be judged by her dancing only. Her husband Alan (Don Percassi) tries to help by finishing all her sentences, resulting in a hysterical duet of sorts. Marvin Hamlisch composed the playful music, and Edward Kleban wrote the clever lyric.

"Sing for Your Supper" is a harmonizing trio that always stops the show when sung in *The Boys From Syracuse* (1938) by Richard Rodgers (music) and Lorenz Hart (lyric). The rhythm number was sung by Muriel Angelus, Wynn Murray and Marcy Westcott as they compared their plight to that of the canary who gets by because of his music; after all, they agree, songbirds always eat.

"Sing Happy" is a desperately joyous number from *Flora, the Red Menace* (1965), the first Broadway score by John Kander (music) and Fred Ebb (lyric). Flora Meszaros (Liza Minnelli) has just been fired from her job because Communist literature has been found in her locker; so she's not putting up with any sad songs, only happy ones.

"Sing Me a Song With Social Significance" was the theme song for the topical labor revue *Pins and Needles* (1937) by Harold Rome. The ensemble sang this self-kidding love song that captured the cheery, satirical tone of the long-running revue. With mock determination, the cast proclaimed that love without social impact is now passé and that all the songs in this revue are fraught with sociopolitical meaning.

"Sing Me Not a Ballad" is a playful character song from the short-lived *The Firebrand of Florence* (1945) by Kurt Weill (music) and Ira Gershwin (lyric). The Duchess of Florence (Lotte Lenya) made her grand entrance on a sedan chair and sang this witty number where she asks not for poetry, music, jewels or even romance; rather, "just, oh just make love!" Lenya recorded the number in the 1950s.

"The Siren's Song" is an alluring number from *Leave It to Jane* (1917), the early college musical by Jerome Kern (music) and P.G. Wodehouse (lyric). In order to recruit footballer Billy Bolton (Robert G. Pitkin) to play for Atwater College, coeds Jane (Edith Hallor) and Bessie (Ann Orr) entice him with this song that tells the legend of Lorelei, the Rhine maiden whose siren call lured fishermen to their destruction. Wodehouse's lyric is playful, and Kern's music is slow and dreamy, yet with a syncopated, swinging strain that keeps it fresh and modern. For other songs using the same legend, see "The Lorelei."

"Sit Down, John" is the pungent chorus number that opens *1776* (1969) and establishes the character of the fiery John Adams (William Daniels) and the sluggish members of the Continental Congress. While Adams urges a declaration of independence from Britain, the members complain about the humid Philadelphia weather and ask for some peace and quiet from Adams. Sherman Edwards wrote the music and lyric, which have a Gilbert and Sullivan flavor to them.

"Sit Down, You're Rockin' the Boat" is the show-stopping revival number from *Guys and Dolls* (1950) that may be the most vivacious eleven o'clock number of the American theatre. Forced by a gambling debt to give testimony at the Save-a-Soul Mission, bookie Nicely-Nicely (Stubby Kaye) tells about a dream he had that led him to confess his sins and reform his ways. The Frank Loesser song hardly advances the plot, but with all the gamblers and mission workers joining in, it does allow for one of the musical theatre's most joyous production numbers.

"Sitting Pretty" is the charming title song from the 1924 musical by Jerome Kern (music) and P.G. Wodehouse (lyric) that has the same sort of romantic silliness as "Tea for Two." Horace Peabody (Dwight Frye) turns from a life of crime to the arms of Dixie Tolliver (Queenie Smith), and they sing this cheery love song in which all they want out of life is to sit together in a chair "that fits just two." Ironically, the number was cut before opening because Frye had a slight lisp that was magnified by the lyric's many "s" sounds. Jason Graae and Judy Blazer made a recording of the reconstructed duet in 1989.

"Six Months Out of Every Year" is the caustic opening number from *Damn Yankees* (1955) by Richard Adler and Jerry Ross. Meg (Shannon Bolin) and the other housewives in Washington, D.C., complain how they lose the attention of their husbands from April to September each year because of the baseball season. Then, in a counterpoint melody, Joe (Robert Shafer) and the husbands sit in front of their television sets and sing of their frustration at the losing season by the Washington Senators.

"Sixteen Going on Seventeen" is the sweetly naive duet between Liesl (Laurie Peters) and Rolf (Brian Davies) in *The Sound of Music* (1959). The Richard Rodgers (music) and Oscar Hammerstein (lyric) song is used to establish this secondary pair of sweethearts in the show and then is reprised in the second act, with a different lyric, by Maria (Mary Martin) and her new stepdaughter Liesl as a way of strengthening their relationship.

"Skid Row (Downtown)" is a breezy doo-wop number from *Little Shop of Horrors* (1982) with an uncomfortable subtext. The cast sings this descriptive song about being stuck in the no-win situation of skid row, where depression is the status quo. Alan Menken composed the 1960s-like pop music, and Howard Ashman wrote the succinct lyric.

"Skip the Build-Up" is a sassy, sexy duet from the musical farce *Ankles Aweigh* (1955) by Sammy Fain (music) and Dan Shapiro (lyric). Betty Kean and Lew Parker sang the saucy number, which suggested that one dispense with the small talk and get right to the loving.

"Sleep Peaceful, Mr. Used-to-Be" is a poignant lullaby-torch song from *St. Louis Woman* (1946) by Harold Arlen (music) and Johnny Mercer (lyric). Lili (June Hawkins) has shot her former lover Biglow Brown (Rex Ingram) when she saw him beating up his new mistress Della (Ruby Hill) and Lili sings this touching farewell song as she gazes upon the dead body of Biglow.

"A Sleepin' Bee" is a sensual yet innocent song from *House of Flowers* (1954) by Harold Arlen (music) and Truman Capote (lyric). The young Haitian Ottilie (Diahann Carroll) sings of the island superstition that says that if a girl catches a bee and it doesn't sting her, then it is a sign that she will soon find true love. Ottilie is joined in the song by three of the "flowers" from the local brothel: Pansy (Ada Moore), Tulip (Enid Mosier) and Gladiola (Dolores Harper). Arlen's melody, which was written earlier for a film and never used, is unconventional in its stark opening, its developing rich harmonies later in the number, and a base line that uses the pedal to create a humming dissonance reminiscent of a bee. Tony Bennett, Julie Wilson, Mel Tormé, Julie Andrews, Jessye Norman and Arlen himself are among those who recorded the unusual ballad.

"Small Craft Warnings" is a wry song about the oncoming of infidelity from *Romance, Romance* (1988). Barb (Deborah Graham) and Lenny (Robert Hoshour) sing the ominous song of warning about Sam (Scott Bakula) and Monica (Alison Fraser) whose platonic friendship is getting a little too romantic for safe sailing. Barry Harman wrote the piquant lyric, and Keith Herrmann composed the enticing music.

"The Small House of Uncle Thomas" is the brilliant dance-drama showpiece from *The King and I* (1951) that utilized character, movement and narrative in an enthralling way. The Burmese slave Tuptim (Doretta Morrow) writes and narrates the dance spectacle as an entertainment for the European visitors to Siam, retelling Harriet Beecher Stowe's tale in Eastern terms. Unlike most ballets from musicals at the time, the music for "The Small House of Uncle Thomas" is original rather than a rehash of other melodies from the score. Trude Rittman, the show's dance-music arranger, used fragments of Richard Rodgers' "Hello, Young Lovers" and "A Puzzlement," but the rest of the music is new and reflects the shifting moods of the piece. Oscar Hammerstein wrote a lyric that uses Tuptim's halting English, chanting repeated phrases until they take on an occidental quality. Of course, the true star of the ballet was Jerome Robbins, who conceived and choreographed it.

"Small World" is a touching and atypically quiet ballad for Ethel Merman in *Gypsy* (1959) by Jule Styne (music) and Stephen Sondheim (lyric). Rose

(Merman) meets candy salesman Herbie (Jack Klugman) and points out all the things they have in common, ending up with a manager for her act and a romantic partner as well. The ballad was made popular by a best-selling Johnny Mathis recording.

"Smile" is a tender song with a frustrated subtext from the Off-Broadway musical *I'm Getting My Act Together and Taking It on the Road* (1978) by Gretchen Cryer (lyric) and Nancy Ford (music). Pop singer and soap opera star Heather Jones (Cryer) recalls how all her life men (her father, her husband, her manager) have been telling her to smile and use her feminine charm to succeed in life.

"Smile" is the tuneful, engaging title number from the 1986 musical satire about beauty contests. The lively Marvin Hamlisch (music) and Howard Ashman (lyric) number was sung by Dick Patterson and the contestants of the Young America Miss Pageant.

"Smiles" is the popular favorite many know from its alternate title "There Are Smiles That Make Me Happy." Lee S. Roberts (music) and J. Will Callahan (lyric) wrote the song for *The Passing Show of 1918*, where it was sung by Neil Carrington and the girls' chorus. The song immediately became popular with an America in the final days of World War One who took to the lyric's gentle optimism. "Smiles" became the biggest hit of the season, with over three million copies of sheet music sold. It became the theme song for the Ipana Troubadors on early radio, and years later Judy Garland made a hit recording of it. In the Broadway revue *Tintypes* (1980), it was sung by Jerry Zaks, Catherine Wright and the company as the finale.

"Smoke Gets in Your Eyes" is the haunting ballad from *Roberta* (1933) that saved the show and went on to become one of Jerome Kern's most popular songs. He wrote it with lyricist Otto Harbach for the expatriate Russian princess Stephanie (Tamara) to sing as she accompanied herself on the guitar. The number so impressed audiences that soon it was heard on national radio, and the fumbling *Roberta* was a hit. Kern wrote the melody as a soft-shoe number for *Show Boat* (1927) but it was never used. For *Roberta*, Kern wrote the song with a brisk, marchlike beat in keeping with the rest of the swinging 1930s musical, and in rehearsals it was a failure. Harbach suggested that it be played at a more leisurely tempo and wrote the enchanting lyric, which he based on an ancient Russian proverb. It is Harbach's finest work, a mysterious piece with the unforgettable image of lost love being like a dying fire with smoke that stings your eyes. As for Kern's music, musicologist David Ewen described it best when he wrote, "The diatonic skips in the broad upward sweep of the melody and the seductive change of key in the release that follows never seem to lose their capacity to win the ear and heart." Tamara recorded the ballad in 1933, and it was continually recorded over the decades, including a haunting interpretation by Sarah Vaughan, a rock and roll version by the Platters in 1958 that sold over a million records, and a 1972 best-seller by the English group Blue Haze. Elisabeth Welch sang the song in the Broadway revue *Jerome Kern Goes to Hollywood* (1986).

"So Am I" is a lyrical duet from the otherwise very jazzy score of *Lady, Be Good!* (1924). Adele Astaire and Alan Edwards sang the simple, melodic number as they echoed each other's praises and endearments. George Gershwin composed the lovely melody, and Ira Gershwin wrote the charming lyric.

"So Far" is a romantic ballad from the conceptual musical *Allegro* (1947) by Richard Rodgers (music) and Oscar Hammerstein (lyric) that managed to become fairly popular despite the show's disappointing run. Gloria Wills, as a girl dating the musical's hero Joe, introduced the number about how their relationship is only beginning and they have, so far, nothing to remember.

"So in Love," the hit ballad in *Kiss Me, Kate* (1948), is Cole Porter at his most operatic. Unlike the same show's "Wunderbar," which mocks old-time operetta, "So in Love" is a lovely and sustained piece of writing in the old style. The lyric is heartfelt and lacks the usual Porter cynicism. As for the music, it builds in intensity by having each section rising one note at the climactic moment. Patricia Morison introduced the song as Lilli Vanessi realizing that she still loves her ex-husband Fred (Alfred Drake). Later in the show, Fred reprises the number when he comes to the same conclusion. Patti Page's recording of the song was a best-seller, and Dinah Shore, Gordon MacRae and Drake himself had success with their recordings of the ballad.

"So Long, Dearie" is an eruptive, comic farewell for Dolly Levi (Carol Channing) as she dismisses Horace Vandergelder (David Burns) in the second act of *Hello, Dolly!* (1964). Jerry Herman wrote the Sophie Tucker-like pastiche number with such electric self-mockery that it was clear to all that Dolly's goodbye was very temporary. The silly aria is also an interesting counterpart to the earlier-sung title song of the show.

"So Long, Letty" is the vibrant title song from the 1919 musical by Earl Carroll. The effervescent Charlotte Greenwood, who played Letty, introduced the number with Sydney Grant and the chorus.

"So Long, Mary" is the catchy farewell song from George M. Cohan's *Forty-Five Minutes From Broadway* (1906) that is both cheerful and endearing. When the New Rochelle maid Mary Jane Jenkins (Fay Templeton) arrives at the small-town railroad station to go to New York, the local residents bid her farewell and she returns the tuneful compliments. In the bio-musical *George M!* (1968), the number was sung by Joel Grey, Harvey Evans, Loni Ackerman, Danny Carroll and Angela Martin.

"So What?" is one of the most German-sounding numbers in *Cabaret* (1966), a Kurt Weill-like song that was made all the more potent by the fact that it was sung by Lotte Lenya, Weill's widow. Fraulein Schneider (Lenya) has survived a war and a depression and has learned to roll with the punches. She sings this calliopelike "I am" song by John Kander (music) and Fred Ebb (lyric) to the new boarder Cliff Bradshaw (Bert Convy), taking his money and not expecting anything more out of life.

"Soft Lights and Sweet Music" is a rapturous romantic ballad by Irving Berlin that was one of the standards to come out of *Face the Music* (1932). The music is among Berlin's most haunting, with its gentle shifts in key and minimal number of notes, and his bewitching lyric uses the image of music as an incentive for romance. Katherine Carrington and J. Harold Murray introduced the number in a dazzling scene that director Hassard Short devised using mirrors.

"Softly, as in a Morning Sunrise" is an impassioned ballad from the operetta *The New Moon* (1928) by Sigmund Romberg (music) and Oscar Hammerstein (lyric). In a New Orleans tavern, Phillipe (William O'Neal) sings to his friend about women's lack of fidelity and how love creeps in as quietly as a sunrise, but soon the vows of love are broken. Romberg's music and Hammerstein's lyric are equally enthralling, though more than one critic has pointed out the redundancy in the title, asking what other kind of sunrise there can possibly be. A decade later Artie Shaw and His Orchestra made a hit recording of the song.

"Soliloquy" is the tour de force character song for Billy Bigelow in Rodgers and Hammerstein's *Carousel* (1945), an ambitious seven-minute stream-of-consciousness piece of musical theatre craftsmanship that has rarely been equaled. Billy (John Raitt) has just learned that his wife is expecting their first child, and his reactions range from pride to worry to the resolve to make something of his life. Oscar Hammerstein spent two weeks creating the extended number, then gave it to Richard Rodgers, who in two hours wrote the musical sequence with eight different melodic sections within it. Although far from a traditional theatre song, "Soliloquy" has remained well known due to recordings by Frank Sinatra, Mandy Patinkin and others.

"Some Day" is a rapturously melancholy song of longing from the operetta

The Vagabond King (1925) by Rudolf Friml (music) and Brian Hooker (lyric). The aristocratic Parisian Katherine de Vaucelles (Carolyn Thomson) loves, of all people, the poet-outlaw Francois Villon, so she has need to sigh and sing this lovelorn ballad. The song had a revival of interest in the 1950s due to recordings by Tony Martin and Frankie Laine.

"Some Enchanted Evening" is arguably the most famous love song Richard Rodgers (music) and Oscar Hammerstein (lyric) ever wrote together. It was sung in *South Pacific* (1949) by Ezio Pinza, as the French planter Emile de Becque, to the American nurse (Mary Martin) he loves. The ballad is unusual in two ways: it is an indirect marriage proposal that tells the story of how they met. Also, Emile's lyric is written in the second person ("somehow *you* know . . . once *you* have have found her"), which somehow distances the two characters, showing the gulf that exists between them. Mary Martin reprised "Some Enchanted Evening" in the second act, and the song has been popular with female as well as male singers. Pinza and Perry Como each made recordings that sold over a million copies. Other popular recordings were made by Jo Stafford, Frank Sinatra, Bing Crosby, in 1965 by Jay and the Americans, and by Jane Olivor in the 1970s.

"Some Other Time" is a lovely quartet from *On the Town* (1944) by Leonard Bernstein (music) and Betty Comden and Adolph Green (lyric). Sailors Chip (Cris Alexander) and Ozzie (Adolph Green) are coming to the end of their twenty-four-hour leave in New York City, and, with their newfound girlfriends Claire (Betty Comden) and Hildy (Nancy Walker), they reflect on how all their dreams will have to be completed some other time. The lyric is one of the gentlest and most flowing that Comden and Green ever wrote, and Bernstein's music, with its enticing ascending and descending phrases and its unforgettable drop of an octave for the resigned "oh well," is a marvel of musical construction. Mabel Mercer and Barbara Cook each made memorable recordings of the song.

"Some People" is one of the strongest "I am" songs of the musical theatre, a dynamic credo of ambition for Rose (Ethel Merman) in *Gypsy* (1959). In what is essentially a list song, Rose describes all the characteristics of "humdrum" people she despises and vows to get more out of life than playing bingo and paying rent. Jule Styne composed the surging music, and Stephen Sondheim wrote the biting lyric.

"Some Sort of Somebody" is a lilting song with a feet-on-the-ground lyric from the Princess Theatre musical *Very Good Eddie* (1915). When the dashing Dick Rivers (Oscar Shaw) tries to woo Elsie Lilly (Ann Orr), she is not easily persuaded, for she knows Dick only too well, and it seems he always has "some sort of somebody" that he's in love with. Jerome Kern (music) and Elsie

Janis (lyric) wrote the song for the short-lived *Miss Information* earlier the same year, and Janis sang it with little success. But when the number was put into the *Very Good Eddie* score unchanged, it became an audience favorite.

"Somebody" is the ambitious "I am" song for the allegorical figure called Angel in the Tom Jones (lyric) and Harvey Schmidt (music) musical *Celebration* (1969). Angel (Susan Watson) is young and pretty and knows that this is the time to use her talents to become a somebody.

"Somebody Died Today" is a captivating folk song of protest from the pioneering rock musical *The Last Sweet Days of Isaac* (1970) by Gretchen Cryer (lyric) and Nancy Ford (music). Isaac (Austin Pendleton) and Alice (Fredricka Weber) are in jail for protesting, and, in this surreal sequence, they see Isaac's accidental death on television. C. David Colson sang the song which says that a little piece of every person dies when a protester is silenced.

"Somebody Loves Me" is the early jazz-age classic by George Gershwin (music) and B.G. DeSylva and Ballard MacDonald (lyric) that was first heard in *George White's Scandals of 1924*. The song was given an elaborate staging, with Winnie Lightner singing it as she is wooed by such diverse heroes as Mark Anthony, Romeo, Harold Lloyd and William S. Hart. The melodic song has a nebulous harmony that is charming, and Gershwin puts a blue note on the word "who" in the refrain that is distinctive. The oft-recorded song was a hit for Paul Whiteman's Orchestra and for Marion Harris, as well as a recurring favorite in Blossom Seeley's nightclub act.

"Somebody, Somewhere" is a lovely arialike solo from Frank Loesser's operalike *The Most Happy Fella* (1956). Amy (Jo Sullivan) is a lonely waitress in a big city, but a love letter left at one of her tables brings her joy as she realizes that someone needs her.

"Somehow I Never Could Believe" is a passionate aria from the operatic *Street Scene* (1947) by Kurt Weill (music) and Langston Hughes (lyric). Mrs. Maurrant (Polyna Stoska) recalls the faded dreams of her youth and looks at her unhappy marriage, determined to find a better future. The solo is very Puccini-like yet has elements of jazz and even some Germanic harmonies but it all works beautifully for this tragic urban character.

"Someone Else's Story" is a fascinating song from the British import *Chess* (1988) by Benny Anderssen and Bjorn Ulvaeus (music) and Tim Rice (lyric). Chess player Florence (Judy Kuhn) thinks back on how she got romantically involved with the temperamental champion Freddie (Philip Casnoff) and sees not herself but someone else.

"Someone in a Tree" is an ambitious musical sequence from *Pacific Overtures* (1976) in which Stephen Sondheim wrote a musical *Rashomon* situation that relates an event from different viewpoints. In 1853 Commodore Perry and the Americans met with the Japanese and held a secret conference in Kanagawa. But no one knows exactly what occurred in the historic meeting. The Reciter (Mako) sings to the audience about the event, but he is interrupted by an Old Man (James Dybas) who, as a young boy (Geede Watanabe), was up in a tree and saw the meeting. Then a Samurai Warrior (Mark Hsu Syers) enters and explains that he was hidden under the floor of the meeting house and heard what happened. What follows is a provocative quartet in which each spectator gives details of the event as he recalls them, but none has the complete story. At one time Stephen Sondheim stated that "Someone in a Tree" was his favorite of all his songs.

"Someone in April" is a poignant musical scene from the unsuccessful *Carmelina* (1979) by Alan Jay Lerner (lyric) and Burton Lane (music). Carmelina Campbell (Georgia Brown) explains to her maid Rosa (Grace Keagy) that many years ago, when she was only seventeen, she fell in love and made love with three different American soldiers, all in the same month. What could have been a crude joke number turns into a lovely confessional song as Carmelina describes her state of mind at the time and her loneliness after each one deserted her.

"Someone Is Waiting" is a melancholy ballad from *Company* (1970) that is flowing and melodic but, at the same time, pathetic and disarming as well. The bachelor Robert (Dean Jones) fantasizes about the kind of woman he'd like to marry, only to find that she is a combination of all the better qualities of his friends' wives. Stephen Sondheim wrote the graceful music and the dreamy lyric that does not complete the long melodic lines, showing the fragmentary nature of Robert's reverie.

"Someone to Watch Over Me" is one of the Gershwins' most beloved and popular ballads, a wistful number that was forever associated with Gertrude Lawrence, who introduced it in *Oh, Kay!* (1926). Kay Denham (Lawrence), disguised as a maid to get into a Long Island mansion, finds out that the one she loves is engaged to another. Alone on the stage, Kay cuddles a rag doll and sings the warm and entrancing song of yearning. George Gershwin had originally written the music as a rhythm song to be danced to but when he was playing the melody one day and took the tempo down to a slower, ballad pace, the music came to life. Ira Gershwin wrote the tender lyric, although the title came from Howard Dietz, who aided in the score's lyrics when Ira was hospitalized for an operation. Lawrence recorded the ballad in 1926 and again in 1927, and more recently Lena Horne, Barbra Streisand, Willie Nelson and Linda Ronstadt have made memorable recordings of it. Jodi Benson, as the prairie girl

Polly Barker, sang it in the "new Gershwin musical comedy" *Crazy for You* (1992). "Someone to Watch Over Me" remains one of the Gershwins' most recorded songs and seems never to be dated.

"Someone Wonderful I Missed" is a breezy country-western ballad from *I Love My Wife* (1977), the musical about wife swapping in New Jersey by Cy Coleman (music) and Michael Stewart (lyric). Wives Monica (Joanna Gleason) and Cleo (Ilene Graff) use the pop country style to express their musical musings about the special someone whom they never met.

"Something Seems Tingle-Ingleing" is a delightful piece of nonsense from *High Jinks* (1913) by Rudolf Friml (music) and Otto Harbach (lyric). The giddy song was sung at different intervals throughout the show. Dick Wayne (Burrell Barbaretto) sang it about about the sensation he is feeling for Sylvia Dale (Mana Zucca), but the song also described the effects of a druglike perfume when sprayed near the ear.

"Something Sort of Grandish" is the whimsical comic number from *Finian's Rainbow* (1947) that serves as the "I am" song for the leprechaun Og (David Wayne). Having come to America to retrieve his stolen pot of gold, Og is losing his magic powers and is beginning to turn mortal. When he meets the lovely Sharon (Ella Logan), feelings he's never felt before are awakened, and they sing this quixotic duet about these new sensations. Burton Lane composed the playful, gavottelike music, and E.Y. Harburg wrote one of his most famous lyrics: a scintillating series of words and phrases with "ish" endings that create a magical and pixilated silliness. This mastery of inventive suffixes would surface throughout Harburg's career, but never with more frivolity than in "Something Sort of Grandish."

"Something to Remember You By" is a melodic ballad by Howard Dietz (lyric) and Arthur Schwartz (music) from the revue *Three's a Crowd* (1930). Libby Holman sang the flowing farewell song to a sailor (Fred MacMurray) who stood with his back to the audience. Schwartz had written the melody years earlier as a lively chorus number, and it was Dietz who suggested that he slow the number down to a ballad tempo. Holman made a hit recording of the song, as did Dinah Shore and others.

"Something Very Strange" is a love song of wonderment from the nautical musical *Sail Away* (1961) by Noël Coward. Elaine Stritch, as the social director on a Mediterranean cruise ship, sang the number as she noticed that everyone around her looks different since she fell in love.

"Something Wonderful" is the stirring inspirational ballad that Lady

Thiang (Dorothy Sarnoff) sings about the King in *The King and I* (1951) by Richard Rodgers (music) and Oscar Hammerstein (lyric). Thiang sings of the King's remarkable potential for good in order to convince Anna (Gertrude Lawrence) not to leave Siam. The number is reprised at the end of the musical when the King dies, suggesting the greatness that the young new king will bring to his country. Lynne Wintersteller sang the ballad in the Broadway revue *A Grand Night for Singing* (1993).

"Something You Never Had Before" is a lilting ballad in the Jerome Kern style from *The Gay Life* (1961), the musical about Viennese high society by Howard Dietz (lyric) and Arthur Schwartz (music). Liesl (Barbara Cook) sings of her doubts about her upcoming marriage to the undependable Anatole (Walter Chiari). The lovely song is perhaps the last notable achievement by the celebrated team of Dietz and Schwartz.

"Something's Coming" is the evocative "I am" song for Tony (Larry Kert) in *West Side Story* (1957) by Leonard Bernstein (music) and Stephen Sondheim (lyric). Tony is losing interest in the Jets, a gang he helped start, and he sings this song of expectation filled with restless, eager music and a dreamy lyric. The number was a late addition to the score; the authors felt that Tony's solo "Maria" later in the act would serve as his musical introduction, but in rehearsals it became clear that the hero's character had to be established from the start. "Something's Coming" is one of the finest "I am" songs of all integrated musicals.

"Sometimes I'm Happy" is an exciting rhythm ballad by Vincent Youmans that became a hit in *Hit the Deck!* (1927) after having been in and out of two other musicals first. With a lyric by Oscar Hammerstein and William Cary Duncan, the melody was called "Come on and Pet Me," written for *Mary Jane McKane* (1923) but cut out of town. With a new lyric by Clifford Grey and Irving Caesar, the song was retitled "Sometimes I'm Happy" and put in *A Night Out* (1925), a show that closed before it reached Broadway. It was finally heard in *Hit the Deck!* where the sailor Bilge (Charles King) and coffeehouse owner Looloo (Louise Groody) sang the lively duet about how one's moods are determined by the other person. The number is one of Youmans' loosest, most carefree melodies, which is remarkable because it has a range of less than an octave. When Benny Goodman's Orchestra recorded it in 1935, it became his first hit. Trumpeter Bunny Berrigan and Florence Mills also made a hit record of the song, Blue Barron and His Orchestra made it their theme song in the 1930s, and it has long been a favorite of jazz musicians. In 1967 Tony Bennett recorded a slower and more intimate version of "Sometimes I'm Happy" that was very effective.

"Somewhere" is the poignant love duet from *West Side Story* (1957) that led into Jerome Robbins' dream ballet sequence foreshadowing the musical's tragic conclusion. Tony (Larry Kert) and Maria (Carol Lawrence) sing brief sections of the song before and after the ballet; the main body of the lyrical number was sung by Reri Grist as an offstage voice. At the end of the musical, Maria reprises part of the song to the dying Tony. Leonard Bernstein composed the flowing melody, and Stephen Sondheim wrote the graceful lyric. Len Barry, P.J. Proby and Barbra Streisand were among the many who recorded the song.

"Somewhere That's Green" is a campy yet touching "I am" song from *Little Shop of Horrors* (1982) by Alan Menken (music) and Howard Ashman (lyric). The beat-up blonde Audrey (Ellen Greene) is stuck with a sadistic boyfriend and a no-advance job in skid row, so she dreams of a life in the suburbs.The lyric is filled with allusions to popular names and products of the late 1950s and early 1960s, which gives the song a nostalgic flavor that is both humorous and accurate.

"The Song Is You" is an ardent, operatic song from *Music in the Air* (1932) by Jerome Kern (music) and Oscar Hammerstein (lyric). In Munich, the opera librettist Bruno Mahler (Tullio Carminati) sings the elegant aria to his mistress, the prima donna Frieda Hatzfeld (Natalie Hall), as she is being fitted for a new dress by her dyspeptic maid. The scene is farcical, but the song is entrancing. Hammerstein's lyric is expansive but sincere, and Kern's music moves higher and higher to an overwhelming climax. The song became very popular, and among its many recordings were best-sellers by Tommy Dorsey and His Orchestra and by Frank Sinatra. It was sung by the ensemble in the Broadway revue *Jerome Kern Goes to Hollywood* (1986).

"Song of Love," the new-old hit from the operetta *Blossom Time* (1921), was adapted by Sigmund Romberg from the first movement of Schubert's Unfinished Symphony. Dorothy Donnelly wrote the lyric for the waltzing number, and it was sung by Olga Cook and Bertram Peacock.

"Song of the Flame" is the entrancing title song from the 1925 musical in which both George Gershwin and Herbert Stothart composed the music for a set of lyrics by Otto Harbach and Oscar Hammerstein. Tessa Kosta (as the Russian rebel known as "the Flame"), Greek Evans and the "Russian Art Choir" sang the number. The music for this song is probably Gershwin's, unique for what Gerald Bordman described as an "unusual coupling of his clipped, clean-cut musical line with central European harmonies." Popular recordings were made by the Ipana Troubadors, Vincent Lopez and His Orchestra and the Victor Light Opera Company.

"Song of the Vagabonds" is a stirring call-to-arms number from the swashbuckling operetta *The Vagabond King* (1925) by Rudolf Friml (music) and Brian Hooker (lyric). Poet-outlaw Francois Villon (Dennis King) led his "rabble of low degree" to save France in the rousing number.

"Song of the Woodman" is a hilarious specialty number for Bert Lahr that he performed in the revue *The Show Is On* (1936) and that remained one of his most celebrated numbers throughout his career. Harold Arlen (music) and E.Y. Harburg (lyric) wrote the prankish song in which Lahr, as an unlikely woodsman with the requisite ax and toupee, sang boldly and ridiculously about the glories of spring and how he loves to chop down trees. The song then moves on to list all the things that can be made out of wood, from a smoking pipe for dad to toothpicks for the patrons at Lindy's. Throughout the daffy number Lahr was intermittently pelted with wood chips from offstage.

"Sons" is an extended musical sequence from *The Rothschilds* (1970) by Jerry Bock (music) and Sheldon Harnick (lyric). The number starts with the newly married Mayer Rothschild (Hal Linden) dreaming of having sons to carry on the family name. Four boys are born in succession, and we next see Mayer training the four youngsters (Lee Franklin, Robby Benson, Michael Maitland and Mitchell Spera) in the business, his dream coming true.

"Soon" is the romantic duet for the young lovers in the satirical Gershwin musical *Strike Up the Band* (1930). Jim Townsend (Jerry Goff) and heiress Joan Fletcher (Margaret Schilling) sing the duet that anticipates happiness together very soon. George Gershwin wrote the endearing music, and Ira Gershwin provided the optimistic lyric. In the "new Gershwin musical" *My One and Only* (1983), aviator Billy Buck Chandler (Tommy Tune) sang "Soon" as he anticipated meeting the aquatic star Edith Herbert (Twiggy). Note: for the Stephen Sondheim song titled "Soon," see "Now/Later/Soon."

"Soon It's Gonna Rain" is the dreamy, pastoral love duet from *The Fantasticks* (1960) by Tom Jones (lyric) and Harvey Schmidt (music). Matt (Kenneth Nelson) and Luisa (Rita Gardner) are in the throes of first love, and all the natural elements that surround them add to the romantic atmosphere. Particularly memorable in the fragile song are the many nature images in the lyric and the lovely raindrop effect by the harp in the musical accompaniment. Barbra Streisand recorded the song early on and helped make it popular.

"Sorry-Grateful" is a thoughtful ballad about the ambivalent nature of marriage from *Company* (1970) by Stephen Sondheim. When bachelor Robert (Dean Jones) asks Harry (Charles Kimbrough) if he's ever sorry he got married, Harry responds with this tender song that reflects on the contradictory elements of a longtime relationship. His sentiments are echoed by the other husbands in the show. Sondheim's music has a gentle waltz rhythm, and the lyric structure is very restrained, with both positive and negative arguments about marriage getting equal time. Stephen Collins sang "Sorry-Grateful" in the Off-Broadway revue *Putting It Together* (1993), and Mandy Patinkin and Betty Buckley have made recent recordings of the song.

"The Sound of Music," the title song that the whole Western world knows because of the movie version of the 1959 Broadway musical, is very close to Rodgers and Hammerstein's earlier "Oh, What a Beautiful Mornin'" from *Oklahoma!* (1943); both songs start their shows with a quiet but exuberant celebration of nature. Curly sings that the earth is filled with sounds that are like music; it is practically a cue for "The Sound of Music" sixteen years later. Postulant Maria (Mary Martin) starts the song sitting in a tree, then proceeds to deliver the number as a traditional ballad on an empty stage. The song is reprised by the Von Trapp family later in the show and is used to warm up the icy relationship the Captain has with his children. Richard Rodgers' music is slightly Viennese, and Oscar Hammerstein's lyric is a bit gushing, but this is, after all, an Austrian nun-to-be singing. Patti Page had a hit recording of "The Sound of Music" in 1960.

"South America, Take It Away" is a show-stopping number from the revue *Call Me Mister* (1946) by Harold Rome that helped propel Betty Garrett to fame. As a rhumba-weary canteen hostess, Garrett and a quartet of GIs sang the animated song about the invasion of all the Latin dances that were sweeping the country. The song itself swept the country, thanks to popular recordings by Xavier Cugat (with a Buddy Clark vocal) and Bing Crosby with the Andrews Sisters that sold over a million records.

"South American Way" is the vivacious rhumba standard that was popular on the radio in the 1940s. The sassy Jimmy McHugh (music) and Al Dubin (lyric) song was introduced as the first-act finale of *The Streets of Paris* (1939). It was sung by Carmen Miranda (on platform shoes and wearing a colossal fruit headdress) with Ramon Vinay, Della Lind and the Hylton Sisters. Miranda recorded the number and it became her signature song. The Andrews Sisters also made a hit recording, as did such bandleaders as Desi Arnaz, Ray Noble (vocal by Larry Stewart) and Ozzie Nelson (vocal by Harriet Hilliard). "South American Way" was among the songs that fostered a trend for Latin-flavored music during the war years.

"Speak Low" is the hit song from *One Touch of Venus* (1943), a haunting and melancholy ballad that has a Cole Porterish beguine quality but was written by German immigrant Kurt Weill (music) and humorist Ogden Nash (lyric).

Mary Martin, as the goddess Venus, sang the number to the reluctant barber Rodney Hatch (Kenny Baker), whom she is trying to lure away from his possessive fiancée. As a seduction song it is very unusual: the music is brooding, and the lyric (based on a passage from *Much Ado About Nothing*) has more of a torch-song quality to it. Guy Lombardo and the Royal Canadians (vocal by Billy Leach) made an early hit record of the song, Weill's widow Lotte Lenya recorded it, Carmen McRae made a sensuous version in 1955 and more recently Barbra Streisand recorded it. "Speak Low" was sung by the ensemble in the Off-Broadway revue *Berlin to Broadway With Kurt Weill* (1972).

"Spread a Little Sunshine" is the sly comic number for the devious mother Fastrada (Leland Palmer) in *Pippin* (1972) by Stephen Schwartz. As she plots to destroy her husband Charlemagne and his son Pippin so that her favorite son Lewis can take the throne, Fastrada ironically sings about spreading joy and happiness to all her brethren. The song led into a frenzied dance solo staged by Bob Fosse that was reminiscent of the kind of specialty numbers he used to choreograph for Gwen Verdon.

"Spring Is Here," a Rodgers and Hart standard that came from *I Married an Angel* (1938), contains one of Lorenz Hart's most heartbreaking lyrics: the season for new life has come, but the lack of true love makes it hollow. The ballad avoids the melodramatic and settles for a numb, disillusioned point of view that makes the song almost unbearably poignant. Richard Rodgers' unfussy melody and harmony use an eight-note triplet that is both disarming and satisfying: all in all, a small masterwork of a song. "Spring Is Here" was sung in the show as a duet by Vivienne Segal and Dennis King. The ballad ought not to be confused with an earlier and different Rodgers and Hart song written for a show called, appropriately, *Spring Is Here* (1929).

"The Springtime Cometh" is a hilarious character song for a genie in the satirical *Flahooley* (1951) by Sammy Fain (music) and E.Y. Harburg (lyric). The genie Abou Ben Atom (Irwin Corey) sings this puckish number celebrating the arrival of spring and the blossoming of sexual activity. Like the leprechaun in *Finian's Rainbow*, Abou speaks a language of his own, and this song is filled with "eth" endings that are both whimsical and saucy.

"Stan' Up and Fight" is the thrilling "Toreador Song" from Georges Bizet's opera *Carmen* as Americanized for the Broadway musical *Carmen Jones* (1943). Librettist-lyricist Oscar Hammerstein set the story in a small Southern town and turned the opera's toreador Escamillo into Husky Miller (Glenn Bryant), a popular prize fighter. At Billy Pastor's cafe, Husky sings of his pugilistic talents before his many admirers, who join him in singing one of the world's most recognized pieces of music. Hammerstein's lyric is vivid and right in keeping with the rousing music.

"Standing on the Corner" is the most popular song to come from Frank Loesser's operatic *The Most Happy Fella* (1956) even though the song is squarely in the musical comedy mold. The jocular quartet, a playful testament to girl watching, was sung by Shorty Long, Alan Gilbert, John Henson and Roy Lazarus in a mock-hillbilly style with fun harmonies. The Mills Brothers, Dean Martin and the Four Lads each had recordings of the song on the charts in 1956.

"Starlight Express" is the magical title song from the 1987 British import by Andrew Lloyd Webber (music) and Richard Stilgoe (lyric). The forlorn engine Rusty (Greg Mowry) sings the beguiling song about a mythical train that he's heard about all his life. El DeBarge had a best-selling recording of the number.

"Starting Here, Starting Now" is an entrancing ballad by David Shire (music) and Richard Maltby, Jr., (lyric) about finding new beginnings in a relationship. It was sung by the ensemble of three (Loni Ackerman, George Lee Andrews and Margery Cohen) in the 1977 Off-Broadway revue of the same title. Barbra Streisand made a popular recording of the song before the revue opened.

"Stay Well" is a sensitive torch song from *Lost in the Stars* (1949) by Kurt Weill (music) and Maxwell Anderson (lyric). Irina (Inez Matthews) sings the lovely song as she thinks of her lover who is in jail, hoping that he is all right and praying that he will return someday. Weill's widow Lotte Lenya, Andrea Marcovicci and Dawn Upshaw each made memorable recordings of "Stay Well."

"Staying Young" is a wistful character song from *Take Me Along* (1959) by Bob Merrill that is not unlike the Weill-Anderson "September Song" in some ways. Family patriarch Nat Miller (Walter Pidgeon) sings that everyone around him seems to be growing older except him. In the second act he reprises the number and admits that he too is not getting any younger.

"Steal With Style" is the vigorous "I am" song for the outlaw Jamie Lockhart (Barry Bostwick) in the musical folktale *The Robber Bridegroom* (1976) by Robert Waldman (music) and Alfred Uhry (lyric). Jamie explains that he is no ordinary bandit and that his methods have more than a touch of the dashing romantic to them.

"Steam Heat" is the jazzy hit song from *The Pajama Game* (1954) that is awkwardly tacked on to the plot but never fails to stop the show. The union workers at the factory put on an evening of amateur theatricals in which the sexy secretary Gladys (Carol Haney) sang and danced this rhythmic number with Buzz

Miller and Peter Gennaro. Bob Fosse's choreography, with the dancers in black suits and derbies and twisting and contorting themselves, launched his career and defined the Fosse style. Although "Steam Heat" was added to the show late, it was an old song that Richard Adler had written years before when he had locked himself in a bathroom and vowed he wouldn't come out until he'd written a song. The dripping of the water faucet and the hissing of the bathroom radiator gave him the idea for the song, and he wrote the music and lyric. Later Jerry Ross helped him add a release, and they showed it to Fosse, who was looking for an offbeat sound for the variety-show scene. Patti Page made a best-selling recording of the song.

"Step to the Rear" is a contagious march number from *How Now, Dow Jones* (1967) by Elmer Bernstein (music) and Carolyn Leigh (lyric) that has the feel of a political campaign song and has indeed been used for that purpose since the Broadway run. The young businessman Charley (Anthony Roberts) is cheered up by Mrs. Millhausen (Charlotte Jones) and the other widows who think he's a real winner.

"Stereophonic Sound" is Cole Porter's musical commentary on the wide-screen, sound-enhanced movies that were a fad in the 1950s. The lively number was sung in *Silk Stockings* (1955) by Gretchen Wyler as a Hollywood star in Paris making a movie using all the latest technology.

"The Story Goes On" is an expansive song of self-realization from *Baby* (1983) by David Shire (music) and Richard Maltby, Jr., (lyric). Lizzie (Liz Callaway) is pregnant and in love and now sees herself as part of a continuing family story that encompasses all life.

"The Story of Lucy and Jessie" is a jazzy pastiche number from *Follies* (1971) that echoes Cole Porter's brash swinging style of the 1930s. Stephen Sondheim wrote the sparkling number for the Loveland fantasy section of the show, where it was performed by Phyllis (Alexis Smith) and a chorus of boys in red tuxedos. The number is a schizophrenic character song in which Phyllis describes her former self (the young, optimistic but naive Lucy) and her present self (the mature, wealthy but hardened Jessie) and relates how one wants to be the other. The song replaced a similarly schizophrenic song called "Uptown, Downtown" that was later heard in the Off-Broadway revue *Marry Me a Little* (1981).

"Stouthearted Men" is the contagious march from the operetta *The New Moon* (1928) by Sigmund Romberg (music) and Oscar Hammerstein (lyric). In eighteenth-century New Orleans, Robert Misson (Robert Halliday) recruits men to join in his revolutionary cause with this rousing chorus number. The song became a popular choral favorite and was often recorded, even by Barbra Streisand, who sang it as a ballad in a 1967 recording.

"Strange Music" is the soaring duet from *Song of Norway* (1944), the bio-musical about Edvard Grieg that uses his music for the score. Grieg (Lawrence Brooks) proposes to the village girl Nina Hagerup (Helena Bliss) and she accepts as the two sing this melodic number. Robert Wright and George Forrest wrote the romantic lyric and adapted Grieg's "Nocturne" and "Wedding Day at Troldhaugen" into a popular theatre song. Bing Crosby, James Melton and Larry Ross made the most successful of the many recordings of the song.

"Stranger in Paradise," the exotic Alexander Borodin melody that most people knew, was turned by Robert Wright and George Forrest into a song everybody knows. It was written for the *Arabian Nights* musical *Kismet* (1953), where the Caliph (Richard Kiley) and the poet's daughter Marsinah (Doretta Morrow) sang the number as a love-at-first-sight duet. Wright and Forrest adapted Borodin's "Polovtsian Dances" from *Prince Igor* and added an entrancing lyric that matched the music effectively. Among the many recordings of the song, the Four Aces and Tony Bennett each made a hit single of it in the 1950s.

"The Streets of New York" is a rollicking showstopper by the unlikely composer of operetta, Victor Herbert. He wrote the comic song for *The Red Mill* (1906), one of his least operatic works but one of his most popular. In faraway Holland, the two American tourists "Con" Kidder and "Kid" Conner (played by comedians Fred A. Stone and David Montgomery) recall their Manhattan home where the "peach crop is always fine." Henry Blossom wrote the lyric for Herbert's Tin Pan Alley-like melody that had a limited range to suit the comedians' singing talents. The song is sometimes titled "In Old New York."

"Strike Up the Band" is the rousing title song for two musicals by the Gershwin brothers. In 1927 the show *Strike Up the Band* closed before reaching New York. The first-act finale was this militaristic march that was sung by Max Hoffman, Jr., and the ensemble. George Gershwin's music was fervently patriotic-sounding, but Ira Gershwin's lyric, in keeping with the satirical nature of the show, was a bit sarcastic, with hyperbolic images and silly onomatopoeia throughout. With some new songs and a much-revised libretto, a different *Strike Up the Band* opened on Broadway in 1930 and was a hit. The title song was now sung by Jim Townsend (Jerry Goff) and the ensemble as the United States goes to war with Switzerland over a tariff on Swiss chocolate. Decades later Tommy Tune sang the song as a solo as the first-act finale of the "new Gershwin musical" *My One and Only* (1983). In 1936 Ira Gershwin, at the request of the University of California at Los Angeles, wrote a new lyric for the song and called it "Strike Up the Band for U.C.L.A." It became the university's official fight song at sports competitions.

"Strong Woman Number" is a seriocomic number from *I'm Getting My Act Together and Taking It on the Road* (1978), the Off-Broadway musical by Gretchen Cryer (lyric) and Nancy Ford (music) about a pop singer who tries to put her life together while rehearsing her new act. Heather Jones (Cryer) has learned to be independent and strong and self-reliant, which men admire, but it makes it all the easier for them to leave her. She sings the tangy rock song with her backup singer Alice (Margot Rose), and the two conclude that what they really need is a "wife."

"The Subway Song" is a comic lament about the plight of urban love from the revue *Make Mine Manhattan* (1948) by Richard Lewine (music) and Arnold B. Horwitt (lyric). Sid Caesar sang the amusing number about a boy who lives in the Bronx who is in love with a girl who lives in Brooklyn, and the subway commute is starting to dampen their romance.

"Suddenly Seymour" is an offbeat but moving duet from *Little Shop of Horrors* (1982) by Alan Menken (music) and Howard Ashman (lyric). The nerdy Seymour Krelbourn (Lee Wilkof) and the dizzy Audrey (Ellen Greene) find that they are in love and express their joy and surprise in this expansive number with the help of three backup singers (Sheila Kay Davis, Leilani Jones and Jennifer Leigh Warren). Although the number starts as a camp 1960s song, it soon develops into an effective duet with a sincere subtext.

"Sue Me" is a hilarious comic duet from *Guys and Dolls* (1950) by Frank Loesser, a clever contrapuntal number for Nathan Detroit (Sam Levene) and Miss Adelaide (Vivian Blaine). While she shrilly lists all of his broken promises and many faults, he groans an apologetic "sue me" and asks for forgiveness. The silly, delightful number is the couple's only duet in the show and captures their lopsided romance beautifully. The number is also the only time in the score in which Nathan is called upon to sing a solo part; Levene could not carry any of the songs Loesser wrote for him, but he managed to fake through this one by talk-singing it. In fact, Loesser had to write a five-note ascending phrase for "call a lawyer and" in order for Levene to find the correct pitch for the climactic "sue me" in his part.

"Summer Is" is a memorable ballad from the unsuccessful musical about boxing, *The Body Beautiful* (1958), by Jerry Bock (music) and Sheldon Harnick (lyric) in their first collaboration. Kathie Forman introduced the song, which, for awhile, was a popular audition piece for aspiring performers.

"Summer Nights" is a pastiche number from *Grease* (1972) that lampoons the summer love and beach songs of the 1950s. Sandy (Carole Demas) sings to the girls about her dreamy summer romance with Danny (Barry Bostwick) while Danny sings to the guys about his hot fling with Sandy. Jim Jacobs and Warren Casey wrote the breezy music and amusing lyric.

"Summertime" is the wistful lullaby that opens the folk opera *Porgy and Bess* (1935) and is sung by the Catfish Row resident Clara (Abbie Mitchell) to her baby as she rocks it to sleep. A bit later she reprises the song against the rough sounds of "The Crapshooters' Song." George Gershwin composed the delicate music, and DuBose Heyward wrote the simple but poetic lyric. Billie Holiday made the first of many popular recordings of the lullaby and Bob Crosby and His Orchestra made it their theme song. In the 1960s Herb Alpert and the Tijuana Brass, Billy Stewart, Janis Joplin, Big Brother and the Holding Company all made successful recordings of "Summertime." Cleo Laine and Ray Charles recorded it in 1976 and most recently Michael Crawford made a personalized recording of the song.

"Summertime Love" is an exuberant love song by Frank Loesser from the unsuccessful *Greenwillow* (1960). Gideon Briggs (Anthony Perkins) has fallen in love with Dorrie (Ellen McCown) in the summer of his youth, but, contrary to what people tell him, he vows to be faithful to her throughout all the seasons of his life. The music has some unusual tempo changes that dramatize Gideon's resolve in an effective way.

"The Sun Shines Brighter" is a swinging song of optimism from the Jerome Kern (music) and P.G. Wodehouse (lyrics) college musical *Leave It to Jane* (1917). The cheery number was sung by the secondary comic characters Stub (Oscar Shaw) and Bessie (Ann Orr).

"Sunday" is the scintillating song from *Sunday in the Park With George* (1984) by Stephen Sondheim that is the centerpiece for one of the modern musical theatre's most unforgettable production numbers: the stirring finale of Act One in which George Seurat (Mandy Patinkin) completes his famous painting "Sunday Afternoon on the Island of La Grande Jatte." As George arranges the people on the island into the famous composition, they sing short, lyrical phrases about visual details in the painting. The lyric pieces come together and climax as the rising music does, just as the stage picture comes together visually and all the production elements combine to make a new whole.

"Sunday in Cicero Falls" is a complex production number from *Bloomer Girl* (1944) that takes a satirical look at small-town life. In this second act opening number, the citizens of the sleepy town of Cicero Falls, New York, lazily tread off to church on Sunday morning. Then the suffragettes, led by Evelina Applegate (Celeste Holm), march down the street advertising their upcoming production of the controversial *Uncle Tom's Cabin*. The police arrive to arrest the bothersome feminists, a fight ensues, and they are dragged off to jail as the gentry emerge from church to spend another dull Sunday. Harold Arlen composed the engaging music that shifted beautifully to tell the story, and E.Y. Harburg wrote the sly lyric that both celebrates and chastises the qualities of small-town life.

"Sunday in the Park" is an appealing song about Central Park as a haven for the working class who cannot afford to leave the city when the heat strikes. Harold Rome wrote the dreamy number for the labor revue *Pins and Needles* (1937), where it was sung by the ensemble as the first-act finale. The song became very popular, was a favorite on the "Hit Parade" radio show, and Rome himself recorded it.

"Sunday in the Park With George" is the delightful soliloquy and title number from the 1984 musical by Stephen Sondheim. The model Dot (Bernadette Peters) stiffly stands in the hot sun while her lover, the artist George Seurat (Mandy Patinkin), sketches her. Dot's thoughts wander from complaints about the difficulty of modeling to her love for George. The song starts out stiff as well, with staccato music and short, blunt lyric phrases. Then Dot's imagination takes off, she steps out of her confining Victorian dress, and the music and lyric run on freely and melodically.

"Sunny" is the catchy title song from the 1925 Jerome Kern musical and one of the hits from the show. The American tourist Tom Warren (Paul Frawley) and the male chorus sang the lilting number about the beautiful circus bareback rider Sunny Peters (Marilyn Miller) and gave her such bohemian advice as "never comb your hair, Sunny!" Otto Harbach and Oscar Hammerstein collaborated with Kern for the first time and wrote the sassy, colloquial lyric.

"Sunrise, Sunset" is the theatre song used at more weddings than any since "Oh, Promise Me!" from *Robin Hood* (1891). In *Fiddler on the Roof* (1964), the hymnlike number was the wedding song for the marriage of Tzeitel and Motel that came near the end of the first act. Tzeitel's parents (Zero Mostel and Maria Karnilova) and the ensemble sang the simple but knowing Jerry Bock (music) and Sheldon Harnick (lyric) song that looks at the passing of time with bittersweet reflection. Eddie Fisher, Perry Como and pianist Roger Williams each made popular recordings of "Sunrise, Sunset" and it is still a hit at thousands of weddings each year.

"Sunset Tree" is a tender duet for mature lovers from the short-lived

Darling of the Day (1968) by Jule Styne (music) and E.Y. Harburg (lyric). The working-class widow Alice Chalice (Patricia Routledge) and the famous artist Priam Farll (Vincent Price), who has been living incognito as a butler, have fallen into a December romance and sing this warm song about love in the sunset years of one's life.

"Superstar" is the hit single that led to the concept album that eventually became the Broadway show *Jesus Christ Superstar* (1971). Andrew Lloyd Webber (music) and Tim Rice (lyric) wrote the provocative number that mixed rock with revival gospel and took a passionate, if unconventional, approach to dramatizing the gospels. While fragments of the song are heard throughout the "rock opera," it is sung in its entirety by Judas (Ben Vereen) and the ensemble as Jesus (Jeff Fenholt) is being led to his crucifixion.

"Supper Time" is a passionate, penetrating song that Irving Berlin wrote for Ethel Waters in the revue *As Thousands Cheer* (1933). A black woman prepares supper for her family, but her husband has been lynched by a white mob, and her thoughts range from despair to bitterness to wondering what she will tell her children. Berlin's terse, truthful lyric and hauntingly painful music were his most ambitious efforts up to that point in his career. The release, for example, is among the most expansive in the whole Berlin repertoire. *As Thousands Cheer* was pretty much an escapist entertainment for Depression audiences, and "Supper Time" was nearly cut, but Waters' rendition overrode any doubts the creators had. Waters later stated that the song portrayed the black experience better than any other she ever sang. Surprisingly, "Supper Time" had two popular early recordings: one by Leo Reisman's Orchestra (with a Clifton Webb vocal) and one by Gertrude Niesen. Opera singer Eileen Farrell made a memorable recording in 1959, and later Barbra Streisand recorded a passionate rendition of the song.

"Suppertime" is a razzle-dazzle song and dance showstopper for Snoopy (Bill Hinnant) in *You're a Good Man, Charlie Brown* (1967) by Clark Gesner. The singing-dancing canine celebrates the arrival of his supper dish with Al Jolson-like enthusiasm and showmanship.

"Surabaya Johnny" is a haunting torch song from *Happy End* with music by Kurt Weill and lyric by Bertolt Brecht, translated by Michael Feingold for the 1977 Broadway premiere of the 1929 German musical. Salvation Army worker Hallelujah Lil (Meryl Streep) sings the heartfelt song about her love for a world-roaming scoundrel who destroyed her innocence and then left her. Weill's music is intoxicating, and the Brecht/Feingold lyric is hard and pungent rather than self-pitying. Long before the 1977 American production of *Happy End*, the song was well known through Marlene Dietrich's many performances of it in her nightclub act and Lotte Lenya's recording of it. "Surabaya Johnny" was first heard on a New York stage in the Off-Broadway revue *Berlin to Broadway With Kurt Weill* (1972), where Judy Lander sang it. Soon after, Bette Midler made a popular recording of the song.

"The Surrey With the Fringe on Top" is a small masterpiece of music drama, a little scene set to music with fully realized characters and shifting action and moods. The song is performed early in Rodgers and Hammerstein's *Oklahoma!* (1943) when the cowboy Curly (Alfred Drake) sings to Laurey about the rig he's going to drive to the box social. The number starts out as a list song as he describes the surrey in detail; then it moves into a rhythm song as Richard Rodgers' music uses repeated notes to suggest the clip-clop of the horse on the prairie road. Oscar Hammerstein's lyric then shifts into a love song as Curly paints a picture of the two lovers riding along together. Finally, as the stars appear and the surrey and its occupants return home in the moonlight, the number becomes a lullaby. Near the end of his life, Hammerstein stated that "The Surrey With the Fringe on Top" was his favorite of all the hundreds of songs he'd written; the expectation and joy that could result from such a simple thing as a ride in a buggy, he said, always brought a tear to his eye. Lena Horne gave a distinctive rendition of the song in her one-woman Broadway show *Lena Horne: The Lady and Her Music* (1981) and Jason Graae sang it in the Broadway revue *A Grand Night for Singing* (1993).

"Swanee" was George Gershwin's first hit song, and no other song he wrote after it surpassed it in popularity. He and lyricist Irving Caesar wrote the Southern-style ballad for the *Demi-Tasse Revue* (1919), where it was sung by Muriel De Forest but seemed to get little reaction. When Al Jolson heard the number and added it to his 1919 tour of *Sinbad*, the song caught on and in a year's time sold over two million copies of sheet music. Although loosely inspired by Stephen Foster's "Swanee River," the Gershwin-Caesar song was very contemporary, with a syncopated beat and a lively rhythm that was quite novel.

"Sweet and Low-Down" is an exhilarating rhythm song from the Gershwins' *Tip-Toes* (1925) that provided for a thrilling Palm Beach party scene. George Gershwin wrote the high-voltage music, and Ira Gershwin provided the vibrant lyric for this jubilant salute to a jazz cabaret. Andrew Tombes, Lovey Lee, Gertrude McDonald and the ensemble sang and danced the number with their own kazoo and trombone accompaniment. In the "new Gershwin musical" *My One and Only* (1983), the song was sung and danced by Tommy Tune and Twiggy with a tap-dancing philosopher called Mr. Magix (Charles "Honi" Coles). Ira Gershwin invented the title phrase, combining "sweet and low" and "low-down"; the expression has since gotten around and appears in the *American*

Thesaurus of Slang.

"Sweet Thursday" is a festive number from *Pipe Dream* (1955), Rodgers and Hammerstein's only outright flop show. Opera star Helen Traubel, as the crusty Madame Fauna, sang the lively song and then broke into a snappy cakewalk with two children. Johnny Mathis made a hit recording of the song in 1962. The song's title comes from the John Steinbeck novel that served as the basis for the musical.

"The Sweetest Sounds" is the most memorable song to come from *No Strings* (1962), the only musical for which Richard Rodgers wrote both music and lyrics. This entrancing song was sung by Diahann Carroll and Richard Kiley, at opposite sides of the stage, in the prologue before the lovers meet and at the end of the show after they have separated.

"Sweethearts" is the waltzing title song from the 1913 operetta by Victor Herbert (music) and Robert B. Smith (lyric). The heroine Sylvia (Christie MacDonald) and the chorus sang this romanticized description of ideal love and lovers. Herbert's music, based on a compositional fragment he'd written and discarded seventeen years earlier, is unusual in its wide range (nearly two octaves) and its rhythmic pulse.

"Sword, Rose and Cape" is an appealing character song from *Carnival* (1961) by Bob Merrill. Marco the Magnificent (James Mitchell), the magician for a run-down carnival troupe, recalls the days of fantasy and adventure and, with the roustabouts, sings a playful tribute to swashbucklers of yore.

"Sympathy" is the sweeping waltz duet from the operetta *The Firefly* (1912) by Rudolf Friml (music) and Otto Harbach (lyric). It was not the musical's pair of lovers that sang the duet, though. Geraldine Van Dare (Audrey Maple) seeks the comfort of "uncle" John (Melville Stewart), and together they find sympathy for one another.

"The Syncopated Walk" is the theme song for *Watch Your Step* (1914), the first Broadway musical with a full score by Irving Berlin. The show was a vehicle for Vernon and Irene Castle, who danced the number together with the ensemble. There is actually very little syncopation in the music; it is more a bizarre pattern created by stressing weak beats as strong beats. But the new sound captivated Broadway audiences and brought ragtime music and theatre together with great success.

T

"T.E.A.M. (The Baseball Game)" is the rousing cheer song from *You're a Good Man, Charlie Brown* (1967) by Clark Gesner that makes up an entire musical scene. While Lucy (Reva Rose) leads the team in the optimistic chant, Charlie Brown (Gary Burghoff) sits to the side and sings a letter to his pen pal describing his version of what happened at the baseball game.

"Take Back Your Mink" is the sly and sexy takeoff of a nightclub number from *Guys and Dolls* (1950) by Frank Loesser. Miss Adelaide (Vivian Blaine) and the Hot Box Girls, clothed in furs, proceed to return the favors given to them by insincere men, thereby creating a mock striptease number. The song, made all the funnier by the bubble-headed innocence of the lyric, was a late addition to the score and was written during the Philadelphia tryouts. As the second-act opener it has never failed to bring down the house.

"Take Care of This House" is a moving ballad from the short-lived *1600 Pennsylvania Avenue* (1976) by Leonard Bernstein (music) and Alan Jay Lerner (lyric). Abigail Adams (Patricia Routledge) and President John Adams (Ken Howard) sing the poignant song to the black servants at the White House, asking them to tend it well, for the house is the hope of the struggling nation. Angelina Reaux and David Love Calloway recorded the duet in 1981.

"Take Him" is a sassy, cynical duet for the two women who loved Joey Evans (Gene Kelly) in *Pal Joey* (1940) by Richard Rodgers (music) and Lorenz Hart (lyric). Vivienne Segal and Leila Ernst sang the number that illustrated the hardened and jaded nature of this tough-as-nails musical.

"Take Me Along" is the infectious old-fashioned title song from the 1959 musical by Bob Merrill. Family patriarch Nat Miller (Walter Pidgeon) and his boozy brother-in-law Sid (Jackie Gleason) sang the tuneful number and broke into an irresistible soft-shoe, and the song became a popular favorite for years.

"Take Me Back to Manhattan" is one of Cole Porter's many anthems to New York City, this one sung by Frances Williams in *The New Yorkers* (1930). Porter wrote the song during the Philadelphia tryouts to entertain some friends visiting from New York. It went over so well that he added the song to the show. "Take Me Back to Manhattan" is often interpolated into revivals of Porter's *Anything Goes*, where it actually makes more sense than in *The New Yorkers*, where everyone is already in Manhattan.

"Take the Moment" is a sweeping ballad from *Do I Hear a Waltz?* (1965) by Richard Rodgers (music) and Stephen Sondheim (lyric). The poignant number was sung by Sergio Franchi as a Venetian shop owner who must convince the wary American spinster Leona (Elizabeth Allen) to fall in love with him. Tony Bennett's recording of the song made it somewhat popular in the late 1960s.

"Taking a Chance on Love" is the famous bluesy ballad from *Cabin in the Sky* (1940) and one of the most popular songs Vernon Duke ever wrote. He and lyricist Ted Fetter had written a number called "Fooling Around With Love" years before, but for the "Negro fable" *Cabin in the Sky* lyricist John Latouche revised it into the sterling song known today. The new number was added only three days before the New York opening, but it turned into the hit of the show. Ethel Waters, as the ever-patient Petunia Jackson, sang the ballad and later in the show reprised it with her husband Joe (Dooley Wilson). Helen Forrest (with Benny Goodman's Orchestra) recorded the song soon after the show opened. Of the many subsequent recordings, one by Barbra Streisand in the 1960s is the smoothest and most enticing.

"The Tale of an Oyster" is an off-color song oddity that was inserted in and out of a few Cole Porter musicals before Helen Broderick sang it in *Fifty Million Frenchmen* (1929) and caused something of an uproar. Some critics and audience members found the song to be offensive, and it was soon deleted. In the show Broderick played an American tourist in Paris who was buying copies of James Joyce's banned novel *Ulysses* to send home to her children. "The Tale of an Oyster" was a novelty number added to bolster Broderick's role. It tells of a lonely oyster who is caught, is served to a millionairess at a fancy New York restaurant, disagrees with her and, while on her yacht, regurgitates itself back into Oyster Bay; but the oyster is happy because it has now had a taste of high society and vice versa. The song was rescued from obscurity many years later by Ben Bagley, who made a recording of Kaye Ballard singing the comic number, and Kay McClelland sang it in the 1991 reconstructed recording of the show.

"Talking to You" is a specialty number for the immortal clown Beatrice Lillie for *High Spirits* (1964), the musical version of Noël Coward's *Blithe Spirit*. As the madcap psychic Madame Arcati, Lillie sang this comic song as she was communing with the dead through the use of a Ouija board. Also memorable about the number is the outrageous series of curtain calls Lillie took after she sang it, each one an uproarious mockery of all the clichéd bows and curtsies that grandiose stage stars have used in the past. Timothy Gray and Hugh Martin wrote the merry song.

"The Tattooed Man" is a delicious comic number from the early Victor Herbert operetta *The Idol's Eye* (1897) and a specialty number for the beloved clown Frank Daniels. The Herbert (music) and Harry B. Smith (lyric) song was sung by the "aeronaut" Abel Conn (Daniels) and described the contented wife of a tattooed circus attraction who had exotic places and wonderful stories all over him. The number was so popular that Herbert wrote another vehicle for Daniels called *The Tattooed Man* that opened on Broadway in 1907.

"Tea for Two," still one of the most recognized tunes in American culture after seventy years, was the biggest hit to come out of *No, No, Nanette* (1925), the archetypal 1920s musical comedy by Vincent Youmans (music) and Irving Caesar (lyric). "Tea for Two" is the best in a long line of songs in which the lovers imagine a simple but blissfully happy life together. In this case, it is the young ward Nanette (Louise Groody) and her beau Tom (John Barker). After they express their humble fantasies, the chorus enters, and an exhilarating production number ensues. The song was a last-minute addition to the score (most of which had lyrics by Otto Harbach), but, because of the long pre-Broadway run of the musical in Chicago, "Tea for Two" was a popular hit nationwide by opening night in New York. Youman's music is unusual, especially in the refrain, where almost all the notes are dotted quarter or eighth notes, yet the melody is far from monotonous. As for Caesar's lyric, it is the most famous "dummy" lyric in the American theatre. A dummy lyric is a rhythmic but nonsensical collection of words a lyricist quickly dashes off to help him remember the cadence of the music until he writes the polished lyric. In the case of "Tea for Two," Caesar, so the story goes, improvised the refrain's repetitive wordplay, then went and wrote a finished one. But Youmans liked the dummy lyric better, so, with a few slight revisions, it was retained and has been sung that way ever since. Among the early recordings of the song were popular ones by Marion Harris, the Benson Orchestra and Ben Bernie and His Orchestra. Over the years there have been hundreds of recordings in dozens of languages. There was even a cha-cha version by Warren Covington in 1958 that was a hit.

"The Tea Party" is an extended musical sequence from *Dear World* (1969) that contains some of composer-lyricist Jerry Herman's most ambitious writing.

Attending the tea are three of Paris's most notorious madwomen: Countess Aurelia (Angela Lansbury), Gabrielle (Jane Connell) and Constance (Carmen Matthews). In the course of the party, various ideas, memories, illusions and solutions for curing the world of evil are presented in contrasting melodies and lyric set pieces. The number was sung by Dorothy Loudon, Leslie Uggams and Chita Rivera in the Broadway revue *Jerry's Girls* (1985).

"The Telephone Hour" is the silly, irresistible chorus number from *Bye Bye Birdie* (1960) that captures the sounds and attitudes of the period's teenagers. Charles Strouse (music) and Lee Adams (lyric) wrote the animated song in which the teens of Sweet Apple, Ohio, use the phone to spread the news about Kim and Hugo going steady. As delightful as the song itself was director Gower Champion's staging of the number on a honeycomb set, with the teenagers lounging in boxes representing bedrooms all over town.

"Tell Me It's Not True" is the powerful finale of the British import *Blood Brothers* (1993) by Willy Russell. With her twin sons both shot to death, Mrs. Johnstone (Stephanie Lawrence) cannot comprehend how such a thing came to happen and sings this ballad of denial, comparing life's greatest miseries to an old movie that isn't true at all. The company joins her in singing the heartrending song.

"Tell Me, Little Gypsy" is a charming Irving Berlin song that John Steel sang to six lovely fortune tellers in the *Ziegfeld Follies* (1920), asking if he'll ever find his true love. Art Hickman and His Orchestra made a popular recording of the song as did Steel himself.

"Tell Me on a Sunday" is a telling ballad from *Song and Dance* (1985) by Andrew Lloyd Webber (music), Don Black and Richard Maltby, Jr., (lyric). The English girl Emma (Bernadette Peters) comes to New York to be a hat designer and falls for the all-American Joe. But the affair is quickly fading, and before he can brush her off with the same old "song and dance," Emma sings this number stating that a letter or a phone call is not how she wants to hear the bad news; she insists he take her to a park on a Sunday afternoon and tell her then. Betty Buckley made a recording of the number.

"Tell Me, Pretty Maiden (Are There Any More at Home Like You?)" is the double-sextet number from the notorious *Florodora* (1900) that was the first hit to come from Broadway that was not sung by any of the principals in a show. Six lovely ladies, soon known as the *Florodora* sextet, entered in delicate finery and twirling parasols and coquettishly reacted to six handsome men who asked the title question. So famous were the six ladies that all New York followed their movements like celebrities. (Most of the girls ended up marrying millionaires.) *Florodora* was a British import, and the music was by Leslie Stuart with a lyric by Frank Clement, Paul Rubens and Stuart himself. The following year the song was parodied in *The Sleeping Beauty and the Beast* (1901) as "Tell Me, Dusky Maiden."

"Ten Cents a Dance" is the torchy hit song that Ruth Etting sang in *Simple Simon* (1930), stopping the show nightly and adding another memorable lament to her repertoire. The song was written by Richard Rodgers (music) and Lorenz Hart (lyric) and is one of their most potent narrative ballads. "Ten Cents a Dance" is the catch phrase for a weary taxi dancer at the Palace Ballroom who reveals her disgust of her patrons and her hope for a better life someday. Both music and lyric suggest a sordid, languid quality. Yet in *Simple Simon* Etting sang the number seated atop a small piano that was pedaled about the stage on a bicycle by Ed Wynn. Etting's recording of the song was a best-seller.

"Terrace Duet" is a beguiling and complex duet from the British import *Chess* (1988) by Benny Anderssen and Bjorn Ulvaeus (music) and Tim Rice (lyric). The Russian chess champion Anatoly (David Carroll) and Florence (Judy Kuhn), his opponent's second, meet to discuss a compromise but are drawn to each other even though they don't trust each other politically. During the musical scene we hear the thoughts of each character and the ambivalent emotions taking place within the two people.

"Tevye's Dream" is one of the most potent examples of dance, character, song and storytelling combining in such a way that each is indistinguishable from the other. This amazing musical sequence from *Fiddler on the Roof* (1964) was as much the concept of choreographer-director Jerome Robbins as it was librettist Joseph Stein and the songwriters' creation. Tevye (Zero Mostel) must convince his wife Golde (Maria Karnilova) to let their daughter marry a poor tailor whom she loves rather than the rich butcher Lazar Wolf, so he invents a dream in which Golde's grandmother (Sue Babel) and Wolf's deceased wife (Carol Sawyer) appear and insist that the marriage be called off. Jerry Bock composed a series of ethnic and surreal melodies to go with Sheldon Harnick's lyric and Stein's narrative, and Robbins staged the number as a comic nightmare worthy of the German expressionists.

"Thank Your Father" is one of the oddest of love songs, a roundabout paean to a girl's apparent illegitimate birth. B.G. DeSylva and Lew Brown (lyric) and Ray Henderson (music) wrote the number for *Flying High* (1930), in which mail pilot Tod Addison (Oscar Shaw) praises Eileen Cassidy (Grace Brinkley) for her somewhat questionable conception. Helen Kane, Fred Waring, Al Goodman and the Knickerbockers all made successful recordings of the song.

"That Certain Feeling" is a rhythmic discovery of love that manages to be sentimental and swinging at the same time. The sparkling number is from *Tip-Toes* (1925), where Queenie Smith, as the hoofer "Tip-Toes" Kay, and Allen Kearns, as the wealthy glue manufacturer Steve Barton, sang the duet. George Gershwin composed the catchy music that utilizes repeated notes that bounce up the scale, and Ira Gershwin wrote the playful lyric.

"That Dirty Old Man" is a comic lament from *A Funny Thing Happened on the Way to the Forum* (1962) by Stephen Sondheim. The overbearing Domina (Ruth Kobart) knows that her lecherous husband is up to no good and sings this farcical soliloquy about her ambivalent feelings for the dirty old man she married. Sondheim's music is mock arioso, and his lyric is very clever as Domina alternates between pent-up passion and vengeful fury.

"That Great Come-and-Get-It Day" is the rousing production number that closes the first act of *Finian's Rainbow* (1947) by Burton Lane (music) and E.Y. Harburg (lyric). When the impoverished citizens of Rainbow Valley find out that the mail-order house Shears and Robust has extended unlimited credit to them, labor organizer Woody Mahoney (Donald Richards) leads the ensemble in this vibrant song celebrating economic freedom. Lane's music mixes black revival rhythms, western hoedown and Broadway razzle-dazzle, while Harburg's lyric is both joyous and sarcastic.

"That's Him" is a scintillating character song from *One Touch of Venus* (1943) by Kurt Weill (music) and Ogden Nash (lyric) that Mary Martin, in her first starring role on Broadway, stopped the show with. The goddess Venus (Martin) lists all of her loved one's simple qualities using unromantic similes (he's like a toothache that stops hurting, a plumber when you need one, woolens in winter and so on) and everyday metaphors (autumn, fresh bread, a new hairdo). The presentation of the song in the original production was unique: Martin pulled a chair down to the footlights and delivered the number sitting and conversationally confiding in the audience. Margery Cohen also sang "That's Him" in the Off-Broadway revue *Berlin to Broadway With Kurt Weill* (1972), and Dawn Upshaw made a stylish recording of it in 1994.

"That's How You Jazz" is an invigorating number from *Jelly's Last Jam* (1992), the conceptual bio-musical about jazz pioneer Jelly Roll Morton. On his way to Chicago, Jelly (Gregory Hines) and his friend Jack the Bear (Stanley Wayne Mathis) teach the crowd at a dance hall about the new form of music. Susan Birkenhead wrote the lyric to Morton's own music.

"That's How Young I Feel" is an exuberant chorus number from *Mame* (1966) in which the heroine (Angela Lansbury) demonstrates that she's as young at heart as all her nephew Patrick's friends. Although the song is essentially a dance piece, Jerry Herman's lyric is quite expert and his music is in the swinging boogie-woogie mode, very atypical for his work. The number was sung and danced by Chita Rivera, Anita Ehler and Joni Masella in the Broadway revue *Jerry's Girls* (1985).

"That's Life" is a comic specialty number written for the great clown Bobby Clark in the revue *Walk a Little Faster* (1932) by Vernon Duke (music) and E.Y. Harburg (lyric). Clark and his stooge Paul McCullough sang the succinct number that slyly chronicles a man's life from birth through school to romance to a job to the economic crash to death, all in nineteen short lines of verse, six of which consist of the simple commentary "that's life." The number is noteworthy for being one of Harburg's earliest efforts in writing songs for comic stars, something he would later excel in, particularly for Bert Lahr.

"Then You May Take Me to the Fair" is a quick-witted song from *Camelot* (1960) in which Queen Guenevere (Julie Andrews) convinces three of the kingdom's best knights (Bruce Yarnell, John Cullum and James Gannon) to challenge the pompous Lancelot at the jousts. Alan Jay Lerner wrote the witty lyric that employs some outlandish arch rhymes, and Frederick Loewe composed the sprightly music. During *Camelot*'s troublesome tryouts, this long musical scene was cut in an effort to reduce the show's extreme length; the number was later restored and, some time after opening, it was cut again. The song is sometimes used in revivals of the show, too often not; but luckily it was recorded when the original cast album was made.

"There Ain't No Flies on Me" is an exhilarating chorus number and a dandy pastiche of a turn-of-the-century sing-along from *New Girl in Town* (1957) by Bob Merrill. The denizens of the New York waterfront sang and danced the jovial song about various local characters who got dressed to the nines and proclaimed "there ain't no flies on me." Director George Abbott and choreographer Bob Fosse used the number to create a unique theatrical moment: as Gwen Verdon led the dancing chorus, the first-act curtain fell before the number was finished. After the intermission the curtain rose on the dance in progress, as if it had continued throughout the break.

"There Are Days and There Are Days" is a bluesy ballad from the short-lived musical *The First* (1981) about Jackie Robinson, the first black player in baseball's major leagues. The song by Bob Brush (music) and Martin Charnin (lyric) was sung by Lonette McKee as Robinson's wife Rachel.

"There Are Worse Things I Could Do" is one of the few serious moments in *Grease* (1972), a painful ballad sung by Betty Rizzo (Adrienne

Barbeau) when she discovers she's pregnant and refuses the sympathy of Sandy (Carole Demas). Jim Jacobs and Warren Casey wrote the intriguing character song.

"There But for You Go I" is a solemn ballad from *Brigadoon* (1947) that looks at love as the only way to avoid despair and loneliness. Tommy Albright (David Brooks) sings to Fiona (Marion Bell) about three different men he saw, each one lost and lonely; then he thought of his love for Fiona and concluded that he would be like those men if it weren't for her. Alan Jay Lerner wrote the provocative lyric, and Frederick Loewe composed the sensitive music.

"There Is Nothin' Like a Dame" is perhaps Rodgers and Hammerstein's finest list song, a dandy collection of arguments for the irreplaceability of the gentle sex. The zestful number was sung by Luther Billis (Myron McCormick) and the Seabees in *South Pacific* (1949) who long for female companionship rather than lame substitutes such as volleyball, movies or Tokyo Rose broadcasts. Richard Rodgers' music is alternately raucous and sincere, and the lyric is among Hammerstein's funniest.

"There Must Be Someone for Me" from *Mexican Hayride* (1944) is one of Cole Porter's more accomplished list songs. June Havoc introduced the clever catalogue of all the people and animals in the world who have found a mate; hence the optimistic hope stated in the song title.

"There Must Be Somethin' Better Than Love" is a show-stopping comic song that Pearl Bailey sang in the Revolutionary War musical *Arms and the Girl* (1950). As the house servant named Connecticut, Bailey philosophized about romance and wondered that if there was something better, would anyone want it? Morton Gould wrote the appealing music, and Dorothy Fields provided the amusing lyric. Recordings of the number were made by both Bailey and Artie Shaw (with a vocal by Mary Ann McCall).

"There Once Was a Man" is an energetic mock-western song written by Richard Adler and Jerry Ross for *The Pajama Game* (1954). Factory superintendent Sid Sorokin (John Raitt) and union organizer Babe Williams (Janis Paige) admit that they love each other, then break into this furious hoedown song. The number was originally meant for Poopsie (Rae Allen) to sing, but the lovers needed to loosen up, and this song fit the bill perfectly.

"There She Is" is a dramatic trio from the short-lived *A Doll's Life* (1982), the musical sequel to Henrik Ibsen's *A Doll's House* with music by Larry Grossman and lyrics by Betty Comden and Adolph Green. Over a game of billiards, Johan (George Hearn), Eric (Edmund Lyndeck) and Otto (Peter

Gallagher), three men involved in the life of Nora, reveal their love and jealous emotions about the elusive, independent woman.

"There Won't Be Trumpets" is a captivating song that was cut from the experimental *Anyone Can Whistle* (1964) by Stephen Sondheim. It is a driving number arguing that true heroes do not enter one's life with the blaring of trumpets. The song was later heard in the Broadway revue *Side by Side by Sondheim* (1977), where it was sung by Millicent Martin, Julia McKenzie and David Kernan; and in the Off-Broadway *Marry Me a Little* (1981), where Suzanne Henry sang it. More recently, Dawn Upshaw made a distinctive recording of the song.

"There's a Boat Dat's Leavin' Soon for New York" is the jazzy seduction song from *Porgy and Bess* (1935) in which the drug dealer Sportin' Life (John W. Bubbles) convinces Bess (Anne Brown) to leave Catfish Row and travel north with him. George Gershwin composed the lurid-sounding music, and Ira Gershwin wrote the sleek and sultry lyric. Ray Charles made a memorable recording of the song in 1976.

"There's a Great Day Coming, Mañana" is a tongue-in-cheek song of optimism from *Hold on to Your Hats* (1940) with music by Burton Lane (his first full score for Broadway) and lyric by E.Y. Harburg. Al Jolson sang the rousing yet satirical number that promised prosperity for all, listing impossibly wonderful things that will happen, but not till tomorrow.

"There's a Hill Beyond a Hill" is a bright and cheerful marching song from *Music in the Air* (1932) by Jerome Kern (music) and Oscar Hammerstein (lyric). In the Bavarian hills and dales, Hans (Edward Hayes) and members of the Walking Club sing the lively number as they travel to Munich.

"There's a Small Hotel" is perhaps the best of Broadway's many songs in which the lovers sing of escaping to some out-of-the-way place together. Richard Rodgers (music) and Lorenz Hart (lyric) wrote the charming ballad for *On Your Toes* (1936) about a dreamy honeymoon in a country hotel. The melody was from a song cut from *Jumbo* the year before, but one can hardly blame Rodgers for holding on to such a perfectly enchanting piece of music. Hart's lyric is romantic as well as descriptive; one can just about smell and touch the old inn. The song was sung as a duet by Ray Bolger and Doris Carson, then later in the show was reprised by Luella Gear and Monty Woolley with a comic lyric. The oft-recorded song was also heard in three movie musicals.

"There's Always One You Can't Forget" is an entrancing torch song from the short-lived *Dance a Little Closer* (1983) by Charles Strouse (music) and Alan Jay Lerner (lyric). Nightclub performer Harry Aiken (Len Cariou) thinks that he is over his long-past love affair with Cynthia (Liz Robertson) but, with haunting sincerity, realizes he'll always remember. Strouse's music is delicately hypnotic, and Lerner's lyric, in this his last Broadway show, is as graceful and penetrating as the love songs he wrote for *Brigadoon* thirty-six years earlier. Andrea Marcovicci made an expert recording of the number.

"There's Gotta Be Something Better Than This" is a determined trio from *Sweet Charity* (1966) by Cy Coleman (music) and Dorothy Fields (lyric). Fed up with working as dance-hall hostesses at the run-down Fan-Dango Ballroom, Charity (Gwen Verdon), Nickie (Helen Gallagher) and Helene (Thelma Oliver) sing this song of comic frustration in which they each imagine themselves in a better line of work.

"There's No Business Like Show Business" is the unofficial anthem for the entertainment business, though one cannot imagine what the "official" one would be. Irving Berlin wrote it for *Annie Get Your Gun* (1946) but, after playing it for producers Rodgers and Hammerstein and others, thought it lacking and discarded it. When Rodgers finally convinced Berlin to keep it in the score, no one in his cluttered office could find the song. (A secretary finally located it under a phone book.) Although the song seems a simple, singable number, it is musically quite complex. The main melody is straightforward, but then the bridge becomes a scale that wavers uncertainly as the lyric conjures up the agony of a flop. Holding it all together is a syncopated beat (a favorite devise of Berlin's in the 1910s and 1920s) that gives the song a pulsating tempo and a sense of urgency. In *Annie Get Your Gun*, the number was done in front of a drop as the scenery was being changed backstage. William O'Neal (as Buffalo Bill), Ray Middleton (as sharpshooter Frank Butler) and Marty May sang it to Ethel Merman (Annie Oakley) in their efforts to convince her to join the Wild West Show. She accepted their offer and joined them in singing it. People have been singing it ever since.

"There's Nothing Like a Model T" is a merry period number from *High Button Shoes* (1947) by Jule Styne (music) and Sammy Cahn (lyric). In 1913 New Brunswick, New Jersey, con man Harrison Floy (Phil Silvers) and the chorus sing a musical tribute to the newfangled invention, the horseless carriage.

"These Charming People" is a delectable comic trio from the Gershwins' *Tip-Toes* (1925) that illustrates the developing wit of lyricist Ira Gershwin. Vaudevillian "Tip-Toes" Kaye (Queenie Smith) is stranded in Florida with her two show-business uncles (Harry Watson and Andrew Tombes), so they adjust to the new environment and pose as members of the upper class. George

Gershwin's music is playful, with what musicologist David Ewen called, "subtly insinuating accentuations." But it is Ira Gershwin's lyric, filled with fun triple rhymes and funny allusions to posh society, that makes the number distinctive.

"They Call It Dancing" is Irving Berlin's musical spoof of the dance-crazy 1920s, much of which he was responsible for with all of his syncopated songs on Broadway. The comic number was featured in the first edition of the *Music Box Revue* (1921), where Sam Bernard and Rene Riano did a wild dance filled with haywire contortions.

"They Call the Wind Maria" is the tantalizing hit ballad from *Paint Your Wagon* (1951) by Alan Jay Lerner (lyric) and Frederick Loewe (music). Steve Bullnack (Rufus Smith), a lonely gold prospector who left his wife behind to seek his fortune, and the other miners sing the penetrating song about the forces of nature and how the wind reminds them of the past. The song was immediately popular and it enjoyed renewed fame in the 1960s with Robert Goulet's hit recording.

"They Didn't Believe Me," perhaps more than any other song, pointed out the direction that the American musical theatre would take as it broke away from European operetta. The timeless Jerome Kern (music) and Herbert Reynolds (lyric) ballad was interpolated into the British import *The Girl From Utah* (1914). Una Trance (Julia Sanderson) flees her Mormon husband and goes to London, where she and Sandy Blair (Donald Brian) sing the unforgettable song that is both tender and resolute. Although few critics pointed out the song in their praise for the show, "They Didn't Believe Me" was not lost on audiences, and over two million copies of sheet music were sold. Grace Kerns and Reed Miller made an early recording of the number. The song is one of the most beloved of theatre pieces, and much has been written analyzing its unique accomplishments: the unusual harmonic influence on the melody, the use of quarter notes in the refrain to build up to the climax that is a key change, and a melody line that is, as musicologist Alec Wilder stated, "as natural as walking." All analysis aside, "They Didn't Believe Me" is one of the very few theatre songs that sounds unique and fresh in no matter what decade it is sung.

"They Like Ike" is a simple little ditty from Irving Berlin's *Call Me Madam* (1950) in which three congressmen (Pat Harrington, Jay Velie and Ralph Chambers) discuss the possibility of General Eisenhower running for president. Once Ike became an actual candidate, the radio networks wouldn't broadcast the song because of equal-time restrictions. Berlin rewrote some of the lyric, and as "I Like Ike" it became the Republican campaign song. Although the lyric is strained and the music a bit strident, the number has all the cheery mindlessness that made it ideal for political conventions and fundraisers.

"They Say It's Wonderful" is the hit ballad from Irving Berlin's *Annie Get Your Gun* (1946), a show loaded with hits. Berlin's music is hesitant and very innocent, and the lyric for the naive Annie Oakley is beautifully restrained; the dangling "and" in the refrain is a superb piece of musical theatre craftsmanship. Ethel Merman and Ray Middleton introduced the warm duet, and it had popular recordings by Perry Como, Frank Sinatra, Andy Russell, Doris Day, Tony Bennett, Bing Crosby and others.

"They Were You" is a quiet duet of maturing love from *The Fantasticks* (1960) by Tom Jones (lyric) and Harvey Schmidt (music). Matt (Kenneth Nelson) and Luisa (Rita Gardner) have been hurt by the cruelties of the world and reunite with this lovely song in which they realize that life's greatest gift was each other. The subdued waltz is a marked contrast to the lovers' earlier bombastic "Metaphor" duet, for the metaphors used in "They Were You" are gentle and simple.

"They're Playing My Song" is the self-congratulatory duet sung by two songwriters from the Marvin Hamlisch (music) and Carole Bayer Sager (lyric) musical *They're Playing Our Song* (1979). Composer Vernon Gersch (Robert Klein) is in a nightclub with lyricist Sonia Walsk (Lucie Arnaz) when one of his tunes is played, and he launches into a frenzied celebration of his own fame. When one of Sonia's songs is then heard, she does likewise until the two egocentric songwriters are caught in a duet together. At the end of the musical the number is reprised by the company of six as "They're Playing Our Song."

"Thief in the Night" is an intriguing lament from the revue *At Home Abroad* (1935), a self-aware torch song that manages to be as sly as it is heartbreaking. Ethel Waters sang the Howard Dietz (lyric) and Arthur Schwartz (music) song in which a tormented lover sings of the man who came like a thief in the night and stole her heart.

"Thine Alone" is the intoxicating duet from Victor Herbert's Irish-flavored operetta *Eileen* (1917) with lyrics by Henry Blossom. The Irish freedom fighter Captain Barry O'Day (Walter Scanlan) and his beloved Eileen Mulvaney (Grace Breen) sing the ardent duet filled with Irish melody and harmony that made it one of Herbert's most successful ballads. Unfortunately the song became popular as a solo piece, especially in a recording by Mario Lanza, so Herbert's individual musical phrases that were characteristic of each of the lovers were lost in most subsequent performances.

"Things" is the show-stopping comic number for Bert Lahr in the revue *Life*

Begins at 8:40 (1934) by Harold Arlen (music) and Ira Gershwin and E.Y. Harburg (lyric). The song and Lahr's rendition of it spoofed formal opera, operetta, serious music and the concert stage all in one fell swoop. Lahr entered in a tuxedo and an outrageous hairpiece, poised himself in a recital position and introduced the song with highbrow nonsense. Then he sang the verse explaining that of all the dreams and wishes that mankind has sought, his has always been . . . things. The refrain, taking on the rhapsodic quality of "Ah! Sweet Mystery of Life," waxes poetic about all sorts of "things," never getting very specific and getting more and more absurd as it moves to a hilarious climax with Lahr fighting to out-sing the orchestra and keep his wayward hairpiece in place. The specialty number would probably not work for anyone else, but Lahr made it the comic highlight of the season, and it propelled his blossoming career.

"Things I Learned in High School" is an astute and touching song from *Is There Life After High School?* (1982) that explores the sometimes painful realizations made during adolescence. Craig Carnelia wrote the knowing song, and it was sung by Harry Groener. Carnelia himself recorded the number in 1991.

"Think of the Odds" is a shrewd and insightful song about platonic relationships from *Romance, Romance* (1988) by Barry Harman (lyric) and Keith Herrmann (music). Sam (Scott Bakula) and Monica (Alison Fraser) have been friends since college, but their spouses Barb (Deborah Graham) and Lenny (Robert Hoshour) are wary as they sing and consider the possibility of friendship turning into romance.

"Think of the Time I Save" is a farcical number for Eddie Foy, Jr., in *The Pajama Game* (1954) by Richard Adler and Jerry Ross. The efficiency expert Hines (Foy) at the Sleep-Tite Pajama Factory expounds on his theories of time management and describes the techniques he uses in his private life to save minutes here and there.

"Thinking of You" is a durable ballad from *The Five O'Clock Girl* (1927) by Harry Ruby (music) and Bert Kalmar (lyric). Mary Eaton, as a humble worker in a cleaners shop, and Oscar Shaw, as a wealthy society gent, introduced the romantic number. Eddie Fisher had his first chart record with the song, Sarah Vaughan and Don Cherry also made successful recordings of it, and "Thinking of You" became the theme song for Kay Kyser and His Orchestra.

"Thirteen Collar" is a show-stopping comic number from the Princess Theatre musical *Very Good Eddie* (1915) by Jerome Kern (music) and Schuyler Greene (lyric). Eddie Kettle (Ernest Truex) is a man small in stature and in courage, and he sings regretfully that he wears only a size thirteen collar. The song is sometimes listed as "When You Wear a Thirteen Collar."

"This Can't Be Love" is an exuberant Rodgers and Hart song from *The Boys From Syracuse* (1938) that recalls the team's earlier "It's Got to Be Love" in its use of negatives to come to the same positive conclusion. In the number the lovers proclaim that they feel so happy that they question the validity of their love free from anguish. Richard Rodgers' sprightly music and Lorenz Hart's light-footed lyric makes "This Can't Be Love" one of their most joyous love songs. Antipholus (Eddie Albert) is falling for his supposed sister-in-law Luciana (Marcy Westcott), and they sing this duet together. Memorable recordings of the number were made by Ella Fitzgerald, Julie Andrews, Nat "King" Cole and, years later, his daughter Natalie Cole.

"This Funny World" is a marvelous but lesser-known Rodgers and Hart ballad from the unsuccessful *Betsy* (1926) that disappeared for twenty-five years until singer-arranger Matt Dennis rediscovered it and performed it on the nightclub circuit. The song, introduced by vaudeville favorite Belle Baker in *Betsy*, is a hauntingly painful lament about how the world laughs at your dreams. Lorenz Hart's lyric is very cynical, but also fragile and uneasy. Richard Rodgers, never one to take the easy way out, manages to create a lonely, aching temperament while keeping the music in an unexpected major key.

"This Is All Very New to Me" is an expansive song of romantic joy from *Plain and Fancy* (1955) by Albert Hague (music) and Arnold B. Horwitt (lyric). The Amish farm girl Hilda (Barbara Cook) has met the New York writer Dan King (Richard Derr) and interprets his charming small talk as a declaration of love. Hilda sings of the new experience, and the ensemble joins her in the jubilant number.

"This Is My Holiday" is an appealing ballad from *The Day Before Spring* (1945) by Alan Jay Lerner (lyric) and Frederick Loewe (music). Irene Manning sang the waltzing number about a married woman who has discovered new love in an old flame.

"This Is New" is a fervent realization of love at first sight from one of the dream sequences in *Lady in the Dark* (1941). Liza Elliott (Gertrude Lawrence) meets the handsome movie star Randy Curtis (Victor Mature), and both declare that the world is changed. Kurt Weill wrote the rhapsodic music, and Ira Gershwin provided the hyperbolic lyric. The number was intended as a solo for Randy, but Mature's singing voice was so weak that it was turned into a duet for him and Lawrence, then eventually a solo for Lawrence. Helen Forrest recorded "This Is New" with Benny Goodman's Orchestra, Lawrence herself made a single of it, and years later Julie Andrews recorded the song.

"This Is the Army, Mr. Jones" is the crowd-pleasing title number (sort of) from Irving Berlin's all-soldier revue *This Is the Army* (1942). The song was sung by the selectees (all cast members were actually in the armed forces) and some Minstrel Men, opening the show with a bizarre but energetic military minstrel show.

"This Is the Life" is a complex musical soliloquy from the experimental *Love Life* (1948). Sam Cooper (Ray Middleton) has separated from his wife and two kids and has taken up residence in a hotel. The stream-of-consciousness song chronicles his fluctuating elation at being free and his somber reflections and memories of the past. Kurt Weill composed the intricate music that moves through three distinct melodies, and Alan Jay Lerner wrote the fascinating lyric.

"This Is the Life" is a breezy tribute to the sweets of success from the boxing musical *Golden Boy* (1964) by Charles Strouse (music) and Lee Adams (lyric). Billy Daniels sang the smooth, bluesy song, then was interrupted by Sammy Davis, Jr., and the ensemble with a rap section, perhaps the first ever heard in a Broadway musical. Also of interest in the list song are the many items mentioned in the lyric that signaled success in the mid-1960s but are now gone or passé.

"This Nearly Was Mine" is arguably Rodgers and Hammerstein's finest torch song, an elegant, heartfelt solo aria for Emile de Becque (Ezio Pinza) in *South Pacific* (1949). The number, in many ways, is a disillusioned counterpart to Emile's earlier "Some Enchanted Evening." Oscar Hammerstein's lyric is passionate without being purple, and Richard Rodgers' music is very European (Emile is a transplanted Frenchman) and operatic. Also of note is how Robert Russell Bennett's original orchestrations include musical fragments of the show's "Bali Ha'i," "Some Enchanted Evening" and "A Wonderful Guy" with certain instruments in the accompaniment. Martin Vidnovic sang the ballad in the Broadway revue *A Grand Night for Singing* (1993).

"This Plum Is Too Ripe" is a jazzy quartet from the Off-Broadway phenomenon *The Fantasticks* (1960) by Tom Jones (lyric) and Harvey Schmidt (music). At the beginning of the second act, with the bright sunlight melting away the romantic moonlight of the previous act, the lovers Matt (Kenneth Nelson) and Luisa (Rita Gardner) are just as disillusioned with each other as the two fathers (William Larsen and Hugh Thomas) are with their old friendship. Schmidt's music is erratic: the melody moves up a half step every sixteen bars, and the dissonant chords create a sense of awkwardness.

"Those Canaan Days" is a raffish pastiche of a French cafe song from *Joseph and the Amazing Technicolor Dreamcoat*, the British musical that finally reached Broadway in 1982. Reuben (Robert Hyman) and his ten brothers sit around and drink wine as they recall the prosperous life they once led. Andrew Lloyd Webber composed the Gallic music, and Tim Rice wrote the amusing lyric.

"Those Were the Good Old Days" is a dandy soft shoe number for the devil in *Damn Yankees* (1955) by Richard Adler and Jerry Ross. The devilish Mr. Applegate (Ray Walston) is discouraged with how his plans to get Joe Hardy's soul are going, so he takes comfort in remembering the disasters and villainous figures of the past three hundred years. The song has a slow vaudeville rhythm to it that humorously contrasts with the comically wicked lyric.

"Thou Swell" remains one of Rodgers and Hart's most delightful duets, a delicious mixture of mock-medieval phrasing and modern slang. This mixture makes sense considering that Richard Rodgers (music) and Lorenz Hart (lyric) wrote it for *A Connecticut Yankee* (1927), the musical version of Mark Twain's fantasy. William Gaxton, as the twentieth-century Martin who dreams he is back in King Arthur's Camelot, sang it with Constance Carpenter, as the beautiful Dame Alisande who loves him despite his strange speech and manners. Memorable recordings of "Thou Swell" were made by Julie Andrews, Ella Fitzgerald, Nat "King" Cole and, years later, his daughter Natalie Cole.

"Thousands of Miles" is a flowing song of optimism from *Lost in the Stars* (1949) by Kurt Weill (music) and Maxwell Anderson (lyric). Stephen Kumalo (Todd Duncan) decides to leave his South African village to travel to Johannesburg to find his son. As he tells his wife in the moving song, the miles and days that separate a parent and a child cannot hold them apart. At the end of the musical the song is reprised by the chorus as Kumalo grieves for his dead son.

"Thousands of Trumpets" is a funny march song that laments all those school band instruments hidden away in closets ever since high-school graduation. Craig Carnelia wrote the clever number that was sung by James Widdoes and the company in *Is There Life After High School?* (1982).

"Three Sunny Rooms" is a charming character duet from the short-lived *Rags* (1986) by Charles Strouse (music) and Stephen Schwartz (lyric). The middle-aged Arram (Dick Latessa) is wooed by the wily widow Rachel (Marcia Lewis), who has a nice apartment facing the street and an eye for matrimony. The charm song ends with the two December lovers agreeing to share the three sunny rooms.

"The Thrill Is Gone" is a haunting torch song by Lew Brown (lyric) and

Ray Henderson (music) written for the 1931 edition of *George White's Scandals*. The entrancing number was sung in the revue by Everett Marshall with Rudy Vallee and Ross McLean. That same year Bing Crosby recorded it with the Boswell Sisters, and the song became very popular. In 1942 Marshall and Vallee reunited in the studio to record the song with Ella Mae Morse and Eddie Slack's Band. Other notable recordings were made by B.B. King and Andrea Marcovicci.

"The Thrill of First Love" is a quick-witted comic duet from *March of the Falsettos* (1981) in which the lovers Marvin (Michael Rupert) and Whizzer (Stephen Bogardus) argue, fight, disagree and insult, all in the hopes of recapturing the early thrill of their romance. William Finn wrote the stimulating music and lyric.

"Through the Years" is the haunting title song from the short-lived 1932 musical by Vincent Youmans (music) and Edward Heyman (lyric). The lengthy, hymnlike ballad was sung by Moonyeen (Natalie Hall), the spectre of a woman long dead. "Through the Years" was Youmans' favorite of the many songs he wrote throughout his career. The ballad achieved some popularity years after the show's twenty-performance run.

"Tickle Toe" is one of those songs that introduced a new dance step during the dance craze early in the century. This one was written by Louis Hirsch (music) and Otto Harbach (lyric) for the aviation musical *Going Up!* (1917), where it was sung and danced by the gushing sweetheart Grace Douglas (Edith Day) and the ensemble. The number is sometimes listed as "Ev'rybody Ought to Know How to Do the Tickle Toe."

"Till Good Luck Comes My Way" is a boastful song of confidence for the swaggering riverboat gambler Gaylord Ravenal (Howard Marsh) in *Show Boat* (1927). Jerome Kern (music) and Oscar Hammerstein (lyric) wrote the breezy number in which Gaylord and the men's chorus dismiss the bad fortune they might experience today because they know tomorrow will be their lucky day. Robert Merrill made a fine recording of the song in 1956.

"Till the Clouds Roll By" is the beloved Jerome Kern (music) and P.G. Wodehouse (lyric) song from *Oh, Boy!* (1917) that was the hit of the popular show and a durable favorite that epitomizes the vibrant style of the Princess Theatre musicals. It was sung by the show's hero, George Budd (Tom Powers), and the plot's comedienne, Jackie Sampson (Anna Wheaton), who pledge platonically to help each other out as they wait for the rainstorm to "roll by." The song is melodically very simple (Kern said that it was suggested by an old German hymn), with a minimal number of notes and no key changes in the refrain. Yet it is totally captivating and is one of those rare early songs that do not seem to date at all. Surprisingly, none of the critics singled out the number in the original production, but audiences knew better, and it became very popular. Two early recordings are of particular interest: Wheaton recorded it with James Harrod a month after the opening, and the original London cast members (Powers and Beatrice Lillie) made a recording a year later.

"Till There Was You" is the hit ballad from *The Music Man* (1957) by Meredith Willson but it is the least typical song in the show, being more in the Broadway mode than in the flavor of 1912 rural America. Professor Harold Hill (Robert Preston) and librarian Marian Paroo (Barbara Cook) sing the rhapsodic duet on the romantic footbridge in the park where the town's lovers like to go. The oft-recorded song had its biggest success with the Anita Bryant single that sold over a million copies, and even the Beatles recorded a rock and roll version in 1963.

"Till Tomorrow" is an enticing waltz number from *Fiorello!* (1959) that was used to create a nostalgic moment from the past without becoming mere pastiche. The lovely song was sung by Thea (Ellen Hanley) as a farewell for LaGuardia (Tom Bosley) and the other soldiers who are going off to fight in France in 1917. Jerry Bock composed the elegant music that mixes a sense of sadness with its melodic sweep, and Sheldon Harnick's lyric is heartfelt but restrained.

"The Time and the Place and the Girl" is a Victor Herbert standard from the operetta *Mlle. Modiste* (1905) with lyrics by Henry Blossom. The young French captain Etienne de Bouvray (Walter Percival) expresses his regret and frustration that he never finds the three elements of the song's title together.

"Time Heals Everything" is Jerry Herman's finest torch song, a gripping, deeply felt number from *Mack and Mabel* (1974) that failed to become popular because of the show's short run. Bernadette Peters, as silent-movie actress Mabel Normand, sang the bluesy song about her love for movie director Mack Sennett (Robert Preston). The number was sung by Dorothy Loudon in the Broadway revue *Jerry's Girls* (1985), and Barbara Cook made a lovely recording of it.

"Time on My Hands" is a gentle ballad from the short-lived *Smiles* (1930) that managed to become popular long after the show closed. Vincent Youmans (music) and Harold Adamson and Mack Gordon (lyric) wrote the flowing song, and it was sung by the doughboy Dick (Paul Gregory) and the French waif (Marilyn Miller) whom he adopts. As often happened in the 1930s, "Time on My Hands" became well known in England long before it found fame in its homeland.

"Times Like This" is a funny, touching ballad about the preference for the security and affection of a dog over that of a human. Stephen Flaherty (music) and Lynn Ahrens (lyric) wrote it for the Off-Broadway musical farce *Lucky Stiff* (1988). Animal-rights advocate Annabel Glick (Julie White) sings the quiet aria during a moment of emotional insecurity amidst the show's madcap confusion.

"T'morra, T'morra" is a dandy character song from *Bloomer Girl* (1944) that impatiently questions waiting for tomorrow for what you ought to get today. The feisty maid Daisy (Joan McCracken) is anxious for love and sex and freedom, not necessarily in that order, and can't understand why everyone keeps telling her to wait and be patient. What society calls Utopia or the Hereafter are also too far away for Daisy, and she merrily demands happiness now. Harold Arlen composed the surging music, and E.Y. Harburg wrote the antic lyric that contains delightful arch rhymes and wordplay.

"To Be Alone With You" is a memorable ballad from *Ben Franklin in Paris* (1964) and the visual highlight of the less-than-successful musical. Franklin (Robert Preston) and his old flame Countess Diane de Vobrillac (Ulla Sallert) sang the romantic duet in a hot-air balloon floating over Paris. Oliver Smith's inventive scenery, in which the backdrops rolled up and down to give the illusion of the balloon's drifting with the breeze, made the number unique. The show's score was by Mark Sandrich, Jr., (music) and Sidney Michaels (lyric), but "To Be Alone With You" was one of the two songs Jerry Herman wrote for the troubled musical during previews.

"To Each His Dulcinea" is the enchanting ballad from *Man of La Mancha* (1965) that was popular with recording artists in the 1960s and 1970s. The Padre (Robert Rounseville) sang the dreamy song that described each man's need for an ideal to keep him from despair. Mitch Leigh composed the haunting music, and Joe Darion wrote the alluring lyric.

"To Keep My Love Alive" is the last lyric that Lorenz Hart wrote, a stinging comic number as fresh and as brash as his early college songs. It was written for the 1943 Broadway revival of the earlier *A Connecticut Yankee* (1927) by Richard Rodgers (music) and himself. The song is a comic tour de force for Queen Morgan le Fay, who recounts how she murdered all of her many husbands in order to "keep my love alive." Rodgers' music is lighthearted and deceptively trivial. Hart's lyric is devastatingly funny, rhyming "appendectomy" with "horse's neck to me" and "fratricide" with "at my mattress side." Vivienne Segal, playing Morgan le Fay, stopped the show with her devilish rendition of the song. Pearl Bailey and Ella Fitzgerald each made fun recordings of the comic number.

"To Life (L'Chaim)" is the most robust song from *Fiddler on the Roof* (1964) and the musical's only concession to a big, traditional song and dance number. At the local inn, Tevye (Zero Mostel) and Lazar Wolf (Michael Granger) celebrate the proposed marriage between the butcher Wolf and Tevye's eldest daughter. Other men join in the song, including some Russian gentiles who salute the couple in their own ethnic manner. The zestful drinking song was written by Jerry Bock (music) and Sheldon Harnick (lyric), and Jerome Robbins devised the rousing Hebrew-Russian choreography that stopped the show each evening.

"Together, Wherever We Go" is a frolicsome trio from *Gypsy* (1959) by Jule Styne (music) and Stephen Sondheim (lyric) that became popular due to its zesty music and sprightly lyrics. Rose (Ethel Merman), her daughter Louise (Sandra Church) and their manager Herbie (Jack Klugman) sing the tongue-in-cheek pledge of unity to cheer themselves up in a Texas desert where the vaudeville act is "between engagements."

"Tomorrow," the unabashedly optimistic ballad from *Annie* (1977), is the most popular song to come from a Broadway show for many a season even though it was hated by as many as loved it. In the context of the Depression-era musical, the song's naive mawkishness is very appropriate as the orphan-on-the-run Annie (Andrea McArdle) befriends the stray dog Sandy and looks hopefully to the future. Charles Strouse wrote the pleasant music, and Martin Charnin provided the simple lyric. This kind of optimism was satirized later in the show with the pastiche number "You're Never Fully Dressed Without a Smile."

"Tomorrow Belongs to Me" is the chilling anthem representing the rise of the Nazi Party in Germany in *Cabaret* (1966) by John Kander (music) and Fred Ebb (lyric). The number was sung by Robert Sharp leading a group of idealistic waiters, and then the Master of Ceremonies (Joel Grey) joined them in singing the ballad. At the end of the first act the song was reprised by Fraulein Kost (Peg Murray), Ernst Ludwig (Edward Winter) and other Nazi supporters. Although the lyric is rather innocent and utilizes nature imagery, the folk song builds until both music and lyric become powerful and threatening.

"Tonight" is the soaring love duet from *West Side Story* (1957) by Leonard Bernstein (music) and Stephen Sondheim (lyric) that serves as the musical's equivalent to the *Romeo and Juliet* balcony scene. Tony (Larry Kert) and Maria (Carol Lawrence) sing the number on an alley fire escape, but the song's imagery transports them to a world of romance and beauty. Originally the creators planned for the lovers to sing "One Hand, One Heart" for the scene and then changed it to "Somewhere." But when Oscar Hammerstein, Sondheim's mentor, saw an early rehearsal, he suggested that a more rhapsodic ballad was needed, and the team then wrote "Tonight." Of the many recordings of the song, a two-piano version by Ferrante and Teicher and a vocal by Eddie Fisher were the most successful.

"Tonight at Eight" is a tingling song of anticipation from *She Loves Me* (1963) in which Georg (Daniel Massey) looks forward to meeting his anonymous "dear friend," with whom he has been corresponding by mail. Jerry Bock composed the energetic music that races up and down the scales, and Sheldon Harnick wrote the lyric that reflects Georg's fluctuating joy and dread.

"Tonight Quintet" is much more than a reprise of *West Side Story*'s ballad "Tonight" by Leonard Bernstein (music) and Stephen Sondheim (lyric). This complex number for five soloists and chorus builds on the music and lyric of the initial song to create one of the musical theatre's finest uses of opera convention for a serious scene. Several numbers from the Gershwins' *Of Thee I Sing* (1931) and Bernstein's earlier *Candide* (1956) had skillfully used mock opera for satirical effect but the "Quintet" is powerful theatre music with no apologies necessary. The sequence includes Riff (Mickey Calin) and the Jets and Bernardo (Ken Le Roy) and the Sharks anticipating the rumble that will occur tonight; Tony and Maria each reprising sections of the earlier song's refrain as each looks forward to seeing the other that night; and Anita (Chita Rivera) conjuring up visions of the lovemaking she will engage in after the fight. As the number progresses, the music takes on a more sinister and uncomfortable tone. By the climax of the song, with all five parts singing simultaneously, dark and dissonant chords pervade the piece, and the air is heavy with expectation.

"Too Close for Comfort" is a swinging ballad from the Sammy Davis, Jr., vehicle *Mr. Wonderful* (1956) that was popular in the 1950s. Davis introduced the number, in which he admitted that his resistance to romance failed when he was close to the lady in question. The smooth lyric is by Larry Holofcener and George Weiss; Jerry Bock, in his pre-Sheldon Harnick days, wrote the absorbing music. Eydie Gorme made a popular recording of the song.

"Too Darn Hot" is Cole Porter's attempt to create a hot jazz number à la Gershwin; he only partially succeeds in the jazz department, but the song is a sensational opportunity for dance and became the choreographic highlight of *Kiss Me, Kate* (1948), where it was introduced. "Too Darn Hot" is the least integrated number in the show; it is used to open the second act by showing the chorus dancers from the musical version of *The Taming of the Shrew* cooling off in the alley outside during the intermission. The number was led by three black specialty dancers, Lorenzo Fuller, Eddie Sledge and Fred Davis, who sang of the heat that discourages lovemaking. Evidently dancing was not out of the question, though, for Hanya Holm's choreography for "Too Darn Hot" was very energetic.

"Too Good for the Average Man" is a cunning character song from *On Your Toes* (1936) by Richard Rodgers (music) and Lorenz Hart (lyric). A Russian impresario (Monty Woolley) and an American patroness of the arts (Luella Gear) engage in a comic duet about the excesses of the excessively rich, stating how the finer things in life (supper clubs, psychiatry, birth control and so on) are not for the masses. Pianist-singer Ramona made a successful recording of the song.

"Too Many Mornings" is a romantic ballad from *Follies* (1971) that has a dreamy, unreal quality to it because the couple singing it are more in love with memories of what they were like than with the way they really are. Stephen Sondheim wrote the rich, melodic number, and it was sung by Ben Stone (John McMartin) and his old flame Sally (Dorothy Collins). In the Broadway revue *Side by Side by Sondheim* (1977), the duet was sung by David Kernan and Julia McKenzie.

"Too Many Rings Around Rosie (Will Never Get Rosie a Ring)" is a delightfully sassy number from *No, No, Nanette* (1925) that is pure 1920s. Lucille Early (Josephine Whittell) and the chorus sing the spirited song about how flirting and marriage proposals usually do not go hand in hand. Vincent Youmans composed the zippy music, and Irving Caesar wrote the witty lyric.

"Toot, Toot, Tootsie!" is the popular farewell song that Al Jolson made famous when he sang it in his 1921 extravaganza *Bombo*. The vivacious number was written by Ernie Erdman, Dan Russo and Gus Kahn and has remained a nonsensical favorite over the years. A recording by Pearl Bailey is particularly memorable.

"Totem Tom Tom" is a rhythmic number from the operetta *Rose-Marie* (1924) with a silly lyric and far-from-authentic Indian music, but it was one of the most spectacular production numbers seen on Broadway in its day. The squaw Wanda (Pearl Regay) led a chorus of dozens of girls dressed as totem poles who marched to the song's incessant beat. Both Rudolf Friml and Herbert Stothart collaborated on the music, Otto Harbach and Oscar Hammerstein wrote the lyric, and David Bennett staged the memorable number.

"The Touch of Your Hand" is a compassionate song of farewell from the Jerome Kern (music) and Otto Harbach (lyric) musical *Roberta* (1933). The lovely number was sung as a duet by the expatriate Russian princess Stephanie (Tamara) and her countryman Ladislaw (William Hain). The Harbach lyric is achingly beautiful, and Kern's music is enthralling, with its unique structure and two distinct melodies for the refrain.

"Toyland" is the soothing ballad that describes a magical land for children and is the theme song for the Broadway extravaganza *Babes in Toyland* (1903) by Victor Herbert (music) and Glen MacDonough (lyric). Bessie Wynn, in the trousers role of Tom Tom, sang the lullabylike song with the men's chorus. Carolyn Mignini sang it in the Broadway revue *Tintypes* (1980).

"Tradition" is the unforgettable opening musical sequence from Bock and Harnick's *Fiddler on the Roof* (1964), one of the great pieces of musical exposition in the American theatre. The local dairyman Tevye (Zero Mostel) leads the company in the sequence that is actually the "I am" song for the Russian village of Anatevka, the musical's true central character. "Tradition" describes the makeup of the village, identifies the roles that the fathers, mothers, sons and daughters play in daily life, and explains the precepts that govern the characters. All the events of the musical that follow are made more potent due to this vivid introductory song. Jerry Bock's music has both an ethnic and a show-business feel, and Sheldon Harnick's lyric captures the folklore quality of the Sholom Aleichem stories that serve as the basis for the musical.

"Train to Johannesburg" is a powerful song from *Lost in the Stars* (1949), the ambitious musical drama about South Africa by Kurt Weill (music) and Maxwell Anderson (lyric). At a train station in a small village, a family of Zulus sing farewell to one of their own number who is going to the big city to work in the mines. The Chorus Leader (Frank Roane) wishes him well, and the Zulus sing that when white men go to Johannesburg, they soon return; but when black men go, they rarely come back. Weill's music has an African folk song quality, but the agitated melody and the rhythmic pattern like that of a train give the number an unsettling feeling.

"Tramp! Tramp! Tramp! (Along the Highway)" is the male marching song that became the prototype of many others to follow. It was written by Victor Herbert (music) and Rida Johnson Young (lyric) for the operetta classic *Naughty Marietta* (1910), where it was sung by Captain Dick Warrington (Orville Harrold) and the Rangers.

"Trina's Song" is a moving and ambiguous ballad from *March of the Falsettos* (1981) by William Finn. Trina (Alison Fraser) has remarried, but she is having trouble adjusting to a cheerful man whose love is so easily forthcoming. The revealing song is also identified by its first line "I'm Tired of

All the Happy Men Who Rule the World."

"A Trip to the Library" is an endearing character song from *She Loves Me* (1963) by Jerry Bock (music) and Sheldon Harnick (lyric). The uneducated Miss Ritter (Barbara Baxley) tells of her adventures the previous evening when she decided to see what a library was like. She was intimidated by all the books until she met a gentle optometrist who invited her back to his flat and, to her amazement, read to her all night long.

"Triplets" is a jocular specialty number from *Between the Devil* (1937) and arguably the finest comic song by the renowned team of Howard Dietz (lyric) and Arthur Schwartz (music). In the show the song was a cabaret number that had nothing to do with the plot. A trio billed as the Tune Twisters sang the riotous number about the aggravations of being born triplets, and Dietz packed the song with a wordy lyric that suggested infant and adult points of view at the same time. The songwriters wrote the number for their earlier revue *Flying Colors* (1932), but it wasn't used until they needed a specialty number for this musical. Kim Criswell, Judy Kaye and George Dvorsky recorded the trio in a 1992 restored version using the original orchestrations and Mandy Patinkin made a recording in which he sang all three parts.

"Trouble" is the thrilling patter song that Professor Harold Hill (Robert Preston) sings in *The Music Man* (1957). The con man Hill arrives in the small Iowa town of River City and launches into this fast-talking sermon about the evils that will inevitably follow from the opening of a pool hall in town. The townspeople gradually join in, and the song turns into a vibrant revival-like chorus number. Meredith Willson wrote the music and lyric for the famous tour de force solo, utilizing more a rhythmic cadence than a traditional melody with rhyming verse. The number is reprised later in the show as Hill works the crowd up to present his idea of a boys' band to solve the "trouble" he's invented. The song is also known as "Ya Got Trouble."

"Trouble Man" is an indelible torch song by Kurt Weill (music) and Maxwell Anderson (lyric) from *Lost in the Stars* (1949), the powerful musical about South Africa. Irina (Inez Matthews) sings this penetrating soliloquy about the torment of being in love with a destructive man. Although he is in jail for murder, she dreams of his returning home, knowing that trouble will follow. Anderson's lyric is both stark and lyrical, and Weill's haunting music is like a cry of pain and anguish. Weill's widow Lotte Lenya made a superb recording of "Trouble Man," and in the Off-Broadway revue *Berlin to Broadway With Kurt Weill* (1972), the song was sung by Judy Lander.

"The Trouble With Women" is a dandy barbershop quartet number from *One Touch of Venus* (1943) that actually takes place in a barbershop. Rodney Hatch (Kenny Baker) has been having women problems, being henpecked by his fiancée and chased by the goddess Venus. Three customers at his barbershop (John Boles, Teddy Hart and Harry Clark) join him in this comic lament about the inconsistency of the female sex, concluding that the true trouble with women is men. Kurt Weill composed the pleasing music, and Ogden Nash wrote the nimble lyric.

"Try Me" is the musical plea of the hyperactive errand boy Arpad (Ralph Williams) in *She Loves Me* (1963) by Jerry Bock (music) and Sheldon Harnick (lyric). The young Arpad hopes to convince his boss to make him a full-fledged clerk at Maraczek's Parfumerie by acting out a furiously gracious encounter with an imaginary customer.

"Try to Forget" is a tearful ballad of farewell from *The Cat and the Fiddle* (1931) by Jerome Kern (music) and Otto Harbach (lyric). It was sung by the American Shirley Sheridan (Bettina Hall), who is in Brussells with her brother Alec (Eddie Foy, Jr.) and her sister-in-law Angie (Doris Carson).

"Try to Remember" is the signature song for the long-running *The Fantasticks* (1960) and one of the musical theatre's most endearing ballads. The narrator El Gallo (Jerry Orbach) opens and closes the little musical with this poignant song that asks the members of the audience to recall their youth and innocence so that the events of the play can be seen in the proper light. Tom Jones wrote the graceful lyric that uses flowery but appropriate imagery, soft alliteration and soothing internal rhymes. Harvey Schmidt's music is warm and evocative, with a subtle key change before the last verse to give it a satisfying finality. The song was originally written as a solo for El Gallo; it was musical arranger Julian Stein who suggested that members of the cast sing the echoing "follow, follow, follow" that gives the ballad a uniquely hypnotic flavor. Roger Williams, Harry Belafonte, the Brothers Four and Gladys Knight and the Pips are among the many who recorded the song, but the most popular was Ed Ames's single in 1965 that helped make the musical known outside of New York.

"Tschaikowsky" is the famous specialty number that made Danny Kaye a Broadway star. The comic list song was written by Kurt Weill (music) and Ira Gershwin (lyric) for the "Circus Dream" sequence in *Lady in the Dark* (1941). In the midst of the Big Top activities, the ringmaster (Kaye) steps forward, announces that he loves Russian music, and proceeds to sing this tongue-twisting song that mentions forty-nine actual Russian composers in thirty-nine seconds. (One of the names sung was Dukelski, a friend of Gershwin's more commonly known for his popular music written under the name Vernon Duke.) Kaye made a successful recording of the song and sang it on request for the rest of his life.

"Tulip Time in Sing Sing" is a wry comic number from *Sitting Pretty* (1924) that stopped the show each evening with its pious, tearful salute to prison as if it were an old college alma mater. Jewel thief Uncle Jo (Frank McIntyre) and his nephew Horace (Dwight Frye) sang the tongue-in-cheek number by Jerome Kern (music) and P.G. Wodehouse (lyric). The song is actually a more refined version of "Put Me in My Little Cell," which was the first lyric Wodehouse ever wrote. "Tulip Time in Sing Sing," which is sometimes listed as "Dear Old-Fashioned Prison of Mine," was recorded by Merwin Goldsmith in a restored version by John McGlinn in 1989.

"Turn Back, O Man" is a sultry revival number from the biblical *Godspell* (1971) by Stephen Schwartz. Sonia Manzano, as a reformed sinner who hadn't changed her musical style, sang the comic vamp song beseeching the audience to repent and change their wicked ways.

"'Twas Not So Long Ago" is a simple but effective number that composer Jerome Kern went so far as to label a "folk song." It was suggested by an old Viennese song and Oscar Hammerstein wrote a straightforward lyric for it that eschewed the ornate. The number was used as a kind of leitmotif throughout *Sweet Adeline* (1929), where Helen Morgan, as saloon singer Addie Schmidt, sang it at three different points in the show, and it was reprised by the chorus at the finale.

"Twenty Million People" is the funny and informative opening number from *My Favorite Year* (1992), the musical about the early days of television by Stephen Flaherty (music) and Lynn Ahrens (lyric). Young comedy writer Benjy Stone (Evan Pappas) and the ensemble sing of the glory and anxieties of putting on a live TV show each week before millions of viewers. The enjoyable number is interrupted with brief scenes introducing all the major characters at the studio and climaxes with the beginning of yet another weekly edition of the comedy show.

"Twenty-Four Hours of Lovin' " is a rousing gospel number sung by the housekeeper Jewel (Delores Hall) in *The Best Little Whorehouse in Texas* (1978) about what she plans to do on her day off. Carol Hall wrote the vibrant music and lyric, and the "girls" at the bordello joined Jewel in the song.

"Twilight in Barakeesh" is the dreamy Victor Herbert standard from *Algeria* (1908) with a lyric by Glen MacDonough. Ida Brooks Hunt, as the Sultana Zoradie, sang the atmospheric song of reflection, which enjoyed a popularity far beyond the show's short run.

"Twin Soliloquies (Wonder How I'd Feel)" is a breathtaking duet for Nellie Forbush (Mary Martin) and Emile de Becque (Ezio Pinza) in the first scene of *South Pacific* (1949); yet it is not a true duet since the two characters never sing together in the number. Richard Rodgers (music) and Oscar Hammerstein (lyric) knew that pairing the belter Martin with the opera basso Pinza would be disconcerting to an audience used to the traditional soprano-baritone combination, so the characters sing their private thoughts as alternating soliloquies. The number is unified lyrically by Hammerstein's rhymes matching in each other's sections, thereby having each character, in a way, complete the other's thought. Also unusual about the song is how the music climaxes in the orchestra rather than on the stage; the two singers are silent, gazing at each other, when in operatic fashion they should be singing their high notes together. Martin and Pinza do sing together much later in the show when the authors felt that the audience had accepted the couple emotionally and musically.

"Two by Two," the title song from the 1970 musical by Richard Rodgers (music) and Martin Charnin (lyric), is not about wedding couples marching down the aisle but about pairs of animals entering Noah's Ark. Danny Kaye, as Noah, and his biblical family sang the lively list song that encouraged various species to procreate. Both the melody and the rhythm of "Two by Two" are uncomfortably similar to the earlier Jerry Herman song "Elegance" from *Hello, Dolly!* (1964), which, in turn, is rumored to have been written by Bob Merrill.

"Two Ladies" is a farcical trio performed at the Kit Kat Klub in *Cabaret* (1966) by the Master of Ceremonies (Joel Grey) and two chorus girls (Mary Ehara and Rita O'Connor). John Kander wrote the delightful honky-tonk music, and Fred Ebb provided the shrewd lyric that celebrates the sexual benefits of a ménage à trois.

"Two Ladies in de Shade of de Banana Tree" is the calypsolike rhythm song from *House of Flowers* (1954) by Harold Arlen (music) and Truman Capote (lyric). In Port-au-Prince, Haiti, two "flowers" from the local brothel, Pansy (Ada Moore) and Tulip (Enid Mosier), sing about how delectable they can be. Arlen's swinging music uses variations of only two notes sustained over eight measures, yet, instead of getting monotonous, the song grows in intensity.

"Two Little Babes in the Wood," one of Cole Porter's early efforts, was written for the *Greenwich Village Follies* (1924) but dropped before opening. The novelty number was later interpolated into *Paris* (1928), where Irene Bordoni sang it and soon recorded it, but the song was not published and the recording was never released. The song was not rediscovered until 1982, when it turned up in a Warner Brothers warehouse in Secaucus, New Jersey.

"Two Little Babes in the Wood" is a sly narrative about two orphans who are abandoned in a forest by a wicked uncle, only to be found by a wealthy New Yorker who takes them to the big city, where they discover gin and fast cars and become the toast of the town.

"**Two Lost Souls**" is a merrily bewitching duet from *Damn Yankees* (1955) by Richard Adler and Jerry Ross. Baseballer Joe Hardy (Stephen Douglass) and temptress Lola (Gwen Verdon) go to a nightclub together to seek refuge from the power of the devilish Mr. Applegate. The number has a lazy, bluesy quality to it, with some delicious arch rhymes in the lyric. Perry Como and Jaye P. Morgan had a successful recording of the number in 1955. In the 1994 Broadway revival the duet was sung by the characters Lola (Bebe Neuwirth) and Applegate (Victor Garber).

"**Typical Self-Made American**" is a Gilbert and Sullivan pastiche number from the Gershwins' *Strike Up the Band* (1930). American chocolate manufacturer Horace J. Fletcher (Dudley Clements) sings how he rose to the top of his business in much the way Sir Joseph Porter boasted in Gilbert and Sullivan's "When I Was a Lad." George Gershwin composed the frolicsome music, and Ira Gershwin wrote the clever lyric.

"**Typically English**" is the wry "I am" song for Evie (Anna Quayle) in the British import *Stop the World -- I Want to Get Off* (1962) by Leslie Bricusse and Anthony Newley. Evie introduces herself as a product of pure English stock, breeding, schools and lifestyle, but she is "Pygmalion bored!" The same melody, with a different lyric and tempo, is used to introduce the other women in the hero's life, all played by Quayle: Anya's "Glorious Russian," Ilse's "Typische Deutsche" and Ginnie's "All-American." All of the songs are hilariously witty, each one building on the ideas presented in the previous ones.

U

"U.N.C.O.U.P.L.E.D." is the prankish spoof of the country-western hit "D.I.V.O.R.C.E." as sung by three train cars who have split from their engines in the British import *Starlight Express* (1987). Dinah (Jane Krakowski), Ashley (Andrea McArdle) and Buffy (Jamie Beth Chandler) sang the playful pastiche song written by Andrew Lloyd Webber (music) and Richard Stilgoe (lyric).

"Under the Bamboo Tree" is the early ragtime classic that was heard in several Broadway shows at the turn of the century. Bob Cole and J. Rosamond Johnson wrote the silly rhythmic number in which a Zulu and a maiden sing of a merry life together in the jungle. The popularity of the song started a trend for other period songs about primitive life in the wild. Marie Cahill heard the song in a vaudeville act and interpolated it into *Sally in Our Alley* (1902), where she sang it for the first of many times throughout her career. It was also heard in *Alphonse and Gaston* (1902), *Zig-Zag Alley* (1903) and *Nancy Brown* (1903), where Cahill sang it again. Songwriters Cole and Johnson, the story goes, were looking for a number for their vaudeville act and considered singing the spiritual favorite "Nobody Knows de Trouble I See." Instead they wrote the new lyric, inverted the melody from the spiritual, and came up with the new song. "Under the Bamboo Tree" was a highlight of the 1944 film musical *Meet Me in St. Louis*, and the number was retained for the 1989 Broadway version, where it was sung by Donna Kane and Courtney Peldon. The song is also known by its first line: "If You Lak-a Me Like I Lak-a You."

"Unexpected Song" is an enthralling ballad from the British import *Song and Dance* (1985) by Andrew Lloyd Webber (music), Don Black and Richard Maltby, Jr., (lyric). The Englishwoman Emma (Bernadette Peters) comes to New York and falls head over heels in love with a "cowboy" named Joe. She describes her surprise and elation in this lovely song, in which the best kind of love is that which comes when least expected. Betty Buckley and Michael Crawford each made recordings of the ballad.

"The Union League" is a satirical song about "old money" from the unsuccessful *Let 'Em Eat Cake* (1933) by George Gershwin (music) and Ira Gershwin (lyric). In a stuffy Victorian library of an exclusive club, whiskered old gentlemen doze in easy chairs and sing languidly about their ancestry and their philosophy of avoiding action on any issue whatsoever. They claim that Rip Van Winkle is their idol and demonstrate their solidarity by all falling asleep at the end of the song. Because of the short run of *Let 'Em Eat Cake*, "The Union League" was not published until 1959 (and then it was only the lyric) and not recorded until 1987, when the Brooklyn Academy of Music recorded virtually the entire score for the first time.

"Unlikely Lovers" is a heartbreaking quartet from *Falsettoland* (1990) about the closeness of friends and lovers. As Whizzer (Stephen Bogardus) lies in the hospital dying of AIDS, he and his companion Marvin (Michael Rupert) quarrel, then marvel at how they ever became lovers. Their friends Cordelia (Janet Metz) and Dr. Charlotte (Heather MacRae), the "lesbians from next door," join them, and all four reflect on themselves as lovers and friends. William Finn wrote the delicate music and the poignant lyric.

"Unworthy of Your Love" is a disturbing duet from the controversial *Assassins* (1991) in which Stephen Sondheim pastiches the pop songs of the 1970s. In a basement rec room of his parents' house, John Hinckley (Greg Germann) and Lynette "Squeaky" Fromme (Annie Golden) sing about their love for someone so great they will kill a president to demonstrate that love. Hinckley expresses his infatuation with movie actress Jodi Foster and Fromme hers for murderer Charles Manson. Sondheim uses a simple guitar accompaniment for the gentle folklike music and a lyric that is chillingly sincere.

"Up, Up in My Aeroplane," one of the first theatre songs written about air travel, was a dazzling production number in the Follies *of 1909*. Lillian Lorraine sang the Gus Edwards (music) and Edward Madden (lyric) song as she rode in a little airplane that actually went out and circled over the heads of the audience.

"Use Your Imagination" is one of Cole Porter's most charming ballads, though it never became a standard. The song was written for *Out of This World* (1950), where it was sung by the messenger god Mercury (William Redfield), who, with Priscilla Gillette, entreated the audience to only imagine and their dreams will come true. Jimmy McPartland and his combo made a moderately popular recording of the song.

"The Usher From the Mezzanine" is a starry-eyed song for the Hollywood hopeful Hope Springfield (Carol Burnett) in *Fade Out -- Fade In* (1964) by Jule Styne (music) and Betty Comden and Adolph Green (lyric). Hope has been an usherette at a movie palace, but now she's been signed to be in a film and rejoices in the realization that she'll move from the mezzanine to the silver screen itself.

V

"The Varsity Drag" is a frenzied song from *Good News!* (1927) by B.G. DeSylva and Lew Brown (lyric) and Ray Henderson (music) that, like their earlier "Black Bottom," started a dance craze of sorts. At Tait College, the students neglect their studies to do the latest dance step. Choreographer Bobby Connolly devised the footwork that, according to the song's lyric, required one to stay down on the heels while keeping up on the toes. The comic flapper Flo (Zelma O'Neal) led the college students Ruth Mayon, Don Tomkins and Wally Coyle in singing and dancing the infectious number.

"Very, Very, Very" is an acerbic comic number from *One Touch of Venus* (1943) by Kurt Weill (music) and Ogden Nash (lyric). Paula Lawrence, as the wisecracking Molly Grant, sang this song about the very, very, very rich who marry well, live well and don't have to pay their bills. Humorist Nash managed to carry over his prankish light verse style to songwriting with sparkling success.

"Violets and Silverbells" is a loving wedding song from the Civil War musical *Shenandoah* (1975) by Gary Geld (music) and Peter Udell (lyric). At the marriage ceremony, Jenny (Penelope Milford) and Sam (Gordon Halliday) join the Reverend Byrd (Charles Welch) in leading the ensemble in this tender song filled with rustic imagery.

W

"The Wages of Sin" is an ingenious pastiche of a Victorian morality song from the music-hall show *The Mystery of Edwin Drood* (1985) by Rupert Holmes. The Princess Puffer (Cleo Laine), who runs a London opium den, cautions the audience about the evils of the world, both in the gutter and in high society. Then, in true music-hall fashion, she entreats the audience to sing along with the last line of each refrain.

"Wagon Wheels" is a western ditty that was featured in the *Ziegfeld Follies* (1934), where it was sung by Everett Marshall in blackface. The melancholy lyric was written by Billy Hill, and Peter De Rose composed the melody which was based on a 1922 song called "Goin' Home," that itself was taken from the largo of Dvořák's "From the New World" symphony. Paul Robeson and Frank Luther were among those who recorded the song, and there were successful orchestral recordings by George Olson, Spade Cooley, Sy Oliver and Tommy Dorsey.

"Wait 'Til We're Sixty-Five" is an amusing character number from *On a Clear Day You Can See Forever* (1965) by Alan Jay Lerner (lyric) and Burton Lane (music). Warren (William Daniels) explains to his fiancée Daisy (Barbara Harris) about all the medical benefits and retirement compensation his new job will provide them in the future. Lane's cheery music and Lerner's unromantic lyric make the song disturbingly funny.

"Wait Till the Cows Come Home" is the bucolic song favorite that was the hit of *Jack o' Lantern* (1917) by Ivan Caryll (music) and Anne Caldwell (lyric). Helen Falconer and Douglas Stevenson sang the number, about a milkmaid who makes a romantically eager city slicker wait for her while she tends to her chores. The number is also known as "Won't You Wait Till the Cows Come Home?"

"Wait Till You See Her" is a sweeping love song in waltz time that Richard Rodgers (music) and Lorenz Hart (lyric) wrote for *By Jupiter* (1942). It was sung by Ronald Graham, as the Greek hero Theseus, and the ensemble and was arguably the finest moment in the show. But the number was cut one month after the opening in order to tighten up the script, and the song might have fallen into obscurity had not Mabel Mercer sung it for years in her act and eventually made it popular.

"Waitin' for My Dearie" is the lilting "I am" song for Fiona MacLaren, the Scottish lassie, in *Brigadoon* (1947). Marion Bell, a former opera singer, and the girls of the village of Brigadoon sang the dreamy Alan Jay Lerner (lyric) and Frederick Loewe (music) song about waiting for the right love to come along rather than just waiting for marriage.

"Waitin' for the Evening Train" is a pleasantly old-fashioned number from the unsuccessful *Jennie* (1963) by Howard Dietz (lyric) and Arthur Schwartz (music) in their last Broadway show. The actress Jennie Malone (Mary Martin) and her husband-manager James O'Connor (George Wallace) sing this catchy song early in the show, capturing the turn-of-the-century flavor that is the musical's setting.

"Waitin' for the Light to Shine" is a poignant character song from *Big River* (1985), the *Huckleberry Finn* musical by country-music composer Roger Miller. Huck (Daniel H. Jenkins) sings the reflective number as he wonders what to expect from life. Near the end of the musical, Huck and the chorus sing a rousing gospel version of the song when he decides to set the slave Jim free and damn the consequences.

"Waiting for Life" is the enthralling "I am" song for Ti Moune (La Chanze), an orphan blessed by the gods, in the musical fable *Once on This Island* (1990). Stephen Flaherty (music) and Lynn Ahrens (lyric) wrote the thrilling number in which Ti Moune asks the gods to bring adventure and love into her life.

"Waiting for the Girls Upstairs" is an absorbing musical scene from *Follies* (1971) that displays the past and the present in a remarkable blend of dialogue and song. The former *Follies* girls Sally (Dorothy Collins) and Phyllis (Alexis Smith) and their husbands Buddy (Gene Nelson) and Ben (John McMartin) recall the old days when they were dating and the boys used to pick up the girls backstage after a performance. Their recollections are bright and cheery at first, then the younger versions of themselves enter and act out what it was really like, and the naive optimism of the youngsters depresses the present characters. They conclude the song with a more sour and painful subtext. Stephen Sondheim wrote the provocative music and lyric for the pure music theatre sequence.

"Walk Him Up the Stairs" is the scintillating revival hymn for the funeral service that opens and concludes *Purlie* (1970) by Gary Geld (music) and Peter Udell (lyric). The black congregation members of the Big Bethel Church in rural Georgia, led by soloist Linda Hopkins, sing this gospel number at the funeral of white plantation owner Cap'n Cotchipee, but the solemn occasion soon erupts into a jubilant celebration of the dying of the old order. At the end of the musical, preacher Purlie (Cleavon Little) leads the congregation in a reprise of the number.

"Walking Away Whistling" is a hauntingly beautiful ballad from the unsuccessful *Greenwillow* (1960) by Frank Loesser. Dorrie (Ellen McCown) loves Gideon Briggs (Anthony Perkins), who is doomed to wander, and she cannot do anything to keep him from "walking away whistling." Loesser's music has a sad but magnetic quality to it, and his lyric is the voice of a woman wistful but resigned.

"Walking Happy" is the jaunty title song from the 1966 musical by James Van Heusen (music) and Sammy Cahn (lyric). Bootmaker Will Mossop (Norman Wisdom) and his wife Maggie (Louise Troy) lead the ensemble in this spirited song and dance about how one's inner feelings are reflected in the way you walk. The authors had written the number seven years earlier for a Fred Astaire film that was never made, and the song was the only one from *Walking Happy* to enjoy any popularity.

"Wand'rin' Star" is the recurring theme song in *Paint Your Wagon* (1951), the musical by Alan Jay Lerner (lyric) and Frederick Loewe (music) about gold prospecting in California. Crusty old Ben Rumson (James Barton) and the other miners sing the beguiling folk song about how they are forced to keep moving to find their dream. At the end of the musical, Ben reprises part of the song on his deathbed. Lee Marvin's growly recording of the song sold over a million copies in 1970.

"Waning Honeymoon" is a wistful song that Harriet Burr sang in *The Time, the Place and the Girl* (1907) and it was very popular in its day. Joe Howard wrote the lovely music, and Will M. Hough and Frank R. Adams provided the touching lyric.

"Wanting You" is a sweeping duet from the operetta *The New Moon* (1928), generally considered the last great example of the genre that lost favor once the Depression hit. The New Orleans aristocrat Marianne (Evelyn Herbert) and the nobleman-turned-revolutionary Robert Misson (Robert Halliday) admit that they love one another and sing this song of longing. Sigmund Romberg composed the graceful music, and Oscar Hammerstein wrote the demonstrative lyric.

"Warm All Over" is an entrancing ballad from Frank Loesser's operatic *The Most Happy Fella* (1956) about the warmth that comes with love. Jo Sullivan, as Rosabella, introduced the song, and Barbra Streisand is among the many who have recorded it over the years.

"Watching the Big Parade Go By" is a gentle but stimulating march sung by a woman who feels honored and thrilled to be a spectator. David Shire (music) and Richard Maltby, Jr., (lyric) wrote the tuneful number, and it was sung by Margery Cohen in the Off-Broadway revue *Starting Here, Starting Now* (1977).

"Way Down Yonder in New Orleans" is the American song favorite by Turner Layton (music) and Henry Creamer (lyric) that has retained its recognition over the years. It was written for *Strut Miss Lizzie* (1922), but was cut before opening. The song was interpolated into *Spice of 1922*, where Layton and Creamer sang it, and it immediately caught on. The number's popularity can also be attributed to Blossom Seeley, who recorded it and sang it often in vaudeville. In 1960 it was a hit all over again for Freddy Cannon whose recording made the Top Ten.

"Way Out West (On West End Avenue)" is Rodgers and Hart's mock-cowboy song that celebrates life in the city, a sort of hillbilly "Manhattan." The dandy song was written for *Babes in Arms* (1937), where it was sung by Wynn Murray, Alex Courtney, Clifton Darling, James Gillis and Robert Rounseville. Richard Rodgers came up with a silly cowpoke melody, and Lorenz Hart's witty lyric has all sorts of fun with puns and urban references.

"We Beseech Thee" is a spirited revival-like number from the long-running Off-Broadway musical *Godspell* (1971). Jeffrey Mylett led the ensemble in the bouncy song that asked Jesus to hear their prayers. Stephen Schwartz wrote the invigorating music and, with the help of the original gospel authors, the fervent lyric.

"We Could Be Close" is a prankish duet from *Sugar* (1972) by Jule Styne (music) and Bob Merrill (lyric) that gets a lot of mileage out of a farcical situation. Jerry (Robert Morse), disguised as a female musician in order to escape from the mob, finds himself on the night train to Miami sharing a sleeping berth with the beautiful Sugar Kane (Elaine Joyce). The double entendres fly fast and furiously as the two sing a song of girlish friendship.

"We Dance" is the electric opening number of the Caribbean musical *Once on This Island* (1990) by Stephen Flaherty (music) and Lynn Ahrens (lyric). As they wait out a violent tropical storm, the peasants re-enact a story of love that occurred "once on this island."

"We Kiss" is a swinging 1940s pastiche from the Off-Broadway musical *Hello Again* (1994) by Michael John LaChiusa. A World War Two-era Soldier (David A. White) and a Nurse (Judy Blazer) sing a big band number with backup help from the ensemble.

"We Kiss in a Shadow" is the clandestine duet for Tuptim (Doretta Morrow) and Lun Tha (Larry Douglas) in *The King and I* (1951). The Richard Rodgers (music) and Oscar Hammerstein (lyric) hymnlike number was staged with the lovers on opposite sides of the stage, kneeling as if in prayer, looking not at each other but out to the audience. Their love must remain a secret from the King, and this song is the way in which they communicate with each other. Martin Vidnovic sang the song in the Broadway revue *A Grand Night for Singing* (1993).

"We Make a Beautiful Pair" is a country-flavored duet from the Civil War musical *Shenandoah* (1975) by Gary Geld (music) and Peter Udell (lyric). Anne (Donna Theodore) and Jenny (Penelope Milford) sing the infectious number about the two men they are in love with.

"We Need a Little Christmas" is the durable holiday song from Jerry Herman's *Mame* (1966), one of the few theatre songs to become a seasonal standard. In the show it is sung by Mame Dennis (Angela Lansbury), her young nephew Patrick (Frankie Michaels), Agnes Gooch (Jane Connell) and Ito (Sab Shimono) as they decide to celebrate Christmas early because the Depression has got them all depressed. Later in the scene the wealthy Beauregard (Charles Braswell) eases their plight and joins them in a reprise of the song.

"We Open in Venice" is the inviting opening number of the musical within the musical *Kiss Me, Kate* (1948). The Cole Porter ditty was sung by Alfred Drake, Patricia Morison, Lisa Kirk and Harold Lang as a quartet of strolling players on the tour circuit of northern Italy.

"A Weekend in the Country" is one of the Stephen Sondheim songs that devotees cite to disprove the complaint that his music is not hummable. This ensemble number from *A Little Night Music* (1973) is a miniopera in which various characters plan and prepare a visit to a country estate. The complex musical scene closes the first act of the musical, and because of its contagious melody and many refrains, audiences actually hum it as they head for the lobby for intermission.

"Welcome Home" is a gentle and engaging aria from *Fanny* (1954) that was sung by the opera favorite Ezio Pinza. Harold Rome wrote the delicate song in which Cesar (Pinza) welcomes back his son Marius (William Tabbert) after many years absence, by singing of all sorts of objects that seem to come to life and say "welcome home."

"Welcome to Brooklyn" is an enjoyable chorus number from *My Favorite Year* (1992), the musical about the early years of TV by Stephen Flaherty (music) and Lynn Ahrens (lyric). When comedy writer Benjy Stone (Evan Pappas) brings the movie star Alan Swann (Tim Curry) to his Brooklyn home for dinner, the celebrity is greeted by Benjy's mother (Lainie Kazan) and stepfather (Thomas Ikeda) and then is swamped by Uncle Morty (David Lipman), Aunt Sadie (Mary Stout) in her wedding dress and all the neighbors.

"Welcome to Holiday Inn" is a tangy character song for the flaky Gittel Mosca (Michele Lee) in *Seesaw* (1973). When out-of-town lawyer Jerry Ryan (Ken Howard) stays at her apartment overnight, Gittel sings this comic list song slyly offering all sorts of special amenities. Cy Coleman composed the bossa nova music, and Dorothy Fields wrote the sparkling lyric.

"Welcome to Kanagawa" is a decadent comic number from *Pacific Overtures* (1976) by Stephen Sondheim. With the arrival of Americans on the shores of Japan, a Madam (Ernest Harada as a woman in Kabuki dress) is forced to recruit farm girls to keep her brothel well stocked. In this song she tries to teach the novice prostitutes how to welcome the foreigners and how to please them with various sexual techniques. The musical number is interrupted by quotations of haiku poetry that wryly comment on the Madam's instructions.

"Welcome to the Theatre" is a mordant tribute to the stage, a sort of caustic version of "There's No Business Like Show Business." Charles Strouse wrote the foreboding music, Lee Adams provided the stinging lyric, and it was sung by the veteran actress Margo Channing (Lauren Bacall) as the first-act finale in *Applause* (1970). More than any other number in the show, "Welcome to the Theatre" captured the acerbic quality of the film *All About Eve* that was the basis for the musical.

"Well, Did You Evah!" is the song that introduced Betty Grable to Broadway, but she didn't stay long; when the movie scouts saw her perform it in *DuBarry Was a Lady* (1939), she was whisked off to Hollywood. The Cole Porter song is a comic duet (Grable sang it with Charles Walters) that lists a series of disasters, then drolly comments on them in a very upper-class way.

"We'll Go Away Together" is a surging romantic duet from the operatic *Street Scene* (1947) by Kurt Weill (music) and Langston Hughes (lyric). Rose (Anne Jeffreys) and Sam (Brian Sullivan) dream of escaping from their suffocating New York City neighborhood and making a better life together.

"A Well Known Fact" is a debonair soft-shoe song and dance from *I Do! I Do!* (1966) in which the pompous Michael (Robert Preston) explains to his wife (Mary Martin) that men get more attractive with age, while women, on the other hand, "go to pot." Tom Jones wrote the puffed-up lyric, and Harvey Schmidt composed the jaunty music.

"We'll Take a Glass Together" is an exhilarating drinking song from *Grand Hotel* (1989) sung by the Baron (David Carroll) and the bookkeeper Otto (Michael Jeter), who break into a raucous Charleston that stopped the show each night. Robert Wright and George Forrest wrote the spirited music and tangy lyric.

"Wells Fargo Wagon" is a tuneful chorus number from Meredith Willson's *The Music Man* (1957) that musically captures the small-town enthusiasm that makes the show so memorable. When the delivery wagon of the Wells Fargo Company is seen approaching River City, all the citizens come out to welcome it and sing of all the wondrous things it brings. For Winthrop (Eddie Hodges) and the other boys in the town, it brings the musical instruments and band uniforms they've anxiously been waiting for.

"We're Alive" is the dynamic opening number in *Juno* (1959) that captured all the bitterness and passion of Sean O'Casey's drama *Juno and the Paycock* (1924), on which the operatic musical was based. The people of Dublin sing optimistically of their belief in survival despite streets "runnin' red" with Irish blood. Then, in the midst of the number, a Republican Army soldier is tracked down and shot by the British. Marc Blitzstein wrote the potent music and lyric, and Agnes de Mille choreographed the stunning number.

"We're Gonna Be All Right" is a cynical duet sung by a married couple (Stuart Damon and Julienne Marie) whose marriage is on the rocky side in *Do I Hear a Waltz?* (1965). Richard Rodgers composed the lively melody, and Stephen Sondheim wrote the acerbic lyric. In fact, it was a bit too acerbic for

Rodgers' tastes (particularly a reference to the husband's occasional homosexuality), and he insisted on a tamer lyric. This from the man who wrote with Lorenz Hart for twenty-four years?

"We're Gonna Have a Good Time" is the contagious gospel number that concludes *Your Arms Too Short to Box With God* (1976), the retelling of the Gospel of St. Matthew as presented at a black revival meeting. Micki Grant wrote the vibrant song, and it was sung by Clinton Derricks-Carroll and the company.

"We're on Our Way to France" is the patriotic song that served as the finale of the 1918 all-soldier revue *Yip, Yip, Yaphank* by Irving Berlin. The entire ensemble, made up of actual military personnel (including Berlin himself), sang the song as they marched off the stage, down the aisles and out the front of the theatre. On the last performance of the benefit show, the cast marched out as usual but continued down the street to the troop ship that was to take them to the French battlefield.

"Were Thine That Special Face" is Petruchio's wooing song in the musical version of *The Taming of the Shrew* being staged in Cole Porter's *Kiss Me, Kate* (1948); it is also actor Fred Graham's attempt to woo back his former wife Lillie. Alfred Drake introduced the operatic ballad that repeatedly uses the archaic "thine" to give the song a pseudo-Elizabethan flavor. The title phrase comes from Shakespeare's text, but it is from a speech by Bianca, not Petruchio.

"What a Blessing (To Know There's a Devil)" is a sweetly sly musical soliloquy that Frank Loesser wrote for the unsuccessful *Greenwillow* (1960). The merry Reverend Birdsong (Cecil Kellaway) confesses in pleasing waltz form that there is a little bit of the devil in each of us; yet he admits that he's thankful for the fact, it being a relief to know someone else is responsible for our faults.

"What a Night This Is Going to Be" is an exciting quartet from the Sherlock Holmes musical *Baker Street* (1965) by Marian Grudeff and Raymond Jessell. Holmes (Fritz Weaver) has enlisted the aid of the American actress Irene Adler (Inga Swenson) in his plan to apprehend Dr. Moriarty. As they get into their disguises, Holmes and Dr. Watson (Peter Sallis) at 221B Baker Street and Irene and her maid (Virginia Vestoff) in her flat, they all sing with anticipation about the excitement that awaits them that evening.

"What Am I Doin'?" is a frenzied comic song sung by a man going out of his mind with love. David Shire (music) and Richard Maltby, Jr., (lyric) wrote it for a musical never produced but it was later heard in the Off-Broadway revue *Closer Than Ever* (1989), where it was sung by Brent Barrett.

"What Can You Do With a Man?" is one of Rodgers and Hart's most delightful comic duets. It was sung by the henpecked slave Dromio (Teddy Hart) and his forceful wife Luce (Wynn Murray) in *The Boys From Syracuse* (1938). Lorenz Hart's lyric is filled with fun anachronisms, and Richard Rodgers' music manages to be funny all on its own.

"What Can You Say in a Love Song?" is a comic song that questions the possibility of saying anything new in a romantic song. The number was written by Harold Arlen (music) and Ira Gershwin and E.Y. Harburg (lyric) for the revue *Life Begins at 8:40* (1934), where it was sung by Josephine Huston, Bartlett Simmons and the ensemble. Like the Gershwins' "Blah, Blah, Blah," this song substitutes meaningless sounds for tender romantic words, arguing that there isn't anything you can say that hasn't been said before. Joey Nash recorded the number in 1934.

"What Causes That?" is a sparkling Gershwin brothers song that only recently has been getting the attention it deserves. It was written for the short-lived *Treasure Girl* (1928), where Clifton Webb and Mary Hay sang the comic number by George Gershwin (music) and Ira Gershwin (lyric) as a quasi-romantic duet. He lists all the dire actions he's been considering (e.g., suicide by jumping off the Brooklyn Bridge), and she adds to his list before he comes to the conclusion that loving her is the reason for his odd behavior. After *Treasure Girl* flopped, the song was neither published nor recorded and seemed to disappear. Michael Feinstein, who helped Ira Gershwin catalogue his archives during his last years, found the song and recorded it in 1987. "What Causes That?" was put in the score for the "new Gershwin musical" *Crazy for You* (1992), where it was performed by hoofer Bobby Child (Harry Groener) and impresario Bela Zangler (Bruce Adler) as a duet sung by two suicidal males who realize that "loving her is what causes that." In 1992 the song was published for the first time.

"What Chance Have I?" is a witty character song from Irving Berlin's *Louisiana Purchase* (1940). Victor Moore, as the investigating Senator Oliver Loganberry, sang this fun list song in which he outlined the fate of the world's great lovers and questioned what his odds at success would be. Michael Feinstein revived interest in the song with his 1987 recording of it.

"What Did I Ever See in Him?" is a feisty duet for two women disillusioned by love in *Bye Bye Birdie* (1960). The eruptive Charles Strouse (music) and Lee Adams (lyric) song was sung by Chita Rivera, as the adult Rose Grant furious at her longtime fiancé Albert, and Susan Watson, as the teenager Kim McAfee who has broken up with her steady Hugo.

"What Did I Have That I Don't Have?" is an unusual torch song from *On a Clear Day You Can See Forever* (1965) by Alan Jay Lerner (lyric) and Burton Lane (music). Daisy Gamble (Barbara Harris) discovers that psychiatrist Mark Bruckner is not in love with her but with Melinda, an eighteenth-century woman who has been reincarnated as Daisy. Aside from its bizarre premise, the song is also unique in the way Lerner uses harsh-sounding one-syllable words with Lane's very flowing melody.

"What Do the Simple Folk Do?" is a bittersweet duet for King Arthur (Richard Burton) and Queen Guenevere (Julie Andrews) in *Camelot* (1960) by Alan Jay Lerner (lyric) and Frederick Loewe (music). The royal marriage is collapsing, but the married couple find a moment of comfort as they imagine what the common people do to brighten their lives. Arthur reports that they whistle, sing and dance (and the royals attempt each of these with little satisfaction), but concludes that mostly they sit around and try to guess what royalty do.

"What Does He Want of Me?" is a lovely, reflective ballad from *Man of La Mancha* (1965) by Mitch Leigh (music) and Joe Darion (lyric). The sluttish Aldonza (Joan Diener) is confused by Don Quixote's gracious treatment of her and in her bewilderment sings this tender song. Although the number was included in the original New York and London productions, it is not in the script versions of the musical and often is omitted in revivals. The song has also been recorded as "What Do You Want of Me?"

"What Good Would the Moon Be?" is a touching ballad that approaches an opera aria from *Street Scene* (1947) by Kurt Weill (music) and Langston Hughes (lyric). Rose Maurrant (Anne Jeffreys) has been propositioned by the slick Mr. Easter (Don Saxon) to set her up as his mistress but she questions whether a life of luxury without love is really for her. Freddy Martin's Orchestra (vocal by Murray Arnold) made a successful recording of the song.

"What I Did for Love" is the only hit to come out of the record-breaking *A Chorus Line* (1975) by Marvin Hamlisch (music) and Edward Kleban (lyric). The ballad was sung by Diane (Priscilla Lopez) and the auditioning dancers in answer to the question "What would you do if you couldn't dance anymore?" The consensus of the chorus-line hopefuls was that dance, like love, is something that you always carry with you and that can never be regretted. Jack Jones had a successful recording of the ballad.

"What Is a Man?" is a character song for the wealthy, jaded Vera Simpson in *Pal Joey* (1940) by Richard Rodgers (music) and Lorenz Hart (lyric). The question in the title is one of idle curiosity since Vera picks up and discards men on a regular basis. Vivienne Segal introduced the acerbic number, which originally had a different lyric with the title "Love Is My Friend." Soon after the show opened, Hart changed the lyric and the title, arguing that Vera and love are not friends.

"What Is a Woman?" is a quiet and reflective little ballad from *I Do! I Do!* (1966) by Tom Jones (lyric) and Harvey Schmidt (music). Agnes (Mary Martin) returns from the wedding of her only daughter and starts to question her role in life now that she seems to be no longer needed. Robert Goulet was among those who recorded the song from the male point of view.

"What Is the Stars?" is a robust comic duet from *Juno* (1959), Marc Blitzstein's operatic version of Sean O'Casey's *Juno and the Paycock* (1924). Braggart "Captain" Jack Boyle (Melvyn Douglas) and his crony Joxer (Jack MacGowran) sing the raucous tribute to a sailor's life far away from all women, though neither of them has ever been to sea.

"What Is There to Say?" is a slick duet in which the lovers are more resigned to love than ardently committed to it. Vernon Duke composed the appealing music, and E.Y. Harburg wrote the piquant lyric that concludes with the lovers in "deadlock," so they decide to face wedlock. Jane Frohman and Everett Marshall sang the witty duet in the *Ziegfeld Follies of 1934*, and the song was recorded by the orchestras of Artie Shaw, Jack Jenny, Bud Freeman and Bobby Hackett.

"What Is This Thing Called Love?" is one of Cole Porter's most straightforward love songs, with a conventional lyric but a unique melody, especially in the refrain, where it shifts from major to minor chords at the least likely of places. Porter once said that he got the melody from a native dance in Marrakesh. The song was sung by Frances Shelley and danced by Tilly Losch in *Wake Up and Dream* (1929), having been introduced earlier that year in the London revue of the same title.

"What Kind of Fool Am I?" is the hit ballad from the British import *Stop the World -- I Want to Get Off* (1962) and one of the most popular songs of the early 1960s. Leslie Bricusse and Anthony Newley wrote the soul-searching song, and Newley sang it as Littlechap, the English Everyman who has loved too many women and finds out too late that the only person he really loved was himself. Among the best-sellers of the oft-recorded song were versions by Newley, Robert Goulet, Sammy Davis, Jr., and, in 1982, Rick Springfield. Like Bricusse and Newley's other hit ballads ("Once in a Lifetime" and "Who Can I Turn To?" in particular), "What Kind of Fool Am I?" starts low and continually climbs throughout the song until it ends in a chilling falsetto range that was a specialty of Newley's, who sang all three songs on stage.

"What Makes Me Love Him?" is a tender ballad from *The Apple Tree* (1966) by Jerry Bock (music) and Sheldon Harnick (lyric) that was sung by Barbara Harris in "The Diary of Adam and Eve" musical playlet. The touching song consists of Eve's listing the less-than-admirable qualities of Adam and trying to rationalize her affection for him. Sarah Brightman recorded the song in 1989.

"What Takes My Fancy" is a show-stopping hoedown number from *Wildcat* (1960), the musical about oil-well drilling by Cy Coleman (music) and Carolyn Leigh (lyric). The scheming Wildcat Jackson (Lucille Ball) and the comic recluse Sookie (Don Tomkins) sang the foot-stomping rouser.

"What Will It Be?" is a tender soliloquy from the operatic *Regina* (1949), Marc Blitzstein's musicalization of Lillian Hellman's *The Little Foxes* (1939). The young Alexandra (Priscilla Gillette), on the verge of womanhood, wonders what love, both emotional and physical, will be like. The song contains one of Blitzstein's most harmonious melodies.

"What Would I Do?" is a penetrating duet from *Falsettoland* (1990) by William Finn. Marvin (Michael Rupert) asks himself what his life would have been like if he'd never met his lover Whizzer (Stephen Bogardus), who has died from AIDS. Then, in a vision of how he was in life, Whizzer enters and echoes Marvin's sentiments, joining him in a moving duet.

"What Would We Do Without You?" is an energetic song and dance pastiche number from *Company* (1970) that the ensemble sang as a vaudeville comic romp complete with hats and canes. Stephen Sondheim wrote the flag-waving, exuberant music and the clever lyric that takes the form of a series of rhetorical questions. The married couples ask how they could survive without their best friend Robert (Dean Jones) and go into a mock kick line rather than search for any real answers. The song was also sung by the cast of the Off-Broadway revue *Putting It Together* (1993).

"What You Don't Know About Women" is a resourceful duet from *City of Angels* (1989) in which two different women have the same complaint about two different men. Gabby (Kay McClelland) sings of her frustration with her husband-writer Stine, who doesn't understand her concern about his wasting his talent. At the same time, in the movie version of Stine's novel, the secretary Oolie (Randy Graff) sings of her frustration with her boss, the private eye Stone, who doesn't understand that her concern for him goes beyond the professional. Cy Coleman composed the 1940s-like music, and

David Zippel wrote the double-edged lyric.

"Whatever Lola Wants (Lola Gets)" is the song that made Gwen Verdon a Broadway star. She sang it in *Damn Yankees* (1955) as the sexy devil's assistant Lola while she tries to seduce baseballer Joe Hardy (Stephen Douglass) in the players' locker room. The siren's song is set to a tango rhythm, and choreographer Bob Fosse staged it as an amusing striptease. Richard Adler and Jerry Ross wrote both the music and lyric. Dinah Shore and Sarah Vaughan each made a best-selling recording of the song.

"What'll I Do?" is one of Irving Berlin's most beloved ballads, a durable favorite that has retained its popularity for over seventy years. Another of Berlin's potent "loss of love" songs, "What'll I Do?" is distinguished by its intricate but subtle internal rhymes and a haunting melody that remains quietly hypnotic as it waltzes along with suspenseful hesitations throughout. Grace Moore and John Steel sang the number, which was interpolated into the 1923 edition of *The Music Box Revue* after opening and the song went on to sell over a million copies of sheet music. Popular recordings have been made over the years by Paul Whiteman, Art Lund, Nat "King" Cole, Frank Sinatra, Judy Holliday, Gisele MacKenzie, Johnny Mathis and others; more recently it has been recorded by Barbara Cook, Linda Ronstadt, Michael Feinstein and Karen Akers.

"What's Goin' On Here?" is a spirited character song from *Paint Your Wagon* (1951), the Alan Jay Lerner (lyric) and Frederick Loewe (music) musical about the California gold rush. Jennifer Rumson (Olga San Juan) and her father Ben (James Barton) move into a mining camp to seek their fortune; but it turns out that Jennifer is the only young girl in the town, and the bewildering behavior of all the men toward her has got the girl perplexed.

"What's New at the Zoo" is a silly sort of 1960s bubblegum song from *Do Re Mi* (1960) that Tilda Mullen (Nancy Dussault) and the "Animal Girls" sing to promote their new pop record. Jule Styne (music) and Betty Comden and Adolph Green (lyric) wrote the snappy number that vocalized the thoughts and comments of animals in a crowded zoo.

"What's the Use?" is a clever quartet from *Candide* (1956) about the flow of money in the criminal world. At a gambling house in Venice, Signora Sofronia (Irra Petina) is a shill for the boss but sings that she never gets to keep the money she supposedly wins. Then the casino owner (William Chapman) complains about how he must pass most of his earnings to the Prefect of Police (Norman Roland), who in turn sings how he must pay off blackmailers to keep from being exposed. Finally, the blackmailer (Robert Mesrobian) sings how he loses all his money playing roulette at the casino. All four conclude the number by asking "What's the Use?" when you have to pass it along. Leonard Bernstein composed the silly, flowery melody, and Richard Wilbur wrote the wry lyric.

"What's the Use of Wond'rin'?" is the delicate ballad from *Carousel* (1945) in which the troubled Julie (Jan Clayton) defends her love for the hard and misunderstood Billy Bigelow. Richard Rodgers' music is both casual and earnest, and Oscar Hammerstein wrote a succinct lyric that captures Julie's New England resolve. Hammerstein always maintained that the song never became as popular as it could have because he ended each refrain with a hard sound ("that," "talk") instead of an open vowel that singers could hold longer. Hit or no hit, the abrupt endings are in character for the piece and make the song distinctive.

"When a Fellow's on the Level With a Girl That's on the Square" is a zesty George M. Cohan song from *The Talk of New York* (1907), a sequel of sorts to his *Forty-Five Minutes From Broadway* (1906), with Victor Moore again playing the wisecracking New Yorker Kid Burns. Moore sang the lively number about his sweetheart Geraldine Wilcox (Emma Littlefield).

"When Did I Fall in Love?" is a clearheaded love ballad in which the singer rationally tries to determine how she got in this state. It was sung in *Fiorello!* (1959) by Thea (Ellen Hanley), who married LaGuardia (Tom Bosley) without love, but as time has passed she feels she is finally in love with him. Jerry Bock wrote the delicate music, and Sheldon Harnick provided the knowing lyric.

"When I First Saw You" is a complex and moving ballad from *Dreamgirls* (1981) by Henry Krieger (music) and Tom Eyen (lyric). The show-business agent Curtis Taylor, Jr., (Ben Harney) sings the song to Deena Jones (Sheryl Lee Ralph), his lover and member of his act the Dreams, when she tells him she wants out of both arrangements.

"When I'm Not Near the Girl I Love (I Love the Girl I'm Near)" is the famous comic song from *Finian's Rainbow* (1947) that the leprechaun Og (David Wayne) sings about his inconsistent behavior toward women. Og, who is losing his magical powers and becoming mortal, is discovering the sexual attraction he has for Sharon and then for Susan. His confusion and joy express themselves in this brilliant character song by Burton Lane (music) and E.Y. Harburg (lyric). Wayne's rendition of the farcical number made him a star, but the song is so perfectly written that even on paper it never fails to amuse. Lane wrote a lively waltz for the number, and Harburg constructed one of the most intricate lyrics ever written for a theatre song. Never more playful than in this number, Harburg twists the words and phrases about in gymnastic fashion to get different meanings at every turn. The lyric also has some memorable arch rhymes and Harburg-invented words that seem right for a leprechaun in love. "When I'm Not Near the Girl I Love" is a comedy classic and, as Stephen Sondheim once stated, the best eleven o'clock number in the American musical theatre.

"When Irish Eyes Are Smiling" is the perennial favorite that was beloved by Irish immigrants (and everyone else) in the years before World War One, and it remains a standard today. Ernest R. Ball wrote the flowing melody, and Chauncey Olcott and George Graff, Jr. provided the sentimental lyric. Olcott sang the number in the musical melodrama *The Isle o' Dreams* (1913), recorded the song and performed it throughout his career. In addition to its many recordings and sheet music sales, the song was a featured favorite on Morton Downey's popular radio show.

"When It's Apple Blossom Time in Normandy" was a popular ballad of domestic joy that Nora Bayes sang in the Weber and Fields burlesque *Roly Poly* (1912). Tom Mellor, Harry Gifford and Huntley Trevor wrote the song, borrowing heavily from Beethoven's Minuet in G, and it was interpolated into the show, where Bayes turned the number into a hit. Early recordings were made by Edna Brown (aka Elsie Baker) with James F. Harrison, and Harry MacDonough with Marguerite Dunlap. Five years later Jerome Kern (music) and P.G. Wodehouse (lyric) spoofed the popular song in *Oh, Boy!* (1917), with their number "Nesting Time in Flatbush."

"When the Boys Come Home" is the opening number from *Bloomer Girl* (1944), a waltzing chorus number sung by the daughters of hoopskirt manufacturer Horace Applegate as they wait for their traveling salesmen husbands to return home. At the end of the show the song is sung by the waiting wives and daughters of Civil War soldiers. Harold Arlen composed the graceful period music, and E.Y. Harburg wrote the telling lyric that develops from a mournful chant to joyous anticipation of how much better life will be when the men return.

"When the Children Are Asleep" is the sweet but silly duet from *Carousel* (1945) where the ambitious Enoch Snow (Eric Mattson) and his fiancée Carrie (Jean Darling) imagine what married life together will be like. The Richard Rodgers (music) and Oscar Hammerstein (lyric) song starts out with pleasant domestic images, then escalates in a hyperbolic manner until the couple owns a fleet of ships and a bevy of kids, both of which come true later in the show. Jason Graae and Victoria Clark sang the duet in the Broadway revue *A*

Grand Night for Singing (1993).

"When the Idle Poor Become the Idle Rich" is a riotous production number from *Finian's Rainbow* (1947) that is also a satirical jab at the double standard of class consciousness. When the impoverished citizens of Rainbow Valley get unlimited credit from the mail-order company Shears and Robust, they order outrageously unnecessary clothes and other items. On delivery day, the members of the ensemble appear dressed in their newfound finery and sing this comic song about high living. Earlier the same crowd satirized the wealthy, but now they have exceeded their own insulting exaggerations. Burton Lane composed the twinkling music that slips into a mock madrigal near the end, E.Y. Harburg wrote the quick-witted lyric that is wickedly stinging at times, Eleanor Goldsmith designed the unique costumes, and Michael Kidd choreographed the antic dance that went with the number.

"When the Kids Get Married" is a playful comic duet from *I Do! I Do!* (1966) in which the middle-aged couple Michael (Robert Preston) and Agnes (Mary Martin) imagine all the fun things they'll do together once the children marry and move out of the house. The number was topped by Preston playing the saxophone and Martin performing on the violin in an amateurish fashion that delighted audiences. Tom Jones wrote the jocular lyric, and Harvey Schmidt composed the hoedown music.

"When the Ships Come Home" is a haunting song of yearning from the Princess Theatre musical *Oh, Lady! Lady!!* (1918) by Jerome Kern (music) and P.G. Wodehouse (lyric). The betrothed Mollie (Vivienne Segal) and the women's chorus sang the gentle song that has an old-fashioned sentimentality to it but avoids being cloying.

"When the Spring Is in the Air" is a lively, upbeat number from the "modern" operetta *Music in the Air* (1932). Jerome Kern wrote the rapturous melody that used repeated notes effectively, Oscar Hammerstein provided the optimistic lyric, and it was sung by the Bavarian heroine Sieglinde (Katherine Carrington).

"When There's No One" is the moody, heartfelt solo for Betty Buckley from the infamous musical flop *Carrie* (1988). The creepy but touching song by Michael Gore (music) and Dean Pitchford (lyric) is the mother's lament when Carrie goes off to the prom.

"When You Meet a Man in Chicago" is a smooth and stylish soft-shoe number from *Sugar* (1972) by Jule Styne (music) and Bob Merrill (lyric). It is the Roaring Twenties and any guy from Chicago is possibly a gangster, or so it seems in this musical farce. The tingling number was sung by Jerry (Robert Morse), Joe (Tony Roberts), Sugar Kane (Elaine Joyce), bandleader Sweet Sue (Sheila Smith) and her all-girl band.

"When Your Lover Says Goodbye" is an amusing if cynical character song from *Coco* (1969) by Alan Jay Lerner (lyric) and Andre Previn (music). The worldly-wise Parisian Louis Greff (George Rose) sings to a downhearted young man that the end of a romance is always a blessing in disguise, for there are no words sweeter than hello except, perhaps, goodbye.

"When You're Away" is a beguiling waltz from the operetta *The Only Girl* (1914) and one of Victor Herbert's most famous love songs. A composer named Ruth Wilson (Wilda Bennett) sings the number after the audience has heard strains of it from the orchestra previously, representing the gradual development of the melody in Ruth's head. Henry Blossom wrote the romantic lyric, but it is Herbert's simple music, which avoids repetition but gradually rises to a higher melodic level, that makes the song so memorable.

"When You're Good to Mama" is the facetious "I am" song for the prison Matron (Mary McCarty) in *Chicago* (1975) by John Kander (music) and Fred Ebb (lyric). In a vaudeville "red hot mama" style, the Matron sings this wry number about how to please her so that Mama will be "good to you." The heavy Kurt Weill-like melody offsets the pseudo-friendly lyric, making it clear that no one messes with the Matron.

"When You're Right, You're Right" is an amusing duet from *Woman of the Year* (1981) by John Kander (music) and Fred Ebb (lyric). Television personality Tess Harding (Lauren Bacall) and cartoonist Sam Craig (Harry Guardino), who start out as adversaries before they end up as lovers, match wits in this entertaining duet.

"Where Am I Going?" is a song of indecision for Charity Hope Valentine (Gwen Verdon) in *Sweet Charity* (1966) by Cy Coleman (music) and Dorothy Fields (lyric). She loves the neurotic Oscar (John McMartin) but is afraid she'll lose him if she tells him the truth about her job as a dance-hall hostess. Her confusion about what path to take results in this appealing ballad. Barbra Streisand made a best-selling recording of the song in the late 1960s.

"Where Did Robinson Crusoe Go (With Friday on Saturday Night)?" is a popular novelty song that Al Jolson introduced in *Robinson Crusoe, Jr.* (1916). George W. Meyer wrote the music, Sam M. Lewis and Joe Young provided the comic lyric, and Jolson, who played Friday in the fantasy section of the show, had a hit recording of the song.

"Where Did the Night Go?" is a lovely ballad from *Wish You Were Here* (1952), the musical about an adult summer camp by Harold Rome. Law student and waiter Chick Miller (Jack Cassidy) and Brooklyn secretary Teddy Stern (Patricia Marand) were joined by the ensemble in singing the dreamy ballad.

"Where Do I Go?" is the delicate ballad that ends the first act of *Hair* (1968), the "tribal love-rock musical" by Galt MacDermot (music) and Gerome Ragni and James Rado (lyric). The soaring musical question was sung on Broadway by Claude (Rado) and the ensemble; in the 1967 Off-Broadway production Claude was played by Walker Daniels. Both Carla Thomas and the Happenings made hit single recordings of the song.

"Where-Has-My-Hubby-Gone? Blues" is a mock torch song from *No, No, Nanette* (1925) by Vincent Youmans (music) and Irving Caesar (lyric). Lucille Early (Josephine Whittell) does not have the most solid of marriages, but she takes it in her stride and sings this sassy number with hardly a tear showing.

"Where in the World" is an emotional lament from *The Secret Garden* (1991) sung by the tormented Archibald Craven (Mandy Patinkin), who travels the world trying to escape from the memory of his deceased wife Lily. In Paris the distraught husband sees his wife's face everywhere and asks where he could possibly go where he can "live without your love?" Lucy Simon composed the surging music, and Marsha Norman wrote the absorbing lyric.

"Where Is Love?" is the simple cry for affection from the orphan Oliver Twist (Bruce Prochnik) in the British import *Oliver!* (1963). Taken from the workhouse and "sold" to Mr. Sowerberry the undertaker, Oliver sings this plaintive song alone in a room full of empty coffins. Later in the show the song is reprised by the loving Mrs. Bedwin (Dortha Duckworth), who is caring for Oliver in his benefactor's house. Lionel Bart wrote the touching music and lyric.

"Where Is the Life That Late I Led?" is perhaps Cole Porter's finest musical soliloquy. It is sung by the pompous Petruchio (Alfred Drake) on his wedding night when his bride has locked him out of the bedroom in *Kiss Me, Kate* (1948). Porter's music is sweeping and filled with mock-Italian opera touches, including a patter section set to mandolins. As for the lyric, it is possibly the funniest in the superior *Kiss Me, Kate* score. The internal rhymes as Petruchio recalls the Italian women in his past are particularly triumphal. The song's title comes directly from Shakespeare's Petruchio.

"Where Is the Warmth?" is an intriguing ballad about sex without love from the unsuccessful *The Baker's Wife* (1976), which closed before its New York opening. Genevieve (Patti LuPone) has left her husband and run off with the handsome Dominique (Kurt Peterson) to a hotel where they have been enjoying torrid lovemaking for several days. But as she looks at the sleeping Dominique, Genevieve asks herself why she feels so cold; the fire is there, but there is no warmth in their relationship. Stephen Schwartz wrote both the entrancing music and the provocative lyric.

"Where, Oh Where?" is that rare thing: a Cole Porter waltz. The rapturous number was sung in *Out of This World* (1950) by Barbara Ashley as a gold digger who seeks eternal love and affection with a millionaire.

"Where or When" is the beguiling Rodgers and Hart ballad about déjà vu that Mitzi Green and Ray Heatherton sang in *Babes in Arms* 1937). The lovers seem to recognize each other but can't quite put their finger on just where or when it was. Philip Furia, in his study of lyrics to popular songs, suggested that the song could also be an "alcoholic's groping efforts to recall a black-out," an idea that seems more than plausible considering Lorenz Hart's lifestyle. In either case, "Where or When" is a wonder of a song with a succinct lyric, and Richard Rodgers' music dramatically climbs the scale a whole octave and a fourth to reach its climactic end. The oft-recorded song got an early recording by Hal Kemp and His Orchestra (vocal by Skinnay Ennis) that became a best-seller, and Dion and the Belmonts had a hit with it in 1960.

"Where Would You Be Without Me?" is a dandy vaudeville turn from the allegorical musical *The Roar of the Greasepaint -- The Smell of the Crowd* (1965) by Leslie Bricusse and Anthony Newley. The aristocratic Sir (Cyril Ritchard) and the have-not Cocky (Newley) perform the soft-shoe number with all the debonair panache of a sophisticated Palace Theatre team even though they are dressed in rags and the lyric is highly cynical.

"Where You Are" is a dazzling fantasy number from *Kiss of the Spider Woman* (1993) in which the movie star Aurora (Chita Rivera) sings and dances with the male chorus about escaping the reality of where you are for the silver screen. In Harold Prince's powerful staging, the song is interspersed with the torture of prisoners and with Molina (Brent Carver) advising Valentin (Anthony Crivello) not to look at the real world. John Kander composed the exhilarating music, and Fred Ebb wrote the ironically cheery lyric.

"Where's That Rainbow?" is a bittersweet torch song that Richard Rodgers (music) and Lorenz Hart (lyric) wrote for the expressionistic musical *Peggy-Ann* (1926). Helen Ford introduced the cynical but heartfelt musical plea of a woman searching for optimism and love.

"Where's the Mate for Me?" is the arresting "I am" song for riverboat gambler Gaylord Ravenal in *Show Boat* (1927). Jerome Kern (music) and Oscar Hammerstein (lyric) wrote the smooth, carefree number in which Gaylord (Howard Marsh) relishes his freedom and independence as he drifts through life, but once in a while he has to stop and ask if there will ever be a true love for him. Jerry Hadley sang the number in John McGlinn's comprehensive 1988 recording of the *Show Boat* score.

"Wherever He Ain't" is a gritty, funny character song for silent-screen star Mabel Normand (Bernadette Peters) in *Mack and Mabel* (1974). Jerry Herman wrote the sassy number in which the furious Mabel leaves her lover Mack Sennett (Robert Preston), vowing to go anywhere he isn't. Chita Rivera sang the song in the Broadway revue *Jerry's Girls* (1985).

"Whip-Poor-Will" is the melodic romantic duet that was one of the hits from *Sally* (1920) by Jerome Kern (music) and Clifford Grey (lyric). Humble dishwasher Sally (Marilyn Miller) and wealthy Blair Farquar (Irving Fisher) sing this airy recollection of their first meeting set to the sounds of birds singing. Kern's music is unique in its unexpected harmonies and sudden octave jumps that subtly suggest the calling of birds.

"Whistle It" is a comic trio from the operetta *The Red Mill* (1906) by Victor Herbert (music) and Henry Blossom (lyric). Two Americans traveling in Europe (Dave Montgomery and Fred Stone) team up with a Dutch innkeeper's daughter (Ethel Johnson) in lamenting the plight of women who, because of a double standard, can only vent their anger by whistling.

"Who?" is the hit romantic ballad from Jerome Kern's *Sunny* (1925) and one of the most unique songs in musical theatre songdom. As was his way, Kern composed his melody before any title or lyric was written. For the two lovers he wrote a surging, spirited melody whose refrain starts with a single note sustained for two and a quarter measures (nine beats), then repeats the same musical phrase five times later in the song. Lyricist Oscar Hammerstein, collaborating with Kern on their first score together, was given the music and, realizing that no phrase could be effectively sung on one note for nine beats, looked for a single word that would be singable, understandable and appropriate. The result was the famous "Who . . . . stole my heart away?" that is so distinctive and so right. The song became very popular, and Kern attributed its success to that magic word "who." The number was sung in *Sunny* as a duet between circus performer Sunny Peters (Marilyn Miller) and the American tourist in London, Tom Warren (Paul Frawley). Among the many recordings of "Who?" was a unique trio version with George Olsen's band that sold over a million copies and started a vogue for trio arrangements of popular songs.

"Who Are You Now?" is a tender and reflective ballad from *Funny Girl* (1964) by Jule Styne (music) and Bob Merrill (lyric) that is too little known. Fanny Brice (Barbra Streisand) knows that her husband's business failures are ruining their marriage, but she doesn't know what to do to keep their love intact. Michael Feinstein recorded the song in 1991.

"Who Can I Turn To (When Nobody Needs Me)?" is the hit ballad from the allegorical musical *The Roar of the Greasepaint -- The Smell of the Crowd* (1965) by Leslie Bricusse and Anthony Newley. When the lowly Cocky (Newley), who represents the have-nots of the world, is at his lowest, he sings this painful query filled with despair. Yet the song is somehow exhilarating and became a hit before the show opened in New York because of a best-selling Tony Bennett recording. While the ballad is usually interpreted as a romantic torch song, it is often forgotten that in the musical Cocky delivers it to God.

"Who Cares?" is a rhythm ballad from *Of Thee I Sing* (1931) that is used as a satirical putdown in one scene and, with the same lyric, an affectionate love song in another. President John Wintergreen (William Gaxton) and his wife Mary (Lois Moran) sing the number as a glib response to the reporters heckling them about the woman Wintergreen jilted. Later in the show, with impeachment at hand, John and Mary sing the song at a slower tempo, and it becomes a touching testament to their love. The George Gershwin (music) and Ira Gershwin (lyric) song had hit recordings by Judy Garland, the Arden-Ohman Orchestra and the Benny Goodman Orchestra (vocal by Fred Astaire). It has also been a longtime favorite of jazz musicians.

"Who Couldn't Dance With You?" is an enticing foxtrot number from *Grand Hotel* (1989) with music and lyric by Robert Wright and George Forrest. The Baron (David Carroll) and the stenographer Flaemmchen (Jane Krakowski) hit it off on the hotel's dance floor, each claiming that the other is an ideal dancing partner. Then, at the Baron's request, Flaemmchen dances with the ailing bookkeeper Otto Kringelein (Michael Jeter), and they echo the same sentiments.

"Who Is Sylvia?" is the only song from *Two Gentlemen of Verona* (1971), the rock version of Shakespeare's play, that uses the original text for a musical number. Galt MacDermot wrote the arresting music for the Shakespearean lyric, and it was sung by Julia (Diana Davila) and the ensemble.

"Who Will Buy?" is a captivating number from the British import *Oliver!* (1963) by Lionel Bart. The orphan Oliver Twist (Bruce Prochnik) is put in the care of a wealthy benefactor and, looking out from his new home at the street vendors, he wonders if his good luck can continue. The musical cries of the vendors blend with Oliver's plea for permanent happiness in a highly effective musical scene.

"Whoever You Are" is a beguiling ballad from *Promises, Promises* (1968) by Burt Bacharach (music) and Hal David (lyric). Fran Kubelik (Jill O'Hara) is attracted to the funny young Chuck Baxter (Jerry Orbach) but still loves the already-married executive J.D. Sheldrake (Edward Winter), and her confusion on the matter reveals itself in this lovely song.

"A Whole Lotta Sunlight" is a poignant ballad from *Raisin* (1973), the musical version of Lorraine Hansberry's *A Raisin in the Sun*. Lena Younger (Virginia Capers) finds hope in a little potted plant that she places on the window sill of her Chicago tenement. The moving song was written by Judd Woldin (music) and Robert Brittan (lyric).

"The Whole World's Waitin' to Sing Your Song" is an electric song and dance from the concept musical *Jelly's Last Jam* (1992) based on the music of Jelly Roll Morton. In New Orleans the young Jelly (Savion Glover) sings this song of determination with the street crowd while the adult Jelly (Gregory Hines) joins in, the two aspects of the same character blending in a riveting number. Susan Birkenhead wrote the lyric for the Morton music.

"Who's Been Sitting in My Chair?" is a comic lament from *Goldilocks* (1958) in which the film actress Maggie Harris (Elaine Stritch) sings her troubles to a film extra in a bear costume. In answer to all the Goldilocks questions (who's been sitting my chair? eating my porridge? sleeping in my bed?), Maggie sadly responds "just me." Leroy Anderson wrote the pleasant music, and Joan Ford and Walter and Jean Kerr provided the dandy lyric.

"Who's Got the Pain (When They Do the Mambo)?" is a show-stopping number from *Damn Yankees* (1955) that is scarcely integrated into the plot but was a crowd pleaser all the same. Gwen Verdon, as the siren Lola, and Eddie Phillips sang and danced the stylish, energetic number choreographed by Bob Fosse and Verdon. Richard Adler and Jerry Ross wrote both the music and lyric together. In the mid-1950s the mambo was the latest fad, and Perry Como had a hit song called "Papa Loves the Mambo" in the same year *Damn Yankees* opened. It was Adler's idea to spoof the mambo in a song when director George Abbott asked for a Latin specialty number for Verdon.

"Who's That Girl?" is a deliciously satiric pastiche number from *Applause* (1970) with music by Charles Strouse and lyric by Lee Adams. Actress Margo Channing (Lauren Bacall), who was a young starlet in 1940s movies, catches one of her old films on the late late show on TV and mocks the naive youngster she used to be. The song has a wartime boogie-woogie sound with less-than-complimentary lyric; interpreted by Bacall, who was herself a 1940s glamour girl, the number was provocative and telling.

"Who's That Woman?" is one of the most exhilarating and devastating production numbers of the postwar American musical theatre. The pastiche revue song from *Follies* (1971), written by Stephen Sondheim and staged by Harold Prince and Michael Bennett, was a lavish splash of irony rarely seen in a musical before or since. At a *Follies* reunion, the aging hoofer Stella Deems (Mary McCarty) and five other ex-dancers re-create their old revue number that asks the identity of the swanky, sad woman in the mirror. As the six veterans struggle through the remembered lyric and dance steps, six ghosts from the past dance behind them in mirror image, showing what the ladies looked like long ago. As the number builds, the young dancers intermingle with the older ones as past and present merge in dazzling musical confusion. The song lyric takes on an ironic edge as the present tries to recognize the past, and the number climaxes with the realization that they are indeed the same.

"Why Can't the English?" is perhaps the most Shavian song in *My Fair Lady* (1956), a sparkling character song for Henry Higgins (Rex Harrison) as he defends the integrity of the English language. Lyricist Alan Jay Lerner took many of the ideas and even some of the phrases directly from George Bernard Shaw's *Pygmalion* (1914), and Frederick Loewe wrote an appealingly pompous melody to back up all the wordage.

"Why Can't the World Go and Leave Us Alone?" is a straightforward lyrical duet for a homosexual couple in *Dance a Little Closer* (1983), the first serious attempt to treat the subject without fuss in a Broadway musical. Charles Strouse (music) and Alan Jay Lerner (lyric) wrote the delicate song, and it was sung by Charles (Brent Barrett) and Edward (Jeff Keller) as the gay couple who get married later in the show. *Dance a Little Closer* closed after one performance; three months later *La Cage aux Folles* opened and was much more successful with its homosexual love story.

"Why Can't You Behave?" is the musical plea of Lois Lane (Lisa Kirk) as she confronts her gambling boyfriend Bill Calhoun (Harold Lang) in Cole Porter's *Kiss Me, Kate* (1948). The ballad has a sultry, "low-down" quality that makes Lois' plea sexy as well as poignant.

"Why Did I Choose You?" is a tender duet from the three-performance flop *The Yearling* (1965), the musical version of Marjorie Kinnan Rawlings' novel by Michael Leonard (music) and Herbert Martin (lyric). Ora Baxter

(Dolores Wilson) has doubts about herself and poses questions to her husband Ezra (David Wayne), who answers them and gently reassures her of his love.

"Why Do I Love You?" is the romantic duet for the lovers in *Show Boat* (1927) once they have matured and the blush of young love is gone. Magnolia (Norma Terris) and Gaylord (Howard Marsh) are married and living in Chicago, but they are in debt and their marriage is being tested. Yet the two still love each other and sing this straightforward duet that uses none of the romanticized embellishments of their earlier "Make Believe." The song is also sung by Magnolia's parents, Andy (Charles Winninger) and Parthy (Edna May Oliver), and the chorus and later is reprised by Magnolia's daughter Kim (also played by Norma Terris) and some 1920s flappers. Jerome Kern wrote the entrancing music, which effectively repeats its initial five-note phrase throughout the song, and Oscar Hammerstein provided the direct, questioning lyric. Dorothy Kirsten and Robert Merrill made a superb recording of the duet in 1949. In the 1988 recording of the complete *Show Boat* score, the duet was sung by Jerry Hadley and Frederica Von Stade.

"Why Do the Wrong People Travel?" is a prankish song by Noël Coward from *Sail Away* (1961), the musical set aboard a Cunard ship touring the Mediterranean. Mimi Paragon (Elaine Stritch), the ship's social director, privately reveals her dislike for all the passengers, wondering why they are the ones traveling when the "right people stay back home." Barbara Cason and Jamie Ross sang the comic number in the Off-Broadway revue *Oh Coward!* (1972).

"Why Him?" is a playful character song from the short-lived *Carmelina* (1979) by Alan Jay Lerner (lyric) and Burton Lane (music). Carmelina Campbell (Georgia Brown) loves the unexciting cafe owner Vittorio (Cesare Siepi) and sings of his many faults; so why, she asks herself, him? The amusing song was reprised later in the show as a duet for Carmelina and Vittorio in which he asked "Why Me?"

"Why Shouldn't I?" is among the gems overlooked in Cole Porter's *Jubilee* (1935), and it took a while for this lovely ballad to gain recognition. Margaret Adams, as a mythical princess traveling incognito in her kingdom, sang it as she contemplated romance. Later the song was recorded with great success by Paul Whiteman's Orchestra (vocal by Ramona), Jimmy Dorsey (vocal by Kay Weber), Artie Shaw, Mary Martin and Bobby Short.

"Why Was I Born?" is the famous torch song that Helen Morgan sang in *Sweet Adeline* (1929) and that was forever after associated with her. Jerome Kern (music) and Oscar Hammerstein (lyric) wrote the song of utter devotion that Addie Schmidt (Morgan) sings about the sailor Tom (Max Hoffman, Jr.), who loves Addie's sister instead of her. Hammerstein's lyric consists of a series of terse questions ending with "Why was I born to love you?" Kern's music, that ingeniously uses a series of repeated notes without becoming predictable, has a delicate blues flavor in the harmony which makes the number very beguiling. "Why Was I Born?" became very popular and was often recorded, but the song always belonged to Morgan.

"Wild Rose" is a hauntingly romantic ballad from *Sally* (1920) by Jerome Kern (music) and Clifford Grey (lyric) that is musically very unique. The song starts with a whole note at C, the sixth interval of the scale. No song, particularly a ballad, has ever begun in such a way, and Kern's melody returns to that C and even jumps to the C an octave above to bring home his startling innovation. Also, the melody is so simple and fulfilling that no harmony is really needed; instead, only four chords are used in the entire song's harmony. "Wild Rose" is a poetic description used by Sally (Marilyn Miller) to explain to the guests at a ritzy party that she's lowly bred and as unpedigreed as a wild rose.

"Wildflower" is the title song from the 1923 musical that boasted an early and memorable Vincent Youmans score. Guy Robertson sang the adoring serenade that had a lyric by Otto Harbach and a very young Oscar Hammerstein. Ben Bernie and His Orchestra made a popular recording of the enchanting song.

"Will He Like Me?" is a thoroughly entrancing character song from *She Loves Me* (1963). Amalia Balash (Barbara Cook) is finally going to meet her anonymous "dear friend" with whom she has been corresponding, but she is filled with doubts. Jerry Bock's music is charming, and Sheldon Harnick's lyric is fragile and intoxicating.

"Will You Remember?" is the evocative ballad that runs throughout the operetta *Maytime* (1917) as a kind of leitmotif for the three generations of family in the plot. Its most stunning version was the waltzing duet sung by the lovers Richard Wayne (Charles Purcell) and Ottillie (Peggy Wood), who must part forever. Sigmund Romberg composed the soaring music, and Rida Johnson Young wrote the romantic lyric. Because the refrain begins with the famous "sweetheart, sweetheart, sweetheart," the song is often mistaken for Victor Herbert's "Sweethearts" from the 1913 operetta of that name.

"William's Song" is a powerful character song from *The Tap Dance Kid* (1983) that is both touching and disturbing. The successful black lawyer William (Samuel E. Wright) wants his family to escape from the prejudiced clichés of the past and forbids his young son to train to become a professional tap dancer like his uncle. Henry Krieger (music) and Robert Lorick (lyric) wrote the provocative number that presents William as a complex man torn between pride for his race and love for his son.

"Willkommen" is the cheery but sleazy song that introduces *Cabaret* (1966), one of the most potent opening numbers in the American theatre. The hypnotic Master of Ceremonies (Joel Grey) greets the patrons of the Kit Kat Klub (and the audience, for they are the same) in German, French and English, urging them to forget their everyday troubles and enjoy the show. Despite his praises, it is clear that the orchestra and the girls are far from beautiful and that tonight's entertainment will be less than wholesome and carefree. At the end of the musical the emcee reprises "Willkommen" and the company reappears to repeat its opening song and dance, but the heavy dissonant strains in the music make the number sour and uncomfortable. John Kander composed the Germanic oompah-pah music, and Fred Ebb wrote the ironic lyric.

"Willomania" is the contagious chorus number that sings of the many talents of Will Rogers (Keith Carradine) in *The Will Rogers Follies* (1991) by Cy Coleman (music) and Betty Comden and Adolph Green (lyric). Ziegfeld's Favorite (Cady Huffman) and the ensemble sing the tuneful song that celebrates the Rogers phenomenon on radio, in the movies, in the newspapers and on stage in the *Ziegfeld Follies*.

"Windflowers" is a poignant ballad from *The Golden Apple* (1954) by Jerome Moross (music) and John Latouche (lyric). The faithful Penelope (Priscilla Gillette) patiently waits for her husband Ulysses (Stephen Douglass) to return home from his adventures. In the heart-rending number she even decides that the world is round and that no matter how far he strays, he will eventually return. The song is sometimes listed as "When We Were Young."

"Wintergreen for President" is arguably the shortest song ever written for a Broadway musical, a four-line chorus number that opened *Of Thee I Sing* (1931). A chorus of campaigners sang the eighteen-word song about their candidate who loves "the Irish and the Jews." George Gershwin composed the peppy march melody and inserted musical phrases from "Stars and Stripes Forever" and "Hail, Hail, the Gang's All Here" as well as Irish and Hebrew rhythms. Ira Gershwin wrote the succinct lyric that, Oscar Hammerstein once commented, is impossible to see or hear without mentally singing the melody in one's head.

"Winter's on the Wing" is a tantalizing song of welcoming spring from *The Secret Garden* (1991) by Lucy Simon (music) and Marsha Norman (lyric). Dickon (John Cameron Mitchell), a Yorkshire lad who has a special affinity with nature, sings the intoxicating chant about spring.

"Wint's Song" is a witty character song with exceptional lyric craftsmanship from *Take Me Along* (1959) by Bob Merrill. The lecherous college student Wint (Peter Conlow) outlines the pleasures of sin to the impressionable Richard (Robert Morse) and convinces Richard to accompany him to the local whorehouse, which he describes with hypnotic panache.

"Wish You Were Here" is the best-selling title song from the 1952 musical by Harold Rome about an adult summer camp in the Catskills. Chick Miller (Jack Cassidy), a law student who works as a waiter and dancing partner at the summer resort, sings the enticing song of yearning with the men in the camp. While the musical delayed its opening to work out its many problems, an Eddie Fisher recording of the song was released and sold a million copies, helping to make the show a hit despite lackluster reviews. Jane Frohman, with Sid Feller's Orchestra, also made a popular recording of the ballad.

"With a Little Bit of Luck" is one of the musical theatre's favorite music-hall turns, a delightful production number from *My Fair Lady* (1956) by Alan Jay Lerner (lyric) and Frederick Loewe (music). The philosophical dustman Alfred Doolittle (Stanley Holloway) describes how one can go through life shirking all responsibility if you use your wits and the little luck that comes your way. He was aided in the Edwardian-style pub song by two of his cronies (Gordon Dillworth and Rod McLennan) and the ensemble. Ironically, the number was not playing well in rehearsals, and the authors seriously considered shortening it or cutting out the song altogether. But from the first tryout preview it stopped the show and has continued to thrill audiences ever since. Despite the overtly British flavor of the song, "With a Little Bit of Luck" became a popular hit in America with recordings by Percy Faith and His Orchestra and by Jo Stafford with Paul Weston's Orchestra.

"With a Song in My Heart" is an atypical Rodgers and Hart song, but one of their most popular ones all the same. Richard Rodgers' music is soaring and rhapsodic, rather in the style he would later adopt with Oscar Hammerstein. Lorenz Hart's lyric is lush and seriously hyperbolic; there is not a trace of cynicism or wit to counter the full-throttle emotion. The song was first heard in *Spring Is Here* (1929), where it was sung by Lillian Taiz and John Hundley. Despite the passionate "With a Song in My Heart," Hundley didn't get the girl; he was the second lead, and Glenn Hunter, the leading man, did. But Hunter couldn't hit the ballad's high notes, so Hundley got the hit song if not the girl.

"Without a Song" is a highly lyrical ballad from the short-lived *Great Day* (1929) by Vincent Youmans (music) and Billy Rose and Edward Eliscu (lyric). The plantation slave Lijah (Lois Deppe) sang the warm number about how living, working and even loving are not possible without music in your heart. Willie Nelson made a hit recording of the song in 1983.

"Without You" is Eliza Doolittle's frantic but eloquent aria sung to Professor Higgins near the conclusion of *My Fair Lady* (1956). Julie Andrews delivered the seriocomic number to Rex Harrison, explaining how she has grown independent of him and can see through him and his ways. Frederick Loewe wrote the animated music, and Alan Jay Lerner devised the succinct lyric that drew on George Bernard Shaw's climactic confrontation scene in *Pygmalion* (1914). Eddie Fisher made a hit recording of the song.

"The Woman for the Man (Who Has Everything)" is a sly, egotistical character number from the musical comic strip *It's a Bird, It's a Plane, It's Superman!* (1966) by Charles Strouse (music) and Lee Adams (lyric). Newspaper columnist Max Mencken (Jack Cassidy) tries to seduce Lois Lane (Patricia Marand) by pointing out that she deserves the best, which is himself.

"A Woman Is a Sometime Thing" is a satiric lament on the fickleness of women from the folk opera *Porgy and Bess* (1935). Jake (Edward Matthews) takes his baby from Clara (Abbie Mitchell), who has been singing the lullaby "Summertime" to it, and sings this jazzy number warning the child about the whims and wishes of the female. He is joined by Mingo (Ford L. Buck), Jim (Jack Carr), Sportin' Life (John W. Bubbles) and the ensemble, who echo Jake's sentiments. A bit later in the musical Porgy (Todd Duncan) joins the group and reprises the number briefly. George Gershwin composed the breezy music, and DuBose Heyward wrote the caustic lyric. Ray Charles made a distinctive recording of the song in 1976.

"A Woman's Prerogative" is an amusing character song from *St. Louis Woman* (1946) by Harold Arlen (music) and Johnny Mercer (lyric). The barmaid Butterfly (Pearl Bailey) has long declined the amorous advances of no-luck jockey Barney (Fayard Nicholas); but now that he has started winning races, she reconsiders, reminding him that it is a woman's "prerogative" to change her mind.

"A Wonderful Day Like Today" is a sprightly song of boundless optimism from the allegorical musical *The Roar of the Greasepaint -- The Smell of the Crowd* (1965) by Leslie Bricusse and Anthony Newley. The sunny number was sung by the aristocratic Sir (Cyril Ritchard) and the urchins near the beginning of the highly symbolic show. The catchy song became quite popular and had a hit recording by Sammy Davis, Jr.

"A Wonderful Guy" is Nellie Forbush's exuberant musical declaration to her fellow nurses in *South Pacific* (1949) that she is in love with Emile de

Becque. Richard Rodgers wrote an unbridled, joyous melody, and Oscar Hammerstein provided the expert lyric that uses repetition and lighthearted imagery in a contagious manner. Nellie (Mary Martin) is not clever or witty, but she is vivacious and thrilling; the number captures her character beautifully. The song is also known as "I'm in Love With a Wonderful Guy."

"Won't You Charleston With Me?" is an infectious pastiche number from the British import *The Boy Friend* (1954) that celebrates the joy of the 1920s dance craze without mocking it. Sandy Wilson wrote the snappy song, and it was sung and danced by Bobby Van Husen (Bob Scheerer) and Maisie (Ann Wakefield).

"Won't You Marry Me?" is an ardent declaration of love from the Sigmund Romberg (music) and Dorothy Donnelly (lyric) operetta *My Maryland* (1927) set during the Civil War. Confederate officer Jack Negly (Warren Hull) courts the plantation heroine Barbara Frietchie (Evelyn Herbert) with the lyrical song.

"Wood" was a comic specialty number for Jimmy Durante that was interpolated into Cole Porter's *The New Yorkers* (1930) as the first-act finale. Durante wrote the song himself and performed it with his partners Lou Clayton and Eddie Jackson. The three gangsters sang of the glory of wood, as they cluttered up the stage with all sorts of wood products.

"Woodman Woodman, Spare That Tree" is a sad-comic ditty that Irving Berlin wrote for the great black performer Bert Williams. A beleaguered husband laments the loss of the forest, not because he loves nature but because he needs a place to escape from his shrewish wife. Williams first sang the song in the *Ziegfeld Follies* (1911) and used it in his act for many years after.

"The World Belongs to the Young" is a determined character song for Gabrielle Chanel (Katharine Hepburn) in the bio-musical *Coco* (1969) by Alan Jay Lerner (lyrics) and Andre Previn (music). Though considered too old and out-of-date by some, designer Coco decides to re-enter the fashion world and, in this acerbic number sung with her staff, challenges the young and trendy to watch what she'll come up with. Lerner's lyric is particularly provoking and somewhat autobiographical: he too was considered too old and out-of-date by many in the business.

"The World Is in My Arms" is the love ballad from *Hold on to Your Hats* (1940), a breezy number in which a roaming lover decides not to explore the globe because the girl he's dancing with is all the world to him now. Burton

Lane wrote the tuneful music, E.Y. Harburg provided the warm lyric, and it was sung by Jack Whiting and Eunice Healey.

"The World Is Your Balloon" is a frolicsome number from the satire *Flahooley* (1951) by Sammy Fain (music) and E.Y. Harburg (lyric). When toy inventor Sylvester Cloud (Jerome Courtland) and his girlfriend Sandy (Barbara Cook) are despondent over the failure of Sylvester's latest product, they are cheered up by some puppets at the toy factory, and all sing this merry, optimistic song.

"World Weary" is a droll Noël Coward number from the revue *This Year of Grace* (1928), which was imported from London. Beatrice Lillie sang the lethargic number about a woman tired of big-city life as she sat on a stool and ate an apple. Bobby Short made a memorable recording of "World Weary" and Barbara Cason, Roderick Cook and Jamie Ross sang the wry song in the Off-Broadway revue *Oh Coward!* (1972).

"Worlds Apart" is a captivating duet from *Big River* (1985), the *Huckleberry Finn* musical by Roger Miller. Huck (Daniel H. Jenkins) and the runaway slave Jim (Ron Richardson) reflect on how they feel the same about so many things, but their race keeps them "worlds apart."

"The Worst Pies in London" is an energetic comic number from *Sweeney Todd, the Demon Barber of Fleet Street* (1979) that is also the "I am" song for the predatory Mrs. Lovett (Angela Lansbury). When Sweeney Todd (Len Cariou) enters her meat pie shop, Mrs. Lovett pounces upon him to try her wares even though she admits that they are the worst in town. Stephen Sondheim wrote the frantic, jaunty song, and Harold Prince directed the sequence in which Lansbury had a gesture, punch or slap for each musical phrase as she made up more uneatable pies.

"Wouldn't It Be Loverly?" is Eliza Doolittle's naive but charming "I am " song from *My Fair Lady* (1956) by Alan Jay Lerner (lyric) and Frederick Loewe (music). Julie Andrews, with the ensemble, introduced the lyrical number. It was often recorded, sometimes with the cockney "loverly" corrected to "lovely" (which is harder to sing).

"Wouldn't You Like to Be on Broadway?" is a light jazz number from the operatic *Street Scene* (1947) by Kurt Weill (music) and Langston Hughes (lyric). The slick Mr. Easter (Don Saxon) sings the breezy song to Rose (Ann Jeffreys), claiming he can get her into show business, but it's obvious that this is just a line he is using to seduce her. The song fulfills the same purpose as the jazzy "There's a Boat Dat's Leavin' Soon for New

York" in *Porgy and Bess* (1935).

"The Writing on the Wall" is the stirring finale to *The Mystery of Edwin Drood* (1985) by Rupert Holmes. The youthful Edwin, played in music-hall fashion by a woman (Betty Buckley), surprises everyone by seemingly returning from the grave. He explains, in a rousing recitative introduction, that he was not murdered, but an attempt was made on his life, so he disguised himself in order to find the culprit. Then Edwin launches into an enthralling marchlike song proclaiming that, having come so close to death, he has seen "the writing on the wall" and realizes how precious life is.

"Wrong Note Rag" is a delicious pastiche of a turn-of-the-century rag from *Wonderful Town* (1953) with 1930s jazz thrown in to help set up the Depression-era story. Sisters Ruth (Rosalind Russell) and Eileen (Edith Adams) go to the Village Vortex in lower Manhattan, where they lead the nightclub patrons in a frenzied tribute to life in New York. Betty Comden and Adolph Green wrote the silly, nonsense lyric, and Leonard Bernstein composed the jubilant music, complete with a dissonant jarring wrong note that sets the whole number askew.

"Wunderbar" is Cole Porter's spoof of Viennese operetta, the kind of musical entertainment he and his "jazz-age" colleagues put out of fashion in the 1930s. In *Kiss Me, Kate* (1948), the stage stars Fred Graham (Alfred Drake) and Lilli Vanessi (Patricia Morison) recall an old operetta they performed in years ago. The waltz starts off mockingly with a lyric that is ridiculous (they remember looking "down on the Jungfrau," which is quite a feat because it is the highest mountain in Europe), but then the number gets quite romantic in a schmaltzy way and the two rekindle a long-lost love. The melody, filled with Strauss-like phrasing, is one of Porter's most recognizable pieces of composition.

Y

"Ya Got Me" is a furious pseudo-Latin number from *On the Town* (1944) by Leonard Bernstein (music) and Betty Comden and Adolph Green (lyric). Sailors Chip (Cris Alexander) and Ozzie (Green) and their girlfriends Hildy (Nancy Walker) and Claire (Comden) have brought the lovelorn Gabey (John Battles) to a nightclub to cheer him up. When the feature attraction proves to be a dreary torch singer, the friends take over the show and attempt to pep up Gabey with this wild number.

"The Yama Yama Man" is an odd, comic number that was one of the hits from *Three Twins* (1908) and made a star of Bessie McCoy. The Karl Hoschna (music) and Collin Davis (lyric) song was interpolated into the score late in rehearsals and proved to be a showstopper. Molly Sommers (McCoy) sang the childish number wearing a satin clown outfit and a cone hat; it made such an impression that McCoy became known as the "Yama Yama Girl." Ada Jones and the Victor Light Opera Company recorded the song.

"The Yankee Doodle Boy" is the boastful George M. Cohan song known today by its altered title "Yankee Doodle Dandy." It was written for *Little Johnny Jones* (1904), Cohan's first hit show, and the number became the signature song for the composer-lyricist-actor-producer-director. "The Yankee Doodle Boy" is the "I am" song for the jockey Johnny Jones (Cohan), which he proudly sings on his first entrance. Arriving in England to ride his horse Yankee Doodle in the Derby, Johnny tells a chorus of lovely ladies to place their bets on him and they won't be disappointed. Joel Grey and the company of *George M!* (1968) sang the song as "Yankee Doodle Dandy," and Jerry Zaks and the ensemble of the revue *Tintypes* (1980) sang it with the original title.

"Yellow Drum" is a gamesome march from the offbeat musical *The Grass Harp* (1971) by Claibe Richardson (music) and Kenward Elmslie (lyric). Spinster Dolly Talbo (Barbara Cook) recalls a victory march her grandfather used to sing, and when she decides to move out of her sister's house and live in a treehouse in the backyard, she sings the rousing number with her nephew Collin (Russ Thacker) and her servant-companion Catherine (Carol Brice).

"Yenta Power" is a stinging comic number about the monstrous ladies who book theatre parties for Broadway shows. The Charles Strouse (music) and Lee Adams (lyric) song was sung by Anne Francine and the ensemble in the single-night flop *A Broadway Musical* (1978).

"Yes" is the life-affirming finale of *70, Girls, 70* (1971), the short-lived musical about old folks by John Kander (music) and Fred Ebb (lyric). The recently deceased Ida (Mildred Natwick) appears overhead on a crescent moon to observe the wedding of Eunice (Lucie Lancaster) and Walter (Gil Lamb) and encourages all the folks at the home to accept life, take risks and say yes to new opportunities. Liza Minnelli, who sang the song in her concert tour and on television, also recorded the exhilarating number.

"Yesterdays" is the tender, evocative ballad from *Roberta* (1933) that the beloved Fay Templeton sang near the end of her career. The aging Aunt Minnie (Templeton), who owns the Paris dress shop called Roberta, recalls times past in this simple but captivating number by Jerome Kern (music) and Otto Harbach (lyric). Billie Holiday made a distinctive recording of "Yesterdays," the song got an interesting new interpretation in a Barbra Streisand recording in the 1960s, and it was sung by Liz Robertson and Scott Holmes in the Broadway revue *Jerome Kern Goes to Hollywood* (1986).

"Yip-I-Addy-I-Ay!" is a delightful nonsense song from *The Merry Widow Burlesque* (1908) that was interpolated later in the run and became the hit of the show. George V. Hobart wrote the score for the spoof using Lehar's original music (with his permission), but "Yip-I-Addy-I-Ay!" was written by John H. Flynn (music) and Will Cobb (lyric). Broadway star Blanche Ring heard the song performed in a nightclub, and added it to the mock-operetta when she replaced Lulu Glaser as the widow of the title. Ring recorded the number in 1908 and it became quite popular.

"You and I" is the soaring love song from the British import *Chess* (1988) by Benny Anderssen and Bjorn Ulvaeus (music) and Tim Rice (lyric). Russian chess champion Anatoly (David Carroll) and the Hungarian refugee Florence (Judy Kuhn) sang the engaging number as Anatoly's wife Svetlana (Marcia Mitzman) added her sentiments for a disturbing effect.

"You and the Night and the Music" is a smoldering love duet in the operatic mode from *Revenge With Music* (1934) by Howard Dietz (lyric) and Arthur Schwartz (music). The Spanish gentleman Carlos (Georges Metaxa) and his wife Maria (Libby Holman) sang the ardent duet. Despite the show's unprofitable run, the song became very popular. Holman recorded the number in 1934.

"You Are Beautiful" is one of Rodgers and Hammerstein's most rhapsodic ballads, a languishing number from *Flower Drum Song* (1958) that captures an Eastern mood in the Western operetta form. The Richard Rodgers (music) and Oscar Hammerstein (lyric) song was introduced by Ed Kenney and Juanita Hall as a Chinese poem about looks of love exchanged on a flower boat going down a river. Johnny Mathis made a popular recording of the song.

"You Are Free" is a enraptured duet interpolated into the "modern" operetta *Apple Blossoms* (1919) that became the hit of the show. Fritz Kreisler scored the operetta but Victor Jacobi wrote the old-style music, and William Le Baron provided the Victorian lyric for "You Are Free." The duet was introduced by Wilda Bennett and John Charles Thomas.

"You Are Love" is the most operatic number in *Show Boat* (1927), an expansive duet with a waltzing tempo in the music by Jerome Kern and a passionate lyric by Oscar Hammerstein. The song is sung by Magnolia (Norma Terris) and Gaylord (Howard Marsh) near the end of the first act when they decide to wed. The duet is later reprised at the musical's poignant finale when the aged Gaylord and the estranged Magnolia are reunited. Patrice Munsel and Robert Merrill's 1956 recording of the duet is arguably the finest of the many recordings.

"You Are Never Away" is a dreamy ballad from the experimental, unsuccessful *Allegro* (1947) by Richard Rodgers (music) and Oscar Hammerstein (lyric). It was introduced by John Battles as Joe, a medical student at college, who recalls his hometown girlfriend Jenny. The number was unusual in that the intimate song was also sung by the large chorus who acted as Joe's alter ego, musicalizing his thoughts. Successful recordings of the song were made by Buddy Clark, Charlie Spivak (with a Tommy Mercer vocal) and Clark Dennis.

"You Are Woman, (I Am Man)" is a sly song of seduction from *Funny Girl* (1964) that turns into more a comic number rather than a romantic one. Dashing gambler Nick Arnstein (Sydney Chaplin) wines and dines the naive Fanny Brice (Barbra Streisand) with this smooth lesson about the sexes, but her comic asides during the seduction make the scene a hilarious farce. Jule Styne composed the smooth music, and Bob Merrill wrote the quick-witted lyric.

"You Can Always Count on Me" is a self-mocking solo for two different characters played by the same actress in *City of Angels* (1989). In the private-eye movie being made, the girl Friday named Oolie (Randy Graff) sits alone in her bedroom and reflects on how she is always so faithful to her boss and everyone else, yet she is always overlooked by men. The song is immediately reprised by the studio secretary Donna (also played by Graff) alone in her bedroom, who is having similar thoughts about herself. Cy Coleman wrote the tangy music, and David Zippel provided the acrid lyric.

"You Can Dance With Any Girl" is one of the many vivacious numbers from the archetypal 1920s musical comedy *No, No, Nanette* (1925). Lawyer Billy Early (Wellington Cross) and his wife Lucille (Josephine Whittell) have a rocky marriage, and before he goes off on a business trip, Lucille makes it clear she trusts him, so he can go out dancing for all she cares. The duet that follows is sassy, witty and full of twenties charm. Vincent Youmans composed the invigorating music, and Irving Caesar wrote the crafty lyric.

"You Cannot Make Your Shimmy Shake on Tea" is Irving Berlin's topical song about the newly passed Volstead Act of 1919 that introduced Prohibition. The silly number was sung by the renowned black comic Bert Williams in the *Ziegfeld Follies* (1919).

"You Can't Get a Man With a Gun" is a delicious character song for Annie Oakley (Ethel Merman) from Irving Berlin's *Annie Get Your Gun* (1946). Annie realizes that her sharpshooting skills are no help in matters of romance, particularly in winning the heart of her rival Frank Butler. Although the number seems an unlikely candidate to travel outside the context of the show, the song was quite popular.

"You Could Drive a Person Crazy" is a hilarious pastiche of a 1940s sister-act song from the landmark musical *Company* (1970) by Stephen Sondheim. The bachelor Robert (Dean Jones) conjures up the memory of three of his ex-girlfriends - Marta (Pamela Myers), Kathy (Donna McKechnie) and April (Susan Browning) - who appear together and berate Robert for his lack of commitment. They sing their insults in a swinging Andrews Sisters style filled with scat sounds, syncopated rhythms and a jazzy patter section. Yet the music has a dissonant quality to it, and the lyric is contemporary, with 1970s slang throughout. The trio was also sung by Millicent Martin, David Kernan and Julia McKenzie in the Broadway revue *Side by Side by Sondheim* (1977). The lyric was changed to "I Could Drive a Person Crazy" for the Off-Broadway revue *Putting It Together* (1993), where it was sung by Christopher Durang and the ensemble.

"You Could Never Shame Me" is a touching ballad from *Kiss of the Spider Woman* (1993) in which Molina's mother (Merle Louise) appears to him in a morphine hallucination and tells him that she has never been ashamed of his homosexuality and the disgrace his sexual offense has brought them both. Molina (Brent Carver) joins her in the delicate song as the fantasy turns into a lovely duet. John Kander composed the graceful music, and Fred Ebb wrote the tender lyric.

"You Did It" is a brilliant musical scene from *My Fair Lady* (1956) that manages to do the impossible: to have characters relate an offstage event in a manner that is more vibrant than the actual showing of the episode would have been. Henry Higgins (Rex Harrison) and Colonel Pickering (Robert Coote) tell the housekeeper Mrs. Pearce (Philippa Bevans) and the servants what happened with Eliza (Julie Andrews) at the Embassy Ball, describing in hilarious detail how the Hungarian Karpathy tried to expose the cockney Eliza, only to conclude that she was a princess of Hungarian blood. Alan Jay Lerner's dazzling lyric and Frederick Loewe's energetic music both change gear twice to accommodate the different moods of the story being told. The focal point throughout the song is Eliza herself, whom no one acknowledges and who says nothing throughout the jubilant celebration.

"You Do Something to Me" is the most famous song to come out of Cole Porter's *Fifty Million Frenchmen* (1929) and the one that first displayed his talent for romance and wit cohabiting comfortably in a single lyric. His internal rhyming of "voodoo," "do do" and "you do" all in one line is still a marvel of lyricwriting. William Gaxton, as a playboy millionaire disguised as a Paris tour guide, and Genevieve Tobin, as his heart's desire, introduced the ballad, which later had successful recordings by Leo Reisman's Orchestra, Marion Harris and Marlene Dietrich. In the 1991 reconstructed recording of the score, the duet was sung by Howard McGillin and Susan Powell.

"You Gotta Have a Gimmick" is a comic trio from *Gypsy* (1959) that regularly stops the show with one of the funniest eleven o'clock numbers in the American musical theatre. The three strippers, Tessie Tura (Maria Karnilova), Mazeppa (Faith Dane) and Electra (Chotzi Foley), teach Louise (Sandra Church) that there is more to burlesque than bumping and grinding; you've got to have that something special that makes your act unique. Jule Styne composed the vampy music, and Stephen Sondheim wrote the hilarious lyric. The number was performed by Debbie Shapiro, Faith Prince and Susann Fletcher in the revue *Jerome Robbins' Broadway* (1989).

"You Made Me Love You (I Didn't Want to Do It)" is Al Jolson's first hit song and the one that established the onstage persona he would portray in shows and films throughout his career. The James Monaco (music) and Joseph McCarthy (lyric) song is a quiet and tender number that Jolson delivered with robust affection in the musical extravaganza *The Honeymoon Express* (1913). Playing the comic valet Gus, Jolson performed in blackface, an image he would forever be associated with. His 1913 recording of the song sold over a million disks, and later there were two recordings by Harry James that were also very popular.

"You Must Meet My Wife" is an amusing duet from *A Little Night Music* (1973) that manages to be operatic and antiromantic at the same time. When the lawyer Fredrik (Len Cariou) finds himself in the boudoir of his old flame Desiree (Glynis Johns), all he can do is sing the praises of his young wife Anne. Since the marriage is not off to a good start, the praises are hollow and full of contradictions, and Desiree's wry interjections destroy any romanticism left in the situation. Stephen Sondheim wrote the piquant lyric and the waltzing music that work nicely against each other. In the Broadway revue *Side by Side by Sondheim* (1977), the duet was sung by David Kernan and Millicent Martin.

"You Mustn't Be Discouraged" is a silly pastiche number from *Fade Out -- Fade In* (1964), the musical about Hollywood in the 1930s by Jule Styne (music) and Betty Comden and Adolph Green (lyric). Movie-star hopeful Hope Springfield (Carol Burnett) and the unemployed Lou Williams (Tiger Haynes) sang and danced this chipper number dressed like and imitating filmdom's little Shirley Temple and Bojangles Robinson.

"You Naughty, Naughty Men" is the only song from *The Black Crook*, considered by many the first American musical comedy, that we know was part of the score on that fateful opening night on September 12, 1866. Since the landmark entertainment had no official score but rather was a collection of songs already available, the musical numbers changed throughout the show's astonishing 475-performance run. But the *New York Times* critic mentioned "You Naughty, Naughty Men," and subsequent sheet-music copies boldly advertised that the song was part of the famous production. The sassy little ditty, filled with risqué (for its time) sexual innuendos, was sung by the saucy maid Carlina (Millie Cavendish) as she boasted that she could see through the male sex, who only flirt and marry for money rather than love. G. Bicknell (music) and T. Kennick (lyric) wrote the number, which was typical of music-hall songs of the period.

"You Never Knew About Me" is a warm comic duet from the Princess Theatre musical *Oh, Boy!* (1917) by Jerome Kern (music) and P.G. Wodehouse (lyric). The young lovers Lou Ellen (Marie Carroll) and George (Tom Powers) wryly imagine the fun they would have had making mud pies, raising rabbits and so on if they had known each other as children. Kern's melody is particularly rich and unique in that in all the refrain's eighteen measures, only one musical sentence is ever repeated.

"You Said Something" is the hit love song from *Have a Heart* (1917), a memorable ballad with a sprightly, catchy melody by Jerome Kern and a direct, no-nonsense lyric by P.G. Wodehouse. Ted (Donald MacDonald) and Lizzie (Marjorie Gateson), a young couple at a seaside resort, introduced the rhythmic number, which was recorded soon after opening night by Harry MacDonough and Alice Green.

"You Say the Nicest Things, Baby" is the hit ballad from *As the Girls Go* (1948), the musical about the first woman president of the United States by Jimmy McHugh (music) and Harold Adamson (lyric). Kenny Wellington (Bill Callahan), the lady president's son, and his sweetheart Kathy Robinson (Betty Jane Watson) sing the appealing duet. Because of an ASCAP strike at the time, none of the songs from the show were recorded for some time, but Jerry Wayne's eventual single version of this number made it very popular.

"You, Too, Can Be a Puppet" is a sly song calling for mindless conformity from the offbeat *Flahooley* (1951) by Sammy Fain (music) and E.Y. Harburg (lyric). In this opening number, the Bil Baird Marionettes joined the chorus in singing of the advantages of abandoning the human race and becoming a puppet. Fain's music is gleeful, and Harburg's lyric is wickedly sarcastic: a bizarre beginning for a bizarre show.

"You Took Advantage of Me" is the hit song from *Present Arms* (1928) by Richard Rodgers (music) and Lorenz Hart (lyric), and it remains one of their most recognized efforts. The lively rhythm song, filled more with sass than with regret, was introduced by the show's secondary characters, played by Joyce Barbour and Busby Berkeley (who also choreographed the musical). A Morton Downey recording popularized the song, and years later Ella Fitzgerald and Linda Ronstadt each made memorable recordings of it. "You Took Advantage of Me" was interpolated into the 1954 Broadway revival of Rodgers and Hart's *On Your Toes*, where it was sung by Elaine Stritch.

"You Were Dead, You Know" is an outright facetious romantic duet in the operatic mode from *Candide* (1956). In Paris, the lovers Candide (Robert Rounseville) and Cunegonde (Barbara Cook) are temporarily reunited despite the fact that each thought the other dead. What would have been the subject of a tragic dirge in grand opera becomes an outlandish mockery with Leonard Bernstein's trilling music and John Latouche's idiotically fervent lyric.

"You Were Meant for Me" is the appealing duet from the British import *Andre Charlot's Revue of 1924* that was written by the Americans Eubie Blake (music) and Noble Sissle (lyric). When the West End revue *London Calling!* (1923) was being put together, the producer included the Americans' song, the only foreign interpolation in the show. When Andre Charlot put together his first import revue for Broadway, he included "You Were Meant for Me" and gave the song to Gertrude Lawrence and Jack Buchanan, and it became a hit.

"You Wouldn't Fool Me, Would You?" is the love song from *Follow Through* (1929), the musical about golf by B.G. DeSylva and Lew Brown (lyric) and Ray Henderson (music). Women's golf champion Lora Moore (Irene Delroy) and her beloved Jerry Downs (John Barker) sang this playful duet in the course of their less-than-smooth romance. Annette Hanshaw and Hal Kemp (vocal by Skinnay Ennis) each made a popular recording of the song.

"You'd Be Surprised" is one of Irving Berlin's funniest and raciest songs, a tribute to a shy, unassuming Johnny who manages to get all the girls. Eddie Cantor sang the delightful number in the *Ziegfeld Follies* (1919), and his recording of it that same year sold over a million disks. It is rare for a comic song to become a best-seller, but "You'd Be Surprised" also sold three quarters of a million copies of sheet music within the first year of publication and thousands of piano rolls as well. With its sly humor and lively double entendres, the song is still hilarious today.

"You'll Never Get Away From Me" is a sprightly charm song from *Gypsy* (1959) by Jule Styne (music) and Stephen Sondheim (lyric). Show-business manager Herbie (Jack Klugman) brings up the possibility that he might quit both the act and Rose (Ethel Merman), but she gets him dancing and confidently tells him otherwise. The song's melody had been written years before for a movie that was never produced, and Styne used it again for a television special. Not knowing this, Sondheim came up with the playful new lyric, and no one recognized the old tune.

"You'll Never Walk Alone" is the simple but powerful hymn from *Carousel* (1945) that is one of Rodgers and Hammerstein's most inspirational efforts. The song is sung by Nettie Fowler (Christine Johnson) to Julie (Jan Clayton) to encourage her to keep living after the death of her husband Billy. At the end of the musical it is sung by the chorus at his daughter's graduation ceremony with the deceased Billy looking on. Oscar Hammerstein's lyric is innocent and perhaps a bit too simple, but Richard Rodgers' melody builds magnificently to a moving climax. Frank Sinatra and Judy Garland each made popular early recordings of the song, and over the years it was a hit for such diverse artists as Roy Hamilton, Patti LaBelle and the Blue Belles, Gerry and the Pacemakers, Elvis Presley and the group Brooklyn Bridge.

"Young and Foolish" is the only popular song to come out of *Plain and Fancy* (1955), the musical about the Pennsylvania Dutch by Albert Hague (music) and Arnold B. Horwitt (lyric). Katie (Gloria Marlowe) is betrothed to the farmer Ezra, but when Ezra's brother (David Daniels) returns to the Amish community, they are attracted to each other and recall when they were "young and foolish" together. The duet became one of the most popular songs of the season and helped keep the musical running for a year.

"A Younger Man" is an appealing character song for Daddy Warbucks (Harve Presnell) from the Off-Broadway sequel *Annie Warbucks* (1993). Charles Strouse (music) and Martin Charnin (lyric) wrote the heartfelt ballad in which billionaire Warbucks sings about his love for his secretary Grace, but feels she deserves a younger man than himself.

"Younger Than Springtime," the popular ballad from *South Pacific* (1949), was the only song not written directly for the show. Richard Rodgers had composed the music years earlier and had pretty much forgotten it; his daughter Mary recalled it and suggested the number for *South Pacific*. Oscar Hammerstein wrote an operatic lyric for Lieutenant Cable (William Tabbert) to sing to Liat (Betta St. John), the Polynesian girl he has just made love to.

"Your Arms Too Short to Box With God" is the title song from the 1976 retelling of the Gospel of St. Matthew as presented at a black revival meeting. When Jesus is brought before Pontius Pilate, Delores Hall and the company defend his innocence with this vibrant gospel number telling the Roman not to mess with the son of God. Alex Bradford wrote the invigorating music and lyric.

"Your Eyes" is a rhapsodic ballad from the romantic swashbuckling operetta *The Three Musketeers* (1928). Rudolf Friml composed the lush music, P.G. Wodehouse and Clifford Grey wrote the fervent lyric, and it was sung by d'Artagnan (Dennis King) and his beloved Constance (Vivienne Segal).

"Your Land and My Land" is the stirring song of nationalism that served as the finale for the Civil War-era operetta *My Maryland* (1927). Sigmund Romberg composed the compelling music, Dorothy Donnelly wrote the driving lyric, and it was sung by Nathaniel Wagner and the entire company.

"You're a Builder-Upper" is the popular paradoxical love song by Harold Arlen (music) and Ira Gershwin and E. Y. Harburg (lyric) that was first heard in the revue *Life Begins at 8:40* (1934). The delightful number chronicles the inconsistent behavior of a pair of lovers, one minute building each other up with praise, the next tearing down egos with insults. Gershwin, the master of inventive contractions, and Harburg, with his penchant for playful suffixes, combined their talents in this song and filled it with such expressions as "sap-a-roo," "give in-er," "take-on-the-chiner" and the title's "builder-upper." The song was introduced by Ray Bolger, Dixie Dunbar and the ensemble, and successful recordings were made by Ethel Merman, Joey Nash, Leo Reisman's Orchestra and Glen Gray and the Casa Loma Orchestra (vocal by Pee Wee Hunt).

"You're a Grand Old Flag" is the classic George M. Cohan patriotic favorite and one of the first theatre songs to sell over a million copies of sheet music. Cohan wrote it for *George Washington, Jr.* (1906), and it was sung by the ardent title character (played by Cohan) as he battled the Anglophile Americans who were down on their own country. Originally the title of the song was "You're a Grand Old Rag," based on a quote by a Civil War veteran who lovingly called the flag a "rag" but patriotic groups protested, so the lyric was changed after opening night and has remained "flag" ever since. The song was performed by Joel Grey and the company in the bio-musical *George M!* (1968) and by the ensemble of the Broadway revue *Tintypes* (1980).

"You're a Queer One, Julie Jordan" is Carrie Pipperidge's reaction to her girlfriend's strange behavior regarding the carousel barker Billy Bigelow in *Carousel* (1945). The Richard Rodgers (music) and Oscar Hammerstein (lyric) duet is more musical dialogue than traditional song and captures the brittle New England cadence in both its rhythms and vocabulary. Jean Darling introduced the number, with Jan Clayton as the dreamy Julie.

"You're an Old Smoothie" is the breezy popular song of restrained affection from *Take a Chance* (1932) that was sung by Jack Haley and Ethel Merman. The lighthearted duet was written by Richard Whiting and Nacio Herb Brown (music) and B.G. DeSylva (lyric) for another show that closed out of town. Lee Wiley made a popular recording with Victor Young's Orchestra. The group Babs and Her Brothers recorded it, changed its name to the Smoothies and used the number as its theme song.

"You're as English as . . ." is an acute character song from *Kwamina* (1961), the short-lived musical about modern Africa by Richard Adler. Dr. Eve Jordan (Sally Ann Howes) confronts Kwamina (Terry Carter) about his European education and how he has more in common with British aristocracy than his native people. The acerbic list song employs a European flavor in contrast with the African rhythms used throughout most of the score.

"You're Devastating" is a haunting song of affection from *Roberta* (1933) by Jerome Kern (music) and Otto Harbach (lyric). It was sung by the bandleader-sidekick Huckleberry Haines (Bob Hope) and reprised by Princess Stephanie (Tamara). The song had originally been heard in the London musical *Blue Eyes* (1928), where it was called "Do I Do Wrong, Dear?"

"You're Gonna Love Tomorrow" is a joyously optimistic pastiche number from *Follies* (1971) in which Stephen Sondheim captures the bounciness of a Vincent Youmans melody and the playfulness of an Ira Gershwin lyric. The cheery duet was sung by Young Ben (Kurt Peterson) and Young Phyllis (Virginia Sandifur) in the Loveland fantasy sequence of the musical and was reprised contrapuntally with another pastiche song, "Love Will See Us Through."

"You're Here and I'm Here" is an early hit song by Jerome Kern that sold thousands of copies of sheet music and was a popular favorite with dance bands. Harry B. Smith provided the lyric for the rhythmic number that points to Kern's break from the European operetta mold. The sheet music was advertised as being the hit song from six different shows and it was no exaggeration: Kern and Smith wrote it for *The Marriage Market* (1913), but it didn't get noticed until it was interpolated into *The Laughing Husband* (1914), which led to its placement in other shows in New York and London. It is also worth pointing out that when the young George Gershwin heard "You're Here and I'm Here," it showed him the direction he wanted to go with his own composing.

"You're Just in Love" is Irving Berlin's most famous contrapuntal duet, a showstopper that Ethel Merman and Russell Nype sang in *Call Me Madam* (1950). Newcomer Nype was delivering his material so well in previews that Berlin wanted to write a new song for him to sing in the second act but feared that the show's star would object. So he devised this exhilarating duet in which Ambassador Sally Adams (Merman) advises her lovestruck assistant (Nype) about his symptoms. The snappy number got seven encores on opening night and continued to stop the show throughout the run. Berlin's two distinct melodies blend in a marvelous way, and both singers get lively, engaging lyrics to sing; it is, as biographer Laurence Bergreen stated, the "last great song of Berlin's." Popular recordings were made by Perry Como with the Fontane Sisters, Rosemary Clooney and Guy Mitchell, Ethel and Dick Haymes, and Merman with Donald O'Connor.

"You're Lonely and I'm Lonely" is an Irving Berlin ballad from *Louisiana Purchase* (1940) that proved to be the hit of the show. Vera Zorina, as the seductive Marina Van Linden, tries to compromise the investigating Senator

Oliver Loganberry (Victor Moore) by using all her charms, including this entrancing duet.

"You're My Everything" is the hit ballad that came from the Ed Wynn vehicle *The Laugh Parade* (1931). Harry Warren wrote the expansive melody, Mort Dixon and Joe Young provided the romantic lyric and the number was sung as a duet by Jeanne Aubert and Lawrence Gray.

"You're Never Fully Dressed Without a Smile" is an entertaining pastiche number from *Annie* (1977) that satirized the kind of bubble-headed songs that were heard on the radio during the Depression. Charles Strouse composed the snappy music, Martin Charnin wrote the tongue-in-cheek lyric, and it was sung in the format of a radio broadcast by Donald Craig, Laurie Beechman, Edie Cowan and Penny Worth. The number was in turn satirized by the six orphans (Diana Barrows, Robyn Finn, Donna Graham, Danielle Brisebois, Shelley Bruce and Janine Ruane) who were listening to the broadcast at the Municipal Orphanage.

"You're Nothing Without Me" is a duet for two personifications of the same person in *City of Angels* (1989). The screenwriter Stine (Gregg Edelman) and his fictional creation, the private eye Stone (James Naughton), hold a musical battle of wits in which each claims to be responsible for the other's fame. At the end of the musical, Stone, Stine and his wife Gabby (Kay McClelland) reprise the number as "I'm Nothing Without You." Cy Coleman composed the jazzy music, and David Zippel wrote the playful lyric.

"You're the Cream in My Coffee" is the popular favorite from *Hold Everything* (1928), the musical about boxing by B.G. DeSylva and Lew Brown (lyric) and Ray Henderson (music). Welterweight contender "Sonny Jim" Brooks (Jack Whiting) and his girl Sue Burke (Ona Munson) sing the delectable song as a duet, using everyday metaphors with great panache. The oft-recorded song had particularly successful singles by Ben Selvin (vocal by Jack Palmer) and Ruth Etting.

"You're the Top" is Cole Porter's most accomplished list song; indeed, it is probably the finest list song in the American theatre. Only Porter could contrive a list of the most unlikely items, from the Colosseum to cellophane to broccoli, and make the whole thing playfully romantic. The song was introduced by William Gaxton and Ethel Merman in *Anything Goes* (1934), and while some of the references have grown obscure ("the eyes of Irene Bordoni"), "You're the Top" is as delicious today as it was in that Depression-be-damned musical.

"You've Got a Hold on Me" is a bluesy ballad from *What's Up?*

(1943), the first Broadway score by the team of Alan Jay Lerner (lyrics) and Frederick Loewe (music). Gloria Warren sang the Cole Porterish number in the original production, and Ann Hampton Callaway made an intriguing recording of it in 1992.

"You've Got Possibilities" is the only song from the camp musical *It's a Bird, It's a Plane, It's Superman!* (1966) to achieve any sort of popularity. The temptress Sydney (Linda Lavin) tried to seduce the square-cut, meek and mild Clark Kent (Bob Holiday) with this sexy and alluring number written by Charles Strouse (music) and Lee Adams (lyric).

"You've Got That Thing," one of Cole Porter's sexier romantic duets, allowed Jack Thompson and Betty Compton to exchange hyperbolic compliments in *Fifty Million Frenchmen* (1929) while making references to Adam and Eve, Samson and Delilah and Helen of Troy. The song's double entendres were not lost in subsequent recordings by Maurice Chevalier, Ted Lewis, Libby Holman, Bobby Short and, in the 1991 complete recording of the score for *Fifty Million Frenchmen*, by Jason Graae.

"You've Got to Be Carefully Taught" is a short (about one minute long), terse song that is the thematic essence of *South Pacific* (1949). Lieutenant Cable (William Tabbert) has left the Polynesian girl Liat because he cannot shake his own prejudices and narrow-minded upbringing. His cowardice, he insists, is something that was ingrained in him. There was some talk of cutting the song before opening, but authors Richard Rodgers (music) and Oscar Hammerstein (lyric) insisted that Cable's bitter musical tirade was what the show was all about. The number was retained, but it was never as popular as the rest of the score, and touring companies of *South Pacific* had difficulty performing the song in the South. Rodgers' melody starts out as a bouncy, childlike ditty; then it turns harsh and dissonant. Hammerstein's lyric repeats the "you've got to be taught" phrase so that the song takes on the feel of a schoolroom lesson. The result is a stinging piece of musical theatre that is packed with difficult and unresolved ideas. Also unresolved is the title; the song is also known as "Carefully Taught" and "You've Got to Be Taught" in various listings.

"You've Got to Pick a Pocket or Two" is a musical lesson in crime from the British import *Oliver!* (1963) by Lionel Bart. The underworld entrepreneur Fagin (Clive Revill) and his boys sing the spirited number to newcomer Oliver Twist (Bruce Prochnik), teaching him the importance and methodology of the pickpocket trade. The music's wide range and exaggerated rises and falls make the number a delightful mock arioso that Revill performed with gusto.

"You've Got What I Need" is a dandy vaudeville-style duet for the two villains in the musical comic strip *It's a Bird, It's a Plane, It's Superman!* (1966) by Charles Strouse (music) and Lee Adams (lyric). The conniving Max Mencken (Jack Cassidy) and the evil scientist Dr. Abner Sedgwick (Michael O'Sullivan) sing and dance the animated number as they plan to destroy Superman.

Z

"Zigeuner" is the romantic narrative ballad about a German princess who falls for a dashing gypsy. It was heard on Broadway in the British import *Bitter Sweet* (1929), an operetta by Noël Coward. The widowed Marchioness of Shayne (Evelyn Laye) sang the number as a song her late husband had written when he was only sixteen years old. Jeanette MacDonald's recording of the ballad is superb.

"Zing! Went the Strings of My Heart!" is the tangy song of romantic realization that came from the revue *Thumbs Up!* (1934). Hal Le Roy and Eunice Healey sang and danced the lighthearted, syncopated song by James Hanley. Judy Garland made a best-selling recording of it when she was only sixteen years old, and in 1972 there was a popular disco version by the Trammps.

"Zip" is the wonderfully droll showstopper from *Pal Joey* (1940) that was sung by Jean Casto as a reporter who recalls her interview with Gypsy Rose Lee. The Richard Rodgers (music) and Lorenz Hart (lyric) comic number follows the thoughts of the famous stripper in a stream-of-consciousness manner, her often-highbrow observations punctuated by the "zip" of her undressing.

Alternate Song Titles

Titles of theatre songs vary from the playbill program to the conductor's score to the printed sheet music to the recorded title. Listed below are some of the most common alternate titles for songs discussed. The alternate title is followed by the title used in this book.

The Abduction Song	It Depends on What You Pay
All the Clouds'll Roll Away	Liza
The Ballad of Uncle Sam	Ballad for Americans
Birdie's Aria	Lionnet
Bongo, Bongo, Bongo	Civilization
Blue Heaven	The Desert Song
The Blue Pajama Song	I Guess I'll Have to Change My Plan
Buddy's Blues	The God-Why-Don't-You-Love-Me Blues
Carefully Taught	You've Got to Be Carefully Taught
Dear Mother, In Dreams I See Her	Lullaby
Dear Old-Fashioned Prison of Mine	Tulip Time in Sing Sing
Do I Do Wrong, Dear?	You're Devastating
Do You Love Me?	D'Ye Love Me?
Drink, Drink, Drink	Drinking Song
Emmett's Lullaby	Lullaby
Ethel Levey's Virginia Song	I Was Born in Virginia
Everything's Up to Date in Kansas City	Kansas City
Ev'rybody Ought to Know How to Do the Tickle Toe	Tickle Toe

The Flesh Failures — Let the Sunshine In
Franklin D. Roosevelt Jones — F.D.R. Jones
Go to Sleep, My Baby — Lullaby
The Gorilla Song — If You Could See Her
Gotta Lotta Livin' to Do — A Lot of Livin' to Do
He Touched Me — She Touched Me
How Do You Solve a Problem Like Maria? — Maria
I, Don Quixote — Man of La Mancha
If — If You Hadn't, But You Did
If You Lak-a Me Like I Lak-a You — Under the Bamboo Tree
I'm in Love With a Wonderful Guy — A Wonderful Guy
I'm Tired of All the Happy Men — Trina's Song
In Old New York — The Streets of New York
In the Land of My Own Romance — The Land of My Own Romance
It's Beginning to Look a Lot Like Christmas — Pine Cones and Holly Berries
I've Been Alone Too Long — Alone Too Long
Jonah Man — I'm a Jonah Man
Kailua — Ka-lu-a
Listen to My Song — Johnny's Song
Little Church Around the Corner — The Church Around the Corner
Mary — Mary's a Grand Old Name
May We Entertain You — Let Me Entertain You
Moritat — Mack the Knife
Mumbo Jumbo Jijiboo J. O'Shea — I've Got Rings on My Fingers
My Rainbow Girl — The Rainbow Girl
Napoleon's a Pastry — Napoleon
Neverland — Never, Never Land
Only Make Believe — Make Believe
Overhead the Moon Is Beaming — Serenade
Play a Simple Melody — A Simple Melody
The Rape Song — It Depends on What You Pay
Reuben, Reuben — Reuben and Cynthia
Rosie, You Are My Posie — Ma Blushin' Rosie
Sailor Tango — Sailors' Song
Some Girl Is on Your Mind — A Girl Is on Your Mind
The Song of Brown October Ale — Brown October Ale
Stairway to Paradise — I'll Build a Stairway to Paradise
Starfish — Seagull, Starfish, Pebble
Sunny Side of the Street — On the Sunny Side of the Street
Theme From *Carnival* — Love Makes the World Go Round
Theme From *The Threepenny Opera* — Mack the Knife

There Are Smiles That Make Me Happy	Smiles
This Is My Lucky Day	Lucky Day
Venice Gavotte	Gavotte
Waltz Hugette	Hugette Waltz
We're Going to Be Pals	A Pal Like You
What Do I Do Now?	Gooch's Song
What Do You Want of Me?	What Does He Want of Me?
When I Marry Mr. Snow	Mr. Snow
When We Were Young	Windflowers
When You Wear a Thirteen Collar	Thirteen Collar
Wonder How I'd Feel	Twin Soliloquies
Won't You Wait Till the Cows Come Home?	Wait Till the Cows Come Home
Why Can't a Woman Be More Like a Man?	A Hymn to Him
Ya Got Trouble	Trouble
Yankee Doodle Dandy	The Yankee Doodle Boy
You Gotta Have Heart	Heart

Musicals

The Act (1977) 233 performances
Arthur in the Afternoon
Little Do They Know

Ain't Misbehavin' (1978) 1,604 performances
Handful of Keys
Lounging at the Waldorf

Ain't Supposed to Die a Natural Death (1971) 256 performances
Come On Feet Do Your Thing
Put a Curse on You

Algeria (1908) 48 performances
Rose of the World
Twilight in Barakeesh

All American (1962) 80 performances
If I Were You
I've Just Seen Her
Nightlife
Once Upon a Time

Allegro (1947) 315 performances
A Fellow Needs a Girl
The Gentleman Is a Dope
Money Isn't Everything
So Far
You Are Never Away

Americana (1932) 77 performances
Brother, Can You Spare a Dime?

America's Sweetheart (1931) 135 performances
I've Got Five Dollars

Andre Charlot's Revue of 1924 (1924) 298 performances
Limehouse Blues
March With Me
Parisian Pierrot
You Were Meant for Me

Angel (1978) 5 performances
Railbird

Angel in the Wings (1947) 308 performances
Civilization

Animal Crackers (1928) 191 performances
Hooray for Captain Spaulding

Ankles Aweigh (1955) 176 performances
Here's to Dear Old Us
Kiss Me and Kill Me With Love
Skip the Build-Up

Annie (1977) 2,377 performances
Easy Street
It's the Hard-Knock Life
Little Girls
Tomorrow
You're Never Fully Dressed Without a Smile

Annie Get Your Gun (1946) 1,147 performances
Anything You Can Do
Doin' What Comes Natur'lly
The Girl That I Marry
I Got Lost in His Arms
I Got the Sun in the Morning
I'm an Indian, Too
Moonshine Lullaby
There's No Business Like Show Business
They Say It's Wonderful

You Can't Get a Man With a Gun

Annie Warbucks (1993) 200 performances (Off Broadway)
It Would Have Been Wonderful
Leave It to the Girls
The Other Woman
A Younger Man

Anya (1965) 16 performances
If This Is Goodbye
Little Hands

Anyone Can Whistle (1964) 9 performances
Anyone Can Whistle
Come Play Wiz Me
Everybody Says Don't
Me and My Town
A Parade in Town
Simple
There Won't Be Trumpets (dropped before opening)

Anything Goes (1934) 420 performances
All Through the Night
Anything Goes
Be Like the Bluebird
Blow, Gabriel, Blow
Easy to Love (dropped before opening)
I Get a Kick Out of You
You're the Top

Applause (1970) 896 performances
Applause
Fasten Your Seat Belts
Welcome to the Theatre
Who's That Girl?

Apple Blossoms (1919) 256 performances
You Are Free

The Apple Tree (1966) 463 performances
Feelings
Friends
Oh, to Be a Movie Star

What Makes Me Love Him?

Arms and the Girl (1950) 134 performances
Nothin' for Nothin'
There Must Be Somethin' Better Than Love

As the Girls Go (1948) 420 performances
I Got Lucky in the Rain
It Takes a Woman to Take a Man
You Say the Nicest Things, Baby

As Thousands Cheer (1933) 400 performances
Easter Parade
Harlem on My Mind
Heat Wave
How's Chances?
Lonely Heart
Supper Time

Aspects of Love (1990) 377 performances
The First Man You Remember
Love Changes Everything

Assassins (1991) 25 performances (Off Broadway)
Another National Anthem
The Ballad of Booth
The Ballad of Guiteau
Everybody's Got the Right
Gun Song
Unworthy of Your Love

At Home Abroad (1935) 198 performances
Get Yourself a Geisha
Hottentot Potentate
Love Is a Dancing Thing
Thief in the Night

Babes in Arms (1937) 289 performances
Babes in Arms
I Wish I Were in Love Again
Imagine
Johnny One-Note
The Lady Is a Tramp

My Funny Valentine
Way Out West
Where or When

Babes in Toyland (1903) 192 performances
I Can't Do the Sum
March of the Toys
Toyland

Baby (1983) 241 performances
The Bear, the Tiger, the Hamster and the Mole (dropped before opening)
Easier to Love
Fatherhood Blues
I Want It All
Patterns (dropped before opening)
The Story Goes On

Bajour (1964) 232 performances
Love-Line
Move Over, New York

Baker Street (1965) 313 performances
Finding Words for Spring
A Married Man
What a Night This Is Going to Be

The Baker's Wife (1976) closed out of town
Chanson
Gifts of Love
Meadowlark
Proud Lady
Serenade
Where Is the Warmth?

Ballroom (1978) 116 performances
I Love to Dance

The Band Wagon (1931) 260 performances
Dancing in the Dark
High and Low
Hoops
I Love Louisa
New Sun in the Sky

Barnum (1980) 854 performances
Bigger Isn't Better
The Colors of My Life
Love Makes Such Fools of Us All
Museum Song

Beauty and the Beast (1994) still running 12/1/94
Human Again
If I Can't Love Her
Me

Bells Are Ringing (1956) 924 performances
Drop That Name
I'm Going Back
It's a Perfect Relationship
It's a Simple Little System
Just in Time
Long Before I Knew You
The Party's Over

Ben Franklin in Paris (1964) 215 performances
Hic Haec Hoc
To Be Alone With You

Best Foot Forward (1941) 326 performances
Buckle Down, Winsocki
Just a Little Joint With a Jukebox

The Best Little Whorehouse in Texas (1978) 1,584 performances
The Bus From Amarillo
Hard Candy Christmas
No Lies
The Sidestep
Twenty-Four Hours of Lovin'

Betsy (1926) 39 performances
Blue Skies
This Funny World

Between the Devil (1937) 93 performances
By Myself
I See Your Face Before Me
Triplets

Big Boy (1925) 176 performances
If You Knew Susie
It All Depends on You
Keep Smiling at Trouble

Big River (1985) 1,005 performances
Free at Last
Leavin's Not the Only Way to Go
River in the Rain
Waitin' for the Light to Shine
Worlds Apart

The Big Show (1916) 425 performances
Poor Butterfly

Billie (1928) 112 performances
Billie

Bitter Sweet (1929) 159 performances
If Love Were All
I'll See You Again
Zigeuner

The Black Crook (1866) 475 performances
Amazons' March
The Broadway, Opera and Bowery Crawl
You Naughty, Naughty Men

Blackbirds of 1928 (1928) 518 performances
Diga Diga Doo
Doin' the New Low-Down
I Can't Give You Anything But Love

The Blonde in Black (1903) 35 performances
I Don't Care

Blood Brothers (1993) still running 2/1/95
Easy Terms
I'm Not Saying a Word
Marilyn Monroe
Shoes Upon the Table
Tell Me It's Not True

Bloomer Girl (1944) 654 performances
The Eagle and Me
Evelina
I Got a Song
It Was Good Enough for Grandma
Right as the Rain
Sunday in Cicero Falls
T'morra, T'morra
When the Boys Come Home

Blossom Time (1921) 516 performances
Serenade
Song of Love

The Blue Paradise (1915) 356 performances
Auf Wiedersehn

The Body Beautiful (1958) 60 performances
All of These and More
Summer Is

Bombo (1921) 219 performances
April Showers
California, Here I Come
Toot, Toot, Tootsie!

The Boy Friend (1954) 485 performances
The Boy Friend
Fancy Forgetting
I Could Be Happy With You
It's Never Too Late to Fall in Love
A Room in Bloomsbury
Safety in Numbers
Won't You Charleston With Me?

The Boys From Syracuse (1938) 235 performances
Dear Old Syracuse
Falling in Love With Love
The Shortest Day of the Year
Sing for Your Supper
This Can't Be Love
What Can You Do With a Man?

Brigadoon (1947) 581 performances
Almost Like Being in Love
Come to Me, Bend to Me
The Heather on the Hill
I'll Go Home With Bonnie Jean
The Love of My Life
My Mother's Wedding Day
There But for You Go I
Waitin' for My Dearie

A Broadway Musical (1978) 1 performance
Yenta Power

By Jupiter (1942) 427 performances
Ev'rything I've Got
Nobody's Heart
Wait Till You See Her

By the Beautiful Sea (1954) 270 performances
Alone Too Long
Coney Island Boat
Hang Up
The Sea Song

Bye Bye Birdie (1960) 607 performances
Baby, Talk to Me
How Lovely to Be a Woman
Hymn for a Sunday Evening
Kids
A Lot of Livin' to Do
One Boy
Put on a Happy Face
The Telephone Hour
What Did I Ever See in Him?

Cabaret (1966) 1,165 performances
Cabaret
Don't Tell Mama
If You Could See Her
It Couldn't Please Me More
Married
Meeskite
So What?

Tomorrow Belongs to Me
Two Ladies
Willkommen

Cabin in the Sky (1940) 156 performances
Cabin in the Sky
Honey in the Honeycomb
Taking a Chance on Love

Call Me Madam (1950) 644 performances
The Best Thing for You
The Hostess With the Mostes' on the Ball
It's a Lovely Day Today
Marrying for Love
They Like Ike
You're Just in Love

Call Me Mister (1946) 734 performances
The Face on the Dime
The Red Ball Express
South America, Take It Away

Camelot (1960) 873 performances
Before I Gaze at You Again
Camelot
C'est Moi
How to Handle a Woman
I Loved You Once in Silence
I Wonder What the King Is Doing Tonight
If Ever I Would Leave You
The Lusty Month of May
The Seven Deadly Virtues
The Simple Joys of Maidenhood
Then You May Take Me to the Fair
What Do the Simple Folk Do?

Can-Can (1953) 892 performances
Can-Can
C'est Magnifique
I Love Paris
It's All Right With Me

Candide (1956) 73 performances
Auto Da Fe (What a Day) (1974 revival)
The Best of All Possible Worlds
Bon Voyage
Gavotte
Glitter and Be Gay
I Am Easily Assimilated
Life Is Happiness Indeed (1974 revival)
Make Our Garden Grow
My Love
Oh, Happy We
What's the Use?
You Were Dead, You Know

Carmelina (1979) 17 performances
It's Time for a Love Song
One More Walk Around the Garden
Someone in April
Why Him?

Carmen Jones (1943) 502 performances
Beat Out Dat Rhythm on a Drum
Dat's Love
Dere's a Cafe on de Corner
My Joe
Stan' Up and Fight

Carnival (1961) 719 performances
Grand Imperial Cirque de Paris
Humming
Love Makes the World Go Round
Mira
Sword, Rose and Cape

Carnival in Flanders (1953) 6 performances
Here's That Rainy Day

Carousel (1945) 890 performances
Blow High, Blow Low
If I Loved You
June Is Bustin' Out All Over
Mister Snow
Soliloquy

What's the Use of Wond'rin'?
When the Children Are Asleep
You'll Never Walk Alone
You're a Queer One, Julie Jordan

Carrie (1988) 5 performances
When There's No One

The Cat and the Fiddle (1931) 395 performances
The Night Was Made for Love
She Didn't Say "Yes"
Try to Forget

Cats (1982) still running 2/1/95
Bustopher Jones
Grizabella
Macavity
Memory
Old Deuteronomy

Celebration (1969) 110 performances
Celebration
I'm Glad to See You've Got What You Want
It's You Who Makes Me Young
Somebody

The Charlot Revue of 1926 (1925) 140 performances
A Cup of Coffee, a Sandwich and You
Poor Little Rich Girl

Charlotte Sweet (1982) 102 performances (Off Broadway)
A-Weaving
Forever

Chess (1988) 68 performances
I Know Him So Well
One Night in Bangkok
Someone Else's Story
Terrace Duet
You and I

Chicago (1975) 898 performances
All I Care About

All That Jazz
Cell Block Tango
Class
Mr. Cellophane
Nowadays
Razzle Dazzle
When You're Good to Mama

Chin-Chin (1914) 295 performances
Goodbye Girls, I'm Through

The Chocolate Dandies (1924) 96 performances
Dixie Moon

A Chorus Line (1975) 6,137 performances
At the Ballet
Dance: Ten; Looks: Three
I Can Do That
The Music and the Mirror
One
Sing!
What I Did for Love

City of Angels (1989) 878 performances
Lost and Found
What You Don't Know About Women
You Can Always Count on Me
You're Nothing Without Me

Closer Than Ever (1989) 288 performances (Off Broadway)
The Bear, the Tiger, the Hamster and the Mole
If I Sing
Life Story
Miss Byrd
Patterns
What Am I Doin'?

Coco (1969) 332 performances
The Money Rings Out Like Freedom
When Your Lover Says Goodbye
The World Belongs to the Young

The Cocoanuts (1925) 276 performances
Always (dropped before opening)

Company (1970) 706 performances
Another Hundred People
Barcelona
Being Alive
Company
Getting Married Today
The Ladies Who Lunch
The Little Things You Do Together
Marry Me a Little (dropped before opening)
Side by Side by Side
Someone Is Waiting
Sorry-Grateful
What Would We Do Without You?
You Could Drive a Person Crazy

A Connecticut Yankee (1927) 418 performances
I Feel at Home With You
My Heart Stood Still
Thou Swell
To Keep My Love Alive (1943 revival)

Conversation Piece (1934) 55 performances
I'll Follow My Secret Heart

The Cradle Will Rock (1937) 108 performances
The Cradle Will Rock
Joe Worker
Nickel Under the Foot

Crazy Quilt (1931) 79 performances
I Found a Million Dollar Baby

Dames at Sea (1968) 575 performances (Off Broadway)
Dames at Sea
The Echo Waltz
Raining in My Heart

Damn Yankees (1955) 1,019 performances
The Game
Goodbye, Old Girl

Heart
A Little Brains -- A Little Talent
Near to You
Shoeless Joe From Hannibal, Mo.
Six Months Out of Every Year
Those Were the Good Old Days
Two Lost Souls
Whatever Lola Wants
Who's Got the Pain?

Dance a Little Closer (1983) 1 performance
Another Life
Dance a Little Closer
He Always Comes Home to Me
Mad
There's Always One You Can't Forget
Why Can't the World Go and Leave Us Alone?

Dancin' Around (1914) 145 performances
It's a Long Way to Tipperary

Darling of the Day (1968) 32 performances
Butler in the Abbey
Let's See What Happens
Sunset Tree

The Day Before Spring (1945) 167 performances
The Day Before Spring
God's Green World
I Love You This Morning
A Jug of Wine
My Love Is a Married Man
This Is My Holiday

Dear Sir (1924) 15 performances
A Mormon Life
My Houseboat on the Harlem

Dear World (1969) 132 performances
And I Was Beautiful
Dear World
Each Tomorrow Morning
Kiss Her Now

The Tea Party

Dearest Enemy (1925) 286 performances
Bye and Bye
Here in My Arms

The Defender (1902) 60 performances
In the Good Old Summer Time

Demi-Tasse Revue (1919) c.12 performances
Come to the Moon
Swanee

The Desert Song (1926) 471 performances
The Desert Song
It
One Alone
The Riff Song

Do I Hear a Waltz? (1965) 220 performances
Do I Hear a Waltz?
Moon in My Window
Take the Moment
We're Gonna Be All Right

Do Re Mi (1960) 400 performances
Adventure
I Know About Love
Make Someone Happy
What's New at the Zoo

A Doll's Life (1982) 5 performances
Learn to Be Lonely
There She Is

Don't Bother Me, I Can't Cope (1972) 1,065 performances
Don't Bother Me, I Can't Cope
Fighting for Pharaoh
Questions

Doonesbury (1983) 104 performances
I Can Have It All

Drat! The Cat! (1965) 8 performances
She Touched Me
She's Roses

Dreamgirls (1981) 1,522 performances
And I Am Telling You I'm Not Going
Cadillac Car
One Night Only
When I First Saw You

DuBarry Was a Lady (1939) 408 performances
But in the Morning, No
Friendship
It Ain't Etiquette
Katie Went to Haiti
Well, Did You Evah!

The Earl and the Girl (1905) 148 performances
How'd You Like to Spoon With Me?

Earl Carroll Vanities (1932) 215 performances
I Gotta Right to Sing the Blues

Eileen (1917) 64 performances
Eileen
Thine Alone

El Capitan (1896) 112 performances
El Capitan's Song

The Enchantress (1911) 72 performances
The Land of My Own Romance

Erminie (1886) c.53 performances
Lullaby

Ernest in Love (1960) 111 performances (Off Broadway)
A Handbag Is Not a Proper Mother

Everybody's Welcome (1931) 139 performances
As Time Goes By

Evita (1979) 1,567 performances
Another Suitcase in Another Hall
Don't Cry for Me, Argentina
High Flying Adored
I'd Be Surprisingly Good for You
A New Argentina
On This Night of a Thousand Stars

Face the Music (1932) 165 performances
I Say It's Spinach
Let's Have Another Cup of Coffee
On a Roof in Manhattan
Soft Lights and Sweet Music

Fade Out -- Fade In (1964) 271 performances
The Usher From the Mezzanine
You Mustn't Be Discouraged

Falsettoland (1990) 215 performances (Off Broadway)
The Baseball Game
Everyone Hates His Parents
Holding to the Ground
Unlikely Lovers
What Would I Do?

Fanny (1954) 888 performances
Be Kind to Your Parents
Fanny
Welcome Home

The Fantasticks (1960) still running 12/1/94 (Off Broadway)
I Can See It
It Depends on What You Pay
Metaphor
Much More
Never Say No
Soon It's Gonna Rain
They Were You
This Plum Is Too Ripe
Try to Remember

Fiddle-Dee-Dee (1900) 262 performances
Ma Blushin' Rosie

Fiddler on the Roof (1964) 3,242 performances
Do You Love Me?
Far From the Home I Love
If I Were a Rich Man
Matchmaker, Matchmaker
Miracle of Miracles
Sabbath Prayer
Sunrise, Sunset
Tevye's Dream
To Life
Tradition

Fifty Miles From Boston (1908) 32 performances
Harrigan

Fifty Million Frenchmen (1929) 254 performances
Find Me a Primitive Man
Paree, What Did You Do to Me?
The Tale of an Oyster
You Do Something to Me
You've Got That Thing

Fine and Dandy (1930) 255 performances
Can This Be Love?
Fine and Dandy

Finian's Rainbow (1947) 725 performances
The Begat
How Are Things in Glocca Morra?
If This Isn't Love
Look to the Rainbow
Necessity
Old Devil Moon
Something Sort of Grandish
That Great Come-and-Get-It Day
When I'm Not Near the Girl I Love
When the Idle Poor Become the Idle Rich

Fiorello! (1959) 795 performances
Gentleman Jimmy
I Love a Cop
Little Tin Box
The Name's LaGuardia

Politics and Poker
Till Tomorrow
When Did I Fall in Love?

Fioretta (1929) 111 performances
Old Wicked Willage of Wenice

The Firebrand of Florence (1945) 43 performances
A Rhyme for Angela
Sing Me Not a Ballad

The Firefly (1912) 120 performances
Giannina Mia
Love Is Like a Firefly
Sympathy

The First (1981) 37 performances
There Are Days and There Are Days

The Five O'Clock Girl (1927) 280 performances
Thinking of You

Flahooley (1951) 40 performances
Flahooley
Here's to Your Illusions
He's Only Wonderful
The Springtime Cometh
The World Is Your Balloon
You, Too, Can Be a Puppet

Flora, the Red Menace (1965) 87 performances
All I Need
Not Every Day of the Week
A Quiet Thing
Sing Happy

Florodora (1900) 553 performances
Tell Me, Pretty Maiden

Flower Drum Song (1958) 600 performances
Don't Marry Me
A Hundred Million Miracles
I Am Going to Like It Here

I Enjoy Being a Girl
Love, Look Away
You Are Beautiful

Flying Colors (1932) 188 performances
Alone Together
Louisiana Hayride
A Shine on Your Shoes

Flying High (1930) 357 performances
Red Hot Chicago
Thank Your Father

Follies (1971) 522 performances
Ah, Paris!
Beautiful Girls
Broadway Baby
Can That Boy Foxtrot (dropped before opening)
Could I Leave You?
The God-Why-Don't-You-Love-Me Blues
I'm Still Here
In Buddy's Eyes
Listen to the Rain on the Roof
Live, Laugh, Love
Losing My Mind
Love Will See Us Through
One More Kiss
The Right Girl
The Road You Didn't Take
The Story of Lucy and Jessie
Too Many Mornings
Waiting for the Girls Upstairs
Who's That Woman?
You're Gonna Love Tomorrow

Follies of 1908 (1908) 120 performances
Shine On, Harvest Moon

Follies of 1909 (1909) 64 performances
By the Light of the Silvery Moon
Up, Up in My Aeroplane

Follies of 1910 (1910) 88 performances
Goodbye, Becky Cohen
Nobody

Follow Me (1916) 78 performances
Oh, Johnny! Oh, Johnny! Oh!

Follow the Girls (1944) 882 performances
I Wanna Get Married

Follow Thru (1929) 403 performances
Button Up Your Overcoat
I Want to Be Bad
My Lucky Star
You Wouldn't Fool Me, Would You?

The Fortune Teller (1898) 40 performances
Always Do As People Say You Should
Gypsy Love Song
Romany Life

Forty-Five Minutes From Broadway (1906) 90 performances
Forty-Five Minutes From Broadway
I Want to Be a Popular Millionaire
Mary's a Grand Old Name
So Long, Mary

The French Doll (1922) 120 performances
Do It Again

Fritz, Our Cousin German (1870) c.26 performances
Lullaby

Funny Face (1927) 244 performances
The Babbitt and the Bromide
Funny Face
He Loves and She Loves
High Hat
My One and Only
'S Wonderful

Funny Girl (1964) 1,348 performances
Don't Rain on My Parade

His Love Makes Me Beautiful
I Want to Be Seen With You Tonight
I'm the Greatest Star
The Music That Makes Me Dance
People
Sadie, Sadie
Who Are You Now?
You Are Woman

A Funny Thing Happened on the Way to the Forum (1962) 964 performances
Comedy Tonight
Everybody Ought to Have a Maid
Free
Love Is in the Air (dropped before opening)
Lovely
Pretty Little Picture
That Dirty Old Man

The Garrick Gaieties (1925) 211 performances
Manhattan
Sentimental Me

The Garrick Gaieties (1926) 174 performances
Mountain Greenery

Gay Divorce (1932) 248 performances
After You, Who?
I've Got You on My Mind
Night and Day

The Gay Life (1961) 113 performances
Come A-Wandering With Me
Magic Moment
Something You Never Had Before

Gentlemen Prefer Blondes (1949) 740 performances
Bye, Bye, Baby
Diamonds Are a Girl's Best Friend
I Love What I'm Doing
A Little Girl From Little Rock

George Washington, Jr. (1906) 81 performances
All Aboard for Broadway

I Was Born in Virginia
You're a Grand Old Flag

George White's Scandals (1922) 88 performances
I'll Build a Stairway to Paradise

George White's Scandals (1924) 192 performances
Somebody Loves Me

George White's Scandals (1926) 424 performances
The Birth of the Blues
Black Bottom
The Girl Is You and the Boy Is Me
Lucky Day

George White's Scandals (1931) 202 performances
Life Is Just a Bowl of Cherries
The Thrill Is Gone

George White's Scandals (1939) 120 performances
Are You Havin' Any Fun?

The Girl Behind the Counter (1907) 260 performances
The Glow-Worm

Girl Crazy (1930) 272 performances
Bidin' My Time
Boy! What Love Has Done to Me!
But Not for Me
Could You Use Me?
Embraceable You
I Got Rhythm
Sam and Delilah

The Girl Friend (1926) 301 performances
The Blue Room
The Girl Friend

The Girl From Utah (1914) 120 performances
Same Sort of Girl
They Didn't Believe Me

The Girl Who Came to Supper (1963) 112 performances
Here and Now
London Is a Little Bit of All Right

Godspell (1971) 2,124 performances
All for the Best
By My Side
Day by Day
Turn Back, O Man
We Beseech Thee

Going Up! (1917) 351 performances
Going Up
Tickle Toe

The Golden Apple (1954) 125 performances
By Goona-Goona Lagoon
Doomed, Doomed, Doomed
It's the Going Home Together
Lazy Afternoon
Scylla and Charybdis
Windflowers

Golden Boy (1964) 569 performances
Don't Forget 127th Street
I Want to Be With You
Lorna's Here
Night Song
This Is the Life

Golden Rainbow (1968) 383 performances
I've Got to Be Me

Goldilocks (1958) 161 performances
The Beast in You
I Can't Be in Love
I Never Know When
Who's Been Sitting in My Chair?

Good Boy (1928) 253 performances
I Wanna Be Loved by You

Good Morning, Dearie (1921) 347 performances
Ka-lu-a

Good News! (1927) 551 performances
The Best Things in Life Are Free
Good News
Just Imagine
Lucky in Love
The Varsity Drag

The Goodbye Girl (1993) 188 performances
A Beat Behind
I Think I Can Play This Part

Goodtime Charley (1975) 104 performances
Goodtime Charley

Grand Hotel (1989) 1,077 performances
I Waltz Alone
Love Can't Happen
Maybe My Baby Loves Me
Roses at the Station
We'll Take a Glass Together
Who Couldn't Dance With You?

The Grand Tour (1979) 61 performances
I'll Be Here Tomorrow
Marianne
One Extraordinary Thing

The Grass Harp (1971) 7 performances
The Babylove Miracle Show
Chain of Love
Marry With Me
Yellow Drum

Grease (1972) 3,388 performances
Alone at a Drive-In Movie
Beauty School Dropout
Freddy, My Love
It's Raining on Prom Night
Look at Me, I'm Sandra Dee
Summer Nights

There Are Worse Things I Could Do

Great Day (1929) 36 performances
Great Day
More Than You Know
Without a Song

Greenwillow (1960) 95 performances
Could've Been a Ring
Faraway Boy
Never Will I Marry
Summertime Love
Walking Away Whistling
What a Blessing

Guys and Dolls (1950) 1,200 performances
Adelaide's Lament
A Bushel and a Peck
Fugue for Tinhorns
Guys and Dolls
If I Were a Bell
I'll Know
I've Never Been in Love Before
Luck Be a Lady
Marry the Man Today
More I Cannot Wish You
My Time of Day
The Oldest Established
Sit Down, You're Rockin' the Boat
Sue Me
Take Back Your Mink

Gypsy (1959) 702 performances
All I Need Is the Girl
Everything's Coming Up Roses
If Momma Was Married
Let Me Entertain You
Little Lamb
Mr. Goldstone
Rose's Turn
Small World
Some People
Together, Wherever We Go

You Gotta Have a Gimmick
You'll Never Get Away From Me

Hair (1968) 1,750 performances
Ain't Got No
Aquarius
Easy to Be Hard
Frank Mills
Good Morning Starshine
Hair
I Got Life
Let the Sunshine In
Where Do I Go?

Half a Sixpence (1965) 512 performances
Half a Sixpence
If the Rain's Got to Fall
Money to Burn

Hallelujah, Baby! (1967) 293 performances
Being Good
Feet, Do Yo' Stuff
Hallelujah, Baby!
My Own Morning
Not Mine
Now's the Time

The Happiest Girl in the World (1961) 97 performances
Adrift on a Star

Happy End (1977) 75 performances
The Bilbao Song
Sailors' Song
Surabaya Johnny

Happy Hunting (1956) 412 performances
Mutual Admiration Society

The Happy Time (1968) 286 performances
Among My Yesterdays
A Certain Girl
The Happy Time
I Don't Remember You

The Life of the Party
Seeing Things

Have a Heart (1917) 76 performances
And I Am All Alone
Napoleon
You Said Something

Hazel Flagg (1953) 190 performances
Every Street's a Boulevard in Old New York
How Do You Speak to an Angel?

Heads Up! (1929) 144 performances
A Ship Without a Sail

Hello Again (1994) 101 performances
Hello Again
Listen to the Music
We Kiss

Hello, Broadway (1914) 123 performances
Barnum and Bailey Rag
Down by the Erie Canal

Hello, Dolly! (1964) 2,844 performances
Before the Parade Passes By
Elegance
Hello, Dolly!
It Only Takes a Moment
Put On Your Sunday Clothes
Ribbons Down My Back
So Long, Dearie

Henry, Sweet Henry (1967) 80 performances
Nobody Steps on Kafritz

Her First Roman (1968) 17 performances
Just for Today

Her Soldier Boy (1916) 198 performances
Pack Up Your Troubles in Your Old Kit Bag

Here's How (1928) 71 performances
Crazy Rhythm

Here's Love (1963) 334 performances
Here's Love
Pine Cones and Holly Berries

High Button Shoes (1947) 727 performances
I Still Get Jealous
On a Sunday by the Sea
Papa, Won't You Dance With Me?
There's Nothing Like a Model T

High Jinks (1913) 213 performances
Something Seems Tingle-Ingleing

High Spirits (1964) 375 performances
Talking to You

Higher and Higher (1940) 104 performances
It Never Entered My Mind

Hit the Deck! (1927) 352 performances
Hallelujah!
Sometimes I'm Happy

Hitchy Koo (1917) 220 performances
I May Be Gone a Long, Long Time

Hold Everything! (1928) 413 performances
You're the Cream in My Coffee

Hold on to Your Hats (1940) 158 performances
Don't Let It Get You Down
There's a Great Day Coming, Mañana
The World Is in My Arms

The Honeymoon Express (1913) 156 performances
You Made Me Love You

Honeymoon Lane (1926) 317 performances
The Little White House

Hooray for What! (1937) 200 performances
Down With Love
God's Country
In the Shade of the New Apple Tree
Moanin' in the Mornin'

Hot Chocolates (1929) 228 performances
Ain't Misbehavin'
Black and Blue

House of Flowers (1954) 165 performances
House of Flowers
I Never Has Seen Snow
A Sleepin' Bee
Two Ladies in de Shade of de Banana Tree

How Now, Dow Jones (1967) 213 performances
Step to the Rear

How to Succeed in Business Without Really Trying (1961) 1,417 performances
Been a Long Day
Brotherhood of Man
Coffee Break
The Company Way
Grand Old Ivy
I Believe in You
Paris Original
A Secretary Is Not a Toy

I Can Get It for You Wholesale (1962) 300 performances
A Gift Today
Have I Told You Lately?
Miss Marmelstein

I Do! I Do! (1966) 560 performances
Flaming Agnes
The Honeymoon Is Over
I Love My Wife
My Cup Runneth Over
A Well Known Fact
What Is a Woman?
When the Kids Get Married

I Love My Wife (1977) 872 performances
Hey There, Good Times
I Love My Wife
Lovers on Christmas Eve
Someone Wonderful I Missed

I Married an Angel (1938) 338 performances
At the Roxy Music Hall
I Married an Angel
Spring Is Here

I'd Rather Be Right (1937) 290 performances
Have You Met Miss Jones?

The Idol's Eye (1897) c.35 performances
The Tattooed Man

I'm Getting My Act Together and Taking It on the Road (1978)
    1,165 performances (Off Broadway)
Dear Tom
Old Friend
Smile
Strong Woman Number

In Dahomey (1903) 53 performances
I'm a Jonah Man

In Trousers (1979) 24 performances (Off Broadway)
I'm Breaking Down

Inside U.S.A. (1948) 399 performances
Haunted Heart
Rhode Island Is Famous for You

The International Revue (1930) 95 performances
Exactly Like You
On the Sunny Side of the Street

Into the Woods (1987) 764 performances
Agony
Children Will Listen
Giants in the Sky
I Know Things Now

No One Is Alone
On the Steps of the Palace

Irene (1919) 670 performances
Alice Blue Gown
Castle of Dreams
Irene

Irma la Douce (1960) 524 performances
Our Language of Love

Is There Life After High School? (1982) 12 performances
Diary of a Homecoming Queen
The Kid Inside
Things I Learned in High School
Thousands of Trumpets

The Isle o' Dreams (1913) 32 performances
Mother Machree
My Wild Irish Rose
When Irish Eyes Are Smiling

It's a Bird, It's a Plane, It's Superman! (1966) 129 performances
It's Superman
The Woman for the Man
You've Got Possibilities
You've Got What I Need

Jack o' Lantern (1917) 265 performances
Wait Till the Cows Come Home

Jamaica (1957) 558 performances
Ain't It de Truth?
Cocoanut Sweet
Leave de Atom Alone
Monkey in the Mango Tree
Napoleon
Push de Button

Jelly's Last Jam (1992) 569 performances
Lovin' Is a Lowdown Blues
That's How You Jazz
The Whole World's Waitin' to Sing Your Song

Jennie (1963) 82 performances
Before I Kiss the World Goodbye
Waitin' for the Evening Train

Jesus Christ Superstar (1971) 720 performances
I Don't Know How to Love Him
King Herod's Song
Superstar

John Murray Anderson's Almanac (1953) 227 performances
Merry Little Minuet

Johnny Johnson (1936) 68 performances
Democracy March
Johnny's Song

The Jolly Bachelors (1910) 84 performances
Has Anybody Here Seen Kelly?

Joseph and the Amazing Technicolor Dreamcoat (1982) 747 performances
Any Dream Will Do
Close Every Door
One More Angel in Heaven
Those Canaan Days

Jubilee (1935) 169 performances
Begin the Beguine
Just One of Those Things
A Picture of Me Without You
Why Shouldn't I?

Jumbo (1935) 233 performances
Little Girl Blue
The Most Beautiful Girl in the World
My Romance

Juno (1959) 16 performances
Bird Upon the Tree
I Wish It So
We're Alive
What Is the Stars?

Katinka (1915) 220 performances
Allah's Holiday
Rackety Coo

Kid Boots (1923) 479 performances
Dinah

The King and I (1951) 1,246 performances
Getting to Know You
Hello, Young Lovers
I Have Dreamed
I Whistle a Happy Tune
My Lord and Master
A Puzzlement
Shall I Tell You What I Think of You?
Shall We Dance?
The Small House of Uncle Thomas
Something Wonderful
We Kiss in a Shadow

Kismet (1953) 583 performances
And This Is My Beloved
Baubles, Bangles and Beads
Night of My Nights
Sands of Time
Stranger in Paradise

Kiss Me, Kate (1948) 1,077 performances
Always True to You in My Fashion
Another Op'nin', Another Show
Brush Up Your Shakespeare
I Hate Men
I've Come to Wive It Wealthily in Padua
So in Love
Too Darn Hot
We Open in Venice
Were Thine That Special Face
Where Is the Life That Late I Led?
Why Can't You Behave?
Wunderbar

Kiss of the Spider Woman (1993) still running 12/1/94
Anything for Him

Dear One
Dressing Them Up
Gimme Love
Kiss of the Spider Woman
Where You Are
You Could Never Shame Me

Knickerbocker Holiday (1938) 168 performances
All Hail the Political Honeymoon
How Can You Tell an American?
It Never Was You
September Song

Kwamina (1961) 32 performances
Another Time, Another Place
The Cocoa Bean Song
Nothing More to Look Forward To
One Wife
Ordinary People
You're as English as . . .

La Cage aux Folles (1983) 1,761 performances
The Best of Times
I Am What I Am
A Little More Mascara

La Strada (1969) 1 performance
Seagull, Starfish, Pebble

Ladies First (1918) 164 performances
The Real American Folk Song

Lady, Be Good! (1924) 330 performances
Fascinating Rhythm
The Half of It, Dearie, Blues
Little Jazz Bird
The Man I Love (dropped before opening)
Oh, Lady, Be Good!
So Am I

Lady in the Dark (1941) 467 performances
Girl of the Moment
My Ship

The Saga of Jenny
This Is New
Tschaikowsky

The Last Sweet Days of Isaac (1970) 485 performances (Off Broadway)
I Want to Walk to San Francisco
My Most Important Moments Go By
Somebody Died Today

The Laugh Parade (1931) 231 performances
You're My Everything

Leave It to Jane (1917) 167 performances
Cleopatterer
Just You Watch My Step
Leave It to Jane
The Siren's Song
The Sun Shines Bright

Leave It to Me! (1938) 291 performances
Get Out of Town
Most Gentlemen Don't Like Love
My Heart Belongs to Daddy

Legs Diamond (1988) 64 performances
The Music Went Out of My Life

Lend an Ear (1948) 460 performances
Doin' the Old Yahoo Step

Les Misérables (1987) still running 2/1/95
Bring Him Home
Empty Chairs at Empty Tables
I Dreamed a Dream
Master of the House
One Day More

Let 'Em Eat Cake (1933) 90 performances
Blue, Blue, Blue
Down With Everyone Who's Up
Mine
On and On and On
The Union League

Let's Face It! (1941) 547 performances
Farming
Let's Not Talk About Love

Lew Leslie's Blackbirds (1930) 61 performances
Memories of You

Life Begins at 8:40 (1934) 237 performances
Fun to Be Fooled
Let's Take a Walk Around the Block
Things
What Can You Say in a Love Song?
You're a Builder-Upper

Li'l Abner (1956) 693 performances
The Country's in the Very Best of Hands
If I Had My Druthers
I'm Past My Prime
Jubilation T. Cornpone
Namely You

Little Jessie James (1923) 453 performances
I Love You

Little Johnny Jones (1904) 52 performances
Give My Regards to Broadway
Life's a Funny Proposition After All
The Yankee Doodle Boy

Little Mary Sunshine (1959) 1,143 performances (Off Broadway)
Colorado Love Call
Look for a Sky of Blue

Little Me (1962) 257 performances
Be a Performer!
Boom-Boom
Deep Down Inside
I Love You
I've Got Your Number
Real Live Girl

The Little Millionaire (1911) 192 performances
Oh, You Wonderful Girl

Little Nellie Kelly (1922) 276 performances
Nellie Kelly, I Love You

A Little Night Music (1973) 600 performances
Bang! (dropped before opening)
Every Day a Little Death
The Glamorous Life
It Would Have Been Wonderful
Liaisons
The Miller's Son
Now/Later/Soon
Send in the Clowns
A Weekend in the Country
You Must Meet My Wife

Little Shop of Horrors (1982) 2,209 performances (Off Broadway)
Dentist!
Skid Row
Somewhere That's Green
Suddenly Seymour

The Little Show (1929) 321 performances
Can't We Be Friends?
Hammacher Schlemmer, I Love You
I Guess I'll Have to Change My Plan
Moanin' Low

A Lonely Romeo (1919) 87 performances
Any Old Place With You

Look, Ma, I'm Dancin' (1948) 188 performances
I'm the First Girl in the Second Row

Lost in the Stars (1949) 273 performances
Cry, the Beloved Country
Lost in the Stars
Stay Well
Thousands of Miles
Train to Johannesburg
Trouble Man

Louisiana Purchase (1940) 444 performances
Fools Fall in Love

It's a Lovely Day Tomorrow
Louisiana Purchase
What Chance Have I?
You're Lonely and I'm Lonely

Love Life (1948) 252 performances
Economics
Green-Up Time
Here I'll Stay
Love Song
Progress
This Is the Life

Lucky Stiff (1988) 15 performances (Off Broadway)
Good to Be Alive
Nice
Times Like This

Lute Song (1946) 142 performances
Mountain High, Valley Low

Mack and Mabel (1974) 65 performances
Hundreds of Girls
I Won't Send Roses
Look What Happened to Mabel
Time Heals Everything
Wherever He Ain't

The Mad Show (1966) 871 performances (Off Broadway)
The Boy From . . .

Madame Sherry (1910) 231 performances
Every Little Movement
Put Your Arms Around Me, Honey

Make Mine Manhattan (1948) 429 performances
Anything Can Happen in New York
My Brudder and Me
The Subway Song

Mame (1966) 1,508 performances
Bosom Buddies
Gooch's Song

If He Walked Into My Life
It's Today
Mame
The Man in the Moon
My Best Girl
Open a New Window
That's How Young I Feel
We Need a Little Christmas

Man of La Mancha (1965) 2,328 performances
Dulcinea
I Really Like Him
I'm Only Thinking of Him
The Impossible Dream
Man of La Mancha
To Each His Dulcinea
What Does He Want of Me?

Man With a Load of Mischief (1966) 240 performances (Off Broadway)
Come to the Masquerade
Hulla-Baloo-Balay
Little Rag Doll
Man With a Load of Mischief

March of the Falsettos (1981) 170 performances (Off Broadway)
Four Jews in a Room Bitching
The Games I Play
I Never Wanted to Love You
March of the Falsettos
The Thrill of First Love
Trina's Song

The Marriage Market (1913) 80 performances
You're Here and I'm Here

Marry Me a Little (1981) 96 performances (Off Broadway)
Bang!
Marry Me a Little
There Won't Be Trumpets

Mary (1920) 219 performances
The Love Nest

May Wine (1935) 213 performances
I Built a Dream One Day

Maytime (1917) 492 performances
Jump Jim Crow!
The Road to Paradise
Will You Remember?

Me and Juliet (1953) 358 performances
The Big Black Giant
Intermission Talk
It's Me
Marriage Type Love
No Other Love

Me and My Girl (1986) 1,486 performances
The Lambeth Walk
Leaning on a Lamp Post
Once You Lose Your Heart

The Me Nobody Knows (1970) 586 performances
Dream Babies
If I Had a Million Dollars
Light Sings

Merrily We Roll Along (1981) 16 performances
Bobby and Jackie and Jack
Franklin Shepard, Inc.
Good Thing Going
Like It Was
Not a Day Goes By
Now You Know
Opening Doors
Our Time

The Merry Widow Burlesque (1908) c.136 performances
Yip-I-Addy-I-Ay!

Mexican Hayride (1944) 481 performances
I Love You
There Must Be Someone for Me

The Midnight Sons (1909) 257 performances
I've Got Rings on My Fingers

Milk and Honey (1961) 543 performances
Chin Up, Ladies
I Will Follow You
Let's Not Waste a Moment
Milk and Honey
Shalom

Miss Liberty (1949) 308 performances
Homework
Just One Way to Say I Love You
Let's Take an Old-Fashioned Walk
Mr. Monotony (dropped before opening)
Only for Americans
Paris Wakes Up and Smiles

Miss Saigon (1991) still running 2/1/95
The American Dream
I Still Believe
If You Want to Die in Bed
The Last Night of the World
The Movie in My Mind

Miss Springtime (1916) 224 performances
My Castle in the Air

Mlle. Modiste (1905) 202 performances
I Want What I Want When I Want It
Kiss Me Again
The Mascot of the Troop
The Time and the Place and the Girl

The Most Happy Fella (1956) 676 performances
Big "D"
Happy to Make Your Acquaintance
How Beautiful the Days
Joey, Joey, Joey
My Heart Is So Full of You
Somebody, Somewhere
Standing on the Corner
Warm All Over

Mother Goose (1903) 105 performances
I Want to Hear a Yankee Doodle Tune

Mr. President (1962) 265 performances
Empty Pockets Filled With Love
Let's Go Back to the Waltz

Mr. Wonderful (1956) 383 performances
Mr. Wonderful
Too Close for Comfort

The Mulligan Guards' Ball (1879) 153 performances
Mulligan Guard

Music Box Revue (1921) 440 performances
Everybody Step
Say It With Music
They Call It Dancing

Music Box Revue (1922) 330 performances
Crinoline Days
Lady of the Evening
Pack Up Your Sins and Go to the Devil

Music Box Revue (1923) 273 performances
What'll I Do?

Music Box Revue (1924) 184 performances
All Alone

Music in the Air (1932) 342 performances
In Egern on the Tegern See
I've Told Ev'ry Little Star
The Song Is You
There's a Hill Beyond a Hill
When the Spring Is in the Air

The Music Man (1957) 1,375 performances
Gary, Indiana
Goodnight, My Someone
Lida Rose
Marian the Librarian
Piano Lesson

Rock Island
Seventy-Six Trombones
Till There Was You
Trouble
Wells Fargo Wagon

My Fair Lady (1956) 2,717 performances
Ascot Gavotte
Get Me to the Church on Time
A Hymn to Him
I Could Have Danced All Night
I'm an Ordinary Man
I've Grown Accustomed to Her Face
Just You Wait
On the Street Where You Live
The Rain in Spain
Show Me
Why Can't the English?
With a Little Bit of Luck
Without You
Wouldn't It Be Loverly?
You Did It

My Favorite Year (1992) 37 performances
If the World Were Like the Movies
Larger Than Life
My Favorite Year
Twenty Million People
Welcome to Brooklyn

My Maryland (1927) 312 performances
Silver Moon
Won't You Marry Me?
Your Land and My Land

My One and Only (1983) 767 performances
Blah, Blah, Blah

The Mystery of Edwin Drood (1985) 608 performances
Both Sides of the Coin
Don't Quit While You're Ahead
Moonfall
Off to the Races

Perfect Strangers
The Wages of Sin
The Writing on the Wall

Naughty Marietta (1910) 136 performances
Ah! Sweet Mystery of Life
I'm Falling in Love With Someone
Italian Street Song
Naughty Marietta
'Neath the Southern Moon
Tramp! Tramp! Tramp!

New Faces of 1952 (1952) 365 performances
The Boston Beguine
Monotonous

New Girl in Town (1957) 431 performances
Flings
It's Good to Be Alive
On the Farm
There Ain't No Flies on Me

The New Moon (1928) 509 performances
Lover, Come Back to Me
One Kiss
Softly, as in a Morning Sunrise
Stouthearted Men
Wanting You

The New Yorkers (1930) 168 performances
I Happen to Like New York
Let's Fly Away
Love for Sale
Take Me Back to Manhattan
Wood

Nick and Nora (1991) 9 performances
Is There Anything Better Than Dancing?
Look Who's Alone Now

The Night Boat (1920) 313 performances
Left All Alone Again Blues

Nine (1982) 732 performances
Be Italian
Be on Your Own
A Call From the Vatican
Guido's Song
My Husband Makes Movies
Only With You
Simple

9:15 Revue (1930) 7 performances
Get Happy

No, No, Nanette (1925) 321 performances
I Want to Be Happy
I've Confessed to the Breeze (dropped before opening)
No, No, Nanette
Tea for Two
Too Many Rings Around Rosie
Where-Has-My-Hubby-Gone? Blues
You Can Dance With Any Girl

No Strings (1962) 580 performances
Loads of Love
No Strings
Nobody Told Me
The Sweetest Sounds

Nymph Errant (1982) 32 performances (Off Broadway)
The Physician

Of Thee I Sing (1931) 441 performances
Because, Because
The Illegitimate Daughter
Jilted
Love Is Sweeping the Country
Of Thee I Sing
The Senatorial Roll Call
Who Cares?
Wintergreen for President

Oh, Boy! (1917) 463 performances
Nesting Time in Flatbush
An Old-Fashioned Wife

A Pal Like You
Till the Clouds Roll By
You Never Knew About Me

Oh! Calcutta! (1969) 397 performances (Off Broadway)
Coming Together, Going Together

Oh, Kay! (1926) 256 performances
Clap Yo' Hands
Do Do Do
Maybe
Someone to Watch Over Me

Oh, Lady! Lady!! (1918) 219 performances
Before I Met You
Bill (dropped before opening)
When the Ships Come Home

Oh, Look! (1918) 68 performances
I'm Always Chasing Rainbows

Oh, Please! (1926) 75 performances
I Know That You Know

Oklahoma! (1943) 2,212 performances
All 'er Nothin'
The Farmer and the Cowman
I Cain't Say No
Kansas City
Lonely Room
Many a New Day
Oh, What a Beautiful Mornin'
Oklahoma
Out of My Dreams
People Will Say We're in Love
Pore Jud Is Daid
The Surrey With the Fringe on Top

Oliver! (1963) 774 performances
As Long As He Needs Me
Consider Yourself
I'd Do Anything
It's a Fine Life

Reviewing the Situation
Where Is Love?
Who Will Buy?
You've Got to Pick a Pocket or Two

Olympus on My Mind (1986) 207 performances (Off Broadway)
At Liberty in Thebes
The Gods on Tap
Heaven on Earth

On a Clear Day You Can See Forever (1965) 280 performances
Come Back to Me
Hurry! It's Lovely Up Here
Melinda
On a Clear Day You Can See Forever
On the S.S. Bernard Cohn
Wait 'Til We're Sixty-Five
What Did I Have That I Don't Have?

On the Town (1944) 463 performances
Come Up to My Place
I Can Cook Too
I Get Carried Away
Lonely Town
Lucky to Be Me
New York, New York
Some Other Time
Ya Got Me

On the Twentieth Century (1978) 449 performances
Babette
Our Private World
Repent

On Your Toes (1936) 315 performances
Glad to Be Unhappy
The Heart Is Quicker Than the Eye
It's Got to Be Love
On Your Toes
Quiet Night
There's a Small Hotel
Too Good for the Average Man

Once on This Island (1990) 469 performances
The Human Heart
Mama Will Provide
Waiting for Life
We Dance

Once Upon a Mattress (1959) 460 performances
In a Little While
Man to Man Talk
Shy

110 in the Shade (1963) 330 performances
Everything Beautiful Happens at Night
Little Red Hat
Love, Don't Turn Away
Melisande
Old Maid
Raunchy
Simple Little Things

One Touch of Venus (1943) 567 performances
Foolish Heart
Speak Low
That's Him
The Trouble With Women
Very, Very, Very

The Only Girl (1914) 240 performances
When You're Away

Orange Blossoms (1922) 95 performances
A Kiss in the Dark

Out of This World (1950) 157 performances
From This Moment On (dropped before opening)
I Am Loved
Nobody's Chasing Me
Use Your Imagination
Where, Oh Where?

Pacific Overtures (1976) 193 performances
A Bowler Hat
Chrysanthemum Tea

Please Hello
Poems
Pretty Lady
Someone in a Tree
Welcome to Kanagawa

Paint Your Wagon (1951) 289 performances
Another Autumn
I Still See Elisa
I Talk to the Trees
They Call the Wind Maria
Wand'rin' Star
What's Goin' On Here?

The Pajama Game (1954) 1,063 performances
Hernando's Hideaway
Hey There
I'll Never Be Jealous Again
I'm Not at All in Love
Once-a-Year-Day!
Seven-and-a-Half Cents
Steam Heat
There Once Was a Man
Think of the Time I Save

Pal Joey (1940) 374 performances
Bewitched
Den of Iniquity
I Could Write a Book
Take Him
What Is a Man?
Zip

Panama Hattie (1940) 501 performances
Let's Be Buddies
Make It Another Old-Fashioned, Please

Pardon My English (1933) 46 performances
Isn't It a Pity?
The Lorelei

Paris (1928) 195 performances
Let's Do It

Let's Misbehave (dropped before opening)
Two Little Babes in the Wood

The Parisian Model (1906) 179 performances
It's Delightful to Be Married

Park Avenue (1946) 72 performances
Don't Be a Woman If You Can

The Passing Show of 1917 (1917) 196 performances
Goodbye Broadway, Hello France

The Passing Show of 1918 (1918) 124 performances
Smiles

The Passing Show of 1922 (1922) 95 performances
Carolina in the Morning

Passion (1994) 340 performances
Farewell Letter
Happiness
I Read
I Wish I Could Forget You
No One Has Ever Loved Me

Peggy-Ann (1926) 333 performances
Where's That Rainbow?

Peter Pan (1954) 152 performances
Captain Hook's Waltz
I Won't Grow Up
I'm Flying
I've Gotta Crow
Never, Never Land
Oh, My Mysterious Lady

The Phantom of the Opera (1988) still running 2/1/95
All I Ask of You
Masquerade
The Music of the Night
The Phantom of the Opera
Prima Donna

Pickwick (1965) 56 performances
If I Ruled the World

The Pink Lady (1911) 312 performances
By the Saskatchewan
Donny Didn't, Donny Did
The Kiss Waltz
My Beautiful Lady

Pins and Needles (1937) 1,108 performances
Chain Store Daisy
Four Little Angels of Peace
Nobody Makes a Pass at Me
One Big Union for Two
Sing Me a Song With Social Significance
Sunday in the Park

Pipe Dream (1955) 246 performances
All at Once You Love Her
Everybody's Got a Home But Me
The Man I Used to Be
Sweet Thursday

Pippin (1972) 1,944 performances
Corner of the Sky
I Guess I'll Miss the Man
Magic to Do
Morning Glow
No Time at All
Spread a Little Sunshine

Plain and Fancy (1955) 461 performances
City Mouse, Country Mouse
This Is All Very New to Me
Young and Foolish

Porgy and Bess (1935) 124 performances
Bess, You Is My Woman Now
I Got Plenty o' Nuttin'
I Loves You, Porgy
I'm on My Way
It Ain't Necessarily So
My Man's Gone Now

Oh, Bess, Oh Where's My Bess?
Oh, I Can't Sit Down
Summertime
There's a Boat Dat's Leavin' Soon for New York
A Woman Is a Sometime Thing

Present Arms (1928) 155 performances
You Took Advantage of Me

The Prince of Tonight (1909) closed out of town
I Wonder Who's Kissing Her Now

The Princess Pat (1915) 158 performances
Love Is the Best of All
Neapolitan Love Song

Promises, Promises (1968) 1,281 performances
I'll Never Fall in Love Again
Knowing When to Leave
Promises, Promises
She Likes Basketball
Whoever You Are

Provincetown Follies (1935) 63 performances
Red Sails in the Sunset

Purlie (1970) 688 performances
First Thing Monday Mornin'
I Got Love
New Fangled Preacher Man
Purlie
Walk Him Up the Stairs

Putting It Together (1993) 59 performances (Off Broadway)
Country House

Queen High (1926) 378 performances
Cross Your Heart

Rags (1986) 4 performances
Blame It on the Summer Night
Children of the Wind
For My Mary

Rags
Three Sunny Rooms

Rainbow (1928) 29 performances
I Want a Man

The Rainbow Girl (1918) 160 performances
The Rainbow Girl

Raisin (1973) 847 performances
Man Say
Measure the Valleys
A Whole Lotta Sunlight

The Ramblers (1926) 291 performances
All Alone Monday

Red, Hot and Blue! (1936) 183 performances
Down in the Depths
It's De-Lovely
Red, Hot and Blue!
Ridin' High

The Red Mill (1906) 274 performances
Because You're You
Every Day Is Ladies' Day With Me
The Isle of Our Dreams
Moonbeams
The Streets of New York
Whistle It

Redhead (1959) 452 performances
Erbie Fitch's Twitch
Look Who's in Love
Merely Marvelous
Pick-Pocket Tango

Regina (1949) 56 performances
The Best Thing of All
Lionnet (Birdie's Aria)
What Will It Be?

Reilly and the Four Hundred (1890) 202 performances
Maggie Murphy's Home

Revenge With Music (1934) 158 performances
If There Is Someone Lovelier Than You
You and the Night and the Music

Rex (1976) 49 performances
Away From You
Christmas at Hampton Court
No Song More Pleasing

Right This Way (1938) 14 performances
I Can Dream, Can't I?
I'll Be Seeing You

The Rink (1984) 204 performances
All the Children in a Row
The Apple Doesn't Fall
Chief Cook and Bottle Washer
Colored Lights
Marry Me
The Rink

Rio Rita (1927) 494 performances
If You're in Love, You'll Waltz
The Rangers' Song
Rio Rita

The Roar of the Greasepaint -- The Smell of the Crowd (1965)
    232 performances
Feeling Good
The Joker
Look at That Face
My First Love Song
Nothing Can Stop Me Now
Where Would You Be Without Me?
Who Can I Turn To?
A Wonderful Day Like Today

The Robber Bridegroom (1976) 145 performances
Love Stolen
The Pricklepear Bloom

Riches
Steal With Style

Roberta (1933) 295 performances
I'll Be Hard to Handle
Smoke Gets in Your Eyes
The Touch of Your Hand
Yesterdays
You're Devastating

Robin Hood (1891) 40 performances
Brown October Ale
Oh, Promise Me

Robinson Crusoe, Jr. (1916) 130 performances
Where Did Robinson Crusoe Go?

Roly-Boly Eyes (1919) 100 performances
Ida, Sweet as Apple Cider

Roly Poly (1912) 60 performances
When It's Apple Blossom Time in Normandy

Romance in Hard Times (1989) 6 performances (Off Broadway)
All Fall Down

Romance, Romance (1988) 297 performances
I'll Always Remember the Song
It's Not Too Late
Romantic Notions
Small Craft Warnings
Think of the Odds

Rosalie (1928) 335 performances
How Long Has This Been Going On?
Oh, Gee! Oh, Joy!

Rose-Marie (1924) 557 performances
The Door of Her Dreams
Indian Love Call
The Mounties
Rose-Marie
Totem Tom Tom

The Rothschilds (1970) 507 performances
In My Own Lifetime
One Room
Sons

Runnin' Wild (1923) 213 performances
Charleston

Sail Away (1961) 167 performances
Sail Away
Something Very Strange
Why Do the Wrong People Travel?

Sally (1920) 570 performances
The Church Around the Corner
Look for the Silver Lining
The Lorelei
Whip-Poor-Will
Wild Rose

Sally in Our Alley (1902) 104 performances
Under the Bamboo Tree

Saratoga (1959) 80 performances
A Game of Poker
Love Held Lightly

The Secret Garden (1991) 706 performances
If I Had a Fine White Horse
Lily's Eyes
Race You to the Top of the Morning
Where in the World
Winter's On the Wing

Seesaw (1973) 296 performances
It's Not Where You Start
Nobody Does It Like Me
Seesaw
Welcome to Holiday Inn

The Serenade (1897) 79 performances
The Angelus
Cupid and I

I Love Thee, I Adore Thee

Sergeant Brue (1905) 152 performances
Put Me in My Little Cell

Set to Music (1939) 129 performances
Mad About the Boy

Seven Lively Arts (1944) 183 performances
Ev'ry Time We Say Goodbye

1776 (1969) 1,217 performances
Cool, Cool, Considerate Men
Is Anybody There?
Molasses to Rum
Momma, Look Sharp
Sit Down, John

70, Girls, 70 (1971) 36 performances
Boom Ditty Boom
Broadway, My Street
Coffee in a Cardboard Cup
Do We?
The Elephant Song
Go Visit
See the Light
Yes

She Loves Me (1963) 301 performances
Dear Friend
Grand Knowing You
Ice Cream
She Loves Me
Tonight at Eight
A Trip to the Library
Try Me
Will He Like Me?

Shenandoah (1975) 1,050 performances
Next to Lovin'
Over the Hill
The Pickers Are Comin'
Violets and Silverbells

We Make a Beautiful Pair

Sherry! (1967) 65 performances
Sherry!

Show Boat (1927) 572 performances
Bill
Can't Help Lovin' Dat Man
I Might Fall Back on You
Life Upon the Wicked Stage
Make Believe
Mis'ry's Comin' 'Round (dropped before opening)
Ol' Man River
Till Good Luck Comes My Way
Where's the Mate for Me?
Why Do I Love You?
You Are Love

Show Girl (1929) 111 performances
Liza

The Show Is On (1936) 237 performances
Buy Yourself a Balloon
By Strauss
Song of the Woodman

Shuffle Along (1921) 504 performances
Bandana Days
I'm Just Wild About Harry
Love Will Find a Way

Silk Stockings (1955) 478 performances
All of You
It's a Chemical Reaction, That's All
Paris Loves Lovers
Stereophonic Sound

Simple Simon (1930) 135 performances
Dancing on the Ceiling (dropped before opening)
He Was Too Good to Me (dropped before opening)
Ten Cents a Dance

Sinbad (1918) 164 performances
Avalon
My Mammy
'N' Everything
Rock-a-Bye Your Baby With a Dixie Melody

Sing for Your Supper (1939) 60 performances
Ballad for Americans

Sing Out the News (1938) 105 performances
F.D.R. Jones

Sitting Pretty (1924) 95 performances
Bongo on the Congo
The Enchanted Train
Sitting Pretty (dropped before opening)
Tulip Time in Sing Sing

1600 Pennsylvania Avenue (1976) 7 performances
Duet for One
Lud's Wedding
The President Jefferson Sunday Luncheon Party March
Take Care of This House

Skyscraper (1965) 241 performances
Everybody Has the Right to Be Wrong

Smile (1986) 48 performances
Disneyland
In Our Hands
Smile

Smiles (1930) 63 performances
Time on My Hands

So Long, Letty (1916) 96 performances
So Long, Letty

Something for the Boys (1943) 422 performances
By the Mississinewah
Hey, Good-Lookin'

Song and Dance (1985) 474 performances
Tell Me on a Sunday
Unexpected Song

Song of Norway (1944) 860 performances
Now!
Strange Music

Song of the Flame (1925) 219 performances
Song of the Flame

The Sound of Music (1959) 1,443 performances
Climb Ev'ry Mountain
Do-Re-Mi
Edelweiss
How Can Love Survive?
The Lonely Goatherd
Maria
My Favorite Things
No Way to Stop It
Sixteen Going on Seventeen
The Sound of Music

South Pacific (1949) 1,925 performances
Bali Ha'i
A Cockeyed Optimist
Dites-Moi
Happy Talk
Honey Bun
I'm Gonna Wash That Man Right Outa My Hair
Some Enchanted Evening
There Is Nothin' Like a Dame
This Nearly Was Mine
Twin Soliloquies
A Wonderful Guy
You've Got to Be Carefully Taught
Younger Than Springtime

Spice of 1922 (1922) 73 performances
Way Down Yonder in New Orleans

Spring Is Here (1929) 104 performances
With a Song in My Heart

St. Louis Woman (1946) 113 performances
Any Place I Hang My Hat Is Home
Come Rain or Come Shine
I Had Myself a True Love
Legalize My Name
Sleep Peaceful, Mr. Used-to-Be
A Woman's Prerogative

Starlight Express (1987) 761 performances
Only You
Starlight Express
U.N.C.O.U.P.L.E.D.

Starting Here, Starting Now (1977) 120 performances (Off Broadway)
Crossword Puzzle
Flair
Starting Here, Starting Now
Watching the Big Parade Go By

Stepping Stones (1923) 241 performances
Once in a Blue Moon

Stop! Look! Listen! (1915) 105 performances
The Girl on the Magazine Cover
I Love a Piano

Stop the World -- I Want to Get Off (1962) 556 performances
Gonna Build a Mountain
Once in a Lifetime
Typically English
What Kind of Fool Am I?

Street Scene (1947) 148 performances
Ain't It Awful the Heat?
I Got a Marble and a Star
Lonely House
Moon-faced, Starry-eyed
Remember That I Care
Somehow I Never Could Believe
We'll Go Away Together
What Good Would the Moon Be?
Wouldn't You Like to Be on Broadway?

The Streets of Paris (1939) 274 performances
South American Way

Strike Up the Band (1930) 191 performances
I've Got a Crush on You
Soon
Strike Up the Band
Typical Self-Made American

The Student Prince (1924) 608 performances
Deep in My Heart, Dear
Drinking Song
Golden Days
Serenade

Subways Are for Sleeping (1961) 205 performances
Be a Santa
Comes Once in a Lifetime
Girls Like Me
I Just Can't Wait
Ride Through the Night

Sugar (1972) 505 performances
November Song
We Could Be Close
When You Meet a Man in Chicago

Sunday in the Park With George (1984) 604 performances
Children and Art
Color and Light
Everybody Loves Louis
Finishing the Hat
Move On
Putting It Together
Sunday
Sunday in the Park With George

Sunny (1925) 517 performances
D'Ye Love Me?
Sunny
Who?

Sweeney Todd, the Demon Barber of Fleet Street (1979) 557 performances
The Ballad of Sweeney Todd
By the Sea
Epiphany
Green Finch and Linnet Bird
Johanna
A Little Priest
Not While I'm Around
Pretty Women
The Worst Pies in London

Sweet Adeline (1929) 234 performances
Don't Ever Leave Me
A Girl Is on Your Mind
Here Am I
'Twas Not So Long Ago
Why Was I Born?

Sweet Charity (1966) 608 performances
Baby, Dream Your Dream
Big Spender
If My Friends Could See Me Now
There's Gotta Be Something Better Than This
Where Am I Going?

Sweethearts (1913) 136 performances
Angelus
Jeanette and Her Little Wooden Shoes
Pretty as a Picture
Sweethearts

Take a Chance (1932) 243 performances
Eadie Was a Lady
Rise 'n' Shine
You're an Old Smoothie

Take Me Along (1959) 448 performances
I Get Embarrassed
Little Green Snake
Promise Me a Rose
Staying Young
Take Me Along
Wint's Song

The Talk of New York (1907) 157 performances
When a Fellow's on the Level With a Girl That's on the Square

The Tap Dance Kid (1983) 669 performances
Fabulous Feet
Like Him
William's Song

Tell Me More (1925) 100 performances
Kickin' the Clouds Away

Tenderloin (1960) 216 performances
Artificial Flowers
Good Clean Fun
How the Money Changes Hands
Little Old New York
The Picture of Happiness

They're Playing Our Song (1979) 1,082 performances
I Still Believe in Love
They're Playing My Song

The Third Little Show (1931) 136 performances
Mad Dogs and Englishmen

This Is the Army (1942) 113 performances
I Left My Heart at the Stage Door Canteen
I'm Getting Tired So I Can Sleep
This Is the Army, Mr. Jones

This Year of Grace (1928) 158 performances
A Room With a View
World Weary

Three Guys Naked From the Waist Down (1985) 160 performances
    (Off Broadway)
Don't Wanna Be No Superstar
I Don't Believe in Heroes Anymore

The Three Musketeers (1928) 318 performances
Ma Belle
March of the Musketeers
My Sword and I

Your Eyes

Three Postcards (1987) 22 performances (Off Broadway)
Cast of Thousands
The Picture in the Hall

Three Twins (1908) 288 performances
Cuddle Up a Little Closer, Lovey Mine
The Yama Yama Man

The Threepenny Opera (1954) 2,611 performances (Off Broadway)
Jealousy Duet
Mack the Knife
Pirate Jenny

Three's a Crowd (1930) 272 performances
Body and Soul
Something to Remember You By

Through the Years (1932) 20 performances
Drums in My Heart
Through the Years

Thumbs Up! (1934) 156 performances
Autumn in New York
Zing! Went the Strings of My Heart

The Time, the Place and the Girl (1907) 32 performances
Waning Honeymoon

Tip-Toes (1925) 194 performances
Looking for a Boy
Sweet and Low-Down
That Certain Feeling
These Charming People

Too Many Girls (1939) 249 performances
Give It Back to the Indians
I Didn't Know What Time It Was

Treasure Girl (1928) 68 performances
Feeling I'm Falling
I Don't Think I'll Fall in Love Today

I've Got a Crush on You
K-ra-zy for You
What Causes That?

A Tree Grows in Brooklyn (1951) 270 performances
He Had Refinement
I'll Buy You a Star
I'm Like a New Broom
Look Who's Dancing
Love Is the Reason
Make the Man Love Me

A Trip to Chinatown (1891) 657 performances
After the Ball
The Bowery
Reuben and Cynthia

Twirly Whirly (1902) 244 performances
Come Down, Ma Evenin' Star

Two by Two (1970) 352 performances
I Do Not Know a Day I Did Not Love You
Two by Two

Two Gentlemen of Verona (1971) 627 performances
Bring All the Boys Back Home
Night Letter
Who Is Silvia?

Two Little Girls in Blue (1921) 135 performances
Oh Me! Oh My!

Two on the Aisle (1951) 281 performances
Give a Little, Get a Little
If You Hadn't, But You Did

The Unsinkable Molly Brown (1960) 532 performances
Are You Sure?
Belly Up to the Bar, Boys
I Ain't Down Yet
I'll Never Say No

Up and Down Broadway (1910) 72 performances
Chinatown, My Chinatown

Up in Central Park (1945) 504 performances
April Snow
The Big Back Yard
Close as Pages in a Book

The Vagabond King (1925) 511 performances
Hugette Waltz
Love for Sale
Love Me Tonight
Only a Rose
Some Day
Song of the Vagabonds

Very Good Eddie (1915) 341 performances
Babes in the Wood
Nodding Roses
Some Sort of Somebody
Thirteen Collar

Very Warm for May (1939) 59 performances
All the Things You Are
Heaven in My Arms
In the Heart of the Dark

Wake Up and Dream (1929) 136 performances
What Is This Thing Called Love?

Walk a Little Faster (1932) 119 performances
April in Paris
That's Life

Walking Happy (1966) 161 performances
Walking Happy

Wang (1891) 151 performances
Ask the Man in the Moon
A Pretty Girl

Watch Your Step (1914) 175 performances
A Simple Melody

The Syncopated Walk

Welcome to the Club (1989) 12 performances
At My Side
In the Name of Love

West Side Story (1957) 732 performances
America
A Boy Like That/I Have a Love
Cool
Gee, Officer Krupke!
I Feel Pretty
Jet Song
Maria
One Hand, One Heart
Something's Coming
Somewhere
Tonight
Tonight Quintet

What Makes Sammy Run? (1964) 540 performances
The Friendliest Thing
My Hometown
A Room Without Windows

What's Up? (1943) 63 performances
My Last Love
You've Got a Hold on Me

Where's Charley? (1948) 792 performances
At the Red Rose Cotillion
Make a Miracle
My Darling, My Darling
The New Ashmolean Marching Society and Students' Conservatory Band
Once in Love With Amy

Whoopee (1928) 379 performances
Love Me or Leave Me
Makin' Whoopee

Wildcat (1960) 171 performances
Hey, Look Me Over!
What Takes My Fancy

Wildflower (1923) 477 performances
Bambalina
Wildflower

The Will Rogers Follies (1991) 973 performances
Give a Man Enough Rope
My Big Mistake
Our Favorite Son
Willomania

Wish You Were Here (1952) 598 performances
Don Jose of Far Rockaway
Where Did the Night Go?
Wish You Were Here

The Wiz (1975) 1,672 performances
Be a Lion
Ease on Down the Road
Everybody Rejoice
Home
If You Believe

Woman of the Year (1981) 770 performances
The Grass Is Always Greener
It Isn't Working
One of the Boys
When You're Right, You're Right

Wonderful Town (1953) 559 performances
Conga!
Conversation Piece
A Little Bit in Love
Ohio
One Hundred Easy Ways
A Quiet Girl
Wrong Note Rag

Working (1978) 25 performances
All the Livelong Day
Brother Trucker
Cleanin' Women
Fathers and Sons
It's an Art

Just a Housewife
The Mason
Nobody Tells Me How

A World of Pleasure (1915) 116 performances
Pretty Baby

The Yearling (1965) 3 performances
Why Did I Choose You?

Yip, Yip, Yaphank (1918) 32 performances
Mandy
Oh! How I Hate to Get Up in the Morning
We're on Our Way to France

You Never Know (1938) 78 performances
At Long Last Love

Your Arms Too Short to Box With God (1976) 427 performances
We're Gonna Have a Good Time
Your Arms Too Short to Box With God

Your Own Thing (1968) 933 performances (Off Broadway)
The Middle Years

You're a Good Man, Charlie Brown (1967) 1,597 performances
  (Off Broadway)
Book Report
Happiness
Suppertime
T.E.A.M.

Ziegfeld Follies (1911) 80 performances
Woodman, Woodman, Spare That Tree

Ziegfeld Follies (1912) 88 performances
Row, Row, Row

Ziegfeld Follies (1915) 104 performances
Hello, Frisco!

Ziegfeld Follies (1919) 171 performances
I've Got My Captain Working for Me Now

A Pretty Girl Is Like a Melody
You Cannot Make Your Shimmy Shake on Tea
You'd Be Surprised

Ziegfeld Follies (1920) 123 performances
Tell Me, Little Gypsy

Ziegfeld Follies (1921) 119 performances
My Man
Second Hand Rose

Ziegfeld Follies (1922) 541 performances
Mr. Gallagher and Mr. Shean

Ziegfeld Follies (1927) 167 performances
Shaking the Blues Away

Ziegfeld Follies (1934) 182 performances
The Last Round-Up
I Like the Likes of You
Wagon Wheels
What Is There to Say?

Ziegfeld Follies (1936) 115 performances
He Hasn't a Thing Except Me
I Can't Get Started

Zorbá (1968) 305 performances
The First Time
Happy Birthday
Life Is
No Boom Boom
Only Love

Bibliography

General Works on the American Musical Theatre

Abbott, George. *Mister Abbott*. New York: Random House, 1963.

Alpert, Hollis. *Broadway: 125 Years of Musical Theatre*. New York: Arcade Publishers, 1991.

Atkinson, Brooks. *Broadway*. Rev. ed. New York: Macmillan Publishing Co., 1974.

Banham, Martin. (ed.) *The Cambridge Guide to Theatre*. New York: Cambridge University Press, 1992.

Baral, Robert. *Revue: The Great Broadway Period*. Rev. ed. New York: Fleet Press Corp., 1970.

Bell, Marty. *Broadway Stories: A Backstage Journey Through Musical Theatre*. New York: Limelight Editions, 1993.

The Best Plays. 77 editions. Editors: Garrison Sherwood and John Chapman (1894-1919); Burns Mantle (1919-1947); John Chapman (1947-1952); Louis Kronenberger (1952-1961); Henry Hewes (1961-1964); Otis Guernsey, Jr. (1964-1994). New York: Dodd, Mead & Co., 1894-1988; New York: Applause Theatre Book Publishers, 1988-1993; New York: Limelight Editions, 1994.

Bloom, Ken. *Broadway: An Encyclopedic Guide to the History, People and Places of Times Square*. New York: Facts on File Publications, 1991.

Blum, Daniel, and John Willis. *A Pictorial History of the American Theatre, 1860-1980*. 5th ed. New York: Crown Publishers, 1981.

Bordman, Gerald. *American Musical Comedy: From Adonis to Dreamgirls*. New York: Oxford University Press, 1982.

_____. *American Musical Revue: From The Passing Show to Sugar Babies*. New York: Oxford University Press, 1985.

_____. *American Musical Theatre: A Chronicle*. 2nd ed. New York: Oxford University Press, 1992.

_____. *American Operetta: From H.M.S. Pinafore to Sweeney Todd*. New

York: Oxford University Press, 1981.

_____. *The Oxford Companion to American Theatre*. 2nd ed. New York: Oxford University Press, 1992.

Botto, Louis. *At This Theatre: An Informal History of New York's Legitimate Theatres*. New York: Dodd, Mead & Co., 1984.

Bowers, Dwight Blocker. *American Musical Theater: Shows, Songs, and Stars*. Washington, DC: Smithsonian Institution Press, 1989.

Burton, Jack. *The Blue Book of Broadway Musicals*. Rev. ed. Watkins Glen, NY: Century House, 1974.

Drone, Jeanette M. *Index to Opera, Operetta and Musical Comedy Synopses in Collections and Periodicals*. Metuchen, NJ: Scarecrow Press, 1978.

Engel, Lehman. *The American Musical Theater: A Consideration*. New York: CBS Legacy Collection Books, 1967.

Ewen, David. *New Complete Book of the American Musical Theatre*. New York: Henry Holt & Co., 1976.

Fields, Armond, and L. Marc Fields. *From the Bowery to Broadway: Lew Fields and the Roots of American Popular Theatre*. New York: Oxford University Press, 1993.

Ganzl, Kurt, and Andrew Lamb. *Ganzl's Book of the Musical Theatre*. New York: Schirmer Books, 1989.

_____. *Ganzl's Encyclopedia of the Musical Theatre*. New York: Schirmer Books, 1993.

Goldman, William. *The Season: A Candid Look at Broadway*. New York: Harcourt, Brace and World, 1969.

Gottfried, Martin. *All His Jazz: The Life and Death of Bob Fosse*. New York: Bantam Books, 1990.

_____. *Broadway Musicals*. New York: Harry N. Abrams, 1980.

_____. *More Broadway Musicals*. New York: Harry N. Abrams, 1991.

Green, Stanley. *Broadway Musicals of the 1930s*. New York: Da Capo Press, 1982.

_____. *Broadway Musicals Show By Show* 3rd ed. Milwaukee: Hal Leonard Publishing Corp., 1990.

_____. *Encyclopedia of the Musical Theatre*. New York: Dodd, Mead & Co., 1976.

_____. *The World of Musical Comedy*. New York: A.S. Barnes & Co., 1980.

Grubb, Kevin Boyd. *Razzle Dazzle: The Life and Work of Bob Fosse*. New York: St. Martin's Press, 1989.

Guernsey, Otis L. (ed.). *Curtain Times: The New York Theatre, 1965-1987*. New York: Applause Theatre Book Publishers, 1987.

Henderson, Mary C. *Theater in America*. New York: Harry N. Abrams, 1986.

Hirsch, Foster. *Harold Prince and the American Musical Theatre*. New York: Cambridge University Press, 1989.

Hischak, Thomas S. *Stage It With Music: An Encyclopedic Guide to the American Musical Theatre*. Westport, CT: Greenwood Press, 1993.

Ilson, Carol. *Harold Prince: From Pajama Game to Phantom of the Opera*. Ann Arbor: UMI Research Press, 1989.

Jackson, Arthur. *The Best Musicals From Show Boat to A Chorus Line*. New York: Crown Publishers, 1977.

Kislan, Richard. *Hoofing on Broadway: A History of Show Dancing*. New York: Prentice-Hall, 1987.

_____.*The Musical: A Look at the American Musical Theater*. Englewood Cliffs, NJ: Prentice-Hall, 1980.

Laufe, Abe. *Anatomy of a Hit: Long-Run Plays on Broadway from 1900 to the Present Day*. New York: Hawthorn Books, Inc., 1966.

_____. *Broadway's Greatest Musicals*. New York: Funk and Wagnalls, 1977.

Leiter, Samuel L. *The Encyclopedia of the New York Stage, 1920-1930*. Westport, CT: Greenwood Press, 1985.

_____. *The Encyclopedia of the New York Stage, 1930-1940*. Westport, CT: Greenwood Press, 1989.

_____. *The Encyclopedia of the New York Stage, 1940-1950*. Westport, CT: Greenwood Press, 1992.

_____. *Ten Seasons: New York Theatre in the Seventies*. Westport, CT: Greenwood Press, 1986.

Lerner, Alan Jay. *The Musical Theatre: A Celebration*. New York: McGraw-Hill Book Co., 1986.

Little, Stuart W. *Enter Joe Papp: In Search of a New American Theatre*. New York: Coward, McCann and Geoghegan, Inc., 1974.

Mandelbaum, Ken. *A Chorus Line and the Musicals of Michael Bennett*. New York: St. Martin's Press, 1989.

_____. *Not Since Carrie: Forty Years of Broadway Musical Flops*. New York: St. Martin's Press, 1991.

Mates, Julian. *America's Musical Stage: Two Hundred Years of Musical Theatre*. Westport, CT: Greenwood Press, 1985.

McSpadden, J. Walker. *Operas and Musical Comedies*. New York: Thomas Y. Crowell Co., 1958.

Mordden, Ethan. *Better Foot Forward: The History of American Musical Theatre*. New York: Grossman Publishers, 1976.

_____. *Broadway Babies: The People Who Made the American Musical*. New York: Oxford University Press, 1983.

Morehouse, Ward. *Matinee Tomorrow: Fifty Years of Our Theater*. New York: McGraw-Hill Book Co., 1949.

Morrow, Lee Alan. *The Tony Award Book*. New York: Abbeville Press, 1987.

Nelson, Stephen. *Only a Paper Moon: The Theatre of Billy Rose*. Ann Arbor: UMI Research Press, 1987.

Peterson, Bernard L. *A Century of Musicals in Black and White*. Westport, CT:

Greenwood Press, 1993.

Porter, Susan L. *With an Air Debonair: Musical Theatre in America, 1785-1815*. Washington, DC: Smithsonian Institution Press, 1992.

Prince, Hal. *Contradictions: Notes on Twenty-Six Years in the Theatre*. New York: Dodd, Mead & Co., 1974.

Rosenberg, Bernard, and Ernest Harburg. *The Broadway Musical: Collaboration in Commerce and Art*. New York: New York University Press, 1993.

Salem, James M. *A Guide to Critical Reviews: The Musical, 1909-1989*. Metuchen, NJ: Scarecrow Press, 1991.

Schlundt, Christena L. *Dance in the Musical Theatre: Jerome Robbins and His Peers, 1934-1965*. New York: Garland Publishing, 1989.

Sheward, David. *It's a Hit: The Back Stage Book of Longest-Running Broadway Shows, 1884 to the Present*. New York: Watson-Guptill Publications-BPI Communications, Inc., 1994.

Simas, Rick. *The Musicals No One Came to See*. New York: Garland Publishing, 1987.

Smith, Cecil, and Glenn Litton. *Musical Comedy in America*. 2nd ed. New York: Theatre Arts Books, 1981.

Suskin, Steven. *Opening Night on Broadway: A Critical Quotebook of the Golden Era of the Musical Theatre*. New York: Schirmer Books, 1990.

Swain, Joseph P. *The Broadway Musical: A Critical and Musical Survey*. New York: Oxford University Press, 1990.

Theatre World. 48 editions. Editors: Daniel Blum (1944-1964); John Willis (1964-). New York: Greenburg, 1944-1957; Philadelphia: Chilton, 1957-1964; New York: Crown Publishers, 1964-1990; New York: Applause Theatre Book Publishers, 1991.

Toll, Robert C. *On With the Show: The First Century of Show Business in America*. New York: Oxford University Press, 1976.

Traubner, Richard. *Operetta: A Theatrical History*. Garden City, NY: Doubleday & Co., 1983.

Woll, Allen. *Black Musical Theatre: From Coontown to Dreamgirls*. Baton Rouge: Louisiana State University Press, 1989.

Works on Theatre Songs and Songwriters

Adler, Richard, with Lee Davis. *You Gotta Have Heart: An Autobiography*. New York: Donald I. Fine, 1990.

Armitage, Merle. *George Gershwin: Man and Legend*. New York: Duell, Sloane and Pearce, 1958.

Arbold, Elliot. *Deep in My Heart: Sigmund Romberg*. New York: Duell, Sloane and Pearce, 1949.

Bach, Bob, and Mercer, Ginger, (eds.) *Our Huckleberry Friend: The Life, Times and Lyrics of Johnny Mercer*. Secaucus, NJ: Lyle Stuart, 1982.

Barrett, Mary Ellin. *Irving Berlin: A Daughter's Memoir*. New York: Simon and Schuster, 1994.

Bergreen, Laurence. *As Thousands Cheer: The Life of Irving Berlin*. New York: Viking Press, 1990.

Bernstein, Leonard. *Findings*. New York: Simon and Schuster, 1982.

Bloom, Ken. *American Song: The Complete Musical Theatre Companion, 1900-1984*. New York: Facts on File Publications, 1985.

Bordman, Gerald. *Days to Be Happy, Years to Be Sad: The Life and Music of Vincent Youmans*. New York: Oxford University Press, 1982.

————. *Jerome Kern: His Life and Music*. New York: Oxford University Press, 1980.

Brahms, Caryl, and Ned Sherrin. *Song By Song: The Lives and Work of 14 Great Lyric Writers*. Egerton, Bolton (U.K.): R. Anderson Publications, 1984.

Burton, Humphrey. *Leonard Bernstein*. Garden City, NY: Doubleday & Co., 1994.

Citron, Stephen. *Noel and Cole: The Sophisticates*. New York: Oxford University Press, 1993.

————. *The Wordsmiths: Oscar Hammerstein II and Alan Jay Lerner*. New York: Oxford University Press, 1995.

Cohan, George M. *Twenty Years on Broadway*. New York: Harper and Brothers, 1924.

David, Lee. *Bolton and Wodehouse and Kern*. New York: James H. Heineman, Inc., 1993.

Dietz, Howard. *Dancing in the Dark*. New York: Quadrangle Books/New York Times Book Co., 1974.

Donaldson, Frances. *P.G. Wodehouse: A Biography*. New York: Alfred A. Knopf, 1982.

Drew, David. *Kurt Weill: A Handbook*. Berkeley: University of California Press, 1987.

Duke, Vernon. *Passport to Paris*. Boston: Little, Brown, 1955.

Eells, George. *The Life That Late He Led: A Biography of Cole Porter*. New York: G.P. Putnam's Sons, 1967.

Engel, Lehman. *Their Words Are Music: The Great Theatre Lyricists and Their Lyrics*. New York: Crown Publishers, 1975.

Ewen, David. *American Songwriters*. New York: H. W. Wilson Co., 1987.

————. *George Gershwin: His Journey to Greatness*. Westport, CT: Greenwood Press, 1977.

————. *Richard Rodgers*. New York: Holt, 1957.

————. *The World of Jerome Kern*. New York: Holt, 1960.

Fordin, Hugh. *Getting to Know Him: A Biography of Oscar Hammerstein II*. New York: Random House, 1977.

Freedland, Michael. *Irving Berlin*. New York: Stein and Day, 1974.

_____. *Jerome Kern*. New York: Stein and Day, 1981.

Furia, Philip. *The Poets of Tin Pan Alley: A History of America's Great Lyricists*. New York: Oxford University Press, 1990.

Gershwin, Ira. *Lyrics on Several Occasions*. New York: Viking Press, 1973.

Gordon, Eric A. *Mark the Music: The Life and Work of Marc Blitzstein*. New York: St. Martin's Press, 1989.

Gordon, Joanne. *Art Isn't Easy: The Achievement of Stephen Sondheim*. Carbondale: Southern Illinois University Press, 1990.

Gottfried, Martin. *Sondheim*. New York: Harry N. Abrams, 1993.

Grafton, David. *Red, Hot and Rich: An Oral History of Cole Porter*. New York: Stein and Day, 1987.

Grattan, Virginia L. *American Women Songwriters: A Biographical Dictionary*. Westport, CT: Greenwood Press, 1993.

Green, Benny. *P.G. Wodehouse: A Literary Biography*. New York: The Rutledge Press, 1981.

Green, Stanley. *Rodgers and Hammerstein Fact Book*. Milwaukee: Lynn Farnol Group/Hal Leonard Publishers, 1986.

_____. *The Rodgers and Hammerstein Story*. New York: John Day Co., 1963.

Guernsey, Otis L. (ed.). *Broadway Song and Story: Playwrights, Lyricists, Composers Discuss Their Hits*. New York: Dodd, Mead & Co., 1985.

_____. *Playwrights, Lyricists, Composers on Theatre*. New York: Dodd, Mead & Co., 1974.

Hamlisch, Marvin, with Gerald Gardner. *The Way I Was*. New York: Scribner, 1992.

Hammerstein, Oscar, II. *Lyrics*. Rev. ed. Milwaukee: Hal Leonard Books, 1985.

Hart, Dorothy, and Robert Kimball (eds.) *The Complete Lyrics of Lorenz Hart*. New York: Alfred A. Knopf, 1986.

Hart, Dorothy. *Thou Swell, Thou Witty: The Life and Lyrics of Lorenz Hart*. New York: Harper & Row, 1976.

Hischak, Thomas S. *Word Crazy: Broadway Lyricists From Cohan to Sondheim*. New York: Praeger Publishers, 1991.

Hodgins, Gordon W. *The Broadway Musical: A Complete LP Discography*. Metuchen, NJ: Scarecrow Press, 1980.

Hummel, David. *The Collector's Guide to the American Musical Theatre*. Metuchen, NJ: Scarecrow Press, 1984.

Hyland, William G. *The Song Is Ended: Songwriters and American Music, 1900-1950*. New York: Oxford University Press, 1995.

Jablonski, Edward. *Gershwin*. Garden City, NY: Doubleday & Co., 1987.

_____. *Harold Arlen: Happy With the Blues*. Garden City, NY: Doubleday & Co., 1961.

Jablonski, Edward, and Lawrence D. Stewart. *The Gershwin Years*. Garden City,

NY: Doubleday & Co., 1958/1973.

Kahn, E.J. *The Merry Partners: The Age and Stage of Harrigan and Hart.* New York: Random House, 1955.

Kasha, Al, and Joel Hirschhorn. *Notes on Broadway: Conversations With the Great Songwriters.* Chicago: Contemporary Books, 1985.

Kaye, Joseph. *Victor Herbert.* New York: Crown Publishers, 1931.

Kendall, Alan. *George Gershwin: A Biography..* New York: Universe Books, 1987.

Kimball, Robert (ed.). *Cole.* New York: Holt, Rinehart and Winston, 1971.

_____. *The Complete Lyrics of Cole Porter.* New York: Alfred A. Knopf, 1983.

_____. *The Complete Lyrics of Ira Gershwin.* New York: Alfred A. Knopf, 1993.

Kimball, Robert, and William Bolcom. *Reminiscing With Sissle and Blake.* New York: Viking Press, 1973.

Kimball, Robert, and Alfred Simon. *The Gershwins.* New York: Atheneum, 1973.

Lees, Gene. *Inventing Champagne: The Worlds of Lerner and Loewe.* New York: St. Martin's Press, 1990.

Lerner, Alan Jay. *The Street Where I Live.* New York: W.W. Norton & Co., 1978.

Lerner, Alan Jay, and Benny Green (ed.). *A Hymn to Him: The Lyrics of Alan Jay Lerner.* New York: Limelight Editions, 1987.

Lewine, Richard, and Alfred Simon. *Encyclopedia of Theatre Music.* New York: Random House, 1961.

_____. *Songs of the Theater.* New York: H. W. Wilson Company, 1984.

Loesser, Susan. *A Most Remarkable Fella: Frank Loesser and the Guys and Dolls in His Life.* New York: Donald I. Fine, 1993.

Lynch, Richard Chigley. *Broadway on Record: A Directory of New York Cast Recordings of Musical Shows, 1931-1986.* Westport, CT: Greenwood Press, 1987.

McCabe, John. *George M. Cohan: The Man Who Owned Broadway.* Garden City, NY: Doubleday & Co., 1973.

McGuire, Patricia. *Lullaby of Broadway: The Life of Al Dubin.* Secaucus, NJ: Citadel Press, 1983.

Meyerson, Harold, and Ernie Harburg. *Who Put the Rainbow in The Wizard of Oz? Yip Harburg, Lyricist.* Ann Arbor: University of Michigan Press, 1993.

Mordden, Ethan. *Rodgers and Hammerstein.* New York: Harry N. Abrams, 1992.

Morehouse, Ward. *George M. Cohan: Prince of the American Theater.* Philadelphia: J.B. Lippincott, 1943.

Morley, Sheridan. *A Talent to Amuse: Noel Coward.* New York: Doubleday, 1970.

Nolan, Frederick. *The Sound of Their Music: The Story of Rodgers and Hammerstein*. New York: Walker & Co., 1978.

_____. *Lorenz Hart: A Poet on Broadway*. New York: Oxford University Press, 1994.

Peyser, Joan. *Bernstein: A Biography*. New York: Ballantine, 1988.

_____. *The Memory of All That: The Life of George Gershwin*. New York: Simon and Schuster, 1993.

Raymond, Jack. *Show Music on Record*. New York: Frederick Ungar, 1981.

Rodgers, Richard. *Musical Stages: An Autobiography*. New York: Random House, 1975.

Root, Deane L. *American Popular Stage Music, 1860-1880*. Ann Arbor: UMI Research Press, 1987.

Rose, Al. *Eubie Blake*. New York: Schirmer Books, 1979.

Rosenberg, Deena. *Fascinating Rhythm: The Collaboration of George and Ira Gershwin*. New York: Dutton, 1991.

Sanders, Ronald. *The Days Grow Short: The Life and Music of Kurt Weill*. New York: Holt, Rinehart and Winston, 1980.

Schwartz, Charles. *Cole Porter: A Biography*. New York: Dial Press, 1977.

_____. *Gershwin, His Life and Music*. Indianapolis: Bobbs-Merrill Co., 1973.

Shivers, Alfred. *The Life of Maxwell Anderson*. New York: Stein and Day, 1983.

Suskin, Steven. *Show Tunes (1905-1985)*. New York: Dodd, Mead & Co., 1986.

Taylor, Deems. *Some Enchanted Evenings: The Story of Rodgers and Hammerstein*. New York: Harper and Brothers, 1953.

Taylor, Theodore. *Jule: The Story of Composer Jule Styne*. New York: Random House, 1979.

Waters, Edward. *Victor Herbert: A Life in Music*. New York: Macmillan, 1955.

Whitcomb, Ian. *Irving Berlin and Ragtime America*. New York: Limelight Editions, 1988.

Wilk, Max. *They're Playing Our Song*. New York: Atheneum, 1973.

Willson, Meredith. *But He Doesn't Know the Territory*. New York: G.P. Putnam's Sons, 1959.

Wodehouse, P.G., and Guy Bolton. *Bring on the Girls! The Improbable Story of Our Life in Musical Comedy*. New York: Simon and Schuster, 1953.

Zadan, Craig. *Sondheim and Co*. 2nd ed. New York: Harper and Row, 1986.

Works on American Popular Music

Cooke, Deryck. *The Language of Music*. New York: Oxford University Press, 1959.

Ewen, David. *All the Years of American Popular Music*. Englewood Cliffs, NJ: Prentice-Hall, 1977.

_____. *American Popular Songs*. New York: Random House, 1966.

_____. *The Life and Death of Tin Pan Alley: The Golden Age of American Popular Music*. New York: Funk & Wagnalls, 1964.

Ferrara, Lawrence. *Philosophy and Analysis of Music: Bridges to Musical Sound, Form and Reference*. Westport, CT: Greenwood Press, 1991.

Gammond, Peter. *The Oxford Companion to Popular Music*. New York: Oxford University Press, 1991.

Hamm, Charles. *Yesterdays: Popular Song in America*. New York: W.W. Norton, 1979.

Lax, Roger, and Frederick Smith. *The Great Song Thesaurus*. 2nd ed. New York: Oxford University Press, 1989.

Lissauer, Robert. *Lissauer's Encyclopedia of Popular Music, 1888 to the Present*. New York: Paragon House, 1991.

Morris, James R., J.R. Taylor and Dwight Blocker Bowers. *American Popular Song: Six Decades of Songwriters and Singers*. Washington, DC: Smithsonian Institution Press, 1984.

Murrells, Joseph. *Million Selling Records From the 1900s to the 1980s*. New York: Arco Publishing, Inc., 1984.

Paymer, Marvin E. (Gen. ed.) *Facts Behind the Songs: A Handbook of American Popular Music From the Nineties to the 90s*. New York: Garland Publishing, 1993.

Popular Music: An Annotated Index of American Popular Songs, 18 volumes. Editors: Nat Shapiro (1964-1973); Bruce Pollock (1984-1994). New York: Adrien Press, 1964-1973; Detroit: Gale Research, 1984-1994.

Robinette, Richard. *Historical Perspectives in Popular Music: A Historical Outline*. Dubuque, IA: Kendall-Hunt, 1980.

Smith, F. Joseph. *The Experiencing of Musical Sound: Prelude to a Phenomenology of Music*. New York: Gordon and Breach, 1979.

Spaeth, Sigmund. *A History of Popular Music in America*. New York: Random House, 1948.

Stambler, Irwin. *Encyclopedia of Popular Music*. New York: St. Martin's Press, 1965.

Wilder, Alec. *American Popular Song: The Great Innovators, 1900-1950*. New York: Oxford University Press, 1972.

Index

About the Author

THOMAS S. HISCHAK is Professor of Theatre History and Criticism at the State University of New York College at Cortland. He is the author of *Word Crazy: Broadway Lyricists From Cohan to Sondheim* (Praeger, 1991) and *Stage It With Music: An Encyclopedic Guide to the American Musical Theatre* (Greenwood, 1993). He lives in Cortland, New York, with his wife and two children.

About the Foreword Author

GERALD BORDMAN is the author of many books on theatre, most recently the second edition of *The Oxford Companion to American Theatre*. His works on musical theatre include *Jerome Kern: His Life and Music* (Oxford, 1980), *Days to Be Happy, Years to Be Sad: The Life and Music of Vincent Youmans* (Oxford, 1982) and the second edition of the comprehensive *American Musical Theatre: A Chronicle* (Oxford, 1992).